American
Economic Development Council
Educational Foundation

PRACTICING
ECONOMIC DEVELOPMENT
3rd Edition

Edited by Robert L. Koepke
PhD, CED
FM, HLM

ISBN
0-9616567-8-6

Contents

PRACTICING ECONOMIC DEVELOPMENT

CASE EXAMPLES

BIBLIOGRAPHY

Preface

The American Economic Development Council Educational Foundation is pleased to present to the economic development profession this third edition of *Practicing Economic Development.*

As was the case for the first and second editions, this third edition of *Practicing Economic Development* has been prepared for several audiences.

The primary audience is the individual who is attending one of the Economic Development Courses accredited by the American Economic Development Council. This publication is designed to provide support material for the twelve economic development topics that comprise the core of this educational effort and most of the elective subjects that are presented at these various Courses.

A second audience is the local community leader who wishes to understand economic development and especially how to plan and implement an economic development program tailored to his/her area.

A third audience is the student in a formal class at a college or university who wishes to learn what economic development is and how it is done. As a collection of material written largely by practitioners, this publication should provide valuable insights into the challenges facing the economic developer and how he/she responds to these opportunities. As such, it generally will be a useful complement to the information presented in the higher education classroom.

This third edition illustrates the rapid growth that has taken place in the economic development profession in the three years since the second edition. For example, new information on a variety of subjects is included, including the use of technology in economic development, the role of incentives. retail development, and the professional development of the practitioner (including tips on passing the Certified Economic Developer exam!).

The American Economic Development Council Educational Foundation is pleased and honored to make this document available to those who wish to learn about economic development and especially to those who desire to use this information to engage in — to practice — economic development in their area.

Harry G. Foden, CED, FM, HLM
Chair, American Economic Development Council Educational Foundation

Frank A. O'Donnell. CED. FM
Immediate Past Chair, American Economic Economic Development Council Educational Foundation

From the Editor

This third edition of *Practicing Economic Development* is substantially a new publication.

It is larger than the currently out-of-print second edition that it replaces. At 296 pages, the third edition is half again as large as the 188 page second edition. Not surprisingly, it contains nearly half again as much material; this third has sixty-six manuscripts, while the second had forty-six.

It contains different manuscripts. Forty-four of the sixty-six manuscripts in this publication are included in *Practicing Economic Development* for the first time. Only twenty-two manuscripts from the second edition are also included in this third edition.

It contains material on topics of current interest. Examples of such new "hot" topics are technology approaches to economic development and professional development.

It is more tightly organized. While still focusing on the "core topics" of the American Economic Development Council accredited Economic Development Courses, the material in it is arranged according to the major issues facing economic developers. These critical topics are "perspectives on economic development" (must know the mission and general composition of e.d.), "addressing the fundamental components" (must know the basics and be able to do them well), "creating the competitive community" (the first job of the economic developer), "marketing the competitive community" (where the rubber hits the road), professional development (learning is a continuous process), and case examples (helpful to see what others have done). A number of subtopics support most of these major elements.

It is also a team effort. It was produced by a group of knowledgeable practitioners who were representatives of the many parts of the AEDC educational community that have an interest in seeing that a useful document is produced. These people, who played a vital role in the creation of this publication, include: Patrick Vercauteren representing the AEDC Educational Foundation, Kjell Knustern, Ken Shakoori, and Charles Strang for the Economic Development Course Directors, Joy Pooler and Daisy Stallworth for the Economic Development Institute, Michael Reese for the Certification Board, Linda Leonard for the Editorial Board, and E. Eugene Handley and Marion Morgan of the American Economic Development Council staff. These individuals actively participated in the development of this publication by reviewing several lists of possible manuscripts and the final mock-up of this third edition. Their assistance contributed greatly to the overall worth of this third edition of *Practicing Economic Development*.

Finally, thanks to the American Economic Development Council for allowing the Foundation to reprint material from its *Economic Development Review* and to the American Economic Development Council Educational Foundation, and its current chair Harry Foden and its immediate past chair Frank O'Donnell, for supporting the preparation of this document.

Robert L. Koepke, PhD, CED, FM, HLM
Editor

Principles Of Total Community Development

Richard Preston, C.E.D., FM. HLM

INTRODUCTION

Three words are basic to economic development. They are:

Growth — Development — Community.

The term "growth is by no means as popular as it was but a few years ago. Some people have come to fear and to oppose growth.

But the truth of the matter is that as long as we continue to have children and as long as we desire to improve our individual standard of living, growth is inevitable.

Once we accept the fact that growth is inevitable, our task becomes to define and attain a growth that is desirable and in tune with all basic needs. Today and in the future, only growth that promotes environmental quality is acceptable.

Think of it this way — a weed patch represents growth — wild, uncontrolled and unpredictable. A garden also represents growth but it is planned, nurtured and desired.

And so we come to development as we use that term today — growth undeveloped is a weed patch; growth properly developed is a garden.

As for the word "community," it has several meanings. Here we are talking about a city or town; the community that is a geographical place.

TOTAL ENVIRONMENT

The total community development that we are considering, therefore, is achieved by planning and developing the balanced growth of the city or town's social, economic, political and natural environments — its total environment.

The socioeconomic environment, so called, has three major components: the social, the economic, and the political.

Social environment refers to housing, health, education, welfare, employment, amenities, recreation, crime prevention and such elements of the community.

Economic environment embraces human resources, natural resources, markets, transportation, utilities, and commerce.

Political environment is composed of the governmental structure of a community; the legislative, the executive and the judicial branches. The government affects the total environment through its mature development and implementation of laws.

The community's natural (or physical) environment has several components; principle among them being air, land, water, other natural resources, ecological systems, aesthetics, and wildlife.

It follows that the development of the total community and of its total environment depends upon many elements, especially those elements concerned with economic development of the community. Why so:

ECONOMIC DEVELOPMENT — ORGANIZATION

Because, these elements, when drawn together through an economic development organization, are committed to a mission of enhancing the quality of life for all people in the community through:

❏ the generation of productive employment opportunities and the

❏ expansion of the economic base.

In so doing, the organization pays close attention to the impact of its operations upon the total environment of both the community and the area of which it is a part.

In carrying out its mission, the economic development organization's objective is to obtain from management its calculated decision to make a consequential capital investment in the identified potentials of the constituent area.

Consider this statement closely, for it presents several important principles of total community development as well as the principles of a sound economic development operation.

To Obtain. This requires sales or marketing. It requires that the total community, the city or town, be a quality product which is capable of continually making a favorable impression upon the capital investment market.

From Management. The private or public source of capital investment. This is usually known as "the suspect or prospect" in economic development terminology.

Its calculated decision. No prospective source of capital investment worthy of the attention of the economic development organization will invest a cent without careful consideration of all of the foreseeable factors involved. This facility planning process of management considers in greatest depth the quality of the social, the economic, the political and the natural environment of the city or town which is seeking to obtain its carefully calculated decision.

Consequential Capital Investment. It must be a mutual long term benefit to the investor and to the community. Since development must be made in the context of environmental quality, we should better define that word "consequential."

The consequence of investing private capital must be a competitive profit for the investor. He/she must realize a fair return upon his/her investment in the "immediate present" and over the years.

Consequential capital investment further requires that the city or town's total environment benefits. A major investment of any type will have a lasting impact. It is, therefore, imperative that natural as well as socioeconomic factors be considered in depth by the economic development organization.

The identified potentials is also a very important phrase. The potentials of a community must be ascertained, evaluated and assigned priorities for development. They must then be reviewed from time to time.

The potentials include both the assets and the liabilities of the city or town. For example, there may be potential for manufacturing industry which could be an asset. On the other hand, inadequate housing or municipal services may be counter balancing liabilities. Therefore, the priority fields for capital investment will be in housing and in municipal services before the potential from manufacturing industry can be realized.

In other words, the economic development organization must do its homework. It must research and plan before it establishes policy upon which to base its program of operations.

In the light of all these principals, it becomes evident that the economic development effort must concern itself deeply with development of the total community, not simply with the development of one or another element in the community.

This being the case, it follows that the economic development organization must be representative of the various segments or groups that make up the larger community. Its executive should be a professional economic developer whenever possible. The organization should have a team of well educated, dedicated men and women who are willing and able to work over a period of time with capital investors to achieve the development goals of the city or town.

If the community is to be successful in achieving balanced growth, it must be in itself a quality product capable of successful sale in the highly competitive marketplace of capital investment.

In view of the fact that the economic development organization must market this quality product, it follows that it must become involved in achieving and maintaining quality.

CONSEQUENTIAL

Earlier the word "consequential" was used. It is a key word in the principles of total community development, not only for the reasons expounded before, but because

today and for the future we must build the consequences of our programs into their original design.

Anything that an economic development organization does and does well or does not do or does poorly has an impact upon the socioeconomic and the natural environment of the community. Furthermore, that impact is of lasting consequence and, therefore, any operations undertaken by the economic development organization must consider carefully what might be termed the "cost/benefit" of any particular project.

One of the best ways in which to ascertain the cost/benefit is to undertake an objective study of what impact a particular development will have upon the major elements of the social, the economic and the natural environment of the community. Such a study will permit the economic development organization indeed to build the consequence of its program into the original design.

There are several methods by which this may be done. Of them, the most recent is the environmental impact study. Indeed, it is required by federal law in many development situations and by an increasingly large number of states, provinces and other governmental jurisdictions.

The environmental impact study/assessment is a useful tool for any economic development organization for, among many other functions, it demonstrates both to the community and to prospective capital investors that its program is concerned with total environmental development.

Such a study, however, is more often than not a complicated process requiring the services of several expert consultants. The tool, therefore can be an expensive one which is, more often than not, beyond the financial capabilities of a community's economic development organization. This does not mean, however, that the *issues* involved should be ignored.

It is well within an organization's capabilities to be prepared. This may be done by carefully reviewing federal, state or other laws and regulations pertaining to the preparation of such studies and then compiling appropriate data. Needless to say, this information, maintained in up-to-date files, is of value for the organization's day-to-day economic development operations and

for other elements concerned with the community's total development.

SUMMARY

In review there are several major elements which must be considered in total community development.

There must be an economic development organization which is knowledgeable, dedicated and applies modern principles in its programming and its operation.

It must work in cooperation with the components of the economic, the social and the political environment in its city or town and area.

It must be concerned with the protection and development of the natural environment.

It must strive to make its city and town a quality product which, in turn, requires it to become involved in developing and sustaining the following:

a. A positive, collective community attitude toward balanced growth which require, in effect, that all of the communities which make up the total community understand that the development which is being undertaken is development with environmental quality;

b. A civic awareness that is representative of the communities within the collective community;

c. A progressive and representative government organization;

d. Housing plan for all income group levels — present and future;

e. Health facilities capable of serving a growing community and efficient "protective services": police, fire, etc.;

f. A broad gauged educational program which includes vocational training and technical assistance;

g. A trained manpower reserve;

h. A realistic land use plan supported by realistic zoning and building ordinances which reflect that the community as a whole appreciates the need to implement comprehensive planning by "development with environmental quality;"

i. Public utilities such as electricity, gas, water, sewage, waste disposal, etc. which can meet both present and projected demands;

j. Public services adequate to accommodate expansion of residential, commercial, manufacturing and recreational facilities;

k. A transportation network commensurate with the development goals;

l. A healthy business community that reflects public appreciation of what private enterprise means to a community;

m. A sense of responsibility towards the area and region of which it is a part.

Total community development, to succeed, requires that many principles of economic development be followed and adhered to on a daily basis.

Three basic principles that encompass all others are:

❑ The community must be a quality product.

❑ "Desirable growth" occurs when the total environmental quality is made the goal of economic development.

❑ Total community development must become the standard process for present and future economic development.

A community that follows these general principles and their specific procedures will be successful in developing as a total community.

Building Viable Communities - The Essence Of Economic Development

Mark D. Waterhouse, C.E.D., FM

I.D., E.D. and C.D.

Development philosophers spend a great deal of time trying to explain, and in some cases, vigorously debating the relationship among the three developments — industrial, economic and community. Creating employment opportunities or expanding tax bases are not the mission of the economic development profession; building better communities is. Let's think about it.

Industrial, economic and community development are similar development concepts, distinguished primarily by the variety of activities included. To provide a basis for understanding each, the distinctions between the three warrant quick exploration.

Industrial development deals primarily with the manufacturing sector of the economy. It involves the value-added process in which some type of operation is performed on a raw material or input component, causing some modification to that material or component, resulting in a product or output component more valuable than that with which we started.

Economic development involves anything which creates new employment opportunities or broadens the tax base. Agriculture, tourism, services and a whole realm of other activities create new jobs and provide new tax revenues, but are in no way industrial in nature.

Commercial development is a primary example. The addition of a major shopping center to a community is instantly recognized for the multitude of new jobs it will create, and the additional dollars it will pay into the coffers of the appropriate taxing bodies. Many states have been recognizing the same benefits in horse and dog tracks, jai alai frontons and casinos, and Indian reservations are well known for "high stakes bingo."

Other activities may provide either the jobs or tax benefits but not both and are still a great asset to the area in which they are located. Yale University pays little or no taxes to the City of New Haven; they are, however, the largest employer in the City, and through the multiplier effect the disposable income of the Yale faculty and staff supports other jobs in the service and retail sectors. On the other hand, utilities are well known in many areas because of the taxes they pay on a major amount of equipment — water mains, for example — while there may be few, if any jobs involved.

The realm of economic development activities which can benefit a location by the jobs and/or taxes it provides is large and widely varied. It is not nearly so multifaceted as the field of which it is a part — community development.

What exactly is community development? If there is one thing it definitely isn't, it isn't "exactly" anything. By its very nature, the distinctive markings of the field of community development are quite nebulous. To understand why, it is perhaps best to adopt a definition of sorts which provides a foundation for the discussion that follows.

First, it is necessary to define what is meant by "development," since this term figures prominently in all three of the fields under discussion. Generally, when we speak of development as it applies to a location or a business, we actually mean growth. In this case, development means the act of getting bigger. Equally important, however, is the concept of development as change, which may or may not involve growth. In fact, development in this instance can mean diminishment — the act of getting smaller rather than larger. Thus, for the purposes of this discussion, "development" should be considered to mean any change from or modification in the current situation.

What, then, is meant by the term "community?" Most people probably use the word to refer to a geographical entity — a location or place which can be identified by name. Of course, the thing that really makes a community is the people living there. From this viewpoint, a community is also a social entity. It is a group of people, living in a general location, and sharing common wants, needs, goals and problems.

If we now recombine "community" with "development," what we are talking about is any change which affects the people living in some location. It is the lack of precision of this definition which has made it difficult for economic developers to realize they are really community developers. It is this same lack of hard and fast guidelines which makes each day at the office different from all the other days and exceptionally exciting, no matter which title you claim.

Can Economic and Community Development Be Separated?

A "success story" for the economic developer usually involves an attracted, expanded, retained or created business in his or her area of operation. Each such story has all sorts of effects on the community involved. The new manufacturing plant or shopping center brought into town by the economic developer will not only create new jobs and pay new taxes, it will also bring new families with additional children for the school system, increased housing demands, increased traffic and congestion and pollution in town.

For the economic developer to take the attitude that his/her job is to bring in the jobs and taxes, and someone else can worry about all the other aspects, many potentially negative, is a disservice both to the profession and to the involved community. Surely, there are many in the economic development profession who are keenly aware of the multiplicity of side-effects their actions have. But it has been the experience of many in the profession to meet more than a few professional peers who admittedly and willingly wore blinders to anything other than jobs and taxes.

Further, this attitude is often fostered by elected officials or directors of economic development agencies who fail to recognize the interrelationships involved and who make it clear to their staff people that unless the jobs and taxes roll in at a suitable rate, employment should be sought elsewhere. The basic nature of the bureaucracy contributes to the problem, where between boards and commissions, and even between staff people who work together every day, there is often a competitiveness, lack of communication and protectiveness of each one's sphere of influence. He who would dare make comment or take action in someone else's rightful territory is branded as power-hungry, out-to-steal-someone's-job, or a maverick who refuses to follow accepted chains of command and divisions of responsibility.

Thus, the economic developer who points out an impending need for a new school because of a major company bringing many people to town, may be told to mind his/her own business by the school board. Even worse, the economic developer who suggests that the community not allow a proposed shopping center because of the horrible traffic congestion it will cause in a nearby residential neighborhood, may be at serious odds with the Chamber of Commerce, and many of the residents of the community (except those who live in the affected neighborhood).

The necessity for the economic developer to consider more than just jobs and taxes creates a precarious situation; yet it is a situation which must be confronted. It is monstrously complex; it will likely get worse. It can be horribly frustrating; but to help a community develop in a way that will not diminish and very well may improve its quality can be exceptionally satisfying and rewarding.

Beyond this satisfaction, however, is a necessity. "The key factor of all economic development comes out of the mind of man."[1] Thus, if economic development is to continue with a maximum benefit and minimum detriment to people and communities, it will require man, the economic and community developer, to keep a watchful eye on *all* the consequences of economic development activity — not just jobs and taxes. The answer to the question, "Can Economic and Community Development be separated?" is a resounding "NO."

The Current Situation: A Lack of Information and Understanding

The image of the economic developer sometimes has been likened to the white hat on the white horse, who comes into an area and frees it from the grasp of evil by providing new jobs, broadening the tax base and generally doing a good deal more to improve the quality of life and keep our country strong. This view is not univer-

sally shared. Others accuse those who confess to being an industrial or economic developer of encouraging the fouling of our water and air, aiding the despoliation of irreplaceable land resources, and generally doing their darndest to make this a less attractive world in which to live.

If those in the second category are not growing more numerous, they are certainly growing more vociferous. Their viewpoint carries validity based on historical fact. It also carries a lot of votes in Congress and the decision-making bodies at all other levels of government.

Nonetheless, economic development will continue, for our way of life is tied inextricably to it. Those in the economic development field who will be most successful are those who recognize that such development cannot and should not be isolated from other aspects of community development. To attempt such a distinction is to invite opposition to our activities, and indicates the mentality of an ostrich, or one who doesn't care what the impact of his or her actions is.

Most who have been in the field for any length of time have already learned the lesson, often through the harrowing experience of unfriendly public hearings, media coverage, and confrontations with angry citizens. The ivory tower and the degrees and letters it confers does not provide the experience factor required for a completely rounded exposure to any occupational field. On the other hand, for the fledgling economic developer, the efficacy of trial by fire is also in question.

So where, then, does the economic developer who wishes to learn more about community development go for that knowledge? Simple; read the community development parts of the economic development literature or vice versa. Good luck. The instances of such cross-referencing are few, and generally not in any detail. Part of the problem is that neither field has historically had a particularly large selection of literature. A brief review of the literature for the two fields indicates that the amount of available literature on the relationship of economic and community development is limited[2]. Furthermore, it is much easier for a community developer to read and learn about economic development than vice versa.

This cannot be allowed to continue if those in the economic development profession are to be expected to meet the goals being set for our industrialized society. These goals are that:

1. Economic development must continue in order to meet the needs for jobs and taxes;

2. The development of each community must be well-planned, orderly and of high quality;

3. Adequate consideration must be given to all possible impacts of development, so that "the people" may recognize not only the benefits but also the costs of a particular action, and may have the opportunity to voice their opinions.

It is this last goal which, increasingly, has brought industry and those working with industry into confrontation with other segments of society. Conflicts concerning the environment are well-known, will continue, and will become more complex. Such topics as solid and hazardous waste disposal, clean-up and reuse of contaminated sites or super-lien requirements — all of which carry both economic and environmental impacts — are a relatively new area of the legal profession.

A current concern of the economic developer is the growing body of legislation which makes development more difficult. Yet the longer such conflicts as that between economic growth and environmental preservation continue, and the more they must be resolved by the court system, the greater the likelihood of intervention by legislation. Congressional and state legislative consideration of economic growth planning, regulations concerning plant relocations and the like have become commonplace in the last decade. While the passage of a new law is usually an attempt to codify the good sense that people all have but fail to use, each new law also adds to a regulatory system which is the antithesis of efficiency.

THE MANY HATS OF THE ECONOMIC DEVELOPER

The Economic Developer: Specialist or Generalist?

There is a simple way to ensure that this condition will become an increasingly impenetrable jungle — and that it will result in ever greater infringements on the free enterprise system. That is to continue the present situation which, while not universal, is all too commonplace: like many other fields, the development field is witnessing a sacrifice in efficiency to overspecialization. The economic developer is in charge of finding and keeping jobs and taxable business; the environmentalist is in charge of clean air and water; the legislator is in charge of setting policy; the city planner is in charge of land use; the educator is in charge of preparing youth for a productive role in society.

Certainly, one person cannot be an expert in all things related to development. On the other hand, it is contraproductive to rely completely on different individuals for each aspect of development. The logical alternative, from the point of view of the economic development profession, is for the economic developer to be a development generalist with a concentration on building sound and enjoyable communities. Like most doctors, he/she will have a specialty in which he/she is particularly strong — economic development — but should also have the education, expertise and outlook of a general practitioner.

In other words, the economic developer must have as much of an allegiance to the community into which he/she is attempting to bring a business as to the business he/she is attempting to bring there. He/she must have a broad-based background, interests and concerns. He/she must wear many hats, and must try them all on each time he/she considers taking some action which will affect the community. The discussion which follows considers some of these hats in more detail.

The Economic Developer As Environmentalist

Conflicts between developers and environmental groups are commonplace. The resulting legislation and possible future adjudication are decried by developers as overly regulatory, and a contradiction to the free enterprise system. Yet, a demonstrated concern for the environment is one of the most important postures the economic developer can take.

E.F. Schumacher wrote in 1973 that because economic growth had no discernable limits, it would necessarily run into "decisive bottlenecks" from the environmental sciences.[3] Indeed, the current situation often finds or is at least perceived as the economic developer on one side, giving no thought to the environment, and the environmentalist on the other side, giving no thought to the economy. This polarization contravenes production or protection of the environment about which both sides are really concerned — the human environment. The statement was made many years ago that "conservation in city affairs (not to be confused with conservation or preservation of wilder-

ness areas) is a crutch that can be used effectively to beat developers into a compromise."[4]

When viewed in terms of the human environment, there is little disagreement between the two sides. The environmentalist generally does not question that adequate income for both individuals and governments is required to support the lifestyle and provide the services sought by most people, and that economic growth is the means to providing that income. Similarly, the economic developer cannot argue in favor of smog, undrinkable water, deafness caused by excessive noise, or resource depletion which will prohibit future production.

The economic developer who makes consideration of environmental impacts of a proposed development a routine part of the overall scheme of doing things will have gone far toward assuaging the fears of the environmentalists simply by showing that he/she hasn't forgotten their viewpoint and is acting responsibly to minimize adverse impacts. While conflicts and confrontations never will be eliminated, the existence of a continuing dialogue between the two "sides" is a primary requisite to meeting the goals of both.

An Environmental Impact Assessment can be a useful tool for the developer; generally it is viewed as a form of harassment. The Assessment should not be confused with a full Environmental Impact Statement, which is much more voluminous, technical, detailed and expensive. The Assessment can usually be done in 5 to 10 single-spaced pages and provides a very basic consideration of all possible environmental effects of a proposed activity.

Much of the information included in the Assessment is the same information a business may often request during its consideration of a site: for example, soil characteristics and drainage, presence of wetlands, traffic counts and the like. Thus the Assessment is really little extra work, and provides a useful tool to the developer.

Conservation and environmental concerns such as those addressed by the Assessment are being recognized more and more by people at the neighborhood level. A common characteristic of neighborhood conservation efforts is a tendency to be skeptical about professionals. If the professional economic developer is not to be hampered by such skepticism, he/she must demonstrate to potential skeptics that he/she is aware of their concerns, is able to

give rational consideration to their viewpoint — and does so. This should be done as a matter of normal procedure designed to provide the highest quality development with the maximum benefit and minimum detriment to the people of his/her community.

The economic developer must accept that most environmentalists are not frivolous, but are deeply concerned with what our world will be like in the future. Economic developers must also show environmentalists that they are not rapists of nature, and share the same concern for the future of our world.

The Economic Developer as Planner

Another area in which the economic developer often is criticized is in the realm of long-range development planning. The argument is that the economic developer is trying to lead the community from the present to the future without a roadmap and is running the risk of getting everyone lost. The alternative to having an economic development plan which sets forth how much, what kind and how fast, is to play the game "Surprise," a variation on Russian roulette, in which a community may find itself undergoing more economic development than it can handle, of kinds it doesn't want, and all at once.

Not all economic development in an area may be good for it. While industrial location in a rural community may bring employment, population growth and economic prosperity, these benefits do not come automatically or in every instance. "More often the industry clearly gains while having a negligible or even negative effect on the host community over the long run."[5] Traffic congestion, air pollution, the need for new schools or public safety services are all possible downsides to the jobs and taxes upside.

From the community's point of view, the real problem is a lack of information on the possible consequences of industrial development, and the subsequent inability to take action to prevent serious problems from occurring. The economic developer, wearing a "Planner's Hat," should fill this role. A fiscal impact analysis should be a normal part of considering a proposed development of any appreciable site.

The economic developer and his/her community should have an economic development or growth plan. This is *not* a fancy, thick and expensive tome prepared by a consultant. On the other hand, it is not merely the existence of zoning regulations which say "This land is zoned for heavy industry and this is what you can and can't put here." The economic development professional has discovered the value of strategic planning. Unfortunately, may development agencies haven't made the effort to prepare one.

The economic development plan combines the expertise of the economic developer with the consensus of desires of the citizenry to make some prognostications on what the community's economic base will someday look like.

The economic development plan and the planning process itself are not difficult to understand[6]. A great deal of literature describing the process, particularly as relates to economic development, is available.[7,8]

An economic development plan makes some fairly simple statements which are probably based on a great deal of homework by the economic developer and his/her economic development commission, agency, board, or other form of community input. The plan analyzes future needs for economic development; may identify specific types of business which would be most suitable for the community and take maximum advantage of its resources; and may identify certain problem areas.

The fact that these problems have been identified now, means that they can be solved ahead of time rather than in a crisis situation, and that any expenses entailed can be spread over a longer period. As economic developers know, this investment will pay dividends in attracting new businesses, for it shows that the community is really interested. However, this fact is often difficult for other people to appreciate, particularly if the community has not experienced first-hand a similar situation. The investment of money "in the hopes that we might land a big one" is seen as an unwarranted gamble, when "we can always do the work when we know we've got one on the line." It must be the economic developer's job, not only to identify problem areas and suggest solutions, but also to convince the community that the likelihood of landing that big one they're after is higher if they get a stronger line and use attractive bait. The economic developer who is an active participant in, if not a leader of, a broad based planning effort is more likely to be listened to than one who merely points out problems from the sidelines.

Unfortunately, too often, the identification of problems and the suggestion of solutions are left to others — the experts or those designated as such for the particular area — unless they have a direct bearing on a prospect or project. For the economic developer concerned with building a better community, this cannot be. Here are some simple examples.

1. Transportation. That the movement of goods, from raw materials to finished products, is the concern of the economic developer is widely recognized. The movement of people is an equivalent concern and has increased in importance, as labor supply has tightened. The economic developer should be interested in an adequate public transportation system. Where traffic congestion is high, public mass transportation can reduce it, improve employee morale by eliminating the necessity of fighting through aggravating traffic jams, and increase productivity by allowing more working time and less commuting time. Two of the contributing factors to Hartford's high office vacancy rate are a lack of adequate downtown parking, coupled with a poor public transportation system. This results in horrible rush hour traffic and very expensive parking, which is motivating office relocation to the suburbs.

Often of importance to corporations is the ability to get executives to other parts of the country or get other companies' executives into town. Adequate nearby air service is necessary, preferably with scheduled service. This is not always feasible, and the alternative is a good general aviation airport which can at least accommodate company planes and charter flights. The economic developer may become involved in developing such a facility, and this activity may even be outside his/her community if a suitable area is not available there.

2. Recreation. While the economic developer may be disposed to thinking of recreational amenities as a selling point for a community, recreation people are not as apt to be aware of this relationship. The provision of these facilities should be a concern of the economic developer. Such facilities serve a dual purpose, for not only do they meet the recreational needs of an area, they may also form part of the economic base of that area. Ski areas, equestrian centers, marinas, fishing piers — even amateur jai alai parlors — are all parts of some communities' recreational opportunities and economic base.

3. Education. An adequate educational system concerns the business person for two reasons. First, the intellectual development of his or her children is a common parental worry; that of employees' children is similarly considered. Secondly, the business person is sensitive to the education and training of those to be hired from an area. The relationship of continuing scientific and technological education to the recruitment of technology oriented businesses is well recognized. Therefore, the economic developer must take an active role in assuring that his/her community's educational system is a good one, providing an adequate general education, a sufficient background for higher education, and solid vocational and technical training responsive to the needs of the area's businesses.

4. Housing. No matter what the nature of an area's economic base, the need for adequate housing opportunities is inescapable. Usually, a variety of both types and costs is advisable in order to satisfy both human preference and different income levels. The economic developer, in the concern to provide a well-rounded community, must be as concerned with the roof over peoples' heads as with the roof over businesses' heads. As with recreational opportunities, the provision of adequate housing may serve a second purpose through the creation of jobs in and tax revenue from the construction industry.

5. Public Health and Safety. The majority of people prefer living in a place where they can be assured of adequate care when ill or injured and protection from crime and hazards to themselves or their property. Business shares these concerns.

The provision of health services varies greatly between areas, from strictly privately provided, to large municipal hospitals and clinics. For a community with an insufficient number of medical personnel, the obvious solution is to recruit more. The recruitment of doctors is not unlike the recruitment of a new business — after all, being a doctor is a form of business — and the information a doctor wants to see about a possible new community includes much of the same material a prospective new business requires. Who is better equipped to provide this information than the economic/community developer? With the "graying of America" underway, the provision of adequate health services is considered to be a future growth industry.

Public safety services generally come under the purview of a unit of government, and in an era of rising crime statistics, business would prefer greater service; business pays substantial taxes, and would like substantial protection. While government cannot always provide the level of service business would like, the economic developer must try to ensure that business receives "a dollar's worth of services for a dollar's worth of taxes."

The Economic Developer
As Policy Shaper

One of the key areas where the economic development profession has been remiss is in the shaping of policies within which communities — from the smallest town to the national community — develop. For all too long, economic developers have complained about the rules of the game, but done little to change those rules or to show others what modifications are needed. While this situation is beginning to change, it needs underlining and emphasizing.

Politics has been regarded as a dirty word, and the political arena a place to be avoided, yet it is within this arena that policies are shaped which set the bounds within which development must take place. If the economic developer is not willing to take an active role in shaping these policies, he/she has no right to complain about them afterwards.

While organizations of developers have begun to stress involvement at the national and state levels, the same should hold true at the local and other sub-state levels. In addition, the strictly political arena is not the only place where policy-shaping should take place; for example, the plans and policies which emanate from the various regional planning agencies can have a significant bearing on development.

The economic developer's role as a community development policy shaper has two facets — active and reactive. The active includes the advocacy of particular policies which the economic developer believes are wise or necessary for healthy development. The reactive includes a variety of possibilities all related to some else's proposed policy: review and comment, testimony and other input, support or opposition.

It should be noted that the higher the level at which such activity takes place, the more advisable it is that the policy-shaping efforts should be focused through a group, as well as being carried out by the individual members of that group. The

individual attempting to oppose a bill in Congress, especially when that bill may have been submitted by some rather influential people, will be "a voice crying in the wilderness." Large numbers of voices shouting in unison are necessary, and affiliation with a group sharing similar interests can provide the required coordination.

Increasingly, the existing groups, councils and associations in the economic development field are recognizing that they have an important role to play in this area. Many, such as the American Economic Development Council, have discovered that lobbying-type activity is not prohibited in their charter, bylaws, or otherwise as had been believed. Recognizing that the viewpoint of the economic developer is essential in shaping balanced development, they are considering procedures which will allow them to speak out actively on issues of concern as long as the establishment of such a position is not opposed by a significant portion of the membership.

The ability of the economic development professional to speak out on the issues indicates that he/she is not satisfied with leaving the establishment of the parameters within which the community may develop, to someone else. This ability also pleases and assists the business person, who on the one hand may want to speak out very badly, but on the other hand recognizes that businesses' credibility may be low, and that any position espoused by business seems to be suspect automatically. Therefore, the task of speaking out must be taken up by those sensible parties who believe that economic activity and growth is essential to community stability.

An important consideration relative to policy shaping by the economic developer — or in any field for that matter — is to avoid falling into the mold of those who find it easy to oppose and criticize someone else's proposal, but never offer a constructive alternative. Those who propose legislation generally do so with the belief that the legislation is necessary to ensure healthy and progressive development. Therefore, those who oppose the legislation without presenting adequate reasons for the opposition appear to be obstructionists. The economic/community developer, interested in the same healthy and progressive growth as the legislator but finding different means to be a more acceptable approach to the same end, is not an obstructionist and should do whatever

necessary to keep from being labeled as such. This requires reasoned arguments and alternative solutions.

Certainly, "educating" our legislators on the intricacies of economic development is important. So too must legislators be made to see that development of healthy communities cannot be considered without taking into account the economic development of that community.

Equally important — perhaps more so — is education of the general public. Legislators are generally sensitive and responsive to what they perceive are the viewpoints of their constituencies. They can hardly be otherwise, for it is that constituency — the voters — that must decide periodically to "rehire" that legislator.

The fact that many legislators appear to be anti-business reflects a lack of educational activity on two fronts. First, it is obvious that the legislators have not been schooled adequately on the importance of economic development; that is, the businessperson and economic developer are not seen to be as important a part of the constituency as "the general citizenry."

The difference in viewpoints attributed to "the economic development faction" and "the general citizenry" is brought about by the second lack of educational activity. The public often does not appreciate or understand the role of business in our society. Most individuals do not think about business beyond whether or not they have a job, or if they do, whether or not that job is allowing them and their families to live comfortably. The fact that taxes keep going up is usually seen only as government spending too much, with little thought to the fact that the tax base may not be growing fast enough because of a failure to broaden the business portion of that tax base.

In a nutshell, "We have a tremendous responsibility to communicate the facts. What we are doing (fostering economic development) is good for society. We should not be ashamed to tell our story." Unfortunately, "the development industry has shirked its duty of educating the public on the value of economic growth."[9] Even more unfortunately, this statement is as true today as it was when it was made in 1976.

The design of such an educational program would be multifaceted and too complex to deal with adequately here. Suffice it to say that such a program is essential, and would go far toward fulfilling the role the economic developer must play as a policy shaper.

The Economic Developer As Catalyst and Convener

The role of economic development was described many years ago as "exert[ing] a positive influence on private investment so that the quality of life in the community is enhanced." Little thought is needed to realize that this process involves business, government and people. The liaison between all three segments of the community should be the economic/community developer.

If each of these three segments was to proceed on its own with no necessity for interaction with the other two, the actions each took and the subsequent results would probably be markedly different from what actually occurs. In the "real world" however, progress is often a product of compromise.

That the world is constantly changing and life is becoming more complex is a generally accepted viewpoint. In the past, the three segments of the community previously mentioned were not seen nearly as closely intertwined as they are today. New problems, increased complexity and a broadened view of what economic development is and means, have all led to a changed role for the departments of economic and community development. Therefore, the economic developer must "recognize that the nature of development problems today make our 'turf' everyone's 'turf,' and that to exercise mandated leadership and initiative in development matters means that the [economic developer's] role has, in part, to be that of catalyst and convener."[10]

In practice, what do these words mean? For one thing, they mean the educational process already mentioned, through which each segment of the community can better understand how they all relate to economic development.

A critical factor is the building of a better bridge between business and government. It often seems that the two are barely on speaking terms. Too many in government (and the general population as well) think business considers itself above the law and will try to get away with anything it can. Too many in business think of government as totally inflexible, unsympathetic to the needs of business, and purposely obstructionist in its actions.

Both viewpoints are stereotypes and are inaccurate descriptions of many of those to whom they are applied. This is wrong, and is detrimental to our ultimate goal of developing healthy communities. Distrust and suspicion are not ingredients of a healthy climate. The economic developer must work to change this situation.

Equally wrong, however, is the fact that, like most stereotypes, these are grounded in some degree of truth. The credibility of business is low on several accounts. Thomas A. Murphy, former Chairman of the General Motors Corporation, once stated:

Too often we rail against government regulation — that is, except regulation to protect us against foreign competition. We oppose government handouts — except those used to bail out particular companies or particular industries. We are dead set against controls on prices — but wage controls might be worth a look . . . Credibility requires that we in business should not ignore or excuse demonstrated instances of questionable practices such as misleading advertising and misrepresented warranties. We cannot overlook the admitted wrongdoings of some of our country's largest and most respected corporations. No one believes that business is blameless in every respect. For us to try to make it seem blameless suggests that we can no longer distinguish between what is right and fair and honest and what is not.[11]

Where business is unjustly accused, the economic developer must be ready to support, defend, and work however necessary to let the public know the truth. Where business has erred, the economic developer must call the error to businesses' attention for correction. Where business refuses to correct its error, integrity and future credibility demand that the economic developer take whatever other action is necessary to correct the situation.

On the opposite side of the coin, government *can* be a tremendous pain in the neck. The plethora of government-created laws and regulations is undeniable and getting worse. If there is ever a paper shortage, the greatest single cause will probably be government-mandated reports. Constructing a new building can be a real challenge, what with all the departments, boards, plans, codes and regulations involved. Government does little to make dealing with it easier, and appears to work hard at being the antithesis of efficiency.

The economic developer can provide an important service to the businessperson by assisting him/her in dealings with the bureaucracy. Providing a "guide service" so that the businessperson deals with all the necessary agencies in the appropriate order, and has come prepared to comply with all the requirements of each agency, will reduce markedly the confusion and time spent in making it through the system. If the economic developer is employed within government, his/her very presence should expedite matters. Even if he/she is an "outsider", continued dealings with those in government on development matters and a reputation for doing things properly, efficiently, and in accordance with the rules, are advantages the economic developer has in dealing with bureaucrats, which the businessperson may not have. The individual in government generally appreciates efficiency; the inefficiency stems from the system itself — the standard operating procedures — more often than it does from individuals.

The economic developer and his/her business contacts can often recommend to government more cost-effective ways to do things, something which elected officials in particular are often happy to implement. Where government is efficient and reasonable to deal with, the economic developer should let the businessperson know this, commend government for it, and make sure the situation doesn't change.

The economic/community developer can also function in the catalyst and convener role between business and the public. Most people have little idea of what goes on inside the industries in their own town. They are not aware of the safety precautions taken to protect employees or the pollution controls used to protect the public. It is difficult to appreciate something you don't know about. As a minimum, the economic developer should see that this important segment of the community receives suitable publicity. Even better, with the cooperation of the local businesses, tours and open houses can be conducted. Such familiarization will bring about a greater appreciation and pride about the community, and community pride is an important resource in attracting and retaining businesses.

Business can make a significant contribution to its community through the sponsorship of various activities. Some communities have been the recipients of major parks through the generosity of the business community. This can work to the advantage of business by making a charitable donation and by reducing the amount of land on which taxes are being paid, particularly when that land may be unusable because it is wetlands. Business also sponsors programs, scholarships, and just about any other community improvement that can be thought of.

Often the majority of the public may not realize that such generosity is occurring. The economic developer should work to rectify the situation. Conversely, where local business is not supporting its community in this fashion, the economic/community developer is a key person in initiating such programs.

While there is certainly a monetary cost to business in supporting community projects, there is also a gain in good will, which benefits are intangible and impossible to measure but are nonetheless there. Another benefit to a business which is respected in its community is the fact that the residents will support the business by buying its products or services if that is possible. The economic developer who can foster this type of business-citizenry relationship will be providing an important service to the community.

Besides the business-government and business-citizenry liaisons, there is a business-business relationship which must be of concern to the economic developer. Bringing a new business into an area may not be to the advantage of those already there. Businesses that compete for the same labor pool or market may create disruptive internal pressures in a community. The economic developer must ask "what will the community gain by bringing in a new business which causes an already established business to leave or go out of business?"

The ideal relationship between businesses in an area is a symbiotic one. The presence of each supports the others through purchase of goods and services. Where employment is cyclical in nature, complementary hiring cycles for similar skills can minimize area unemployment and also minimize the amount of training required for new employees. New businesses brought into town are those which can supply necessary goods and services to those already there, utilize the goods and services of those already there, or provide employment for underutilized skills. An area seeking to diversify its employment base may bring in businesses

completely different from existing business.

Certainly the economic developer cannot advocate that each area business have a monopoly in its field. A certain amount of competition is a healthy and strengthening factor in the evolution of an area's economic base. A community should not be expected to nurture an obsolete company merely because it has been in town for a long time; companies that are unwilling or unable to adapt to modern requirements should be replaced with those that can give the area a healthier future. Who is in a better position that the economic developer to perceive how the community must develop in order to have the strongest economic base? And who is in a better position to work with both existing and potential businesses to make sure the economic sector of the community's existence is healthy? No one.

Similarly, the economic developer can serve as a catalyst in helping business to get problems solved. Almost every business has problems; most do not know what problems others have. The economic developer, who should be finding out what these problems are, is in the best position to identify trends and problem areas and bring these to the attention of the appropriate powers for correction. Where an individual business may have little success in getting the problem solved, the "strength in numbers" approach can bring about improvements which are to everyone's advantage.

Thus, the economic/community developer, as the hub of a wheel which includes the spokes of business, government and citizenry, is in a critical position of influence on the development of an area. He/she must recognize this position and use it wisely.

COMMUNITY DEVELOPMENT + ECONOMIC DEVELOPMENT = A QUALITY ENVIRONMENT FOR PEOPLE AND BUSINESS

A quality environment, otherwise known as a "good place to live," is a goal shared by both people and business. While they differ somewhat on defining that good place — for instance, we don't usually need a rail siding next to our home, but business often does — they also agree on many other areas, some of which have already been explored.

One of the primary goals of the economic and community developer, whether

these areas are handled by separate individuals, or the same person wearing more than one hat, has to be the provision of that quality environment. This environment is composed by: (1) charting a course of rational growth and development; and (2) attaining or maintaining a high quality of life. A secondary consideration, but of personal concern to the development professional, is that where people are happy about the first two areas, there will be (3) a minimum of opposition to the developer and his/her activities.

The economic developer who maintains a community development predilection in the conduct of daily activities will have success in all three areas by fostering more rational growth, contributing to a higher quality of life, and having the least opposition possible. These areas are considered further below.

More Rational Growth

One of the key factors in defining "rational growth" is the minimizing of "sprawl." Sprawl is another one of the concepts in community development which cannot be defined completely. While its presence is usually indicative of a lack of, or poor quality of planning, poor or no planning does not necessarily result in sprawl.

Sprawl results in inconvenience because of greater than necessary distances between residential, commercial and industrial areas. It usually means less than efficient road and utility networks, and a higher cost to provide these services. For residential areas, these extra costs are generally borne by government, but in reality, they are borne by the families and businesses that pay taxes to that government. Business actually feels the brunt twice, for where the cost of living, including taxes, goes up, pressure is brought to bear to increase wages accordingly.

Where local costs increase too much, business may leave, causing an increased tax burden on those who remain. Ever rising tax costs in an area will also be felt by a business considering that area, for the owner of that piece of land the business wants to buy is going to ask a price which will compensate for the taxes paid all these years; where taxes keep rising, so does the cost of the land.

Certainly, there are numerous other factors besides the cost of sprawl which figure in this inflationary spiral. Nonetheless, if these increasing costs can be lessened by the economic developer by working to ensure more rational growth and development of the total community, it is his/her responsibility to do so.

Beyond reduced sprawl and less cost is a third benefit of this type of effort: more foreseeable growth trends. If current development is taking place by happenstance, it is very difficult to predict what future development will be. Anxiety about the unknown is a common feeling, and it should apply no less to what our community will look like twenty years from now than it does to how we're going to pay for the kids to go to college.

Neighborhood opposition to a proposed zone change nearby or to allowing an unusual use is really an expression of concern over what this precedent is going to mean to the character of the neighborhood in the long run. Often, this opposition would not occur if the uncertainty was not there.

Business, as a common practice, attempts to project what it will look like at some point in the future; it projects how big it is going to be, its activities, its costs and its revenues. There is no reason why a community cannot do similarly. By so doing, the community will be much more at ease with itself. Those who join the community in the future will not be able to complain later that how the community is developing is not what they expected. Much needless opposition to that development will be avoided. The "no growth" syndrome should be averted, or at least minimized.

Perhaps most importantly, a sense of community will be fostered. Sociologists tell us that a lack of this sense of community is an important contributing factor to many of the ills in our society: crime, pollution, inadequate services at too high a cost, and general discontent.

A Higher Quality of Life

In order for the economic developer to appreciate how his/her activities relate to the quality of life of a community, he/she must consider three measures of that quality of life: economics, environment, and daily activities, as they pertain to people, both individually and in groups. The economic developer who views his/her job as community development as well as matching sites and businesses and solving the businessman's problems, will maximize the level of all three of these measures.

The economic component of the quality of life is perhaps the easiest to appreciate, for it is the one most often talked about — jobs and taxes. People are happiest where there is a high level of income and services with low unemployment, taxes and other costs. A healthy economic base accomplishes all of these.

An adequate number of good jobs means more people are working and have more disposable income, which supports more service businesses, encouraging lower prices through competition and higher volume. More businesses means more and better service provided by government at a lower tax rate for all, which again contributes to more disposable income, or perhaps higher investment in savings allowing lower interest rates for borrowing. The whole process is cyclical in nature.

A higher quality of the community environment is another result. Environment does not mean merely things related to air, water, noise, litter and natural resources; rather it means everything that is related to "what kind of place is this to live?" Certainly, the importance of air, water, noise, litter and natural resources cannot be minimized. The economic developer who can build a strong economic base while minimizing environmental pollution and resource depletion will be in a utopian situation, and this portion of the environmental quality of life will be difficult to improve upon.

However, these advantages will be minimized where the other components of the environment are inferior. People are much more willing to tolerate a belching smokestack if the alternative is unemployment. Crystal clear water may be very important to the fisherman, but is not nearly so valuable to those who would like other recreational outlets which are unavailable. Most of us would rather live in an area with good schools, a variety of cultural and recreational activities and a low level of litter, than in an area which can only claim to be litter-free.

These other things, which contribute so substantially to our daily activities, are equally important as the more commonly considered aspects of a good environment in defining what we mean by a high environmental quality of life. The economic developer who takes a community development approach to his/her job may be involved in this area because of the realization that it will make the community more attractive as a location for business. Be that as it may, it will also make the community more attractive for people, and it is that type of attractiveness that is the primary determinant in selecting where one is going to live.

A Minimum of Opposition

The economic developer's existence will never be free from conflict and opposition. Each additional person in a community increases the likelihood of a difference of opinion and an ensuing debate. But even if the economic developer was the only person in the place, this type of debate should go on in his/her own head, for a debate is merely the consideration of various points of view in order to reach a rational decision on an issue.

He who takes the "Damn the torpedoes; full speed ahead!" approach, is asking for torpedoes. Conversely, those who make the extra effort to consider viewpoints other than their own will have much less opposition to their final decision, no matter with whom they agree. The opportunity to be heard is often as important as having someone agree with you. Furthermore, the economic developer may find his/her opinion changing after listening to others' thoughts on a matter. Whatever the final decision, it is certainly less susceptible to challenge if other viewpoints have been considered, than if they were ignored.

Expertise is partly knowledge about a topic, and partly how good at your job others believe you are. No matter how much you may know about that topic, it will carry little weight if those around you have little confidence in you. Lack of confidence is most often manifested in skepticism and sometimes outright opposition. A common indicator of expertise is thoroughness. The ability to consider all the variables, anticipate all of the questions and have answered them already, is generally associated with success, no matter what the endeavor. Preparedness comes from attention to details. More and more, such thoroughness in the field of economic development entails the myriad of community development considerations discussed above.

SUMMARY

The role of the economic developer has changed markedly over the past several years. Confronted as the economic development profession is today with burgeoning control by legislation and regulation, survival is a very real issue, and sensitivity to the changing demands of society may decide whether those now in the profession still have a profession ten years from now.

No longer will society blindly accept smoke-spewing, water-contaminating factories merely because they provide jobs. Nor will communities be tolerated whose sole personality is that of the old mill town, with none of the amenities we expect today in the place we live. When people are dissatisfied, and their problems are not dealt with voluntarily, someone will attempt to provide the solution by a law or regulation. Where people believe that a proper job is being done, governmental meddling is minimized.

The proper job for the economic developer today is not just a concern for business, jobs, taxes and economics. Healthy, viable communities must be the ultimate goal, and all efforts must be focused in that direction.

There are some who argue that economic development is a zero-sum game; that economic developers don't influence what happens, but merely where; and that money spent on the effort is largely a waste. No one can argue that building better communities is not a worthy pursuit.

FOOTNOTES

[1]E.F. Schumacher, *Small is Beautiful: Economics as if People Mattered* (New York: Harper & Row, 1973), p. 72.

[2]American Economic Development Council, *A Bibliography of Recent Literature in Economic Development*, Rosemont, IL, July, 1987.

[3]Schumacher, *op. cit.*, p. 27.

[4]Sherwood Stockwell, "Seven Fantasies of City Planning," *Nation's Cities*, February 1975, p. 39.

[5]Gene F. Summers and Jean M. Lang, "Bringing Jobs to People: Does It Pay?" *Small Town*, 7 (September 1976): 4-11.

[6]Mark D. Waterhouse and Paul J. Hockersmith, "Economic Development Strategic Planning through 'SMEAC'", *Economic Development Review*, Spring 1990.

[7]David R. Kolzow, *Strategic Planning for Economic Development* (Rosemont, IL: AEDC, 1988).

[8]*Economic Development Review* (Rosemont, IL: AEDC, Spring 1990).

[9]William A. Pate, "A Decade of Changes Poses New Problems For Balanced Growth," *Area Development*, May 1976, pp. 62, 101-103.

[10]Ibid

[11]Thomas A. Murphy, "Businessman, Heal Thyself," *Newsweek*, December 20, 1976, p. 11.

Skills Needed by The Economic Developer

Jerold R. Thomas

In today's and tomorrow's competitive environment, economic developers require and will need certain skills to compete. This article focuses on five broad skill areas that economic developers (or any professional for that matter) should develop and maintain to be able to compete. These skills are really nothing new. They have always been around. Because of the many changes taking place, however, successful adoption and mastering of them has now become critical. These five skill areas are: leadership, theoretical, practical, political, and change skills. Because these are broad skill areas, the reader will find that many of the items listed in one area are interchangeable with other areas.

LEADERSHIP SKILLS

Leadership skills are discussed first, because without them the other skills cannot be implemented. Leadership skills are the skills needed to be successful in life. The basic leadership skills that all economic developers should try to acquire include communicating, planning, decision making, boardsmanship, consensus building and group dynamics, and delegation.

Communicating
The economic developer needs to be an effective communicator to several audiences, including government agencies, boards, prospects, and the public. To address these audiences, the economic developer must learn to write in various styles and learn to be an effective public speaker.

Planning
To be both efficient and effective, the economic developer needs to develop planning skills. These include time management and project management.

Decision making
The economic developer is faced with a dazzling number of decisions every day. There are proven techniques that can be used to help people make logical decisions.

Boardsmanship
Committees are a way of life. The economic developer likely answers to one and works with many. Knowing proper operating procedures and skills will save much time and frustration and can produce committees people look forward to serving on.

Consensus building and group dynamics
Economic developers are involved with many projects that require the participation of various groups, often including volunteers. Being able to help these groups reach a common consensus and then work together on various projects requires patience and tact. These skills need to be acquired.

Delegation
To remain sane and be effective, the economic developer needs to develop the skill of delegation. While delegation sounds simple and straight forward, most of us are reluctant to turn parts of our pet project over to someone else. To be effective, one must learn to trust others. Don't be surprised if someone develops a new and different way of completing the project!

Obtaining the skills
These are the basic leadership skills. There are others, but these are a good start. Most economic developers have some of these skills. They can be gained or improved upon from a number of sources. Many areas offer leadership courses. Universities, community schools, and private companies offer many of these courses as well. There are many self-help books, tapes, and videos available today. They can be found at libraries and book stores. Role models are excellent sources of information.

THEORETICAL SKILLS

Theoretical skills include those concepts that have been proposed, but may not have been universally applied to the practice of economic development. While theories are often shunned by "practical people", they are generally the starting point for all policies that are implemented. Since we will all run the risk of becoming slaves to theory, it behooves us to attempt to understand it. An understanding of various theories helps one to better understand the world and the changes impacting it. This allows one to do a more effective job of planning and adapting.

Since the actions taken are often a result of the theories one believes in, it is a healthy practice to keep abreast of other theories and challenge our own. Current theoretical areas the economic developer should be aware of include globalization of the economy, general development theories and specific economic development strategies.

Globalization of the economy
While this is reality and not theory, there are various theories as to why this has happened and where we are headed. Investigating these theories may change the economic developer's outlook; at the least, it can reaffirm current opinions.

General development theories
Current debate abounds on what will make the economy grow. Various topics include job training, tax abatement, the money supply, free trade, and industrial policy. Each of these areas impacts economic development. The astute economic developer learns all he can about these theories to determine what they may mean locally.

Specific economic development strategies
There are various economic development strategies. The ones most commonly practiced are industrial attraction and retention/expansion. There are various pro and con opinions on both. Other theoretical strategies also exist, including tourism, retail development, service sector development, attraction of retirees, and the so call "third wave economic development strategies". An awareness and understanding of these strategies can help the economic developer formulate his/her own polices and strategies.

Staying current

To keep abreast on current economic development theories, economic developers can read the existing economic development literature. This includes *Economic Development Review, Economic Development Quarterly, Economic Development Commentary*, and *The Journal of the Community Development Society*. Current books are often reviewed in these publications. Attending conferences and workshops sponsored by AEDC and other economic development related groups can also provide insight. For a cross-fertilization of ideas, a good exercise is to spend a few hours cruising the periodical racks at a nearby university. You will be surprised at the specialized journals you will find.

PRACTICAL SKILLS

Practical skills are directly applicable to the everyday operations of the economic developer. They are the skills that allow the economic developer to apply theoretical skills. Leadership skills are a type of practical skills, but here the focus is on more direct technical skills. Practical skills are skills such as computer skills, management skills, salesmanship, and grantsmanship.

Computer skills

To be without a computer today is unthinkable. Most economic development offices have at least one, but not all economic developers know how to use them. Besides the basic programs for word processing, data bases, and spreadsheets, microcomputers can run sophisticated targeting, salesmanship, organizational, and mapping programs. By using on-line services and the Internet (our current international information highway), the economic developer can have contact with a multitude of services, data, and people. Faxes can be sent and received on the computer. Phone messages can be recorded on the computer. Even if one does not plan to use the programs, one at least needs to know what the programs can do. A subscription to a non-technical (or at least low-tech) computer magazine is a cheap investment to help keep one up to date on the latest hardware and software. Saving the magazines provides a data bank of information.

Management skills

Economic developers often have to manage resources - people, budgets, and equipment. To do so requires a variety of skills. Some of these skills are leadership skills, especially for interpersonal relations. Skills are also needed in the areas of budgeting/accounting, employees rights and benefits, hiring people, marketing, purchasing equipment, maintenance of equipment, and liability.

Salesmanship

This has been a traditional economic development skill, to the extent that many people compare economic developers to used car salesmen. There are many techniques involved with salesmanship and the closely related field of customer relations. In today's competitive world, appropriate usage of these services is expected.

Grantsmanship

Economic developers usually have experience in writing grants or developing other means of creating "innovative financing". For better or worse, many industries today expect some kind of subsidy. The economic developer must be aware of the various funding available and be prepared to work with industries to meet their needs.

This is nothing new. What is new to many economic development agencies is that because of budget cutbacks at all levels of government, today's economic developer may need to become a grant writer to fund his organization. There are various foundations, donors, and yes, even some grants available for those who inquire and know how to prepare proposals and applications. In times of limited resources, grantsmanship is not a bad skill to have.

POLITICAL SKILLS

If things were perfect, one would live in a non-political world. Unfortunately, things definitely are not perfect. We live a life of politics. These include office politics, local government politics, politics among local agencies and organization, and politics among our peers. Simply saying we hate politics does not help much, no matter how true it might be. So what can one do to address the situation? This following questions and comments are at least a starting point.

What is the mission of your organization?

All politics aside, the mission of one's organization should be the key driving force. It should be used to guide the economic developer and to inform others of what he/she is trying to accomplish.

Who funds you?

Who pays the bills? One must retain the respect and the sense of usefulness of the funding source. The funding source does not have to like the economic developer (although that is a tremendous help), but they do have to be assured that he/she is doing what he/she is supposed to be doing.

Who provides oversight and direction to your efforts?

This might not be the funding agency. Make sure you make a good impression with these folks. It is important to have friends who can speak for you. Do the same for them.

What agencies or groups do you compete with?

Try to approach this positively. If possible, share responsibilities - there is almost always more than enough work to go around. Always make sure you can document your work and results, and show any impacts if possible.

If you cannot work with the other organization(s), handle yourself professionally. Do not act spiteful or vengeful. Expressing these feelings makes you look immature and unprofessional. Do make your side of the story known and keep your board and supporters informed.

What other agencies receive funding from the same source you do?

Keep abreast of these organizations. Again, handle yourself professionally. Be aware of any rumors or signs of favoritism. Keep one's accomplishments before the funding source. Even more important, have one's supporters talk to the funding source about the accomplishments. But, use caution in selecting who represents you, and remember that anyone who talks to the funding source may comment positively or negatively about you!

Develop a good network

Do this both locally and at regional, state, national, and even international levels. One never knows when one might need something. One person I know keeps an index card on everyone he knows. When he has a problem, he finds a person who has faced it before and can provide assistance. Be willing to help your peers when they contact you.

Take credit when you deserve it

If you do not, someone will. Be ready to share that credit with politicians and others. Just make sure that you get some credit.

Try not to get intimidated by politics. At the other end of the spectrum, do not let it be the sole driving force behind your efforts. If this is the case, something is out of balance. Use common sense and professionalism in your actions.

CHANGE SKILLS

Change skills are an attitude, an attitude that should become a way of life. Change skills are how one uses the other skill areas to survive and manage change. Change will happen; how one handles it is up to the individual. Some ways to think about it are to become a lifelong learner, be willing to give up past ways of doing things, and keeping abreast of current events.

Become a lifelong learner

This is the number one skill one must develop. Technically all of us are lifelong learners: we all learn something new everyday. What is referred to here, however, is a more proactive role -- making an effort at learning. It may be by reading more, by talking with experts in a given field, by developing a hobby or by attending lectures. Although the economic developer must be a lifelong learner of economic development, he/she should not limit him/herself to this one field. In the first place, the field involves many schools of thought. Secondly, reading in other fields (what is sometimes called developing a liberal education) provides a cross fertilization of ideas and different ways of viewing the world. The more ways one sees the world, the more ways one can deal with change.

Be willing to give up past ways of doing things

Just because one has always done something a certain way does not mean that this

needs to continue. Re-examine the old way. Maybe it's still the best way. If it is, keep it; if not, change. Do not hang on to sacred cows for sentimental reasons. Likewise, do not implement change for change's sake. Evaluate the situation and make a decision.

Keep abreast of current events

What are the current theories? What new technologies are being developed? Once again, read well and widely. Challenge oneself to create various scenarios of the future. This mental exercise can prepare one for possible changes ahead, and make accepting them easier - they are no longer surprises.

CONCLUDING COMMENTS

As mentioned at the beginning of this article, most of these skills are not new. The problem lies in implementing them and then sticking with them. The economic developer who does both will have a definite advantage.

Site Selection: Corporate Perspective and Community Response

Phillip D. Phillips, Ph.D.

The primary goal of economic development programs is to influence corporate site selection decisions. Influencing the site selection decision is vital to attracting new investment and employment from outside an area and is just as important to creating new businesses and retaining existing businesses. How and why businesses choose where to locate is without doubt the most frequently discussed topic in economic development; it is also one of the most misunderstood. This article will specifically discuss the following questions from both the perspective of the corporate site seeker and the response by the community economic developer:

❑ What types of site selection decisions do businesses make?

❑ What factors control these decisions?

❑ What steps does a business go through in selecting a site?

❑ At what points in the process can a community development organization influence the site selection decision?

❑ How can an economic developer best have a positive influence on an area's chances in the site selection process?

An understanding of these topics is a prerequisite to knowing what an area's true strengths and weaknesses for economic development are and for designing an action program to improve its development prospects. Failure to understand the site selection process leads development organizations to spend a great deal of time and money doing things that will not materially improve their prospects for attracting and retaining businesses while ignoring important programs and initiatives. Failure to understand the site selection process can also lead to needless bickering and recrimination over opportunities that were lost through no fault of the development or-

ganization. Last but not least, an understanding of what factors are important in business site selection and what makes an area an attractive location is as important for retaining and creating businesses as it is for attracting outside businesses development.

TYPES OF SITE SELECTION DECISIONS

Start-up

All companies face at least one site selection decision during their corporate history: where should the business be established? This is true of retail businesses, manufacturers, wholesalers, high-tech businesses—all businesses. Because the start-up decision is made by all businesses and because it influences so many decisions that follow, this undoubtedly is the most important of all site selection decisions.

The start-up decision is, unfortunately, often ignored by economic developers. Generally entrepreneurs choose to start a new business in their home town, wherever that may be. Just think of the difference it would have made if Henry Ford had been from St. Louis rather than from Detroit! One important job of community economic development organizations is to help new business start-ups by making it easier for them to find financing, facilities, and all of the other things a new business needs.

Expansion

The second most common site selection decision is expansion—all growing companies must make this decision sooner or later. Expanding on-site at a business's current location is always easiest, yet it may not always be possible or desirable. Some businesses cannot expand because of the physical limitations of their current building site—there is simply nowhere to grow. Other businesses may locate expan-

sion elsewhere for a variety of reasons, often to be nearer their customers.

Businesses often expand at new locations because of the strong "pull" of operating advantages, such as lower wages, lower utility costs, or tax incentives. Unfortunately, some businesses also choose to expand in new locations because of the "push" of operating difficulties in their current location. As many midwestern and northeastern communities discovered, expansion by local manufacturing companies in Sunbelt and foreign locations with better operating conditions and costs was only the first part of a two-step process. Expansion at a new location was followed by contraction—and perhaps complete closure—of facilities in old locations. Bit by bit, they lost companies that had been the mainstay of the community. In business retention the community must make certain that it does not "push" any local business to locate elsewhere because of avoidable cost or operating difficulties.

Relocation

A one-time, complete relocation of a business, meaning simply pulling up stakes in community A and moving to community B, is rare. Yet this aspect of site selection receives a great deal of attention, partly because it is dramatic compared with the establishment of a small new firm. There were no newspaper headlines on the day when General Motors, IBM, or almost any other company was founded, despite their future importance. A relocation also gets a great deal of attention because it puts the issues of site selection and economic development—operating costs, operating conditions, business climate, and incentive—into clear perspective.

The nature of a site selection decision also varies with the type of company. Franchise restaurants make these decisions on a continuous basis: new locations are how they grow. Public utilities, on the other hand, are assigned their service territory by government regulation and so cannot relocate.

Major multinational corporations make site selection decisions within the context of an ever-changing "portfolio" of products and locations. A branch plant for such a company is part of a much larger strategy involving many different products, functions, and locations. For most manufacturing companies which are small or mid-size, the site selection decision is a rare and often traumatic occurrence.

CONTROL FACTORS IN SITE SELECTION

While many factors influence site selection, only a few are strong enough to really control the location process. A first and overriding control factor is familiarity and knowledge. For any company, a site is chosen from among those locations with which it is familiar. This is why most new companies are started in the founder's home town—the location he or she knows best. The goal of economic development marketing to outside companies is, above all else, to make them aware that a community exists so that it can become a possible candidate location.

COST FACTORS

Cost factors are generally the starting place in a site search, and for good reason. A business cannot succeed if it does not make a reasonable profit. Once profitability is assured, a business may consider quality of life and other operating conditions. Specific cost factors are described in more detail below.

Markets and Raw Material Sources

Market proximity is a major location factor for most firms. A few companies are termed "footloose" because their product does not involve major transportation costs for bringing in raw materials and shipping out the finished product. But even theoretically footloose companies—computer manufacturers are a good example—have many reasons to be near and easily accessible to their customers so that they can understand and respond to their needs. For retail, service, and wholesale firms, market proximity is the heart of the site selection process. For a fast food restaurant, the right location is one that has the maximum possible number of customers within a nearby area. Other decisions such as finding an available piece of property on a major thoroughfare, are purely tactical.

For some firms, access to raw materials is a key. This relationship is clear for a grain miller who must be near the farmers who supply the raw material. It can also be important for other types of firms for reasons that might not be so obvious. For example, many new food additives and pharmaceutical products are produced by fermentation processes that use the by-products of wet grain milling as their feed-stock, that is, their raw material. Thus, for many of these firms, being near a wet-grain milling center is a major location factor and this can be an important aspect of the economic development strategy for a community with grain milling facilities. Community developers must always look for "forward linkages," that is, for firms using locally produced products as raw materials.

Labor

Traditionally, labor has been the most important single cost and location factor for most businesses. This is still true today, although automation, rising energy and transportation costs, higher land and building costs, and other factors have made labor less dominant in the cost picture than it once was. To be successful, an area must still be competitive in terms of labor costs.

Increasingly, labor supply, productivity, quality, skills, and work ethic are becoming more important in a firm's site selection decision that simple hourly wage rates. Some of the reasons for this are demographic and economic. The number of new workers entering the labor force is rapidly declining. This decline, when combined with the impact of eight years of continued economic expansion in the 1980s has put a real squeeze on the labor supply. This is especially the case in areas such as New England which have seen rapid growth in the last several years.

Also, the increasing incorporation of technology in virtually every type of job from auto mechanics to clerical work to traditional manufacturing calls for better reading and mathematical skills and a generally higher level of employee competence. Education, literacy, and numeracy (the ability to handle arithmetic and mathematics) rather than low cost have become the new buzzwords in describing what employers are looking for in workers.

Unionization, which was a major factor in site selection in the 1960s and 1970s, has faded in importance in the 1980s for several reasons. Labor unions are weaker and less aggressive now than they were ten or twenty years ago, although this could certainly change in the future. Also, the sectors of the economy that are expanding most rapidly—services, clerical, and high-tech—are generally the least unionized. Site selectors have also become more sophisticated. No longer is the level of unionization viewed as a simple litmus test of community's labor-management climate. Rather, educational levels, strike history, absenteeism, turnover rates, and other pro-ductivity-related labor factors are more closely analyzed.

Utilities

Utility costs have become a more important site selection factor over the last two decades as basic energy costs have risen. Electric and natural gas rates have also become much more complex, with many specialized rates and with negotiated rates for larger users. For site selectors, utility territories have become "invisible states," and for companies using large amounts of electricity or natural gas the cost differences between these "states" can be far more significant than the more generally recognized tax cost differentials.

Sewer and water costs are only minor location factors for the vast bulk of firms, but there are exceptions. For example, food processors may require large amounts of water and may discharge tremendous amounts of organic matter, creating high BOD (biologic oxygen demand) loadings in their wastewater. For these firms, both cost and availability of water supply and wastewater treatment are important site selection factors. There is no more effective way for a community to halt economic development than to have a sewer moratorium.

Increasingly, high quality, high capacity telephone service is a location factor. Some facilities, such as order fulfillment centers, need high volume, voice-grade communications, while others, such as branch manufacturing plants, depend on data transmissions of everything from orders to payroll. Smaller communities and rural areas—especially those not served by major telephone companies—are at a disadvantage in trying to attract or retain the increasing proportion of companies having sophisticated telecommunications needs.

Transportation

Transportation costs are an important factor for manufacturing firms. Just how a community measures up in terms of transportation costs for a particular firm will, of course, depend on the firm's sources of materials and markets.

For a firm distributing its product from a single location to a national consumer market, there is a very regular pattern of transportation costs, with the lowest costs being in Kentucky, Tennessee, southern Illinois, Indiana, and Ohio. It is no wonder that most of the "transplant" foreign auto producers such as Mitsubishi, Honda, Nissan and Isuzu have located in just this region. After all, a freight cost differential of $100 per car will add up to $100 million in five years for a plant producing 200,000 cars per year. Yet many small communities from Minnesota to Texas to Florida worked hard to lure the General Motors Saturn plant and the Japanese transplant assembly facilities.

Taxes and Business Climate

Taxes are a much less important and a more complex site selection factor than is commonly recognized. Taxes generally account for only a few percent of the total operating cost of a facility and can be easily overwhelmed by other cost factors, but taxes are discussed a great deal, for two reasons: (1) they are visible—a company gets a bill, and (2) they are negotiable—a company can try to lower this cost factor through incentives.

Because businesses vary tremendously, no single "best tax climate" exists. Some states and communities tax real property heavily, which is a problem for a manufacturing firm with very expensive plant facilities, but not a problem for a computer software firm that has few real property assets. Other states tax corporate income heavily, which is more of a problem for established, profitable firms than new start-ups. Franchise taxes, inventory taxes, and a host of others also influence different firms — or even different facilities of the same firm — differently. Thus a site search must carefully evaluate how the tax structure of a particular state and community relates to the corporation's specific characteristics and the nature of the specific facility being located.

Municipal, township, special district, and county taxes especially influence site selection when the issue gets down to particular parcels. At this point, as a firm is comparing site A in a community to site B in a community a few miles away, local taxes and tax incentives can become an important factor even though locally variable taxes are generally only a fraction of a percent of total costs. The site selection process narrows the field of communities under consideration to only those locations that score very well on other cost and operating condition factors and as a result even a relatively small tax cost difference can be decisive in site selection.

NON-COST FACTORS

Non-cost factors are also important in site selection. Most significant among them are access to specialized suppliers, access to training facilities, environmental regulations, and quality of life.

Specialized Suppliers

Lack of specialized suppliers and services is one of the biggest hurdles that many communities must face in attracting businesses. Many manufacturing firms need specialized services, such as anodizing or heat treating. For non-manufacturing firms, general-business services such as accounting or specialized maintenance can be important site selection criteria.

Access To Training Facilities

For many firms, access to community college training programs is an important factor and will be evaluated with special care. A few firms are also highly concerned about the availability of college training and postgraduate education for managerial personnel. Given the increasing need for high quality, well-educated employees, virtually all firms are now closely scrutinizing the quality of local primary and secondary education, especially in terms of providing basic skills in reading and mathematics.

Environmental Regulation

Environmental regulations are not a controlling factor for the overwhelming majority of site selection decisions. But they are crucial for a few decisions and are likely to become more important in the next several years. Environmental questions center around four issues: (1) air emissions, (2) wastewater discharge, (3) solid waste, and (4) disposal of toxic and hazardous wastes. The issue of environmental regulation is far too complex to deal with in detail here, but a few general comments are relevant and possible.

The environment is likely to become a more important issue in site selection in the future for several reasons. The U.S. Environmental Protection Agency continues to develop more stringent standards for control of pollution and toxic substances. This, however, may be less important than the fact that many target dates for attaining various environmental standards established over the last twenty years are now coming due. Also, increasing use of technology in manufacturing has resulted in the increasing use of exotic and often highly toxic chemicals.

Rural areas and small communities are frequently at an advantage in having less severe existing environmental problems. Often they do not face the increasingly draconian limitations on development such as those placed on air quality nonattainment areas. On the other hand, small communities and rural areas have often been less sophisticated in dealing with environmental hazards. As a result, these areas are finding that they are the scene of toxic waste disposal sites and "midnight dumping." In a few cases, unscrupulous businesses have attempted to take advantage of a small community's lack of sophistication and desire to create jobs to operate hazardous facilities, although state and federal environmental regulations make this increasingly difficult.

Quality of Life

Finally, quality of life is an important site factor for almost any facility. Discussion of this factor has been saved until last because that is where it generally falls in the site selection process. In corporate site selections, a firm reduces its number of choices to a handful of "best" locations based on operating cost and operating conditions because there is no point for a firm to consider a location in which it cannot be financially competitive. While quality of life may have contributed to getting down to this short list, it is rarely the most important factor. In the end, however, a site selector is faced with several locations, all of which look good on paper in terms of cost and operating conditions. Needless to say, if the designated facility manager or other personnel who are to be transferred to a new location are on site selection team they will be especially concerned about quality of life.

Two exceptions to this generalization are high-tech facility locations and corporate headquarters. Because top technical and managerial talent is so rare and because these persons are so important to the future value of the company, the site selection decisions for these facilities are (or at least should be) primarily recruitment decisions. The location that will do the most to help recruit the best people is the best location, with cost factors being of only secondary importance.

Intangible Factors

The author's experience in site selection taught him that one cannot go strictly by the numbers. Communities that are indistinguishable based on statistical data can be vastly different places on the ground. One community may be neat and tidy, while another is unkempt and ill-planned, even though they have nearly identical income levels. Some communities have a high degree of community spirit, others are contentious. A field inspection of the communities and a meeting with civic leaders quickly reveal these differences.

No matter how unique and wonderful one may think his or her community is, it looks just like many others on paper. The difference between being the bride and the bridesmaid—between being number 1 and number 2 in site selection—is often quality of life and community cooperation. Remember, too, that community cooperation is more than just giving incentives; it is also instilling confidence. When a company "buys the product" by selecting a community as a location, it is placing tremendous faith in the town, its community leaders' truthfulness, and their ability to keep promises as well as to make them.

STEPS IN THE SITE SELECTION PROCESS

Any site selection, whether it is a branch plant location, a new business start-up, a relocation, or an expansion, goes through a predictable series of steps. Though the details will vary among types of firms, the basic outline is the same. Sometimes the order of the steps changes, and often a firm will go back and rework an earlier step because of new information gathered during the site selection process. In many cases a "no go" decision will be made at some point. The selection process will then be terminated, generally either because of changing economic conditions for the firm (declining sales or profits, higher interest rates, and the like) or because the firm learns that it had unrealistic expectations about the potential market for its product or what kind of costs or operating conditions could be obtained.

Often site selection is a stop-and-go process, which can be maddening for communities working with firms, whether they are local companies planning an expansion or outside companies considering a location. One day representatives of the firm are in a tremendous hurry—they want information or commitments and they want them by tomorrow. Then these corporate representatives disappear for six months while the project is put on hold, waiting for better market conditions, financing, or approval at a higher level of management. All one can do as an economic developer is respond as best as possible to requests for information and suppress the natural human urge to strangle someone who asks for the impossible by tomorrow and then appears to lose interest or disappears for several months.

Distilled below are the author's observations on the steps in the site selection process, based on working with many firms as a site selection consultant, along with comments about what a community's economic developers can or cannot do to influence the process. Just remember that not all site selections go by the book and that it is difficult to know just where a firm is in its decision-making process. Often even the identify of an outside prospect is not known early in the process, which will add a little mystery and intrigue to life. The steps presented here are for a manufacturing facility.

Step 1: Defining the Facility

This is probably the most important step in the entire process for a community's success in attracting or retaining a facility, because during this phase firms define both what they will produce and the basic requirements to produce it. Unfortunately, this is also a step that takes place behind closed doors far from the eyes of economic developers.

Within this general phase a company or entrepreneur will define the following:

❑ The product or mission of the facility

❑ Managerial and technical skill needs to operate the facility

❑ Overall anticipated employment levels and skill needs

❑ Utility requirements (water, sewer, electric, and natural gas)

❑ Site and building requirements

❑ Supplier and service requirements

❑ Environmental constraints (water or air pollution, solid waste generation)

❑ Relation to other corporate and competitor facilities.

It is common for the definition of the facility to change during the site selection process as the company learns more about not only its own needs, but also what is reasonably available in the real world. Many companies begin with an impossible wish list of desires that they will never be able to meet in one location. For example, they want highly skilled workers and low wages or to be in a major metropolitan area but also to be in an area with a low level of unionization. As they continue through the site selection process, companies have to decide what is most important and make choices based on these decisions.

Step 2: Geographic Analysis of the Market

New facilities are often built to serve new markets. This was the primary reason for the growth of the Sunbelt in the 1980s. Growth of this region in the 1960s and 1970s created new demand and companies moved in or were established to meet that demand. Also, different facilities will serve different markets. In the example of the auto manufacturers given earlier, the market is the United States. Other facilities might serve a market region ranging from the local community (especially for retail facilities), to a multistate region, to the world. The local market is typically most important for retail operations, while regional and national markets are most important for manufacturers. A company will generally also try to forecast the level and geographic distribution of demand for some future planning time, perhaps five years, and will take this into account in determining the size and location of a new facility.

Step 3: Deciding to Do a Site Search

That a site search should be undertaken may appear to be self evident, but that is far from the case. In fact, many if not most considerations of building a new facility do not ever lead to a formal site selection process. Even if a company concludes that new product lines or expanding markets require more production capacity, there are a variety of ways of achieving this end. A company may renovate and automate an existing facility or build onto it rather than seeking a new facility. Increasingly, companies seek to gain new production capacity by acquiring operating facilities or entire companies. In some cases, however, the most reasonable solution is to search for a new location, whether that is starting from scratch on a "greenfield" site or buying a vacant existing building.

Of course, a business expansion or retention decision is simply a site selection process from the point of view of the community where a firm is currently located. The job of the economic developer is to convince local companies that they already have the best possible site and that they cannot find better operating costs and conditions elsewhere. One must also make sure that the basic requirements for expansion—good sites, utility capacity, trained labor, etc.—are available in the area.

Step 4: Freight Cost Analysis

An early step in a site search for a manufacturing facility is generally a freight cost analysis. In the analysis, the company can compute the inbound cost of raw materials at various sites as well as the outbound shipping cost to customers. This allows the company to narrow its region of research by finding a least freight cost location and determining the additional cost that would be incurred in moving away from that location.

The least freight cost point is of interest, but even more important is the range of possible locations allowed by the cost penalty of moving away from this location. Very high freight cost penalties are not likely to be overcome by savings in other areas such as labor or taxes, so high freight cost areas can be eliminated from consideration. For nonmanufacturing companies, other cost factors may serve the same basic role as freight. For example, for a corporate office with a great deal of personal travel, the cost and time required for executive travel is a major consideration.

Step 5: Defining the Search Area

Based on freight costs and market area a firm usually defines a search area for facility. A few examples are:

❑ Between 50 and 150 miles from Chicago—for a manufacturer of steel shelving

❑ Illinois, Indiana, Ohio and Kentucky—for an automotive component supplier

❑ In a city of more than 250,000 with excellent flying weather—for an aircraft manufacturer

❑ Towns of fewer than 25,000 within a triangle bounded by Houston, Dallas, and San Antonio, Texas—for a furniture manufacturer.

If a community is outside the area of search or does not meet the basic site criteria of a company, it will not be considered, much less selected, as the facility location.

Step 6: Initial Screening

Even within these delimited search areas, however, there are likely to be hundreds if not thousands of communities that can be considered as potential locations. At this stage, site selection is a ruthless process of winnowing the locations under consideration down to a manageable number that can be screened more thoroughly. This screening phase usually concentrates on several "knockout" factors, any one of which will eliminate a community from

further consideration. Knockout factors could include a minimum size of the local labor force, distance to an interstate highway, available sewer capacity, or any one of dozens of other items that are important for the particular facility.

Often the criteria used in initial screening are quite arbitrary. This screening is typically done without directly contacting community development organizations, because the information is readily obtained from the state, utility companies, or a computerized database. Despite its brief and arbitrary nature, this preliminary screening tends to be final; that is, communities do not reenter the site search at a later stage once they have been dropped.

A fatal problem for communities in the initial screening phase is lack of information. If a data sheet or computer database indicates "no data available" or simply has a blank for sewer capacity, a firm generally drops the community from consideration. Filling in gaps in data requires time and effort on the part of the site selector and lack of data is viewed as an indication of a potential problem or at least a community's lack of commitment to provide information; hundreds of other communities do provide complete information so there are plenty of other choices remaining.

Economic developers must recognize that at this phase a site selector's interest is either unknown to him/her or is very limited. When a prospect asks for certain specific information during an initial contact, it is usually for screening purposes. It is very important that one provide all of the information requested and to make it readily accessible. Site selectors do not want to wade through a four-inch-thick pile of information they did not request just to find the eight facts they did request. Thus, "jumbo" packets of unrequested information are often left unexamined and piled in a corner of the site selector's office in unopened express delivery packages. He or she will concentrate on those communities providing requested data in a concise form and will review massive data packets "when I have more time," which is generally never.

Step 7: Second-Round Screening

Beginning with a list of hundreds of communities and several knockout factors, the site selector can quickly narrow the field to 10 to 20 communities for more intensive investigation. It is often at this point that the site selector will first make direct contact with community development officials. The community developer

should recognize that his/her area is still probably only one of many areas under consideration and that the real work has just begun.

Often an important factor at this point in the process is evaluation of available sites and buildings. They do not call the process "site selection" for nothing! Unfortunately, many communities, including some very large ones, do a poor job of gathering and presenting information on sites. They have elaborate color brochures on the quality of life and a fly-specked hand drawings of sites and buildings. Care should be given to providing complete site and building information and to presenting it in a professional fashion.

Information on sites should include not only standard data on size and utilities, but also an asking price. Nothing is more exasperating to a site selector than a community or developer who is coy about price. A blank is not an answer to the question "site price," nor is the term "negotiable." Any firm worth dealing with knows that the price is negotiable. The question is: at what price is the seller beginning the negotiation process?

Step 8: Field Visits

Generally, a professional site selector will narrow the field of communities under consideration down to three or four on the basis of secondary screening and will then undertake field visits. A company doing its own site selection without a consultant will usually visit more communities, perhaps five, seven, or even ten. Often this is the first view the site selector will have of a community. Therefore it is important that everyone in the relatively large cast involved in local economic development do a good job and know his or her part.

A site visit is usually brief, ranging from a few hours to two days. During that time the site selector or selection team will want to meet with local employers in larger firms and firms within their particular business. These visits are most informative, because through them a site selector can learn a great deal more than factual information.

After a few interviews, community attitudes begin to come through clearly. Local businesspersons may tell prospects some things you would rather they did not hear but businessperson to businessperson discussions are the most important single factor in evaluating a community. Only a very naive site selector would not expect and want to hear the bad as well as the good and to hear it sooner rather than later. During a site visit a prospect will also typically meet with local elected officials and utility representatives and will look at promising sites and available buildings.

Several words of caution are in order in dealing with site visits:

❑ Don't try to hide anything. Problems will usually come out eventually, and if you have tried to hide them, your credibility is gone.

❑ Show the prospects what they want to see, not what the community wants to show them. Time is short in a site visit, and people do not like to have their time wasted.

❑ Be well prepared and use development allies. The power company representative will have the best grasp of electric rates; the real estate sales companies will know the sites best; the state commerce department representative will have the best grasp on how incentive programs work; and the wastewater treatment plant operator will know those trickling filters like no one else.

❑ Don't wear your prospects out. Many communities seem to try to attract firms by overkill and exhaustion. Scheduling too many interviews does not allow enough time for any of them and invites problems. Prospects who are kept going from dawn to midnight without a break will not be happy when they leave that community.

Step 9: Ranking Alternatives

In ranking alternative locations, prospects have the problem of choosing between apples and oranges. One community has low freight costs, the second a good labor force, the third good living conditions. How to choose? At this point, a firm must decide which factors are really the most important, because one community never has all of the advantages.

Eventually, however, the communities are ranked and the site selection recommendations will be made. These rankings may be based on an apparently rigorous weighting of factors and ranking of communities for each factor to produce an overall community rank. Often, selection of a site is a compromise among different individuals and interests; for example, the engineer who wants a level site, the freight specialist who wants good access and the designated plant manager who wants good housing and schools. These competing interests are not readily measured on a point value scale. The decision may just be a gut reaction by the corporate owner or CEO.

One way or another candidate locations will be ranked.

Step 10: Engineering Analysis, Legal Analysis, and Options

It is a long way from a recommendation to a facility. A company may take out an option on a site or building but this is hardly an assurance that they will be coming to the community. Prudent site selectors will option sites in more than one community so that they are not left out in the cold by an unforeseen problem.

Two subjects require special attention. First, an engineering analysis of the site should be made to assure that the drainage, soil-bearing characteristics, and other factors are acceptable. Second, a legal analysis is also important, because a flaw in the title or an unexpected easement can eliminate a site. Problems in either of these two could knock a site and possibly a community out of the running. A well prepared community will have soil surveys, title checks and other standard purchase procedures taken care of in advance in order to eliminate these as possible concerns for the site selector and move their community along in the selection process.

Step 11: Implementation

Even after the groundwork has been laid, all the analysis done, and all of the recommendations made, many site selection decisions stall out for long periods or fizzle out completely. Why? The most important reason is probably money or, more accurately, the lack of it. Obtaining financing is often time-consuming and uncertain for smaller companies; obtaining internal approval in large corporations can be just as time-consuming because approvals are often required from a board of directors and even if the company has plenty of money there are also many other competing demands for it. During this phase and the previous one, incentives will be negotiated. Superior state and local incentive packages can often tip the balance at this point if (as is likely) the first and second or third choice locations are similar in terms of costs and operating conditions.

As the time approaches for making a final site decision that may influence the future of the entire company—not to mention the individuals on the site selection team—many of the basic questions reassert themselves. Is the new facility really a good idea? Corporate politics may also enter the picture: some people oppose a facility within a company because they

think the product it will make is a mistake or because they believe the money could be spent more wisely for other things. In more than one case opponents of a new product have tried to kill the product by muddling and delaying the site selection. Perhaps market conditions have changed. Thus, there are often delays ranging from a few weeks to several months or even years during the final phases of the site selection process while these issues are resolved. Site options are renewed and re-renewed until either the project is undertaken or—all too often—dropped.

Step 12: Start-up

Even after the "go" decision has been made, there is a long process in getting a facility into production. A new facility must be constructed or an existing building must be modified to meet the company's specific needs, personnel must be transferred in or hired locally, and machinery and equipment must be set up. All of these stages can benefit from local assistance to assure a smooth start-up. Success is a smoothly operating facility, not an announcement. Even when the facility is up and running, your job as an economic developer is not over. It has merely changed from attraction to retention!

CASE STUDY

The best way to understand the dynamics and intracacies of the site selection process is to look at an actual example. A detailed description of the location criteria for a furniture manufacturing plant based on an actual site search is provided in Exhibit 1. This is a relatively large facility and an elaborate facility description, providing a good example of many issues you are likely to face in responding to a manufacturing company's site selection needs. Note that this is not a purely hypothetical example; these are the actual site location requirements of a company that was evaluating communities in North Carolina and Georgia for a facility location. An office or retail site selection would involve a very different list of site selection criteria and would require substantially different data from the community.

By the time the community receives a set of site criteria such as those presented in Exhibit 1, the firm will most likely have gone through the first five steps of the site selection process: that is, it will have defined the facility, analyzed its market, decided to begin a site search, done a freight cost analysis, and defined the search area. It may also have completed step 6, initial site screening, without the knowledge of communities involved. Most community developers do not recognize the amount of work that prospects or consultants have done before they ever contact the community.

A company may change its site criteria as it gains new information on markets or production processes and engineering, but one will not talk them out of a major criterion simply because the community does not meet it. If the firm wants a 20-acre site, one will not convince them that the town's 10-acre parcel is good enough.

In the example furniture manufacturing plant, the community responding to an information request would have a great deal of data to provide and would do well to consider some larger issues to determine if the community is right for the plant. For example:

☐ Is the labor market in the area able to provide 280 hourly workers? What impact will this have on existing employers?

☐ Does the local work force have any experience with a three-shift operation and will it be accepted?

☐ Does the community have trucking service capable of handling the very large inbound and outbound freight requirements?

☐ Does the community have a good available site or building?

☐ Does it have the utility services (electric, natural gas, water, and sewer) needed for a plant of this size?

☐ Are all the industrial supplies and services available in or near the community?

If it is decided that the community meets the major site criteria for the facility, getting answers to all of these questions takes a good deal of legwork, and typically a prospect or consultant will want information in a few days or at most in a few weeks. Thus, before going to the trouble of responding, make a "first cut" decision as to whether the community meets the site selection criteria. This does not imply a perfect match. No community is ever perfect for a facility, which is what makes site selection so difficult. For example, a company is not likely to find an existing building that meets its needs; the one in this case study did not. But there should be a reasonably good match between your community and the facility, and it should be a business you believe would be a good neighbor to existing business.

EXHIBIT 1
Example of a Facility Description
Furniture Manufacturing Plant

Product:
Laminate on chipboard furniture and furniture hardware (casters, pulls, etc.).

Labor (number):
Salaried personnel (includes accounting, engineering, sales, and general management). 50

Hourly Personnel

Receiving, shipping and inspection	40
Toolroom and maintenance	20
Casting, forming, and finishing	60
Assembly	160
Total hourly	280

Note: This would be a three-shift, five day-a-week operation.

Inbound Freight (lb/yr):

Zinc and zinc alloying block	3,000,000
Steel coil	2,600,000
Wire	1,600,000
Chipboard and plastic laminate	10,000,000
Other fabricated metal components	3,500,000

Additional materials, including corrugated cardboard boxing and plastic for packaging, would be obtained from local sources.

Outbound Freight:
Approximately 22,250,000 lb/yr to be shipped nationwide by LTL (less than carload) common carrier.

Scrap to Be Recycled (lb/yr):

Zinc	230,000
Steel	980,000
Plastic	Quantity Unknown

Site:
Approximately 20 acres.

Building:
Desire existing building of 280,000 sq. ft. including 75,000-100,000 sq. ft. of warehouse space and 15,000-20,000 sq. ft. of office space. Warehouse portions should have 16-20 ft. ceiling.

Electric Power:
Monthly usage 40,000-450,000 Kwh. Power factor .97. Three-phase current required.

Natural Gas:
2,000 Mcf per month. Noninterruptible service highly preferred.

Water:
Approximately 70,000 gallons per day, primarily for process cooling. Prefer municipal supply.

Sewer:
Prefer municipal system.

Solid Waste:
Zinc, steel, and plastic to be handled by a scrap dealer; chipboard to be handled by a landfill.

Environmental:
Will pretreat wastewater.
No known air emission problems.

Noise:
No problems at property line.

Industrial Services and Supplies:
Reasonable proximity (100 to 150 miles) to a variety of industrial supplies and services will be required. These include:
Mill supply
Platers (zinc, chrome, brass, nickel, oxide)

Packaging fabricator
Plastic injection molding (250-450 ton range)
Tool and die shop (steel stamping, injection die cast, and injection plastic molding)
Stamping shop (250 tons)
Rubber molding shop
Heat treating
Batch tumbling
Screw machine shop
Vacuum metalizing
Plastic laminate
Chipboard
Zinc, steel, and plastic scrap dealers

Community:
Should be within 50 miles of a hub airport.
A small community of about 10,000 population is preferable. The community should have excellent labor-management relations and a good supply of labor at reasonable wage rates.
Favorable state and local tax codes are important.

Responding to these site specifications emphasizes the importance of data as the primary community marketing tool. As an exercise for development groups, try putting together a response packet indicating how the community can meet the various facility needs outlined in Exhibit 1. Who will provide the various types of information needed? For example, who will provide information on the size, skills, and quality of the local labor force? How long will it take to assemble the needed data? Who will handle these duties as a backup if your first choice person is out of town, ill or otherwise unavailable?

CONCLUSION

The best way for a town's leaders to succeed in locating a facility is to think not in terms of the community's interests and not even as an economic developer, but rather as a prospect. By recognizing the site selector's motivations and needs and by understanding the site selection process, the economic developer can avoid many pitfalls—for example spending time and effort trying to attract a firm when the area has virtually no chance of success, providing not enough or too much information, or not meeting the prospect's needs. A more widespread understanding of the steps in the site selection process and the many reasons that a company may choose another community that best meets its needs can also help to prevent needless recrimination and bickering among those involved in economic development in those many instances when your community is not chosen.

The Role Of Service Activity in Regional Economic Growth

J. Craig Davis, Ph. D.
Thomas A. Hutton, Ph. D.

We do not yet understand much about the service economy: what does it do? what is its relation to material production? what are its forms of institutional organization? what is its relation to international trade: how is its productivity to be measured? and what, for goodness sake, are all those people doing in those burgeoning metropolitan downtowns? (Alonso 1989: 225)

INTRODUCTION

Many urban areas in North America were established as manufacturing centers in the nineteenth century and subsequently matured during the high point of mass production toward the middle of the present century. In this period the classic "industrial city" (e.g., Pittsburgh, Chicago, Detroit in the U.S.; Toronto, Montreal, Hamilton in Canada) were clearly in ascendance. This relationship between industrial expansion and urban growth had a naturally powerful influence on models of urban and regional development and, in turn, on development policy and practice.

Over the past quarter century, however, the economies of most North American cities have been fundamentally transformed by processes of structural change that have been characterized by a long term shift of capital and labour from standard production to high technology industry and, in particular, service activities. In a report summarizing a two-year study of the role of tertiary (or service) industries in metropolitan growth and development. Daniels (1990: 5) observed that:

It has always been assumed that the tertiary sector has an essentially benign status in the evolution of metropolitan economies...[service industries] have been considered as only indirectly contributing to their eco-

nomic and social well-being. This is now an out-dated and erroneous assessment. During the last decade the tertiary sector has undergone substantial restructuring. This has brought about a fundamental re-evaluation of its contribution to metropolitan development; the tertiary sector has become a catalyst rather than a parasite.

Accordingly, the role of services in regional economic development and in regional development policy is now in a period of reappraisal.

In an effort to contribute to this reappraisal, this article cursorily reviews the role of services in one of the leading models of regional growth and offers an analysis of the potential contributions of services to the metropolitan or regional growth process in terms of a simple model. Empirical evidence for one of the principal contributions, direct exports, is presented from the results of a survey of selected service firms in the metropolitan economy of Vancouver, British Columbia. The discussion is concluded with some suggestions as to how the public sector might promote the further development of metropolitan service activities.

METROPOLITAN ECONOMIC GROWTH THEORY

At present there is no single, generally accepted theory of regional or metropolitan growth. In his survey of the state of regional growth theory, for example, Richardson (1973) includes export base models, neoclassical models, cumulative causation models, econometric models and input-output models. Mills and MacDonald (1992) list as "five leading theories" export base theory, neoclassical growth theory, product cycle theory, cumulative causation theory and disequilibrium dynamic adjustment theory. In discussing metropolitan

growth and the role of services we will briefly review the role of services in what is perhaps the oldest and most popular of the principal theories, export base.

Export base theory has long been held to be one of the cornerstones of urban and regional economics. In its simplest form, base theory divides the local economy into two sectors: the *basic* sector which is composed of all economic activity whose ultimate market lies outside the local economy and the *non-basic* sector which contains the remaining activities, i.e., those activities serving markets within the local economy. Exports are defined as all sales outside the local economy (the economy of the geographic area under study) and thus include more than sales to foreign nations.

Implicit in this two-fold division of economic activity is a cause and effect relationship. The basic sector is assumed to be the active sector, the non-basic, the passive or dependent sector. External demand for the region's exports is the primary economic engine of the local economy. Basic employment and income expand directly with increases in the demand for the region's exports. In turn, non-basic employment and income are assumed to vary directly with that of the basic sector. As the basic sector expands output to meet an increase in external demand, more money flows into the local economy through the payment of wages and salaries to local employees (and, perhaps, profits to locally owned enterprises). A portion of this expanded income is spent on products and services offered in the local retail market (non-basic sector), thus expanding income and employment in this sector as well. Because of the primary role export activity plays in the economy, it is considered as "basic."

Thousands of economic [export] base studies of varying degrees of sophistication have been completed for regions and localities. Frequently, the economic base study divides the activity in the region into basic and nonbasic activities simply by industry type. For instance, all manufacturing activity is considered basic and all services, retail trade, and local government activities are nonbasic. Crude as this may appear, the technique has been used to provide economic base studies for hundreds of areas (Emerson and Lamphear 1975: 130).

Because exports are so intimately linked in the minds of many with goods production, the nonbasic sector in a number of export base studies is referred to as the "service" sector. From this perspective, stimulation of regional economic growth originates solely in the goods sector, which consists of primary (agriculture, mining, forestry and fishing) and secondary (manufacturing) activities. Services are then stimulated by the spending from the increased incomes earned in the goods sector.

This view of service activity as passive and as primarily responsive only to changes in the export of goods production has undergone substantial revision in the past decade. To a large degree this reconsideration of the role of service activity has been prompted by the continuing process of economic restructuring which has occurred throughout the developed world on the national and, in particular, the metropolitan levels.

Reexamination of the role of services in regional development has emphasized the heterogeneity of the service activity and has led to the current view that particular service activities make important direct and indirect contributions to export development. Empirical research on regional economies in recent years has strongly supported this view and, moreover, contributed significantly to its formulation.[1]

SERVICES AS AN ENGINE OF METROPOLITAN ECONOMIC GROWTH

Because of the increasing attention directed to service activities, a number of taxonomies have been proposed by economists (see, e.g., Bailly et al., 1987; Coffey, 1991; Harrington, 1992). For our purposes, the taxonomy established by the Economic Council of Canada is sufficient in that it emphasizes both the diversity of the service sector and distinguishes those services that are the principal contributors to the economic growth process.

Table 1 divides service activities into three major groups, each of which has its own distinctive characteristics, employment pattern, and role in the economic growth process. The principal divisions are the dynamic services, the traditional services, and the nonmarket services.

TABLE 1
A Typology of Service Activities

Dynamic services
Finance, Insurance and Real Estate
Business Services
Transport & Storage
Communication and Utilities
Wholesale trade

Traditional services
Retail Trade
Accommodation, Food and Beverage
Amusement and Recreation
Personal Services

Nonmarket services
Education
Health Services
Social Services
Public Administration

Source: Economic Council of Canada, 1991.

The dynamic services are composed of the producer services (finance, insurance and real estate; business services) and the distributive services (transport and storage; communications and utilities; wholesale trade). These services have been labeled "dynamic" by the Economic Council because they are generally the high value-added, high growth industries that are involved in globally competitive markets. They are increasingly exported and shape to a considerable degree the international competitiveness of goods production.

In the Council's view the traditional services are the more "garden variety" commercial services. Compared to the dynamic services, they tend to be lower value-added, less subject to technological change, and less rapidly expanding. While this observation applies to the services as a group, there are exceptions (e.g., the fast-food industry, electronic home shopping, and tourism services in some areas).

The nonmarket services are those service activities that are primarily generated outside the market place under the control and supervision of the public sector. While these services are not directly subject to the competitive pressures of the private sector, increasing attention is being directed to the influence of management practices, technological change and productivity growth in these activities.

In light of this typology of service activities, the potential contributions of service activities to the regional growth process may now be considered in terms of the following simple model:

$$Y = \frac{v}{1 - cs}$$

where
Y = regional income
v = the volume of dollar inflow to the region;
c = the marginal propensity to consume locally; and
s = the marginal propensity of local business to generate local income per dollar of sales.

Two basic determinants underlie the generation of income in a regional economy. The first is the amount of money flowing into the region, v. The second is the regional income multiplier, $1/(1 - cs)$, i.e. the average number of times each dollar inflow changes hands within the economy before it "leaks" from the local respending process in the form of savings, imports or taxes. Regional income Y varies directly with the volume of monetary inflow (i.e., with v) and with the regional income multiplier (i.e., with c and s).

The External Demand for Services

Traditionally, public policy has turned to the stimulation of manufacturing and resource extraction as means of expanding exports and thus the inflow of dollars into the local economy. In terms of the equation above, such action is directed toward increasing regional income Y by increasing v. There is a growing body of empirical evidence, however, to support the proposition that services, particularly the dynamic services, are becoming increasingly exportable (Daniels, 1990). The decline in many advanced nations of the ability of manufacturing exports to finance import demand is causing these nations to consider expanding exports via their comparative advantages in services (Marquand, 1983; Riddle, 1986; Petit, 1986; Daniels, 1987). Changes in the composition of international trade has to a large degree paralleled the shift in importance of service activities within developed nations. Trade in services, although relatively small in comparison with merchandise trade, is growing in significance.[2] An estimate of Canadian international trade in producer services is shown in Table 2.

At the provincial level, Stabler and Howe (1988) used detailed provincial input-output data provided by Statistics Canada for the years 1974 and 1979 to analyze service exports for the four western provinces, Manitoba, Saskatchewan, Alberta and Brit-

TABLE 2
Exports of Canadian Producer Services and Dependent Employment, 1988

	Export Share of Total Output	Export-Dependent Employment
	(Percent)	(In Thousands)
Transportation		
Air	5.0	3
Rail	31.9	24
Truck	21.2	24
Other Trans. & Storage	20.3	42
Communication	2.2	5
Electric Power	11.8	10
Other Utilities	0.9	1
Wholesale Trade	11.8	65
Finance, Ins. & Real Estate	1.1	7
Business Services	8.7	45
TOTAL		228

Source: McRae (1989) as cited in Economic Council of Canada (1990).

ish Columbia. The authors found that for the four provinces combined, service exports, which were between 22 and 44 percent of total (direct plus indirect) exports in 1974, rose to a level between 38 and 53 percent in 1979. In terms of absolute gain, the increase in value added generated by service exports exceeded that resulting from goods exports in Manitoba and Saskatchewan and was approximately three-quarters of the increase in value added by goods for the other two provinces.

At the regional and urban level, services have been regarded for many years as constituting the passive economic sector oriented toward meeting local rather than external demand. As previously discussed, the common expression of this view is found in the frequently employed economic base model which has traditionally focussed on extractive and manufacturing activities as the principal generators of economic development. In contrast, service activities have been traditionally thought to constitute the principal portion of the passive sector in the model (frequently referred to as the "service" sector), expanding only in response to increases in the exports of tangible commodities.

In the last ten years, however, empirical evidence of the export of services, particularly the dynamic services from the metropolitan regions, has continued to accumulate (Beyers and Alvine, 1985; Keil and Mack, 1986; Gilmer et al., 1987; Coffey and Polese, 1987; Ley and Hutton, 1987; Austrian and Zlatoper, 1988; Michalak and

Fairbairn, 1988; Gilmer, 1990; Davis and Hutton, 1991; Harrington et al., 1992.) The evidence is now overwhelming that service activities are increasingly exported from urban economies, thus directly contributing to the monetary flows into these economies. While it is the dynamic services and the tourism-linked traditional services that are the primary service activity exports, the contribution to the volume of cash inflows by the services demanded by those on retirement income is likely to become an increasingly important factor as the aver-

age age of the Canadian population continues to rise (Bender, 1987; Hodge, 1991).

Recent empirical evidence of service exports from the metropolitan Vancouver economy is presented in a later section.

Services and the Regional Income Multiplier

In addition to their contribution to direct exports, service activities generate income in the local economy through the income multiplier, the total regional income generated per dollar inflow to the region. The magnitude of the multiplier is a function of the technical and consumption linkages in the economy.

Technical linkages are the input-output or sales-purchase relationships between producing sectors in the economy. For example, when there is a direct export from the economy of a particular good or service, the exporter purchases a number of inputs from the local economy in order to produce and deliver the product. The local suppliers of these inputs must in turn purchase inputs in order to make their supporting production, which leads to further rounds of purchases. Each successive round is smaller in magnitude than the immediately preceding round because of leakages from the local economy (imports, savings and taxes).

Among the service activities, it is the dynamic services that provide the greater portion of the technical linkages. A comparison of the first round linkages of the dynamic, traditional and nonmarket serv-

TABLE 3
Direct Purchases of Services Inputs by All Sectors of the Metropolitan Vancouver Economy, 1971

	Intermediate Purchases	Percent
Primary Industries	11,368	1.2
Goods Industries	503,432	52.9
Dynamic Services (less wholesale trade and transport)	146,544	15.4
Traditional Services (less retail trade)	30,908	3.2
Nonmarket Services	50,958	5.4
Trade and Transport	209,128	22.0
TOTAL	952,338	100.1

Source: Davis (1976). Wholesale trade, retail trade, and transport are aggregated in the trade and transport sector.

ices in the metropolitan Vancouver economy can be seen from Table 3.

Over the two decades that have passed since the input-output study was completed, the direct linkages provided by the dynamic services have undoubtedly increased.

The second set of linkages on which the magnitude of the regional income multiplier depends is the consumption linkages. Consumption linkages are the sales of goods and services to local consumers. While the dominant contribution among the services to the technical linkages are the dynamic services, it is the traditional services that are of relatively greater importance in forming the consumption linkages, as can be seen from Table 3.

The magnitude of the regional income multiplier is increased whenever the technical or consumption linkages are increased. An expansion of linkages may result from product innovation (new sets of technical and consumption linkages) or from import substitution (the replacement of linkages to external economies with linkages to the local economy). In either case, the regional income multiplier is expanded by an increase in the magnitude of c, the marginal propensity to consume locally, in the equation given earlier.

Services and Productivity

Services constitute a large and critical portion of the inputs both to goods and service activities (*Statistics Canada, 1991*). Complexity in production processes continues to increase, i.e. the linkages between economic activities continue to expand (Cohen and Sysman, 1987). Services, particularly the dynamic services, are vital among these linkages. Increases in the productivity and quality of these services will in turn increase the productivity of the economic activities to which they serve as inputs. In the long run, the competitiveness of a region's production vis-a-vis other regions will depend in large part on the productivity of its expanding employment in the services.

In its study of sectoral interdependencies, the Economic Council of Canada (1991: 39) concludes that:

goods producers are highly dependent on services as large and important sources of intermediate inputs. Consequently, the quality (and cost) of those service inputs will have a critical impact on the competitiveness of the goods sector, and that competitiveness will ultimately determine whether the goods sector grows.

The argument applies as well to the dynamic services themselves. For example, the increases in productivity of these service activities shown in Table 3 are undoubtedly attributable in large part to the infusion of computer and telecommunications technology into these services. Productivity in the legal, management consulting, accounting, engineering spheres — to name but a few — has been enhanced by the various applications of computer hardware and software. Advances in the quality (i.e., productivity) of these particular goods are the results of improved information services (the services of engineers, programmers, lawyers, accountants, consultants, etc.) that are inputs into the production process. The dynamic services are increasingly a key factor in the determination of economic growth across all sectors.

The growth of producer services in part of the process of capital deepening in society which has been the source of ever-increasing productivity and living standards in Canada. In particular, the accumulation of human capital in the form of education and of knowledge in the form of technical know-how has been accompanied by the growth of specialized firms and professionals. These agents sell their services to others who use them to increase the productivity of their factor inputs. Seen in the broad context of overall development…, the process of capital deepening is typically accompanied by increased specialization, of which service sector growth is an important manifestation (Gruebel and Walker 1989:258)

In terms of the equation above, increases in productivity originating in the service sector can increase regional income Y in two principal ways. If the beneficiary of the increased labour productivity is serving the local market, an increase in s, the propensity to generate a dollar of income per dollar of local sales, may result. If increased productivity occurs in a local firm serving the export market, Y may be expanded by the increase in v, the volume of cash inflow. The augmented inflow in this case is increased export revenue and perhaps, as well, an increased inflow of investment funds.

REGIONAL SERVICE EXPORTS: EMPIRICAL EVIDENCE FROM VANCOUVER, B.C.

Metropolitan Vancouver with a current population of 1.8 million is Canada's third largest urban area (behind Toronto and Montreal) and is the largest metropolitan area in the province of British Columbia. The regional economy of Vancouver encompasses a diversity of activities but is distinguished from other regions of the province by its complex of interdependent producer or 'corporate' services, e.g., engineering, computer services, management consultants, accounting, financial, and legal services (Davis and Hutton, 1989; Ley and Hutton, 1987). In contrast, the metropolitan economy of Victoria, the provincial capital, is based primarily on the public-sector activities of education, health and social services, and government administration. The regions in the remainder of the province are distinguished by a relative dependence on resource-based, primary industries (forestry, mining, agriculture and fishing).

Although there is evidence that economic ties between Vancouver and the rest of the province remain very strong (Davis 1993), there has undoubtedly been a substantial reorientation of the Vancouver economy from its traditional role as a service centre for the rest of the province to its position in the increasingly interdependent urban nodes of the emerging economy of the Pacific Rim. As its service sector has gained in prominence (see Table 4), Vancouver has experienced a steadily expanding share of total provincial employment. By January 1991, 55 percent of the jobs in the province were in the metropolitan Vancouver economy, up from 53 percent a year ago. This trend has been relatively steady since 1984, when Vancouver's share of provincial employment was 48%.

TABLE 4
Growth of Selected Vancouver Service Activities, 1981-1991

	Employment 1991 (1000)	Percent Change 1981-1991
Bus. Serv.	72.5	65.5
Accom./Food	54.0	57.4
Health	78.4	50.2
Education	52.8	36.4
Trade	52.0	19.3
F.I.R.E.	55.7	16.8
TOTAL ECONOMY	812.9	26.4

Source: Adapted from Kunin and Knauf (1992: 16).

In 1990 an effort was made to determine the proportion of output exported from selected sectors of the Vancouver economy, as well as the destinations of the exports. A questionnaire survey by post was jointly undertaken by the City of Vancouver Economic Development Office and the University of British Columbia School of Community and Regional Planning.[3] The survey was of several hundred firms, principally producer services and technology-intensive manufacturing. The results reported here focus on the 251 responses from the producer services.

A principal focus of the survey was engineering services, a sector of the economy which has not received the attention in studies of restructuring compared with other producer services such as finance, real estate and insurance, legal services, advertising, accounting, and management consulting. Like the other producer service activities, however, engineering services are experiencing economic globalization and are increasingly exported.

Present Markets

An estimation was requested of the approximate percentages of current sales to clients located in metropolitan Vancouver, Victoria, the remainder of British Columbia, the rest of Canada, U.S., U.K./Western Europe, Asia-Pacific, and elsewhere. The responses of the firms surveyed, shown in Table 5, indicate the extent of the export orientation of the producer service firms in the Vancouver economy. The ratio of exports to total sales ranges from 24 percent for advertising services to 84 percent for computer services.

Engineering and advertising in Table 5 show less of a dependence on the local market and a great proportion of sales internationally. Table 5 also shows the greater importance of Asia as a market for the selected service exports relative to Europe, a result consistent with the ongoing reorientation of the Vancouver economy toward the Pacific Rim (Hutton and Davis 1990).

The results are particularly striking when compared with the geographic distribution of exports for service activities in the metropolitan Vancouver economy two decades ago. In the early 1970s, producer services were predominantly oriented toward the facilitation and administration of natural resource activity in the provincial economy. Exports of producer services were thus overwhelmingly to the rest of the province (Davis 1976). By 1990 a complex of interdependent corporate services was

beginning to emerge that weakened, relatively if not absolutely, the traditional tie between the Vancouver economy and that of the remainder of the province. Stronger links with the U.S. and the Asia Pacific had evolved and the direct exports of producer services to these regions have formed a critical part of these new ties.

The evolving links via producer services with the economies of the Pacific Rim are also evident from a comparison of the Vancouver service exports with those of Edmonton. For a sample of 173 producer service firms in the Edmonton metropolitan area, Michalak and Fairbairn (1988) found that slightly over a third of their production was exported from the region. Of total sales, 27.2 percent was to Alberta, 5.9 percent to Canada and only 3.2 percent was destined for markets outside Canada. Similar to the Vancouver study, the Edmonton survey was restricted to the commercially oriented producer services or

business services. The significantly greater proportion of exports from the Vancouver service activities, in particular to foreign markets, is undoubtedly attributable to the City's status as a major Pacific port and its expanding role within the system of increasingly interdependent Pacific Rim economies.

Future markets

Firms surveyed were asked in which of the above regions they expected to register their greatest sales increase over the next five to ten years. Table 6 shows the number of firms that listed each geographical market as a market in which a significant increase in sales is foreseen. Several firms listed more than one region.

What is striking about these figures in the context of service-led urban economic growth is the strong export expectations of each of the four sectors. In the Engineering sector, more firms listed the U.S. than

TABLE 5
Geographical Distribution of Sales by Vancouver Service Activity

(Percent)

Service Activity	No. of Firms	Van. CMA	Vic. CMA	Rest of B.C.	Rest of Can.	U.S.	Eur.	Asia	Other
Engineering	148	42.5	5.4	22.4	10.1	10.5	0.8	4.3	4.0
Advertising	49	76.3	6.6	5.2	6.0	4.0	0.3	1.0	0.7
Mgmnt. Consult.	35	54.1	2.5	11.8	21.3	5.6	0.8	3.6	0.2
Computer	8	16.3	1.9	25.9	16.9	19.0	5.0	15.0	0.0
TOTAL	240								

Source: Davis and Hutton (1991).

TABLE 6
Area of Expected Major Increase in Sales over the Next Five to Ten Years by Vancouver Service Activity

(No. of firms)

Service Activity	No. of Firms	Van. CMA	Vic. CMA	Rest of B.C.	Rest of Can.	U.S.	Eur.	Asia	Other
Engineering	155	33	1	30	25	39	6	32	17
Advertising	50	23	4	12	8	16	0	4	0
Mgmnt. Consult.	38	11	1	10	12	13	2	7	1
Computer	8	0	1	0	1	5	2	3	0
TOTAL	251	67	7	52	46	73	10	46	18

Source: Davis and Hutton (1991).

Vancouver as the major growth area. The latter was listed by only one more firm than was Asia. Perhaps reflecting the incipient talks regarding the North American Free Trade Area, six engineering firms indicated Mexico as the prime growth area for sales (included as "Other" in Table 6), equal to the number which look to Europe. Overall, it is clear from the Table that for the selected producer services the growing importance of the Asian market, particularly in relation to the European market, is expected to continue.

SERVICES AND PUBLIC POLICY

In view of the growing importance of service activities in the metropolitan economy, greater emphasis needs to be assigned these activities in the formulation of economic development policy. In this regard there are a number of ways in which the public sector might respond.

First, government may facilitate in various ways the export of services. It may do so directly by organizing trade missions abroad and by gathering and disseminating information regarding export opportunities and the steps necessary to exploit these opportunities. In the longer run, government may promote export development in a more indirect manner by working with local educational institutions, including the media.

Second, in its various efforts at promoting the urban area to attract new investment, local government might advertise the service activities, providing significant information on the development, operation and future prospects of these activities. The public sector might also support the targeted service activities by promoting trade shows, articles in trade magazines, and promotional films. Such efforts may facilitate not only financial investment in the sector, but as well the in-migration of skilled personnel.

Third, government might take action to promote the sharing of information and experience within the industry (Satterthwaite, 1992). Government might do this by assisting in the development of local trade and professional associations and the networking of such organizations with their counterparts elsewhere.

Fourth, government may support the development of programs that will impart skills to the work force that firms will increasingly demand as the process of globalization continues and international competition increases. In his assessment of producer services in the U.S., Beyers (1992:

16) concludes that regional development policy should:

> support the education and training system needed to provide workers with the skills needed in the more technical, professional, and managerially oriented economy that appears to be coming in this country. In addition, support for research that continues the evolution and development of information processing and telecommunications technologies, as well as support for the creative application of these technologies in industries in various communities, would appear to be high priorities. This would include assistance in marketing for small "niche" firms, allowing them to engage in the market extension process needed to take advantage of new possibilities for economies of scale in the provision of services.

The current status of regional economic development policy in the province of British Columbia is similar to that of many other regions: policy still largely favours the enhancement of resource-based primary activities and the development of secondary manufacturing. There is, however, a continuously increasing body of theoretical argument and empirical evidence in support of the contribution of service activity to regional development (Swan, 1985; McRae, 1985; Browne, 1986). Service activities are seen to play critical roles in creating local economic linkages that increase the magnitude of the local income and employment multipliers, while simultaneously adding to the diversity and stability of the local economy; in contributing to the productivity, and hence the competitiveness, of primary and secondary activities; and, in an increasing number of instances, in generating revenue through direct exports. Comprehensive and effective regional policy can no longer be formulated without an explicit accounting of the active contributions to regional development rendered by service activities.

NOTES

[1] Like export base theory, neoclassical agglomeration theory has traditionally focused on goods production activity and has been the basis for the development of industrial complex analysis of industries such as steel and petrochemicals (Isard 1975). Also like export base theory, it has not been until recently that agglomeration theory has been reexamined with a view to reassessing the role of service activities, which has largely been overlooked see, e.g., Henderson 1988; Mills and MacDonald 1992). Service activity has also traditionally played a secondary role in other regional growth theories such as product cycle theory and cumulative causation theory.

[2] World trade in services is now estimated to have reached $770 billion (U.S.) annually (Economist, 1991: 62).
[3] Since data are not generated with regard to regional exports, a quicker and less expensive method of estimating such exports compared with the survey approach is the calculation of location quotients. For example, in their consideration of services as employment generators, Polse and Stafford (1982) used location quotients to estimate the principal service exports of Canadian metropolitan areas in 1971. In constructing the elements of a location model with specific reference to producer services, Coffey and Polse (1987) also constructed location quotients as indicators of export activity. The same technique was adopted by Keil and Mack (1986) to identify export potential for service activities in urban economies in the U.S. Midwest. However, the shortcomings of the location quotient approach, in particular its tendency to overestimate export activity, are well known (see, e.g., Davis, 1990).

REFERENCES

Alonso, W. 1989. "Deindustrialization and Regional Policy," in Rodwin, L. and Sazanami H. *Deindustrialization and Regional Economic Transformation*. Boston: Unwin Hyman.

Austrian, Z. and Zlatoper, T.J. 1988. "The Role of Export Services," *REI Review* (Case Western Reserve University): Fall: 24-29.

Bailly, A. Roulianne, L., Mailat, D., Rey, M. and Thevoz, L. 1987. "Services and Production: For a Reassessment of Economic Sectors," *Annals of Regional Science* 21:45-59.

Bender, L.D. 1987. "The Role of Services in Rural Development Policies," *Land Economics* 63:62-71.

Beyers, W.B. and Alvine, M.J. 1985. "Export Services in Post-Industrial Society," *Papers of the Regional Science Association* 57: 33-45.

Beyers, W.B. 1992. "Producer Services and Metropolitan Growth and Development," in Mills, E.S. and McDonald, J.F. (eds). *Sources of Metropolitan Growth*. New Brunswick, N.J.: Center for Urban Policy Research.

Browne, L.E. 1986. "Taking In Each Other's Laundry — The Service Economy," *New England Economic Review* July/August: 20-31.

Coffey, W. 1991. "High Order Services in the Ottawa Region: Location Factors and Elements of a Development Strategy," Paper presented to the North American Meetings of the Regional Science Association, New Orleans, Louisiana.

Coffey, W. and Polse, M. 1987. "Intrafirm Trade of Producer Services: a Canadian Perspective," *Environment and Planning* A 19:597-611.

Cohen, S. and Zysman, J. 1987. *Manufacturing Matters: The Myth of the Post-Industrial Economy.* New York: Basic Books.

Daniels, P.W. 1987. "The Geography of Services," *Progress in Human Geography* 11:433-447.

Daniels, P.W. 1990. *Change and Transition in Metropolitan Areas: The Role of Tertiary Industries.* Report prepared for Metropolis '90, Melbourne, Australia.

Davis, H.C. 1976. *An Interindustry Study of the Metropolitan Vancouver Economy.* Report No. 6. Urban Land Economics, Faculty of Commerce, University of British Columbia.

Davis, H.C. 1993. "Is the Metropolitan Vancouver Economy Uncoupling from the Rest of the Province?" *BC Studies* (forthcoming).

Davis, H.C. 1990 *Regional Economic Impact Analysis and Project Evaluation.* Vancouver: UBC Press.

Davis, H.C. and Hutton, T.A. 1989. "The Two Economies of British Columbia," *BC Studies* 82: 3-15.

Davis, H.C. and Hutton, T.A. 1991. "An Empirical Analysis of Producer Service Exports from the Vancouver Metropolitan Region," *Canadian Journal of Regional Science* 14: 375-394.

Economic Council of Canada. 1990. *Good Jobs, Bad Jobs*. Ottawa: Supply and Services Canada.

Economic Council of Canada. 1991. *Employment in the Service Economy*. Ottawa: Supply and Services Canada.

Economist. 1991. "GATT and Services," August 3.

Emerson, M.J. and Lamphear, F.C. 1975. *Urban and Regional Economics*. Boston: Allyn and Bacon, Inc.

Gilmer, R.W. 1990. "Identifying Service-Sector Exports from Major Texas Cities," *Economic Review*, Federal Reserve Bank of Dallas, July: 1-16.

Gilmer, R.W., Keil, S.R. and Mack, R.S. 1987. "Export Potential of Services in the Tennessee Valley," *Regional Science Perspectives* 17:15-23.

Gruebel, H.G. and Walker, M.A. 1988. *Service Industry Growth: Cause and Effects*. Vancouver: The Fraser Institute.

Harrington, R., J.W. 1992. "Information-Intensive Services and Local Economic Development," Paper presented to the annual meeting of the Southern Regional Science Association.

Harrington, J.W., MacPherson, A.D. and Lombard, J.R. 1992. "Interregional Trade in Producer Services: Review and Synthesis," *Growth and Change* (forthcoming).

Henderson, V.J. 1988. *Urban Development: Theory, Fact, and Illusion*. New York: Oxford University Press.

Hodge, G. 1991. "The Economic Impact of Retirees on Smaller Communities: Results from Three Canadian Studies," *Research on Aging* 13: 39-54.

Hoover, E.M. 1971. *An Introduction to Regional Economics*. New York: Alfred A. Knopf.

Hutton, T.A. and H.C. Davis. 1990. "Vancouver's Emergence as a Pacific Rim City: Issues, Implications and Responses." Paper presented at the Conference of the Association of Major Metropolises, Melbourne.

Isard, W. 1975. *Introduction to Regional Science*. Englewood Cliffs, N.J.: Prentice-Hall.

Keil, S.R. and Mack, R.S. 1986. "Identifying Export Potential in the Service Sector," *Growth and Change* 17: 1-10.

Kunin, R. and Knauf, J. 1992. "Skill-Shifts in our Economy: A Decade in the Life of British Columbia," Vancouver: Canada Employment and Immigration Commission.

Ley, D.F. and Hutton, T.A. 1987. "Vancouver's Corporate Complex and Producer Services Sector: Linkages and Divergence within a Provincial Staples Economy," *Regional Studies* 21(5): 413-424.

McRae, J. 1985. "Can Growth in the Service Sector Rescue Western Canada?" *Canadian Public Policy* 11: 351-53.

McRae, J. 1989. "An Exploratory Analysis of Canada's International Transactions in Service Commodities." Paper prepared for the Economic Council of Canada.

MacDonald, J.F. 1992. "Assessing the Development Status of Metropolitan Areas," in Mills, E.S. and McDonald, J.F. (eds). *Sources of Metropolitan Growth*.

New Brunswick, N.J.: Center for Urban Policy Research.

Marquand, J. 1983. "The Changing Distribution of Service Employment," in J.B. Goddard and A. G. Champion (eds.) *Urban and Regional Transformation of Britain*. London: Methuen, 99-134.

Michalak, W.Z. and Fairbairn, K.J. 1988. "Producer Services in a Peripheral Economy," *Canadian Journal of Regional Science* 11:353-372.

Mills, E.S. and McDonald, J.F. (eds). 1992. *Sources of Metropolitan Growth*. New Brunswick, N.J.: Center for Urban Policy Research.

Petit, P. 1986. *Slow Growth and the Service Economy*. London: Frances Pinter.

Polse, M. and R. Stafford. 1982. "Une Estimation Des Exportations de Services des Regions Urbaines: L'application d'un Modele Simple au Canada," *Canadian Journal of Regional Science* 5: 313-331.

Richardson, H.W. 1973. *Regional Growth Theory*. London: The MacMillan Press Ltd.

Riddle, D. 1986. *Service-led Growth: The Role of the Service Sector*. New York: Praeger.

Satterthwaite, M.A. 1992. "High-Growth Industries and Uneven Metropolitan Growth," in Mills, E.S. and McDonald, J.F. (eds). *Sources of Metropolitan Growth*. New Brunswick, N.J.: Center for Urban Policy Research.

Stabler, J.C. and Howe, E.C. 1988. "Service Industries and Regional Growth in the Postindustrial Era," *Journal of Regional Science* 28: 303-315.

Statistics Canada. 1991. *The Labour Force*. Catalogue No. 71-001. Ottawa: Minister of Supply and Services.

Swan, N.M. 1985. "The Service Sector: Engine of Growth?" *Canadian Public Policy* 11 (Supplement): 344-350.

When Does Retail Count as Economic Development?

Robert H. Pittman,, Ph.D.
Rhonda P. Culp

Economic development means different things to different people. To some people, a new shopping center in the community is economic development. Certainly real estate developers would be inclined to include shopping centers in their definition of economic development. If a new shopping center "creates jobs" in the tenant stores, does this not count as economic development just like a new manufacturing firm moving into town?

The answer to this question depends on one's definition of economic development. A new shopping center certainly generates construction jobs and income, and conveys a sense of growth and prosperity. But does a new shopping center meet the more rigorous definition of economic development which includes the creation of permanent new jobs and income in the community? The answer to this question is maybe. Depending on the situation, retail development can create permanent new jobs and income in a community, or it can simply redistribute income which is already present in the community with very little net impact.

This article identifies a basic litmus test to answer the question of when retail "counts" as economic development. To lay the groundwork for this discussion, however, it is helpful to review briefly how local economies function. The economic base model of local economic activity is presented as a simple yet effective tool to analyze local economies. The article concludes with examples of retail activities which clearly count as economic development by creating permanent jobs and income.[1]

REGIONAL GROWTH

There has been a great deal of research and debate among scholars and practitioners over the past few decades concerning the determinants of regional growth and development.[2] In the most basic formulation, regional growth can be analyzed through the "Keynesian" model taught in Economics 101 which postulates that regional (or national) income and economic activity can be divided up into the following components:

❏ Purchases of local goods by private individuals in the area (consumption);

❏ Purchases of local goods by private businesses in the area (investment);

❏ Purchases of local goods by government organizations in the area; and

❏ Net purchases of local goods by individuals, businesses, or governments *outside* of the area (net exports).

In this simple model, income and jobs in a region can grow if area households start saving less and buying more, businesses increase their investment expenditures, or government agencies increase their procurement of local goods. While fluctuations in local household, business and government expenditures to occur, there is a limit to how much these local expenditures will change. No rational economic developer would advocate that households in an area should spend all their income and save nothing in order to increase the employment level in the community.

The real key to sustained community growth, then, is the fourth component of the local economy listed above; net purchases of local goods and services by persons or organizations outside of the region. When consumers in Chicago purchase electronic products made in Meridian, Mississippi, income in Meridian is increased, generating employment and population growth. The key for sustained community growth is to bring in expenditures from outside of the area and not simply redistribute expenditures that are already present in the area.

Reliance on outside expenditures for sustained economic growth explains why manufacturing firms are highly prized catches for communities. Manufacturing firms export much, if not most, of their products to other communities, states, or countries, which brings in outside expenditures. However, other types of firms can also bring in outside expenditures. For example, the economies of many major cities are heavily based on non-manufacturing activities such as corporate headquarters and professional services (finance, legal, insurance, etc.) which attract expenditures from consumers and businesses outside of the region.

It should be noted that to experience growth from an increased demand for local products from outside purchasers, a community must be capable of expanding local production. In other words, there must be no constraint on increased production such as inadequate labor supply, land availability problems, or facilities expansion difficulties. Most communities do not suffer from supply-side growth constraints. For most communities, growth is constrained by outside demand for local products and services.

ECONOMIC BASE MODEL

In the economic base model, activities such as manufacturing and advanced services which bring outside expenditures into a community are called export base or economic base activities, while other activities which do not bring in outside expenditures are called non-basic activities. Examples of non-basic activities include activities which are patronized mainly by local customers such as retail (including restaurants) and professional services (e.g. accounting, legal, medical). These activities usually do not bring in outside expenditures. Instead, they compete for a share of the income and expenditures which are already in the community. This is not to say that the services they provide are not valuable. The quality of life in communities is improved by the presence of strong and diversified retail and service sectors.

The non-basic activities in a community are ultimately dependent upon the basic activities. The basic activities bring in outside expenditures, which support the non-basic activities such as restaurants and retail stores.

The ratio of employment (or income) in basic activities to non-basic activities is used to calculate the economic base multiplier. The multiplier is then used to estimate the increase in total income in a community generated by an increase in income in the economic base sector. For example, if the economic base multiplier in a community is 1.5, then an increase of $100,000 in income generated by the economic base sector (say manufacturing) would lead to a total increase of $150,000 in community income as another $50,000 of non-basic activity (e.g. retail) is supported by the new $100,000 of income in the manufacturing sector.

The economic base approach has its limitations as a model of regional economic activity, especially in larger metro areas with significant service sectors. However, it generally serves as a very useful tool for analyzing the jobs and income impacts of local economic activity.

If a new retail establishment catering only to local residents opened in a community without an increase in basic economic activity, that new establishment would most likely not increase total income in the community. In this case, current expenditures in the community would simply be redistributed among existing similar retail establishments, assuming that the new establishment did not entice consumers in the community to buy locally what they had been buying out of the area, hence plugging a retail *leakage* which drains local income out the community.[3]

Now we are in a position to answer the question posed by the title of this article: "When does retail count as economic development?" The simple litmus test is that retail counts as economic development when it increases the amount of money available in the community. This occurs when retail brings outside expenditures into the community, that is, when it is a basic economic activity. In addition, new retail establishments which entice residents to buy locally what they had been buying outside the community, thereby reducing retail leakage and keeping more income in the community, also counts as economic development. In addition to the creation of new permanent jobs and income in the community, retail economic development benefits the community through increased sales and property tax revenues. Some com-

munities rely heavily on sales taxes in municipal budgets and increased sales tax revenue can be a powerful incentive to generate interest among local politicians and citizens in a retail economic development program.[4]

EXAMPLES OF RETAIL ECONOMIC DEVELOPMENT

Common examples of retail activities which fit the criteria given above for economic development are discussed below. These examples of retail economic development are not intended to be exhaustive. There are many other situations where retail counts as economic development. The litmus test is whether the retail activity brings in expenditures from outside of the community or reduces or eliminates retail expenditure leakages from the community.

Regional Malls
Typically, regional malls have in excess of 500,000 square feet of space and two or more major department store anchors. Regional malls, as the term implies, bring in shoppers and expenditures from outside of the immediate community or county. In more rural areas, regional malls can pull in customers from as far away as 50 to 75 miles (or much further in states where population density is quite low).

The community containing the regional mall "exports" retail services to consumers in other places. Of course, regional malls also redistribute some expenditures already in communities away from existing retail establishments. Vacant storefronts in the downtown business districts of many communities where regional malls are developed are a testimony to this effect.

Community Centers
Smaller than regional malls, community centers generally have between 150,000 and 300,000 square feet of space and include a junior or discount department store such as Wal-Mart. Power centers containing "category killers" such as Toys "R" Us are included in this classification. Community centers usually draw customers from outside the immediate community, but the geographic trade area is more limited since a smaller population base is necessary to support a community center compared to a regional mall. In more densely populated areas, community centers may serve only

local customers and not draw in outside expenditures.

Below community centers in the retail hierarchy are neighborhood centers (80,000 to 150,000 square feet of space, typically anchored by a grocery or drug store) and strip/specialty centers (50,000 square feet or less usually without an anchor tenant). These retail centers serve only local customers (except in the smallest of communities) and therefore usually do not attract outside expenditures.

Outlet Centers
More and more national consumer product companies are bypassing the typical retail outlets and selling direct to the customers through outlet stores. Typically, outlet stores are clustered together in outlet centers, which usually function in a manner similar to regional malls. According to Gruen (1994), between 1988 and 1993 the number of outlet stores and outlet centers in the United States more than doubled. As of January 1, 1993, there were 9,151 outlet stores and 275 outlet centers in the United States.

Outlet centers are often located on interstate highways or other major transportation arteries to attract the business of motorists who pass by on a daily basis. Outlet centers may locate in smaller communities with good interstate highway access, bringing in outside retail expenditures to these communities which they would otherwise not capture.

Tourism-Related Specialty Retail
Tourism and retail development go hand-in-hand. Tourists drawn to a community for whatever reason spend money on lodging, food, recreation and retail products of various descriptions. In some cases, a cluster of specialty retail stores can become one of the major reasons tourists visit the area. Restored historic districts with specialty retail stores attract tourists and outside expenditures in many communities across the nation.

For example, Duluth, Minnesota brought new vitality to an economically depressed downtown by creating a program to restore historic waterfront properties and create a tourist/retail destination (see Rodne, 1991 for a discussion). In a variation of this theme, the small town of Helen in the mountains of North Georgia transformed itself into a significant tourist/retail destination by adopting a Bavarian Alps motif.

Most of the retail and restaurant establishments there feature Alpine architectural treatment and many specialize in Alpine-related products and gifts.

National Retail Specialty Stores and Restaurants Which Reduce Leakage

Many small- to medium-sized communities experience leakage of retail expenditures as local citizens drive to a neighboring town to shop at national retail chains (e.g. PayLess Shoes, PepBoys auto supply) or eat at national restaurant chains (e.g. Red Lobster, Applebee's). Attracting such national retail chain stores and restaurants to a community can prevent this type of expenditure leakage and create local jobs.[5]

Local Retail Stores Which Reduce Leakage

Reducing expenditure leakage does not necessarily involve attracting a national retail store or restaurant. Local retail stores and restaurants can prevent expenditure leakage also. For example, local consumers might be traveling to neighboring communities to purchase specialty clothing or jewelry when the local market could actually support these specialty stores. Thus, communities should make every effort to facilitate the development of local specialty stores where the local market is sufficient to support them.

Local retail stores and restaurants carry the additional advantage that any profits accrue to local owners, who are more likely to spend this additional income in the community. Profits from local units of national retail stores and restaurants are usually transferred out of the community to the corporate headquarters location.

RETAIL ANALOGIES TO INDUSTRY RECRUITMENT, RETENTION AND NEW BUSINESS DEVELOPMENT

In standard economic development parlance, industry recruitment refers to the attraction to a community of a new or relocating manufacturing or service company which is export based. Retention and expansion refers to keeping firms (especially the export based facilities) in the community satisfied with their current location so they will not relocate and hopefully expand at their current site. Finally, new business development refers to establishing and growing new business in the community through incubators, small business development centers, revolving loan funds, or whatever mechanisms are appropriate.

As an aid to understanding and classifying the above examples of retail economic development, analogies can be drawn between these retail facilities and the standard economic development terms. Retail developments such as regional malls, outlet centers and community centers with national stores correspond to recruitment of manufacturing or service firms because both activities export "products" to consumers outside of the area.

Retail activities which eliminate or reduce local expenditure leakages, including some national specialty stores and restaurants and some local specialty retail stores, correspond to industry retention because they retain income already created in the community. Finally, the start-up of a local retail establishment to eliminate or reduce expenditure leakage in a certain retail category corresponds to new business development. Just as a start-up manufacturing firm generates new permanent jobs and income from exporting its products, a new local retail establishment which prevents expenditure leakage creates new jobs and income for the community.

CONCLUSION

Retail counts as economic development when it draws in expenditures from persons or organizations outside of the area and when it reduces or eliminates leakages of expenditures by local consumers. Examples of retail economic development activities include regional malls, some community shopping centers, some national retail stores or restaurants, and retail stores which reduce local expenditure leakage. In addition to creating permanent jobs and income, retail economic development activities offer the additional benefit of increasing sales and property tax revenues.

Since retail economic development can generate the same benefits as "traditional" economic development based on recruitment or retention of manufacturing or service firms, it behooves the economic developer to consider implementing a retail economic development program alongside the traditional manufacturing and service firm program. Such a balanced program might generate more "bang for the buck" than a program which concentrates solely on traditional manufacturing and service firm job creation. A first step is for the economic developer to assess the local potential for creating export-based retail activity, and therefore new permanent jobs and income in the retail sector.

REFERENCES

Brammer, Rick and Tomasik, Jack. "Retail Potential Analysis for Local Economic Developers." *Economic Development Review*, Spring, 1995.

Devine, James. "Glendale Arizona's Retail Sales Tax Maximization Program." *Economic Development Review*, Fall 1993.

Gruen, Nina. "Revolutionary Changes in Retailing." *Western City*, May 1994.

Krikelas, Andrew. "Why Regions Grow: A Review of Research on the Economic Base Model." *Economic Review*, Federal Reserve Bank of Atlanta, July/August 1992.

O'Neill, Ann and Delmerica, Jennifer. "Analyzing Retail Potential in Rural Communities." *Economic Development Review*, Spring, 1995.

Rodne, Kjell. "Duluth's Revival." *Public Management*, March 1991.

NOTES

[1]This article does not attempt to cover activities such as tourism, recreation, sporting events, and other related activities which may also be legitimate economic development functions, even though they are related to retail. However, a few observations are made concerning tourism-related retail development.
[2]Krikelas (1992) summarizes in a non-technical way some of this research and debate on economic growth.
[3]See Brammer and Tomasik (1995) and O'Neill and Delmerico (1995) for a discussion of retail leakages.
[4]An example is the community of Glendale, Arizona. See Devine (1993) for a discussion.
[5]In international trade and economics, this is referred to as "import substitution" since local goods and services are being substituted for ones that were formerly imported or consumed elsewhere.

Community Power Structures

Robert W. Shively, CED, FM, HLM

Economic developers cannot function effectively unless they can answer the question, who runs their towns? Who REALLY runs them?

"Your town is run by a handful of people." When conducting workshops the author asks participants to raise their hands if they think that statement applies to them. The reaction is predictable: a few snickers, some nervous glances around the room, a shifting of feet. Two or three brave souls will raise their hands, then a few more, and finally almost every hand in the room will come up and the nervous smiles will turn into broad grins.

The inescapable conclusion is that every town is run by a small group of community leaders known collectively as the power structure. Webster's New Collegiate Dictionary defines it as "A group of persons having control of an organization: Establishment. The hierarchial interrelationships existing within a control group."[1] The author prefers a simpler definition: The leaders/decision-makers in an organization, more especially a community. This article will discuss community power structures from the vantage of personal observations over a 40-year career.

FORMAL AND INFORMAL POWER STRUCTURES

All power structures including those in a community have two components, formal and informal.

Formal Structure

The formal power structure is readily identifiable and includes elected officials, appointed government officials and leaders of civic organizations such as a chamber of commerce. The formal power structure is characterized by easy entry and high turnover. Like the tip of an iceberg, the formal part of a power structure is the part that shows.

Informal Structure

Existing simultaneously with the formal power structure is an informal power structure which may have far greater influence on the course of a community's development. Its members are hard to identify and usually shun publicity. They may move in and out of the formal power structure from time to time, but will retain their position in the informal power structure during their term of public office. Entry into the informal power structure is restricted and there is little turnover.

Dr. Roger Schmenner, professor of economics at Duke University refers to the informal power structure as the "town fathers" and writes, "Some manufacturers are less interested in the elected officials, who come and go, as they are in the town's establishment, the movers and shakers who frequently stand behind the elected officials and who may largely determine their fate . . . The view here is that the town fathers will determine how progressive the town is."[2]

Entry into an informal power structure is generally achieved by one of four routes.

☐ Status - These people attain their influence by virtue of family prominence, positions held, past achievements or personal prestige.

☐ Wealth - Never underestimate the role of money in attaining influence.

☐ Expertise - Lawyers, bankers, entrepreneurs, accountants, etc., are influential because of their specific knowledge and abilities. They do not inherit influence; they earn it.

☐ Charisma - Some leaders gain power and influence by having such unique qualities of personal magnetism that people naturally follow them, often with blind devotion.

Community leadership, which is strongly linked to the composition of the informal structure, generally runs in generational cycles of 20 to 25 years. A generation of strong leaders is usually followed by a generation of weak leaders and vice versa. Although the author knows of no empirical research that supports this conclusion, it makes sense. Informal power structure members are usually of the same age group. They know each other socially, belong to the same clubs and have similar life styles. Acceptance into an informal power structure is difficult; members support each other and do not like dilution of their power. Consequently, their successors have little opportunity to experience inner circle leadership. When the old generation passes the torch, if they do at all, the new leaders flounder as they wade in unfamiliar waters.

Identifying Informal Power Structure Members

Economic developers must be able to identify the town's informal leaders. This is no easy task, particularly if the economic developer is new to the community. The North Central Regional Extension Service (in Iowa) has identified four methods of identifying community power actors.[3]

☐ Positional Method - This method merely involves making a list of key positions in local government and leading organizations, compiling a list of incumbents and updating the list as changes occur. This is an easy method of identifying the formal power structure, but it has two weaknesses. It assumes the people in the positions actually exercise power, and it does not identify those power actors who operate behind the scenes and function on the basis of personal influence.

☐ Reputational Method - Ask knowledgeable citizens to list the most influential people in the city. If the "knowledgeables" have been selected correctly, many of the names will appear on several lists. People to interview include chamber of commerce executives, city managers, city clerks, utility managers, media executives and one's predecessor economic developers. It should be noted that some leaders may be single issue power actors. A person influential with the school board may not have an interest in city government, for example.

☐ Decision-Making Method - Study the history of several important community decisions to determine the power actors who participated in these decisions. Sources of information include reading minutes, reviewing press reports and interviewing participants in the decision. The same names will frequently appear on several issues, giving the economic developer a pool of leaders. By reviewing a number of decisions, it is possible to determine members of a general power structure and whether specialized power structures exist that deal with single issues.

☐ Social Participation Method - Develop a list of the active participants (officers, committee chairs, etc.) in voluntary associations in the city. It assumes that activists in organizations will be the same people who are active in community decision making. In other words, the power to affect community decisions is acquired through participation in the community's voluntary organizations. This method may be better used to determine future community leaders, that is, those working their way up through volunteer participation. The assumption that leaders of community organizations comprise the informal power structure is questionable.

UNIFIED AND SEGMENTED POWER STRUCTURES

Another way to increase one's understanding of a community's power structure is to determine whether it is unified or segmented.

Unified Power Structures

A unified power structure can be represented best by a triangle, with people forming the base and rising to a single apex of power (Figure 1). The apex may be a company, an individual, or a small group of people who tightly hold power in a community. A unified power structure is essentially a totalitariat, with all segments of the community subordinated to a single center of power.

The extreme example of a unified power structure is a "company town," usually found in the coal mining regions of Appalachia and the western lumber areas. The company controls the source of jobs and owns the homes of workers and the company store. All decisions affecting the community are made by the company.

A community may be dominated, but not owned by, a major employer. Robert and Helen Lynd studied Muncie, Indiana, in the 1930's and concluded that the Ball family, owners of the Ball Jar Company, dominated the decision-making process in Muncie. Ball Jar was the city's major employer, and the Ball family had extensive real estate holdings and major interests in all financial institutions in the town. They controlled the Republican Party and had considerable influence in the Democratic Party. The Lynds concluded that one family could control change in Muncie and shape the city's growth.[4]

There are many examples of cities with a dominant employer. Bartlesville, Oklahoma, population 35,000, is the home of Phillips Petroleum Company. It is reasonable to assume that little happens in Bartlesville without the blessing of Phillips Petroleum. Ponca City, Oklahoma (Conoco) and Rochester, Minnesota (Mayo Clinic) are other examples of cities where a dominant employer has considerable influence if not outright control of community decisions.

Sometimes a community is dominated by a single individual. The person usually controls money or publicity, a powerful banker or newspaper publisher, for example. In these communities, there is no question "who runs this town".

These are extreme examples. More often a unified power structure consists of a small group of individuals who tightly hold power in a community. They will agree on major issues. Differences are worked out privately. Once a course of action is adopted, it will be supported by all. The power structure is seldom challenged unless it gets far out of touch with its constituents. On the rare occasions when this happens, aroused citizen groups may change the leadership's direction through petition, referendum, public protest and boycott. When a power structure loses on a specific issue, it usually retains its power but will be more attentive to popular opinion in the future.

The author has observed a gradual decline of unified power structures and attributes this to several factors. Company towns are no longer profitable. The company can better invest its money in new machinery, modern plants and expansions than in employee housing and company stores. Many family-owned industries have been acquired by national firms that have little desire to control the local political scene. They are managed by professional executives with few ties to the community. They desire to be good citizens rather than masters.

Individuals comprising a unified power structure are, with few exceptions, stakeholders in the community, i.e., owners of businesses and real estate. Local businesses are being acquired by out-of-town firms with increasing frequency, especially banks, newspapers and retail stores. The managers of these businesses owe their loyalty to the firm, not the community. They are transitory and seldom aspire to leadership positions in the town. The remaining local businesses lack the resources, desire or ability to control the city's destiny.

Segmented Power Structures

A segmented power structure consists of two or more groups with parallel and roughly equal authority, each with its own leaders. It is illustrated by a series of partially overlapping triangles, each with its own base and rising to its own apex of power (Figure 2).

These groups, although having overlapping memberships, owe no allegiance to each other and go their own directions. Their leaders seldom consult with each other except when trying to form a coalition or when an external force or major internal problem threatens the community.

The triangles in Figure 2 are of equal size and height. This is for illustrative purposes only. In real situations, the groups will vary in size and power, and their relative strength will change over time.

Modified Segmented Power Structures

An extension of the segmented power structure is called a modified segmented power structure (Figure 3). When an external threat arises or an internal crisis occurs, the various power groups may temporarily unite behind a common leader. Coalescence under a single leader is temporary and holds together only until the common problem is resolved.

Clustered Segmented Power Structures

Unified, segmented and modified segmented power structures are relatively simplistic vehicles for community leadership. As cities become larger and more diverse, their problems and their decision-making processes increase in complexity. Power structures in most metropolitan areas have evolved into a further extension of a segmented power structure which the author calls a "clustered segmented power structure." Figure 4 illustrates the complex inter-relationships that exist in major cities.

The outer triangle represents the entire metropolitan area. The large inner triangle represents the central power structure, a relatively small group of leaders who are most influential in the affairs of the city.

FIGURE 1
Unified Power Structure

power

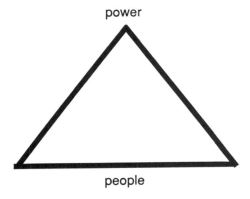

people

FIGURE 2
Segmented Power Structure

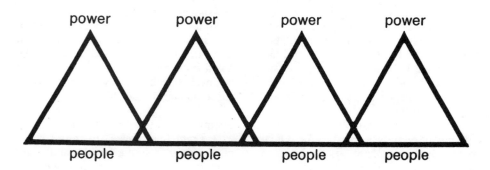

FIGURE 3
Modified Segmented Power Structure

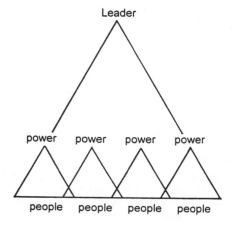

FIGURE 4
Clustered Power Structure

The small triangles represent organizations, ethnic groups, political subsets and other entities that comprise the city, each with its own leaders.

Consider each angle of each triangle as an arrow indicating the direction of the flow of influence among the different groups. Power can flow toward the central triangle or away from it. The central power structure can serve as the catalyst for uniting the city because it interfaces with all parts of it. It can also divide the community by separating its several parts. It can provide a means of access to the leadership, or it can frustrate citizen participation.

Sometimes a dynamic, charismatic or manipulative individual can unify the elements of a clustered power structure. Chicago under the leadership of Mayor Richard J. Daley functioned successfully, if somewhat arbitrarily, because Mayor Daley was a genius at manipulating the many power blocks in the city.

CONCLUDING COMMENTS

No type of power structure can claim moral superiority over another. No consensus exists over which is the best, the most

efficient or the most public-minded. The quality of the leadership in a city is more important than the type of power structure it has.

Understanding a community's power structure and the relationships that energize it, however, will help economic developers achieve their goals and the goals of their organizations. Successful economic development cannot be accomplished without the active participation of the power structure. In summary, the economic developer should:

❑ Identify the members of the power structure, both formal and informal.

❑ Determine the type of power structure in the city, unified or segmented.

❑ Get to know the players. Establish rapport. Gain their confidence.

❑ Discover relationships within the group. Which ones are friends? Which ones despise each other? Who can twist whose arm?

❑ Learn what motivates each member. Is it lust for power? Money? Political ambition? Recognition? A highly developed sense of social responsibility?

❑ Seek their counsel and advice. Obtain their support before pursuing a course of action. Fighting a power structure is an exercise in futility and greatly erodes an economic developer's job security and ability to perform.

❑ Never back them into a corner. Always provide a face-saving way for them to join up after initially opposing you.

NOTES

[1]Webster's Ninth *New Collegiate Dictionary*, (1989).
[2]Richard W. Schmenner, *Making Business Location Decisions*, (Englewood Cliffs, NJ: Prentice-Hall, Inc., 1982) 141.
[3]North Central Regional Extension Bulletin 59, *Identifying the Community Power Actors: A Guide for Change Agents*, (April 1982), by J. Tait, J. Bokemeier, and J. Bohlen, Ames, IA.
[4]Robert S. and Helen Merrell Lynd, *Middletown in Transition: A Study in Cultural Conflicts* (New York: Harcourt, Brace and World, 1937).

Power, Influence And the Development Professional

Eric P. Canada

When is an economic development professional like the President of the United States?

When he/she charges into a town built on tradition, riding a wave of excitement and expectation . The inauguration is past, Congressmen are judging Clinton. They are measuring his strengths and zeroing in on his weaknesses. They are quietly testing his determination and pressing to find out if he is willing to say no.

Clinton has the bigger job. He is trying to get a quick reading on every member of Congress. He is sorting the decision makers and leaders from the blowhards and obstructionists. Their independent decisions will form the base for relationships that will lead to success or failure for the new Clinton administration.

COMMUNITY POWER POINTS

All of life is said to be a game of power. The object of the game is simple enough: to know what you want and how to get it.

Knowing is one thing. Getting it is quite another matter. Generally, your interests are nobody else's concern, your gain is inevitably someone else's loss, and your failure someone else's victory.

This paradox is the source of a great deal of anxiety for the economic development professional. The anxiety flows from the struggle to *GUESS* other people's agendas and their relative positions of power relative to the desired change.

> Will _____ be for or against the project?
> Does it matter if we have _____'s support?
> What will it take to bring them "on board"?
> Where will the opposition come from for this project?
> Who should be involved to make this happen?
> Why is ____ dragging his / her feet on this?

All of your success as a development professional will be determined by your ability to answer these questions. To do that, you must first accurately identify the decision makers, influence peddlers, power brokers, and ringers in your community and understand their agendas. Every community has them. As a development professional, your job is first to be able to tell the difference and secondly to learn everything you can about the leadership.

There are at a minimum three separate power structures for the development professional to master:

> inside the organization
> in the political parties
> in the community

It takes time to learn these power points. However, without investing the time, you will be *GUESSING* where opposition will come from, who the supporters will be, or, who ultimately makes the decision that determines the fate of your project or program.

RULES OF THE GAME

"The only way to learn the rules of this game of games is to take the usual prescribed courses, which require many years; and none of the initiates could ever possibly have any interest in making these rules easier to learn."[1]

Herman Hesse was absolutely correct, it is a complex game and those in power do not want to make it easy to understand. Yet, as a development professional, we do not have years to figure out a community. My introduction to the community decision making process was at a U.S. Chamber Academy class. This class provided my first formal exposure to the practical aspects of community power structure analysis. This course and a lot of mistakes have helped me figure out the basic rule:

The development professional's influence is solely related to the job.

The essential distinction is the difference between power and influence.

❑ POWER the ability to make a decision and have other abide by the decision.

❑ INFLUENCE indirect power, the ability to sway people in authority.

Like the President of the United States, the development professional has a unique status in the community. Residents have the advantage of being their first. They have established positions. Many have family and/or economic roots in the community. And, the majority will be there to welcome the next person to fill your job.

This insiders' view of the development executive's role was driven home to me while working with a client group forming a new development organization. The members of the board had been picked. The by-laws had been written. We were meeting to determine how the executive would be selected. Soon after the meeting began, the head of a prominent family business offered the name of a local man for consideration. He presented the candidate's credentials as an "agreeable man, who will take advice."

The clear implication was that the candidate had no power base of his own and would follow direction from this man and those in power in the community.

The development professional indeed holds has a position of influence. The decisions impacting the community's future will be made by the community's leadership. The professional's role is one of advice, counsel, and support to these decision makers. Overstepping this line to make and enforce decisions has cost numerous development professionals their job.

POWER

Expanding on the definition, power is:

❑ the ability to make a decision and have others abide by the decision.

❑ the acts of going about the business of moving others to act in relation to themselves.

When a person has real power, all others want is *the* person. He or she walks in empty-handed because what they're bringing is not expertise, or information, but *the right to say yes or no.*

When I started in the business, almost 20 years ago, there were several generally recognized power points in every community.

❑ Bankers
❑ Industrialists

☐ Publishers
☐ Local wealth

Bankers had power because they decided who got money and how much. In many cases, their families owned the bank. They filled prominent positions in local business and social activities. Interstate banking laws, holding companies, and acquisitions have dramatically changed the role of bankers in the community. Today, few have true lending authority. Lending decisions are made by established company policy. Policy set somewhere outside the community without regard for community needs.

Similarly, the corporate merger and acquisition wave of the 80's has removed many industrialists and publishers from the power structure of our communities. Like their associates in the banks, they are now managers who must look to someone outside the community for approval. Such executive managers have weak roots in the community. These weak roots limit their role to one of influence.

As bankers, industrialists, and publishers have lost power, new leaders have emerged. New leaders include lawyers, doctors, and accountants who's business activities and networks make them prominent in the community. These constitute the power base of many a community along with the remaining successful family business leaders.

Another component of a community's power base is political power. Local elected officials frequently play prominent roles in local decisions. Generally behind every elected official is a political party organization. Sometimes, people within the political organizations are equally or more powerful than the elected official because they pick and help elect the candidates.

LEADERSHIP INVENTORY

To be effective, the development professional must identify the participants in the community's power structure fairly quickly and accurately. In addition to the decision makers, it is necessary to identify their advisors, confidants, sources, and obstructionists.

The larger the community, the more complex this process becomes. Since it is impossible to keep all this information in one's head, I find it useful to develop a matrix of players, their interests, and interrelationships. The matrix or leadership inventory looks like a highway mileage chart. All names are repeated on both the top and the left. Information, in code form, is placed in the cells where two names intersect. The legend explains the codes, i.e. R/republican, C/confident, N/neighbor, A/adversary, etc. (Figure 1).

An organized process will help shorten the time it takes to gather and verify the information for the matrix. Keep in mind the process of investigating the power structure is a sensitive matter. Recently, while working to develop a leadership inventory in a major metropolitan county, I had a fascinating dream in the form of a two panel cartoon.

First panel . . . 60's flower child tripping through a meadow gayly picking flowers.

FIGURE 1
Sample Leadership Inventory Matrix

	1	2	3	4	5	6	7	8	9	10	11	12	13	14
1 R	- -	AL		N	O		C		RSL	O			B P A	
2 D	AL	- - -												F
3 D			B - - -						R D					
4 D				IS - - -										
5 R	O				- - -						B P N			
6						B OL						AL		
7 d					AL		- -					AL		
8 D								IS - -						
9 r	R B		R D						- - -				S P	
10 0	O									- - -				
11 R					B P N						- - -	N		
12 R					AL	AL					N	- - -		
13 DB P	B P								S P				- - -	
14 d		F												- - -

Leaders
1. David White, Mayor, V.P. Kennet, Inc.
2. Winston Davis, Attorney
3. Claire White, President, White Trucking
4. Gary Maitland, Auto Dealer
5. Ed Burk, Councilman, Stock Broker
6. Typer Keith, Keith Farms
7. Eric Curtin, President, White Insurance
8. Cassy Burnside, Owner, Travel Source
9. Victoria Nolan, Socialite
10. Charles Sorenson, Owner, Structural Engineering
11. Jacoby Dickers, President, Lake Side Banks
12. Tom Acres, President, First National Bank
13. Daniel Levy, Attorney, Developer
14. Tom Ping, President, Topdeck Manufacturing

Legend
Politics: Republican, Democrat, lower case inactive
Advisor
Relative: Son, Daughter, Brother, Sister, Cousins, Spouse
Confidant
Ally
Information Source
Neighbor
Networker
Business Partner
Friend
Opponent
Opinion Leader
Benefactor

Second panel...control center, intruder alarms flashing all over the room as the flowers are disturbed. Guards frantically calling superiors.

Before the dream, I had spent two days breaking all the rules of discretion by innocently asking about people, their power bases, and relationships. Subconsciously the flowers represented secrets. I was imagining every person I called calling two or three other people to alert key people in their network of the inquiry, find out why these questions were being asked, and identify the intruder.

As consultants, we have even less time to learn a community's power structure. In this case, we had only a couple of weeks to construct a basic leadership inventory. The short time frame forced us to violate some of the rules of conduct.

BACKGROUND INFORMATION

The leadership inventory technique has worked for me over the years. It is built on careful information gathering. The first step in building a leadership inventory is to identify potential players. Sources of this background information include:

❑ personal interviews with officers and staff members

❑ news accounts and organizational records

❑ board lists and overlapping members
 — chamber
 — economic development
 — hospital
 — civic organizations
 — corporate
 —financial
 —associations
 — cultural
 — charitable
 — educational institutions

❑ governmental commissions or committees

❑ building fund campaigns

❑ members of boards for local companies

❑ exclusive club memberships

❑ family business leaders

❑ political office holders

❑ political party leaders

❑ locally controlled corporations

❑ political contributors lists (state board of elections)

❑ charitable contributors

❑ neighbors

❑ informal breakfast and coffee groups

PERSONAL INTERVIEWS

After identifying prime leadership candidates, it is necessary to determine what role if any they play in the local decision process. The best way to learn this is through personal conversations. You can never talk to too many people. But, it is more than talk. The process of constructing a leadership inventory is an investigation. There are specific types of information needed. The goals of constructing an inventory are:

❑ Verify players and their personal agendas

❑ Identify confidants and advisors

❑ Isolate obstructionists

❑ Trace information networks and how information moves through the community.

As a development professional you are on the phone or in meetings almost constantly. Use these chance encounters to investigate relationships. Bring up names in conversation. Ask how an individual helped with a specific project. Ask who was involved in a recent community project. Ask how important recent decisions have been made. Ask about the circumstances behind the decisions and the people involved. Limiting yourself to a few questions and using casual conversations help to reduce the perception of probing.

Arrange personal get-acquainted meetings with the people who's names surface most frequently. Resist probing too deeply in the first meeting. Asking "who can make things happen?", or, "who can stop a project from going forward?" will put your contact on guard. Unless the person volunteers this detail it is best not to pursue it until you have an established relationship. But, feel free to ask about people and relationships generally. Such inquiries are expected during the early months of a new job.

Also, remember that most people do not think in terms of decision makers and leadership. Therefore, if you ask who the decision makers are you will probably only hear about the most visible community activists. Frequency of mention is an indicator of a power point but it is not a firm indicator. The true power player often prefers a less visible role.

Make notes as soon as possible after every conversation. Then, transfer information to the leadership matrix. Note other questions as they occur for inquiry later.

Research indicates that people generally do not reach their power peak until after the age of fifty. The exceptions are those who derive their power base from a prominent family business or family wealth. But, as you observe the power structure, watch for the emerging leaders. At times, tension develops between younger power seekers and those who have the power. Major power shifts occur occasionally in a community as one generation relinquishes power and a new generation takes over.

Some communities try to identify and train future leaders. Many chambers of commerce run leadership training programs to help prepare executives for future leadership roles. When organized programs are not available, future leaders are polishing their skills in community based organizations like the Jaycees, Rotary, United Way, and a host of other civic organizations.

COACHES

Just as development professionals rely on technical advisors, it is helpful to identify people who are familiar with the power structure and willing to help. These advisors, coaches, or mentors can save valuable time understanding the power structure of a community.

The role of the coach(s) is to:

❑ provide and interpret information about the situation, influences, risks, and rewards.

❑ explain the nature of the players, supporters, opposition, and their relative strengths and weaknesses.

The coach can help:

❑ Ask the right questions

❑ Look in the right places

❑ Access the right people

❑ Provide an early warning system.

Begin the search for coaches by using development board members. But, do not be surprised if some will have little information to offer. Many executives are "non-political." Non-political does not refer here to party politics. Many business executives are not tuned in to the local power structure, i.e. non-political.

I have found executives with social services organizations and sometimes foundation executives can be very helpful during the early stages of defining the leadership structure. Like the development professional they are not members of the power structure. Yet, their jobs require them to identify and work with leadership. By virtue of their position, they take a more analytical view of the community than local business executives. Their role in the community also lowers the risk of asking the wrong person a sensitive question.

Gradually, expand your group of advisors to include others in the community who demonstrate a willingness to help. Select advisors carefully. Create an informal, personal board of advisors.

TESTING

Decision makers are people of dominance, power, and influence. They want to know who they are dealing with. Consequently, some will devise tests to evaluate your sincerity, loyalty, motives, and will.

On one large project, the mayor was a critical decision maker. The project team I was on decided to involve the mayor's brother who had political standing of his own as a county official. After the first meeting, he submitted a list of typed questions for our response. He used the questions to test our responsiveness. He wanted to know how we would respond and how quickly.

In another example, a friend took a position in a large midwestern community. Part of his decision to take the position was the personal support of the mayor. Shortly after taking the position, the mayor's assistant, who had also been involved in the selection process, informed the new executive that if he wanted something from the mayor, "You go through me." Since this was a new condition, the new executive decided to check with the mayor. The mayor claimed to be unaware of the condition the assistant had created. But, he did not offer to correct the problem. The mayor said, "you handle it." The new executive challenged the assistant's "authority" and proceeded to work directly with the mayor. Yet, overtime, the exec and the mayor's assistant became close friends. The mayor continued to be supportive. The new executive passed both tests.

CONCLUSION

Development professionals must work with and through community leadership. Development professionals need the help and support of members and the community leaders to implement the organization's agenda. To that end, the professional must be aware of the players and their interests. Time and experience in a community provides this awareness. However, a development executive does not have the luxury of time. Action requires preparation. The leadership inventory process outlined here is an excellent tool for gathering critical information in a compressed period of time.

Many power players prefer to operate behind the scenes, getting what they want with the minimum of publicity and fuss. This makes them harder to identify. Then there are others who want everyone to believe they make all the major decisions. These are two of the reasons a leadership inventory is useful to the development professional. Other benefits of a leadership inventory include:

❏ Identifying power base constituencies

❏ Identifying potential winners and losers

❏ Pinpointing sources of support

❏ Providing historical perspective

❏ Developing a sense of who talks to who

❏ Knowing where to test ideas.

Maintain the leadership matrix, notes, questions and related information in a ring binder. Over time, you will find it an invaluable resource.

After creating the leadership inventory, it is an excellent practice to cross check your board members. Is the organization sufficiently linked to the community's power base? Are the right people on the board? Are emerging leaders being represented?

Using this technique and information that surfaces as you interact with community leaders will quickly give you an excellent view of the community's decision structure.

The point of a leadership inventory is knowing who leads on which issues. This information allows the development professional to use time more constructively. Waiting until the information is needed is always too late. Waiting forces the anxiety of *GUESSING* other people's agendas and their relative position of power.

NOTES

[1]Herman Hesse, *THE GLASS BEAD GAME*. translation by Richard and Clare Winston. New York: Holt, 1969. 558 pages.

Organizational Models For Economic Development

William T. Whitehead
Robert M. Ady

INTRODUCTION

Over 10,000 organizations are presently involved in the sponsorship of economic development programs nationwide. How well these organizations accomplish their economic development goals depends on the availability of a number of key elements, including capable volunteer leadership, adequate funding, skilled professional staff, and a clearly defined action plan.

Underpinning each of these key elements, however, is the need for a sound organizational structure. A sound organizational structure provides the foundation essential for mobilizing support and developing fiscal resources. The experience of Fantus in dealing with communities throughout the United States clearly indicates that *there is no single organizational structure that is suitable for all communities*. Rather the organization of development efforts must reflect the needs of the community, the inherent strengths and weaknesses of existing public and private development efforts, and the particular history of development in the area.

Within this context, it is possible to discern key organizational similarities and differences, an understanding of which can aid in establishing the most effective economic development organization possible for a community.

This article suggests a framework for analyzing economic development organizations. Three distinct organizational models are identified. Particular attention is given to the public/private partnership model because of its prevalence today among economic development organizations.

The article also provides information and advice on two important organizational issues: the benefits of piggybacking a new economic development organization on an existing non-profit or government agency and the types of tax-exempt status for non-government economic development organizations.

ORGANIZATIONAL MODELS

Most community-based economic development organizations have a somewhat similar overall structure, consisting of a governing board that establishes policy direction and an administrative staff that carries out the board's directives. Within this overall framework, however, there is considerable variation.

A useful way to categorize economic development groups is based on the degree of private sector and public sector involvement in the economic development organization. At one end of the spectrum is the private sector model; at the other end of the spectrum is the government agency model; and falling in between these two is the public/private partnership model, representing a blend of private sector and public sector participation.

Private Sector Model

The private sector organization draws its funding and board of directors solely from those involved in private enterprise. Private individuals, businesses and local industry provide financial support. Organization board members typically include bankers, attorneys, accountants, industrialists, small business owners, real estate brokers, developers, and others involved in non-government activities. Many, although not all, chambers of commerce are examples of the private sector model. The board of directors establishes economic development policies which are carried out by an administrative staff. Exhibit I profiles a typical private sector model organization.

The private sector model offers three significant operational advantages. Its activities are not restricted by political boundaries. It allows maintenance of confidentiality on important issues. And it can speak effectively for the business sector's interests.

The major disadvantage of the private sector model is the lack of control over certain development activities that are growing in importance and require local government involvement. These include investment incentives (tax abatement, UDAGs, etc.) and infrastructure improvements (roads, sewer line extensions, etc.). Less than ten percent of the respondents to a AEDC organizational survey of 55 economic development organizations were private sector model organizations.

Government Agency Model

At the other end of the spectrum is the economic development organization directed and funded solely by the public sector. Many city and county economic development efforts are examples of the government agency model. The mayor and city council (village president and board of trustees in smaller communities) provide policy direction and appropriate all funds for economic development. A government employee (village manager, city manager, economic development director) carries out economic development activities and reports to the mayor and city council. Exhibit I profiles a typical government agency (public sector) model organization.

The major operational advantages of the government agency model are that it allows input from all sectors of the community via elected officials and it ensures direct access to government programs providing incentives and infrastructure improvements.

Two disadvantages of the government agency model are the potential for a lack of continuity in development efforts due to changes in elected leadership and the lack of meaningful involvement by volunteers. The AEDC organizational survey revealed less than ten percent of respondents were government agency model organizations.

PUBLIC/PRIVATE PARTNERSHIP MODEL

As the name implies, economic development organizations falling into this category receive funding and policy direction from *both* the public and private sectors.

Results of the AEDC organizational survey indicate the strong presence of the public/private partnership model among economic development organizations today. Over 80 percent of responding organi-

EXHIBIT I
Profile of Typical Private Sector
And Government Agency Model
Economic Development Organizations

Typical Private Sector Model	Typical Public Sector Model
Major sources of funding:	
Contributions of business, industry, and private individuals	Government funds
Governing body:	
Board of Directors elected by membership	Mayor and City Council elected by public
Legal form:	
Non-profit 501 (c) (6) corporation	Government agency
Economic development functions:	
Engaged in variety of activities creating, retaining, and attracting jobs and capital investment	Engaged in variety of activities creating, retaining, and attracting jobs and capital investment
Operational advantages:	
Not restricted by political boundaries	Direct access to incentives: property tax abatement, UDAG's, etc.
Structure allows maintenance of confidentiality on important issues (e.g., identity of prospects)	Effective in providing development infrastructure: roads, sewer lines, water lines, etc.
Speaks effectively on business sector's interests	Structure allows input from all sectors of community via elected city officials

zations have governing boards with members from both the private and public sector and local government.

The growing presence of public/private partnership organizations reflects a number of factors, but probably has been most strongly influenced by the increasing cost associated with economic development activities. Communities are beginning to realize that public and private resources must be pooled in order to have an adequate budget for various development activities. A conscious desire to combine the operational advantages offered by both the government and private sector models has also contributed to the growth of public/private partnerships.

Public/private partnerships take a variety of forms, depending on the exact blend of public and private participation. Discussed below are three examples representative of the range of approaches, while each is profiled in Exhibit II.

Private Sector Emphasis

The Greater Paducah Economic Development Council (GPEDC) in Paducah, Kentucky is an example of a public/private partnership with a private sector emphasis. Although the GPEDC has its own board of directors and funding, it is organizationally a part of the Chamber of Commerce and is located in the Chamber's offices. An important feature of this approach is that the executive director of the Chamber serves via a contractual arrangement as executive director of the GPEDC, thus allowing economy of scale benefits.

Private sector representatives (bankers, chamber designees, utility service representatives, industrialists) account for approximately 75 percent of the board's 20 members. Public sector representatives include the mayor, county judge executives, and representatives of Murray State University and the local community college. Private sector funding (Chamber contractual fee and private donations) accounts for approximately 85 percent of GPEDC's budget, with city and county government providing the balance.

Public Sector Emphasis

The Aurora Economic Development Commission in Aurora, Illinois is an example of a public/private partnership with a public sector emphasis. The mayor appoints all nine commission members including the commission chairman. The mayor also appoints the commission's executive director who is a city employee. Private sector input is achieved since four of the nine commissioners must be selected by the mayor from a list of nominees submitted by the chamber. In addition, the city and the chamber each contribute 50 percent of the commission's annual operating budget. An interesting feature of the Aurora structure is that the commission is not housed in city hall, but is instead located in the chamber of commerce office.

Balanced Organization

One of the best examples of a balanced public/private organization is the Eugene-Springfield Metropolitan Partnership in Oregon. This organization is a freestanding non-profit corporation which draws its funding and board membership virtually

EXHIBIT II
Examples of Public/Private Partnerships

Name of organization	Greater Paducah Economic Development Council (GPEDC)	Aurora Economic Development Commission	Eugene/Springfield Metropolitan Partnership
Major sources of funding	Business, industry, and personal contributions City of Paducah	Greater Aurora Chamber of Commerce City of Aurora	City of Eugene Eugene Chamber of Commerce City of Springfield Springfield Chamber of Commerce Lane County Private Industry Council Business, industry, and personal contributions
Governing body	18-member board of directors, including mayor of Paducah and McCracken County Judge Executive	Nine-member commission appointed by mayor of Aurora with consent of the city council. Four commission members must come from a list of ten names provided by the Greater Aurora Chamber of Commerce.	44-member board of directors, including mayors of Eugene and Springfield, chairman of Lane County Board, president of University of Oregon, and president of Lane Community College.
Legal form	Part of Paducah Area Chamber of Commerce, a 501 (c) (6) non-profit corporation.	Part of City of Aurora	Non-profit 501 (c) (3)
Other organizational features	GPEDC purchases administrative services from Chamber of Commerce: – GPEDC is located in chamber office – Chamber of commerce executive director is also director of GPEDC – Chamber of commerce provides secretarial and accounting services	Executive director of the commission is appointed by the mayor of Aurora on recommendation of the commission The City of Aurora and the Greater Aurora Chamber of Commerce have entered into a five-year contract, whereby each agrees to provide 50 percent of the commission's funding. Development Commission office is co-located with Chamber of Commerce	Partnership is freestanding non-profit corporation 50 percent of funding from public sector and 50 percent from private sector Partnership is located in office space separate from Chamber or government offices

equally from the public and private sectors. Of the 44 board members, 23 are private sector representatives and 21 represent the public sector. Private sector representatives include chamber officials and their designees, industrialists and professionals. Public sector representatives include the mayors of Eugene and Springfield, the county board chairman, and the presidents of the University of Oregon, the local community college, and the private industry council.

The private sector and public sector each contribute 50 percent of the Partnership's annual operating budget. Private sector contributions come from the chambers of commerce in Eugene and Springfield and private donations. The cities of Eugene and Springfield, the county government, and the private industry council contribute the public sector share.

In contrast to both Paducah and Aurora, the Partnership board of directors has hiring/firing authority over its executive director and its offices are located separate

from any chamber or government offices.

FREESTANDING ORGANIZATION OR "PIGGYBACK"?

If the local situation allows it, piggybacking the new public/private partnership onto an existing organization can be highly advantageous. Two of the more popular approaches are to attach the partnership to the chamber of commerce as was done in Paducah, or to attach it to a local government body, as done in Aurora. Either approach allows the new partnership to use an existing organization as its fiscal agent, and thus avoid the time-consuming process of obtaining non-profit corporation status.

Of course there will be situations where piggybacking on an existing organization is not acceptable or feasible. These circumstances require establishing the public/private partnership as a freestanding non-profit corporation, as was done in Eugene-Springfield. This entails incorporating the organization under the rules of its state. Achieving non-profit incorporation status is not a simple task, and much time and energy can be saved by operating under the auspices of an existing non-profit corporation or government unit.

OBTAINING TAX-EXEMPT STATUS

One of the major hurdles in establishing a freestanding public/private partnership is obtaining tax-exempt status. Tax-exempt status is desirable so that the revenues of the organization are not taxed. More importantly, from a fund raising perspective, tax-exempt status makes certain donations to the economic development organization tax deductible.

In order to qualify for tax-exempt status, application must be made to the Internal Revenue Service. It typically requires the Internal Revenue Service about nine months to render a decision regarding tax-exempt status.

Economic development organizations qualify for tax exempt status under either section 501(c)(3) or section 501(c)(6) of the IRS Code:

501 (c)(3) Tax Exempt Status

This section of the code covers a variety of religious, educational, charitable, scientific and other organizations. Quoting directly from an IRS publication: *Tax Exempt Status for your Organization:* "Aiding a community or geographical area by attracting new industry to the community or area, or by encouraging the development or retention of an industry in the community or area" falls under the purposes of section 501 (c) (3) .

A benefit of 501 (c)(3) designation is that it permits contributors to treat their contributions to an economic development organization as a deduction on their personal income tax returns. However, it should be noted that certain restrictions are imposed on 501 (c)(3) organizations regarding activities to influence legislation.

501 (c)(6) Tax Exempt Status

The tax advantages under this section — the so-called "business league" section — are generally less advantageous than under section 501 (c)(3). Chambers of commerce are one of the groups that qualify for 501 (c)(6) designation. One advantage of a 501 (c)(6) organization is that it may engage in any amount of legislative activity germane to the common business interests of the organization's members.

Of the non-profit corporations responding to the AEDC organizational survey, 55 percent were 501 (c)(3) organizations and 45 percent were 501 (c)(6) organizations. Competent legal counsel should be retained to provide advice on the type of tax-exempt status advisable for your economic development organization.

SUMMARY

Organizational structure is a key element in achieving economic development goals, yet no single organizational structure is suitable for all communities. The organization of development efforts must reflect the needs of the community, the strengths and weaknesses of existing development groups, and the particular history of development in the area.

Three models for categorizing community based economic development organizations can be identified: the private sector model, the government agency model, and the public/private partnership model. A large percentage of community based economic development groups are organized as public/private partnerships. The prevalence of the public/private partnership reflects a number of factors, but probably has been most strongly influenced by the increasing cost associated with economic development activities. The exact blend of public and private participation varies significantly from organization to organization.

New economic development organizations may be created as freestanding non-profit, tax-exempt corporations or may "piggy-back" on an existing non-profit or government agency. Achieving non-profit, tax-exempt status is not a simple task, and much time and energy can be saved by operating under the auspices of an existing non-profit corporation or government unit. Economic development organizations qualify for tax-exempt status under either section 501 (c)(3) or section 501 (c)(6) of the Internal Revenue Service Code. The 501 (c)(3) designation generally has more tax advantages.

Public/Private Partnership: The Economic Development Organization of the 90s

David R. Kolzow, Ph. D.

It is becoming increasingly clear that the economic development process is more complicated than merely setting in motion promotional programs to attract new companies to a community. The slowdown in the rate of economic growth, both nationally and locally, and the major shifts in the nature of this growth are forcing a reevaluation of approaches to stimulating and maintaining a vibrant economic environment.

Certainly, the basic goal of the economic development process has not changed significantly over the past several decades. The purpose of a planned economic development effort is to influence private sector decisions for the benefit of the community. The desired result is the attraction of investors, the retention/expansion/creation of jobs, and the promotion of the community's economic health. Although the ultimate aim of economic development tends to remain the same over time, the means employed to facilitate the process continue to change.

This change can be seen, for example, in the attempts across the nation to redesign the structure of the economic development organization to be more responsive to the new economic environment. The organizational structures of the past are often not adapted to the economic development needs of the present and future. For example, planned economic development initiatives are not likely to be very effective if they are merely an adjunct to the many programs of a local chamber of commerce or just one of the many functions of a local government agency. Successful development programs in today's environment need to be highly focussed and strategically oriented.

Furthermore, many communities have found that their ability to respond promptly and effectively to the needs of industrial prospects and to the local business community is impaired by organizational rivalries. Inevitably, these communities pay the price in the form of lost opportunities for new or additional investments and new jobs.

Within a complex urban environment, no one agency can be entirely responsible for the local economy. This is especially so as local economies become more entwined with national and international economic activity. Resources have to be drawn from a variety of sources to tackle the complex set of socioeconomic problems that a community typically faces. Inter-organizational relationships can be better understood if the natures of both public and private sector agencies are clarified.

PUBLIC SECTOR AGENCIES

The public sector agencies generally focus their economic development approach on what they can do to create a positive environment for the business community. This is accomplished in a number of ways:

❑ They can provide public sources of funding that otherwise would not be available to local projects or activities.

❑ In certain cases, public agencies can provide tax incentives or other incentives that otherwise would not be available to private business.

❑ They can provide assistance with regulations that are often a major stumbling block for new industrial projects.

❑ Public agencies provide assistance in quality-of-life factors, which appear to be increasingly important to business investment decisions. The quality of state and local school systems, access to cultural activities and recreational facilities, the quality and availability of public facilities and infrastructure, and public safety can all have a significant impact on a local decision.

❑ They can provide access to political and professional leadership for major development efforts. Without such support, many investment activities might be more difficult to achieve.

❑ Public agencies can help coordinate the use of resources from state and local government. Generally, most local development policies ultimately are implemented by public agencies. Further, many federal, state, and local resources targeted toward economic development require the approval of state or local governments before they can be used to promote specific projects and activities.[1]

On the other hand, state and local government agencies have both constitutional and statutory limitations. They often are constrained by the laws of the state, county, or city. Most local governments have limits placed on general obligation municipal debt to support private initiatives. States often have constitutional limits on the use of public funds for private gain; these limit the ability of public agencies to use such resources for stimulating private investment. Even where such measures are legal, political constraints frequently make it difficult to use local or state tax dollars for such efforts.[2]

PRIVATE SECTOR AGENCIES

Private economic development organizations generally operate as nonprofit corporations, although they may also be structured as for-profit organizations. Private for-profit and nonprofit corporations are an excellent way to achieve certain economic development goals because they provide flexibility that local public organizations simply do not. For example, they can carry out business-related activities benefitting private parties that public organizations cannot legally perform. The nonprofit private organization may also be able to draw on additional resources and funding sources because it can directly involve the business community, and the tax advantages of a contribution can be attractive to donors.

A private sector organization can enlist the involvement and support of key business and industry leaders in the local economic development process. Far too often, the development agenda of public agencies gets lost in reelection politics, and new administrations move cautiously into redefining development priorities. Involvement of private sector leaders can often provide a continuity in the development process that is more difficult to achieve in the public sector.

Private corporations also have disadvantages. Unlike governmental entities, private organizations cannot apply directly for many federal and state assistance programs even though they may become the beneficiaries of such programs. In addition, they have none of the taxation or regulatory powers that reside in local governments. They may also have serious public relations or political limitations in building public support. Local elected officials might find it much easier than a private association to rally public support behind a particular economic development activity.[3]

GAINING THE BEST OF BOTH WORLDS

What is the "best" way to structure the economic development organization to maximize the advantages of both the public sector and private sector entities? What approach is most effective?" These questions are not easily answered, and every community should attempt to address them on the basis of the strategies that have been chosen to accomplish local economic development goals.

However, an important trend emerging across the country is the effort to cultivate new relationships between the public and private sectors within a framework of cooperation and involvement. A survey of the membership of the American Economic Development Council indicated that the sources of funds supporting the members' organizations are divided approximately equally among public sources, private sources, and a combination of the two. This represents a substantial increase in organizations drawing on both business and government sources to support their efforts. It is the experience of the author that the most effective local and regional economic development programs heavily involve key community leadership and participation from the area's most prominent private corporations, as well as drawing from these sources for the core of their funding.

A public/private partnership in economic development is much more than the public sector merely offering cooperation to the private sector to facilitate the profitability of local firms. It is far more than occasional meetings between the city council or county board of supervisors, and local business organizations, such as the chamber of commerce. While these activities are important, and perhaps integral to good business/government relations, they do not constitute true partnerships among the sectors. Partnerships are shared commitments to pursue common economic goals that are jointly determined by the community's lead-

ership in both the private and public sectors. This collaborative effort can lead to a more rational allocation of both public and private sector resources (including financial) so that these goals are accomplished.

A review of successful public/private partnership efforts suggests the following guidelines:

☐ A positive community culture that encourages leadership and citizen participation, and that is related to the long-term development concerns of the community.

The goals for the development process must reflect the desires and interests of the leaders and residents fo the community. Community organizations that focus on creating jobs and stimulating the economic base can form effective partnerships. On the other hand, those organizations that are primarily self-serving, ambiguous in their purpose, or overly concerned with who gets credit for what, have a difficult time finding a common ground for a partnership.

☐ A realistic and commonly accepted vision of the community that is based on the area's strengths and weaknesses as well as on a common understanding of the potential for the area.

Without a common understanding of what the community is or what it can become, it is difficult to build a better community. Furthermore, unless a realistic vision of the potential for the area is shared by the leadership, the community will never come together to achieve its goals.

☐ An effective community organization that can blend the self-interest of members with the broader interests of the community.

Self-interest is undoubtedly the spark to most action taken by individuals and organizations in a development context. If the individual interests of local leaders and key development organizations can be collectively marshalled through some structure to achieve common ends for the total community, the development process is more likely to work.

☐ A network of key groups and individuals that encourages communication among leaders and facilitates mediation of differences among competing interests.

This network builds respect and confidence in the community. It allows business, labor, and government to work out their differences in private rather than in public. This allows the focus of public discussion to be on the areas of agreement rather than on the problems and misunder-

standings resulting from conflicting relationships.

☐ The ability and desire to nurture entrepreneurship in the community, that is, to encourage the risk-takers and nurture their enterprises.

Without some form of positive intervention, communities generally don't become successful centers of new job-creating ventures. These entrepreneurial centers are usually the result of some active and motivated organizations willing to direct a concerted effort to establish a "climate" that encourages entrepreneurial activity. If local entrepreneurs are not encouraged, then the development process will stop and the community will be the loser.

☐ Continuity of policy, including the ability to adapt to changing circumstances and reduce uncertainty for business and individuals who want to take economic risks.

Too frequently, government, in the absence of any consistent goals, pursues ad hoc policies that are disruptive to the development process. Steps can be taken to minimize this. First, the community should work on a set of development policies that act as a framework for their actions in the development arena. For example, a community might adopt policies to promote the development of highly skilled jobs. Subsequent projects as well as regulations would be examined to see if they met that test. Second, local government and private enterprise, along with representatives of the work force and community groups, should try to determine what kind of community they really want and build social and physical infrastructure accordingly.[4]

These six guidelines form the basis for any organizational structure the community decides to adopt. Essentially, public and private partnerships can provide a bridge of trust that is based on similar goals but that allows for differences in roles. Achieving public/private cooperation is the first step in the establishment of an effective, long-term economic development program. The actions toward accomplishing this cooperation will occur much more easily if the structure is there to facilitate the relationships.

It should be emphasized, however, that it is not enough to merely reorganize the community's economic development organizational structure. Organizations seeking to provide economic development leadership must also employ professionals capable of meeting the challenges of the increasing complexity of the development process. Today's economic developer must stay current with developments within the field, be well aware of national and international economic trends, have well-honed interpersonal skills, understand the community's political environment, and must be able to both educate local leadership as well as effectively involve them in the economic development process.

CHAMBERS OF COMMERCE AS PUBLIC/PRIVATE PARTNERSHIPS

As was stated earlier, there is no one way to structure the public/private partnership. However, it is generally desirable that local economic development functions (particularly outreach) not become entangled with the typical activities and orientation of the chamber of commerce. Certainly, economic development and the services of a chamber of commerce are and should be interrelated. But the inherent inwardness of most chamber duties (i.e., services to members and lobbying or governmental relations) is often in basic conflict with the goal of attracting new firms into the community. Furthermore, it is more difficult for a chamber, given its mission, to enter into a joint partnership with local government.

However, the local Chamber of Commerce can be an effective economic development agency when two characteristics are prevalent:

❑ the chief paid staff member is either an economic development professional or has a strong orientation to that being the Chamber's primary role; or,

❑ the Chamber is organized to make economic development one of its highest priorities, or the economic development function is clearly demarcated within the organization and has a high level of independent action.

Clearly, a smaller community has less flexibility in separating the chamber of commerce and economic development responsibilities. In these circumstances, it is particularly important that the chamber executive and his/her Board have a well-articulated organizational plan to help ensure that important economic development activities don't get lost in the day-to-day requirements of chamber operations.

CONCLUDING COMMENTS

In conclusion, the advantages of teamwork in the local economic development process are becoming increasingly apparent in the face of changing economic trends, budgetary constraints, and the growing need for the combined resources of the private and public sectors. Communities in which the public and private sector band together to form "economic development teams" through an organization structured as a public-private partnership are more likely to experience effective actions and successful results. The turf problems and political in-fighting of the past need to be resolved in an atmosphere of mutually beneficial negotiation rather than one of adversarial conflict. The theme of the 90s and beyond *must* be collaboration, commitment, and "community" concern if our local economies are to survive the competition of the global economy.

NOTES

[1]Luke , Jeffrey S. *Managing Economic Development.* Jossey-Bass Publishers: San Francisco, 1988. Pages 57-58.

[2]Ibid., Page 58.

[3]Ibid., Pages 64-65.

[4]Blakely, Edward J. *Planning Local Economic Development.* Sage Publications: Newbury Park, 1989. Pages 261-263.

Energizing Boards, Commissions, Task Forces, And Volunteer Groups

Paul J. Greeley

THE CHANGING ENVIRONMENT

It is useful to examine what is happening at the board level in the corporate world today and consider the impact these changes are having on the management of non-profit agencies.

According to Ralph Whitworth, President of the United Shareholders Association, directors of national corporations were like house cats:, "the better you treated them the quieter they became". For too long, directors have felt beholden to the gift-giving CEO even when the company was in trouble and the chief executive should have been replaced. Today, the larger shareholders of troubled companies are focusing on what they judge to be the major underlying problem, namely, an ineffective board of directors. Generous compensation, significant perks and benefits should have been a warning signal. "Bad boards are the result," says Neil Minaw, a principal of Cat Lens. John Wilcox, chairman of a proxy solicitation firm reports, "there is a revolution going on in the corporate world and most of it is taking place from within the corporation."

The result of all this is that directors are now responding aggressively, taking bolder action, exercising their responsibilities and getting things done. Examples abound on the positive results of energized corporate directors.

Community and economic development executives, therefore, should become aware of this changing environment. Particularly, they should sense the implications it has for non-profit managers. These changes should not be feared, but rather looked upon as opportunities. Creative ways of capitalizing these opportunities will attract additional dynamic leaders. It will result in quality programs. It will make the organization a "driving force" for balanced economic growth. It will win, for managers, respect and the rewards for jobs well done. Yes, it will require skills and effort and good human relations to influence the behavior of others. A few managers may not be willing to make this effort. They will end up with apathetic boards. Those managers who choose to make it a priority responsibility will reap the rich rewards of forging a strong leadership team, creating relevant action-packed programs, and produce economically healthy communities. To achieve these results, this article makes seven suggestions:

SEARCH DILIGENTLY TO IDENTIFY POTENTIAL LEADERS

Obviously, the first step in the process of building a strong leadership team is to identify potential community leaders. This process is best illustrated with an analogy. Lou Holtz is the successful coach of the Notre Dame football team. Lou is a master at building an energized football squad. But, Lou does not wait for the announcement of the All-American High School Football team before he starts his searching. He sends scouts throughout the countryside ferreting out the players who will fit into his plans for a top flight team. He is identifying future All-Americans. A similar effort should be the first step in building an energized community leadership team. Every community has an abundance of community leadership talent, but not enough effort is put into identifying these potential leaders. We do want to look for specific qualities as we identify the community leaders we need. We look for "advocates". Webster defines an advocate as one who "pleads the cause of another". To put it another way, we want one who has the capability of feeling intensely the mission, the purpose, and the programs of our organization. We look for people who can become intellectually committed to their attainment.

A second skill we look for is "a group problem solver". Solving problems in a group is a more complex process than solving problems individually. Experience in group problem solving is highly desirable.

A third skill is "a group decision maker". The need for people who can participate in a group decision making process and accept the discipline required in building consensus. We should be aware of where such suspects can be found. Frequently, they are already centers of influence in the community. They are making an impact on events, happenings, and crises. They move in circles of social and political power. Their opinion and judgment matters and is frequently sought. They may be found in the constituency groups in the community, in service clubs, fraternal organizations, and neighborhood associations. They appear occasionally at public meetings. They are quoted in the newspaper. They have earned a degree in credibility. They care, and in all likelihood, will be willing and active participants of your leadership team.

RECRUIT VIGOROUSLY TO ATTRACT THE STRONGEST POSSIBLE LEADERSHIP TEAM

The value of a painstaking search can be lost if the actual recruiting effort is not carried out with equal diligence. All too often, the selection of new directors is left to a nominating committee that meets with little preparation, reflects briefly on the prospective candidates, quickly reaches a consensus, and with the best of intentions has some member of the nominating committee extend the invitation with a telephone call. While stressing it is an honor to serve and will not take too much time, this casual process will never produce your strongest possible leadership team.

A more effective method is to provide the nominating committee with the carefully researched candidates list. Additionally, it highlights those special qualities it is desirable for directors to possess. Of paramount importance, it is to be sure the candidates can and will be strong advocates for the organization.

The author acknwledges the financial support of the American Economic Development Council Educational Foundation in the preparation of this article.

How the invitation to serve on the board or commission is extended is critically important. Many have found the most successful way of recruiting a new director is to have two or three influential friends call on the prospect at his or her place of business or, better still, invite the prospect to a luncheon meeting. Such treatment raises the perception of the candidate on the importance attached to this position and has got to be persuasive. While the honor of serving is mentioned, emphasis should be placed on the responsibilities and obligations of those agreeing to serve.

ORIENT THOROUGHLY AND INSPIRE YOUR LEADERSHIP TEAM

The orientation of the new leadership team has two purposes - to inform - and to excite. Obviously, information on the objectives and programs of the organization is necessary. Rarely does a new member come on board aware of the breadth and depth of the activities and programs of your organization. They should hear the full story so to develop a "Big Picture" attitude about the organization and its mission.

Equally important is to emphasize the responsibilities each member of the leadership team accepts when he or she agrees to serve. It is essential that they develop an intellectual commitment to the mission of the organization. With such a commitment, they will become strong advocates and supporters. They will eagerly assist in a share of the responsibility for implementing your program, including marshaling the resources, both financial and material required to get the job accomplished. It will mean the development of a sensitivity for opportunities to advance the cause of economic development, and face up to the challenges of your community.

Other suggestions to make orientations successful are to conduct the session on your own turf and as soon as possible after the invitation to serve has been accepted. Stress the team concept with emphasis. What is needed are team players, not one-man gangs.

Another purpose of the orientation session is to create in the volunteer an intense excitement about the opportunity to participate in the community development process. Help them develop a sincere enthusiasm for your action program.

Do not rely on your mission statement or your program alone to accomplish this. It is their *perception* of your program and it's relevancy to their value system that will more effectively influence their behavior on your board. It is critical, therefore, at orientation, to form in the minds of the volunteers a perception that the role you want them to play in your organization is the best action they can take to serve their own interests and their value system.

ASSIGN SKILLFULLY TO CHALLENGING AND MEANINGFUL ASSIGNMENTS

Asking a volunteer to accept a share of responsibility for one of your projects should be done with great sensitivity. Just as a square peg does not fit into a round hole, neither will volunteers perform at their highest potential when asked to do something that is not perceived by them as contributing to their best interests. The crucial element then is to make sure that the assignment made asks the volunteer to undertake a project that is serving his or her best interests.

Place team players at their best playing positions. Volunteers come with a variety of skills, talents, experiences and interests. Ask volunteers to serve on a task most likely to match their potential. Some consideration might also be given to the interests of the firm for which they work. Volunteers are taking work from their regular employment to fulfill their responsibility to you. When what you want them to do matches both the interests of their employer and themselves, the volunteer can be expected to do a most conscientious and effective job.

It is also important to ensure the assignment is a challenging one. Business leaders are accustomed to facing challenges, they are "risk takers". Accordingly, the community tasks for business leaders should be challenging, but the risk must seem reasonable.

Attention should be carefully given to the "mechanics" of making the assignment. Here is a suggested scenario. Visit the volunteer at his or her place of business. Explain that you have a challenging opportunity for community service which might be of interest to him or her. Outline the importance of the objective of the assignment, suggest a date when it is expected to be completed or a progress report due. Be specific about what resources will be avail-able by way of research, budget and staff. Give the volunteer an opportunity to ask questions. Later, write a "sense of the meeting" memo. Return it to the volunteer and suggest he or she amend, add or delete any specifics. When the volunteer returns the memo with suggested additions, corrections or deletions, you can be confident the assignment is understood and in all likelihood will be fulfilled.

COACH AND TRAIN THE TEAM PLAYERS WITH ENTHUSIASM

Since your board, commission or task force is viewed as a team, you should look upon your role as a coach. Yours is the key role in the development of the game plan and the selection of the strategies to be used. But, let the team players play the game. Be the coach, not the quarterback. Guide, inspire, motivate and prod, but let the volunteers carry the ball.

Help them keep focused on their assignment. As a well-focused camera produces a clear picture, so a well-focused committee will avoid distractions or deviations to cause them to lose sight of the team's ultimate objective. Remember, obstacles will appear whenever you take your eye off the ball.

Coaches also provide training, particularly in two major areas. One area is in "group decision" making. Many boards fall into a set pattern of decision making. The reality is that all group decisions should not be reached in the same manner. There are various models of effective group decision making. These are factors which influence which group decision making model best fits each situation.

Three factors determine which model should be used. These three factors are (1) time -- how much time is there before a decision must be reached, (2) quality -- how important is the quality of the decision and is there sufficient information and data on hand to ensure a quality decision, and (3) commitment -- to what extent are the decision makers going to have to be involved in the implementation of the decision.

There are occasions when time is of the essence. Immediate action is needed. The quality of the decision can be assured either through established practice, policy or tradition or when it can be assumed that others will accept the decision and commit to its implementation. Time, therefore, becomes most important. But there are also decisions when additional ideas or information are necessary. Time for gathering such information is available and there is opportunity to let all the participants share in the decision making process. A third decision making model is appropriate when both the quality of the decision and the commitment from others for successful implementation of the decision become critical. Obviously, there must be time to gather the information and permit adequate discussion. When looking for the consensus of the group, you are obligating them to take responsibility for the successful implementation of that decision. When the commitment of the participants to the decision is crucial, the following guidelines must be followed.

All the members should have opportunity to present their ideas and their reasons for them. Differences of opinion should be openly discussed. Conflict should be managed but not avoided. Team members should modify their opinions based on the discussion. Final decisions should be made after a thorough examination of all the ideas presented. Admittedly, group decision making slows down the progress of action, but it greatly enhances the chances for a successful implementation of the decision.

The second area where training is generally required is group problem solving. When a board is presented with a problem, the tendency is immediately to explore possible solutions to that problem. This is what is called the "aspirin-type" problem solving method. If you have a headache and you take aspirin, the headache may go away but the cause of the headache is still there. So it is when a board faces a problem and develops a solution prior to identifying possible causes of the problem. Group problem solving begins when the problem is stated in a simple declarative sentence with all the participants agreeing on the statement of the problem. This can require considerable discussion until the problem is expressed in a way that all members clearly understand. The next step is to analyze the problem and search for possible causes of the problem. After causes of the problem have been identified, then and only then should the group turn to possible solutions. Implementing the solution will be enhanced when the group has gone through this problem-solving process.

EVALUATE PERIODICALLY BOTH THE STATUS OF THE PROJECT AND THE PERFORMANCE OF THE LEADERSHIP TEAM

A periodic checkup on how things are going is an exigent step in every in-progress project or activity. Provision for a periodic evaluation should be built into the project description. Evaluation might be viewed as a form of criticism if not scheduled.

The purpose of the evaluation is to measure "performance" against "promise". It is also useful to explore the "why" of success or failure. An understanding of the reasons for the progress -- or lack of it -- makes possible the adjustments that get and keep the project on target.

Not only should the project itself be examined, but the performance of the team players needs to be evaluated. Working with volunteers, who have priority responsibilities, can sometimes cause the project to lag and take more time than was anticipated. Team players feel their interest waning and it is then that the batteries must be recharged. Motivation must be rekindled. All individuals strive to satisfy personal goals. However, individual goals vary.

To achieve organizational goals, the executive must understand and cater to the individual's varying goals. Individuals with strong affiliation goals prefer to maintain close relationships with others. They are fearful about disrupting relationship, they do not like to cause hard feelings. Being liked and accepted is important to them. To motivate such individuals, you must keep in contact with the individual more frequently and communicate in terms of feelings, rather than logic. Such people work better in teamwork settings. They avoid being alone. They work hard to reconcile differences among people. Such people should be involved in planning the meetings. They accept the "helping" jobs readily. Individuals who dominate goal is power desire greater personal freedom and opportunities to control others and events. These individuals show concern for their reputation. They seek a position of leadership, frequently will give unsolicited advice, are good at influencing others to perform tasks and are willing to take big risks. Such individuals should be involved in establishing goals and strategies. They are motivated by receiving visibility for their performance. They shy from direct supervision and seek authority in their area of expertise.

Other individuals are motivated by the desire for achievement. They pursue excellence as an end in itself. They constantly seek performance improvement, new methods, long-range planning and pursue career paths. They are particularly good at setting challenging but realistic goals. They look for feedback on their performance. They are not particularly strong at working in teams, tend to be persistent and have a strong career orientation. Motivation for such individuals is enhanced when they are involved in setting goals that are measurable, specific, and challenging. They are skilled in giving feedback and clearly defining specific tasks. They perform at their best when they see the task as an opportunity to advance personal growth and development.

When you perceive the board is experiencing a "let down", then it is time to "motivate". Remembering that individuals have varying dominant goals, these differences must be kept in mind when recharging the batteries of your leadership team.

CONSISTENTLY PRACTICE GOOD HUMAN RELATIONS

There is overwhelming evidence that the higher up you go in your profession and the greater your responsibilities, the more does your success depend upon your skill and ability to get along with people, and less and less on your technical knowledge and know how. It is important, therefore, for the executive coaching leaders to practice at all times good human relations. Here are a few examples of some human relation techniques particularly applicable to the executive of an economic development organization.

Make the people with whom you work feel important. Everybody wants to feel important. It is human nature to do so. Take a look at a group photograph and you will find yourself looking for yourself first. Why? because you believe you are important.

Give honest, sincere appreciation. The deepest craving in every human being is the desire to be appreciated. There are a myriad of ways in which appreciation can be expressed, but sincere appreciation is the fuel that drives people to greater effort.

When giving appreciation, compliment the deed and not the person. Personal compliments are difficult to accept. On the other hand, a compliment sincerely given that praises the deed or the act allows the person being complimented to accept it much more gracefully and is therefore more effective.

Work with enthusiasm. By enthusiasm, we do not mean backslapping and highly animated behavior. Enthusiasm means a "strong spirit within you". You are enthusiastic when you work with an "intense inner feeling". Mark Twain, who was so successful in a number of different endeavors was asked one time, "How come you're so successful?" Mark said, "I was born with excitement." General Eisenhower on D-Day in World War II was asked, "How do you pick men for leadership on the battlefield?" Eisenhower replied, "We have aptitude tests which measure men's ability, but I pick my leaders by those who have enthusiasm." Sire Edward Victor Appleton, knighted by the King of England, when he was awarded the Nobel Prize in physics received a telegram from the New York Times, "Tell us, Sir Knight, to what do you owe your success?" He wired back, "I owe my success 10% on my technical knowledge of physics and 90% for the enthusiasm I have for what I do." Enthusiasm is like the measles, it's contagious. If you want energized directors, leaders and volunteers, develop and use the magic of enthusiasm.

SUMMARY

This article suggests to economic development organization managers some strategies and techniques that will help them cultivate energized and committed leaders in community and economic development. It addresses one of the most common laments expressed by organization managers, "How can I overcome the apathy and indifference of my leadership team?" Admittedly, the material is basic. It contains no magic. It calls for hard work and effort, but remember, the public language of your organization, your mission statements and program of work reports will never energize the behavior of the volunteer to the extent that you desire. The primary method of influencing the behavior of your leaders is to shape their perception of what you do and its relationship to their best interest and their value systems.

Smooth Sailing With Your Board of Directors

David R. Kolzow, Ph.D.

Imagine embarking on a sailing trip. The crew has never worked together before. The captain supposedly is in charge of the ship, but the crew insists on reviewing every decision the captain makes. The destination is some beautiful island, but no one is sure exactly where that is or how to get there. No one on the crew is really clear as to what his or her respective job is. Sailing experience among the crew ranges from fully qualified to non-existent.

Does this sound like a trip you would be eager to be part of? Unfortunately, this is an allegory that rings true with many non-profit organizations such as economic development agencies. Furthermore, it is not always clear just who is the captain and who is the crew. No wonder the trip is often choppy and stormy. This article is meant to stimulate thinking about how to have a smoother sailing organization through better board relations.

THE DYNAMICS OF ORGANIZATIONS

All organizations are constantly being recreated, whether they are aware of it or not. There are bound to be changes over time in circumstances, in staff, in leadership and in priorities. As a result, every organization has a need for periodic review, fine-tuning, and sometimes major changes in the way it is organized and managed.

As the corporate world has discovered, the most appropriate way of dealing with the realities of change and the competitive environment often lies in dramatically altering the way the organization is managed. Major corporations, for example, are discovering that the traditional "hierarchical" management approach no longer meets the pressures of a global economy. We hear and read of "reengineering the corporation," "reinventing the organization," "total quality management," "participatory management," and so on. As faddish as

these management approaches may sound, each corporation attempts to find the right approach for itself, which is usually some adaptation of parts of all of the above or more. Someone once said: "the joy is in the struggle," meaning that the end result may be elusive, but the process of getting there reaps positive dividends for those involved.

The economic development organization, being in most cases a non-profit agency, has the further complications of multiple leadership and constituencies. It must serve industrial prospects, existing business and industry, local leadership, local government officials, in some cases its members, and more ambiguously, the community at large. The relationship with each of these constituencies is an ongoing effort, often made more difficult by many conflicting interests.

Regardless of the difficulty in responding appropriately to changing circumstances, there is growing acceptance of the notion that management is becoming more of a team effort. In a typical nonprofit organization, the board of directors governs and the executive director manages. Given the reality of this structure, one of the key issues is how to integrate more successfully the board of the organization. What roles should they play as part of the economic development team, and what can be done to facilitate better board relations?

THE VALUE OF THE BOARD'S ROLE

Governing boards, whether they are called boards of directors, trustees, or commissioners, are the valuable "steering wheels" of nonprofit organizations and have the primary responsibility for fulfilling their varied and worthwhile missions[1]. In practice, boards carry out extremely important roles that complement the work of the chief executive and his or her staff. These include: establishing contacts, raising funds, enhancing the organization's reputation and

giving it legitimacy, representing it publicly and politically, and giving it advice.

The board also serves as a bridge between the organization's staff and its members, constituents, or clients. A key job of the board is to ensure that the organization is adequately supported by the leadership of the community, and that its performance fully justifies that support. One of the means for accomplishing this is to have the board of the economic development organization work towards a closer coordination with boards of other development-related organizations to build program support and to reduce turf battles.

To help the development organization advance and grow, it is critical to develop a strong, effective, and productive governing board. Key leaders from the community with vision and commitment need to be involved; people who are willing to work collaboratively to contribute their talents and resources to the success of the organization and its mission. As much as is possible, these leaders should represent diverse segments of the community, encompassing such groups as business, industry, government, education and the work force.

GETTING THE BOARD "ON BOARD"

Far too often, new board members receive very little orientation regarding their role or responsibilities. It is assumed that somehow they will pick up on what they are supposed to be about. This generally leads to ambiguity, confusion, and misdirection. A structured orientation of the board is important. It gets members functioning faster as a team; it clarifies levels of authority and expectations; it allows members to begin to feel a part of the group; and it provides individuals with the appropriate tools to help them become more effective in their position of leadership.

Individuals who have indicated a willingness to serve as a board member should do so with full awareness of the obligations that accompany the position. Written job descriptions for the board and its members should help boards strengthen their sense of purpose, their relations with their organization's executive and staff, and their overall performance.

Board members should be given a manual when taking office that consists of at least the following:

- ❑ Articles of incorporation
- ❑ Bylaws
- ❑ The mission statement of the organization
- ❑ Description of the organization's programs
- ❑ Board roster
- ❑ List of committees, with a statement of purpose and duties of each
- ❑ Statement of Board policies
- ❑ Organizational chart
- ❑ Most recent annual report
- ❑ Current budget and financial report
- ❑ Board minutes from the previous year.

CREATING AN EFFECTIVE TEAM

In addition to using the initial orientation to provide key information about the organization and the role of the board, it can also be employed to build a sense of teamwork among the members. This team spirit usually does not happen on its own. Structured exercises using team approaches to problem-solving can help create the necessary cooperative attitude while at the same time fostering a better understanding of the problems faced by the organization.

The problem with leadership in an organization is that there is often a clash of wills and expectations. Simple procedures become complicated as individuals struggle to assert themselves. Differences of opinion become serious conflicts. Negotiations become fights. Precious time and resources are wasted. Critical support is lost, and the credibility of the organization suffers. It is to be expected that leaders have strong opinions and agendas; the problem is how to meld them all together so that the organization can function effectively.

A "team" environment is most likely to occur where the leadership is facilitative rather than dictatorial. For many, the definition of leadership does not include the notion of facilitation. However, in the corporate world, chief executives are discovering how important it is to serve as a facilitator to multiple teams in the organization. This actually results, if done well, in increased productivity and an ability to become more competitive globally.

WHO ARE WE?

Before any organization can structure or restructure its management approach, it must first have a clear idea of who or what it is. A statement of mission and purpose should clearly articulate the organization's goals, means, and primary constituents served. It should explain what makes the organization distinctive and special and should present a compelling reason for individuals, foundations, and corporations to support it financially. In any effective organization, the board is fundamental to the organization's mission. "The board not only helps think through the organization's mission, it is the guardian of that mission, and makes sure the organization lives up to its basic commitment."[2]

The mission should reflect a deeply felt sense for the present as well as for the desirable future of the state of the organization. The mission needs to be understood as both strategic and lofty. It is strategic in the sense that it is realistic and credible. It is lofty to the extent that it is an attractive statement that the stakeholders of the organization can understand and embrace. Finally, the mission must be shared by everyone connected with the organization and those who are its constituents.

It is clearly important that the board members agree about the most fundamental definition of the organization's purpose. In fact, everyone connected directly or indirectly with the organization should understand its reasons for existing -- precisely what it is striving to accomplish. An effective board builds support for the mission of the organization; but to do so, it must first understand and agree upon that mission. Otherwise, it is possible that board members may be working hard but pulling in different directions. Or the board may not be working hard at all because individual board members do not know which way to direct their efforts. Gaining this shared sense of mission requires an ongoing effort; it doesn't happen by default or just during one retreat. It grows out of a continuing process of consensus-building.

BOARDS IN ACTION

Anyone serving as a director of an organization must be aware of what a director is and is not. Board responsibilities are fundamentally the same for all organizations (although nearly everyone feels that his or her organization is unique and special). There is no generic model, however, of board size or composition or organization that has proven itself to be viable in all circumstances. On the other hand, a body of knowledge has evolved that argues for certain structures, policies, and practices that consistently work better than others. A number of these "principles" follow.

Once the board begins functioning, meetings and other aspects of board work should be experienced as gratifying and constructive. To ensure more effective meetings, agendas and tasks should be clear and purposeful, and they should be provided to board members in advance. Generally, it is helpful for the agenda to be organized around three separate kinds of items: information to share, issues to discuss, and actions to take. Information to share includes all the relevant and important data the board should know about. Background budget data, information about key meetings and deadlines, updates on programs and proposals, progress reports on the accomplishment of goals, and all the other kinds of important information should be made regularly available to all board members on a need-to-know basis.[3]

In meetings, it is important for the board to understand the difference between discussing issues and deciding which actions to take. Some issues relevant to the purpose of the organization or the nature of its activity, such as the general approach for funding the organization, need ongoing discussion by board members. Often these broader issues do not require specific actions to be taken, at least not initially. However, once certain issues have been thoroughly discussed and major differences have been resolved, then it may be the time to make decisions regarding the appropriate action steps.

It should be the goal of the board to work toward consensus on issues of importance. However, consensus does not necessarily mean unanimity. The process of consensus-building on a board is meant to ensure that all points of view are heard and that all positions are understood and carefully considered. After all, each member brings to this group unique knowledge, insight, skill, and experience. It is unlikely that there will be agreement on every, or even on most, issues. However, it is the process of sorting through the differences that leads to improved understanding of the issues and how to solve key problems facing the organization.

Boards begin to reach their optimal levels of performance when they exercise their responsibilities primarily by asking good and timely questions rather than by "running" programs or implementing their own agenda. The board should spend most of its time on ends, not means. The board makes policy, the chief executive is the one who carries it out in the day-to-day decisions and actions of the organization.

Policies are rules and procedures. They are ways for nonprofits to set limits and to develop systems for how things are done within the agency. Policies serve as management guidelines so that, when implemented, they accomplish the day-to-day running of the agency without constant board approval.[4]

Board members should not expect to understand or address all the problems affecting every program or activity of the organization. If a board clearly understands its role, it will delegate authority to the director of the organization and minimize meddling. A test of appropriate board involvement in organization issues is to ask if the discussion is focused on "what". If so, the board is doing its job. On the other hand, if the discussion is on the "how" of an issue, the board is doing the executive director's job.[5]

The ultimate question the board should be asking is what it should be doing to improve the organization's involvement in the community. How can it make the organization more effective at stimulating local development? It's greatest concern should be the long term effects of specific areas of need as related to the stated mission of the organization.

Although it may seem obvious, it should be emphasized to board members that they serve the organization as a whole rather than any special interest groups or constituencies. Board members should avoid even the appearance of a conflict of interest that might embarrass the board or the organization and disclose any possible conflicts to the board in a timely fashion. Furthermore, board members should avoid asking for special favors of the staff, including special requests for extensive information, without at least prior consultation with the chief executive, board or appropriate committee chairperson.

An additional key function of the board is to have the final say on who should be the chief executive of the organization. Therefore, it is the board's responsibility to prepare a comprehensive job description for the executive director. It should also be clear from the onset as to how the board will support the chief executive. This should include:

❑ frequent and constructive feedback;

❑ introduction to other community leaders and organizations;

❑ invitations to important social functions;

❑ giving compliments for exceptional initiatives;

❑ encouragement to take professional and personal leave for renewal;

❑ assistance when board members overstep prerogatives or misunderstand their roles;

❑ a feeling that the board is aware of and sensitive to family situations and needs;

❑ a feeling that his or her performance is being assessed in relation to the board's performance.[6]

Once the executive director has been hired, this individual should be given the primary responsibility to staff the operation. Furthermore, the administration of this staff is also the executive director's responsibility. When board members intervene in staff affairs, it sends a confusing message to staff members about who is responsible for what and who is accountable to whom. For example, if the board overturns a discipline decision involving a staff person, it undermines the administrator's role. The result is that his or her authority to manage staff has been seriously damaged.

WHERE DO WE WANT TO GO?

To develop a long term focus for the organization, it is extremely useful to set forth an organizational strategic plan. This plan should present a clear vision for the future activity of the organization, a set of goals to attain that vision, a set of strategies to achieve each goal, and a system for evaluating the results. This planning process is best understood as a complex effort on the part of both the chief executive and board members. The board has a responsibility to ensure that the organization has such an ongoing planning process and that it is working.

The process of planning is often as important as the plan itself. This process, if done correctly, brings key leadership together in ways that facilitate higher levels of communication and consensus-building. A team approach to addressing issues can result in collaborative problem-solving and innovative management and implementation approaches for the organization.

A key role of the board in the planning process is to define the desired results for the organization and to hold the organization accountable for achieving these results. Preferably, these "desired results" should reflect the needs of the community at large rather than any vested interest groups. Once the plan is in place, the board should question whether current and proposed programs and services are consistent with the plan's vision and goals. Given limited resources and unlimited demands on them, the board must help the executive director decide among competing priorities.

In most cases, choosing priorities is the most difficult step in the process. Plans that attempt to make everyone happy result in decisions that please no one. It should also be kept in mind that the priorities of the plan can and are likely to change over time.

Out of the strategic plan should come a clear set of goals, priorities, and strategic actions to guide the operation of the organization and its budget preparation. These goals and priorities should also be clearly reflected in the policies for the organization set forth by the board. If they are highly involved in the strategic planning process, the setting or appropriate policies will be greatly facilitated.

It is the responsibility of the chief executive and staff to prepare a budget that is based on the action agenda contained in the program of work. This proposed budget should be submitted to the board for its approval. However, board members should study it and ask questions, if needed, before voting to approve it.

Although it is not up to the board to develop the program of work and the budget for the organization, it needs to ensure that the organization is effectively implementing them. However, this means monitoring the results of the executive director's spending decisions, not telling him or her how to spend the money. But, the board can only monitor the implementation of the work program and budget if it has clear, intelligible, accurate, and timely financial statements and reports.

The financial health, as well as the finances, of the organization are major concerns of the board. Members have to make sure that adequate income exists to pay for the organizations day-to-day operation, as well as for its long-range goals. Board members are also trustees of the organization's assets, which means that they are ultimately responsible for the bottom line. It is clearly the board's role to raise the funds necessary for the organization's operation. Many boards shrink from this activity, preferring to leave it to the executive director. But he or she does not have the "connections" and "credibility" in the community that the board member has. Furthermore, the time taken by staff to raise money is valuable time taken away from successfully implementing the program.

THE EXECUTIVE DIRECTOR AND THE BOARD

Although the board typically is the legal and hierarchical superior, it is usually very dependent on the chief executive for information and expertise. Successful executive directors have much better information about the organization, its funding sources, and its problems in program delivery than do most board members.

However, just because the chief executive has the information does not mean that he or she does a good job of sharing it. Far too often, the board receives critical information well after the fact. Boards do not like to be surprised! Bad news particularly should be shared quickly and openly. Members of the board should not be embarrassed because they were not aware of something happening that the public or the media would have expected them to be knowledgeable about.

Effective executives facilitate communication and interaction both within the board and between themselves and the board by:

❑ soliciting full participation by all board members;

❑ helping the board achieve consensus about important matters;

❑ helping to resolve differences among members; and,

❑ encouraging collective efforts as well

as prizing individual members' contributions.

Chief executive should work carefully with their boards on important issues before any actions or final decisions are made. They should expect to devote between twenty-five and thirty percent of their time to board relations.[7]

Who should be the organization's spokesperson? There are definite advantages to having an especially articulate board chairperson or volunteer president who can serve this important function. Volunteer leaders who convey their commitment and education through advocacy and a willingness, on behalf of their boards, to get out in front of their chief executives and staffs on the thorny issues command more public attention and respect because they do not receive remuneration. However, no board member should ever use this platform to promote a personal opinion or agenda.[8]

HOW ARE WE DOING?

Increasingly, boards are recognizing their responsibility to the community with respect to the achievements of the organization. Without a systematic and periodic evaluation of performance of staff and programs, it is impossible to know what is working and what is not. Furthermore, it is difficult to tell someone you work with what you do or do not like about his or her performance. A formal evaluation removes this reticence, because it turns the evaluation into an objective, rather than a subjective, process.

The primary purpose of evaluation and review is to help the chief executive and his/her staff to perform more effectively. However, it should not be the responsibility for a board to evaluate day-to-day staff performance. This should remain the responsibility of the chief executive. The board, instead, must constantly pay attention to how well the organization is meeting the needs of it constituents.[9] The final measure of success is whether local stakeholders are satisfied with the services provided and therefore are willing to renew funding.

The assessment of the performance of the organization and its staff should not be done without also considering the impact of the board's performance. Neither can be assessed completely independent of one another because they are so interdependent. This means that the board should also go through a process of reviewing and assessing its performance. This can be accomplished through a committee of leaders from outside the organization. Board evaluation not only identifies core problems, it also points out and reinforces things that it is already doing well.

CONCLUSIONS

It is natural and likely that conflicts will arise within the leadership of any organization, just as they might on the crew of a ship on an extended voyage. Clarification of roles and functions will reduce the amount of conflict and facilitative leadership will find ways to solve problems that would be beneficial to the organization and its mission. Smooth sailing at all times is difficult for any organization but increased attention paid to basic organizational principles should help increase the frequency of its occurrence.

NOTES

[1]Judith Grummon Nelson, *Six Keys to Recruiting, Orienting,* and *Involving Nonprofit Board Members*, Washington DC: National Center for Nonprofit Boards, 1991, p.iii.
[2]Peter F. Drucker, *Managing the Non-Profit Organization*, New York: Harper Business, 1990, p.59.
[3]Robert D. Herman and Richard D. Heimovics, *Executive Leadership in Nonprofit Organizations*, San Francisco: Jossey-Bass Publishers, 1991, p.122.
[4]Susan M. Scribner, *Boards from Hell*, Long Beach CA: Scribner & Associates, 1991, p.22.
[5]1995 Board Member Manual, Gaithersburg MD: Aspen Publishers, 1994, p.31.
[6]Richard T. Ingram, *Ten Basic Responsibilities of Nonprofit Boards*, Washington DC: National Center for Nonprofit Boards, 1988, p.4.
[7]Douglas C. Eadie, "Strengthening Board Leadership and the Board-Chief Executive Partnership," *Economic Development Review*, Summer 1991, p.42.
[8]Richard T. Ingram, op.cit. p.12.
[9]Robert D. Herman and Richard D. Heimovics, op.cit., p.96.

Creating Your Own Economic Development Team

Michael A. Lanava

INTRODUCTION

For most of us, success is marked by milestones—installed one at a time. Bring a great employer to your town, fill a long-vacant building, sell an industrial park lot. After a while, your career may be filled with such markers, and someone calls you successful.

I was asked recently what I feel has made me successful in Fitchburg. Having seen my work as individual milestones—rather than a long road defined by them—I was caught a bit off-guard. But I began to think about the question, and soon realized that success is really built on the basics of economic development. We all know them. Some of the lessons even go back to our childhoods, or to human relations courses we took in school, or books we've read—Dale Carnegie, Dr. Norman Vincent Peale and the like. The problem is, we sometimes forget about those lessons.

Certainly, there are skills that we hone along the way. But if you stick to the basics, you'll find yourself on the right road every time.

So in this article, we'll review "Basics 101", and I'll add a few hints and examples along the way. I hope you'll find yourself nodding in agreement as you move from point to point.

When I was hired for my present job, I had heard of the community, but had visited it for only a few hours before my interview. Clearly, I didn't know a soul, and the first day on the job brought all the normal feelings of uncertainty, nervousness, and doubt about making the right decision.

What did those doubts have to do with being successful in economic development? Those first few days and weeks, I realized, would set the tone for my effectiveness as an economic development professional. I was starting out with a clean slate, and the impression I made at the beginning was in my own hands.

I always remember what my father taught me when we worked together summers at the envelope factory. Always have a smile. Be nice to people. Take an interest in them. Ask their advice and speak to them, not at them. Most of all, remember where you came from.

THE STAFF

So I began by introducing myself to every single department head in the city, and, more importantly, to their secretaries. I smiled a lot, and made sure to know the secretaries' and janitors' names. Sure, I sent letters to all of the "power" people in the community, introduced myself and followed up with a phone call and personal meeting. But it's important to lay the groundwork with the staff. We all know about being nice to secretaries or administrative assistants. But how many of us fail to build these relationships? And how many of us look beyond those key players to the rest of the staff? A janitor, for example, does a lot more than empty wastebaskets. He knows everyone in City Hall, can tell you what's happening, and give you a sense of who the "good guys" are. But more importantly, he lives in the community and can tell you what he thinks is wrong with it—and what to do about it. These opinions and ideas come from his friends and an extensive network of family members—the kind of people you're supposed to be working for. The janitor probably got his job because he knew the Mayor or someone in the City Council, or your boss. Guess who can help you influence people?

Back to secretaries. We all know that a good secretary can make or break your day. So you set out to win over those people in City Hall who influence their bosses. Go to meetings a little early and chit-chat with the secretary—share some personal (but not too personal) information about families, hobbies, vacations, interests. Then, when you call on the phone, you'll stand a better chance of getting through, finding out a good time to catch the boss, or learning what kind of mood he's in.

There are times when I'll bring something small for the secretary or administrative assistant—a bag of apples in the Fall, for example, or a container of hard candies to set on the corner of a desk. No, I'm not trying to buy people—but who among us doesn't appreciate a little thoughtfulness once in a while? Those little things are remembered when I make a phone call and ask for information.

That means that I can respond quickly to my client—and it makes me look good. To put this in another context, think of someone with a friend or relative in a nursing home. Sure, the nurses and aides take care of every patient, but they're short-staffed and overworked. You're the person who develops a good relationship with them—maybe bringing donuts for the whole staff, and being pleasant when you talk to them. Guess whose parents get the extra care?

People want to, and will, help friendly people they like, so it's important to develop these relationships.

DEPARTMENT HEADS

This holds true for the "power" people as well. Meeting over lunch or dinner, I made sure from my first day on the job to pay my own way so that people would see that I can't be "bought" by lunch or a pair of ballgame tickets. This remains my policy. Important people are always getting the bite put on them. If every call you make to them is a request for money, it won't be long before they stop taking your calls. .. and when you have to make that rare call, you want the answer to be "yes".

On the other side of the coin, during the course of a year I take every department head out to lunch, or make sure we have coffee together on occasion—and I make it a point to buy. I listen to all their problems with the public, the front office, and each other. I might agree with them that so-and-so is the problem ... and maybe when I'm with so-and-so I agree with his point of view as well. I don't add to their criticism, I just nod a lot. So when the fire department is mad at the building department for not involving them with a review of a plan for a new project early, and the fire department wants to drag its feet, I can work as the middle man to bring the sides to some workable solution.

My project gets reviewed fast and approved, because each department head doesn't want the other to think he can't do the job. Once I get what I want, I call and thank them and, depending on how big the project or issue is, I provide an updated call and thank them again. Nobody likes to be taken for granted. Everyone likes a little praise. The extra effort on my part helps them "buy into" the project, since they see that they're playing an important role.

For example: It's late in the construction season, and a project needs to get underway before weather delays it until spring, or adds extra costs. A building plan needs to be completed for review. You seek and get approval to submit just foundation plans so construction can start. Without cooperation, you're dead. But because you've done your homework, you get the approval, the contractor is happy, the client is pleased that you and the city want him. He made the right decision. The goodwill lasts a long time.

During the holiday season, I write a letter to all department heads, personally thanking them for their cooperation.

ELECTED AND APPOINTED OFFICIALS

Now—we've talked about the secretary, staff and department heads. But what about your bosses—the Mayor, City Council, and other Board members?

The mayor is your boss. It's simple as that. His job is to get elected. What you do or don't do affects him, which impacts on you. So you have one simple rule: Tell the Mayor you know it's his job to cut the ribbons and get his picture taken for the newspaper... and it's your job to see that it happens. It's also your job to make sure the economic development corner is covered, and he won't be caught off-guard or go to a meeting without being briefed.

Is this extra work? Maybe, but it pays off. He leaves you alone and allows you to do your job. It's a small price, with big dividends. This has worked well for me under five different mayors and city councils. The council works the same way—make sure councillors get invited to ground-breakings, open houses and so on. If a project is in their ward, let them know early. Introduce the client. And never take

their votes for granted. I always ask directly for their votes. If it's a politically-sensitive issue and I don't need their vote, I let them know. I prepare a briefing package before a vote, talk to all of the councilors, and make sure they get all the promotional materials.

THE PRESS

Networking at City Hall is vital, but equally important is your relationship with the press. You're probably all making faces, but be honest—the press can make or break you. Talk with reporters. Return their phone calls. Be honest with them. If you can't release information, tell them you can't say any more, but tell them to call you in a couple of days. They have a job to do, so you might as well work with them. Educate them about your job. Let them become believers. Build a relationship. Meet with the editorial board and provide them with a story. You need the fourth estate as much as they need you.

OTHERS

These same principles that work for you in City Hall apply to business and social networks—the Chamber of Commerce, Rotary Club, YMCA. Economic development is a team effort. You should be constantly working to add people to your team. Think of every person you meet as a potential player on that team, and you'll see that effort pay off throughout the year.

PROFESSIONALISM

Phone calls—from whatever source— are important. Return them. Some calls are going to be trouble, or cause you more work, but you must make them. There are better times to make the calls than other times ... like early in the morning, or late in the afternoon, when you hope the person you're calling isn't in. Once you've returned a call, the obligation shifts back to the other person. If you really need to speak to someone, try around lunch (when the secretary is out), or late evening. Chances are your person will pick up the

phone directly. Listen carefully, ask questions, and if you make commitments, follow up on them.

Use your phone as part of your retention program. While it's always better to visit a company in person, a phone call to check up is useful. Follow up and delivery—no matter how big or small the issue—is critical to your credibility. If you say you're going to send literature, send it. And don't promise things you can't deliver, because you'll lose that credibility quickly.

I would rather have a potential customer go away mad, knowing we can't do what he wants, rather than string him along and ultimately not deliver. Wasted time, money and opportunity will only make him even more unhappy—and that ill will lasts a long time.

Remember, just as you must do what you say you will do, you must also be honest about yourself. Don't try to be anything other than who and what you are. Don't put on airs. Understand the city or town you work for. If you're in a beer town, don't drink champagne.

Your employers want you to be professional and well-educated, but they want someone they can relate to. When you make a public presentation, show your professionalism, but keep the information understandable for everyone in the room. Don't speak down to people, but on the other hand, don't go overboard trying to show them how smart you are. If you know what you're doing, it will be obvious.

CONCLUDING COMMENTS

Treat economic development as if it were your own company, and keep your eye on the road to its success. If you're serious about what you do, economic development will be on your mind with every contact you make, at work or at play.

Why am I successful? Communication, cooperation and consideration are my guiding principles. Try putting them to work for you, and watch those milestones accumulate on your road to success.

Obtaining Technological Resources for the Economic Development Office

Gene B. Lawin,
Donald G. Chaplain, CED

A basic computer system is an essential item in a typical economic development office. Computers can help compose correspondence, track appointments, generate promotional materials based on current information, and manage prospect lists. Many would like to know more about the basic elements of a computer system. This knowledge is particularly useful to those who are contemplating the purchase of a computer. However those who already own a computer may also find this information useful as technology continues to evolve.

When faced with trying to understand computer technology and more importantly, when spending money to obtain it, many people become overwhelmed. This article attempts to remove some of the "fog factor" that surfaces regarding computer terminology. The opinions expressed are those of the authors and are certainly subject to challenge like those of most economic developers.

With rampant technology, there is always the opportunity to try for "bigger, better, faster" in all aspects of computer hardware and software. The critical focus that economic developers need to maintain when considering upgrades or initial purchases revolves around two key questions: What do you want the computer to do? How much of your budget are you willing to spend? Remember your answers to those questions as you consider the options available.

SOFTWARE

Computer systems typically consist of hardware and software components. The majority of this article is going to concentrate on the hardware side of the computer system, but let's briefly discuss what the software can do. Software is a generic term which is applied to any program (some use the term application) which runs on a computer. A typical computer system will utilize software such as an operating system (examples include DOS/Windows, OS/2, and Unix), a word processor , a spreadsheet, a database manager, and various utility programs for maintenance.

Word Processing

The word processing software available today contains some extremely sophisticated features which can really improve the productivity of most offices. Word processors can generate "customized" letters based on a common template, a feature which simplifies the typical correspondence most often found in day-to-day activities of the ED office. A good example is the follow-up letter. A predefined letter can be set up containing the information which remains static or unchanging. This "form" can then be used as a starting point and customized for a particular prospect.

Most word processors also have a mail merge function. Merging is the process of taking data from a list and letting the computer enter that data directly into a "form" letter when the letter is printed. For example, a meeting announcement might be needed for the members of your development board. The announcement document would contain all of the meeting information and some "fill in the blank areas" (typically called fields). The word processor gathers the names and addresses of the board members from an existing list and then generates one letter for each member of the list, placing each member's name and address in the defined field in the document. Mail merging is one of the most time saving uses of a computer system and typically justifies the effort required to maintain common lists of important names and information.

All word processors can check spelling for typical errors and save any unique words back to the dictionary so that the program becomes more intelligent with usage. Additionally, the major word processors can check grammar usage or display a thesaurus for those occasions when you're looking for the "right" word. Graphical word processors such as Amipro or Word allow editing a document on the computer screen which closely resembles the final printed output. For example, text which should be bolded or italicized when printed appears bolded or italicized on the screen. In computer terms the ability for a word processor to display on the screen an accurate image of the printed output is referred to as What You See Is What You Get (WYSIWYG - pronounced whizzy-wig).

Database Managers

Databases are typically the second most useful program in a computer system. A database manager is simply a program which manages lists of information. The database program helps in the creation of the lists by generating forms on the screen which you prompt for the correct information. Database data entry forms can contain validity checks, which are instructions to disallow the entering of data which does not conform to what should be in the database. For example, a particular entry in the database form might be a scheduled meeting date. A meeting usually isn't scheduled for the past and so the database form can compare the current date to the scheduled date. If the scheduled date has already passed, the computer can post a warning message about the possible erroneous date being entered.

Database programs can also generate differing types of sorted lists based on the information in the same database, which makes a properly designed computerized list extremely flexible. For instance, a prospect report can be sorted by zip code, SIC code, lead source, last name, or company name depending on your needs at the time. A computerized list can also be used by a word processor to generate "customized" form letters intended for distribution to many people.

Community profile programs, building/site inventory programs, and contact managers are some examples of customized database programs which are designed to fit particular needs. Contact managers, such as ACT!®, are designed to help organize people, such as economic developers, whose livelihood depends on maintaining communications with many people. Contact managers typically include a simple word processor, scheduling package, and a report generator. The word processor will draw names and addresses from the database to simplify correspondence composition, the scheduler will remind you about appointments and phone calls, and the report generator will generate lists of contacts based on common criteria, such as city, state, or status.

Spreadsheets

Many economic developers will also find a spreadsheet program, such as Lotus 123 or Microsoft Excel extremely useful for office budgeting and the structuring of financial packages. Spreadsheets are very good at organizing numbers or analyzing numerical data from a database. A spreadsheet is a powerful analysis tool and, although less frequently used than a word processor or a database, a very important part of the typical computer system in an economic developers office. The spreadsheet can also be a difficult software for the economic developer to master so taking a class on spreadsheet usage to gain an understanding of the power of a spreadsheet program is highly recommended.

Learning Aids

Modern software packages often include on-line, self-paced tutorials which can be used to gain a basic understanding of the program. After-market books are also available which are typically targeted to most computer novices. An excellent series of books, all having a title of ". . . for Dummies" (such as "DOS for Dummies" or "OS/2 for Dummies") is an acclaimed resource for information about the computer. Above all, you should be aware that the hardware and software purchase price is only a small amount of the total expenditure for a computer system. A great amount of time, and some additional expense, should be budgeted for training.

HARDWARE

The hardware component of a basic computer system typically consists of the computer itself (sometimes called the CPU) and an attached video monitor and printer.

Some additional optional components, such as an internal modem or internal CD ROM drive, may be installed inside the computer case. A peripheral is a computer component item which is attached to the computer rather than installed inside the computer. Printers, monitors, external CD ROM drives, and external modems are all examples of common computer peripherals.

What Should I be Buying Now?

Table 1 provides some common computer configurations available from most manufacturers of equipment. Listed are what the authors believe will be the low end, median, and high end types of systems that will be available when this article is published. (Due to the long lead time of the publishing cycle and the short change period for computer equipment this information should be considered an educated guess rather than a hard fact). Any of the systems listed in Table 1 is capable of running any application an economic developer is likely to be using. The differences between the systems are related primarily to speed and storage capacity. The performance issue becomes important when you are waiting for the word processing program to finish that mail merge to fifty people.

Computer purchasers are typically very concerned about obsolescence due to the rapid evolution of computer technology. In the 80's, the obsolescence factor revolved around the ability of older machines to run newer software. With the introduction of the 80386 processor in 1987, this issue has for the most part disappeared. All software currently written, and yet to be written, for the Intel x86 architecture will run on any of the above systems for the rest of the decade. The obsolescence factor in the 90's is a speed issue. Although any computer purchased today will certainly run most software written through the end of the decade, the computer may perform so slowly that most users will quickly become frustrated by long waits during processing. The best idea when purchasing a computer is to buy the fastest computer with the most storage capacity that will fit in your budget.

Prior to the introduction of Windows

TABLE 1
Typical Computer Configurations

Component	Typical Computer Ad Configurations		
	Low End	Median	High End
CPU	Intel 66 MHz 486 DX/2	Intel 75 MHz Pentium	Intel 90 MHz Pentium
Working Memory (RAM)	8 MB RAM	16 MB RAM, 256 KB cache	16 MB RAM, 256 KB cache
Permanent Storage (Hard disk)	340 MD 13 ms IDE Hard Drive	540 MB 13 ms IDE Hard Drive	1 GB 11 ms SCSI Hard Drive
Disk Drive Interface		Enhanced IDE interface	PCI Fast SCSI interface
Video System	Local Bus Graphics w/1MB	Local Bus Graphics w/1MB	PCI Local Bus Graphics w/1MB
Video Monitors	14" Color SVGA Monitor	15" Color SVGA Monitor	17" Color SVGA Monitor
Floppy Drives	3.5" Diskette Drive	3.5" Diskette Drive	3.5" Diskette Drive
CD ROM Drives	Double Speed CD ROM	Double Speed CD ROM	Triple Speed CD ROM
Case Style	Mini Desktop Case	Desktop Case	Minitower Case
Keyboard and mouse	101-key Keyboard and Mouse	101-key Keyboard and Mouse	101-key Keyboard and Mouse
Operating System	MS DOS 6.2 and and Windows 3.11	PC DOS 6.3 and WFW 3.11	OS/2 3.0
Modem	14.4 kbps Data/ Fax modem	14.4 kbps Data/ Fax modem	14.4 kbps Data/ Fax modem
Additional Bundled Software	MS Works 3.0 CD	MS Office Professional 3.0 CD	Lotus Smart Suite 3.0 CD
Estimated Street Price*	$1,199.00	$2,199.00	$3,199.00

*The prices are given for illustration only and do not reflect actual pricing of any one vendor.

3.0 in 1990, most computer applications used a text mode user interface. A user interface is computer technospeak for the way a person interacts with a computer program. Text mode applications suffer from two major disadvantages when compared to more modern graphical applications. A steep initial learning curve is the biggest drawback of a text mode application and is caused by each text mode computer program requiring you to learn its unique way of performing tasks, such as saving a file. For example, saving a file in the WordPerfect 5.1 word processor and the Lotus 123 spreadsheet programs are accomplished in two entirely different manners. You would have to learn how to do the simplest of things -- saving a file -- two different ways. If you use many applications, the differing instruction sets of each program make using a computer that much more difficult.

The other disadvantage of text based applications is that the printed version of a document or letter usually does not visually match the version that is displayed on the computer screen. A text mode program is only capable of displaying 25 lines of the same sized 80 characters on the computer screen. The actual printed appearance of these characters is often substantially different from the characters seen by the user on the computer screen.

The use of graphical applications creates a computer environment which is much more natural for most people when using a computer. Graphical applications, such as Microsoft's Word for Windows wordprocessor and Lotus' 123 for OS/2 spreadsheet, level the learning curve because many basic functions, such as opening a file, are handled in a similar manner. Another inherent benefit of graphical applications is that the viewed and printed form of a document appear the same to the writer of the document.

However, the arrival of graphical computer programs has eliminated the ability to buy the lowest price equipment and be satisfied with the resulting performance. Graphical applications make the computer much easier to use, but these same applications require more computer horsepower to attain the same performance level as the text based applications. Therefore, the recommended purchasing rule of thumb is "buy as much performance as you can". In essence, the computer is using the additional horsepower that the higher perform-

ance provides to create a more productive and user friendly computing environment.

The need for more computer horsepower leads to the price/performance ratio and the related reliability of various computer systems. Most purchasing decisions are based solely on speed and price because we all want to purchase the fastest computer for the lowest price. This is a natural reaction in the decision making process, but there is a key component of the purchase decision missing. That component is the reliability of the computer system.

The reliability of the computer system and its closely related ability to run more modern computer software should be a major factor in the purchase of a computer system. For the past decade, the reliability of most computers has been based on the machine's ability to execute computer programs in a PC DOS environment with few problems. The PC DOS operating system puts very little stress on most modern computer equipment, so most computers were judged to be reliable if they ran PC DOS programs without failure.

An operating system is the basic software which provides a framework for the different types of programs which run on a computer system. The operating system allows other programs to access the hard disk, share memory, output items to the printer, and otherwise work together. The introduction of more powerful operating systems, such as IBM's OS/2, nullifies the older reliability test of simply running PC DOS programs without failure. Computers now must also reliably run new advanced (commonly called 32 bit mode) computer programs. Recent experience has shown that some low budget systems have achieved the low price point by cutting corners in computer component quality during system design and manufacturing. A computer system should have the ability to run the newest 32 bit programs such as IBM's OS/2 operating system and the Windows 95 operating system when it's released by Microsoft in mid to late 1995. Major vendors will guarantee that computer systems have the ability to run modern 32 bit software.

Microsoft's Windows 95 operating system support cannot be certified at this time by vendors because that operating system has not been released yet; however any machine capable of running IBM's OS/2 should also be able to run Windows 95 without difficulty. Although one may now

prefer only to run the current PC DOS and Windows operating environment on the new computer system, purchasing a computer which will not run the newer advanced operating systems is not recommended.

The best way to buy a reliable computer is to stay with major name vendors. The top tier of these vendors includes IBM, Compaq, and Hewlett-Packard (HP). Dell, Gateway 2000, and AST are second tier manufacturers whose computers sell for lower prices. However, experience has shown that second tier vendor equipment has a higher failure rate than equipment from the top tier companies. In most cases, the failure is not high enough to warrant avoiding the purchase of equipment from a second tier vendor.

Part of the purchase decision process relates to what you want the computer to do. How important is having the best reliability history compared to the cost advantages usually available from the second tier vendors? Will the machine be the only computer in the office or is it an additional one? Do you intend to totally computerize the office or do you anticipate only having certain functions performed on the computer? Focusing on needs before beginning the purchasing process will help determine whether you need to purchase a computer from a top tier or second tier vendor.

Private label brand computers usually inhabit the very low end of the computer cost curve, but they are never the bargain they seem. Private label brand computers are usually either assembled from generic components by a dealer or by a company which pursues a regional market rather than a national market. If the dealer discontinues the product line or the company goes out of business, one will have an "orphaned" computer with no future support in the event something goes wrong. Most private label brands have such a high risk factor of being "orphaned" that the purchase is usually never justified by the low price alone.

Currently there are over 300 computer manufacturers competing in a market which is reaching saturation, and a shakeout is expected in the next few years as operating margins continue to be squeezed by competition in the industry. Smaller computer manufacturers whose sales are under $1 billion annually will not be able to generate enough revenue to design, develop, and support the more complex computer systems the industry is moving to. The smaller vendors are also less likely to develop sales in international markets where future growth would allow the company to survive.

The Computer (CPU)

The central processor unit (CPU) is the brain of the computer system. When most people think of the CPU of a computer system they picture the large case or shell of the computer system, but the CPU is really just one chip (the technical term is integrated circuit or IC) on a circuit board full of IC's inside that case. The type of CPU that a computer system is based on largely determines how much processing "horsepower" the computer system has to work with. The more horsepower a computer system has, the more quickly programs will run and when programs run faster they appear to be more responsive to user input such as keystrokes and mouse movements. Remember, the point is to buy the fastest computer one can budget, because a faster computer will perform more work in a shorter period of time.

A CPU's horsepower rating is positively correlated to two factors, the central processor type and the clock speed rating. The clock inside a computer system is not like the 24 hour time piece we hang on walls or keep on our wrists. The computer's clock is a component of the computer system which keeps all the complex systems inside a computer running in harmony. The clock generates electronic pulses which are measured in millions of cycles per second (called megahertz and abbreviated MHz). As shown in Table 1, some of the available clock speeds are 33 MHz, 75 MHz, and 90 MHz. The clock speed of a computer is similar to the RPM measurement of a car's engine. So it follows that the faster the clock cycle rating in megahertz, the faster the computer will process programs and respond to instructions.

Newer processor designs are usually more powerful than that of their predecessors. For example, a 486 CPU is more powerful than a 386 processor and a Pentium CPU is more powerful than a 486 processor. A nice feature of the IBM PC and compatible line of computers is that while the newer processors are getting faster, they continue to be able to run the programs designed for the older CPU's so you do not have to replace all of the software when you replace a computer with a newer model. The 386 CPU is no longer

manufactured for use in personal computer systems, but some 386 processor computers are available as used equipment. The 486 processor computers are currently positioned at the entry level because they combine good performance with a low price. Pentium processors are the fastest CPUs available today from Intel in a personal computer system, but in the future the Power PC computer may provide real price and performance competition to the Intel family of processors.

Differences between Working Memory (RAM) and Hard Disk Capacity

To fully understand the difference between working memory and hard disk storage, and why both are needed, you need to know how a computer processes and stores information. Think about the process of reading this article. We read the text on the paper into our minds for processing. The paper on which the article is printed can be considered a permanent storage device and your memory (if similar to most) can best be termed temporary (or working) storage.

Similarly, a computer will read the contents of a file from a permanent storage device, such as a hard disk or a floppy disk, into working memory and process it. Therefore, the computer needs both permanent and working storage capacity. There are two forms of storage devices which are incorporated into the design of personal computers to fulfill the differing requirements of permanent storage and working memory. These two devices are called a hard disk drive, which is largely a mechanical device, and Random Access Memory (RAM), which is an electronic device.

In computer design there is a direct tradeoff between the cost and speed of a storage device. The faster information may be read from, or written to, a storage device, the more expensive the device is. For example, 1 MB of storage capacity on a hard disk drive is about $.50 to $1, while 1MB of RAM, which has a transfer speed that is hundreds of times faster than a hard disk, costs about $40. Personal computers need hundreds of megabytes of permanent storage capacity while requiring only a few megabytes of working memory capacity. The permanent storage device doesn't need to have as high a data transfer speed as the working memory device where data transfer speed is vitally important. Therefore, for economic and performance reasons a personal computer uses a hard disk as a

permanent storage device and RAM as the working memory device.

The best attribute of a hard disk drive, the low cost per megabyte of capacity, makes it a good choice for a permanent storage device, while the major disadvantage of a hard disk drive, the information transfer speed, is not an important requirement for permanent storage. A hard disk drive stores information magnetically in the same manner as a tape recorder. In fact, if you ever have a chance to look inside a hard disk, you will see a brown magnetic material similar to the surface on magnetic tape coating the drive's platters.

Hard disk drive capacity is usually described in millions of bytes (megabytes, abbreviated MB). A byte is a unit of information, such as any individual letter on this page, that the computer processes. Hard drive capacities for PC's now range from about 200MB to over 9,000 MG (9 billion bytes). The newer graphical mode applications generally require a great deal of permanent storage space. For example, Amipro, which is a graphical word processor from Lotus Development Corp., requires over 16 MB of permanent storage. Therefore, a personal computer should have at least 300 MB of hard disk capacity available to store adequately a modern operating system, a good set of application programs, and other data.

The best feature of RAM, the fast information transfer speed, makes it a good choice for a working memory device, while the high cost per megabyte of capacity for RAM makes it a poor choice for a permanent storage device. The type of RAM, called volatile RAM, used in a personal computer has another major disadvantage, other than cost, when used as a permanent storage device. The contents of volatile RAM are lost when power is removed or interrupted, thus power would have to be constantly supplied to the computer or all the permanent information would be lost.

RAM capacities are usually measured in megabytes, just like hard disks. The usual amount of RAM installed in a personal computer system, however, is far less than the usual hard disk drive capacity. Installed RAM capacities range from 4MB to 16MB with capacities of greater than 256 MB of RAM possible in more advanced machines. The more advanced programs and computer environments available today, such as computer networking, require more working memory capacity in a personal computer. For example, Windows and OS/2 will run, albeit not quickly, with 4 MB of RAM installed in a computer. A good computer system really needs at least 8 MB of installed RAM to function productively with graphical applications and 16 MB of installed RAM is a good amount for a computer running the OS/2 operating system software or the forthcoming Windows 95 operating system software from Microsoft.

What is a Local Bus?

Notice that all of the systems displayed in Table 1 have either local bus graphics or PCI local bus graphics capability. The bus of a computer system is the highway system through which all information travels in a computer. Any data which needs to go from working memory, permanent storage, or video memory to the processor or back must travel through the system bus to get to its destination. People who add internal modems or other cards which go inside the computer case are all familiar with the sockets that the cards plug into. Those sockets reside on the system bus and plugging the cards into the sockets attaches the cards physically to the system bus.

The system bus that is in use in most personal computers sold today was designed by IBM in 1984 for use in the "AT" series of personal computers. This bus later became known as the "Industry Standard Architecture" (or ISA) bus. The problem is the ISA bus has some pretty severe limitations regarding the amount of data that could cross the bus at one time. An analogy most of us are familiar with is that of a two lane highway which passes less traffic than a four lane highway. A two lane highway will quickly become clogged with a heavy traffic flow which a four lane highway can accommodate with ease. Manufacturers became more aware of this limitation when graphical applications started becoming prevalent on the desktop PC because graphical applications send enormous amounts of data across the bus. Computer engineers came up with several new bus designs to try to provide more data throughput at a faster rate in the computer.

Two initial designs emerged from this effort, the Microchannel Architecture (MCA) found in most IBM PS/2 computers, and the Enhanced Industry Standard Architecture (EISA) found in most other manufacturers' top of the line machines. The MCA and EISA buses were more costly than the ISA buses they were designed to replace and subsequently had poor sales rates. More importantly, the use of high quality video in some graphical programs puts a tremendous load on the personal computer data bus which even the MCA and EISA architectures were not capable of handling quickly enough.

What personal computer customers really wanted was a bus that had a greater reliability and higher speed than the ISA bus provided, but was no more expensive than the ISA bus. The first solution attempted by the industry to fulfill the low cost and high speed criteria was called the VESA Local (VL) bus. The VL bus was designed by a consortium of computer graphics adapter manufacturers primarily to speed up the display of graphics information on a computer screen. Some of the older 486 designs you might see advertised will indicate that a computer model has "local bus" graphics to indicate that the VL bus is used in the computer. The VL bus was initially well received by the computer industry, however, it became quickly apparent that the VL bus was not a good future solution for evolving computer CPU architectures because it was tied too closely to the existing 486 architecture.

Intel designed a bus called the Peripheral Component Interconnect (PCI) bus which was designed to be a more processor "independent" bus than the VL bus. The PCI bus is now the preferred local bus implementation on personal computers and is the smart buy right now. In the future, computer add-in cards for a VL bus computer will become difficult to locate as manufacturers move their product lines to the PCI bus.

The Monitor and Computer Video

A computer video display subsystem is perhaps the most important part of any personal computer system. In fact, it is the incredible performance of the display system in a personal computer which makes personal computers appealing to most of us. In the days when mainframe based computers ruled the world, the cost of the hardware dictated that all of the "CPU power" was to be used for processing purposes only. Any use of valuable "CPU cycles" to make the computer easier for normal humans to use was considered a waste of money. Modern personal computers are so inexpensive that it has become cost efficient to use some of the computer's CPU power to make the computer easier to use. The advent of the graphical user interface (GUI) is only possible because of the low cost of personal computer "CPU cycles" and the power of present day computer display systems.

Most people do not give much thought to their computer displays when purchasing a computer, but a bad computer display system used over an 8 hour day can cause physical discomfort to anyone unlucky enough to be sitting in front of it. Personal computer display systems are composed of two separate, but matched, components. The graphics card inside the computer generates an image that is displayed by the computer monitor. Personal computer video display monitors are rated in categories such as dot pitch, resolution, and refresh frequencies. Computer graphics cards are rated by the resolution that the video card is capable of generating and the number of colors the graphics card is capable of sending to the display at one time.

The image we see on a computer screen is built from very small dots of light. The size of the dots is measured in millimeters (mm) and is called the dot pitch rating of the computer monitor. The larger the size of the dots the less focused an image will appear on the computer screen. A smaller dot pitch rating is better when comparing computer monitors. A good computer monitor will have a dot pitch rating of .29 mm, or less, and the displayed image will be sharp and focused. Some less expensive computer monitors, such as those packaged with a typical low budget computer system will have dot pitch ratings of .39 mm or more. While the size difference of the dots may appear small, to most people a computer display with a .39 mm dot pitch will appear fuzzy and out of focus. After a prolonged session in front of the computer the average user of a large dot pitch monitor will start to experience physical discomfort, usually in the form of tired eyes and headaches from constantly trying to focus on the grainy image.

The resolution that a monitor is capable of displaying and a graphics card is capable of generating is directly correlated to the coarseness, or jaggedness, of that image. Resolution is measured in pixels and the more pixels a graphics card can generate and a monitor can display, the finer the texture of the image the user views on the computer screen. Resolutions are typically denoted in a number such as 640x480 which means the computer display system will present a block of pixels which is 480 pixels high and 640 pixels wide on the computer display. A common term for a computer video resolution of 640x480 pixels is VGA (VGA is an acronym for video graphics array) resolution. The higher resolutions of 800x600, 1024x768, and higher, are referred to as SVGA (super VGA) resolutions.

The video refresh frequency (sometimes called the vertical frequency) rating of a monitor and graphics card is the measurement of the number of times per second that the image on the computer screen is redrawn. For example a refresh frequency of 72 Hz means the displayed image is regenerated 72 times per second. Any refresh frequency above 60 Hz will generate a nice stable image on the computer screen and refresh frequencies below 60 Hz will begin to cause the appearance of flickering similar to that of old home movies. The current recommended standard for the video refresh frequency is 72 Hz.

Most computer display monitors currently on the market, as well as almost all graphics cards packaged in major vendor computers, are capable of displaying VGA and SVGA resolutions. However, if a graphics card generates a higher resolution than the computer monitor can display, the computer monitor can be damaged, so be careful about attaching older computer displays to a new computer system. For example, an older monitor may not be capable of displaying 1024x768 resolution at 60 Hz and will be damaged if connected to a graphics card which is currently generating this resolution and frequency combination. Some new, but really low cost monitors (usually below $275), may also be incapable of displaying 1024x768 at 60 Hz and should be avoided.

The amount of video memory which comes with a computer determines how many colors can be shown on the screen at one time at a given resolution. Most computer systems sold by major vendors today come with 1 MB of video memory which is enough memory to display 256 colors at a 1024x768 resolution. This is an adequate range of colors for anything used in the typical economic developer's office. Machines used in photographic imaging applications typically have a 4 MB of video memory so they can display over 16 million different colors. The capability to display 16 million colors is also called a "true"

color" capability because the human eye can distinguish no more than 16 million colors.

The dot pitch and resolution displayed on a computer monitor are also tied to another ergonomic factor in the display system, the optimal physical size of the computer monitor. The use of higher reso-

lutions to display information on a computer screen allows more information to be presented on the computer screen. For example, spreadsheets will show more rows and columns on a sheet and a word processor can give a wider view of the printable page at a higher video resolution. However, information presented at a resolution

TABLE 2
Printer Technologies

	Dot matrix printers	Ink Jets	Personal/Workgroup laser printers	Departmental laser printers
Pros	Least expensive with lowest cost per page of output. Can print multipart forms and can handle 11" wide paper.	Much quieter than dot matrix, good print quality. Most will print in color.	High quality print. Quiet, compact, more energy efficient than the departmental laser printers. Least expensive laser models.	High quality print. Can handle a high printing volume per month without damaging the printer. Very fast output. Some can handle 11 by 17 inch paper and have multiple paper bins available.
Cons	Lowest print quality, unacceptable for professional correspondence.	Cost per page is higher than dot matrix and slightly higher than laser printers. Poor quality paper will let the ink "bleed" into the paper. Smearing can be a problem, particularly on transparencies.	If shared by more than a few people, the rated volume may be exceeded and void the warranty. Some base units may not be able to print a full graphical page without a memory upgrade.	Setup is more difficult. Printers are generally in a common area where anyone can see the output.
Speed	25 to 150 characters per second (cps).	1 to 3 pages per minute (ppm) depending on content of the printed page.	Personal laser printers, 4 to 6 pages per minute (ppm). Workgroup printers can do 8 to 12 ppm.	16 to 32 pages per minute.
Cost	$100-$300	Monochrome models, $200 - $300. Three color models, $300 - $400. Four color models $500 - $3,000.	Personal models, $400 - $1,000. Workgroup models, $750 - $1,500.	$3,000 - $20,000.
Cost per page	Less than 1 cent.	Monochrome 2 - 8 cents. Color $.20 - $1.20.	1 to 4 cents.	1 to 3 cents.
Output quality	No match for inkjet or laser printer.	Almost, but not quite, laser quality. Special paper will improve the quality. Good for printing business charts. The best do a good job of reproducing photos on special paper.	Excellent, especially from 800 dot per inch (dpi) units. Some vendors now offer color laser printers priced at $7,000 to $10,000.	
Color	Some units have color ribbons, but output is acceptable only for color highlighting text.	Cut sheets, transparencies, labels, envelopes, customized forms.		No departmental laser printers are capable of printing in color yet.
Media	Continuous feed perforated or cut sheets.			

63

of 1024x768 on a 14" monitor can be almost too small to read.

There are common monitor size/display resolution ratios that are considered optimal by the computer industry. A 14" monitor should display information at a resolution of no higher than a 800x600 pixels, while a 15" monitor is the bare minimum for displaying information at a resolution of 1024x768 pixels and a 17" monitor is really the preferred solution at higher resolutions. The problem with using a smaller monitor at a higher resolution is the same as trying to read small type in printed material. A higher resolution will create smaller type (similar to the "fine" print) while a larger monitor will display smaller type as larger characters, similar to using reading glasses to magnify the characters on a page. In fact, if glasses are required to read printed material such as a newspaper, a 17", or larger, computer monitor will make the computer much more comfortable to use ergonomically because it puts less strain on your eyes.

Printers

The annual printer issue of *PC Magazine* is the best source for printer information and should be considered the consumer's guide to printer technology. Table 2 shows most of the relative advantages and disadvantages for different printer technologies and is based on information from the annual printer issue. For more detailed information on specific printers, and particularly if you are contemplating a printer purchase, referring to the annual *PC Magazine* printer issue is highly recommended.

Modems

The most current industry standard for modems which connect across standard phone lines is v.34 which allows a transfer speed between modems of 28,800 bits per second (bps). The standard is set by an international standards committee and is used to insure that any modem which follows the v.34 standard will be able to communicate with other modems which also follow the standard. This number probably will not mean anything to you, but if you purchase a modem make sure the modem is v.34 compliant.

Modems can be purchased either as internal or external units. Internal modems are installed inside the computer and external modems are attached to the computer by a modem cable. External units are generally preferable because there are indicator lights on the modem case which can be used to troubleshoot modem communication problems and the modems are easily moved from one machine to another. Internal modems possess no indicator lights and are not easily moved to another computer, but they are also less expensive and a modem cable is not needed.

A Data/fax modem is a hybrid type of modem which is capable of sending/receiving faxes to/from a standard office fax machine. Special faxing software is needed to use this feature, but that software is readily available (sometimes included free with the data/fax modem) and usually very simple to use.

A useful feature of most faxing software is the ability to act as a "printer" for application programs such as spreadsheets and word processors. One can literally print a document from a word processor, or any program for that matter, to any standard fax machine by simply entering the recipient's fax phone number. Fax software usually allows a received fax to be redirected to a printer which is attached to the computer. This allows faxes to be printed on the plain paper used in inkjet or laser printers rather than the expensive, hard to handle, thermal fax paper many times found in office fax machines.

CD ROM Drives

A large portion of the newest application and game software available today for the PC has grown in size to a point which makes a CD ROM drive a necessity in most economic development offices. For example, OS/2, Microsoft Office, and many prepackaged databases all consume a great deal of space. The most efficient way to install these programs is to use a CD ROM drive. Many databases useful to an economic developer, such as manufacturer directories, are also available on CD ROM.

CD ROM drives can be installed in each workstation individually. However, if the CD ROM drive is to be used for access to databases which may be used by more than one person on a network, a better solution is to install CD ROM drives in the file server where the CD ROM information can be shared by all people connected to the network. If frequent shared access is required for a particular CD ROM database, a good solution is to dedicate a file server attached CD ROM drive to that database.

CD ROM drives come in various forms. The interface (how the drive connects to a computer) can be either IDE or SCSI. IDE interface drives are less expensive than the SCSI interface models. However, only two CD ROM drives can be attached to an IDE interface, while seven drives can be attached to a SCSI interface. For most offices the IDE interface model is sufficient; however, if the CD ROM drives are to be attached to a file server and shared throughout the network, the SCSI type drives are a far more flexible solution.

CD ROM drives are also rated on the speed with which data can be read from them. The first CD ROM drives on the market, and now rarely available, were known as single speed CD ROM drives. A single speed drive spins the CD platter at the same speed as the CD player in a home stereo and achieves a data throughput of 150 kilobytes (KB) per second.

The original, single speed CD ROM drives were considered very slow by computer standards and manufacturers quickly moved to develop faster technology. The most common CD ROM drive available today is known as a "double speed" (or 2x) CD ROM drive. Double speed drives spin the CD platter at twice the speed of the original single speed CD ROM drives and therefore can deliver data at twice the rate of the older drives (300 KB/second).

Triple (3x) and quad (4x) speed CD ROM drives are also available but at a higher cost than the more common double speed drives. By the end of 1995, triple speed CD ROM drives will become the market standard for entry level cost CD ROM drives as manufacturing efficiencies increase. When multimedia and video become prevalent in business PC's, quad speed CD ROM drives will become the standard because a throughput of 500KB/second is required to sustain full screen, full motion video at 30 frames per second. A triple speed drive's throughput (450 KB/second) is not up to the requirements for full screen, full motion video, while a quad speed drive's throughput (600KB/second) will easily handle the data throughput requirements.

Multiple CD ROM capable drives, such as the Pioneer 6 disc drive, are also available. Multi-disc drives can access one CD platter at a time, but they can store several CD ROM's and switch back and forth among them. Multi-disc drives are useful in situations where you may have several CD ROM's that you want to keep "on-line" simultaneously, but which are not shared or accessed frequently. The multi-disc drive needs five to seven seconds to change CD ROM platters, which prevents efficient operation if the CD ROM discs are frequently accessed or shared. Multi-disc drives are currently available in double and quad speed versions.

SUMMARY

In summary, here is a recap of the significant information presented in this article:

❏ Remember to consider the need for reliability of a computer system along with price. Know how important the reliability of this computer will be to your office.

❏ Graphical software and operating systems are the applications which are most likely to be used on a new computer system. OS/2 and Windows applications lower the initial learning curve.

❏ The low end CPU is a 486, 66 MHz computer and the high end is a 100 MHz Pentium. Buy as much performance as you can.

❏ Minimum hard disk capacity you should consider is 300 MG. Again, more is better.

❏ Minimum RAM capacity is 8 MB and 16 MB is desirable.

❏ The local bus in the computer should be the PCI type.

❏ The video monitor should have a minimum dot pitch of .29 or smaller and support a minimum refresh frequency of 72 Hz. Optimal monitor size is 15" for resolutions of 800x600 pixels and 17" for 1024x768 pixels.

❏ The optimal printer depends on usage, purchase price considerations, and operating costs. Before buying a printer try to read the annual *PC Magazine* review of printers.

❏ Modems should be v.34 compliant. External units are preferred.

❏ Double speed CD ROM drives are the basic units with triple speed becoming the standard this year.

One final caution. The one pitfall computer equipment buyers should be wary of is that of buying limitations. Not limitations as pertains to current software, but as to the demands future software will place on computer capabilities. Today's equipment will be limited soon enough, so buying smart (buying as much capacity and speed as you can afford) will help postpone the inevitable obsolescence awhile longer.

Preparing Tailored Fact Books and Prospect Proposals

Rick L. Weddle

INTRODUCTION

To function successfully today, economic developers must communicate effectively in writing to an increasingly sophisticated target audience. Much of the success in working with new business clients is directly related to how well one can deliver the information they need to make good sound business investment decisions. The words written must convey the desired meaning and they must do it quickly. If the written message takes too much of the reader's time to make its point, the reader is unlikely to get to the desired point or to care much upon finally grasping it. To effectively reach the target audience, one must present the information needed and present it in a format that is easy to read, understand, and absorb. Both the contents of the written communications and the manner in which they are presented are critical to getting the message across.

Two important products in the written communication arsenal are tailored fact books and custom proposals. These products have long been key features in the wide range of collateral materials used to present information about a community, a region, and/or a state.

Technology in today's workplace can greatly improve one's ability to communicate via these two vehicles. In recent years, the availability of sophisticated personal computer systems, application software, and printing capability has enabled the practitioner to become much more customer driven and focused in the preparation and delivery of community data and information.

Further, these technology tools have declined in cost to a point that they are readily available to almost all economic development practitioners. No longer are such productivity enhancements available in only the largest and best funded economic development programs. Indeed, the application and use of modern technology is leveling the playing field and narrowing the gap of communication advantages between the largest and the smallest of economic development operations.

This article reviews both customer driven design of tailored fact books and custom proposals and the use of off-the-shelf technology in the preparation of these communication tools. More specifically, it discusses:

❑ Tailored fact books and custom proposals as key communications tools,

❑ Customer driven content, organization and presentation format,

❑ Off-the-shelf technology that can make a real difference in your ability to prepare and deliver written communications, and

❑ Human resource issues associated with using technology in your economic development office.

It is noted that this article does not attempt to be all inclusive or to cover all aspects of modern office technology. Rather it attempts to share the knowledge learned from a decade of practical experience in dealing with rapidly changing technologies in the preparation of written communication materials, or more specifically, tailored fact books and custom proposals. Hopefully fellow practitioners will find the sharing of these experiences to be of value.

TAILORED FACT BOOKS AND CUSTOM PROPOSALS AS KEY WRITTEN COMMUNICATION PRODUCTS

Tailored fact books and custom proposals are similar in design and layout but differ in their use, length and the degree of detail. Both are printed outputs of information maintained in your research library and/or data base. The key to successful development and preparation of fact books and proposals is the degree to which their information content is customer driven and tailored to their specific requirements and needs.

Tailored Fact Books

Fact books have long been one of the practitioner's key information tools. They often present a complete compendium of information about our community, region, or state and function as a community economic development reference book.

Fact books are frequently produced in either a three-ring binder or a comb-bound format. As a collection of loosely assembled information pieces separated by pre-printed tabs, they often resemble a community "scrap book" more than a professionally prepared reference document.

The advent of modern technology has enabled the practitioner to produce and deliver the modern fact book as a highly tailored information piece. A functionally designed and modular format provides topical sections covering basic categories of data requested by clients.

The use of technology enables the practitioner to access automated data bases and output an up-to-date fact book in a standardized format. Adding a detailed table of contents and an index makes it easier to read and use.

Custom Proposals

The tailored fact book and the information base from which it is produced are the foundation for the development and preparation of custom proposals. Custom proposals are also a key element of the practitioner's communications arsenal. Developed in response to a client's specific information request, the custom proposal has grown in use and practical application to become a principal sales tool.

A proposal can be as simple as a few pages of text and related exhibits, or as complex as a fully customized summary of relevant information along with maps, photographs, and graphics. The proposal should cover issues to be resolved for the client to reach a location decision. It may also offer financial incentives along with a call to action suggesting a decision or leading to negotiations. A custom proposal moves from general to specific in presenting the community, region, or state sales pitch.

The typical proposal is presented in a comb-bound format with a cover designed for and addressed to the client. For larger projects, the proposal may involve a more expensive format with a hard-back personalized cover.

CUSTOMER DRIVEN CONTENT, ORGANIZATION, AND PRESENTATION FORMAT

The presentation format of these materials is most directly enhanced by the use and application of modern office technology. It is not enough to simply use modern office technology. One should maximize its advantages by incorporating it directly into the design of the materials. Since the tailored fact book is the foundation upon which custom proposals are based, the discussion that follows addresses the organization, layout and presentation of tailored fact book information.

Planning

Advance planning is essential. Content should be organized with the client in mind and presented in a modular format by functional area of interest.

An organizational tip exists in the information requests received in the past few years. Future clients frequently have interests similar to previous clients. This can help tailor materials to future clients' needs in advance. Examine previous requests to identify areas of information most commonly required. Assemble these into a matrix and one can get a good idea of not only the topics but also the level of detail needed.

This customer driven approach also will give an idea as to what sections or topics to include and, most importantly, the order in which they should be presented.

Components

❑ **Executive Summary.** Always include an executive summary to highlight the area's key features and location attributes. For custom proposals, the executive summary delivers the sales pitch by addressing specific issues or client location requirements. In both documents, the executive summary should call attention to sections that more fully address the client's information needs.

❑ **Section Tabs.** Topical section tabs should be used to make it easier to access randomly specific information. If the bud-get allows, consider pre-printing section tabs for major information categories that might be included in either a tailored fact book or a custom proposal. By doing so, one will have the flexibility of adding or eliminating sections based on specific needs. Another tip to consider is to organize the office informational filing system to correspond with the sections in the fact book. This will help with maintenance of information in between updates of the data base and subsequently the fact book. By cross referencing office informational files with the electronic data base, one will be taking a big step toward full data base/fact book integration.

❑ **Table of Contents.** A good table of contents, sufficiently detailed to include and cover topics within sections, is essential. By using a legal outlining and paragraph numbering format in your document (1, 1.1, 1.1.1, for example) the table of contents can easily lead the reader to the specific information required. Figure 1 is an example of a "user friendly" table of contents format.

❑ **List of Tables, Charts, Graphs, and Illustrations.** Immediately following the table of contents, include a list of tables, charts, graphs, and illustrations.

❑ **Section Presentation and Layout.** Each section covers a functional area of information and should be designed to be presented either as a modular section or as a free-standing information piece. Each section should begin with an executive summary no longer than two or three paragraphs. This summary frames the context within which the data is presented and states the importance of the attribute to the customer or client. Fact book and custom proposal sections should follow a legal outlining and paragraph numbering format to correspond with the table of contents format illustrated in Figure 1.

❑ **Page Layout and Numbering.** Page design should include features to enhance readability (such as primary and secondary headings and extra space between lines and paragraphs). A section header referencing the section topic is also recommended. Another tip is to number each section's

---

FIGURE 1
Example:
Table of Contents Format

Section 1 -- Population Characteristics	Page
1.1. Demographic Trends	1-1
1.2. Educational Levels	1-4
1.3. Income Levels	1-6
1.4. Commuting Patterns	1-7

Section 2 -- Labor Force	
2.1. Active Applicants	2-1
2.2. Employment and Unemployment Trends	2-5
2.3. Employment by Category	2-6
2.4. Wage Rates and Fringe Benefits	2-7
2.5. Employee Turnover and Absenteeism	2-10
2.6. Labor Force and Unionization	2-11
2.7. Training and Retraining	2-13

Section 3 -- Transportation	
3.1. Highways and Major Road System	3-1
3.2. Motor and Rail Service	3-4
3.3. Major Airports and Airline Service	3-6
3.4. Waterways and Deep Water Ports	3-8
3.5. Intermodal Facilities	3-9

Note: The above example is presented to illustrate the level of detail suggested for inclusion in the fact book table of contents.

pages separately. For example, pages in section one would be numbered 1-1, 1-2, 1-3 and so on. Such numbering makes it easier for sections to be rearranged or changed without requiring page re-numbering for the entire document.

APPLICATION OF "OFF-THE-SHELF" TECHNOLOGY

Modern technology has developed systems that enable one to manage and use information more accurately and efficiently than ever before. Today's economic development practitioner must be familiar with these tools and understand basic concepts in the management and use of information systems.

Selecting the Right Information System

There are very simple rules for creating an information system that will stay within budget and get the job done. Remember that technology is a tool for performing work tasks and not an end in itself.

The overall economic development information system must cover a wide range of program needs and capabilities. The system selected must meet the complete needs of the office and program. One should begin with an operational plan describing the services that are currently being performed and outline the specific technological tools required. Without a thorough assessment of operations and goals, some economic development organizations wind up using large and complex systems to accomplish very straightforward and simple tasks. Conversely, some organizations try to do complex tasks with small systems, thereby making the job harder. For example, the best system for tracking an organization's membership may or may not have the capabilities to support the development and preparation of tailored fact books and custom proposals. With a good, clear plan, the information system (and the technology used for it) can be properly selected for particular needs.

Hardware Requirements

Hardware is the physical wiring and machinery that make up computers and their systems. This includes central processing units (CPUs), monitors, keyboards, network interface cards (NICs), CD-ROM, internal modems, and assorted cables. Peripherals and other devices include printers, scanners, plotters, and external mo-

dems, that can be attached to the CPU.

In order to power the software needed to prepare tailored fact books and custom proposals, the hardware system must have certain minimum capabilities. Additionally, the system should be easy to learn and use. For these reasons, a Windows environment is recommended.

Suggested minimum capabilities for a small office with limited budgetary resources (under $5,000) are:

❑ 486 CPU,

❑ 4 to 6 Megabytes of RAM,

❑ Super VGA Color Monitor,

❑ SVGA Video Card capable of displaying 256 colors in 640x480 mode,

❑ Windows 3.1,

❑ Laser Printer capable of 4 to 6 pages per minute.

Larger offices with more sophisticated and demanding requirements may wish to acquire a more advanced system. Recommended capabilities for a more advanced

information system in the budget range of $8-10,000 are:

❑ 90MHz Pentium system or better,

❑ 8-16 megabytes of RAM with ability to further upgrade,

❑ Super VGA color monitor,

❑ SVGA video card with 1 megabyte or more of VRAM,

❑ Double speed CD-ROM drive or better,

❑ 9,600 baud modem as a minimum or preferably a 14,400 baud modem as an upgrade,

❑ Color flat bed scanner,

❑ Windows 3.1 or above,

❑ Laser printer capable of 12-18 pages per minute, and

❑ Ink jet color printer as a minimum or preferably a color laser printer as an upgrade.

Software Requirements

Software drives the system and tells the

FIGURE 2
Example:
Economic Development Computer Applications

1. **Document Creation** (MS Word)
   Letters/memos   Reports
   Mailing lists   Fax Templates
2. **Fact Book/Proposal Template** (MS Word)
   Text/tables   Graphs/graphic drawings
   Aerial photos   Maps/site plans
3. **Spreadsheet** (MS Excel)
   Financial analysis   Graphs
   Economic impact analysis
4. **Desktop Publishing** (PageMaker)
   Brochures/pamphlets   Newsletters
5. **Presentations** (Harvard Graphics/Powerpoint)
   LCD Panel Projection   Color Charts/Graphs
   Transparencies and slides
6. **Mapping** (Atlas GIS)
   Data by geographic area   Color printing/display
   Spatial analysis -- comparing areas/time frames
7. **Database** (Microsoft Access/Act!)
   Mailing list management   Client database
   Business statistics data by gegraphic area
8. **Telecommunications** (ProComm Plus)
   Link to on-line systems and remote databases
9. **Project Management** (ManagePro)
   Action plan goals   Timelines
10. **WorkGroup Tools** (GroupWise/Word Perfect Office)
    Shared access calendar   E-mail/Task manager

computer what to do. Computer programs such as word processors, spreadsheets, and other common business applications are all based on software developed to accomplish certain tasks. Figure 2 shows the computer software applications currently being used in the Toledo Regional Growth Partnership office.

Specific software application tasks needed to prepare tailored fact books and custom proposals include the following:

❑ **Document Creation.** Generally, one should be able to handle all the document creation needs within a standard word processing application. Both Microsoft Word 6.0 and WordPerfect 6.0a for Windows programs have all the power, automation, and integration capabilities to meet document creation needs. Since the document creation function will be the foundation upon which fact books and custom proposals are based, this is the most important software application to consider. Make sure the program selected has the features needed, including the flexibility to work with and integrate with other important applications.

❑ **Spreadsheet Applications.** A wide range of spreadsheet applications exists that can crunch numbers as easily as word processors massage text. Today's spreadsheets are more powerful than ever. Charting capabilities and links to maps enhance the display of data in fact books and proposals. For example, the ChartWizard function of Microsoft Excel 5.0 helps analyze data to choose the most effective graph type. Coupled with strong database support, such spreadsheet programs are essential ingredients in effective fact book and proposal preparation.

❑ **Desktop Publishing.** Fact book and custom proposal text is generally managed in a word processing program. Desktop publishing programs, however, can be effectively used to enhance cover design and other special design needs. Additionally, desktop publishing programs are indispensable if one is going to be designing and producing brochures, newsletters and other materials. Microsoft Publisher 2.0 is an excellent program for beginning desktop publishers. The more advanced user may wish to consider PageMaker or, perhaps, QuarkXPress 3.3, a very powerful program designed specifically for magazine and advertising work.

❑ **Presentation Graphics.** The ability to import charts from Excel and outlines straight from Word makes Microsoft PowerPoint 4.0 for Windows a good choice for a presentation graphics program. It is relatively easy to learn and use.

❑ **Mapping.** The Toledo Regional Growth Partnership currently uses Atlas GIS for mapping. The ability to reference data by geographic area, conduct spatial analysis comparing areas and time frames, and print in color is a tremendous capability that enhances fact books and proposals.

❑ **Database.** The Toledo Regional Growth Partnership also uses Microsoft Access for general database functions because of its flexibility, easy programming, and integration with other programs. Other programs such as Approach Release 3.0 for Windows and Paradox 5.0 for Windows exist as equally capable alternatives. Client database, tracking and sales management functions are handled in our office by the versatile Act! program.

❑ **Telecommunications.** Since the majority of today's critical data resides in systems outside one's information system, it is important that the database program be able to link to external data sources. ProComm Plus 2.0 sets the standard for communications software. It has a new completely standard Windows interface, more powerful scripting language, and new features like drop-down dialing lists, programmable button bars, and the best fax feature of any communications program.

❑ **Project Management.** The ManagePro project management program is a new tool used to enhance custom proposals. This powerful program, usually used to track and manage goals, objectives, and project timelines, can also be easily used to illustrate graphically the critical path associated with an economic development project. The ability to show a client the timelines associated with an expedited permit approval process, for example, is a great custom proposal enhancement.

❑ **Scanning of Images.** Linking a scanner to a system is highly desirable, especially for custom proposals. A scanner enables one to load directly pictures, maps, or even company logos into documents. When selecting a scanner, be sure to look for speed, resolution, detailed gray scale imaging, image fine-tuning before scanning and post-scan editing features. The ScanJet IIcx by

Hewlett-Packard is among the best value priced scanners on the market today.

❑ **Printing.** Document printing today is improving rapidly from both a cost and capability perspective. The best monochrome printers today all run at 600 dpi that is close to magazine and book quality. Features one should look for include automatic port switching, network protocol switching, automatic PCL-to-PostScript switching, fast processing, and flexible paper handling. For monochrome printers, the 12-ppm Hewlett-Packard LaserJet 4M Plus is both versatile and affordable. Color printing capabilities range from a pricey color laser ($8,000 and up) or the more affordable ink-jet ($5-600). An increasing range of ink-jet options has brought color printing within range of most economic development budgets. Epson's Stylus Color printer is a reasonably priced ink-jet printer capable of output at 720-by-720 dpi resolution. A fast monochrome laser printer and a high quality ink-jet color printer are a combination that will significantly enhance your ability to print high quality fact books and custom proposals.

Where and How to Buy Information Systems

With all the technology choices available to the economic development practitioner, the buying decision can get pretty confusing. A local full service computer store is recommended as the best choice for the beginning practitioner or small economic development office. One can expect to receive installation, configuration, testing and troubleshooting services needed to assure that the system works as intended. Unless one has technical support staff in the office, purchasing from a direct mail or warehouse vendor is not recommended. What is saved on the purchase price may not offset the problems experienced getting the system up and running. In either case, establishing a technical support arrangement with a local computer consultant is recommended for ongoing maintenance, troubleshooting, and advanced capability enhancement.

HUMAN RESOURCES ISSUES FOR A TECHNOLOGY BASED OFFICE

Computers are able to do any repetitive task extremely fast and with incredible accuracy. The problem is that they must be instructed to perform their work in exceptional detail and with exact precision. Therefore, staff training is vital. An economic development organization must undertake a continuous process of keeping up with technology to ensure sustained productivity in the modern workplace.

Cross-Train Whenever Possible

There are two major information assets in an economic development office: the information in the computer system and, more importantly, the information in the staff. If there is only one individual in the organization who knows how to use the information systems, the organization may be in for trouble. Because the information systems skill level of many entry level employees may be minimal and technology is changing so rapidly, training in the systems installed is very important. Equally important is the cross-training of as many individuals as possible on the same tasks.

Ongoing training and cross-training will make the whole staff stronger and improve the organization's ability to sustain the quality of all the written communication materials. A professional development plan should be created along with a strategic technology plan and the two should run parallel with each other.

Prepare for Change

One of the basic aspects of any economic development information system is that it grows and changes constantly. Anticipate and plan for this change. Also understand that the system is likely to become out of date rapidly. Even so, this does not mean constantly purchasing a more powerful system. If one sticks with off-the-shelf software, one will have the option of upgrading the software to new and improved versions at a reasonable cost. It will not be necessary to examine the present software every time a new version comes out, but one does need to know when the present version has been superseded by another generation that truly performs better. Upgrades are usually justified not by simple improvements in degrees. Software or system upgrades can best be justified when the improvement results in a significant change in program function or capability. Plan and budget accordingly.

SUMMARY AND CONCLUSIONS

A wide range of new technologies exists to help improve the quality of tailored fact books and custom proposals. Powerful off-the-shelf technologies enable both small and large offices to build customer orientation into their communication materials as never before. In order to take full advantage of such technology, one needs to select the right information system for the identified needs, design full use of the system into the production of materials, understand the human resource issues associated with the effective use of new office technologies, and, importantly, anticipate and plan for continuous change.

Exploring the Internet For Economic Development Opportunities

Michael L. DuBrow, CED

INTRODUCTION

With over 25 million users, explosive growth in business use, and major improvements in organization and content, the Internet is a significant new resource for economic development. Every state and over a hundred communities currently offer a broad range of information through the Internet. They are using it to attract companies, open new markets for local businesses, and increase community access to a vast array of research, support and global information resources.

Dozens of communities use the Internet to provide tourism information, such as what to see and do, and where to eat and stay. But a handful of cities are taking full advantage of the Internet's interactive, multimedia capabilities. These "Net pioneers" offer comprehensive profiles of their communities, local manufacturers, labor force, education, transportation, health care, housing and even weather. St. Louis, one of the more creative Internet "sites," includes full color street maps and a photographic ride to the top of the Arch. Some communities (e.g. Cleveland, Ohio) now operate local "free-nets" to promote access to and use of the Internet.

Unfortunately, many economic development professionals and community leaders still perceive the Internet as an overgrown jungle of technological jargon, media hype and telecommunications hucksterism. Often at the heart of this forest-for-the-trees myopia is a simple lack of information on the nature of the Internet and the basic tools for its exploration and use.

WHAT IS IT?

According to Ed Krol (Krol, 1991), "Getting a handle on the Internet is a lot like grabbing a handful of Jello - the more firm you think your grasp is, the more it oozes down your arm." Over two million computers on more than 30,000 computer networks are connected to the Internet and current percentage growth in the number of users is at least double digit - per month! Dr. Vinton Cerf, one of the developers of the Internet's data transfer protocol, testified before the House of Representatives that "there is reason to expect that the user population will exceed 100 million by 1998." All the major operating systems for PCs will soon include built-in access to the Internet. Commercial enterprises, which were almost non-existent on the Internet two years ago, now account for over fifty-one percent of its growth in usage.

The Internet's vast resources are controlled by no single authority (although a voluntary membership organization does set standards) and no single agency collects usage fees. In many ways it is fair to describe it as "decentralized, free wheeling, chaotic and generally uncontrollable" (Lehman, 1995), something like Los Angeles freeways on a Saturday night.

Yet thinking of the Internet as an "information highway" is akin to characterizing automobiles as "horseless buggies" and train locomotives as "iron horses." This mind-set limits the imagination about what is possible and becomes a source of errors in conceptualization and planning (Niles, 1994).

It is probably more appropriate to think of the Internet as an integral part of a worldwide information ecosystem. An ecosystem is a community of plants and animals in the context of a specific environment of resources. The most extensive communities, such as rain forests and grasslands, are called biomes. The Internet is a man-made ecosystem, a rain forest populated by computer hardware (trees), telecommunication infrastructures (rivers), software for accessing, transferring and finding data (footpaths, furry animals, comic characters and webs), and, of course, people. The latter are made up of numerous species characterized by how they access the Internet (the trees they live in and the rivers they travel) and which tools they use to harvest the Internet's vast resources. Table 1 lists some common characteristics of Internet users.

Like any ecosystem, the inhabitants of the Internet live together in communities. Some of these communities are organized around institutions, i.e. governmental, educational, commercial, nonprofits, military and network providers. Others are established around common interests, such as business, computers, recreation, social issues or debate.

Despite the rich diversity of Internet species and communities, there is a shared "language" and culture. The language, TCP/IP, is what allows the various inhabitants of the Internet "biome" to exchange "energy" - that is information in the form of electronic mail, files, images and sound. It is not necessary for the average user to understand TCP/IP. Interspecies communication is usually handled deftly by computers and software.

The culture of the Internet is based on a kind of unwritten law of the jungle. Even the uninitiated Internet explorer is expected

TABLE 1
Internet Household Characteristics

	Internet	All Households
Average Income	$66,700	$42,400
White Collar Workers	59%	34%
Self-Employed	31%	14%
College Graduate	81%	33%
Own Cellular Phone	31%	15%
3+ Direct Mail Purchases per Year	63%	37%
Purchase Online	24%	2%

Source: 1994 American Information User Survey, FIND/SVP

to know and hew to two of these laws: DO provide information of value and do NOT promulgate unsolicited sales pitches or engage in blatant self-promotion. Violators of these rules, especially the latter, are subject to "flaming" by their peers. Flaming is the process by which violators receive thousands of unwanted electronic mail (e-mail) messages condemning their actions. The sheer volume of mail can incapacitate the receiver's network node, rendering it the Internet equivalent of a toxic waste dump.

INSECTS GALORE

Like bees, ants and other insects, electronic mail (e-mail) is a ubiquitous inhabitant of the Internet biome. It is the most popular and most frequently used of the Internet tools. E-mail is used to send all types of letters and documents. It is available through the greatest variety and number of Internet services, including commercial providers such as America Online, Compuserve and Prodigy.

There are a number of advantages to e-mail. It is:

❏ Fast - messages are often delivered in minutes.

❏ Inexpensive - messages typically cost less than a first-class postage stamp, whether traveling across town or around the world. Many Internet providers charge only a monthly fee; all e-mail messages are free.

❏ Convenient - mail can be read or sent at home, work or on the road; anywhere a computer can be hooked up to a phone line.

❏ Popular - many individuals are including their e-mail address on their business cards, letterhead and promotional literature.

To use e-mail, you need an account with Internet access and an address. Your address is the "place" to send and receive messages, your e-mailbox. E-mail addresses typically have the form:

smdubro@slvaxa.musl.edu

You don't have to understand Internet addresses to use them. But learning about their components will provide you with information about the addressee and how to handle the occasional errors that occur. Table 2 provides a brief overview of e-mail addressing conventions.

A common misconception among Internet beginners is that you have to leave your computer on to receive e-mail. Unlike other Internet tools, e-mail is not an "end-to-end" service: the sending and receiving computers do not need to communicate directly. Like the U.S. Postal Service, it is a "store and forward" service. E-mail is passed from system to system until it arrives in your e-mailbox located on your host system. It will wait there until you log on and retrieve it.

Understanding a few simple rules of e-mail conduct, or "netiquette," can significantly reduce your risk of embarrassment, or worse, being flamed.

❏ Don't send anything via e-mail that you wouldn't want public. Flies often go astray and end up in other people's soup.

❏ Don't send abusive or harassing messages. Messages can usually be traced to their originating system which is liable for user misdeeds. Nobody likes the sound of a mosquito buzzing in their ear.

❏ Be very careful with sarcasm and other '"tone-dependent" messages. There is no body language on the Internet. The recipient of your message may not know you personally. Bugs often zig when you thought they were sure to zag.

❏ Use upper- and lower- case. Uppercase only messages are hard to read, although you can use it for emphasis. Butterflies are beautiful until there are so many they obliterate your view.

❏ Read your message before you send it. What you intended as a casual reply may be interpreted as an irrevocable business commitment. Insects cast-in-stone often end up on public display in museums.

Having e-mail capabilities also allows participation in discussion lists and Usenet news groups. These groups number in the thousands and are e-mail interchanges focused on a particular topic. Some lists and groups are moderated - an administrator will screen "postings" for appropriateness of content and excessive flaming. Unmoderated lists and groups post every message "as is."

FOOTPATHS IN THE JUNGLE

Until recently, two of the most common modes for foraging in the Internet were FTP and telnet. Thousands of files on the Internet are available free to the public through anonymous FTP (File Transfer Protocol). FTP allows you to transfer and retrieve both text and software files, including those generated by word processors, spreadsheets and databases.

In order to use FTP, your host (the Internet service provider's computer) must

---

TABLE 2
Understanding E-Mail Addresses

Sample address:

smdubro@slvaxa.umsl.edu

①   ②   ③ ④

①   Individual's name; may be first and last name or cryptic equivalent, e.g., msb004; may include characters such as %, !, or—;always followed by @.

②   Computer's name; where the mail is collected and stored until read by the recipient

③   Group or organization name; used when several computer's are connected together of which ② (above) is one

④   Domain name; three-letter designator identifying the type of Internet user providing the e-mail account; in foreign countries domain names are often replaced by a two-letter country designator

Computer, group and domain names are always preceded by a period (.).

have FTP software. FTP also usually requires that you have three pieces of information:

❑ The address of the site where the file you want is located.

❑ The subdirectory in which the file is stored.

❑ The name of the file.

FTP commands can be a little cryptic, especially when attempting to transfer binary programs (e.g. executable software). Sites typically provide a list of FTP commands which can be accessed by typing "help" at the FTP prompt.

FTP works well for getting a specific file, but is slow and hit-or-miss when this information is unavailable. Archie (yes, the famous Jughead comic character inhabits the Internet jungle) is a database search system containing the names and locations of files accessible at anonymous FTP sites. To use archie, you will need telnet access to an archie server, where you log in as archie. Gopher and the World Wide Web (below) provide powerful alternatives for searching the Internet.

On the Internet, telnet lets you sit at your computer and logon directly to a remote system across the network. Once there, you can access whatever services that computer provides to local terminals such as library catalogs, databases, search tools and BBSs. In order to use telnet, both your host or service provider's computer and the remote computer must have telnet software installed. In addition, you must either have an account on the remote system or it must allow open access.

SMALL, FURRY ANIMALS

Gopher was invented in the "Gopher State" (Minnesota) at the University with the "Golden Gophers" sports teams. It is an easy-to-use, standardized, menu-based Internet tool for doing what its name implies, to go-fer this and go-fer that, accessing the multitude of Internet files and services. Using gopher allows you to transfer files without having to deal with cryptic UNIX and VAX commands. Accessing gopher requires a dial-up Internet account (see below) and your normal telecommunications software.

Each gopher session begins by accessing a top menu which leads to other menus, submenus and files. An arrow --> indicates which item is highlighted. Simply move the arrow to the item of interest and press <ENTER>. When a user selects a file, the file is retrieved and displayed. If the file is compressed or a binary file, gopher "does the right thing," automatically retrieving the file using the correct protocol. Besides allowing you to read text files online, gopher can find and download sound, graphics and other data.

Gopher menu items can point to files and menus on other systems, as well as other services such as FTP and telnet. This ability makes it as easy to browse a menu in Timbuktu as locally. Using gopher only requires knowledge of a few commands, most of which are listed at the bottom of the screen.

Veronica (yes, another Jughead comic character), the acronym for Very Easy Rodent Oriented Net-wide Index to Computerized Archies, is an index of thousands of Internet gopher menu items. At many gopher sites, the top menu will have an item such as Gopher and other information servers. Selecting this will likely lead to a menu choice to "search" titles in Gopherspace using Veronica. Veronica will request a keyword (or several) for your search. After a few seconds or minutes, the results of Veronica's search will be displayed as a gopher-style menu. From here, you can select any item and move to that gopher.

Gopher cannot take full advantage of graphical presentations nor does it allow links to specific points within a document. Both of these weaknesses are overcome by the Web (below). Table 3 provides a list of some useful gopher sites.

LITTLE MISS MUFFET

Spiders abound in the Internet jungle, as evidenced by its newest and most powerful tool, the World Wide Web (WWW or Web). The Web is growing rapidly as the medium of choice for marketing and advertising. In fact, since the end of 1994, the Web has become the de facto standard for publishing on the Internet. Web documents or "pages" can include hyper-text and -media, marked words that link you to other documents, images and audio files, and other Internet resources. Businesses, community organizations and government agencies use these "slick," full-image capabilities to create promotional materials including brochures, catalogs and product demonstrations.

The Web's Who's Who includes tele-communications companies such as AT&T, MCI and Sprint as well as retailers such as Radio Shack, Pizza Hut, Volvo and Club Med. Merrill Lynch and Bank of America have Web pages, as does the White House. Among the Fortune 500, major industries represented on the Web include computer companies, health care institutions, pharmaceutical companies, financial services, high-tech manufacturing and publishing.

To access the Web, you must have a SLIP or PPP connection to the Internet (described below) and a graphical interface, or Web "browser" such as Mosaic on your terminal. (There are text-based browsers, but they are not as easy to use nor can you see the pretty graphics.)

Web browsers provide such powerful features as:

❑ a mouse-driven point-and-click interface

❑ the ability to display hyper-text and media in a variety of fonts

❑ support for maps, photo-realistic images, sound and movies

❑ the ability to display complex layouts such as bullets, columns and boxes.

In addition, the Web browsers facilitate simple and easy to understand access to FTP and Gopher services.

Netscape, a popular Mosaic Web browser, is free for personal use and available via FTP from ftp.mcom.com in the subdirectory /netscape as NSCAPE09.ZIP. (A commercial license is $99 per user.) One word of caution: graphical image files are large and take a while to download: a 14.4 kbps or faster modem is recommended.

Web sessions begin with access to a "home" page, a unique starting place, from which you can go to a Web-formatted document. These documents have been formatted using the HyperTextMarkup Language, HTML. The link information is embedded in the document and is usually visible as highlighted words or icons. Usually you are given an URL (universal resource locator) address. Often you can enter these URLs to make your connection directly. These addresses typically take the form of:

http://www.ecodev.state.mo.us

Table 4 provides URLs for some of the more interesting and useful Web sites. The World Wide Web Unleashed (December, 1994) is an excellent primer on navigating and weaving Webs.

ECONOMIC DEVELOPER AS INFOCOLOGIST

Despite the rapidly increasing importance of electronic media in commerce, the marketing and organizational opportunities created by Internet remain largely uncharted. In biological ecosystems, developing an understanding of plant and animal interrelationships is the purview of ecologists. In the information ecosystem, the work of developing and sharing that understanding, gathering tools for Internet exploration and assisting communities in the appropriate use of global information resources, will likely fall to the economic development professional acting as information ecologist, or infocologist.

In fact, the job of community infocologist can usefully be divided into three levels or phases:

❑ Awareness - alerting economic development staff, community leaders, local businesses and other organizations to resources and opportunities on the Internet through seminars, newsletters and discussion lists;

❑ Networking - identifying and marshalling Internet tools, resources and expertise for accomplishing specific community objectives such as business attraction, local market expansion, technology dissemination and improvements to quality of life;

❑ Facilitation - providing economic development and information services on the Internet such as community profiles, product finders, catalog shows and facility locators.

GETTING CONNECTED

Developing a community Internet plan is essential before leading your community into the vast and uncharted regions of the information ecosystem. And before you can do that, you need access. There are primarily four ways of connecting to the Internet: gateways, dial-up accounts, SLIP/PPP and dedicated lines (Ellsworth, 1994).

Local BBS services, Fidonet, freenets and online services such as America Online and Compuserve typically provide gateway access to the Internet. These services are most appropriate for personal use as they are often limited to Internet e-mail and involve extra charges for usage beyond a certain minimum. America Online currently charges $9.95 per month for five hours usage, $2.95 for each additional hour, and places limits on incoming message size. As the name implies, these services are not necessarily on the Internet, but simply gateways to some of its features.

Dial-up or shell accounts allow you access to a host computer that is on the Internet and provide e-mail, FTP, telnet and Gopher connections. For accessing these accounts, you need a PC or MAC, modem, phone line and telecommunications software such as Procomm. Using dial-up accounts usually requires knowledge of some basic UNIX or VAX commands.

SLIP (Serial Line Internet Protocol), or PPP (Point-to-Point Protocol), makes use of special Internet software on your computer and a standard phone line. With this type of account you have full access to the Web's multimedia features and other Internet services. IBM OS/2, MAC 7.5 and the forthcoming Windows 95 operating system come with this software and access built-in. In order to take advantage of these features, it's best to have modem speeds of 14,400 baud or higher. SLIP is available from a growing number of commercial providers for as low as $19.95 per month for forty hours of peak (business hours) usage and unlimited off-peak (9PM to 7AM) and weekend usage. SLIP is an excellent

TABLE 3
Gopher Sites of Interest

Site	Address	Description
Census Bureau	bigcat.missouri.edu	Data available as text and in Lotus 1-2-3 format for U.S. cities, counties, metropolitan areas, states and the nation, with comparisons from 1980
Catalog of Federal Domestic Assistance	marvel.loc.gov	Over 1,000 U.S. government assistance programs from more than 50 federal agencies; searchable by keyword
Federal Register	gopher.netsys.com	System limits access by non-subscribers; still a good starting place
State Department Travel Advisories	gopher.stolaf.edu	Arranged by country, provides information on medical facilities, consulates, embassies, crime, drug penalties, registrations and current conditions
State Department Background~Notes	umslvma.umsl.edu /library/govdocs/ bnotes	Arranged by country, information on politics, economy, geography and people
Internet Sources of Government Information by Blake Grumbrecht	gopher.lib.umich.edu	Regularly updated list from the University of Michigan Clearinghouse for Subject-Oriented Internet Resource Guides

solution for many communities.

To make your computer a permanent part of the Internet, that is, a node, you need a dedicated line. Dedicated lines, frequently referred to as 56KB, T1 or T3, are used by large institutions and corporations. These lines are expensive to set up and maintain, and require the purchase or lease of fairly sophisticated minicomputers, disk arrays, routers and personnel time. It used to be necessary to have this type of service in order to use your organizations name as a node name. However, a number of SLIP providers are now allowing companies and organizations to have domain names through the use of mailboxes and aliases (Ellsworth, 1994).

When deciding upon an Internet provider it's useful to consider:

❑ provider restrictions regarding use

❑ type of service needed and provided

❑ kind of equipment you have or will purchase, including modem speed

❑ long distance costs

❑ price: including connect and usage charges, and extras.

TABLE 4
World Wide Web Sites

Site	Address	Description
Census Bureau	www.census.gov	Includes U.S. International Trade in Goods and Services, County Business Patterns, Center for Economic Studies, Trade Statistics
CityLink Project	www.NeoSoft.Com:80/Citylink	Economic development "home" pages for all 50 states and over 100 communities
U.S. Industrial Outlook	umslvma.umsl.edu:70/11/library/govdocs/usio94	1994 report (the last published) of over 350 U.S. industries including current performances, trends and long term prospects
CommerceNet	www.commerce.net	A consortium of Fortune 500 companies; product information and business transactions in real-time!
Norway's Arctic Adventures~	www.oslonett.no/data/advlAAl	Full color photos promote tourism
Downtown Anywhere	www.awa.com	Industrial mall for smaller companies
South Dakota	www.state.sd.us	Government information, including connections with local offices, tourism information, educational resources

EXPEDITIONARY PLANNING

The next step in developing an Internet plan is to explore: there is no substitute for first-hand experience. You may consider hiring a guide for help in mastering some basic navigational techniques and identifying particularly useful resources. The Internet is a fast-changing environment and survival depends on adaptation to those changes.

When choosing a consultant, look for individuals who combine hands-on experience developing and maintaining Gopher or Web sites with solid marketing backgrounds. As Tom Lehman aptly put it, "No one would dream of asking their printing company to design and write direct mail campaigns, but many companies assume computer service [companies] ... can design an effective Internet marketing program" (Lehman, 1995).

The key to a good Internet plan is the development of a strategic vision. Too many communities and organizations get stuck on the technology, building expensive telecommunications infrastructures with no clear idea about applications. Rather the plan should be driven by the community's vision of itself, where it is and where it wants to be. Communicated effectively through the Internet, this vision is likely to strike a chord in firms looking to relocate to a receptive community.

Making information available on the Internet requires an investment of time, money and effort. Materials must be kept timely and accurate. After initial development, these activities may require 5-10 hours per week, in addition to 5-20 hours to process e-mail and requests (although some automated list software can greatly reduce this requirement).

Your plan should also include cross-media promotion activities such as including your Internet address (e-mail, gopher and Web) on your business card, letterhead, magazine advertisements, direct mail flyers and other promotional literature. It is common to automatically include a .sig (read "dot sig") at the end of your e-mail messages. This short addendum may include your organization's name, address and motto. There are also a growing number of online Internet directories and search services where you can list your community's offerings.

FIELD OF DREAMS

One of the first tasks of community infocologists should be to conduct community-wide seminars on the opportunities for commerce on the Internet. Providing local businesses with a competitive edge, especially in global markets, is an important use of the Internet. Because of the lack of national boundaries and distance, and its relatively cheap access, even "cottage industries" can compete in the global marketplace. A bookstore in Portland, Oregon is now selling nationwide; mutual funds are being managed from a ranch in Utah; and a software company with international distribution is supporting customers from the foothills of Appalachia.

There are numerous models for creating a community presence on the Internet, depending on your goals, resources, level of service and expertise. Four common approaches based on commercial models include: billboards, yellow pages, brochures and catalog shows.

Billboards are postings of "come-on" kinds of information, typically directing viewers to the location of more complete information or inviting them to take action. They usually appear as e-mail headers, footers or dot-sigs and are, therefore, the easiest and least expensive to implement.

Communities use *yellow pages* as directories to community organizations and agencies, or as product finders for local businesses such as manufacturers. This approach can be developed for gophers, but most communities are making use of the Web.

The *brochure* approach to providing information can be implemented as a FTP archive, gopher space, Web site or even automated e-mail service. It is currently the most popular model and has been implemented on the Web by all fifty states and over one hundred communities. Champaign County, Illinois (URLhttp://www.prairienet.org /Silicon Prairie/ccnet.html) offers information about local attractions as well as a community profile and history.

The South Dakota Web site's (URLhttp://www.state.sd.us) information is both useful for the state's citizens and at the same time, is intended to attract businesses to relocate to the state. It includes government information with a graphical interface to branches and offices, a tour of the Capitol Complex complete with map and building pictures, and extensive information on education and tourism.

St. Louis, Missouri (http://www. st-louis. mo.us/) makes extensive use of color maps, pictures and interactive buttons to provide one of the most comprehensive community brochures including: county and neighborhood profiles, cultural and tourist attractions, arts and literary calendars, area parks, transportation, local companies, weather, sports, schools, universities, media and a ride to the top of the Arch.

Catalog shows are full information services designed to showcase products manufactured locally and, in some cases, to allow online purchasing and customer support. They include activities from all of the other models and require a heavy investment of time, money and effort to develop and maintain.

Community infocologists can help local companies keep track of industry and government standards, as well as state-of-the-art information on products, materials, best practices and advanced technologies. Discussion lists and Usenet newsgroups are terrific sources of competitive information and focus group-like market feedback. The Internet can also be used to manage and train diverse work forces with its many simulations, manuals, training aid and instructional materials.

PARADIGM SHIFT

Being a successful citizen of the Internet does require a paradigm shift. "Polluting" the Internet biome through mass marketing and unsolicited promotions will not work. The information provided must be timely, responsive, and of demonstrable value to users or it will not be tolerated. The focus needs to be on content and not image, on demonstrating a knowledgeable presence with the targeted client audience.

Communities contemplating a presence on the Internet need to be aware of its unique culture as well as its opportunities and limitations. Economic development professionals who lead their communities onto the Internet are very visible and stand out as pioneers and innovators. Community leaders need a willingness to experiment and adapt in order to take full advantage of the Internet's vast resources and opportunities.

The Internet is likely, in the foreseeable future, to remain a confusing environment, a cacophony of technology and culture. Most communities will benefit from outside support as they make their way through the overgrown jungle of technological jargon, media hype and telecommunications hucksterism. But those who persevere are bound to find the Internet as rich as any rain forest in resources, benefits and adventure.

REFERENCES

December, John and Neil Randall, The World Wide Web Unleashed, Sams Publishing, 1994.

Ellsworth, Jill and Matthew, The Internet Business Book, John Wiley & Sons, 1994.

Krol, Ed, The Whole Internet Catalog & User's Guide, O'Reilley & Associates, Inc., 1992.

Lehman, Tom, "Doing Business on the Internet,." New Telecomm Quarterly, First Quarter, 1995.

Niles, John, Beyond Telecommuting: A New Paradigm for the Effect of Telecommunications on Travel, U.S. Department of Energy, Office of Scientific Computing, September 1994.

Location Quotient: A Basic Tool for Economic Development Analysis

Mark M. Miller, Ph.D.
Lay James Gibson, Ph.D.
N. Gene Wright

INTRODUCTION

The location quotient (L.Q.) is not a new technique; it has been widely used by researchers in economic geography and regional economics since the 1940s. However, it is a technique known to only a relative handful of development professionals. For the most part, it is a technique which is underutilized and largely unappreciated. The purpose of this paper is to illustrate the utility of the L.Q. technique in answering questions frequently asked by development professionals and to describe the series of relatively simple procedures needed to actually produce L.Q. values.

The location quotient is one of the most basic analytical tools available to the economic development researcher/professional. The purpose of the location quotient technique is to yield a coefficient, or a simple expression, of how well represented a particular industry is in a given study region. For example, a state might be compared with some larger reference region such as the United States. With this technique, we can determine whether or not the study region has its "fair share" of some industry, given the experience of the reference region.

Location quotients are measured on a simple numerical scale. A quotient of less than one indicates that an industry is "underrepresented;" i.e., that the study region has "less than its share." A quotient of more than one means that the study region has "more than its share" of an industry. A quotient of one, of course, means that the study region's share of the industry is identical to the reference region's share. It is easy to see why some researchers refer to the L.Q. as the "self-sufficiency ratio."

To illustrate, suppose we are concerned with the representation of furniture manu-facturing in a particular county, compared with the state as a whole. (Alternatively, we might use states versus the entire U.S.) Suppose further that furniture manufacturing accounts for 7.5% of the county's total manufacturing employment, whereas this industry accounts for 10% of the statewide manufacturing employment. The location quotient in this case would be 7.5% ÷ 10% = 0.75. Inasmuch as this L.Q. is less than 1.0, we can conclude that furniture manufacturing is underrepresented (at least by this measure) relative to the state as a whole. By using the L.Q. in the manner just described, the economic developer is given a means of objectively describing the industrial mix of a region.

One of the most significant attributes to the L.Q. technique is its simplicity. This, or course, is good news and bad news. The good news includes the fact the L.Q. can easily be employed with off-the-shelf data from state or federal sources and with technology no more sophisticated than a calculator or electronic spreadsheet. The bad news is that findings cannot always be taken at face value (Isard 1960). By itself, the L.Q. says nothing, for example, about *why* furniture manufacturing is apparently underrepresented in the county, or whether there is any potential for the further expansion of furniture manufacturing there. There may be very good reasons why there is relatively little furniture manufacturing found in the study county. The L.Q. will show where the county stands, but it is still up to the economic developer to evaluate labor limitations, supply or distribution outlets, market access, or other factors which might limit that industry. The user will also be the one to determine whether limitations can be overcome. Despite these caveats and cautions, economic developers continue to use the L.Q. where the cost of developing and utilizing more advanced methodologies is prohibitive, when high resolution data are scarce, or when more subjective approaches are deemed unsatisfactory.

CALCULATING A LOCATION QUOTIENT

The location quotient can be stated as a ratio of ratios. The formula in the furniture manufacturing case would be either

$$\frac{R_i / RR_i}{R / RR} \quad \text{or} \quad \frac{R_i / R}{RR_i / RR}$$

where: R_i equals the number of employees in manufacturing industry i (i.e., furniture manufacturing) located in region R (i.e., the county). Suppose that there are 750 people employed in furniture manufacturing in this county.

RR_i equals the number of employees in manufacturing industry i (i.e., furniture manufacturing) located in reference region RR (i.e., the state as a whole). Suppose that there are a total of 25,000 people in the state employed in furniture manufacturing.

R equals the number of employees in all manufacturing industries in region R, or the county. Suppose that there are 10,000 people total employed in all manufacturing activities in the county.

RR equals the total number of employees in all manufacturing industries in reference region RR, or the state as a whole. Suppose that there are a grand total of 250,000 manufacturing employees in the state.

Then,

$$\frac{R_i / RR_i}{R / RR} = \frac{750 / 25,000}{10,000 / 250,000} = 0.75$$

alternatively,

$$\frac{R_i / R}{RR_i / RR} = \frac{750 / 10,000}{25,000 / 250,000} = 0.75$$

The two formulas yield identical results. Depending on the circumstances, it may be easier to conceptualize an economic development problem in terms of one formula or the other. The technique is very flexible, lending itself to a wide range of variations. For example, we may choose to compare the county only with other similar counties in the state, rather than with the entire state, RR might represent only the southeastern region of the state or only nonmetropolitan counties in the state. Similarly, we might choose to measure industrial representation in terms of employee income (or payrolls) rather than number of employees, or in terms of value added. We might also choose to measure the county's furniture manufacturing relative to raw material manufacturers in the county. In this last case, we would be assessing how well the county appears to be taking advantage of available linkages, either forward or backward, and perhaps identifying opportunities for developing these linkage industries.

SOME EXAMPLES OF LOCATION QUOTIENT APPLICATIONS

We conclude this paper with examples of both the misapplication and appropriate application of the location quotient to economic development analysis.

Economic base analysis

The location quotient has been used frequently (and often inappropriately) as a shortcut method for estimating regional economic base multipliers. In a simple case of this application, location quotients would be calculated for all industrial sectors in a given study region — e.g., city or county — relative to other cities or counties of about the same size (Table 1). If the location quotient for any given industry is greater than one, the assumption is made that the study region exports that industrial product. Stated another way, that industry provides a basic economic activity for that region. An economic development multiplier for that region, in turn, can be calculated from the location quotients of all industries in the region (Blakely 1989, Issermann 1977).

Compared with one obvious alternative — an exhaustive survey approach — this is a tempting methodology. It is simple in concept and calculation, and it is very economical in its data requirements. Unfortunately, Gibson and Worden (1981) found this methodology to be nearly worthless, in an empirical comparison with the "true" multiplier, or the multiplier derived from a survey approach — at least when studying smaller communities. In almost all cases, the multiplier derived from the location quotient wildly and erratically exaggerates the true multiplier. In the case of one study town, for example, the survey multiplier was found to be 1.65, while the location quotient estimates ranged as high as 11.59. On the other hand, there is some evidence to suggest that the L.Q. produces better results in larger study regions, e.g., states.

Gibson and Worden's analysis employed highly aggregated data. Issermann (1977) has suggested that the exaggeration of the multiplier may be reduced, in theory, by the use of disaggregated, three- or four-digit S.I.C. (Standard Industrial Classification) data. We are not aware of conclusive empirical evidence for this. In any case, such a disaggregated analysis to some extent defeats the advantages of the location quotient as a relatively simple and economical methodology.

When all is said and done, the L.Q. can be an appropriate tool for economic base analysis, but it should not be uncritically applied. Further, there are alternative and more complex methodologies for doing things like economic base bifurcations. These alternatives may give more accurate results, but there is a cost. In some cases the L.Q. will be simply the more cost-effective option.

Targeting opportunities for regional economic development and diversification.

We believe that the following case study provides an example of an application which is fully appropriate to both the advantages and limitations of the location quotient. In this case, the location quotient is employed as a simple, objective, analytic basis for a targeting study which draws on the subjective expertise and experience of a community panel. No greater claims are made for the location quotient than can be justified, given the limitations of the methodology.

TABLE 1
Hypothetical Example of the Use of L.Q. in Economic Base Analysis

Sector Two Digit SIC Level	R_i employment in industry i in study region	RR_i employment in industry i in reference region	R employment in all industries in study region	R R employment in all industries in reference region	L.Q.	Basic Empl.
Agriculture, fishing and forestry	50	11,000	4,200	100,000	0.107	0
Mining	25	500	4,200	100,000	1.190	4
Construction	100	9,500	4,200	100,000	0.250	0
Manufacturing	1,000	9,000	4,200	100,000	2.645	622
TCPU *	300	4,000	4,200	100,000	1.786	132
Trade	1,200	17,500	4,200	100,000	1.633	469
FIRE *	75	7,000	4,200	100,000	0.255	0
Services	1,250	21,300	4,200	100,000	1.398	360
Public Administration	200	20,200	4,200	100,000	0.236	0
Total	4,200	100,000	-	-	-	1587

* TCPU = Transportation, Communication, and Public Utilities; FIRE = Finance, Insurance and Real Estate

A county in Arizona was concerned with its apparent overdependence on a single economic base activity (a local military facility). Local economic development leaders were interested in targeting those industries which would be most appropriate and realistic for broadening the county's economic base. Funds for this study were very limited, but a large number of community leaders were willing to lend their time to the project.

We decided to utilize a highly-modified "Delphi" process for this study, in which these local leaders — together with some state economic development authorities — would respond to a short series of questionnaires (Gibson et al 1989 and 1988). The purpose of the Delphi process is, first, to generate as wide a range of relevant observations and ideas as possible and, second, to narrow these ideas down to a set of specific and feasible recommendations which can be generally agreed upon. We also decided to provide all participants in the study with a common pool of objective data on which to base their initial observations. We employed a location quotient analysis as the most useful, easily understood, and economical means of providing these objective data.

The Arizona State Department of Economic Security provided us with data to the four-digit S.I.C. level (subject to confidentiality regulations) for every county in the state. From these data, we calculated a location quotient for every industrial sector. Because we were studying a largely rural county, we decided to compare it only with other nonmetropolitan counties in the state. Using the notation introduced above, the county would be R and the state's 13 nonmetro counties would be RR.

We then classified all industrial sectors in terms of their degree of representation in the county, according to the following categories:

☐ Group I: Very underrepresented industries — those with an L.Q. less than 0.7;

☐ Group II: Moderately underrepresented industries — industries with an L.Q. of 0.71 to 0.90;

☐ Group III: Industries with "average" representation — industries with an L.Q. of 0.91 to 1.10;

☐ Group IV: Industries with moderately high representation — industries with an L.Q. of 1.11 to 1.30;

☐ Group V: Industries with very high representation — industries with an L.Q. of 1.31 or more.

Participants in the study were given a list of all industrial sectors, organized into this classification. Because of confidentiality regulations, some industries could not be reported: i.e., those industries which are represented only by a very few firms. Participants were given a separate list of all these industries which could not be classified, along with a note of explanation.

Study participants were then asked to reclassify all industries into four different categories: (1) those with excellent apparent potential for development in the county (these were put in the highest priority category), (2) those industries with good potential, (3) those with some potential, and (4) those with little or no potential. The participants were instructed to draw on their own expertise, experience, and informed judgement in making these classifications. We also suggested that they utilize the results of the location quotient analysis as a basis for their conclusions. For example, among the industries which are "overrepresented" in the county, is the county already overcrowded with these industries, or does it enjoy strong enough advantages for these industries that they may be able to develop even further? Similarly, among the industries which are "underrepresented" in the county, are there good reasons why these industries are not located widely in the county or do these represent good, underutilized opportunities for development and divesification?

The Delphi/L.Q. combination provided interesting results. If we had been short on time and local participation, we might have focused only on those industries which were clearly underrepresented. Fortunately, we had the local talent necessary to take a more ambitious approach. But even here we might have overwhelmed our local resource people had we not used the L.Q. to arrange our data into five groups of manageable size. In other words, the L.Q. gave us an objective basis for organizing a large mass of data. An application of this sort may not be elegant, but it leads to almost instant results for the development professional who needs to draw bottom-line conclusions from an almost bewildering mass of data.

SUMMARY

The location quotient is one of the most basic analytical tools for the economic development practitioner. It is simple to calculate, using existing data. It is usable in economic base analysis and can be helpful in economic development recruitment targeting activities.

REFERENCES

Blakely, Edward J. 1989. *Planning Local Economic Development: Theory and Practice*. Newbury Park, CA: Sage.

Gibson, Lay James; Mark M. Miller; Sally A. Rusdent; and N. Gene Wright. 1989. *Preemptive Economic Development: A Model Economic Diversification Planning Process for Areas with High Concentrations of Military Employment*. Technical Report issued by The Economic Development Program/ OALS, University of Arizona.

Gibson, Lay James; Mark M. Miller; Sally A. Rusdent; and N. Gene Wright. 1988. *Preemptive Economic Development in Cochise County, Arizona: A Model Economic Diversification Planning Process for an Area with a High Concentration of Military Employment*. Technical Report issued by The Economic Development Program/OALS, University of Arizona.

Isard, Walter. 1960. *Methods of Regional Analysis: An Introduction to Regional Science*. Cambridge, Mass.: M.I.T. Press.

Issermann, Andrew M. 1977. The location quotient approach to estimating regional economic impacts. *Journal of the American Institute of Planners* 43:33-41.

Strategic Alliances For Innovation: Emerging Models of Technology-Based Twenty-First Century Economic Development

Richard F. Celeste

As we approach the next century, technology is driving the key economic development challenges. At the same time, competition has become a daily fact of life at every level of business and government. Consequently, we must design new ways to turn these dynamics to our advantage, much as a private sector company hones its competitive edge with continuous improvement.

Several writers, most notably David Osborne and Rosabeth Moss Kanter, have documented the public/private partnerships born in response to new competitive forces. In this article, I want to highlight new economic development strategies, whose technology focus is making such partnerships deeper and broader.

A recent *New York Times* article described the new Gallatin Steel Company plant in Ghent, Kentucky. Forty percent of its 200 workers have college degrees, mostly in mechanical engineering or metallurgy. Another twenty percent have two-year degrees. The president of this automated facility owned by two Canadian steel companies remarked that "with 200 people we will produce as much steel as it used to take 5000 people to make."

The Gallatin plant shows a "mature" industry -- steel -- reborn as a high tech industry. Significant foreign investment in advanced computer technology has paid off in exponential gains in productivity. Young people with advanced skills are finding careers in steel and other industries, where only a decade ago thousands of workers were losing theirs.

In a recent visit to Navistar, the truck manufacturer, I was struck forcefully by technology's potential to transform prod-
uct in unseen, but profound ways. Using electronic advancements, Navistar will reduce the number of mechanical components controlling its fuel injection system by a factor of ten, and reduce the injector size by half. Navistar has accomplished this while adding performance and emission control capabilities, and reducing total system costs. The new fuel system already meets 1998 federal emission standards, and a subsequent version will be the key to attaining 2004 emission standards before the turn of the century. The Navistar example shows that high regulatory standards can promote technology and product innovation, spurring companies to adopt new technologies ahead of their global counterparts.

These two brief examples underscore the capacity of new technology to transform what seemed to be failing industries. In 1989, when Ohio launched its Steel Futures Fund to support industry collaboration for technology and training, some critics argued money was being wasted on a "doomed" industry. Companies like Republic Engineered Steels, Timken, and others have proved these observers wrong. Building on historic strengths in the manufacturing heartland, steel and other bedrock industries used new technology to upset the expectations of many Wall Street pundits.

But while technology has the power to transform industries, it cannot do so alone. Successful transfer and insertion of new technologies into the workplace are tremendously dependent on other factors, especially an exceptionally skilled workforce willing to suspend conventional practices and recalibrate its skills for new
technologies.

The tremendous explosion in productivity has had a profound impact on economic and industrial developers across the nation. When 200 people do the work of 5000, single projects that are jobs bonanzas will be increasingly scarce. We may still be on the lookout for them, but we must not let them be our main focus.

Instead, we must understand and respect the sheer pace of technology change in products and processes, and the challenge that pace presents to our companies and our communities. In fact, I believe that we, as economic developers, can boost our businesses to lasting success only if we make well-conceived investments that enable our businesses and communities to cope with an accelerating pace of change.

Radical and continuous innovation -- in technology and work methods, and in the structure of companies and industries -- is the hallmark of the emerging twenty-first century economy. It must become the hallmark of twenty-first century economic development as well. In the rest of this article, I'd like to briefly explore the meaning of this challenge, showing examples of how some states and communities are meeting it.

INNOVATING TO COMPETE: THE CHALLENGE TO ECONOMIC DEVELOPMENT

It may not get us many headlines, but those of us working to win a solid footing for our cities, towns, counties, and states in the emerging twenty-first century economy have an immense, and immensely important, task. As never before, the quality of jobs available in our communities depends on the quality of our thought and action. Further, in a time of fewer dollars and close public scrutiny, we are under pressure to show the value of our efforts.

Many industries that were a steady source of high-paying jobs have downsized. Familiar companies have merged, restructured, or disappeared. Communities and individuals have had to reinvent themselves. Competition has become global, with foreign investment and transplants a major source of jobs, innovation, and competition.

As I have said, driving these changes is the technological revolution transforming the American economic landscape. More accurately, these are *revolutions* -- in information, communications, manufacturing, materials, and electronics. These interacting technology revolutions are creating new products and new markets for companies while reducing product planning cycles -- even product life cycles -- to less than a year. Sometimes the pace and scope of change seems too sweeping to comprehend, let alone master. For example, simply keeping up with fast changing information technology is a full time job.

Many phrases have attempted to capture this change -- "the Information Age," "the Knowledge Society," or "the Post-Industrial Economy." Perhaps the most exact is "the innovation economy." In their informative book *Beyond Mass Production*, Martin Kenney and Richard Florida have shown how the integration of intellectual and physical labor, innovation and production, have undermined the mass-production economy on which many past economic development strategies were based. Similarly, in his seminal book *The Competitive Advantage of Nations*, Michael Porter has placed the ability to innovate at the center of contemporary economic success.

Innovation means putting new knowledge to work. New technologies are catalysts for innovation, but not the only one. Innovation occurs at every step from the laboratory to the shop floor, and ranges from small, continuous improvements to revolutionary breakthroughs. It occurs between companies and their suppliers (not only their business suppliers, but also the institutions, schools, banks, and governments) that supply workforce training, capital and services. In other words, innovation is a community responsibility.

In her important new book, *World Class: Thriving Locally in the Global Economy*, Rosabeth Moss Kanter gives a good description of this challenge:

"To avoid a clash between global economic interests and local political interests, businesses must know how to be responsive to the needs of the communities in which they operate even as they globalize. And communities must determine how best to connect cosmopolitans and locals and how to create a civic culture that will attract and retain footloose companies...[T]he best way for communities to preserve their local control is to become more competitive globally."

Whether in services or manufacturing, promoting innovation in both products and processes before and better than competitors is the surest way to long-lasting high wage jobs that build on and strengthen a community's skills and technology base, and its ability to compete.

TECHNOLOGY PARTNERSHIPS: THE RISE OF INNOVATION-BASED COMPETITION

However, encouraging and sustaining such innovation can be difficult. In a recent *Scientific American*, editor John Rennie noted that:

"A good technology must by definition be useful. It must be able to survive fierce buffeting by market forces, economic and social conditions, governmental policies, quirky timing, whims of fashion and all vagaries of human nature and custom."

Over the past decade, with support from state governments, public-private technology partnerships have made this winnowing process more efficient. They have removed some "vagaries" -- like bureaucratic rigidity, lack of information, and the "not invented here" attitude -- that previously slowed the transition of advanced technologies from the laboratory to the marketplace and shop floor.

Many public/private partnerships for technology innovation were created in the early 1980s, in response to the crisis faced by older industries like auto, steel, and machine tools. New "pre-competitive" alliances of companies, state government, and academic and research institutions with common technology agendas were formed to revive older industries or support new ones. (David Osborne gives a vivid account of their origins and goals in his influential book *Laboratories of Democracy*.) They have been huge assets in the Midwest manufacturing renaissance that has made the term "Rust Belt" itself obsolete. Equally important, they remain key nurturers of innovation in their states.

Pennsylvania's Ben Franklin Partnership and Ohio's Thomas Edison Program were among the first to support industry-driven agendas for advanced technologies. Indiana's Manufacturing Technology Service, Maryland's Technology Extension Service, Iowa's Heartland Technology Network and the California Manufacturing Excellence Program are among the programs helping companies adopt new technologies successfully.

The Columbus-based Edison Welding Institute (EWI) is a good example. The largest materials joining center in the Western hemisphere, its comprehensive focus includes welding processes, engineering, materials, quality control and automation. Like many similar efforts, EWI got its initial boost with state dollars. These have been complemented with a $10 million U.S. Navy grant that established a Navy Joining Center to develop and deploy advanced joining technologies for both the navy and civilian companies. EWI members include companies from the automotive, aerospace, primary metals, utilities, heavy equipment, electronic, and welding equipment industries -- some of them keen competitors. Together, these partners are developing and deploying technologies critical for both industrial competitiveness and defense.

Centers like these across the nation now commit about $2 billion annually to science and technology for industrial innovation. (These programs are thoroughly documented in *Partnerships*, a study prepared for the State-Federal Technology Partnership.)

These "pre-competitive" partnerships, formed to share the costs and benefits of new technology and operating methods, serve as important new tools for economic development. But to institutionalize fully innovation in our states and communities, we must deepen and expand the principle of partnership that created them. We need strategic alliances for economic competitiveness.

ECONOMIC DEVELOPMENT: FROM ZERO-SUM TO WIN-WIN

Economic development used to be a lot simpler. Industrial recruitment programs usually competed with tax breaks, cheap loans, even outright grants to lure big manufacturing projects based on mass production methods pioneered early in the century. "Business climate" studies in the 60's and 70's emphasized tax and wage rates almost to the exclusion of other factors.

Even "revolutionary" technological innovation was usually orderly, and occurred at a pace that conventional balance sheets could account for in the "long-term" category. For example, Xerox introduced its first commercial copy machine twelve years after discovering xerography. Except for agricultural extension services, states and local government involvement in technology was limited.

Competition was usually a zero-sum game -- you win, I lose. The goals were worthy -- decent jobs for constituents, an expanded tax base. The costs are also well-known -- massive tax incentives or cash grants to attract footloose companies, and demands for the same incentives from companies already based in the state or community. Despite growing criticism of "beggar thy neighbor" incentive wars, and occasional efforts to limit them, we have all engaged in them. Some of us still do.

But the time has come to lift our competition to a higher and more productive level, one that helps our best firms compete globally. We do this when we understand that, in today's innovation and technology-driven economy, cooperation and competition are not mutually exclusive. New, sometimes unexpected partnerships are developing between the private sector and government at all levels, between businesses and the university and research community, between companies, between states and between communities. The best of these partnerships do not preclude competition; they presuppose it.

Partnerships emerging on the next century's doorstep differ in important ways from those of the past. What is different is their intensity -- their scope, focus, and imagination -- and their ability to put old rivalries to use in the service of competitive excellence.

A recent example. Lincoln, Nebraska, the state capital and home to the University of Nebraska, has historically been a major rival to Omaha, the state's largest city. These cities, only an hour's drive from each other, have often been locked in a "win-lose" combat for new businesses, convinced one city's loss was the other's gain.

However, Lincoln recently engaged in a comprehensive review of its strategic business mission and direction. In so doing, the mayor, civic leadership and the business community realized that it was critically important to pursue a different dynamic with Omaha. The two cities are now piloting a project called "Linc-O" that will focus on issues important to the entire region: labor force skills improvement and recruitment, and regional infrastructure issues such as airport development.

Such cooperation certainly will not mean an end to competition for either city or their businesses, but it will raise their chances to compete on the basis of innovation. That's a "win" for both cities. For the truth is the most serious competition for Lincoln and Omaha is not each other; it is Taiwan and Tallahassee, India and Indianapolis.

STRATEGIC ALLIANCE FOR INNOVATION: EMERGING MODELS, NEW GUIDELINES

The goals of development for innovation are straightforward:

❑ Create long-term jobs that capitalize on raising an area's skills and technology base.

❑ Stimulate sustained private/public investment in strategic technologies.

❑ Make an area's economy more capable of sustained innovation.

Of course, the trick is how to do this. Fortunately, the experience of important strategic technology alliances formed over the last five years suggests several key principles.

Principle One -- Identify opportunities for public/private technology investment and development, beginning with an analysis of your community's basic strengths, or competitive advantage

Developed by Michael Porter in several books, the concept of competitive advantage helps us understand how geographic areas can specialize and excel in certain economic activities, and successfully support clusters of competing firms that conduct them. The competitive advantage framework is being adapted to analyze the technology needs of states, cities, and other geographical areas.

Industry clusters are the basis of sustainable competitive advantage. Competing companies, customers, suppliers, and other supporting institutions like schools and government can comprise a cluster, in which both supportive and competitive relationships spur innovation. Cluster boundaries can change over time. Competition between companies, even within the same community, is desirable since it spurs

innovation, and prepares them to compete in global markets.

Identifying and building clusters that match an area's core competencies -- its endowment of technology resources, workforce skills, or suppliers -- helps a community target its economic development activities and resources better. It begins with these basic questions:

❑ In which technologies and products do the community's companies excel?

❑ Are there new market segments in which they should begin to compete?

❑ What suppliers, customers, or related industries or companies could be attracted?

❑ What are the community strengths that our dynamic companies value, and how do we build them?

The ultimate goal of this analysis is to nurture specialized factors of production -- for example, highly skilled labor, or research facilities focused on a particular industrial cluster; a strong and innovative supplier base; demanding local customers; and domestic competitors. Assets and pressures like these encourage companies to maintain the continual innovation and quality improvement needed to compete globally, and to strengthen market position.

Determining competitive advantage for a state or locality requires assembling an area's key economic, government, and technology leadership -- not to pick technology or industry winners and losers, but to meet the technology-related needs of an area's most dynamic companies, or seek new companies based on the area's technology or skills base.

Principle Two -- Effective public/ private partnerships that identify and invest in opportunities for innovation must be led by the private sector stakeholders

Whether it is the Edison Welding Institute in Ohio, or Project California, their strategic economic analysis and ensuing action agendas need to be rooted in credible data provided by industry, informed by the factory floor perspective of successful firms, and supported by real non-tax dollar investment. This leads to dynamic, surprising partnerships that can usually find a way around bureaucracy, narrow self-interest, and old habits that can hamper dynamic economic growth.

Competitive Advantage in Action: Emerging Models.

Project California is a compelling example of the next generation of state-level programs using technology to promote economic development. It is an ongoing public/private effort launched by the California Legislature, the Wilson Administration, key private sector leaders, and the California Council on Science and Technology.

Project California's mission is to identify and implement actions that boost California's competitive advantage in key advanced transportation technology areas, providing long-term value, added manufacturing jobs to replace lost defense jobs, and improving the state's environment by reducing urban congestion.

A thorough evaluation of California's superb resources in several advanced technology areas: telecommunications; intelligent transportation systems; command, control, and systems integration; electric vehicles; high speed rail; and fuel cells has produced an economic development action agenda for each area. Project California members are now dealing with thorny issues like public procurement processes, regulatory streamlining, communications deregulation, and regulations forcing a fundamentally new form of automotive product and infrastructure.

The Lincoln Partnership for Economic Development is being formed as a result of a comprehensive analysis of its *community* competitive advantage. Although Lincoln, Nebraska is one of the top performers for cities of its size, with large and growing businesses, its political and business leadership is not content with current success. One critical problem is the abundance of highly educated workers from the Lincoln-based University of Nebraska, and the limited number of satisfactory career paths open to them in the Lincoln area.

An intensive strategic assessment resulted in a comprehensive economic development strategy around Lincoln's emerging industrial strengths: pharmaceutical/biotechnology, information technology, and electronics manufacturing. Better leveraging the University of Nebraska-Lincoln's technology resources is a key component of the proposed strategy. Some options under consideration are a public/private venture for electronic manufacturing research and production, an information technology initiative, and capitalizing on biotechnology research at the University of Nebraska's Beadle Center.

This type of comprehensive assessment should lead to better targeting of economic development resources to support technology-oriented companies. For example, during the strategic assessment, city economic developers discovered that an electronics components manufacturer in Lincoln needed strong supplier links to support its long-term growth strategy. With a network of key suppliers and fabrication functions nearby, the company could adopt "just-in-time" inventory management that quickly adjusts product specifications to market needs. Learning this key fact allowed the city's economic development department to partner with businesses to create an appealing long-term approach to this company's suppliers.

Currently, the Long Island Association, the organization of Long Island business leaders, is undertaking a comprehensive analysis of Long Island's technology intensive industries -- electronics, software, biotechnology, and graphics communications -- to decide which industry segments best match the island's core capabilities. As with Project California and Lincoln, this requires a wide-ranging analysis of the market and technology challenges facing each industry, and of each industry's competitive structure.

For example, the Select Panel governing Project California included oil industry executives who agreed to promote electric vehicles because of the industry's great potential value to the state. Further, a panel of cable, TV, telco, cellular, and utility executives overcame longstanding differences to call for a large-scale experiment in complete deregulation of California's communications market.

Principle Three: Serious and sustained CEO involvement is essential to maintain public sector respect and resolve tough issues

CEO involvement means access to private dollars for key tasks, without having to wait for public funds. It means being able to attract the support of other stakeholders for action steps. It provides a built-in test of values and relevance, since CEOs will not sit still for empty studies and endless meetings. It means being able to confront tough issues head-on.

With two funds capitalized with over $100 million, Primus Venture Partners is a remarkable example of a high-level partnership to provide "patient" capital to fund new companies or revitalize mature ones. Initiated by CEOs of major Cleveland-area companies and banks (including several Fortune 500 companies), this unique private/public partnership matches private sector funds with contributions from public sector organizations like the State Teachers Retirement Board of Ohio and the Public Employees' Retirement System of Ohio.

Mal Currie (a former CEO of Hughes Aircraft), Roy Anderson (a former CEO of Lockheed), and Bank of America CEO Dick Rosenberg provided the high-profile private sector leadership guiding Project California through the many difficult debates that concluded in the bold consensus for action I described earlier.

The Edison Polymer Innovation Corporation (EPIC), in Akron, Ohio also shows how high-level CEO participation allows tough issues to be resolved head-on. Formed to promote the development and application of polymer technology, EPIC's membership was at first confined to companies with U.S. ownership. This principle was challenged in 1990 when the Japanese-owned Bridgestone purchased Firestone, and wanted to continue Firestone's previous membership in EPIC. EPIC's leadership agreed that Bridgestone's participation would contribute positively to U.S. based polymer capacities. The private sector leaders of EPIC's Board of Directors understood that the nationality of ownership mattered less in today's economy than the people employed and the competitiveness of production capabilities in their community.

Principle Four: The public sector -- state, regional, and local governments -- should be creative participants in these new alliances

In most of the cases I have cited, states or local governments provided the seed money for the initiative. That early investment helped frame the public purpose around which the private sector could rally. Usually a continuing willingness to provide some public funding is important. But the public sector can be an equally creative partner in the enterprise.

States can spur innovation through regulations, especially when they have firm goals but flexible means. The role in promoting electric vehicle development through both mandates and negotiation of the California Air Resources Board is a good illustration. States can also review how regulation can inhibit innovation. For example, as Richard Florida has noted, banks often use inventory as collateral when making loans to companies -- in direct conflict with low inventory "just-in-time" principles.

Public agencies can also encourage innovation through procurement decisions. For example, through the Council of Great Lakes Governors, the Great Lakes states have combined their huge purchasing power to expand the market for recycled paper and other materials while partnering with key industries, like printing, to prevent pollution with new technologies and practices.

Training resources can also make innovation easier; Iowa's program to train small and medium-sized companies to ISO 9000 quality standards is an example.

SUMMARY

In a globally competitive marketplace, innovation (new technologies, new skills, new systems) is driving the creation of the highest value jobs. The challenge for economic developers is how to cultivate innovation -- you can't "capture" it.

I believe the most promising path for communities in the future is crafting and building "strategic alliances for innovation." These alliances build on existing strengths (competitive advantage); they are driven by the private sector; they require CEO leadership; and they need creative public participation.

The lines between public interest and private initiative are increasingly blurred. I believe responsible leaders in the public and private sectors, working together, can invent exciting new relationships that stimulate growth, create jobs, respond to global competition, and contribute to a healthy "bottom line" for everyone involved.

Economic Development and the Small Community

Jerry L. Wade, Ph.D.

INTRODUCTION

What can be done for the small community is a continuing difficulty for those engaged in rural economic development. Generally, experience suggests that success in economic development is correlated with community size. The argument is that the factors conducive to successful economic development require larger communities. These factors include a variety of infrastructure and organizational variables [1]. One need only look at locational decision research to begin identifying these factors: transportation, water and sewage systems, industrial park, school system, labor force, cultural amenities, low taxes. The obvious conclusion is that the smaller the community, the less likely the necessary elements will be present and, therefore, the lower the probability of success. The logical extension of this argument is that some communities are so small, there is little chance for economic development. Consequently, at worst, we can only accept the community's impending death, and, at best, try to ease the pain.

The premise of this article is that there are extensive opportunities for economic development for a community of any size. The problem is not the community but inadequate conceptualization and methodologies of economic development and the mindset of economic and rural developers.

Rather than continuing the elaborate rationalization for blaming the failure of economic development on the victims, attention should be focused on building an adequate conceptualization and methodology of economic development and on improving practitioners' understanding of how to practice economic development successfully in small communities. A community, size-neutral, conceptualization and methodology of economic development will be presented. Based on experience with the methodology in Missouri, the article will conclude with a discussion of changes that need to occur in the practice of rural economic development.

THE SITUATION

Following W.W.ll, the economies of Europe and Japan lay in devastation while the U.S. industrial machine remained intact. Between the demand for products to rebuild the wartorn European economies and the postponed domestic consumption from the depression, a huge pent-up demand for industrial output existed. The U.S. made the conversion from the war economy to a consumer goods economy and started on an enormous economic boom. From this boom, the final pieces of the industrial paradigm, the way in which the nation's economic activities are organized and managed was put into place. It was an economic system driven by the belief that "bigger is better," i.e., the economies of scale. Production systems were dominated by standardized, large scale basic production and the basic organizational pattern moved toward larger and larger production units controlled by corporations which were themselves shifting from a national to a global organization [2].

Within this context, economic development emerged as an intervention methodology. The initial stimulus was to address two questions germane to those years of economic boom: (1) How is the industrial expansion geographically distributed throughout the country; and (2) How can the "left out" groups get a piece of the action? From the prevailing economic conditions, economic development quite logically emerged as the methodology for increasing the amount of manufacturing in an area. Economic development became synonymous with industrial development. Many of the present characteristics of economic development can be directly traced to that early post-war context.

Sometime in the 1970's, conditions started to change. The economy just did not seem to be working as well. The basic production industries which formed the backbone of the U.S. economy were no longer effective producers of wealth, nor were they maintaining an international competitiveness. Globally, economic patterns and, subsequently, political relationships began undergoing major alteration. For the United States, this has meant widespread and basic changes in the structure of its economics system.

Futurists have characterized the present age in terms of the internationalization of the economic system, the service economy, the communications era, and the post-industrial society. Hidden behind the cliches are hints of the fundamental issues facing communities. The world is undergoing a period of restructuring basic economic organization and reordering economic patterns and techniques. A basic system change is occurring and the old economics no longer fit the current situations [3].

Not surprisingly, the context or environment has changed far more rapidly and extensively than the response. Economic development of the post-war boom became institutionalized and professionalized, with the status structure rewarding activities in external attraction. The challenge now lies in rebuilding and restructuring local economic systems so they become more productive and flexible [4]. The problem is that little experience or knowledge exists on how to do it. Existing concepts, methodologies and programming in economic development are neither appropriate nor adequate. The task is not merely one of delivering what we already have [5]. A reconceptualization of economic development with methodologies that work for any size community is needed.

THE PROBLEM

Most economic development concepts, methodologies and programming today are not only inadequate, but are also inappropriate for the task at hand. This is true not only for the traditional economic development programming still dominated by the attraction methods, but for most new programming that has emerged in the past several years. The rhetoric about economic development is changing, but the content of most economic development training and actual job performance is not. The most prevalent economic development programs and strategies today continue to exhibit the same two basic characteristics as the attraction strategies.

First, the prevalent definition of successful economic development is new, identifiable jobs. The problem with the definition is that it unnecessarily limits the potential for economic development. Economic development is the purposeful intervention into an economy to improve economic well-being. By limiting the focus to jobs, a broad range of activities which strengthen an economy but do not necessarily result in new jobs is overlooked.

Second, most economic development programs presume what the community should do as the appropriate action and specific economic development project. That is, the professionals determine what they believe is needed and develop a program to get the community to act appropriately. In that sense, communities are constantly offered a series of camouflaged answers devised by experts flying under the guise of economic development programming. What is presented as a program to assist the community in economic development is actually a program to get the community to ask the economic development question for which the professional already has the answer. Therefore, much of the program implementation efforts actually involve the "search for the question" to which the program is the appropriate answer. It is as if the television game show "Jeopardy" serves as the program development model. The answer is given; the only problem is to get the community to give a correct question so the programming can proceed. The resultant economic development programs are grounded in a problem-solving orientation and reflect an "expert's" orientation to solution development.

There are several obvious results from continuing this orientation to economic development. First, community responses tend to be confined within the framework of the initial program. The programming

entrance into the community will set the limitations. By and large, it is much easier to move from more general to more specific programs than to go from specific to more general efforts. Once a specific program focus is set, only with great difficulty will communities move to a broader community economic development focus. Consequently, the initial program implemented in a community sets the top limit of generality to which programming can then move. The more specific the program, the more a community's options are limited.

Second, the difficulty for small communities, and the reason that no relevant economic development options appear for them, is that present programming is implicitly size biased. The answers imbedded in the various programs tend to rest on premises that are more apt to hold true for larger communities and require actions more achievable in larger communities. When the programs do not work, there is a tendency to blame those whom the program is supposed to benefit. However, the problem is not with the community. That is begging the question. The challenge is to develop programming which would enable any community to have successful economic development. Consequently, the first question is: what would the characteristics of such programming be?

1. Obviously, it needs to be compatible with the economic conditions and dynamics of today. Therefore, unlike the pre-1970's era where a methodological focus on only one economic development potential was quite appropriate, the effort needs to emphasize a diversity of methodologies.

2. The desired outcome of economic development should be to enhance economic viability rather than to just create jobs. The economic development challenge of today is to build the economic well-being of community residents. Creating jobs is only one way to do that. Other ways include such things as increasing disposable income and improving economic efficiency.

3. Successful economic development activities should result from the programming independent of community size.

4. The "answers" should come from the community's effort rather than be predetermined in the programming. This means that the basic community economic devel-

opment programming should "open up a local economy" and reveal areas of potential. The community decides which avenues to pursue.

If the above criteria are met in the conceptualization and methodologies of economic development, then the size issue becomes mute. The critical question of change is one of the economic developer, not the target audience. Can and will economic developers make the changes to new ways of thinking and behaving? The attempt to develop and test such a methodology and conceptualization has been underway for some time in Missouri. The next section discusses the effort.

RUSTY BUCKET ECONOMICS

"Rusty Bucket" economics provides a conceptualization for a variety of strategies to build a stronger local economy. The emphasis is placed on understanding the local economy and then building the local economy from within [6]. The bucket imagery offers communities a new way of looking at themselves to understand what can be done. How does one do economic development? Stand in the bucket. Where can one reach for more economic activity? Traditional strategies have reached outside the bucket, external to the economic system of concern. The external strategies are still a part of the possibilities; however, an additional set of strategies emerge. Reach back into the bucket, into the local economic system, and get more use out of what is already there. Building on the capacity of what is already in the bucket is the key to the internal strategies of community economic development.

Not everything can be done close to home, but internal development is based on three strategies for using what already exists in e bucket. These strategies increase both the community's level of economic activity and its control over its future. They involve finding ways of creating new jobs and keeping jobs in the community instead of sending them elsewhere.

The following principles are the basic strategies of internal economic development:

IMPORT SUBSTITUTION Liza's musical response to the leaky bucket—then mend it—is the first principle. That is, plug a leak. Look at what goods and services are imported. Identify those that can be provided locally and be economically competitive.

VALUE ADDITION Add economic value to things already produced in the community. Find ways to make them worth more before they leave as exports.

RESOURCE ENHANCEMENT Increase the use of local wealth and talent. Evaluate existing resources to identify those which are either unused or underused. Then use them to support an economic activity increase in efficiency.

In the past, economic development has emphasized expanding the economic base by importing manufacturing, tourism and retailing. The "Rusty Bucket" offers a new perspective with strategies that are more appropriate and productive for communities regardless of size. The emphasis is on building for the future from a community's capacity rather than solving problems, which connect to the past [7]. Look at the local economy, see what can be done to get more out of the wealth already there. The emphasis is on communities making their own decisions and on local wealth and talent working together to bring new life to the community and the American economy. Where can community leaks be plugged? How can value be added to something already produced? Where are under/unused resources? Where can a community find opportunities to make a difference in their economic future? Success depends on identifying and developing ideas for economic activity in the community[8].

CONCLUSION

The Rusty Bucket methodology and conceptualization has been tested and experimented with enough that the author knows it works. The four following Missouri towns are illustrations. In Hamilton, population 1,800, over twenty new businesses, including two manufacturing firms, started in the last two years. Plattsburg has forty-three new business over the past three years with only nine closures, for a net increase of thirty-four. In Jamesport, a town of 680, about twenty-five new businesses opened in the same time. Coffee, with a population of 169, has two, including one manufacturing firm with fourteen employees[9]. The successes are an outgrowth of the application of the Rusty Bucket ideas by the community to itself[10].

Obviously, successful rural community economic development need not be size-specific. Small rural communities can be as successful as large communities, but not necessarily by doing the same things. A growing amount of experience with small communities using the Rusty Bucket methodology points toward the changes which need to occur in most rural economic development efforts.

First, rural economic development efforts must be based on a broader concept of intervention by a community if that community wants to impact its own economic well-being. Projects with the purpose of simply providing jobs are not adequate.

Second, rural economic development programming must use methodologies that enmesh the methodology into the community itself and allow the community to accept responsibility for determining the appropriate community economic development strategies and activities. Prescribed solutions generally do not work and will not allow a community to discover its own unique capabilities and resources and do not foster community-specific economic activities.

Third, economic development must be viewed as a community grounded process involving practical, action-oriented education .

Such an orientation is much broader in scope and involves a very different set of professional skills than the technical assistance orientation. Community economic development educational programming results in informed, responsible community and economic development. The skeleton of the community economic development process looks like this:

• imaging the future
• learning about strategies for local community economic development
• developing short-term goals for community action
• forming a functional organization of task forces
• providing support (educational and technical) to task forces
• evaluating
• restating goals, refining/expanding activities and organizational structure.

It is well to note that the process is not linear nor necessarily sequential. The community will determine its own flow and strict adherence to a step-by-step procedure limits it to becoming simply another prescription.

All of us would do well to remember that successful community economic development does not depend on the size of a community tax base, low taxes, interstate and airport availability, community size, or whether a community can afford to hire a professional economic developer. Rather, successful community economic development results from communities believing that they can affect their own future, commitment to do it, a willingness to look at themselves differently and apply new ways of thinking to themselves, and a lot of hard work. The challenge in economic development is to provide the conceptual framework and educational assistance that enables a community to do its own economic development.

NOTES

[1] An excellent review of the various factors is provided by John P. Blair and Robert Premus, "Major Features in Industrial Location: A Review," in *Economic Development Quarterly*, Vol. 1, No. 1, February 1987, pp. 72-85.
[2] Robert B. Reich. *The Next American Frontier*. New York: Times Books, 1983.
[3] Two excellent discussions of the economic transition are Gar Alperovitz and Jeff Faux. *Rebuilding America*, New York: Pantheon Books, 1984 and Robert B. Reich. *The Next American Frontier*. New York: Times Books, 1983.
[4] The need to think locally within today's global economy is well developed by David Morris, "A Globe of Villages - Not a Global Village," in *Alternative Economic Development Idea Bulletin*, Vol. 2, No. 1, Winter, 1987, pp. 3-4.
[5] A similar conclusion about rural development was reached by Daryl Hobbs, "Toward a More Innovative Rural Missouri," Unpublished paper, March, 1987.
[6] The basic elements of self-reliance and the idea of creating boundaries for the local community is detailed in David Morris, *The New City-States*. Washington, D.C.: The Institute for Local Self-Reliance, 1985.
[7] For a discussion on shifting from an orientation grounded in the past to one focusing on the future, see Jerry L. Wade, "Felt Needs And The Future Of A Community", paper presented at the Annual Meeting of the Community Development Society, Morgantown, West Virginia, 1987. John McDonald, in his paper "Looking at Capacity, Not Deficiency," in Marc Lipsitz (ed.), *Revitalizing our Cities*, The Fund for an American Renaissance and the National Center for Neighborhood Enterprise, 1985 provides a good discussion on a capacity-building vs. a problem-solving orientation.
[8] Two other major community economic development methodologies are the economic renewal project of the Rocky Mountain Institute (RMI) and the Wisconsin community economic development

programming by Glen Pulver and Ron Shaffer. For a discussion of the Wisconsin methodology, see Glen Pulver, "Community Economic Development Strategies," Department of Agricultural Journalism, University of Wisconsin-Madison and Ron Hustedde, Ron Shaffer, and Glen Pulver, *Community Economic Analysis,* North Central Regional Center for Rural Development, Iowa State University, Ames, Iowa, 1984. The RMI work is discussed in two articles in the *Alternative Economic Development Idea Bulletin,* Vol. 2, No. 2, Summer 1987, "RMI: a Sustainable Future," by Mary Simon Leuci and "Community Economic Development - Ingredients for Success," by Hunter Lovins and Michael Kinsley. The Lovins and Kinsley article also discussed successful economic development in small communities.

[9] Hamilton is discussed in Vol. 2, No. 2, Summer 1987 and Jamesport in Vol. 3, No. 1, Winter 1988 of the *Alternative Economic Development Ideas Bulletin.* Additional information on the Coffee project is available in the *Tool Kit for Community Economic Development* by Jerry L. Wade, Carolyn Cook, and Mary Simon Leuci.

[10] The forthcoming publication by Jack McCall, *Community Survival Manual,* to be published by the Department of Community Development, University of Missouri, is based upon and presents the programming details of using the "Rusty Bucket" ideas.

Providing Community Support

Joseph H. Nies

In any business today, competitive advantage is the key to survival. Often it is not necessary that you have a better mouse trap, but it is your ability to respond and react to market needs in an efficient and timely manner. This is especially the case when a situation arises that requires a new start up or the physical expansion of an existing operation. The time and cost involved in locating the correct community, site selection and constructing the actual building, obtaining necessary permits, etc. can consume more time and effort than the marketplace and your competition will allow.

Handling this type of project can traditionally take 12-18 months or longer. It always ties up key resources and capital that is unproductive. In the process you could select a site with cheaper taxes, better access to a highway, nicer community (in general, the perfect location) and totally miss the boat due to delays getting the project completed on time.

In today's market you can not take 12-18 months for a start up or expansion. Six months must be a reality unless you have capital to tie up in a building speculating on the future.

Anyone who has been involved in starting a new operation or a major expansion can give you a long list of horror stories and issues that can delay completion. It is difficult to handle issues within your own company where you have some control, but it can be extremely frustrating when you deal with outside delays with the community, government agencies, utilities. Getting a reading on a potential wet land situation, storm drain permit, etc. can cause long delays and tie up resources. A community with the right person, generally with the title of Director of Economic Development can make all the difference and makes a 6 month goal a reality. The person in this position doesn't complete his duties after the site is selected, taxes are negotiated or an IRB is in place. To be successful, the person needs to carry through to completion the total project and provide support for future expansions. Building a partnership to insure success for your business and in turn the community should be the goal.

Some examples of community support which may be required to make the six month goal a reality are listed below:

❑ *Financing*: Putting together an IRB, SBA 504, or traditional financing. Introduction to the right people within the financial agencies and banking community.

❑ *Utilities*: Identifying the correct contact, the lead time issues (such as power transformers) and pushing when support or lead times are not good enough to meet your needs.

❑ *Permits*: Walking you or your contractor through the process. Identifying areas where delays could occur. Providing general introduction and communicating the importance of your project to the local agencies.

❑ *Introduction to your Neighbors*: Working out conflicts where or when they may occur.

❑ *Supplier Support*: Providing lists of potential suppliers, contractors as well as potential customers.

❑ *Negotiation Point and Negotiation Support*: Contact to negotiate taxes, rebates, or to assist in negotiating utility rates.

❑ *Labor Sources*: Identify potential labor sources, technical training capabilities, technical schools and college level recruiting.

❑ *Export/Import Information Sources*: Know who to contact at State and Federal levels to help expand your business or handle issues within these areas. Introduction to State and Federal Representatives to assist in solving issues.

❑ *EPA/21E Understanding*: Knowledge in regulation issues and correct individuals to contact for information and/or resolutions.

❑ *Site Location/Temporary Space Availability*: Excellent knowledge of available land or building for expansion or temporary needs.

The list could and will go on for your particular situations. The key is that the support is available and provided in a timely manner in both directions.

In conclusion, in today's corporate world, time is almost always a factor. Time for a start up or expansion is often the longest lead time involved in any project. If this is important in your business, make sure you look for the community that really wants your company and has committed the right individual with the know how and relationships that can support you in getting the project completed quickly. A few dollars difference in the tax rate, cost of the land or better access to a major highway may be secondary to producing and capturing the customers prior to your competition. If you are not careful, you can end up with the perfect location or facility and no customers or losses due to delays that may take years to recapture.

TQM Benchmarking For Economic Development Programs: *"Good Is Not Good Where Better is Expected."*

Eric P. Canada

TOTAL QUALITY MANAGEMENT

The quality debate is entering economic development organizations through the board room. Board members engaged in in-plant and in-office quality management programs are asking how development executives can apply total quality management (TQM) principles to development organizations. Consequently, professional conference and seminar programs are beginning to offer introductions to TQM.

A Summary of TQM[1]

❑ Improve process consistency and reduce errors through an on-going, organization wide effort, led from the top, instilling pride in workmanship at the bottom, using staff teams involved in the process and empowered to make changes.

❑ Use measurement tools to track processes and pinpoint problems — compare to the best in the industry.

❑ Focus on increasing customer satisfaction.

❑ Work with partners.

❑ Think long-term; act short term.

"Improving quality is nothing new" as Bob Stoffels, editor, *Telecommunication Engineering and Management* magazine points out. "What is new is the rate at which improvement must take place."[2]

Quality is a subjective judgement based on an individual's perception each time of encounter or use. Performance is pitted against the service, program, or product's ability to meet or exceed expectations.

Eighty percent of a firm's poor quality is due to poor management systems, according to quality consultant V. Daniel Hunt. Only 20 percent of the quality problems result from poor workmanship.[3]

A quality improvement scenario views programs, activities, and services as repeatable processes instead of a cluster of innovative activities reinvented each time they are executed.

The underlying assumption of TQM is that managers have a choice: *continue current administrative practices, or initiate a search for better ways to manage limited resources.*

COMPETITIVE ADVANTAGE

Properly executed, a TQM program can create a sustainable competitive advantage for economic development organizations. This competitive advantage could benefit the organization in comparison to organizations competing for:

❑ funds

❑ industrial investment.

BENCHMARKING

Quality improvement relies on benchmarks which:

❑ accurately identify customer needs

❑ carefully identify and model best practices.

Benchmarking is the cornerstone of TQM management. It is fast becoming a condition of survival in business and will impact economic development organizations dramatically by forcing increasing levels of sophistication and increased performance.

Benchmarking is: "the continuous process of measuring products, services, and practices against the toughest competitors and/or recognized industry leaders.[4]

Noted business consultant, Tom Peters whimsically defines benchmarking as, "stealing from the best with pride."

Benchmarking requires an alternate view of organizational structure. The traditional view of separate units or divisions must be replaced with a systems view. Benchmarking requires the organization to be viewed as a complex set of interactive systems (Figure 1). The importance of this distinction is based on research findings which conclude that only 15 percent of problems impacting quality originate within the group with control. Eighty-five percent of these problems originate elsewhere in the organization, crossing group lines.[5]

MOMENT OF TRUTH PROCESSES

Service-intensive organizations such as economic development are characterized by "moment of truth processes." A.T. Kearney, an international management consulting firm, identifies two categories of processes: operations processes, and moment of truth processes.

Kearney defines an operations process as one which produces the same tangible output, time after time, like a factory, warehouse, or insurance claims processing center. A moment of truth process, on the other hand, produces the same output over and over, in an interpersonal customer service setting like an airline check-in counter or a bank teller station. But unlike operations processes, the output is intangible and the results are difficult to measure and control. *The key to total quality management for moments of truth environments is training and empowering employees to meet customer needs "now."*[6]

Examples of the moment of truth in economic development include: when the prospect calls asking "what can you do for my company?" Or, when the investor (member) asks "what have you done for me lately?" In these and other moment of truth encounters, quality is evaluated (subjectively) on the strength of the response. Proven performance over time is not always considered.

Moment of truth performance is critical in economic development. In one recent case, a midwest company needing space for an east coast operation, sought a location along the Interstate 81 corridor. Twenty-two communities met the initial site criteria and were invited to provide information. Fifteen were selected for serious consideration. The final decision was not made on the basis of the numbers alone. The dominant decision factors were attitude and results. The winning community's economic development professional and community leaders provided the nec-

FIGURE 1
Traditional View of Economic Development Organization

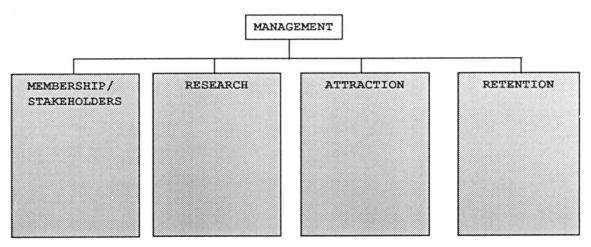

Systems (Horizontal) View of Organizations

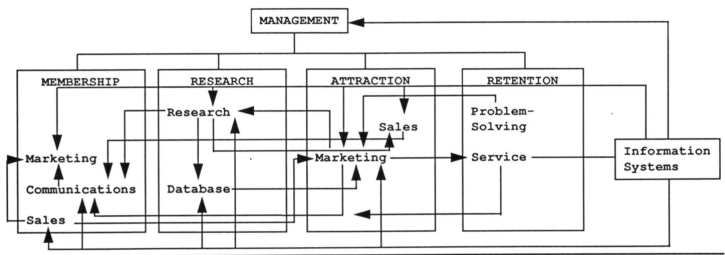

essary information, but *they also demonstrated a willingness and ability to overcome less than desirable circumstances.* The company's real estate executive explained, "You can buy BUD in any bar. Why go in? It's the guy who's pouring."

BENCHMARKING IN ECONOMIC DEVELOPMENT

Economic development organizations and chambers of commerce have always borrowed liberally from others through peer networks like the American Economic Development Council, American Chamber of Commerce Executives Association, The National Council for Urban Economic Development, Mid-America Economic Development Council as well as other regional and state organizations for professionals.

Benchmarking takes this interchange

of information to new levels. Our clients are looking carefully at systems and techniques, not just concepts. We are using proven survey instruments to analyze practices as well as identify and model best practices. We also scout related industries such as real estate, service companies, and unrelated industries like toy design or sports, for insights into how economic development processes can be improved.

By concentrating on the system level and using carefully designed survey instruments, benchmarking allows for meaningful comparisons among organizations. The results provide:

❏ reference points for evaluation

❏ models to be emulated

A typical TQM improvement cycle is shown in Figure 2. The process includes three components: management, planning, and benchmarking. After making a com-

mitment to quality, management and staff must conduct an initial quality evaluation to determine what strengths and weaknesses the organization has when measured against the expectations of customers.

Based on the information gathered during the program evaluation, practices and/or systems producing less than desirable results are identified for improvement. Goals are then set, and individuals involved with these practices are gathered into teams. The first two challenges for the team are to determine who the customers are and their expectations. Then, the team must create tools to measure the performance of the practices against expectations.

The following case study highlights a two stage benchmarking study. A Level 1 review is the first step in identifying best practices for benchmarks and modeling. A

FIGURE 2
TQM Improvement Cycle

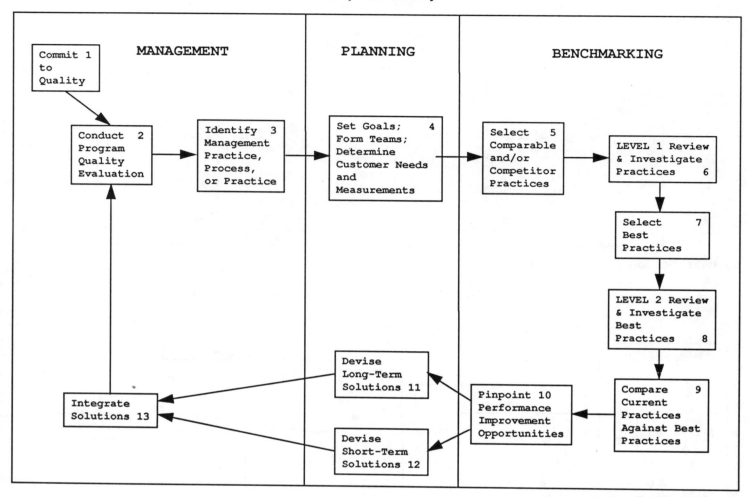

Level 1 review concentrates on a general investigation of a broad range of practices and systems at the proposed benchmark organizations. The purpose is to identify superior performance and the underlying systems and practices. The organization in the case study could easily be identified as an excellent benchmark organization for a volunteer based retention system, but not staffing and management policy.

Level 2 interviews isolate business practices supporting superior performance and collecting data on how they work and the results they produce.

Successful systems for modeling may come from many different models. One of the keys to successful benchmarking is developing comparable results for meaningful comparisons among the benchmark organizations and isolation of best practices.

CASE STUDY: APPLYING THE TQM IMPROVEMENT CYCLE (FIGURE 2) TO AN ECONOMIC DEVELOPMENT MARKETING PROBLEM

Situation

An economic development organization's business attraction results peaked prematurely.

Goal

Increase attraction results.

Management

When the *program quality evaluation* was conducted it was noted that one staff person held the primary responsibility for both business retention and attraction. Other staffers provided support. Support systems including volunteer management,

standardized forms, and computer tracking were in place and very well organized.

The program quality evaluation reviewed:

☐ the retention and attraction programs and supporting systems

☐ goals

☐ staff responsibilities

☐ volunteer responsibilities

☐ policies

☐ management practices

☐ performance reports

☐ staff activity records (time sheets

☐ computer system support (both hardware and software)

Planning

The program quality evaluation concluded: staffing practice combined with retention policy priority effectively capped attraction performance by severely limiting the resources committed to prospect management, contact, and follow-up.

Benchmarking

Criteria for *selecting benchmark organizations:*

❑ stable program

❑ success over time

❑ aggressiveness

❑ similar mission

❑ similar customer needs

❑ lead development organization

❑ regional service area

Level 1 Review interviews focused on retention and attraction goals, policies, staffing skills, assignments, activities, support systems, budget and allocations, and performance. The business retention and attractions of four organizations were benchmarked. Interviews averaged over two hours each, not including follow-up inquiries.

Level 2 Review interviews were conducted with the benchmark organization demonstrating superior performance in specific systems or practices. These interviews probed to greater depth on policies, goals, staffing assignment, staff training, activities, and support systems. They averaged over an hour each.

Performance improvement opportunities (conclusions). Total staffing, funding levels, and allocations were comparable with benchmark organizations. However, best practices strongly suggest success at retention and attraction require different skill sets and personality types, sales training, and increased hardware and software support.

Planning (Revisited)

Short-term solutions. Reduce policy priority for retention, and/or move responsibility for attraction to another staff member, and/or provide sales training, and/or provide more sophisticated electronic support tools, and/or recruit a part-time retired executive with sales experience.

Long-term solution. When filling next staff vacancy, target applicants with skill sets and related personality characteristics for the attraction sales responsibilities.

Management (Revisited)

After *integrating appropriate actions*, the process begins again with a *program*

quality evaluation of marketing practices. Why not benchmark staffing and marketing practices concurrently? When multiple practices are addressed concurrently, it becomes difficult to document the impact of changes on performance. A successful corrective action could be offset by an unsuccessful action. Producing results becomes more frustrating. This increased the probability of failure and return to the status quo.

MEASUREMENT

Comparability of results is dependent on developing tools to accurately gauge performance. Performance measurement tools can be classified in one of two categories, numerical or observation.

Numerical measurements count units, process time, ad responses, number of contacts, errors, costs, completion time, etc. Numerical measurements are straight forward and easy to develop.

Observation measurements present a greater challenge, but they are critical to benchmarking service organizations like economic development—moment of truth processes. These systems do not lend themselves to numerical measurement. In these cases, performance must be measured through observation by capturing and quantifying opinions and attitudes of customer groups. Tools of choice include interviews, surveys, and focus sessions.

INTERVIEW DESIGN

Benchmarking interviews include a combination of closed and open ended questions. The author has developed a core group of standardized questions for customer needs studies and for organizational benchmarking. Situation specific questions are then added to investigate specific issues or problems.

Level 1 benchmark reviews are always conducted by phone with a pre-arranged appointment. Participants are given a brief description of the subjects to be covered to allowing them to gather any necessary resource materials.

Level 2 reviews generally require on-site visits.

Customer needs and preferences require a combination of personal and telephone interviews.

INTERVIEWEE PARTICIPATION

Why do interviewees participate in benchmarking studies? Most of the cus-

tomers of economic development organizations sincerely want to be helpful. They recognize that they benefit when quality improves. Economic development executives who have participated in our benchmarking studies comment about the self-assessment value they receive from participating. The interview questions cause them to ask why certain policies, practices or systems are maintained in their organization. We share summaries of benchmark study results with participants. These summaries allow interviewees to make a comparative assessment of their organization with others included in the study.

INTERVIEW ANALYSIS

The open ended — what, how, and why, questions increase the complexity of evaluating the data. To deal with the large quantity of language data (ideas, opinions, issues, observations, etc.), a technique called affinity analysis is used. Affinity analysis organizes language data into groupings based on the natural relationships between items. Each group is then characterized by the general theme describing the relationship. This is more often a creative process than a logical one.[7]

The extremely small survey samples — as few as four organizations — involved in organization benchmarking calls into question the reliability of the information gathered. There are two means of addressing these reliability concerns: survey design, and a comparative database.

Interviews should never be free-form, but should always be conducted with a carefully prepared survey instrument. The survey instrument should be tightly constructed to focus on questions that circumvent activity and probe support systems. Studies should include a base of core questions to allow for comparability with future studies.

Blane, Canada Ltd. has built two databases for comparison from benchmark interviews. One database contains the results of economic development program interviews. The second contains the results of economic development organization's customer need studies. New benchmark study results are constantly added to the databases. These databases allow a comparison to help recognize abnormal response patterns that could represent a problem or an opportunity. These databases also allow a comparison of program performance and increase the reliability of the analysis.

Both practices, careful survey design and comparative databases, help increase the validity of the results.

CONCLUSION

"Good is not good where better is expected."[8]

In the world of economic development there is little time for trial and error program design. Answers, wherever they are found, must be quickly applied to keep pace with customer expectations.

Total quality management is not about building better products. It is about eliminating problems and mistakes which will inherently result in a better product.

Benchmarking — finding, documenting, and analyzing best practices of others against current practices and customer needs — encourages us to think of the organization as a system and to manage the system, not the people.[9]

NOTES

[1]Monica Alexander, "TQM: a case study," *Talking to the Boss*, December 1992, pp 6-8, 46.

[2]Bob Stoffels, "Quality: What is it? Quality: Telecommunications Password for the '90's", Special Supplement to *Telecommunications Engineering and Management* (TE&M), 1992, pp 6.

[3]V. Daniel Hunt, "Quality in America," *Business One* Irwin, 1992.

[4]David Wilkerson, Anne Kuh, and Tracy Wilkerson, "A Tale of Change," *TQM Magazine*: Benchmarking, July/August 1992, pp. 146-151.

[5]John C. Kohler, "Strategic Quality Management for Today's Business," (speech), College of DuPage Business and Professional Institute, January 1992.

[6]AT Kearney, Inc., "Total Quality Management: A Business Process Perspective," *A.T. Kearney Management Report,* September 1992, pp 9-10.

[7]Michael Brassard, "The Memory Jogger Plus+: Continuous Quality and Productivity Improvement; *GOAL/QPC,* 1989, pp 17.

[8]Thomas Fuller, (1608-61) English clergyman, antiquarian and wit.

[9]Ronald Yates, "GAME PLAN: On the Road With The 'Messiah of Management' As He Tries To Do For His Country What He Did For Japan," *Chicago Tribune Magazine*, February 16, 1992, pp. 19.

Using Strategic Planning in Economic Development

Barbara Francis Keller

STRATEGIC PLANNING: A DEFINITION

Strategic planning and long-range planning are not the same thing. Understanding the difference is important and can be key to a successful planning process. As General Electric Company Chairman John F. Welch asserts:

"Strategy is trying to understand where you sit in today's world. Not where you hoped you would be, but where you are. And [it's trying to understand] where you want to be in 1990. [It's] assessing with everything in your head the competitive changes, the market changes that you can capitalize on or ward off to go from here to there. [And] it's assessing the realistic chances of getting from here to there."[1]

The term strategic planning has to do with the grand design, the major directions for an organization or community. Strategic planning is designed to assist an entity to make the best use of its resources in order to respond effectively to change, to take full advantage of its opportunities, and to avert threats to its existence.

Strategic planning is about direction, not time. It could be either long or short term. It deals with overall organization purpose (or community direction); it focuses on the future; it is concerned with both external and internal environments; and it is innovation oriented. Contrary to most long-range planning, strategic planning is not a simple aggregation of functional plans, an extrapolation of current programs and budgets, or a set of goals and objectives based on wished-for futures. Rather, it asks the fundamental questions of: What is the purpose of the organization? Is it the right purpose? What is likely to happen in the future that will affect the community; that is, what are the opportunities and threats it will face? What are its strengths? Realisti-

cally what are its weaknesses? And what directions should it therefore take? Strategic planning also differs from other forms of planning in its specific recognition and concern for the outside environment. It concentrates on identifying strategic advantages and vulnerabilities in meeting the challenges in the environment.

The essence of strategic planning lies in positioning the organization or community in order to gain major advantage. That is, after careful assessment, to direct the organization's (or community's) limited resources toward a limited number of major directions where the greatest benefit can be realized.[2]

Such strategic decision making is often dominated appropriately by non-quantitative factors. Strategic planning is an art, a creative process that requires analysis and knowledge different from that of long range planning. The key to organizational survival or the economic health of a community lies in the clarity of its strategic thinking.[3]

Intuition is extremely important in strategic thinking and planning, intuition that is, which represents a leap in thinking preceded by very careful analysis of facts. According to Bruce Hendrickson of the Boston Consulting Group:

"For the most significant decisions, the ideal is to be sure that the result is based upon rigorous and painstaking analysis guided and reinforced by intuition based upon experience. Intuition is needed to determine the method of rigorous analysis to be employed, the data collected and the method of analysis. The final decision is intuitive. If this were not so, all managerial problems would be solved by mathematicians."[4]

Strategic planning is designed to structure opportunities for intuition to break loose. A wise planning process uses both

pertinent quantitative analysis and qualitative intuition and judgment. Without both, the process is not strategic planning.

To further distinguish between a strategic and a long range plan, the strategic plan answers the question of what the organization or community intends to be in the future. The long range operational plan answers very specific questions about how to get from here to there. Long and short range planning are both parts of a strategic planning process. What have been too often neglected are the initial strategic decisions about mission, purpose, major services, and clients. It is very much like setting out to drive a thousand miles (a long range plan) without deciding if the goal is to arrive at New York or San Francisco (the strategic destination).[5] Thus strategic planning sets the vision, the framework, and the boundaries for operational planning.

WHY STRATEGIC PLANNING

Strategic planning is a process, and a rather rigorous process at that. So why should an organization or community go to all this work? Simply because it works. It works because it forces concentration on key strategic issues and questions, because the process promotes creativity and innovative thinking, because it forces those involved to face facts they do not like and to ask questions they have lacked the courage or knowledge to ask. It works because, in today's increasingly turbulent, changing environment, the ability to adapt properly is key to survival. It works because it identifies opportunities, because it concentrates, husbands, controls, and directs resources to assure a future consistent with organizational or community interest.[6]

Strategic planning provides an organized way in which a consensus can be developed that allows strategies to be successfully implemented in a community. This is more probable with strategic planning than with other planning processes for two reasons. First, good strategic planning is not an ivory tower, intellectual exercise. It involves key participants in ways that insure their agreement with the final product. Second, the careful analysis of environmental threats and opportunities, internal strengths and weaknesses is more likely to result in successful, implementable strategies. It has been documented that those using strategic planning have been more successful in attaining their goals than those without such a plan. In a report to the Chicago Department of Economic Development, the

Institute of Cultural Affairs, hired by the city to do economic development planning with 46 Chicago agencies, states that "groups that were able to produce the most results were those which had done strategic planning."[7] In a 1970 study of 67 companies, those with strategic planning reported a 38 percent greater sales increase, 64 percent greater earnings per share, and a 56 percent greater appreciation in stock prices during the planned period than those without such a plan.[8] Strategic planning does make a difference.

THE PROCESS

The strategic planning process consists of nine essential elements (see Figure 1): a plan to plan, mission/goals, the situation audit, a strategic analysis, master strategies, long range plans, short range operational plans, intentional allocation of resources, ("budgeting" financial and people resources) and an evaluation system. There might be a tendency, in the midst of the demands of everyday economic development, to shortchange one or more of these steps. This would be a mistake; effective systems require each of the nine elements. Judgment about the steps is needed however. It is crucial to decide on the appropriate depth or intensity of each element for each local situation. And probably just as many mistakes are made insisting on a process that is too complicated for the situation at hand as are made eliminating or short changing steps.

The strategic planning process must be adapted to the local "organizational culture." In economic development this means adapting not only to the style of the leadership of the economic development organization, but it also means creating a comfort level among the citizens of the community. This is particularly important because development strategies are often long term and risky in nature. A correct judgment about who needs to be involved in the decision making process and when can mean greater overall understanding of the economic development process and consequently greater patience with long term results.

COMMUNITY STRATEGIC PLANNING

Step1: Planning to Plan

In a community, selection of the right groups and individuals to participate in the planning process is very important. Can-

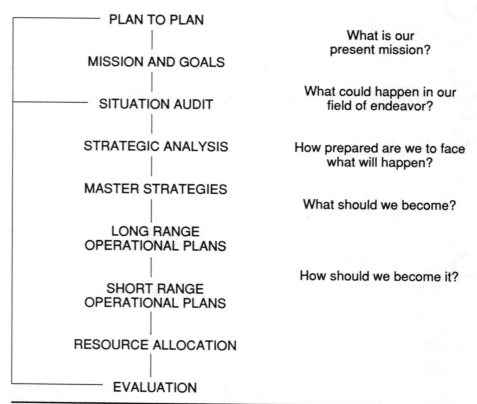

FIGURE 1
Elements of the Strategic Planning Process

PLAN TO PLAN

MISSION AND GOALS — What is our present mission?

SITUATION AUDIT — What could happen in our field of endeavor?

STRATEGIC ANALYSIS — How prepared are we to face what will happen?

MASTER STRATEGIES — What should we become?

LONG RANGE OPERATIONAL PLANS

SHORT RANGE OPERATIONAL PLANS — How should we become it?

RESOURCE ALLOCATION

EVALUATION

didates include persons from government, civic, and private sectors. The first step in any new effort is to create a focal point for the planning process. Typical focal points include: a specific governmental agency, a government committee or commission, a local development corporation, an ad hoc group, and the Chamber of Commerce.

The next action is to select individual participants. Candidates for inclusion from the government sector include: local elected officials, state agencies, council/board representatives, county/ regional government, regional planning groups, education institutions, and publicly owned utilities. Civic group participants can be found in business associations, citizen groups, service clubs, tourist bureaus, taxpayer's associations, foundations, professional associations, women's organizations, or church groups. Private sector candidates include businesses and individuals with an interest in economic development i.e. bankers, realtors, attorneys, developers, retail corporations, industrial corporations, utilities, transportation, service corporations, communications companies, and news media.[9]

The key is to analyze community power

and influence structures to determine who is important to insure the success of the plan.

The group should include people with power to approve the plan, and those who will be needed to see that it is implemented. It is important to look for respected, nonpartisan persons. Both the formal and informal decision makers should be secured for the team. It is important to have needed expertise represented. Persons of authority and charisma can sell the rest of the community on the plan. The group can be small or large, operate through an informal or formal structure, but the persons chosen can make the difference between success and failure of the effort.[10]

There is a pitfall to avoid in designing a timeframe for the plan. The economic developer must carefully judge how long it takes his/her community to make and implement a decision requiring substantial expenditure. This is the "turning radius" of that community. The timeframe for the plan should be at least as long as the turning radius. On the other hand, it is also important to evaluate how long the community will wait patiently for results. If the timeframe demanded for evaluation of results is unrealistic, then the plan could be judged unsuccessful when it is not. For an impatient community, short term interim benefits should be built into the plan. A realistic picture of each of these factors will help in determining an optimum timeframe for the planning cycle.

Step 2: Creating the Mission Statement

The words mission, purpose, charger, role, definition of the business, the grand design have all been used to describe this step in the planning process. This is the first major strategic decision. "If one does not know what game one's playing, it is impossible to know whether to run, dribble, or putt."[11] The concept of a mission/goals statement is not as easy to imagine clearly for a community as it is for an organization. However, conflict in communities often stems from differences in what various citizens want the community to be like in the future. Therefore, the process of sharing views, looking realistically at what is possible, and coming to some form of consensus on the community's hoped-for future, is a very important part of the planning process.

In a community, the mission question is: what is the nature of the community now and what is the community's vision of what it wants to be in the future? The vision may be, for instance, of a sleepy rural town, a regional commercial center, a diversified blue collar industrial city, a wealthy suburb, or a tourist center. Consensus must be forged here before effective economic development strategies can be established. Failure to build this consensus is the source of much community tension, backing up and restarting, even loss of jobs for economic developers.

A mission statement can be developed by the economic developer, submitted to public hearing, and approved by the City Council. However, because of the need for consensus, it is recommended that the mission statement be developed by a planning group representative of the community.

Step 3: Conducting a Situation Audit

The idea that a community needs to do a comprehensive, objective situation audit is relatively new. The need has been created by the competitive environment of economic development today. A credible situation audit can be a great aid to the economic developer in getting the community to face unpleasant facts or to trade wish dreams for real possibilities. It is also extremely important to the process of resolving the strategic weaknesses of a community. Traditionally economic development has looked at factors such as transportation, utility capacities/rates, tax comparisons, other costs of doing business, and industrial site availability. One of the results of today's changes in the business environment is the need to focus on additional factors in this audit. Included among these new issues are skill levels of employees, environmental issues, quality of life, community services, community response time, entrepreneurial potential, and various business retention issues.

A local planning group can gather data through interviews, surveys, public hearings, reading publications, talking to experts, and hiring of consultants as well as through special reports, case studies, feasibility studies, statistics, group brainstorming meetings, and aggregate quantitative analyses. However the analysis is done, the planning data base should include long range futuring projections, analyses of past and current environmental conditions, and internal performance.

Future forecasts are important and should not be neglected, but there is always a danger that community people will view them as promises about the future. Forecasts can be wrong. Education on this point is important to the community's acceptance of changes in the plan made because the external situation shifts. Frequent updates of forecasts and of the planning data base provides for rapid course corrections as our turbulent environment shifts. Conversely, the "environmental scanning" process can confirm decisions to move in the directions already planned. One way to be alert for needed course corrections is to assign members to read various publications regularly in order to be alert for changes that could mean that a shift in the plan is warranted.

The community needs to consider its situation in the following areas. Not all areas will require an indepth analysis in every community. It is important to consider, however, whether each area provides a significant economic development advantage or a significant disadvantage to the community.

Economic trends: international, national, state and local;

Demographic realities: population growth/decline, age distribution;

Business base: type; diversity; trends likely to affect existing businesses; work force (employed, unemployed and potential) — skills, wages, availability, unionization;

Taxes: relative position of the state and community; services provided for tax dollars;

Housing: age, type, condition, gaps, changing expectations;

Physical environment: air and water quality, natural amenities;

Political conditions: strengths and weaknesses, state and local;

Health and safety: crime, fire and police protection, medical services;

Transportation: highway, rail, air water;

Utilities: water, sewer, electric, gas;

Education: childhood, worker training, management training;

Community services: recreation, cultural opportunities, service groups, churches;

Climate;

Industrial/commercial site information;

Current economic development activity;

Entrepreneurial potential;

Business assistance programs/financial resources;

Analysis of external environmental factors;

Central business district evaluation;

Community vitality;

Economic Development Network Analysis: assistance and competition for local efforts.

Step 4: The Strategic Analysis

The strategic analysis focuses the situation audit in relationship to the mission/goals. It involves discerning the community's strategic issues and *strategic* opportunities. It describes the key areas where the limited resources of the community should be focused at this particular moment to realize the greatest benefit. The strategic analysis takes the broad collection of problems and opportunities described in the situation audit and focuses in on those few things that are most worth the community's investment: the key issues that must be resolved to move into the future, and the real opportunities that this community should not miss. It is perhaps the most crucial part of the entire process and the least understood. It requires both disciplined analysis and creative decision making. Developers who stand out are often those that are intuitively good at strategic analysis. Good strategic planning processes use the creativity of all of the members of the development organization at this point.

The strategic analysis should be done by the planning group after reviewing the entire situation audit. There are normally only 5-10 strategic issues and opportunities in a community at any given point in time. It should also be remembered that since economic development is an ongoing process, strategic issues will change as progress is made. They should therefore be reviewed in every planning cycle.

Step 5: Designing Strategies

The word strategy here is used in a sense very similar to military strategy. It is a plan, method, program of action, or series of maneuvers designed to obtain a specific goal or result. Strategies provide a framework that guides day to day tactical actions.

Strategies may be designed to exploit opportunities, to avoid threats, to maximize strengths or to eliminate weaknesses. They are directly related to the strategic analysis. This is a key point. One of the dangers in a strategic planning system is that the parts have not been integrally related. Strategies that don't make use of identified strategic opportunities or resolve strategic issues are not really strategies, they're just nice ideas.

Industrial development has traditionally been interested in growth strategies such as attraction of new industries. Today's economic development organizations and the communities they serve may also need to consider contraction strategies which strip the organization down to its most viable program components. They may need to be involved in product development strategies such as downtown rehabilitation, improving the maintenance of community housing, or developing parklands.[12] The questions asked might include: Which strategies contribute most directly to the goals? What is the employment impact of each strategy? Which strategies are the most expensive? Which strategy brings the most dollars into the community? Which contributes most to the retention of dollars in the community? What are the environmental impacts, social impacts, and community impacts of each strategy? What are the skill and time requirements?

Which appear to be pivotal or catalytic? Which are sequential? Which can be combined? Which are mutually exclusive? Which can be undertaken immediately and create signs of progress? Which strategies are most consistent with the operating principles and philosophy? Which strategies make the best use of strengths? Which strategies eliminate, or minimize weaknesses? Which strategies position the community to exploit opportunities? Which

strategies position the community to avoid threats?

In choosing strategies, it is very important not to sacrifice the comprehensive picture. Wisdom from community development professionals indicates that it is more successful ultimately to deal with all of the problems in a community at the same time. A networking of strategies is important because issues not dealt with often interfere with the overall success of the plan. The word "maneuver" has been used to describe a set of strategies that move in a few intercoordinated directions to get the whole job done with the least resources. To create strategies is to create the maneuvers that will give the organization or community the greatest chance of accomplishing its goals. This is the core and substance of strategic planning.

Communities also need to think about timing. The proper point in time to initiate or conclude an action is the "opportunity window."[13] Being prepared for such a window requires an awareness of place, politics, economics, and technology. Flexibility is required if planning is to be truly strategic. The strategies should be designed in such a way that the organization or community can take advantage of new opportunities as they arise.

Steps 6-8: The Operational Plan

One of the key issues in organizational strategic planning is the translation of strategies into everyday actions. In public sector organizations particularly, too often the budget drives the plan instead of vice versa. It is no less of a problem in communities. The challenge is in having the resources of the community directed toward the plan and not in random directions that may or may not contribute to reaching the goals. City councils have many pressures on them; an effective development plan that they understand enough to defend, and which is carefully translated into operational plans and budgets, can mean less short term random expenditure which may even be detrimental to long term success. Figure 2 (see following page) illustrates the relationship between long range plans and short range objectives.

Step 9: The Evaluation System

Evaluation, the end and the beginning, the most often neglected part of the strategic planning process. Two things need to be evaluated—the results achieved and the "plan to plan."

Review of results provides measures of progress. These become important elements of the situation audit for the next

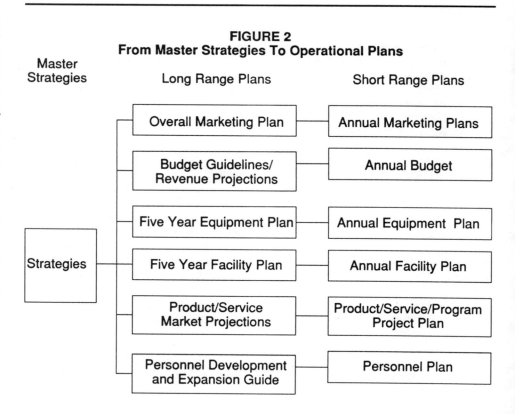

FIGURE 2
From Master Strategies To Operational Plans

Master Strategies	Long Range Plans	Short Range Plans
	Overall Marketing Plan	Annual Marketing Plans
	Budget Guidelines/ Revenue Projections	Annual Budget
Strategies	Five Year Equipment Plan	Annual Equipment Plan
	Five Year Facility Plan	Annual Facility Plan
	Product/Service Market Projections	Product/Service/Program Project Plan
	Personnel Development and Expansion Guide	Personnel Plan

planning cycle. Planning literature indicates that it can take as long as 5 years to develop a satisfactory planning process; review of the process itself is therefore also important.

CONCLUSION

The final key to successful strategic planning is to remember that it is a process. It is more important to create a system that makes community members, boards and councils self-conscious about the impact of their decisions on a long term healthy economy than to have a fancy printed planning document, or a precisely "right" planning process.

For the economic developer, strategic planning can be a valuable tool to educate community leaders about economic development. Strategic planning can be used to generate the creativity and enable the objectivity, to deal with our very competitive and turbulent environment. It can help clarify what's possible and impossible, likely and unlikely, to a community and its leaders. Strategic planning is an important tool for today's economic development professional.

FOOTNOTES

[1] ————. "The New Breed of Strategic Planner," *Business Week*, September 17,1984. p. 66.

[2] Dale D. McConkey, unpublished course materials from "Strategic Planning for Non-profit Organizations, Management Institute, University of Wisconsin-Madison, May 1984.

[3] Benjamin Tregoe & John Zimmerman, "Strategic Thinking: Key to Corporate Survival," The *Management Review,* February 1979, p. 15.

[4] Bruce D. Hendrickson, *Management of Local Planning.* (Washington, DC: International City Management Association, 1984) p. 41.

[5] Dale D. McConkey, unpublished...

[6] Avrom Bendavid-Val, "Local Economic Development Planning: From Goals to Projects," American Planning Association's Planning Advisory Service, #359, (September 1980) Chicago, Illinois, p. 1.

[7] Institute of Cultural Affairs, "Cultivating Strategic Thinking in Local Economic Development," Report to the City of Chicago, Department of Economic Development, June 1986, p. 11.

[8] S.S. Thune & R.J. Howe, "Where Long Range Planning Pays Off," *Business Horizons,* Vol. 13, August 1970.

[9] ————·*Minnesota Star Cities Program: An Economic Development Strategy for Your Community,* Minneapolis: Minnesota Star Cities Program Manual, undated, p. 1-2 to 1-11.

[10] Ibid.

[11] Wm. P. Anthony, "Effective Strategic Planning in Non-Profit Organizations," The *Non-Profit World Report,* July/August 1984, p. 12.

[12] Arthur D. Little and Co., Course Handout, original source unknown.

[13] "Wm. L. Shanklin and John K. Ryans, Jr., *Thinking Strategically, Planning Your Company's Future,* (United *States:* Random House, 1985) p. 21.

Self - Help Strategic Planning For Small Communities

Patricia L. Plugge

INTRODUCTION

When the agricultural economy took a downturn in the early 1980's, many Nebraska communities were quickly affected. Land values plunged, banks closed, main street businesses shut their doors, farm income dropped, factories laid off workers and people left town in search of work.[1] Unemployment went from 2.9% in 1978 to 6.1% in 1982. In the 10-year period between 1970 and 1980, Nebraska lost 12,616 persons to outmigration. This compares to 16,000 persons lost during a 4-year period from 1980-1984. Twenty-seven banks were closed in Nebraska from 1980-1986.[2]

During this time, Nebraska communities could receive training and technical assistance in economic development from a diverse group of public and private agencies. These groups provided assistance through a variety of federal, state and local development resources. "A community development process" was the foundation of the majority of the programs delivered by these agencies. Community improvement programs were being implemented, but fundamental economic development issues were not being addressed. At the same time, federal funds for many of the programs were being reduced. It became apparent to state officials that a modification of the community development process would be needed to offset the economic distress facing Nebraska's rural communities.

It was during this time that the Nebraska Department of Economic Development (DED) and the University of Nebraska at Omaha's (UNO) Center for Applied Urban Research (CAUR) began working jointly on a program to combat the effects the economy was having on Nebraska communities. Strategic planning was chosen as the method to address rural development opportunities and constraints.[3]

The use of strategic planning in economic development in Nebraska has gone through some significant changes since its inception in 1984. It will be the purpose of this study to document the evolutionary process of strategic planning in Nebraska. What started as a consultative-based approach has emerged into a largely self-help approach.

CONCEPT OF STRATEGIC PLANNING

Strategic planning has been defined as "the process by which an organization (or a community) envisions its future and develops the necessary procedures and operations to achieve that future.[4] It was first used by businesses in the 1960's as a way to improve their ability to compete in the private market place. In recent years, communities have found that strategic planning offers a systematic and effective way of taking the local situation in hand and implementing actions that are designed to improve its future prospects. The ability of an area to improve its competitive position and the subsequent economic well-being of its residents involves a more effective use of local resources. Every community would like to have high personal income, low crime rates, an abundance of job opportunities, excellent schools, and so on. However, every community also has a limited resource base from which to work. No community can accomplish everything its citizenry would like to see happen.

As a consequence, priorities have to be given to various elements of the local economic development plan. These priorities often are simply determined by local government or economic development professionals. When these values mirror the values of the public, the people are satisfied. Often though, this is not the case.[5] When using strategic planning in economic development, there is special recognition of the citizen's concerns. They can feel that they have their say in the plan.

According to a guide published by Public Technology Incorporated (PTI), there are seven necessary steps to successfully implement the strategic planning process:

1. Scan the environment to identify the key factors and trends important to the future.

2. Select key issues that must be resolved before it can successfully accomplish its aim.

3. Set mission statements or broad goals to provide overall direction in developing the strategy.

4. Analyze external and internal factors that affect the community.

5. Develop strategies that move the organization in the direction it wishes to go while doing so within the constraints which it has to operate.

6. Develop implementation plan that provides a specific timetable and assign responsibility for accomplishing each action step.

7. Monitor the plan and make adjustments as the local environment changes.[6]

Strategic planning is an important and relevant tool for economic developers and for the communities for which they are working. It allows economic developers the opportunity to obtain community support for actions the citizens feel they had a say in prioritizing. It also gives the community a chance to really understand the economy of their community, and what can realistically be done to improve their competitive position.

INITIAL CONSULTATIVE-BASED APPROACH

In 1986, Nebraska expanded work on a strategic planning pilot program that started in 1984. Eight rural communities with populations between 2,500 and 10,000 were selected to take part in the pilot program.

Preparing and Organizing for Economic Development

The first phase of the process involves each community building on its own existing capacity and forming a solid foundation for a new or revitalized effort in local economic development. This phase could be considered the most critical phase, for if the foundation is not solid the rest of the project will most likely be unsuccessful.

In each community a steering committee and resource team were formed. The steering committee is the "local policy-making group" for economic development. The primary purpose for this group is to unify the various local organizations which already devote some resources to economic development. Representation for this committee should come from various local interests: city government, chamber of commerce, county government, retail merchants, industrial/manufacturing, education, banking and finance, professional and service, and agriculture. Members of the steering committee were to report back to their respective organizations (Chamber Board, City Council, etc.) to give process reports, get input, and build support for the development program.

The local resource team would be providing staff support to the steering committee. Members of the resource team should have skills in organizational development, data collection and analysis, and knowledge of information sources. Examples of possible local resource team members are staff from the chamber of commerce, city or county offices, the local economic development district, local colleges, utilities, or county extension service.

Project staff assisted in identifying potential members for both teams. In addition, a single individual was selected from each community to serve as a local project coordinator. This person would be the primary contact for the overall project staff and would be the local organizer and facilitator for meetings and workshops. In each case, a member of the resource team was the local project coordinator.

Leadership Training

The Nebraska Department of Economic Development (DED) contracted with the Heartland Center for Leadership Development to conduct workshops at each project location on "Developing Skills for Strategic Community Leadership". (Heartland Center is a private, non-profit corporation in Nebraska which provides assistance to public and private clients in organizing and leadership development.) Participants in the leadership training workshop included the members of the steering committee and the local resources committee. Other interested citizens were encouraged to attend. The leadership training phase of the project was to accomplish the following:

1. Conduct "readiness training" for the local participants.

2. Introduce participants to the concepts and techniques of strategic planning.

3. Develop local and area capacity for cooperative working relationships, or team building.

4. Provide an opportunity for existing and emerging local leadership to mobilize and begin planning for the future.

5. Build community support for the project.

Building the Data Base for Economic Development

The local resource team was to have the responsibility of collecting the information about community characteristics. The following is a brief description of the community information needed to develop the strategic plan:

1. Infrastructure information, with questions dealing with the following services: housing, planning, health service, industrial development, fire and police protection, air service, streets, education, parks, water and wastewater, solid waste and library services.

2. Community attitude information, using a survey format.

3. Business attitude information, also using a survey form.

4. Economic data base, including area population, income and employment. Data from 1970 and 1980 were needed so trends could be tracked.

Strategic Planning Exercises

The strategic planning sessions served a central function in the overall local economic development program. At this point in the process, the local community has made a commitment of resources, a substantial amount of information has been gathered on the economic and demographic character of the area, and leaders were ready to initiate efforts. These strategic planning exercises were designed to achieve the following objectives:

1. Help the community focus its resources on a select number of realistic options and development alternatives,

2. Assist the community in identifying a range of development options and selecting those which are achievable,

3. Provide a forum where community leaders could examine and discuss the external and internal factors which impact the area,

4. Begin a process where a plan can be assembled which coordinates the various local development resources towards common objectives.

These strategic planning workshops were planned and facilitated by the staff from DED, UNO and CAUR. Attending the sessions were members of the local resource team, the steering committee and other interested community representatives. During these sessions the community data collected by the local resource team was used. The major work tasks

completed were the following:

1. Environmental scan - Small groups examined the information. The groups were provided with packets of information and given questions or outlines to stimulate discussion and analysis. They were grouped into functional area: infrastructure, attitude surveys, economic base information, and population and labor force data. The groups were then to identify trends and/or factors.

2. External/Internal factors - The full group discussed the findings of the small groups. Negative and positive factors were identified, as well as external and internal factors.

3. Key issue identification - At this point, the participants began the process of "narrowing down". Voting and a matrix exercise were techniques used to focus on a manageable number of issues.

4. Goal and objective development - The group analyzed the smaller collection of issues and began forming objectives to address the issues. This information became the foundation of the action plan.

Forming the Action Plan

The community action plan is an outline of the locally based comprehensive program of economic development. It is the document which provides the basis for focusing resources towards development efforts in the community. The action plan is proactive in nature, not passive like many other plans. Providing a mechanism to identify and pursue opportunities for community and economic development is the foundation of an action plan. The objectives of an action plan are to answer the following questions:

1. What development objectives should be given priority?

2. What projects should be undertaken to reach the objectives?

3. What local group or organization shall have the responsibility for specific projects?

4. What steps need to be taken to complete each project?

5. How long should it take to complete each step?

6. What should be done if the steps cannot be completed?

7. How can the plan be modified to accommodate changes?

Upon completion of the strategic planning sessions in each of the communities, a very rough draft of a community action plan for economic development was assembled by DED.

After the local resource team and steering committee were given opportunities to make changes in the summary, DED and UNO staff prepared a draft of a comprehensive action plan to address those objectives previously identified.

Following the modifications made by the steering committee and resource team, a second draft was prepared by the project staff. The communities were then encouraged to discuss the plan in open public forums, like town hall meetings. This was to help establish local ownership of the project.

Implementation and evaluation of action plan

It is at this stage where the communities had essentially completed the strategic planning and were ready to begin the implementation of the action plan. An action plan is never complete or perfect, therefore the community should be continually evaluating and monitoring the components. Through the project staff, each community was helped in identifying state or regional development resources to help carry out their action plan.

Observations and evaluations

One of the objectives of this pilot project was to refine a process communities could follow if they decided to organize or revitalize a local economic development program. The following observations regarding the components of the strategic planning progress were made.

Preparing and Organizing for Economic Development

The communities need more information on the program before it begins. More precise printed material or possibly a video presentation that would describe what will be expected of the community and an explanation of what strategic planning is would be helpful.

Also, a more formal relationship between the community and the state could give more of a sense of legitimacy to the effort. Because the nature of this project requires substantial commitments of resources and local coordination, legitimacy and public information was an important factor. A simple resolution of support from the city and chamber board may be all that is needed.

Leadership Training

Although the leadership training is considered critical to the overall success of the program, there may be more effective ways to meet the objectives. Several of the local participants expressed the view that the community leaders were ready to begin putting a development plan together, not just learn and talk more about it. It was not that they did not feel the leadership program was needed, but just that they were ready to move aggressively forward. A "readiness checklist" might allow staff to evaluate the community preparedness for economic development.

Building the Data Base

Making the collection of local information convenient and uniform is necessary. A better job needs to be done in identifying the data needed for the planning sessions and the data needed for implementing a long term economic development program. If DED or UNO could provide a software program for the economic data information, most communities would be able to use local computers for the task.

Strategic Planning Exercises

The educational information on the economic base theory should be standardized, as it was found to be very useful to the participants.

Forming the Action Plan

Although the communities made modifications in the first and second drafts of the action plan, because DED formed the drafts the communities did not feel an accurate sense of ownership in the action plan. Although the communities were encouraged to hold an open forum to discuss the plan with the community at large, this was not being done.

Implementation and evaluation

Some of the projects outlined in the action plan did not come as a surprise to the participants. They felt that this information was something they already knew. It needs to be stressed that by the prioritizing done in the strategic planning process, those projects were taken "off the back burner" and brought to the community's attention. Each of these priorities were assigned a responsible person to take action on them.

THE CURRENT S.T.A.R.T. PROGRAM

What started with a pilot project in 1984 has today developed into a largely self-help approach for communities interested in starting or upgrading their economic development program. This program is called S.T.A.R.T., which stands for Strategic Training and Resource Targeting.

Administering the S.T.A.R.T. program is the responsibility of the Center for Public Affairs Research (CPAR), which was formerly known as the Center for Applied Urban Research (CAUR). Requests for this course came mainly from local economic development committees, chambers of commerce, or local governments. This program has been designed primarily for communities with populations between 2,500 and 10,000, although it is presently being altered to include larger communities.

The S.T.A.R.T. program has basically the same format for strategic planning as the pilot program. The seven necessary steps to a successful strategic planning process (as noted earlier) are followed in both programs. But there are some differences that have improved the process in the S.T.A.R.T. program.

When a community contacts the CPAR office requesting information on the program, they are sent an introductory video. The video presentation will help assess the community's readiness for the program. Readiness, in this case, means that sufficient resources are available in order to move on with the program. Once the community has determined their readiness and committed to the program, a local organization (Chamber of commerce, economic development corporation, city, etc.) signs a formal agreement with the providers (CPAR). This agreement tends to legitimize the program.

The local leader, local resource team, and the steering committee make up the citizen participation in S.T.A.R.T., as in the pilot program. The local leader's role and duties remain the same, but the roles have changed somewhat for the local resource team and the steering committee.

The local resource team is made up of 6-10 local leaders. Each person on the local resource team has a defined role or assignment. Those roles are that of a recorder, meeting planner, surveyor, data coordinator, public relations liaison and steering committee liaison. This group will provide the resources for the steering committee to develop the strategic plan.

The steering committee is made up of a cross-section of 25-30 citizens. It is important that a good representation of the community is on this committee. This is one of the ways the community will assume ownership in the eventual finished action plan.

The leadership training concept of the

pilot project has been integrated in the S.T.A.R.T. program. While there is no separate meeting specifically for leadership development, the objectives are being met throughout the different steps in the program.

Building the local data base has been simplified by a software program that comes with the program. Much of the demographic information is already on the disk. There is also a section on the software program that allows the program participants to enter their own survey results into a computer. In the pilot program, project staff did the entering of the community and business attitude information.

The group process of developing and prioritizing key issues has remained the same. Developing the action plan has gone from the responsibility of the project staff to that of the program participants. From rough draft to final draft, the steering committee develops the plan. Task forces are assigned to each of the key issues by the steering committee. It is the responsibility of each individual task force to develop an action plan for their assigned issue.

At the last meeting of the steering committee, a final draft of the community action plan is drafted. The action plan is unveiled to the community by the governor at a town hall meeting. State agencies will accompany the governor to ensure the community is aware of and has access to appropriate state resources and programs to help implement the action plan.

Monitoring the process is the responsibility of the local leader. The local leader will meet regularly with the implementors to assure they stay on track and to assist in adjusting implementation plans to unpredicted changes in the community's environment. This process is ongoing, and may take several years.

CONCLUSIONS AND EVALUATIONS

Nebraska's strategic planning program has evolved from a pilot program with six communities to a total program that has assisted over 20 communities. The written material, facilitator style, and meeting style are constantly being improved as the program matures.

Most of the observations made on the pilot program have been acted upon. Videotape material is currently being used in S.T.A.R.T. program as an educational tool. A software program has been designed to coordinate the community information. A formal town hall meeting, including the governor, is the format used to unveil the finalized action plan. These changes enhance the self-help structure of the program and the perceived community ownership in the plan.

BIBLIOGRAPHY

Kolzow, David R. *Strategic Planning for Economic Development*. USA: American Economic Development Council, 1988.

Nebraska Department of Economic Development. *Nebraska Statistical Handbook*. Lincoln, Nebraska: Nebraska Department of Economic Development, 1987.

Pamphlets
Reed, B.J. and Reed, Chris. *A Guide to Local Economic Development Strategic Planning*, Omaha, Nebraska: University of Nebraska at Omaha, 1986.

Articles
Goldstein, Leonard. "Applied Strategic Planning: A New Model for Organization Growth and Vitality". *Strategic Planning: Selected Readings*. San Diego, University Associated, 1986.

Other
Blair, Bob, Reed, B.J., and Smith, Russel. "Training for Small Town Economic Development: The Case for Strategic Planning." Unpublished report for presentation at the Annual Meeting of the American Society for Public Administration, Portland, Oregon, April 16-20, 1988.

Keller, Barbara. "Strategic Planning in Economic Development." Unpublished thesis for Economic Development Institute, University of Oklahoma, 1988.

Nebraska Department of Economic Development. "Strategic Planning for Community Development." Unpublished report to the U.S. Department of Housing and Urban Development, December, 1988.

ENDNOTES

[1] Nebraska Department of Economic Development, "Strategic Planning for Community Development", (unpublished report to the U.S. Department of Housing and Urban Development, December, 1988, p. 1).

[2] Nebraska Department of Economic Development, *Nebraska Statistical Handbook, 1986-1987* (Lincoln, Nebraska, Department of Economic Development, 1987, pp. 13-47).

[3] Bob Blair, B.J. Reed, and Russel Smith, "Training for Small Town Economic Development: The Case of Strategic Planning", (unpublished report for presentation at the Annual Meeting of the American Society for Public Administration, Portland, Oregon, April 16-20, 1988, pp. 7-8).

[4] Leonard D. Goldstein, "Applied Strategic Planning: A New Model for Organization Growth and Vitality", *Strategic Planning: Selected Readings* (San Diego: University Associated, 1986, p. 2).

[5] David R. Kolzow, *Strategic Planning for Economic Development*, American Economic Development Council, 1988, pp. 8-9.

[6] B.J. Reed and Chris Reed, *A Guide to Local Economic Development Strategic Planning*, Omaha, Nebraska, University of Nebraska at Omaha, 1986, p. 3.

The Interdependence Of Economic Development and Environmental Protection

Raymond B. Ludwiszewski

INTRODUCTION

The intersection of economic development and ecological protection is at the "cutting edge" of the policy debate here in America. To verify that conclusion, one need merely follow recent developments in the 1992 presidential race or read the *Washington Post*. On Earth Day, Democratic Presidential candidate Bill Clinton outlined his environmental policy agenda in Philadelphia. The principal theme of his speech was the very issue addressed in this article — how to best ensure America has a bright future with both a strong economy and a livable environment. Similarly, the April 26, 1992 *Washington Post* ran an Op-Ed column by Jessica Matthews, vice president of World Resources Institute, entitled "It's Not 'Jobs vs. the Earth.'" Her column's premise, following candidate Clinton's reasoning, was that although economics and ecology are two societal goals that are somewhat at tension, they are manifestly *not* mutually exclusive. That same message is presented in this article.

ECONOMIC AND ENVIRON-MENTAL INTERDEPENDENCE

The environment and the economy are two sides of the same coin — they interrelate and are, indeed, highly interdependent. When conflicts develop between environmental groups and economic development forces, both sides tend to forget this close interrelation and, instead, polarize into warring camps. Viewed with some perspective, however, it quickly becomes clear that both sides in these often heated debates profoundly need each other.

Let's analyze that proposition. It is well known that industry, in locating new facilities, often is attracted by "quality-of-life" factors. There are few aspects of quality-of-life more significant than a clean, safe,

attractive environment. Localities which offer such an environment will often win the development sweepstakes and secure the most sought after economic development projects. Similarly, despite the way they sometimes behave, responsible environmentalists must recognize that their cause benefits from a strong economy. When the economy is weak, the everyday citizens, upon whom environmental groups rely heavily for financial and political strength, are often pre-occupied with the immediate stresses that a poor economy creates. A citizen whose economic future is uncertain is less likely to contribute funds or time to environmental causes. For example, during the recent recession, contributions to environmental groups dropped precipitously and the national groups were actually laying off paid staffers. Moreover, congressional sympathy toward environmental issues also fluctuates with the economy.

In light of these facts, all involved (regulators, environmentalists, industry) will be better off the sooner they all recognize the fundamental truth -- society *cannot* have economic growth over the long-term without protecting the environment, nor can the environment be protected to the exclusion of sustainable economic growth in today's competitive world.

The world is replete with examples of the intimate linkage between the economy and the environment. One is the environmental devastation in Eastern Europe and, particularly, in Poland. For approximately 50 years, Poland operated under a system that valued unconstrained economic progress at the expense of environmental values. Did that result in a workers' paradise of plenty? Did Polish industry — freed from environmental control costs — flourish and capture foreign markets? No! The economy stagnated and the environment greatly suffered. Today, the Vistula River,

which runs the length of Poland north to south, is so polluted it cannot even be used for industrial cooling. The discharges of the past 50 years have rendered the Vistula so corrosive that untreated river water will actually eat through machinery. The new democratic Polish government now estimates that the loss of productive capacity from polluted natural resources constitutes a drag on Poland's gross domestic product of at least 15% a year.

One is poignantly reminded of the words of Gifford Pinochet — founder of the U.S. Forest Service at the turn of the century and advisor to our first great environmental president — Teddy Roosevelt. Pinochet said, "A nation that has lost its liberty may win it; a nation divided may reunite. But a nation whose natural resources are destroyed must inevitably pay the penalty of poverty, degradation, and decay." Although a century old, these words ring true across a newly free Poland and a reunited Germany which both face daunting environmental problems.

Similarly, the environment/economy linkage is a major issue in the on-going North American Free Trade Agreement (NAFTA) negotiations with Mexico. Opponents of NAFTA often claim that economic growth in Mexico will lead to environmental degradation in that country. As evidence they usually point to the effect of the "maquiladoras" on the border environment. Maquiladoras are American companies who locate in the economic development zone immediately south of the Mexican-American border. On closer examination, however, this example appears to both belie their claims and make the opposite point. Mexican government studies show that the health of Mexican families near the border is actually better than in the rest of Mexico. Relative economic prosperity in the maquiladoras region has led to relatively better environmental and health benefits. In fact, economic growth is often a precondition for environmental improvement throughout the developing world.

EPA'S ROLE IN THE ECONOMIC/ENVIRONMENTAL BALANCE

If economic progress is essential to environmental progress, is the United States Environmental Protection Agency (USEPA) adjusting its policies to account for the positive contributions that industry could make? The short answer is "yes". Although implementing and enforcing the nation's environmental laws are still vital elements of USEPA's daily work, it is recognized that there is much that industry can and will do for the environment without the threat of congressional compulsion and agency enforcement. Accordingly, built into the policy structure is a large voluntary component centered on the concept of pollution prevention.

Over the past two decades, USEPA has utilized its permitting and enforcement authorities granted under the Clean Water Act, Clean Air Act and other "command and control" statutes to improve dramatically the quality of the nation's land, water and air. These statutes are effective in controlling point source or "end of the pipe" pollution. To attack troublesome "nonpoint" pollution (e.g. stormwater run- off), traditional "command and control" approaches to regulation will not be as effective. Instead, USEPA must work with industry and the public at large to encourage prevention of pollution at its point of origin, before it is released into the environment. A significant part of this effort includes creating voluntary programs encouraging production of less harmful substances and greater energy efficiency.

The first tentative steps into voluntary environmental policy were taken back in the fall of 1989. Administrator Reilly invited Chief Executive Officers of several corporations to discuss the voluntary reduction of toxic air emissions. That initiative turned out to be more successful than anyone had dared hope. The next step was more formal — and, on a far larger scale. Over a year ago, the Administrator announced the Industrial Toxics Reduction project, better known as the 33/50 project. USEPA asked companies to volunteer to make a 33 percent reduction in releases to the environment of 17 chemicals by the end of 1992, and a 50 percent reduction by the end of 1995. It's fair to say that we have been astonished by the response. In the year since the announcement, over 700 companies have signed up for 33/50. They have committed to reduce by 1995 their toxic emissions of the 17 target chemicals by about 300 million pounds per year.

Several companies, in fact, have made public commitments to go beyond 33/50. Monsanto, for example, plans to reduce its releases of all toxic air pollutants by 90 percent by the end of this year, and has set that goal for all its facilities worldwide. Union Carbide, Shell Oil, and Sterling Chemicals all have committed to reducing emissions by more than 50 percent, or to reduce emissions of more than the 17 target chemicals — or both.

Last year, USEPA launched a third voluntary initiative that has not received quite as much press as 33/50, but promises to be equally impressive. In the *Green Lights Program*, the agency is working with public and private organizations to improve the efficiency of lighting in this country and, thus, reduce the pollution associated with powerplants. Businesses, universities, state governments — anybody who uses lighting on a large scale — have been asked to improve their lighting efficiency.

The response to Green Lights has been very encouraging. So far over 160 corporations have signed up as partners in the Green Lights Program. Several corporations, such as Amoco and Shell are enrolled in both Green Lights and 33/50. Counting state governments and other organizations, over 200 partners that occupy about 1.8 billion square feet of building space are now participating in Green Lights.

What is the total estimated pollution reductions that will result from this voluntary initiative?: 6,800,000 metric tons of carbon monoxide, 50,000 tons of sulfur dioxide, and 26,000 tons of carbon monoxide — per year. That's equivalent to the pollution emitted by one and a half million cars in one year. All this has been done *voluntarily*, and the organizations involved are *saving money*.

DEALING WITH OPPOSITION TO ECONOMIC DEVELOPMENT

Assume the premise that the economy and the environment are deeply interrelated is correct. What can economic development professionals do to avoid vociferous local opposition to economic development? There are no perfect solutions, but there are some fairly obvious opportunities.

First and most obvious, look for industries that are "environmentally friendly." There has been phenomenal growth in the environmental protection business over recent years. It is now a $115 billion a year industry — it has quadrupled in size since 1972. Continued growth is expected over the next few years. Indeed, USEPA projects it will be a $200 billion a year industry by the year 2000.

Second, new industry should be encouraged to be open with its new potential neighbors about environmental risks. There is nothing that is more devastating to successful siting of facilities than a local community's sense that they have not been told the entire truth. Great care must be taken in these communications, because even innocent miscommunications can be misinterpreted as dishonesty or deliberate omission. Openness is in the economic developers self-interest for another reason, as well. Almost all of USEPA and state environmental enforcement efforts are a matter of public record. Similarly, Congress has passed Community Right to Know legislation as part of the 1986 Reauthorization of Superfund. This law provides the public a great deal of information about the level of toxic chemicals that major industrial facilities release to the air, water and land. Such information is readily available through a computer database. Accordingly, sophisticated local opposition groups will discover most of what they want to know from publicly available sources. Experience shows that its better that the public hear such information from the developer accompanied by an honest explanation.

Third, and this sounds a bit self-serving at first blush, let it be known that the economic development organization and the proposed project support rigorous EPA and/or state environmental agency review of the project and effective enforcement after the project is operating. Community confidence in a project will be reinforced, and opposition weakened, if a company acknowledges its responsibilities under existing federal and state environmental laws and regulations and commits to compliance with them.

Finally, most responsible corporate citizens these days have at least some positive environmental stories to tell. It might be volunteer participation in one of the USEPA programs mentioned earlier. It might be support for local environmental efforts, such as bike paths or stream clean-ups. It might be something else. One should aggressively market these activities to the community.

CONCLUSION

In conclusion, economic developers face the difficult task of being on the front lines as our society attempts to reconcile the tension between environmental protection and economic growth. A Roper poll conducted last year showed that 74% of people believe that business has a definite responsibility for environmental protection yet, only 36% believe that business was fulfilling that responsibility fully or fairly well. It will take a concerted long-term effort using the suggestions described above and many other creative approaches to close this considerable gap. Rest assured, however, that these problems will be worked through, simply because they must. The American people demand a strong economy and a safe, clean environment and they will count on regulators, environmentalists, and economic developers to provide both.

Tips on Creating An Environmentally and Economically Successful Project

Hans Neuhauser

A recent United Nations report, *Our Common Future,* contained this insightful statement: *continued economic development will be necessary to cure many of the world's problems, but to be successful, that economic development must be done in ways that are both socially and environmentally sustainable.*

It was the recognition of the interdependence between economic development and a quality environment that was at the heart of the success of the recent Crossroads Business Center project described in the previous two articles. Acting diligently on this interdependence resulted in a permit being issued in five months (and even that could have been shortened). Failure to recognize the interrelationships between the economy and the environment can lead to such tragedies as occurred in Guadalajara.

The Savannah Economic Development Authority (SEDA) project is not just an example of sustainable economic development; it is a model. While some of the components that led to SEDA's success are unique, other key elements, or hallmarks are suitable for use elsewhere. In fact, it is strongly recommended that economic developers adopt all of them in your next project.

ENGAGE IN ENVIRONMENTALLY SENSITIVE PLANNING

The first hallmark of SEDA's success was the commitment of Dick Knowlton and his team to the creation of a "class A" industrial park that included environmental enhancements, buffers and other amenities. The SEDA team sought to create an environmentally sensitive project by eliminating environmental problems in the project's master plan.

They identified the environmental criteria in the Section 404 wetlands permitting program as setting the principal planning constraint on the project and they proceeded to design the project to accommodate those constraints.

The primary constraints on other projects may be different. The constraints may be set by other laws such as the Clean Air Act Amendments, the Endangered Species Act, the Historic Preservation Act or the Coastal Zone Management Act. Whatever the law(s) that sets the primary constraints, identify them and then plan to accommodate them in the project.

In the SEDA project, the wetlands constraints called for avoidance and, where avoidance was not possible, mitigation. SEDA avoided wetlands damage by leaving more than half of the tract outside of the development parcels. Some wetlands damage was unavoidable, however. It was compensated for by such actions as encouraging the return of native hardwood wetland species in areas that had been planted in pine, leaving a 50 foot buffer around the hardwood wetlands and protecting the most important wetlands by restrictive covenant. Ian McHarg would regard the project as "designed with nature".

CREATE COOPERATION

The second hallmark of the SEDA project was *cooperation.* The SEDA team considered the alternative — of taking an adversarial approach to the wetlands requirements — but rejected it early in the process in favor of a cooperative approach, working with the key stakeholders in the project through an open process of involvement.

If one treats the regulatory process as an adversarial one, it will be. That's human nature. If one treats some of the key stakeholders as enemies, they will probably return the favor. And since they are key stakeholders, they often have the means to stop the project or at least delay it for years.

A cooperative approach will reduce suspicion and hostility borne out of ignorance. Cooperation will improve communication and that will help the potential opposition understand the project; it will give others positive feelings about the project. This kind of understanding and support can lead to quicker approval and a significant reduction in the likelihood of litigation.

ENGAGE IN EARLY CONSULTATION

The third hallmark of the SEDA project is *early consultation.* The Georgia Conservancy initiated "getting to know you" sessions with SEDA when Dick Knowlton first came to Savannah. Over greasy hamburgers at the beach, we sought to understand one another's interests and concerns, and sought to find ways to work together to accomplish our goals.

These discussions evolved into The Georgia Conservancy being invited to join the Savannah Economic Development Partnership — an entity that, while it does not publicize itself in this way, joins economic development and environmental sustainability together in a community revitalization effort. All of this occurred before the conceptualization of the Crossroads Business Center project had gotten very far along.

It is very important that consultation begin very early in the process. It should begin before one has spent a lot of money on engineering and other site-specific studies. There are even benefits to consultation before one has committed to buy the land. Consult early when one can still change the plans. It is a lot easier to change the plans when one has not committed a lot of money to them. If absolutely necessary, one can request that the early consultations be confidential. The Georgia Conservancy, for example, will treat information as confidential if requested to do so. Try it; you may be able to find representatives of environmental organizations who will agree to participate in confidential discussions.

Traditionally, economic developers consult with allies and likely allies. The SEDA model calls for early consultation with potential adversaries as well. Whose interests will be affected by the project? What agencies will one have to interact with eventually? What local or regional interests might be affected — a wildlife refuge, a park, a historic building, a neighborhood — Who are the key stakeholders? What stakeholders will perceive that the project will damage their interests? Meet with representatives of these key interest groups early to, first, determine what their concerns might be and second, to find ways in which their concerns can be met. Note that the statement is not — find out how their concerns can be overcome or whitewashed over. Find ways to meet the concerns.

ACCOMMODATE CHANGE

This leads to the fourth hallmark of the SEDA project: *accommodation*. Aim the project for a win-win solution, where one achieves one's goals and other key stakeholders achieve theirs as well.

In the case of the SEDA project, one of the key stakeholders was the U.S. Army Corps of Engineers. Overworked, understaffed and being criticized for inordinate delays in issuing permits, the Corps was looking for a way to issue one permit for the entire project rather than piecemeal permitting eleven sites; this was their "win-win" goal.

The U.S. Environmental Protection Agency was another key stakeholder. They were being criticized over the require-ments imposed by the 1989 wetlands delineation manual. EPA wanted to show that even with the 1989 manual, development in an area with a preponderance of wetlands was possible. SEDA was able to accommodate both of these needs and get its permit — a win-win solution.

Accommodation means that one has to be willing and able to change the project to accommodate the concerns of key stakeholders. If you're not, the consultation will be a charade, and efforts to establish meaningful consultation in the future will be damaged.

Why should one be so accommodating? There are a number of reasons. First, you may get some good advice. Others may have local knowledge or suggestions that your design team did not have. These ideas can help make the project better. Second, the improvements should help the environment — which is, after all, the environment of the community in which one lives and is selling. Probably the most impressive reason for accommodation is its effect on the bottom line. By designing a project to meet the environmental constraints, one can turn potential adversaries

who project supporters who can help expedite the approval process. The Georgia Conservancy met with representatives of US EPA and helped persuade them to adopt a favorable attitude towards the SEDA project. We did this before SEDA officials ever met with US EPA. We helped pave the way for rapid permit approval.

Of course, an environmentally sensitive project is a high quality project. As such, it can be more attractive to investors. The final justification for accommodation should be of special importance to professional economic developers. Accommodation creates a positive community image where everyone welcomes environmentally sensitive development. Contrast this to communities and regions of the country where polarized attitudes between developers and environmentalists have become so embittered and intrenched that potential investors are scared away and existing industry may choose to move out.

These four hallmarks of the SEDA project — *environmentally sensitive planning, cooperation, early consultation* and a *willingness to accommodate change* — will work for you.

How to Make an Industrial Site Survey

A community that identifies all local sites suitable for industry and compiles accurate, up-to-date site information enjoys a distinct advantage in the highly competitive quest for new industry and jobs. Failure to develop such factual information—and failure to keep it up-to-date—may jeopardize the area's development effort. The following details how a survey can be made.

WHAT A PROSPECT NEEDS TO KNOW

The value of a thorough industrial site survey for a community is best seen through the eyes of the industrial prospect himself. A manufacturer considering a possible location for a new or branch plant is not convinced by mere assurances of "lots of fine plant sites in town." He/she wants clear evidence that these sites exist and that at least one of the sites is available and suitable for the operation of his proposed plant.

To determine whether or not one of the local sites suits his/her requirements, the manufacturer must know where all the sites are located, their size, cost, topography, grading requirements, and susceptibility to flooding, drainage characteristics and load-bearing capacity of the soil, depth to ground water, zoning designation, tax rate, adjacent land use, existing industrial buildings, and other improvements, and the utilities and transportation facilities by which they presently are or definitely will be serviced by the time a plant would be in operation.

Some brief comments concerning several of these factors may serve to clarify their respective roles in site selection.

Size and Shape

One of the most obvious changes in plant location, over the last few decades, has been the general trend toward larger

*Adapted from a publication of the same name prepared by The Economic Development Administration of the U.S. Department of Commerce.

sites. In most cases, a relatively large lot is sought in order to insure adequate space for deliveries, employee parking, and possible future expansion. Also, a spacious, well-landscaped site makes for better plant appearance than a smaller site and, at the same time, provides greater privacy.

As to shape of site, the usual preference is for a site of regular shape or one otherwise suitable from such standpoints as building layout, access to transportation, parking, and future expansion.

Topography

So far as topography is concerned, the usual preference is for a comparatively level site, with just enough slope to provide good drainage. There are exceptions, however. Some firms may choose a hilltop location because of supposed advantages in appearance and advertising value. In other cases, the type of building preferred by the company may be best adapted to a sloping site. For example, the president of one small company wished to construct his plant on a hill so that shipments and deliveries could be made on two levels.

Utilities

Utilities are always an important consideration in the inspection of individual plant sites. The utilities with which manufacturing establishments are chiefly concerned are electric power, water, natural gas, and sewerage. While utility rates may represent an important cost variable between communities, they are normally uniform within a community. Hence, the principal difference in utility costs between sites in the same community is found in the cost of extending utility lines to the plant site. In many cases, this represents a significant element in the total, developed cost of the site.

Water Supply

An adequate, safe, and reliable source of water is needed for drinking and sanitary purposes. In addition, many industrial plants use large quantities of water in the production process. When this is the case, location near a natural source of water is frequently a necessity, and such characteristics of the water supply as temperature, mineral content, bacterial content, and regularity of flow may be quite important.

Flooding

Whenever flooding is a possibility it should be a major site consideration. If records of previous floods are available, these should be checked over a long period. If not, long-time residents of the area and newspaper accounts of past floods can often provide useful information.

While some firms are willing to incur the risk of occasional flooding to gain other site advantages, the customary policy is to insist on a flood-free site.

Drainage and Soil Conditions

Large areas of standing water on a site indicate that subsurface drainage problems can be expected. It is important to avoid the site that is a natural low spot.

Soil engineers should be consulted, particularly in doubtful situations, for assurance that soil conditions will permit adequate drainage once anticipated site development has been completed.

Soil structure should be investigated, since it may also have a significant bearing on foundation conditions and the cost of developing the site. It must receive special attention if contemplated plant structures or equipment require land with an exceptionally high load-bearing capacity.

Test borings will show graphically where rock is located, whether the groundwater table is high or low, whether the soil will drain easily, and whether there is sufficient topsoil to stabilize the ground surface after construction.

Cost of Development

The cost of a developed site is much more significant than the price of the unimproved acreage. A prospect will consider, not only the original cost of the land, but also the estimated additional costs of grading, filling, drainage, excavation, foundation construction, building access roads, constructing a railroad siding, providing for water supply and waste disposal, and bringing in other necessary utilities. When all development costs are brought into the comparison, the lowest-priced site sometimes turns out to be the most expensive.

Location within the Community

As a site factor, location within the community has various facets. One is accessibility—from the standpoints of employees, customers, and salesmen. Roads, traffic conditions, availability of public transportation, and distance from residential areas must be taken into account in this regard. Another facet is advertising value. Toward this end, a location on a main highway or main-line railroad, or one from which the plant is visible over a large area may be sought. Still another facet of site location concerns the immediate surroundings. Like a family shopping for a new home, the manufacturing firm looks for attractive surroundings and tries to avoid possible community relations problems.

Transportation Facilities

Transportation is a significant factor at each major stage of site selection; that is to say, in the choice of region, community, and specific site. Accessibility of a site to the various modes of local transportation is usually a primary consideration to a prospect. Thus, if the firm plans to use railroad transportation, it must look into the feasibility and cost of constructing a spur or siding. (Some firms like to provide switching facilities, even if little rail shipment is in prospect, so as to allow for possible future use and add to the resale value of the plant.) If it plans to ship by truck, attention must be given to such matters as distance from main highways, type of access roads, roadway requirements within the site, and potential traffic problems. Similarly, other forms of transportation present their own special problems of accessibility.

Many industrial firms require fast transportation, not only for their executives, but for the receipt of raw materials and delivery of their products. These firms are finding the airport-industrial park concept extremely practical. There are an estimated 45,000 private business planes in use now, and the number is growing. The need for an airport to stimulate economic growth will become increasingly more apparent as executive air travel further expands and the air transportation industry assumes a still larger role in moving goods.

In surveying tracts of land as possible locations for an air-industrial park, these points should be considered;
• Access roads and other local means of ground transportation serving an existing airport often can do double duty to serve industrial firms locating near the air facility.
• Any available land located near an airport is likely to be level and therefore often suitable for industrial development. Such land—frequently owned by the community—is ideal for modern, horizontal-type buildings.
• Utilities—water, gas, sewer, electricity—already available at airports usually can be extended to serve adjacent industrial uses.

Site surveys for integrated airport-industrial development should be made in conjunction with discussions with the Federal Aviation Administration. FAA guidance is important in evaluating prospective air-industrial sites in terms of anticipated flight patterns, required clear zones, height restrictions on nearby buildings, and safety regulations in general.

Taxes and Insurance

In site selection, tax considerations are usually centered on property tax rates and assessments.

As regards property taxes, many companies pay as much attention to long-range stability as to the present level of rates.

Fire insurance costs are considered in surveying both communities and sites. In selecting the community, plant locators are interested primarily in insurance ratings. In evaluating sites, the prospect is usually careful to note all factors likely to affect the insurance classification of the plant.

Zoning and Other Legal Aspects

Zoning is a site factor that has often been overlooked in the past. Profiting from the experiences of others, most firms now regard proper zoning as highly essential. A careful check of zoning regulations is desirable for two principal reasons—to avoid litigation, and to protect the new plant against incompatible industrial neighbors or other land use. In addition to zoning, other local regulations, such as building codes, laws relating to waste disposal, smoke, and fumes, and restrictions on highway use need to be checked.

Environmental Conditions

Nowadays, an investor also wishes to know what the site contains, including any wetlands, and how the site has been used in the past.

WHO MAKES A SITE SURVEY?

Many local development organizations have a committee concerned with the needs of existing and potential industrial. To organize and direct a site survey, it is desirable for this committee to obtain the services of people who have skills in determining qualifications of land for various industrial uses. The ideal site-survey team includes representatives of the local or county planning, zoning, engineering, and tax assessment staffs, industrial land realtors, local chamber of commerce officials, area development representatives of utility and transportation firms serving the community, and officials of firms already located in the area. They decide exactly what information to collect on each site and to keep on hand for ready reference.

State agencies and many utilities can provide helpful information and guidance on industrial site surveys, and they should be consulted in the early stages of organizing the surveys.

BASIC TOOLS FOR SITE IDENTIFICATION

Maps and aerial photographs are helpful in identifying potential industrial sites accurately and compiling pertinent data on them that prospects want to know. To start, obtain as large-scale a base map of the area as practicable. Identify on it relevant information, including such major features as industrial zoning boundaries, road, rail, air, and water transportation networks, and major utility lines (wager, sewage disposal, gas, and power). As individual sites are identified, depict them on separate maps covering the above items in detail, together with topographic features, notation of areas subject to flooding, direction of prevailing winds, character of adjacent land uses, and similar data helpful to manufacturers in selecting a plant site.

Particular attention should be given the location of existing industrial buildings or other buildings that can be converted to industrial use. In addition, photographs of these buildings should be made from several angles and combined with floor plans and other pertinent data. This information is of special interest to prospects with priority needs for available building space. Some sources of information are the following.

Land-Use maps are usually prepared by

the planning commission responsible for community planning activities in the area. They are helpful in locating existing tracts of land in industrial use and identifying land uses in sections adjacent to proposed new industrial sites. They also show locations of airports and airstrips.

Zoning maps, available from the town or county zoning office, indicate current zoning of land deemed suitable for industrial sites and point up any need to rezone this land if current zoning is other than industrial. Zoning maps, in showing current zoning adjacent to proposed industrial sites, indicate the type of neighboring development that may be expected in the future.

Street and road maps are generally available from the municipal engineer's office, while **State highway maps** may be obtained from county and State highway departments.

Railroad maps are available from offices of railroads serving the community or from the municipal engineer's office. Large-scale maps showing number of tracks, spurs, and yard and switching limits, are of great interest to users of railroad freight facilities.

Utility maps, indicating the limits of municipal and private water districts, the distribution fo sewage disposal service, and the local of gas and electric power lines, are compiled by local utility companies, the State public service commission, or the local planning commission, and are available from them.

Topographic quadrangle maps of the county or local area, prepared at a scale of 1:24,000, reduce the amount of on-the-site time needed to determine the amount of site grading that is necessary. They also provide information on probably drainage conditions and show waterways and other transit facilities in detail for site-planning purposes.

Aerial photographs are useful to supplement and correct topographic maps, including identification and location of man-made land features developed since the topographic surveys were prepared. They are valuable in determining current land use in areas where existing land-use maps are outdated. They also show the site in relation to nearby transportation facilities, power lines, and community services.

HOW TO IDENTIFY SITES SUITABLE FOR INDUSTRY

After obtaining basic mapping and photographic material, proceed to identify suitable sites as follows.

Preliminary Identification

Referring to topographic maps, outline on the base map those land areas with a slope of approximately 10 percent or less. Referring to recent aerial photographs, land-use maps, and zoning maps, locate vacant tracts with slope of 10 percent or less that are available for industrial use. (Note: zoning boundaries may be changed by official action if it is shown that land currently zoned for other land uses is more suitable for industry.) Referring to transportation maps, draw lines parallel to and about 1 mile from paved highways and railroads (the maximum distance from these transportation facilities that plants will normally be located). Referring to utility maps, plot location of electric transmission lines, gas lines, water supply lines, and sewage disposal systems.

On-Site Inspection and Selection

Once preliminary data have been plotted on the large base map, and those tracts with the best characteristics for industrial use are tentatively identified, the site-survey team can inspect these tracts. Utilizing their combined skills and experience, team members eliminate from consideration any tracts that present serious drawbacks for plant operation and service. They confirm the potential industrial value of other tracts and determine what improvements are required to make them more attractive to manufacturers.

Following this the team must ascertain the availability of the tracts selected and obtain definite price agreements for their acquisition. The industry committee then can quote for prospects firm prices on individual tracts.

READY-REFERENCE SITE MAP AND DATA FILE

The industry committee must be prepared to answer readily all questions prospects may ask about each site market for potential industrial development. Inability to provide essential data, or delay in

making information available, may cause a prospect to look to another community.

A good site data sheet includes such items of information as location, description of property (acreage, shape, grade, mineral rights), utilities (electricity, natural gas, water, sewerage, telephone), transportation (railroad, airport, motor freight, highways), zoning, owner, and remarks. A scale drawing of the site is nearly always included, showing the exact shape and relation to such physical features as rail lines, roads, and streams. Photographs of the site (surface and aerial views) often accompany the description.

Individual maps graphically describing each site, or group of neighboring sites, are helpful to prospects in the evaluation process. From the standpoint of a prospect's plant requirements, each site map should show such characteristics as size, topography, zoning, and relation to transportation facilities and service utilities.

For promotional purposes, similar graphic materials for industrial sites in the area—maps, charts, aerial photographs, and descriptions—can be combined as a brochure. Copies should be sent to a selected list of industrial prospects to the State agency coordinating development activities in your State, State credit corporations or authorities, and to utilities, railroads, and other transportation companies capable of serving your industrial sites.

Complete site-survey files contain a wide range of information and data on each designated site. This information includes not only current conditions and site characteristics, but also scheduled changes expected to improve the site and its ability to serve industrial activities of various kinds. Note should be made where a site appears particularly well suited to a specific industry or industry group. In all instances, data files must regularly be kept up-to-date.

A SUGGESTED INDUSTRIAL SITE-SURVEY CHECK LIST

The check list that follows summarizes the basic data to be compiled on most industrial sites. Special conditions or resources in your own community and area will indicate changes or suggest other categories of information to maintain in your site files.

1. TITLE or other designation of site_____

2. ACREAGE_____

3. LOCATION _____
    a. Distance from community center or center of nearest
       built-up area _____
    b. Present use of land at site_____
    c. Use and character of land adjoining site _____

4. ZONING
    a. Zoning of site _____
    b. Zoning of adjacent properties _____

5. OWNER(S)
Address _____

6. COST: PER ACRE $_____; TOTAL $ _____

7. CHARACTER OF TERRAIN (maximum slope and other
       indicators of
       possible need for grading) _____

8. ESTIMATED GRADING COST $_____

9. ELEVATION (relative to highest known highwater level)
    a. Low point _____
    b. High point _____

10. SOIL AND WATER
    a. Load-bearing characteristics of soil _____
    b. Sub-soil characteristics_____
    c. Depth to bedrock _____
    d. Depth of ground water _____

11. DRAINAGE
    a. Natural runoff capacity _____
    b. Need for artificial drainage facilities _____
    c. Need for flood protection (include existing facilities)

_____

12. PREVAILING WINDS (note seasonal variations)_____

_____

13. UTILITIES
  a. Water
    (1) Company name _____
    (2) Rates $_____
    (3) Size of mains _____
    (4) Pressure_____
    (5) Capacity of treated water_____
    (6) Surplus treated water on peak day_____
    (7) Capacity of untreated water _____
    (8) Surplus untreated water on peak day_____
    (9) Cost of extending to site $_____
  b. Gas
    (1) Company name _____
    (2) Rates $_____
    (3) Nearest lines_____
    (4) Size _____
    (5) Pressure_____
    (6) Cost of extending to site $ _____
  c. Electricity
    (1) Company name _____
    (2) Rates $_____
    (3) Number of lines serving community _____
    (4) Capacity of each line _____
    (5) Cost of extending to site $_____
  d. Sewage
    (1) Rates $_____
    (2) Size of mains _____
      (a) Storm_____
      (b) Sanitary_____
    (3) Capacity of treatment plant _____
    (4) Surplus capacity on peak day_____
    (5) Means of disposal_____
    (6) Cost of extending to site $_____

14. TRANSPORTATION
    a. Roadway access to site
       (designation of location) _____
       (1) Type of road _____
       (2) Surface _____
       (3) Width _____
    b. Cost of providing road
       access if not yet available $_____
    c. Distance of site from
       arterial street or highway _____
    d. Railroads serving site (or area)_____
       (1) Cost of extending service (spur) to site if not yet
         available $ _____
    e. Waterways serving site or area_____

f. Commercial airports serving site or area _____
    (1) Distance to airports _____
    (2) Types of aircraft served _____
g. Public transportation serving site _____

15. IMPROVEMENT SON SITE
    a. Industrial buildings _____
    b. Other improvements _____

16. TAXES
    a. On land _____
    b. On improvements _____

17. ENVIRONMENTAL CONCERNS
    a. Present _____
    b. Past _____

Principles Of the Real Property Development Process

Mark D. Waterhouse, C.I.D., F.M.

Most economic developers, at some point in their careers, come in contact with the real property development process. For some, their role is limited to assisting the private sector developer who is actually undertaking the project. Others — the fortunate ones, I think — actually have the opportunity and responsibility to be the developer on behalf of the communities or agencies they represent.

No matter what the relationship between the economic developer and the project, it is important that some common principles and characteristics of the development process are understood.

THE DEVELOPMENT BUSINESS PLAN

The outline of the real property development process bears a strong resemblance to that of a business plan; in essence, it *is* a business plan for an endeavor which has the potential to be very profitable or the risk of being very costly.

We have all heard the stories about or perhaps met successful developers, who never seem to do more than make a few notes on the back of an envelope before making a few million dollars in a development project. Rest assured that even where there may not be much of a paper trail of the planning process, even the most "intuitive" developer goes through the same checklist of critical variables.

The development process falls into five sequential, though sometimes overlapping, parts:
1. The establishment of the project goals and development philosophies;
2. The market analysis;
3. The planning and engineering analysis;
4. The financial analysis; and
5. The implementation plan.

Each one of these parts is dependent on information created in preceding parts. As a simple example, I can't do the market analysis until I have decided whether I am creating an office park or a shopping center; I should not spend the money on planning and engineering unless the market analysis indicates the project will work; I can't crunch the numbers in the financial analysis until I have revenue projections from the market analysis and cost estimates from the engineering analysis; and there is no sense preparing an implementation plan if the project is not economically viable.

Most developers go through this planning process twice for a project. The first pass is a broad-brush attempt to find major problems with the project; if found, the project is likely to be scrapped. The second pass is more detailed, time-consuming and costly, since it involves the expertise of many specialty disciplines such as landscape architects, engineers, environmental scientists, financial analysts, attorneys and many others. But there is no sense in paying for all these folks if a "quick and dirty" consideration of the project will uncover fatal flaws. Assisting in this front-end evaluation process is an important role for the local economic developer.

GOALS AND PHILOSOPHIES

Developers begin the development process by establishing some ground rules for themselves and the projects they will undertake. The most obvious example is the developer who specializes in a certain type of project (e.g., strip shopping centers) and refuses to become involved with other types of development (e.g., residential subdivisions).

There are other similar decisions which should be made early on; some of these are more applicable to the public sector developer than to the private sector. Examples are:

❑ Quick or Quality? A major crisis in the local economic base, or the developer's desire to turn a quick profit may lead to a decision to develop a lower quality project which will take anyone and be completed rapidly. The insistence on high quality generally means a longer development period.

❑ Jobs or Taxes? An area undertaking a project to provide employment opportunities should probably avoid a pure distribution park, which can chew up a lot of land but not employ many people. Similarly, if tax base is important, the emphasis should be on higher value development.

❑ Industrial Park or District? The level of planning, amenities and management is higher for a park than for a district, which is merely the clustering of similar uses in a certain area. But developer preference, community attitude or the market may make the park a better bet.

❑ Mixed or Single Use? On the one hand, a mixture of potential uses in the same development can speed absorption. On the other hand, it may not be a compatible use for the neighborhood, or even where compatible, acceptable to local zoning officials.

Making these types of decisions has a bearing on exactly what type of project will be scrutinized in the market analysis.

MARKET ANALYSIS

A market analysis is intended to answer the questions "Is there one?" and if so, "What does it look like?" We tend to think of a market analysis as being primarily a dollars-and-cents matter, but there are a wide variety of other areas which must be considered.

Part of the market analysis must be to evaluate the project and project area in the same fashion that potential occupants of the project will. This requires consideration of typical locational determinants such as:

❑ Access to markets

❏ Transportation

❏ Utilities (including availability, capacity and costs)

❏ Labor (including availability, skills and costs)

❏ Availability of raw materials, component parts and support services

❏ Business climate

❏ Community facilities and services

❏ Quality of life characteristics

❏ Capital availability

❏ Available sites and buildings

This last category is particularly important because it represents potential competition. A market analysis must identify that competition and assess its strengths and weaknesses in comparison with the proposed project.

Another "non-number" aspect of the market analysis is a consideration of community attitude toward the project. This is a benchmark of potential support or opposition and must include key elected and appointed officials, planning and zoning commissions, utility departments or public utilities, building officials, tax assessors, environmental groups and the public in general. (And, of course, our friendly local economic development staff, commission or corporation.) Any indication of substantial delays in the planning process because of a hostile public, uncooperative local officials, or unsuitable regulations may result in a "No Go" decision after the market analysis.

Time really *is* money in the development game because the developer is often paying a mortgage or option on a piece of land. Delays in the planning and approval process usually mean that extra design, engineering and legal costs are involved. While a lengthy approval process is not necessarily a deal-killer, it is important for the developer to understand early on what the rules of the game are, so that this can be built into project planning and budgeting.

Finally, there are the numbers. Some are readily available; some can be extracted from data sources; some must be projected, extrapolated, created or crystal-balled. Developers will look at several common types of data in a market analysis:

❏ Demographics of the area (e.g., population, growth and cohort groups; housing patterns; income statistics; labor force characteristics; commuting patterns) which are indicators of development trends.

❏ Local construction activity (how much, what types, new construction vs. expansions vs. rehabilitation; how much land is involved, both in total and by typical lot size; is the source local or from outside the area; what is the value; how many jobs were created?).

❏ Expansion needs (how many local companies need or want to expand, but can't or won't at their current location, either due to market considerations, site limitations or tenancy problems?).

❏ Prospect trends (what is the profile of the annual prospect load in terms of number, types, sizes, desire to own vs. lease, current location, acceptable price, employment?).

❏ Lost opportunities; this is a subset of the prospect category. The distinction is that a prospect is someone we talked to but lost track of and therefore don't know whether the project was ever completed. A lost opportunity is a project which took place elsewhere, and which we can contact to find out what competitive advantages that other area had.

❏ Induced markets; that is, unmet needs or desires within the area which represent a niche or emerging market that has never occurred before.

Results of a market analysis may include any number of considerations which the developer considers relevant; examples include:

❏ Projected annual square feet of construction.

❏ Typical lot sizes and projected annual land absorption.

❏ Estimate of initial sale or lease price and annual escalation.

❏ Probable mixture of uses.

❏ Estimated job creation.

❏ Projected construction value.

❏ Estimated addition to grand list and resulting property taxes.

❏ Other important project characteristics, user needs or amenities.

PLANNING AND ENGINEERING ANALYSIS

This phase of the development process relates a particular piece of property to the desired market characteristics. In some instances, a market analysis will have been prepared to identify the best use of a piece of property already in hand. In other instances, the results of the market analysis will be used by the developer to find a piece of property which best meets the needs of the marketplace. As an example, if the market analysis has found a need for sites for large footprint industrial or distribution facilities, the developer will not be interested in sites with significant topographic limitations.

In any event, the planning and engineering analysis is intended to result in a development plan, on paper, which can be discussed with and perhaps officially submitted to appropriate planning agencies. In some areas an informal discussion is encouraged before official submission; in many instances this is preferable for the developer because less engineering work is required to create a concept or schematic plan than for a full plan for site plan and/or subdivision approval.

Creation of the plan must consider not only the site itself, but also the surrounding area. Topics which may be considered include:

❏ Land uses (what is in the immediate neighborhood and what would be compatible with it; what alternative uses can be made of the site in question or parts of it; treatment of special features such as jogging trails; optimization of attractive natural features such as views or ponds).

❏ Road considerations (improvements needed in roads leading to the site; major "spine" roads and secondary streets; internal and external circulation and traffic; creation of an appropriate project entrance).

❏ Utility considerations (are those available adequate in size and capacity; if not, what must be constructed; what should the internal and external routing of new systems be?).

❏ Physical features of the site (topography; soils; vegetation; drainage patterns and storm water management).

❏ Zoning (are existing regulations and performance standards suitable for the type project envisioned; what changes can reasonably be expected to be obtained?).

❑ Opportunities and constraints (what natural or man-made conditions exist or can be created which enhance the developability of the site; how do these impact building potential? What physical, regulatory or attitudinal limitations may reduce developability?)

❑ Environmental issues (wetlands and water courses; water supply water sheds; hydrogeology; protected or restricted areas; likelihood of prior contamination).

This final aspect — the likelihood of prior contamination — while listed last here, has moved to the top of the list in recent years. Phase I Environmental Audits are increasingly done as a very early step, and sites with even a hint of possible environmental contamination are being avoided by developers. The inclusion of a "clean site contingency" is a standard part of a purchase or option offer. Economic developers interested in expediting development in their areas would be well-advised to encourage landowners in their areas to have Phase I Environmental Audits prepared by reputable firms and on file with some public body.

The end products of the planning and engineering analysis are one or more drawings and supporting narrative showing and describing:

❑ The key features of the development site and surrounding neighborhood;

❑ The intended uses of the site and various portions of it;

❑ The roads and utilities network;

❑ A conceptual subdivision; and

❑ If appropriate, a recommended phasing of development.

FINANCIAL ANALYSIS

As previously noted, the financial analysis is, in part, dependent on project absorption and revenue projections made in the market analysis, and on project development costs estimated in the planning and engineering analysis. As you will note, however, there are other pieces of information in both the revenues and costs categories which must be added into the calculations.

Revenues

While the ultimate success of most projects is measured by how much land sale proceeds exceed expenditures, other sources of financing are usually necessary because development costs hit at the front end of a project while land sale revenue spreads out over the absorption cycle.

It should also be noted that land sale revenue may be somewhat less important in a publicly developed project where the creation of new jobs or additional tax base are seen as more important than one-time land sale dollars.

Typical information about revenue include:

❑ Initial land sales (or leases) including previously negotiated or special "first project" prices which differ from market rate prices.

❑ Annual increases in pricing to reflect inflation and, hopefully, the increasing desirability of the project; this must be multiplied against the annual projected absorption, which typically occurs on a bell-shaped curve, rather than a straight-line projection.

❑ Governmental capital investment. Where the public sector is the developer, or is investing in a private development project (perhaps by paying some of the infrastructure cost in recognition of the tax revenues which will be generated), the amount, terms and conditions of this financing must be included in the financial analysis. Included in this category are both general fund appropriations and a variety of general or special obligation bonds.

❑ Loans, either from conventional (i.e., banks) or less conventional (e.g., state programs, pension funds, insurance companies) sources. Amounts, terms and conditions must be factored in.

❑ Grants. Yes, Virginia, while they are much fewer and farther between than in past years, there are still some sources which are available.

❑ Other sources. Every project will probably have some interest income from cash flow. Each project may have other revenue sources such as park association membership fees or utility company rebates based on actual usage of utilities which the developer initially paid for.

Costs

There are many more possible cost categories than revenue sources. Because it is important to be conservative in the financial analysis, it is probably more important not to forget a cost category than it is to overlook a revenue source. Some cost categories appear only in the start-up, absorption or close-out phase of the project, while others are annual costs which may or may not change over time.

Major cost categories and items which comprise them are:

❑ Site acquisition, including the actual purchase price as well as the cost of appraisals, legal and closing fees, surveys, title insurance, and environmental audits. Real estate commissions paid by the buyer would be included here.

❑ Planning and design costs. The fees of landscape architects, engineers, attorneys, environmental specialists, traffic engineers and any other specialty discipline required to create the plans necessary to obtain all governmental and financing source permits and approvals.

❑ Infrastructure costs. Both on-site and off-site costs of construction, including any escalation which may be caused by project phasing, to provide necessary roads and utilities. Special assessments or impact fees may also be included here.

❑ Soft costs related to project administration, marketing and promotion; insurance; selling/leasing commissions; legal and accounting fees; property management; and annual permit fees. Each project may have other types of soft costs such as special financial consultants.

❑ Financing costs.

The typical financial analysis works all of these revenues and costs into a detailed cash flow analysis showing both how much money has been made or must be obtained during each year of the project, as well as the total profits at the end of the development cycle. A discounted cash flow analysis is used to reflect the time value of money and allow the developer to decide if the rate of return is acceptable.

If the answer is no, the developer must decide whether projections have been too conservative and project revenues or absorption can be increased; project costs can be reduced; outside sources of help can be obtained (e.g., government grants or additional capital investment seeking a rate of return less than borrowing costs); or the project terminated.

IMPLEMENTATION PLAN

This is the step which converts a plan into reality. Much work is still required to make happen what has been put into drawings or narrative. These efforts generally relate to three types of need:

❏ Project design. A summary statement must be created describing what the project is all about and what it is intended to do. This carries over into assuring that zoning regulations and performance standards are the proper ones for the project, and that these are complemented or reinforced by suitable protective covenants.

❏ Marketing strategy. A promotional and marketing program must be created which, if appropriate, builds on any existing marketing effort, and creates its own project-related campaign of advertising, direct mail, personal contact and networking through economic development agencies and the real estate brokerage community. The identification of what will be included in the program must be accompanied by consideration of personnel and budget aspects.

❏ Management and operations. Who will be responsible for doing what? How do these assignments change over time as the project moves from start-up, through the development or absorption phase, to close-out when the project has been completed. A wide range of work is necessary related to general administration, financial management, property management, marketing, and physical development. Planning must identify which of this work will be handled by staff and which by independent contractors and consultants. Any changes in the project budget identified in the implementation plan must be reflected in amendments to the financial analysis. It is the hope of most developers to complete a project and to leave it behind; where there may be ongoing requirements such as maintenance of common areas or enforcement of covenants, consideration should be given to creation of a park association, if appropriate.

CONCLUSION

Despite the current economy and a glut of real estate product in many areas, the development process will continue and can be extremely exciting and rewarding.

It should not, however, be done by the seat of the pants. Successful development, and the ability to avoid catastrophic error, are not so much a matter of having a particular depth of knowledge in one or more fields (you can hire experts to provide that), but rather in having a breadth of knowledge about the development process and the willingness to be methodical and attentive to detail.

Whether your role is to assist a developer or to be one, understanding how the development process typically works is an essential first step.

SUGGESTED READINGS

BUSINESS AND INDUSTRIAL PARK DEVELOPMENT HANDBOOK, Community Builders Handbook Series, Urban Land Institute, 625 Indiana Avenue, N.W., Washington, DC 20004, 1988, (202) 289-8500.

INDUSTRIAL PARKS: A Step by Step Guide, Midwest Research Institute, 4-25 Volker Boulevard, Kansas City, Missouri 64410, 1988, (816) 753-7600.

MIXED-USE BUSINESS PARKS, National Association of Industrial Office Parks, 1215 Jefferson Davis Highway, Suite 100, Arlington, VA 22202, 1988, (800) 666-6780.

REAL ESTATE DEVELOPMENT: Principles and Process, Urban Land Institute, 625 Indiana Avenue, N.W., Washington, DC 20004, 1991, (202) 289-8500.

Prospects, Realtors And Economic Developers: A New Partnership

Rick Thrasher, C.E.D.

INTRODUCTION

The process of attracting companies to a community is both competitive and complex. The successful community, the winner, is often the one that better coordinates its response to the needs of the client company.

By definition, coordination means assembling representatives from a variety of disciplines to provide the client with the necessary services. It often involves elected officials, professionals from public works, engineering, finance, law, utilities, business executive ranks and real estate. Each discipline has a vital role in the recruitment effort.

Because of the need for coordination, the economic development executive strives for a positive ongoing relationship with the community's representatives from the other necessary disciplines. In particular, the relationship between economic development organizations and commercial/industrial real estate agencies should be a win-win situation. And it can be with an efficient adjustment in the typical working relationship.

Few would suggest that the relationship between real estate agencies and economic development organizations is as strong as it should be. While each has different missions and criteria for measuring results, a successful outcome is beneficial to both.

Economic developers are most commonly measured on companies and/or new jobs attracted to the community. E.D. people spend a great deal of time, money and energy trying to recruit those jobs. Unless clients are dropping from the skies and landing in the community without effort, each prospect is a matter of great significance. The level of significance tends to be directly related to the number of jobs the company represents. While each client is very important, the loss of one rarely affects the economic developer's job or income.

The real estate professional, on the other hand, is not measured by jobs and companies. Real estate executives are measured by square footage absorbed, either leased or sold. Square foot absorption is the index that determines a real estate agent's income.

A BASIS FOR COOPERATION

Every company needs real estate in one form or another. This simple fact creates a basis for cooperation between real estate agencies and economic development organizations.

Generally speaking, the greater number of jobs involved, the larger the size of the facility sought. The bigger the project both in jobs and facility, the more there is at stake. And the greater the stake, the more need there is for cooperation. Cooperation is teamwork.

What is the economic developer's typical response to this need for teamwork? Unfortunately, the tendency is to use a technique that separates, rather than unites.

In an effort to maintain neutrality among the local, competing real estate brokerage firms, economic developers are driven to great lengths. Economic development executives think that these lengths will insulate them from the competitive crossfire among competing real estate interests and further, protect the corporate client's confidentiality. Despite these honorable and noble intentions, our traditional approach may actually embroil us rather than insulate us.

THE TRADITIONAL APPROACH

Economic developers tend to spend much effort tracking real estate factors such as land availability, building availability, rental rates and sale prices. This is a colossal task. In many economic development agencies, this assignment requires a full-time position with the associated expenses of salary, fringe benefits, payroll taxes, rent, telephone, supplies etc. In many markets, such an effort could easily cost $20,000 to $30,000 per year. To what purpose? Ironically, local real estate agencies usually have the same material readily available. The real estate professional's income depends on timely, accurate market information. Because the economic development organization's records are seldom complete and often outdated, the emergence of a client drives the economic developer to duplicate the research all over again. But this time, the research is done in a semi-crisis manner.

The client wants the information in a few days. The economic developer has some in the files, but wants to provide the client with a broad variety of options.

So the economic developer collects the appropriate data from the office files, then starts the rapid-fire telephone calls to see what else might be on the market. The economic developer calls several real estate offices and asks for material on appropriate properties. The real estate agents catch the sense of urgency and opportunity, search their own files and amass everything appropriate. Those agents call other agents in the community who individually respond from their records. Every agent who knows about the project is calling the owner of every unlisted property for miles around. The number of telephone calls multiplies exponentially and multiplies and multiplies. And soon they are all calling the economic development office with "the perfect site".

What does all this bring to the effort to land the client? The economic developer ends up with multiple duplications of property, multiple real estate agents calling hoping to be in on the project, area landowners inflating prices, all trying to serve a client.

The economic developer amasses the information from all the canvassed and responding real estate agents and sends it to the client. Now all these real estate agents and land owners join the economic developer in hoping the client's interest continues.

Suppose it does. The client calls and schedules a visit in two weeks. The client outlines the company's needs and the economic developer goes about planning the itinerary: calls of opportunity to some real estate agents, calls of disappointment to others, appointments with education and training officials, dinners with elected and business leaders.

The economic developer schedules several individual real estate agents to show property. Each agent has one or two sites to present. The demands of the itinerary allow only 10-15 minutes for each property.

The surviving real estate agents are excited about the opportunity, but wonder if they can adequately represent the property in such a short time. The agents who did not make the cut are disappointed and have little or no feedback about why their properties are not scheduled for presentation.

The client comes to town and quickly inspects each of the properties. The client meets individually and briefly with several real estate agents. Each agent is trying to sell his/her property. Promoting that specific property becomes the only role the individual real estate agent plays in the community-wide effort to land the client. The agent has no participation in the overall presentation of the community's assets and attractiveness. And the client knows it.

The client usually wants discretion, if not total confidentiality. In the course of the day, the client has seen multiple real estate agents. With only a few minutes each, the real estate people become a blur of nameless, faceless people. No one agent had time to establish any rapport or relationship with the client. The true real estate professional is trained to be a real estate problem solver. With such a short time for a presentation, an agent can easily become overzealous and perhaps overly aggressive. The client is turned off and wonders what happened to discretion. The traditional process reduced a potentially valuable team member to a "carnival barker". Both the client and the economic developer see the real estate agent in a very unfavorable light.

If the community survives this stage and the client selects the community, what is the result? The economic development professional has several disappointed real estate agents and one happy one. The winning agent is delighted. Several thousand dollars in commission accrue to the agency, a large portion of which is the agent's. With only a 10-15 minute involvement in the visit, the agent's role was limited to a very brief presentation of a property. The agent never participated in, or even saw, the ongoing discussion between the client and the economic developer. Because the real estate agent knows only that the client selected his

property, the agent understandably suspects that the whole deal results from a combination of sales talent and real estate product. The agent has gained little knowledge of the comprehensive approach that successful business recruitment requires.

Disappointed real estate agents do not understand why their individual properties were not selected. The inevitable "post game analysis" begins. "Did I have enough time?" "Did other real estate agents get more time?" "I had to show my property at 6:30 a.m. in the dark to a tired and not-yet-awake client." "My property was shown late in the day and the client was tired." "Did that damn economic developer steer him?" It's understandable why the losing real estate agents may be understandably suspicious of future calls from the economic development office. Eventually, the real estate agents say they don't want to put much effort into the economic developer's next project. And depending on the type of economic development organization, the dwindling enthusiasm may be reflected in the local development organization's budget.

This is the typical process between economic development agencies and commercial/industrial real estate brokerage firms. The process started with a common goal, a basis for cooperation. It ended with a contented corporate client, a contented economic developer, one happy real estate agent and several who are cynical and frustrated about the economic development process.

A NEW PARADIGM

There may be a better way, a system that strengthens the relationship between the economic development organization and the industrial/commercial real estate community while serving the client far more productively.

This better system is simply a "lead broker" technique. By definition, it means that the economic development office selects one "lead broker" for each project. This system simplifies and improves the response to the client, provides a much better opportunity for the real estate community to more actively and comprehensively participate in the community-wide recruitment effort and builds a project-long relationship involving the corporate executive, the real estate executive and the economic development executive.

SELECTING THE LEAD

The selection of "the lead" is key to the success of the technique. And there are two parts to that selection. The first part is the selection of the lead real estate brokerage firm. The second is the choice of the lead real estate agent.

There are a number of ways to select the lead broker for a project. If the economic development agency preferred to have only one real estate brokerage firm to deal with, exclusive access could be auctioned for some specific time frame or on a project by project basis. Clearly, this approach would be controversial and a bit extraordinary. If there were several real estate agencies in the community, the economic development office may want to rotate the lead. In this case, a process for rotating has to be selected.

In the Utah experience, the lead broker has been rotated. The Economic Development Corporation is a free standing entity funded by investments from both the public sector and the private sector. Its members include several commercial/industrial real estate agencies that pay an annual fee that enrolls them in the rotation. The rotation is based simply on taking turns with absolutely no consideration of the size of the project, who has what property listed, potential size of commission, seriousness of the client, etc. It is exclusively "take turns."

Currently, there are six commercial/industrial brokerages on the rotation list. Occasionally, one of the firms suggests a revision in the process. The response is simple. The revision must meet one test. It must result in the same or higher total income to The EDC from the participating firms. If that test is successfully met, there is little likelihood that The EDC would object to the revision. By our one test, it is required that all the brokerage firms essentially agree on the revision. If they cannot agree, income to The EDC might be negatively affected and the suggested revision is not implemented.

The most common suggestion is to reduce the number of firms on the rotation list. That means the remaining firms have to provide a larger annual fee to participate. With that criteria, the individual real estate agency has to calculate the value of the rotation. It translates into a market based decision, a pure business decision based on "return on investment." The implementation of the suggestion is a substantive statement that the economic development organization has a value to the real estate community. It is simply the old adage, "money talks."

The selection of the lead real estate agent is very important also. A well qualified agent can enhance the overall presentation of both the real estate and the community.

In Utah, we do not select the individual agent. Rather, we call the managing partner of the real estate brokerage firm whose turn it is. The managing partner chooses the individual agent. The managing partner is motivated by the agency's potential commission, so the managing partner names the agent best able to generate the commission.

This step also puts the managing partner and the economic developer in a degree of professional parity. The appointed agent is subordinate to the goal of each agency, real estate brokerage and economic development.

The real estate industry is quite familiar with the lead broker technique. For example, the Salt Lake Board of Realtors estimates for 1990 that fully 50% of the reported transactions were "cooperative." Cooperative means that the commission was split between participating real estate agencies and agents.

IMPACTS AND BENEFITS

By using a technique already common in the real estate industry, the relationship between the economic development office and the local real estate community is strengthened. This improved relationship translates into better service to the corporate client.

In a lead broker system, the real estate brokerage firm and the individual agent have a much improved opportunity for a commission. This improved opportunity for reward energizes the real estate executive. The lead agent now does the real estate research and presentation. The lead agent will contact the community's other real estate agents in the search for available property that answer the corporate client's needs.

Since access to the client is now available only through the lead agent, the entire real estate community is forced to work cooperatively. The goal becomes a mutual desire to generate a commission by meeting the client's need.

The lead broker system saves time and money for the economic development agency. Since real estate professionals have only product knowledge to sell, they keep current on the market. In most metropolitan areas, each real estate brokerage has its own research department. It is that department that assists the agency and the individual agents stay current on the community's real estate market. That knowledge contributes to a faster response time to the client. The economic development agency no longer needs to exert exhaustive and often frustrating effort to stay current on the local real estate market. And the money the economic development office previously spent on maintaining real estate data can be redirected to more important matters. The economic development agency's research department can use the new found time more productively to provide answers to the other pressing questions from clients.

The lead real estate executive has much greater involvement in the team effort to land the client. Because the selected professional has exclusive access to the client, there is a greater opportunity to build a relationship bigger than the project itself. The greater time involvement affords the lead real estate executive the opportunity to better understand the diversity of the economic development process and also to have a better understanding of the client's real estate requirements. The increased time with the prospect provides opportunity for the real estate executive to hear the questions about education, training, worker productivity, taxation, etc. The economic developer's expertise in these areas will be clearly exposed to the real estate executive. As the two professionals watch each other respond to the client's needs, mutual respect grows.

The client is better served because one of the community's best real estate professionals is on the job. The client has only one real estate professional to deal with and can do that through the economic development office.

The economic development office and the real estate agency are better served. The economic developer's influence in the process is enhanced. Because of the relationship that builds between the economic develop-

ment executive and the lead real estate professional, there is less chance or need for the real estate professional to circumvent the economic developer by making an independent contact with the client. The true real estate professional recognizes that the trusting and respectful relationship being built on the current project can be transferred to future projects. And since most projects take months, if not years, the individual agent is forced to work with the economic development professional throughout the period.

The lead broker system eliminates two of the economic developer's most unpleasant chores. First, the economic development executive does not have to explain to any one real estate agent why a certain piece of property is no longer under consideration. That task now falls to the lead real estate professional. Also, the economic developer avoids the delicate and unpleasant assignment of explaining why any one certain real estate agent is not the lead. Under the rotation system that task now belongs to the managing partner of the lead brokerage house.

For private or public-private economic development agencies, the rotation enhances membership funding also. In most cases, the rotation is limited to real estate agencies that fund the program. For real estate agencies, membership is no longer a charitable contribution; it is now truly an investment. The real estate agency is buying into the system. The economic development agency knows approximately how much commission income the brokerage firm has gained. And the real estate agency knows that the economic developer knows. The fairness and equitability is easily verified. The economic development agency can keep a running record of referrals to use any time there is a question.

SUMMARY

In the Utah experience, the lead broker system has helped build a better and more united economic development team. It has contributed to a positive relationship between the commercial/industrial real estate community and the economic development office. And most important, the system improves the service to the corporate client.

Planning and Developing A Speculative Industrial Building

James Halverson

INTRODUCTION

A Speculative Industrial Building (SIB) program can provide a community with many advantages in its quest to attract new business. In areas that have a limited supply of available industrial buildings or where the existing inventory has serious limitations (e.g., poor location and condition, exorbitant price or lease rate, etc.), a SIB can be beneficial. In addition to increasing the inventory of "quality" industrial buildings, the effort also reflects a sense of commitment to community growth and development.

Although a SIB program has the potential to enhance a community's economic development efforts, it is not a panacea for business attraction and retention. Programs of this nature should be part of a comprehensive economic development approach, not merely an ad hoc method of business attraction.

In the Summer, 1989 edition of the *Economic Development Review*, Jim Reichardt provided an excellent overview on the development of a speculative industrial building program. The objective of this paper is to offer additional guidance in the planning and development of a speculative industrial building. As more communities consider incorporating a SIB program into their overall economic development program, documentation of alternative experiences can be a valuable resource for planning and development purposes.

PRO'S AND CON'S OF SPECULATIVE BUILDING DEVELOPMENT

The potential economic impact resulting from a successful speculative industrial building project is immense. It has the potential to attract and/or obtain jobs add to the tax base, diversify the area economy, and promote the community's willingness to invest in its future and maintain a proactive business attraction effort.

As communities compete to attract industry and jobs, the availability of a well located and well constructed industrial building could mean the difference between a community being placed on the "short list" or being eliminated from the site selection process.

As with any speculative development, there are several potential risks, including the willingness or ability of an organization to assume debt and the potential inability to lease or sell the building. It is critical to consider and evaluate the potential benefits and costs of a project and minimize the risks. For example, a business attorney with experience in negotiating leases can minimize the risk associated with structuring a lease arrangement.

As the organization addresses the issue of whether to initiate the project or not, it is important that the project have adequate support from those involved.

PRELIMINARY RESEARCH: QUALIFYING THE MARKET

Before a SIB project is initiated it is important to measure both the market demand and supply for additional industrial buildings. Often the process involves conducting an inventory of available industrial buildings. Listed below are several criteria to be considered and a description of what to look for:

❏ Building size. Is the size of the building compatible with what most prospective companies are looking for? Are there irregularities relative to building dimensions (e.g., side wall height, expansions occurring in an ad hoc manner, etc.)?

❏ Age and condition of the building. Check for obsolescence, deterioration, lack of maintenance, unique advantages and disadvantages.

❏ Location. Determine all applicable zoning requirements and how they may affect the use of the facility and verify whether adjacent land uses are consistent or inconsistent with the prevailing land use in the area.

❏ Accessibility. Is the building accessible to a variety of forms of transportation such as highway, rail, and commercial airport?

❏ Ability to expand. If the building has limited expansion potential at the current site it could be a potential negative to a prospective buyer.

❏ Cost. How does the asking price of an existing building compare to the cost of constructing a new building? Are the lease or sale terms consistent with prevailing market rates/prices?

As the survey of existing buildings is completed, the information should be thoroughly reviewed and analyzed. Primary considerations should include: the salability of existing buildings — are they overpriced, obsolete, or poorly located? Or, on the other hand, do the building(s) have the potential to attract businesses? If the survey results conclude that the existing inventory of available buildings is inconsistent with the requirements of the marketplace, it is reasonable to proceed to the next phase of the project — development planning.

At this point it is also reasonable to share the market information with private developers that are familiar with the community and/or have been involved in development projects in the area. Meetings such as these are an excellent opportunity to verify survey results and conclusions but more importantly, measure the private developer's interest in pursuing the project. As discussed earlier, it is important to minimize the risk and maximize the benefit. If the private developer expresses an interest in doing the project on an independent basis, the development group's financial liability is either minimized or removed and the market demand for a new building is addressed. Remember that the overall goal of this and related efforts is to create and retain jobs.

Qualifying the market is a critical component to the overall development process. It gives one an opportunity to identify available building(s) and make a determination about the "quality" of the inventory. It also provides an opportunity to define certain building and location characteristics which would be preferred to the existing building inventory.

LOCATION AND BUILDING SPECIFICATION CONSIDERATIONS

Location and "key" building specifications are important to the development of an attractive SIB. It is important to provide a location which is conducive to industrial development and include building specifications which address the general facility requirements of a manufacturer, yet remain competitively priced.

An architect who has significant experience in the design and construction of industrial buildings should be retained. The architect will not only provide advice relative to the design aspects of the project, but also could act as the "project manager." As the "manager" he/she will review work that has been completed, maintain quality assurance, review requests for payment, and perform other related tasks.

Architect's fees are generally based either on a flat (per hour) charge or on a percentage of the total project cost. Prior to working with an architect, be aware of the terms of compensation and get them in writing.

As previously stated, the site should be conducive to industrial development, (e.g., an industrial park). In general, industrial parks have appropriate zoning for manufacturing operations, consistent land use and building design features, and infrastructure required by manufacturers (e.g., electric and gas utility laterals, sewer and water laterals, paved streets, etc.). Additional considerations which specifically relate to the site include: soil composition, site elevation, access to transportation alternatives (e.g., rail, major highway, port, airport), and providing ample acreage to expand the facility.

Protective covenants associated with many private and public industrial parks often require a minimum and/or maximum land-to-building ratio. Subsequently, it is important that the size of the building and the site be determined at the same time.

The initial site should be large enough to facilitate construction of the primary building and associated parking and truck turn-around areas. The site should also be large enough to expand the building at least twice its original size. For example, if the initial structure is 10,000 square feet, then the initial site should be large enough to accommodate a 20,000 square foot building, including all setback requirements, parking and trucking areas.

There are several theories associated with determining the site of the SIB. Many of these include a relationship between the building size and a community's population or basing the size of the building on requests submitted by prospects. Some community organizations construct only two or three walls of the building and allow the buyer/leaser to complete the building based on size and design requirements.

Soliciting information from other communities of similar population and within the same region that have or are also considering a SIB development can help verify building size considerations and market demand.

Once the location, site acreage, and building size have been determined, it is important to identify additional building specifications. Typically these take the form of: truck docks, sidewall height, construction materials to be used, floor type, and sprinkler system. As with determining the size of the building, specifications should be reasonable and serve a purpose. For example, some SIB's are constructed with "at-grade" truck docks as opposed to the "well" type. "At-grade" docks are typically used in areas with harsh winters to avoid the accumulation of ice that often results with the "well" type dock.

Building specifications should also be flexible. For example, many manufacturers require a six-inch, reinforced concrete floor. Although this type of floor should support most types of machinery used by the company, there may be a few exceptions. In cases where certain pieces of machinery require greater floor density, sections of the floor can be removed and reinforced with additional concrete, thereby creating "pads."

There are two important rules to remember when establishing building specifications. First, the SIB should provide amenities that would be attractive for a variety of different industries. In most cases, the design characteristics should not be restricted to the needs of one or a few specific industries. As a rule, the more generic the building, the greater the probability of accommodating several types of industry.

Secondly, be selective about building design specifications. A building which offers several amenities automatically translates into higher per square foot costs. Always be sensitive to the prevailing market price for leasable or salable industrial space. Chances are if there are too many amenities, the per square foot cost will be excessive and limit the building's sale or lease potential.

During this phase of the project it is important to involve the architect, manufacturers and/or developers familiar with the design of industrial buildings. As the building specifications are integrated into the over-all design, the architect will be charged with preparing drawings, and other documents relating to the solicitation of bids.

Once the necessary documents and drawings have been prepared, they should be distributed to general contractors for bidding purposes. The materials should also specify a date, time and place where the bids must be returned. It is also customary to inform the contractors about protocol associated with the review of bids and the selection process.

FINANCING THE PROJECT

Although it is not the intent of this paper to address specific scenarios associated with financing a SIB, several considerations which contribute to this phase of the project are addressed.

Before identifying sources of funds, one must identify all costs associated with the project. In general, these costs can be categorized in four areas:

❑ Site acquisition and preparation. This includes any costs associated with purchasing the site, testing the soil, and/or preparing the site for construction.

❑ Construction cost. This includes any and all costs associated with constructing the building, including utility extensions, paving parking areas and sidewalks.

❑ Professional and Administrative costs. Any legal, architectural, engineering, surveying, or related project fees. As noted earlier, it is good to have a formal agreement specifying the terms of payment, as many times costs of this nature can be based on a flat hourly rate or a percentage of the total project cost.

☐ Contingency. This would include the allocation of funds for unexpected cost(s) which may develop. A contingency of 10 to 15 percent of the total project cost is typical. Although these funds may never be used, it is a good fail-safe measure.

It is critical to identify and define all costs associated with the project, including how frequent requests for payment will be submitted by the contractor(s).

Once all of the costs have been identified, it is time to identify funding sources. If the development of the SIB involves a non-profit development group as opposed to a for-profit development company, funding sources may be restricted to those which are more "community development" in nature. These sources would primarily include: conventional lenders, revolving loan funds (RLF) administered at the local level, local community development group(s) and/or utility, state or local government programs (e.g., industrial revenue bonds), and equity capital.

For example, many SIB's receive capital through several sources, including conventional lenders, revolving loan funds (RLF's), municipal involvement (e.g., donation of land, deferring payment for the site, etc.) and an equity investment from the development group.

Identifying sources of capital is only part of the process, for negotiating the mortgage is also involved. The negotiation process involves four basic criteria: loan amount, term of the note, interest rate and security. Many, if not all of these criteria will be restricted by the policies of the lender.

The amount may be based on a "cap" or a percentage of equity involved in the project. The interest rate is generally at "prime" or somewhat below "prime" because the project is intended to promote community growth. The term of the note is negotiated; however, generally the loan term involves a 10 year payment schedule based on a 30 year amortization. Security refers to the "position" a lender takes if the property goes into foreclosure. In general, all conventional lenders will take nothing less than a first position on the asset(s) and it is assumed that other lender(s) will take subordinated positions.

INITIATING THE CONSTRUCTION PHASE

At this point the bids have been received, financing has been arranged and a general contractor has been hired to construct the building. Now timing becomes important — how long will it be before the building is completed and available for sale or lease?

Both the architect and the general contractor are critical participants in organizing and implementing the construction phase. Initially a project "time line" is established. The time line allows various aspects of the project to be scheduled in an orderly fashion. For example, the site preparation must be completed before the footings and foundation can be started. Typically, the project time line will involve at least four phases: site preparation, construction, leasehold improvements (if any), and the final site work.

Before the project commences, it is important to have the development area insured. "Builder's Risk" insurance is a form of liability insurance used during the construction phase. This type of insurance protects the development group from any liability which may occur on the project site prior to completion of the project.

While the project is underway, be sure that the architect continues to monitor the contractor's work and that his/her observations are documented. This will become very important when requests for payment are submitted. It is customary for the invoice to provide a description of the work completed to date, as well as any material costs the contractor has incurred. Before the payment is authorized, the architect should state, in writing, that the work described in the invoice has been completed.

Before construction commences, be sure that the general contractor and all subcontractors are aware of how payments will be made. Many times invoices will be submitted by the general contractor and include costs of various subcontractors. It is important to know how disbursements will be made and subsequently avoid making double payments.

It is also critical that a signed "lien waiver" proceed every disbursement. A lien is a claim that a creditor has on the property of another as either security for a debt or fulfillment of a financial obligation. The waiver prevents the creditor (e.g., contractor) from placing a restriction on the property for work completed.

DEVELOPMENT OF THE MARKETING PLAN

It is very reasonable for both the construction and marketing phase to occur simultaneously. Generally this "interim" period provides an excellent opportunity to notify targeted market(s) and/or location(s) about the development of this building.

Once the "targeted" areas have been identified, the marketing group should determine "what" the message will be and "how" the message will be disseminated most effectively. The development of a brochure, letter, or advertisement (print, radio, or television) should provide "key" information pertaining to the building and its location (e.g., key building specifications, renderings of the building, community data, contact person and a phone number). If the marketing strategy involves a direct mail piece, a telemarketing campaign should also be implemented.

Depending upon an organization's budgetary situation, there may be several ways of promoting the SIB. Whether it involves direct mail or "word of mouth," it is important that the message be consistent and persistent.

COMPLETION OF THE CONSTRUCTION PHASE

After approximately three to four months, the construction phase will be completed. Typically, the project completion will involve a final review and inspection of the building, verification of any additional work that has not been completed (and when it will be completed), the request for final payment, and addressing future insurance needs.

As in the construction phase, utilize the architect to review the work that has been completed. Before anyone receives payment for completed work, the architect should review and authorize that payment be made and, as suggested earlier, receive a signed lien waiver. If there are any aspects of the project which are incomplete, obtain a detailed description of the incomplete work and an estimated completion date. Obviously, work that has not been completed should not be paid for.

When the project has been completed, the insurance coverage relevant during construction may no longer be valid. For this reason, it is important to qualify any insurance coverage requirements which may be relevant to an existing or anticipated situation. It is recommended that an insurance agent and/or attorney be contacted prior to the completion of construction and address building coverage options.

STRUCTURING THE SALE OR LEASE ARRANGEMENT

Hopefully the building is well located, reasonably priced, and the marketing was so successful that a prospect has been generated. These are good signs, but a lease or purchase agreement must be structured before the deal can be consummated.

There are several considerations associated with structuring a lease and/or sale agreement; however, these suggestions should not be used as a substitution for sound legal advice. It is imperative that an attorney, familiar with negotiating and structuring real estate agreements, be retained.

The most conservative option would involve a "sale" of the land and building. Once the "price" has been agreed upon (generally determined through an appraisal), a purchase agreement is drafted and signed, financing is arranged and title to the property is transferred to the purchaser.

Although this is an oversimplified scenario, the sale may be the preferred alternative because the legal ownership reverts to the buyer. This means that building maintenance, debt service, etc., become the responsibility of the new owner. A lease arrangement represents a substantially different scenario.

A lease arrangement can be structured in several different ways. A "gross," or

"net" lease and leasing with an option to purchase, are just three of the more common types. There are several considerations associated with structuring a lease. These considerations are summarized below:

❑ **Is the prospective tenant credit worthy?** It is imperative that the prospective tenant's ability to pay be determined. This can be derived through conducting a financial analysis of the company/principal(s) and interviewing the principal officer(s).

❑ **Will the lease be a "gross" or a "net" lease?** In a "gross" lease situation the landlord would pay the operating expenses and debt service out of the rent received. Alternatively, a "net" lease would involve the tenant assuming specific building operating costs (e.g., insurance, utilities, taxes, etc.), plus a rental amount to cover debt service and other related costs.

• **Are there modifications to the lease?** Buy-out provisions, amortized lease-hold improvements, etc., must be specifically addressed in the lease instrument. Be specific about how they are structured. For example, if a tenant leaves before the leasehold improvements have been fully amortized, who is responsible for the outstanding balance?

❑ **What will the lease rate be?** Identify all annual costs (e.g., debt service, insurance, taxes, costs that are netted out to the tenant, etc.), and prorate this amount over the square footage that is to be leased.

Selling and leasing a building involves several considerations with far reaching consequences. This emphasizes the importance of soliciting an attorney to help prepare the required documents, negotiate

and structure the lease and perform other related duties.

SUMMARY

The development of a speculative industrial building has great potential in the attraction and retention of industry; however, the process is not without risk. Planning and soliciting the advice of experienced professionals can be the development group's greatest ally.

Economic development groups contemplating the development of a SIB should incorporate the following considerations into the overall development plan:

❑ A SIB should be part of a community's overall economic development marketing program.

❑ Be aware of prevailing market conditions, the cost and availability of money, and the community's inventory of existing buildings.

❑ Create a project development team, including the architect, local business people with experience in building development, an attorney, lender(s) and others who could contribute to the planning process.

❑ Market the building before, during and after the development process.

❑ Be aware of the implications associated with all financial arrangements and establish an accounting system for all disbursements.

❑ Determine the credit history and "ability to pay" of a prospective tenant before proceeding with any financial arrangement(s).

Creating A "SIMPLE" Spec Building Program: The Example of Glendale, Arizona

James A. Devine, C.E.D., FM

The City of Glendale was losing manufacturing and back office prospects because it lacked a key requirement, namely 40,000 to 80,000 square feet of free-standing space. Other communities had this product available, despite the fact that Glendale had some of the best quality and well masterplanned business parks in the metropolitan Phoenix area. This article deals with how Glendale responded to this challenge by creating SIMPLE -- Strategic Industrial Master Plan and Landscape Enterprise.

BACKGROUND

The City's Director of Economic Development was hired in April of 1991. After meeting with brokers, developers and potential users, it was clear that the City lacked available buildings to compete with other communities. In May, during a lunch with a major general contractor, the economic developer was asked by the contractor what the contractor could do to help the City of Glendale, The Director responded, "Build me a spec building." Both laughed, knowing that there was absolutely no financing for this kind of speculative opportunity. After all, Arizona's real estate boom busted and so were most of the Savings and Loans which fueled spec space in the mid-1980's. Nevertheless, the Director challenged the contractor to build a spec building anyway. . . on paper! The Director offered to publicize the spec building program far and wide, if it could be done. Good PR would result. The general contractor took the bait and lined up a large architect and engineering firm to assist, pro bono, of course.

To avoid the perception of favoritism, the City insisted on the ground rule that whatever innovative program resulted, it could be used by the contractor's competitors. All the pro bono work could be lost to the competition despite the up-front work

of both firms. Once the program was up and running, this agreement increased the City's image as a pro-business and neutral business partner. Additional contractor and A & E firm referrals resulted after the program was initiated.

CREATING A "PAPER" SPEC BUILDING

The City of Glendale Department of Economic Development set out to define the configuration and building specs required by the 40,000 to 80,000 square foot users. The department interviewed twenty-one industrial brokers and reviewed all the space requirements of the industrial leads received by the regional marketing agency, The Greater Phoenix Economic Development Council. The ideal building was defined during the summer of 1991.

Meanwhile, the Director of Economic Development assembled the most senior and customer service oriented members of the City's design and development review teams. The disciplines included: landscape architecture, land development, fire, plans examining, and design review and development services. He challenged them to become part of the public and private partnership to make Glendale Number One in the Valley for new space and a new pro-business attitude. The team responded positively, as they seldom had the opportunity to take the time to create their best possible project without time and budget constraints.

Then the Director of Economic Development approached the developers of the best business parks in the City and asked them to submit lots on which to site the speculative building. Initially, most were skeptical. A City asking for a partnership? But after a meeting with the City staff, the contractor, and the A & E firms, they fully understood they had nothing to lose and a lot to gain. They cooperated fully and, when asked, donated $3,000 to publicize

the concept once it was ready to go public.

From the months of October, 1991 through June, 1992, the private sector developers, contractors and public sector team worked hard to design the product. The result was an adaptable design for a spec building which had all the necessary City approvals without actually having to build it! The building is approved in three of the City's major business areas, Glen Harbor Business Park, Eaton Industrial Park, and Talavi Business Park. The private sector partners provided the architectural and engineering brain power behind the project, and the general contractor provided the construction know-how.

OBTAINING APPROVALS

The City staff piloted architectural drawings of the "spec building", preliminary site plans, landscaping and elevations through the approval process with the result being a ready-for-construction, site specific building in any of the City's three major business parks. In addition, the City committed to an expedited construction plan review for these buildings and a rebate of building permit and plan check fees.

THE "BUILDING"

The spec building is 50,000 square feet, expandable to 80,000 square feet, with twenty percent of the space devoted to office use and eighty percent to plant operations. Even these parameters are flexible. The building can be adapted for a smaller or larger building. It can be either single-story or two-story. In addition, if none of the proposed locations is suitable, the City committed to move the building to another site within any of the three business parks. In effect, a "model" home was created to generate inquiries.

Glendale's spec building can compete on both a cost and time basis with retrofitting existing space. It represents significant savings of time and money over the conventional process of designing and building a new facility.

According to the calculations by the City, the contractor and the A & E firm, companies taking advantage of the "SIMPLE" program can save up to eleven weeks design, approval and construction time and up to seventy-five percent of planning costs. Companies using the "SIMPLE" plans also can save up to sixty-five percent of the time and money needed to prepare financing exhibits and up to fifteen percent of their architectural and engineering fees.

Another "SIMPLE" building program advantage is that the company can build a new building in about the same amount of time required to retrofit an existing structure. There also are significant savings of up to fifty percent in the time and money required to prepare financing exhibits, according to the City's calculations.

SPIN-OFF BENEFITS

One of the most important aspects of the project, according to Bernard Deutsch, president of the architectural firm, is being able to work with a municipal government in a positive, problem-solving mode.

"My role as president of Deutsch Associates requires me to spend a lot of time working with City officials on behalf of our clients. For the most part, the officials are very amiable. However, as the process proceeds to staff level, the sense of urgency and helpfulness in assisting the clients often diminishes dramatically, thereby negatively impacting their business plan", Deutsch says.

"Glendale is the *first* City to demonstrate this unique pro-active approach in working with new and existing businesses. As a result of this approach, a positive professional attitude permeates the Glendale staff. This is extremely important to the success of any business venture."

Carol Warner, vice president/business development for Johnson Carlier, says the major challenge for the project team was "to even out the time and costs of the 'SIMPLE' project so Glendale could compete with cities with an inventory of existing space".

"Time is especially critical to negotiations with potential users," says Peggy Kirch, vice president of SunCor, developer of Talavi.

A City government that can offer short-cuts in the approval process and is ready to work with a client to make things happen can make or break a deal. By all standards, Glendale's public/private sector team's efforts were successful. In the process, they also nourished a spirit of cooperation between the City and private enterprise which rarely exists.

RESULTS

While "SIMPLE" was on the drawing board, an existing company in Phoenix learned of the program through the City's on-going sales and public relations efforts. The company, Allied Color Industries, a division of a Fortune 500 company, was sold on the "SIMPLE" concept. They were running out of space and time in their existing location. The City, the developers, the contractor and the A & E firm jumped at the opportunity.

Allied Color Industries received its Certificate of Occupancy in November, 1992 in Del Webb's Glen Harbor Business Park. Bernard Deutsch and Associates performed the architectural services and a different general contractor built the facility.

Currently, two firms are in the pipeline for the SIMPLE program. One is using Deutsch, the other isn't. One firm will employ one hundred and fifty (150) people in an 80,000 square foot facility, and the other will employ twenty (20) people in a 12,000 square foot facility. In addition, seven firms were interested in the SIMPLE program, but did not want to locate in the pre-approved business park locations for various reasons. Of the seven firms, two firms are in the process of locating in Glendale anyway. They will employ two hundred (200) people and absorb 150,000 square feet of existing space. Glendale's SIMPLE program hooked them on Glendale's pro-business attitude.

CONCLUDING COMMENTS

The "SIMPLE" program levels the competitive playing field between Glendale and other cities with a large inventory of existing office and industrial space.

Now, Glendale has a competitive, spec facility for companies attracted by the City's location, lifestyle and low cost of doing business.

It's "SIMPLE".

And "SIMPLE" works.

The SIMPLE program is an excellent marketing tool for attracting firms' attention. Even if they don't locate in the City, it demonstrates:

❏ A pro-business and pro-active City.

❏ A cooperative spirit between the public and private sector.

❏ A City which respects time and money.

Labor Force Surveys and the Economic Development Program

Lay James Gibson*

INTRODUCTION

Economic developers regularly use labor force data in their work. In most cases these data come "off the shelf," i.e., they are secondary data which are routinely collected or estimated by the U.S. Bureau of the Census, the Bureau of Labor Statistics (BLS), a state employment service or some other governmental agency. Data from established sources are easy for the developer to obtain, they are usually accepted as authoritative, and because they are typically collected at regular intervals, they allow the developer the opportunity to build a longitudinal picture of changes and trends.

Such secondary data can indeed provide valuable insights for the economic developer. They describe the structure of the regional economy and can be used to track structural change. Further, it is these "public data" that normally provide the figures on unemployment which are regularly reported in the press. Unfortunately, however, questions raised by prospects, policy makers and others about productivity, turnover, absenteeism, skills, and other characteristics of an area's workforce often require data different than those which are readily available at a low cost. In such cases, the developer will usually be forced to consider generating his own data -- probably by survey. The discussions which follow will initially focus on the questions when to survey, where to survey, and how to survey and then move on to more detailed descriptions of two very different families of surveys -- household based surveys and workplace based surveys.

WHEN TO SURVEY

The answer to this question is relatively straightforward. The developer conducts a labor survey when he has no other choice. Surveys are expensive and they are time consuming. Economic development operations are characteristically short on staff and short on budget. A labor survey is a fairly ambitious undertaking -- it is something only worth doing if the payoffs are substantial. Situations which might justify a survey are those when secondary data are not available to describe specific geographic areas, specific points in time, or specific topics of interest.

Studies of Specific Areas. Secondary data are typically collected for legal entities, i.e. cities, counties, states. Whereas such geographic units have the benefit of being stable over time (because of annexation, cities are often an exception) they frequently come up short as useful units to describe the laborshed or labor market area of individual communities or firms. Most communities or firms, for example, will draw labor from **portions** of one or more counties. A survey allows the developer to determine the reach of a laborshed and eliminate the "noise" which comes when data describing workers from outside the laborshed are included. Survey data can be used to describe the content of **meaningful** areas.

Studies of Specific Times. Secondary data tend to become dated. The Census of Population includes a variety of valuable data on both employment by industry and occupation and on the household characteristics of those who are a part of the current and future workforce. Unfortunately, a full Census is taken only every 10 years and publication may lag collection by three or four years. Especially in rapidly growing or declining areas, data collected in, say, 1980 will have only limited value after three or four years and even less value after 10 years. Survey data can be used to describe the **current** situation in a local region.

Studies of Specific Topics. The number of questions that a developer (or development prospect) might ask about a local labor market are almost infinite. Little wonder then that those who collect "official data" are often unprepared to offer specific answers to specific questions. For example, underemployment may be suspected but secondary data are rarely available to answer questions about skills held but not utilized by local residents. Or, what about special recruitment problems faced by area employers? In either case, surveys can be used to provide direct and **specific** answers to questions such as those which cannot, usually, be answered from secondary data.

Payoffs and Limitations. When the developer does respond to appropriate situations by generating labor market data the payoffs can be handsome.

❑ He is better able to service industrial prospects by providing specific questions.

❑ He has armed himself with solid information that can sharpen his marketing and target industry selection efforts.

❑ He has current and appropriate information upon which to base programmatic efforts to service existing industries and new industries through the correction of existing problems and the exploitation of underdeveloped potentials.

*I would like to thank Bruce Hernandez of Behavior Research Center for his substantial contributions to the survey instruments described in this article and an anonymous EDR reviewer who offered a number of extremely valuable comments and suggestions.

In addition, there is a more cosmetic benefit -- by going to the effort to produce "fresh" labor force information, the developer has added to his image as an aggressive and alert professional.

On the other hand, it is wise to recognize certain potential limitations. First, there may be a credibility issue. Data provided by a federal or state agency are generally perceived as being "believable" whereas locally generated data may be received with a certain (healthy) skepticism. Such concerns can be mitigated by documenting a solid, professional approach or by having the survey conducted by an objective third part, e.g., a university or respected consultant.

Additionally, there is the question of comparability. BLS data, for example, allow comparisons from state to state, county to county, and year to year. Surveys are often one-shot affairs; initially, at least, they do not allow for comparisons from place to place or from year to year. Comparability need not be an issue but if it does appear to be a concern, the true total cost of the survey approach should be carefully evaluated.

WHERE TO SURVEY

In most cases, the developer will select between place of residence and place of work when conducting a survey. If the intent is to identify unused and underused local labor resources, for instance, a household based survey would be appropriate. If, on the other hand, the intent is to describe the experiences of local employees and, perhaps, to identify labor force problems and shortcomings that might be corrected, a place-of-work-based survey might be in order. There are, of course, other places where surveys might be conducted; e.g., union halls and employment offices; the choice of "where" depends on the thrust of the survey and a determination of what constitutes an appropriate location given local circumstances.

Closely related to the questions of where to survey is the question "whom to survey." Household based surveys can, potentially, include responses from all family members. Such an approach may not be practical in many cases. Typically, the head-of-household or some other "responsible adult" will be asked to provide information on all members of the household unit. The latter approach will be less tedious although some will argue that information about other family members might get lost if each individual does not speak for himself.

Similarly, workplace based surveys can be directed either at a company official(s) or they may be directed at individual workers. In the former case, the developer gets the benefit of dealing directly with the region's influential business decision makers and the benefit of "one-stop shopping," i.e., obtaining information on perhaps dozens of individuals by dealing with just one person. As with the household survey, which relies on one informant per household, e.g., the head-of-household, details might be lost.

In short, the questions of "where and whom" must be answered after the developer has determined what he wants to know and how much time and money he is willing to devote to know it. In most cases, it is likely that household surveys will depend upon one mature and knowledgeable respondent per household and that workplace surveys will be directed to key officials (who may farm out certain questions to appropriate subordinates).

HOW TO SURVEY

Two items should be considered here. First, how do you reach respondents? Second, what do you ask them, i.e., what is the content of your survey instrument?

As for the first question, there are several approaches and each has its advocates. Although there are all sorts of variations and combinations, the three basic approaches are phone, mail, and personal interviews. Phone interviews are especially appropriate for household based surveys. They are relatively fast, inexpensive, and content can be effectively controlled by skilled interviewers. Critics point to the fact that precision might be lost because the interviewer does not have the benefit of face-to-face contact and because such surveys are often conducted so rapidly that respondents do not have time to develop thoughtful responses. Proponents, on the other hand, assert that professionally prepared and administered survey instruments can avoid most problems and provide high-quality results. Such arguments are convincing given the widespread use of phone surveys by highly regarded private survey firms and the amount of effort lavished on the improvement of phone surveys by universities and other research institutions.

Personal surveys do permit face-to-face contact but they are usually relatively expensive given the field time (and travel time to the field) that is often involved. If respondents are hard to locate, the face-to-face survey might be especially appropriate although in most cases phone surveys are likely to be more cost effective and superior where it comes to questions of how to control the composition of the survey population.

Mail and other self-administered surveys are often criticized for producing low response rates and because the "interview" is not conducted in a controlled environment. There are, however, certain advantages to this approach. For example, questions which rely on diagrams or data can be offered because the respondent has the opportunity to see and examine such exhibits, detailed questions requiring thought can be asked because the respondent sets his or her own pace and questionnaires can be lengthy because respondents can work at their leisure. (These "advantages" may also help account for the fact that response rates are frequently low.) Mail surveys are especially appropriate for reaching employers in the workplace because they allow the respondent to "research" questions of fact and to provide thoughtful responses to complex questions.

Next, there is the question of content. Needless to say, the opportunities for asking specific questions are endless but for a good many development applications two models will be appropriate. In the first instance, imagine a situation in which you want to be able to tell industrial prospects something about current labor force patterns and potentials in your region. You want to answer such questions as "who works where doing what?", "who are the people who are not now in the labor force but who have the potential to join the labor force?" In short, what are the patterns and potentials of the region's labor pool? Questions of this sort are answered by a household based labor force study using the telephone.

The second scenario assumes that you want to understand something about the labor force recruitment and utilization process as seen through the eyes of the region's employers. You want to know who is working at what and which skills are being utilized. You want to know about prevailing wage rates. You want to know if employers are satisfied with their current labor force and if problems are encountered when they move to expand their workforce. You want to be able to tell industrial prospects about the positive features of your workforce, e.g., high productivity, low levels of absenteeism, based on the experience of those who now utilize local workers, and you want to be able to identify problems that can be corrected to enhance the position of existing industry. The survey instrument to be utilized is a mail survey which is completed by top officials in your region's firms.

Finally, there is the question of validity. A detailed discussion of this topic is beyond the scope of this article. However, we can note that surveys can be divided into two groups -- census surveys and sample surveys. In the former case, the entire universe, e.g., all households in the study area, are surveyed. In the latter case, only a fraction of the potential residents are surveyed. If the person preparing the survey wishes to generalize about an entire population using sample survey results, questions about statistical validity will certainly need to be addressed.

HOUSEHOLD BASED LABOR FORCE SURVEY

A telephone survey of randomly selected area households is suggested. The approach which this writer has employed with good results in the past utilizes a questionnaire composed of several sections which provide general information on all households and then branches to collect specific information on household members with varying employment status.[1]

The household summary section provides data which describe the composition of all households including:

❑ Tenure at current address and in the community;

❑ Status as permanent or seasonal resident;

❑ Age, sex, relation to household head, years of formal education, and employment status of all family members;

❑ Ethnic background, and

❑ Household income.

The second, third, and fourth sections cover employed household members, unemployed household members, and household members not seeking employment. If, for example, there were two household members employed, questions in this section would be asked twice so that each employed member would be fully described. Similarly, the questions describing the unemployed and those not seeking employment should be repeated as often as necessary. To the extent possible, each household members should be allowed to speak for himself. The final result, of course, is a comprehensive profile of each member of the sample household who is 16 years of age or older. Employed adults in the household are asked:

❑ if they are self-employed;

❑ how many employers they work for;

❑ the business or industry of their primary employer;

❑ the type of work they do;

❑ their job title;

❑ the number of years experience that they have with their present occupation;

❑ their pay rate;

❑ the shift that they worked;

❑ whether they belong to a union;

❑ the name of the community in which they work;

❑ the name of the community in which they would prefer to work;

❑ their travel time to work;

❑ the nature of work on a second job;

❑ types of work that the person has done before that he would be willing to do again;

❑ whether the individual is actually looking for another job and why;

❑ to list special skills that would qualify the individual for the current or other jobs;

❑ whether there are special skills that the individual would like to develop;

❑ whether the individual is enrolled or anticipates enrolling in any program to improve job skills;

❑ and finally, whether work options are limited by physical disabilities.

The unemployed are asked questions designed to describe talents and past employment experiences. It is important to note that the definition of "unemployed" used in the survey is more liberal than the definitions used by most governmental agencies. As a result, survey results can be expected to describe those who are "officially" unemployed as well as discouraged workers and even those with tentative plans to enter the workforce. Questions include:

❑ has the individual ever held a job?

❑ why did he leave his last job?

❑ what was the business or industry of the last job?

❑ what sort of work was done?

❑ what was the job title?

❑ how much experience does the individual have with the sort of work most recently done?

❑ when did the last job end?

❑ is the individual looking for the same sort of work done previously?

❑ what sort of work is he looking for?

❑ is the individual looking for full-time or part-time work?

❑ is there a shift preference?

❑ is there a preference for work in a particular location?

❑ any special skills possessed?

❑ are there skills that the individual would like to develop?

❑ are work options limited by physical disabilities?

Finally, to balance the profile of adult household members, questions are asked to describe those not seeking employment. The first seven items are identical to the first seven items asked of the unemployed. Remaining items are:

❑ why is the individual not looking for work?

❑ does he plan to work in the future?

❑ what kind of work might he look for?

❑ will it be full- or part-time?

❑ is there a shift preference?

❑ what skills are possessed?

❑ are there skills which the individual would like to develop?

❑ is the individual enrolled in any skill training program?

❑ is the individual limited by physical disabilities?

The end result of the survey described above is a fascinating profile of an area's adult population. It presents a comprehensive data file describing both those who work and those who do not. Even more significant, it allows insights into the "hidden labor force" -- those who are neither working nor officially unemployed. In short, the household-based labor force study offers the decision maker valuable insights and perspectives that are not available through the variety of channels, for example, the U.S. Department of labor or a state employment service, that produce "regular" labor force data of various sorts. It provides a current look at the population of a region that is defined to meet the specific needs of those with localized development interests. It provides information that can be of tremendous value to those who have a direct financial interest in development; e.g., financial institutions, homebuilders, facility locators, and real estate brokers. Industrial developers, chamber of commerce, and urban planners are armed with data for diagnostic and promotional purposes. Educational planners can use data to program their curriculum devel-

opment efforts, and area employers are given an in-depth picture of the character of the resident labor resource.

WORKPLACE BASED LABOR FORCE SURVEY

A mail survey with telephone follow-up is suggested for this survey. The questionnaire which this writer has used with substantial success and which is outlined below is relatively lengthy and it requires the listing of detailed data. In short, it is not likely that much of the information called for will be at the finger tips of company officials; respondents will need to "dig" to answer many of the questions. Further, because the recommended approach is somewhat intimidating it is suggested that potential respondents be written or called prior to the distribution of the questionnaire to assure them that one's request is of vital importance and that one is "standing by" to help them interpret questions that may come up. A week or 10 days after the questionnaire has been mailed, a follow-up call (perhaps the first of several) to those who have not yet responded will likely improve the response rate.

The recommended format described below was initially developed by Mountain West Research -- Southwest, Tempe, Arizona, for the Arizona Office of Economic Planning and Development/Manpower Division. Field testing, revision, and application were undertaken by Lay James Gibson Associates in cooperation with Behavior Research Center, Inc. of Phoenix. The questionnaire has nine sections or groups of questions designed to provide the sort of information that an economic developer would find useful if he wants ammunition for an industrial recruitment program or insights that might support a labor force improvement program undertaken as part of an industrial retention program.

1. General questions needed to describe the participants in the exercise.

❑ formal name of establishment;

❑ street address and community;

❑ P.O. Box, zip code, phone;

❑ name and title of person providing interview;

❑ principal function of establishment and SIC code;

2. Workforce description.

❑ total employment;

❑ breakdown of full-time and part-time male and female employees;

❑ average number of hours per week worked by part-time employees;

❑ number of shifts;

❑ community of residence of employees;

❑ age of employees by sex;

❑ ethnic status by sex;

❑ number of seasonal employees, duration of employment, and place or origin if they come from outside the region.

3. Wage Scales. For each occupational category, information is requested on number employed, the wage range (high and low hourly figures) and the most common wage. Occupational categories should be selected to fit the sort of industry being surveyed. A survey focusing on manufacturing establishments might include:

❑ *Office and Clerical*
Secretaries, File Clerks

❑ *Professional, Administrative and Technical Support*
Department Managers, Computer Programmers, Draftspersons

❑ *Maintenance*
Maintenance Electricians, Maintenance Mechanics

❑ *Processing and Production*
Machinists, Welders, Assemblers

❑ *Material Management*
Truck Drivers, Shipping Packers, Forklift Operators

❏ *Service and Custodial*
Guards, Janitors, Porters, Cleaners

4. Fringe Benefits

❏ Are various benefits fully paid by company, partially paid by company, fully paid by employee, or not available? Benefits considered might include group insurance (medical, dental, disability), a pension/retirement plan, continuing education and/or training, child care, other "exotic" items such as legal aid.

❏ The number of days of time off for paid vacation, paid holidays, sick leave (paid and unpaid), and maternity leave (paid and unpaid). Additional items might be included, e.g., if maternity leave is unpaid, is it included in sick leave?

❏ Are relocation expenses for transferred or new employees paid by the company?

5. Recruitment Procedures

The procedures considered should be evaluated separately for each of the occupational categories used. Procedures considered might include internal promotion, use of the state employment service, use of local (private) employment agencies, advertisements in local or other newspapers, recruitment from local schools and training programs, and use of the industry network. Respondents should be asked to note the frequency with which these or other recruitment procedures are used.

6. Success of Recruitment Efforts

❏ First, ask respondents to rate the overall success of recruitment efforts in the various occupational categories.

❏ Next, have them comment on the qualifications (education, training, experience) of applicants for each job type.

Additional questions might focus on:

❏ the percentage of recruits for each job type that come from the local labor market;

❏ the level of difficulty involved with hiring say 1 to 3 or 5 to 10 persons in a particular job category;

❏ the percentage of workers currently on the day shift, night shift, and swing shift and the level of difficulty associated with recruiting each shift type;

❏ the extent to which the firm uses specific external training programs, such as those offered by technical schools, community colleges, or professional programs.

7. Performance

This is usually seen as a critical area given the fact that productivity and, eventually, cost per unit of output are a bottom line type concern for most firms.

❏ How does productivity in the study area compare with experiences in other areas (e.g., at other plants operated by your firm or that you have worked at);

❏ How does the study area stack up against other areas in terms of absenteeism (e.g., what rates of absenteeism are currently experienced at our plant, how have these rates changed in the past few years, how do they compare to other plants);

❏ How does turnover in the study area compare with other areas;

❏ What are the attitudes toward shift work;

❏ In general, how does the work force in the study area stack up in terms of skills and qualifications (e.g., in terms of work ethic, ability and willingness to learn new skills);

❏ What portion of the workforce is, or appears to be, disposed toward union membership.

8. Expansion Prospects

❏ How likely is expansion;

❏ If expansion is likely, how many employees and what occupational types might be involved;

❏ What factors would increase the likelihood of expansion;

❏ What factors would decrease the likelihood of expansion.

9. Miscellaneous

The questions listed above are fairly typical of those usually included in a workplace-based survey but by no means do they exhaust the possibilities for describing firms in a region. Depending on the nature of the assignment, other sections might be developed or a few miscellaneous questions might be included in a final section of the questionnaire. In a recent application of the survey instrument, several members of the local economic development advisory committee offered specific questions that were included in a special final section of the questionnaire. Among the questions included were the following:

❏ What are the market areas for major products. This economic base type question contributes to a better understanding of linkages and sources of support;

❏ Where is the firm's personnel office located, e.g. is it in the plant or elsewhere;

❏ Are drugs a problem in your plant;

❏ And, finally, an open-ended question calling for insights on the firms' experiences in the labor market area.

SOME FINAL OBSERVATIONS

Labor force surveys can produce data which yield new insights for the economic development professional and give him a powerful tool to enhance both industrial attraction and industrial retention efforts. Unfortunately, there is a cost, sometimes a substantial cost, that comes with even a relatively modest survey program. In many cases, consultants are retained to conduct the survey. This approach offers a variety of advantages. The work is done by experienced professionals and the developer is spared the interruptions that always come when work of this sort is done in-house. Further, professionally done research may have more objectivity, credibility and prestige associated with it than work done in-house. On the other hand, it will almost certainly cost more than a "homemade" product and there will certainly be at least some demands made on the developer's time -- for review of the survey instrument and procedures and later in the process, for review of study findings.

What if the development professional is unwilling or unable to bite the bullet and come up with the funds for a consultant? A solid survey program can clearly be produced on an in-house basis if the developer decides to commit the required time and effort to producing a quality study in an efficient manner. Tasks which must be programmed include questionnaire development, administration of the survey instrument, data tabulation and editing, and finally, analysis and report writing. This process can place heavy demands on the development professional's schedule and probably his office staff but it will keep hard costs down to an acceptable level even in the leanest development office.

Regardless of who does the labor force survey, there are costs. But a well conceived and executed survey can produce handsome benefits which are far greater than the cost incurred.

NOTES

[1]The questionnaire and research approach described was developed by Behavior Research center, Inc. (Phoenix, Arizona) and Lay James Gibson for the Western Metropolitan Phoenix Labor Force Study.

Obtaining Comparable And Reliable Community Labor Data

Steven R. Warren

INTRODUCTION

An economic developer wears a number of hats, particularly when working at the local level. He/she must contend with the local political situation, therefore becoming a bit of a politician. The economic developer must (or should) be involved in some sort of strategic planning process, therefore being a bit of a planner. An economic developer must be responsible for, or at least be involved in a budgeting and financial accountability process, therefore becoming a financial manager that at times borders on being an accountant (of sorts). The list goes on and on, and that is without listing responsibilities that are directly related to the economic development process - or the activities that lead to the attraction of new investment and the creation of new jobs.

While dealing with the implementation of an economic development program, he/she is functioning as a salesperson and must recognize that the techniques that are to be utilized are similar to those that are used by any salesperson. The prospect is the potential customer, the community (or area) is the product, and the economic developer is the salesperson. A good salesperson has several basic characteristics. Amongst a number of personal qualities, he/she must be aggressive, well organized, market-wise, and probably most important, knowledgeable about the product. This is true whether one is selling cars, shoes, insurance, or business locations. Some products are more intricate than others, thus making this task more difficult for some salespeople.

Unfortunately for economic developers, the product is very complex and the process of becoming thoroughly knowledgeable about the product is extremely difficult and very time consuming. To further complicate things, the product is constantly changing and these changes must be acknowledged. The better that an economic developer can anticipate questions about his or her product, the better the chances of success. To accomplish this task, one must, as best as possible, be aware of and understand the site selection process. Easier said than done. Each industry type considers different factors and weighs them differently. It is unrealistic to attempt to develop a local database that is designed to respond to all the questions that might arise from any and all prospects.

One can approach this difficult and laborious task by first identifying and then addressing those topics that are common to most industry types, or those industries that have been targeted by the community. There are a number of items that arise as part of most dealings with prospects; many of which relate to the "cost of doing business" and the resulting profitability that a firm can expect from locating a facility in a particular community. A good economic developer must recognize this very basic concept and prepare accordingly.

Certainly, information related to the availability and cost of suitable properties, state and local taxes, state and local incentives, and the cost and skills of the area's labor force are but a few of the items that are frequently asked about by most prospects. Although the availability and quality of the information differs from state to state and from community to community, these items must be addressed if a community is to continue to be considered.

The quality of the information is a key to effective prospect handling. There are, of course, a variety of sources for the many database components, depending on the topic or informational need. In addition, and what usually translates to one more headache for the economic developer, is that the reliability of the information is as varied as the topics themselves.

Consider labor data, for example in Illinois and in most other states, where current and comprehensive labor information has been difficult to maintain, particularly when trying to reference an unbiased source. Because of the lack of such a source, the burden of gathering this information has traditionally been shifted to the local level. This too has created several problems. When a prospect, consultant, or other economic development ally is comparing the labor results from one community to that of another, it is in most cases like comparing "apples and oranges". This is because the format, definitions and assumptions of one community may be drastically different from those of another. The reliability of the data can also be questionable, at best. Much work can go into generating labor data that, in the eyes of its audience, is "not worth the paper that it is written on."

OBTAINING COMPARABLE, RELIABLE LABOR DATA

In recent years, the Economic Development staff at Illinois Power Company has had more and more requests for labor information from prospects. This is partially due to the increased level of activity from foreign firms, although domestic firms are also concerned about the local labor environments. Labor costs, skills, availability and productivity have become key criteria in many companies' site selection process. Having recognized (1) the lack of good reliable source of labor data, and (2) the growing need to be able to provide it, Illinois Power developed a labor survey that is currently being utilized throughout the utility's service territory.

The program, itself, was developed to be implemented as a cooperative effort between Illinois Power and the appropriate local economic development organization(s). The cost and time required is divided in a way that helps minimize both organizations' financial and manpower resources. Because Illinois Power is conducting this program with local organizations that range from volunteer groups with little knowledge of economic development to those organizations with sizable staffs and very sophisticated programs, a "Soup to Nuts Kit" was developed. This helps assure consistency in the procedure and it also serves as a cookbook for those local economic development allies that need additional guidance.

A total of 33 areas have been identified and targeted for the study. This initiative began in 1990 when approximately half the surveys were conducted and the remainder were completed in 1991. In addition, each survey is to be conducted biennially. This will help assure that the information is relatively current at any given time. Truly, the secret to this program's success is having this information on all communities served. If any of Illinois Power Company's principal communities had chosen to not participate, it would have severely compromised the value of this program. Fortunately, however, the program was well received and 100% participation was assured.

THE PROCESS

The step-by-step process, as detailed in the labor survey kit, identifies each subactivity or component of the survey. As part of this explanation, responsibility is assigned to either Illinois Power or the participating local organization. This holds true for both task performance and financial responsibility. The process is as follows.

Creating The List of Firms

Once the local organization agrees to participate with Illinois Power in the program, the first step is to identify what companies will be surveyed. It is the responsibility of the local group to identify those that are to be surveyed. Once the list is compiled, Illinois Power reviews the list and compares it against its sources to make sure that the list is complete. All employers with 25 or more employees are the recommended recipients of the survey. This guideline, however, can be altered to reflect the employer base of either smaller communities or unusally large ones. Because the computer program that is used to tabulate the responses can sort and compile the results for "Manufacturing Only", "Non-manufacturing Only" and "Both Manufacturing and Non-manufacturing" respondents, all major employers in the community are targeted. The program's sorting capabilities will be discussed in greater detail later in this article.

Mailing The Survey

The second step involves determining the time frame for the survey to be conducted and the mailing of the survey. Because each step in the surveying process is linked to each other, as outlined in the survey kit, it is important that all target dates are established prior to initiating the survey. A sufficient quantity of standardized questionnaires (with customized covers that include the name of the local economic development organization and the initial return date) are provided to enable the local organization to survey each local company twice. The reason for this will be discussed in the follow-up step. Postage paid envelopes are also provided by Illinois Power. It is the local organization's responsibility to develop a cover letter on their letterhead that is similar to the sample found in the kit. The letter, survey form and return envelope are then mailed to those employers on the survey list. A two week response period is permitted and the return deadline is included in both the letter and on the questionnaire. All responses go directly to Illinois Power for computer input and tabulation.

Follow-up

Two weeks later and we are still waiting. A number of responses have been received at this point, but more are needed. And so begins the follow-up. A second letter that contains an additional survey form and return envelope is mailed to those that did not respond to the initial round of correspondence. Another suggested cover letter is also included in the kit, and this too is to go out under the letterhead of the local economic development organization. Ten additional days are allowed for a response and a second return deadline is established.

The ten days pass and at this point the level of response is either satisfactory or not. In those cases when the response rate is not at an acceptable level, additional follow-up is necessary. Because additional surveys were received during the previous follow-up (hopefully), the number of outstanding respondents is less than it had been. The number of surveys that have not been returned and the amount of time required to make the necessary contact will dictate the manner of the next follow-up. Telephone contact is preferred.

Tabulating the Results

A final deadline is established and all responses received to that point will be included in the results. All responses are entered into the PC and an applications program that utilizes DBASE 3+ is used to calculate the results in the manner that was determined to be most appropriate and of greatest value to Illinois Power, the local organizations and, most importantly, prospects.

The results are tabulated and a customized cover, inside page entitled "About the Survey" and the computer generated survey results are assembled. Copies are then distributed, locally and to other interested parties. As established initially with the local sponsor of the survey, it is their responsibility to distribute copies to the survey participants that requested one.

THE RESULTS

The process described above is not dissimilar to that of other surveys. But the way the results of this survey can be customized to better respond to the specific informational needs of prospects makes it unique. This feature of the program is truly what distinguishes it from other labor surveys and makes it more useful. In most cases, it is appropriate to furnish information that cites the total results of the survey. There are, however, instances when totals are not the best or most accurate way to respond to questions about the local labor force. This fact was recognized when developing this program and several query fields were incorporated into the program that allows the following "sorting" capabilities:

By Type of Respondent

As previously mentioned, both manufacturing and non-manufacturing employers were surveyed. Results can be expressed as totals for manufacturing respondents only, non-manufacturing respondents only and for all respondents. This gives Illinois Power and the local economic development organization the flexibility to provide the results that are most appropriate, given the nature of the prospect's business.

By Size of Employer

Since oftentimes the competition for employees tends to be amongst employers of comparable size, the results can be sorted based on the size of the employer (in terms of the number of employees). This is especially true when the prospect proposes to create a modest number of jobs — say 50. The data can be sorted by entering a "range" for the size of the respondents — say those that reported having between 1 and 100 employees. This is particularly helpful in communities that have one, or a few, large employers that strongly influence or skew the results of the entire survey.

By SIC Code

Results can also be provided that show the aggregate responses for specific industry types by using a 2-, 3-, or 4- digit SIC Code. If a prospect is interested in the results for those businesses or industries that are from similar businesses, a customized response can be easily assembled.

Regional Totals

Since labor results will be maintained for nearly all of Illiois Power Company's entire service territory, a need to provide regional or multi-community data was anticipated. This is used to respond to requests from prospects that will employ a significant number of employees and anticipate drawing workers from other communities. Any or all participating communities can be included in the regional totals.

In addition, the aforementioned sorting tools can be used in conjunction with each other. For example, the results can be tabulated for all non-manufacturing respondents with 100 to 250 employees for a region consisting of six communities. This information can be obtained in less than 15 minutes.

SUMMARY

For a number of years, Illinois Power utilized a virtual hodge-podge of labor data, some good, some not so good. Whether good or bad, the information was inconsistent in the manner that the results were expressed. Not only has this program enabled IP to provide consistent data, the sorting capabilities allows for a customized response to labor data requests.

The availability of this service is also being publicized to a number of non-local allies. They, too, have had difficulty obtaining reliable and consistent labor information. Although it is too early to tell how valuable they perceive this information to be, the hope is that this service will also lead to additional prospect activity.

Career Fair for High School Sophomores

Patrick J. Vercauteren, CED, FM

INTRODUCTION

In order to work toward the sustained development of the skilled workforce needed by firms and organizations in the county, the Johnson County Development Corporation in conjunction with area businesses of the Manufacturer's Network decided that an annual county-wide career fair for high school sophomores would be an efficient, economical, and community-oriented support measure. While only a one-day event, the career fair has proven to be an effective way to pull together education and business to form a partnership having lasting impact on the economic health of the community. This article provides information on this economic development tool.

OBJECTIVES

The objectives of the program all worked together towards the long-term betterment of the local workforces. They are:

❏ to better inform county sophomores of career choices and requirements while they still have time to include job-readiness skills in their academic programs.

❏ to increase communication between area human resource directors and high school guidance counselors so that non-college bound students are receiving more sufficient and more appropriate career information and advice.

❏ to encourage youth to investigate local employment opportunities.

❏ to improve the skills of entry-level workers for local businesses.

❏ to secure for local businesses a steady, well-prepared supply of new workers.

❏ to form a mutually beneficial, lasting partnership between area school districts and local businesses.

ACTION PLAN

The 1994 annual county-wide career fair was executed according to the following timetable with the main components, budget, and costs listed in tables 1 and 2.

It is important to note that while the budget for the event was $5,000, this figure is flexible and could be tailored to fit the human and economic resources of a particular local development corporation. Likewise, the timetable could vary depending on the scope of the fair anticipated by a local development corporation.

RESULTS OF THE PROGRAM

According to available information, the annual county-wide career fair promises to have a significant positive impact on the economic well-being of the community.

In its second year, the fair attracted over 900 sophomores from eight school districts as well as the participation of thirty-eight area businesses in fields as diverse as manufacturing, employment counseling, municipal service, law enforcement, finance, utility service, health care, social services, communications, vocational training, distribution, retail trade, building trades, and library services. Such numbers constitute a twenty-two percent increase in student participation and a sixteen percent increase in business participation in the course of a single year, thus indicating the importance the surrounding community attaches to the program as a means of educating Johnson County's future workforce.

Also, according to an exit survey of sophomores attending the fair, student response was overwhelmingly positive:

❏ 85% agreed that the fair gave them career information that was beneficial

❏ 88% said they would recommend the career fair to other students

❏ 61% of the sophomores agreed that, as a result of the fair, they had a better idea of what courses to take in their last two years of high school

❏ 73% felt that the fair helped them know more about the skills that businesses need in their new employees.

These numbers indicate that the majority of the participating sophomores are likely to be better informed and better prepared entrants into the workforce.

Business participants were also extremely supportive of the fair in their comments, noting that the fair gave them the opportunity to show their commitment to the community in a concrete way through face-to-face discussion with the youth who would one-day be their workers. In this way, business participants saw themselves as mentors who could share their years in and knowledge of the world of work with the sophomores who needed advice on necessary skills, standard workplace expectations, and possible career paths.

While the lasting impact of the annual county-wide career fair cannot yet be known, the initial enthusiastic response to it would indicate that the fair is a positive and effective first step in actively developing the dialogue between education and business that is a prerequisite for building the sort of well-informed and well-prepared workforce necessary for the county's strong, economic growth and development.

DESCRIPTION OF THE PROGRAM TEAM

Truly a community program, the annual county-wide career fair was initiated by the Manufacturers' Network of the Johnson County Development Corporation. This network is composed primarily of area human resource directors from local manufacturers and businesses as well as area educators.

At the suggestion of the Manufacturer's Network, the staff of the Johnson County Development Corporation took on primary responsibility for coordinating with various local community chambers of commerce in developing, promoting, and staging the fair.

The Johnson County Development Corporation staff consists of Executive Director Patrick J. Vercauteren, CED, and Administrative Assistant Phyllis A. Daly,

TABLE 1
Timetable

July 1994	<u>Date of November 16, 1994 selected for fair.</u> Centrally-located Valle Vista Country Club selected as site for fair; Facilities reserved.
August 1994	<u>General promotion of fair begins.</u> High school counselors notified of date and location.
	Businesses notified and requested to participate.
	Participant information materials sent out.
September 1994	<u>In-school promotion of fair begins.</u> Volunteers start attending parent/teacher conferences to hand out promotional brochures and talk with parents about the fair.
October 1994	Pre-fair promotional video made to be shown in schools.
	Promotional posters and video delivered to school.
	Room layout and booth assignments sent to business participants.
	Requests for promotional advertising sponsors go out to Johnson County Development Corporation board members.
November 1994	Volunteers prepare over 1000 student folders to be handed out at the fair. Folders contain business profiles, career-information, interviewing tips, and follow-up essay contest information.
	Career questionnaires and room layout maps with key to participants delivered to high schools.
	<u>Annual county-wide career fair takes place on November 16, 1994, attracting over 900 students and 38 businesses.</u>
	<u>Career fair follow-up.</u> Results of sophomore exit survey compiled. Business participants asked for responses and thanked. Essay contest judged and awards made to winners. Wrap-up publicity monitored.

TABLE 2
Budget and Costs

<u>Career fair budget:</u> $5,000.00
<u>Actual total costs:</u> $4,435.67

	Johnson County Development Corporation contributions	Contributions by participating businesses
Facility	$2,339.92	
Pipe & drape for booths	630.00	
Signs	107.10	
Beverages for exhibitors	115.50	
Pre-fair promotions		$ 421.57 (in kind)
Sign		117.00
Materials and supplies		594.58
Totals	$3,302.52	$1,133.15

Grand Total of all contributions: $4,435.67

demonstrating that coordination of a program such as this does not require a large staff.

SECONDARY BENEFITS

While accomplishing its primary objective of forming a link between business and education capable of aiding today's students to develop into the highly skilled, well-prepared workers increasingly needed by area businesses, Johnson County has experienced other benefits directly attributable to the annual county-wide career fair.

Perhaps one of the most notable secondary benefits of the fair is the strong feeling throughout the business community that the Johnson County Development Corporation truly supports existing local business concerns in addition to attracting new investment. This commitment to the continued health and well-being of existing businesses, as indicated by the career fair in its objective of helping to develop and sustain a superior local workforce, has resulted in increased membership in the Johnson County Development Corporation and its Manufacturer's network as well as increased calls from local businesses asking the Corporation for guidance and assistance.

TRANSFERABILITY

Also noteworthy is the high transferability of this program. While the specifics of such a program, including the organizational structure of a manufacturer's network, the cost of a career fair, the scope of a career fair (one school or several, regional or metropolitan area coverage, and so on), may vary, the structure of the annual career fair developed by the Johnson County Development Corporation is highly flexible and adaptable to any community's human and economic resources.

With some effort, most local development corporations should be able to work to support the equivalent of the Johnson County Manufacturer's Network, an open forum where local businesses discuss issues of importance. In the case of Johnson County, the businesses of the Manufacturer's Network were able to pinpoint the declining number of well-prepared, entry-level workers in the county, the misperception among youth that manufacturing was a second-class career with no opportunity for advancement, and the need to directly interact with educators through a proactive career education event.

Likewise, after the identification of local challenges, most local development corporations should be able to help spearhead needed efforts to enhance business interaction with the community. In the case of Johnson County, this led to the creation of the annual county-wide career fair, an event which is viewed by the manufacturers, school administrators, and counselors involved as a program with lasting and long-term benefits as education and business work together in partnership- for the economic health of the community.

1995 UPDATE

On November 14, the Johnson County Development Corporation held Career Fair '95. For the first time, sophomores from all ten of the invited high schools attended. While the numbers attending varied by high school, it is estimated over 950 students visited the career fair.

A questionaire was developed by the Johnson County Development Corporation for the students to use as an "ice breaker" to start conversations with the business participants. These questionaires were distributed to high school counselors before the fair and passed out to students just before entering the career fair. The questions could be answered only by actually talking with the businesses.

It is evident the repetition of an annual career fair enhances the effectiveness of the business/educator dialogue. Since counselors are now familiar with the intent and purpose of the career fair, this year students were better informed on what to expect and how to best utilize their time at the fair. Business participants were excited about the enthusiasm shown by the students to learn about the workplace and the many opportunities for employment in Johnson County.

SUMMARY

This model of an annual county-wide career fair created by the Johnson County Development Corporation is a strong, transferable example of the sort of efficient and economical program that can be effectively sponsored by local development corporations. Such a program demonstrates to the community and its businesses that the local development corporation is concerned not only with the increasing new investment but is just as committed to reinvesting in the community's existing businesses, citizens, and resources in a substantial and concrete way.

Emerging Trends and Opportunities in Economic Development Financing

Mark Barbash

INTRODUCTION

Economic development professionals have always had to keep a watchful eye on market and political factors. The availability of public sector financing for business development has always depended on decisions made by others, namely elected officials, lenders and the voters.

Recent trends in politics, economics and the banking industry provide an opportunity for economic development decision-makers to fashion public sector solutions with a very strong market focus; programs which will provide real benefit to business and which can be flexible enough to respond to the changes in the private market place.

This article reviews three major trends and opportunities. It will also suggest an approach for decision-makers which can yield longer-term and more stable public sector financing programs.

At the heart of what economic developers are doing should always be the creation of long-term, permanent, private sector jobs. The creation of jobs in the public sector, through direct employment and "last resort" types of programs, is the field of others in this industry.

TREND #1: THE IMPACT OF INCREASED REGULATORY SCRUTINY OF THE BANKING INDUSTRY

The banking industry has been hit hard by three simultaneous events.

First, the collapse of much of the savings and loan industry has focused the regulators on the activities of the nation's banks, in an effort to forestall a similar collapse in the banking industry. Strong emphasis has been placed on bank stability, increasing loss reserves for riskier projects, maintaining control of future credit decisions. Invariably, included in these areas have been economic development projects and small business financing.

Regulators and lenders have also focused on unrealistic real estate values and environmental risks as two collateral problems which have reduced the ability to recover their investment if a loan goes bad. There is now significantly greater reluctance to lend if there is a question about value or environmental liability. This has a very strong negative impact on obtaining financing for the rehabilitation of existing commercial or industrial facilities.

And as before, lenders have always been reluctant to provide funds for critical site preparation needs (demolition, site improvement and infrastructure development, spec building construction) absent any outside credit support, such as from a municipal government or a well-capitalized developer.

Second, the wave of mergers and acquisitions in the banking industry is restructuring many of the lending institutions which have been the mainstay of the private sector economic development financing community. Banks have been evaluating various services to determine their profitability. These include the small business and government program sectors, which have traditionally been more "cost centers" than profit centers. Branches in neighborhood areas are being consolidated or eliminated with an eye towards the bottom line.

Third, bank ratings under the Community Reinvestment Act (CRA), the major legislation governing bank service to the community, are now being publicly disclosed, with the resulting increasing oversight and pressure by community and public interest organizations.

OPPORTUNITY #1: CREATIVE BANKING SOLUTIONS FOR MEETING COMMUNITY REINVESTMENT NEEDS

Bank CDC's and Local Revolving Loan Funds

To encourage lenders to look for creative solutions to their CRA responsibilities, both the Federal Reserve Bank and the Comptroller fo the Currency have been encouraging the establishment of Bank Community Development Corporations within banking institutions.

Individual banks have been reviewing their own published performance under CRA and searching for other ways of interacting more directly with economic development and housing efforts. Local revolving loan funds are being created with the first incentive funds coming from the lending community, not from the public sector.

Program Development for Bank Financing Gaps

Banks with an interest in community economic development can evaluate their own internal financing gaps and help to create programs with the public sector which meet those gaps.

For example, small loans for small businesses ("micro-lending") has traditionally been costly to lenders, due to the time and effort involved in credit underwriting when compared to the income which the loans generate for the bank.

In addition, lending restrictions caused by real estate and environmental issues should encourage lenders to develop creative partnerships with the public sector to meet legitimate job creating needs, such as in the area of infrastructure improvement and environmental cleanup of industrial facilities.

While some of this may be impacted by current regulations under consideration which would remove smaller lenders from some of their obligations under CRA, the structural gaps in bank lending are not likely to change in the near term.

TREND #2: CUTBACKS AND RE-EVALUATION OF GOVERNMENT FINANCING PROGRAMS AS A RESPONSE TO BUDGET DEFICITS

While nevertheless coinciding with an election campaign, the current public/voter concern with the budget deficit has led to increasing scrutiny of government expenditures in the economic development field.

New Governors were elected in a number of eastern and midwestern states. Some of them campaigned against the "give-aways" their predecessors gave to major companies locating large manufacturing plants in their states. Many of these Governors were also quickly confronted with major budget deficits. Among their first responses were to cut back on business financing programs, both for evaluation and for philosophical reasons.

If past history is any measure, economic development financing programs will continue to feel the budget-cutting ax at both the state and federal levels, as witnessed by:

❏ The virtual elimination of the pioneering financing programs created by the Michigan Strategic Fund (MSF).

❏ The elimination of the Urban Development Action Grant program at the federal level, first by budget cuts and second by scandal.

❏ The cutbacks in the federal Community Development Block Grant programs.

❏ The continual battle for the extension of tax exempt Industrial Revenue Bonds.

❏ The annual lobbying effort necessary to extend the programs of the Small Business Administration.

❏ The SBA MESBIC Program (Minority Enterprise Small Business Investment Corporation) has been targeted for major scrutiny which resulted in its being frozen for a time and its operations reviewed.

OPPORTUNITY #2: "DOING MORE WITH LESS" IN ECONOMIC DEVELOPMENT FINANCING

The confluence of the above trends — cutbacks in government dollars, market conditions and regulatory-caused changes — is providing the opportunity to create financing techniques which serve to establish a much stronger practical partnership with private lenders.

Guarantees

Public (non-tax) authority can be used to guarantee private sector debt, instead of (or in addition to) direct loans. For example:

❏ *Common Bond Funds* use non-project related resources to guaranty payment of bonds, often eliminating the need for Letters of Credit for Industrial Revenue Bonds and making the national capital markets accessible to smaller businesses and projects;

❏ *Capital Access Programs,* first tested in depth by the Michigan Strategic Fund, utilize limited government funds to increase the banks' loss reserves for smaller loans and riskier loans;

❏ Existing *Tax Increment Financing (TIF)* laws which allow the use of increased real estate tax revenues to pay for site improvement should be strengthened to allow bonds to be issued more easily prior to the business real estate investment.

Targeting

Direct government funds should be targeted to "non-lendable" capital investment, but which are critical to new business development and attraction, such as infrastructure development, land banking and industrial park improvement.

Reform

Program evaluations should *recognize a need and reform programs* without gutting them. The review of the MESBIC Program has improved oversight and accountability while at the same time streamlining the program's operations to enable it to make the kinds of venture investments for which it was designed.

TREND #3: DEBATE ON POLICY FOCUS FOR ECONOMIC DEVELOPMENT

Policy-makers are once again asking the question: What is the most effective way of promoting job retention and creation?

The debate is similar to the "third wave" debate which prompted the Michigan experiment. What is different this time around is that the question is being increasingly prompted by the fiscal crises at the state and federal levels.

The debate has focused on several key questions:

❏ What is the trade-off between tax abatement and the "loss" of future revenue for education and public services?

❏ Is tax abatement alone (vis-a-vis enterprise zones) sufficient to change the locational decisions of corporations?

❏ Do we need to encourage the "kitchen sink" mentality in offering tax and financing incentives to businesses who are relocating jobs from one state to another? (And increasingly from one municipality to another within the same economic market!)

❏ Is micro-economic development (project-specific investment such as loans or grants directly to businesses) effective and efficient above the local level?

❏ What are the real gaps in private sector economic development investment?

OPPORTUNITY #3: MUCH STRONGER TARGETING OF PROGRAMS

The policy questions being asked offer the opportunity to impact public sector investment in a number of positive ways, if the economic development community focuses its efforts.

Local Flexible Funding

On the theory that "all economic development is local," federal and state agencies should increasingly provide flexible funding to local economic agencies for making loans in their own communities.

At the federal level, such programs have been or are being established in the Small Business Administration (SBA 504 and the Micro Loan Program); Farmers Home Administration (Intermediary Relending Program), and in the Departments of Commerce (EDA) and Housing and Urban Development (revolving loan fund capitalization).

Many states have also adopted this approach as a way of delivering services with reduced state government staff and cultivating stronger relationships with local development leaders. Some of these programs have also targeted the small loan needs of small businesses.

Change Development Environment

Government funds should be targeted towards capital infrastructure investment, land banking and incubator/spec buildings which will change the broader atmosphere for business development, particularly in small communities and within urban areas. Such targeting should not only be through direct expenditure of government funds, but also through credit support for conventional lender investment, through the point in time when the private business investment is made.

Target Specific Groups

Funds should be targeted to assist local public/private partnerships which meet the specific business development needs of minority and women-owned businesses and low income families. Because these needs are as much training and technical assistance as they are financing, local implementation with federal or state resources and oversight is preferred.

A large number of women-owned business demonstration programs are currently being funded through the Small Business Administration. Additional funds for similar purposes are coming from HUD and other federal agencies through state intermediaries.

CREATIVE RESPONSES BY THE ECONOMIC DEVELOPMENT INDUSTRY

Capitalizing on these opportunities can result in economic development financing programs which not only have a stronger impact on job creation/retention, but also can stand the political test of time, being less susceptible to the "budget ax" when the periodic funding crises hit the rest of state government.

In order to take advantage, however, economic development professionals need to take some basic, but critical, steps in the structuring of their development organizations:

❏ Existing public/private partnerships should be reviewed to assure that they are broadly based, including decision-makers in lending, investment banking, foundations, corporate giving coordinators and community organizations.

❏ Practical day-to-day linkages among economic development professionals in neighboring states should be increased and formalized, perhaps with the assistance of professional economic development organizations. Competition between states for business investment should be done on the basis of natural attractions of their eco-nomic climates, rather than on the basis of who can write the biggest check.

❏ There should be more sharing of information among professionals about "programs that work." Reinventing the wheel in the face of budget crises is costly, takes time, and in the end, is rarely successful.

❏ Close attention should be paid to the operational details of existing programs to look for opportunities to "tinker" with the rules to make them more accessible and effective.

❏ Public relations activities on "success stories" should be increased. When the time comes for political decision-making, elected officials should know of the businesses and bankers in their districts who participated with these programs.

How To Analyze Financial Statements*

Henry L. Taylor, Sr.

INTRODUCTION

In the course of working with a prospective industry, the industrial developer will find knowledge of the prospect's financial background of vital importance. This knowledge will help the developer, the prospect, and occasionally even members of the local community. For the developer this awareness may determine whether or not the prospect is legitimate. It could provide the necessary information to rank priority of projects with respect to an overburdened schedule. Knowledge of the company's financial strength should enable the professional developer to evaluate more accurately various options of financial assistance which may be available.

There will also be times when members of the local community will call upon the industrial developer for his assessment of the company. This becomes even more important when the identity of the prospect is known only to the industrial developer. For whatever reasons, an awareness and an understanding of the prospect's financial strength is an important part of the project's development.

The purpose of this article, then, is to present an appropriate method for achieving this insight. The primary source of information from which this knowledge can be obtained is the *corporate financial statement*. Financial analysis involves the examination and interpretation of these reports.

There are two approaches to financial analysis of an industrial prospect. The easier method is the utilization of previously prepared reports and recommendations. Many sources of these reports exist, particularly if the prospect is of sufficient size. However, since all of these sources are not readily available, nor is every new industrial prospect large enough to have published financial data, the burden of the analysis falls on the industrial developer. Given the proper tools to review financial statements, he can perform an analysis sufficient for his needs.

The industrial developer is generally regarded as a "jack-of-all-trades but master of none." At home or on the road, the developer is usually the first contact the prospect has with the local area, and sometimes may be the only contact. In these situations he must be prepared to respond with a wide variety of information. He must know a little about many things and know where to get the additional details if necessary.

This condition also prevails in the financial analysis of an industrial prospect. The developer needs some knowledge of financial statements and some awareness of the prospect's financial condition. He requires the ability to converse intelligently and make reasonably basic judgements. When the time comes for a thorough detailed financial analysis, experts are usually available in the local community.

Within these limitations, the industrial developer must make his analysis. The industrial development financial analysis utilizes each of the other perspectives: credit, investment, and financial management analysis. It tests for liquidity, solvency, and profitability. However, using only these basic tests it does not attempt to be as sophisticated as the analysis in each of these specific areas.

BASIC STATEMENTS

The company's financial statements are the most important source of financial information about the prospect. They are the statistics of the annual report and are the hardest part of the report for the uninitiated person to understand. In addition to the balance sheet and the income report, a complete set of financial statements contains a statement of changes in financial position, accompanying footnotes, and possibly other statements further defining the financial operations of the company. Comprehension of these is necessary for a complete understanding of the prospect's financial condition.

Particular attention should be paid to any footnotes attached to the financial statements. They should be read carefully and considered to be an integral part of the statement. They may relay important information which cannot be abbreviated enough to appear in the statement itself. Although they may be complicated and hard to read, statement analysis is incomplete without complete interpretation of all footnotes.

The two most important and most commonly available financial statements are the *balance sheet* and the *income statement*. They are so important and so generally used in financial analysis that a thorough understanding of them is necessary. All businesses should have at least these two statements. Among the references on interpretation of financial condition, the importance of these two statements appears to be the most universally accepted.

Balance Sheet

The balance sheet, showing what the company owns and what it owes on a certain date, reveals how strong its finances are. The income statement tells how well the company did this year, whether the year was profitable or not and to what degree.

Fundamental to any analysis of a business enterprise is a test of its liquidity and its solvency. Liquidity is a measure of the convertibility of a company's assets into cash. Solvency is a measure of a company's ability to meet creditor obligations as they mature. Showing the money invested in its assets and properties and the source of these funds, the balance sheet is a good indicator of both liquidity and solvency. Since it shows past earning power, the income statement is also used to determine solvency.

A typical balance sheet for a manufacturing company appears as Table 1. Normally a balance sheet appears as a single page; if a division is necessary, it is as shown with assets on one page and liabilities on the other. The balance sheet lists all assets of the company and claims against those assets, as of the last day of the accounting period. Those claims include those of creditors, called liabilities, and those of the owners, referred to as equity or net worth.

The balance sheet is a statement of the basic accounting equation: Assets = Liabilities + Equity. From this relationship, it is easy to see why the sum of all assets equals the sum of all liabilities plus any equity. Another way to express this is: equity is equal to assets minus liabilities.

Before looking at the individual components of the balance sheet, a point of terminology needs to be made. "Current" normally refers to the next twelve months, while "long-term" is greater than one year. Thus, current assets and current liabilities are those converted to cash or payable during the coming year, as opposed to long-term or fixed assets and long-term liabilities.

The balance sheet in Table 1 is divided as to assets, liabilities, and stockholders' equity. Being incorporated, Hi-Tech's equity is comprised of stock and earnings. Assets are subdivided into current assets, plant or fixed assets, and intangible assets. Liabilities are divided into current and long-term.

There are two important terms derived from the balance sheet which surface in later analyses. Working capital, as it may be called, is the difference between total current assets and total current liabilities. Theoretically, it represents the funds available to the company for doing business during the next thirty to ninety days. Net worth or equity capital is equal to the total assets minus total liabilities. Net worth is the owners' share of the business as a result of their investment. As these terms are used often in the business world, it is important to understand their true meaning.

Income Statement

Whereas the balance sheet can be compared to a still picture -- a financial picture of business at the close of operations on the last day of the accounting period -- the income statement is a moving picture of the income and expenses during the accounting period. The income statement may also be referred to as the profit-and-loss statement or a statement of earnings.

The income statement for Hi-Tech, Inc. for the year ended December 31, 1988 is shown in Table 2. Note the first item is always the most important source of revenue and the last item is always the income or profit after all expenses and costs. Standard form usually has income and expenses related to operations separated from those unrelated.

A set of financial statements given the industrial developer by a prospect may include additional statements. Some of the more common are a statement of retained earnings, a statement of changes in financial position, or a statement of source and application of funds. They may be included for good reasons; however, the balance sheet and the income statement are the two primary statements, and it is to these two that the industrial developer should pay the most attention.

TABLE 1
Hi-Tech, Inc.
Balance Sheet
December 31, 1988

ASSETS

Current assets:		
Cash	$450,000	
Accounts receivable	2,000.000	
Inventories	2,700,000	
Total current assets		$5,150,000
Fixed assets:		
Land	$450,000	
Building	3,800,000	
Equipment	1,000,000	
Total fixed assets		5,250,000
Intangible assets		50,000
Total assets		$10,450,000

LIABILITIES

Current liabilities		
Accounts payable	$1,000,000	
Wages payable	200,000	
Est. income tax payable	400,000	
Interest payable	300,000	
Total current liabilities		$1,900,000
Long-term liabilities		3,000,000
Total liabilities		$4,900,000

STOCKHOLDERS EQUITY

Common stock	$4,000,000	
Retained earnings	1,550,000	
Total stockholders' equity		$5,550,000
Total liabilities and stockholders' equity		$10,450,000

ANALYSIS

Types of Analysis

With an understanding of the pertinent financial statements, the industrial developer is able to begin an analysis to interpret those statements and to understand the industrial prospect's financial position.

There are three types of statement analyses, depending upon the perspective of the analyst. The banker employs credit analysis since he is more concerned with liquidity and the company's ability to repay debts in the short-term. The stockholder may employ an analysis to determine the company's solvency and its earning power. The executive employs financial management analysis as a tool to measure cost and efficiency and to derive information to facilitate decision-making.

Credit analysis places more emphasis on an examination of the balance sheet, testing for liquidity and the ability to meet short-term debt. The credit lender is more interested in the relationship of current assets compared to current liabilities and the adequacy of working capital. Although before the Great Depression income statements were rarely requested, today credit lenders examine them. This is a recognition that a lack of earning power can weaken a strong working capital position, while large earnings may reduce the credit risk of a weak current position.

The primary objective of investment analysis is to appraise the prospective earning power of the company from examination of the income statement. Emphasis is placed on predicting the trends of near- and long-term earnings. It calls for an examination of the industry and the caliber of the company's management. It uses the working capital position as a measure of solvency, testing the company's ability to meet debt with reduced earnings and to finance improvements and expand without heavy borrowing.

In financial management analysis the executive is interested in promoting efficiencies, increasing profits, and providing information for sound business decisions. He analyzes the balance sheet to determine the efficiency of the utilization of assets. Comparative analysis is an important technique in which the executive may measure relative efficiency, comparing his corporation's financial statements with others in the industry. He looks for trends in sales, costs, and profit by comparing similar months of different accounting periods and the current annual report with previous ones.

The approach that the industrial developer should use in his analysis of the financial statements depends on the amount of information provided by the prospect. The minimum requirement is the balance sheet and income statement for the most recent accounting period. A comparative statement contrasting the current year with the previous one provides a minimum amount of information. Three years of financial statements make comparative analysis more meaningful. Five years of information is what a banker would prefer to see and is the period required in annual reports. Some annual reports contain a summary of ten years or more, allowing for very meaningful results from trend analysis. However, as in anything else, the developer will have to make the most of what is available.

From the balance sheet the computation of working capital (current assets minus current liabilities) is the most important consideration for the credit analyst. It indicates if adequate funds are available to run the business and its size represents the amount of "cushion" for current creditors in the event of unforeseen difficulties. In comparison with current liabilities and possibly total debt (current and long-term liabilities), working capital should be substantial. Quick assets (the sum of cash and accounts receivable) should be ample enough to cover current liabilities without the sale of any inventories. Comparing net worth (total assets minus total liabilities) with total liabilities reveals the owners' interest in the business as compared to the creditors'. The owners' interest should be at least as large, if not larger, than the creditors'. If significantly smaller, as debt grows the owners may be less inclined to stick it out and tempted to let the business "go belly up."

This analysis can be performed with only one year's balance sheet, but it may not be necessarily a totally accurate assessment. With information from several years, trends can be analyzed. Steady growth in working capital and net worth is encouraging, while continued declines could be forecasting disaster. An upward trend in sales and in net profit is also encouraging.

Examining a single item of only one financial statement has little meaning in itself. The real understanding comes when the item is examined with respect to others. For this reason ratio analysis -- "the process of determining and interpreting numerical relationships based on financial statements" -- is a very important tool in financial analysis. Ratios relate items of the income statement to each other, items of the balance sheet to each other, and items of one statement to items of the other statement.

Ratio Calculations

Calculations of ratios serves three im-

TABLE 2
Hi-Tech, Inc.
Income Statement
For Year Ended December 31, 1988

Sales	$11,000,000
Cost of goods sold	8,000,000
Gross profit on sales	$3,000,000
Operating expenses	1,000,000
Net Income from operations	$2,000,000
Interest expense	300,000
Net income before taxes	$1,700,000
Taxes	700,000
Net income after taxes	$1,000,000

---

portant purposes: (1) as a double check to ensure review of important items in the financial statements, (2) for comparison against similar company or industry standards, and (3) as an indicator of satisfactory or unsatisfactory financial condition.

The value of ratio analysis comes from comparison with a standard. There are four commonly used standards: absolute, past record, company or industry average, and budgeted. The absolute standard is a desirable "rule of thumb" regardless of the industry, time, or stage in the business cycle. Rarely used, the past standard is useful only if the past proves to be indicative of the future. Comparison with another company or an industry standard is the most commonly used technique in financial analysis. The budget standard is used in-house to compare with projections in order to measure accomplishment of goals. Selection of the proper standard is an important element in financial analysis.

Financial ratios have become so important that more and more companies are now including them in their annual reports. A number of published references[1] provide average ratios regularly for all manufacturing industries in the United States. These are useful as a bench mark for evaluating individual industries and companies provided one keeps in mind that particular conditions may cause variances from the industry averages.

With ratio analysis playing such an important part in the financial analysis of a prospect, the industrial development professional needs to know which ratios are best suited for his purposes. With the numerous amounts of information available in the balance sheet and the income statement, an almost infinite number of relationships is possible. However, seven key ratios are recommended by most experts. They are: (1) the current ratio, (2) the quick ratio, (3) debt to net worth, (4) sales to receivables, (5) sales to inventory, (6) net profit to net sales, and (7) net profit to net worth.

With these seven ratios a good insight into the prospect's financial position is available and they are well suited for the inexperienced analyst. They provide the proper test of liquidity (ability to convert assets to cash), solvency (ability to meet debt obligations as they occur), and profitability. The information for their computation is readily available from the two primary financial statements. Industry averages are available for each ratio, but in their absence most of the key ratios have some rule of thumb standards.

The current ratio and the quick ratio are good indicators of liquidity. The *current ratio* is equal to current assets divided by current liabilities, and is one of the best measures of financial strength, it indicates the relationship of current debt and the ability of the firm to meet it. The rule of thumb standard of 2:1 indicates that there are enough current assets available to meet current liabilities with allowance for a margin of safety.

The *quick ratio* is also called the "acid test" and is equal to the quick assets (cash and accounts receivable) divided by current liabilities. It is a better indicator of liquidity since it omits inventories, significant because most other components of current assets are either cash or one transaction from cash. Inventories require two transactions, conversion to accounts receivable and then conversion to cash. A minimum quick ration of 1:1 is recommended. Any ratio less than one means the company could not quickly meet its obligations and this could be indicative of problems.

The *debt to net worth ratio* is the most important test of solvency and is equal to total liabilities divided by net worth (assets minus liabilities). This ratio is used to measure the extent to which company operations are financed by borrowed funds. It represents the relationship of total borrowed capital to total capital invested by owners. A conservative rule of thumb to indicate satisfactory solvency is 2:3 or 66 percent; anything larger is less solvent. A condition of 1:1 indicates the creditors own as much of the business as the owners do. It is a path to bankruptcy when debt grows to the point where creditors are the larger owners of the business, for in almost every bankruptcy, total debt will substantially exceed net worth.

The *sales to receivables* ratio is also referred to as the turnover of accounts receivable. It is equal to sales divided by accounts receivable. A ratio of four, for example, says that accounts receivable were paid or turned over four times during the year. It also says one fourth of the year's sales had not been collected at the end of the accounting period. The average collection period is equal to 360 days divided by the accounts receivable runover.

This average period for collecting accounts receivable can then be compared to the company's terms of sale. In our example, the average collection period is 90 days. Should the company's terms call for 30 days net, management has been lax in collecting the accounts receivable, and this puts a drain on working capital.

Turnover of inventory is another name for the *sales to inventory* ratio. It is equal to sales divided by inventory and represents the number of times the inventory turns over or sells during the accounting period. It is a measure of efficiency, with higher numbers indicating good merchandising and more profits. Inventory turnover varies with the industry and is normally compared against industry standards.

The other two ratios are measures of profitability and can be used by management to measure efficiencies. The *net profit to net sales* ratio is equal to the net profit after taxes divided by net sales. It indicates the number of cents of profit the company made for each dollar of sales. It is often compared with ratios for similar companies or against previous years.

The *net profit to net worth* ratio is often referred to as the return on investment (ROI). It is equal to the net profit after taxes divided by the net worth. This represents the profit generated by the owners' investment in the company, showing cents of profit per dollar of investment. Management reviews the return on investment before making major outlays for new plants and equipment. If it borrows money for expansion, the ROI should exceed the rate of interest. If it utilizes surplus cash, ROI should exceed the interest rate available on the more secure investments.

It should be apparent how important the seven key ratios are in analyzing the financial statements of a company. They provide proper tests of liquidity, solvency, and profitability. They are easy to calculate and compare with standards. Finally, they serve to ensure that important items of the financial statement have been examined by the analyst.

THE BOTTOM LINE

Steps in the Analysis

The first step in the industrial developer's analysis is to secure financial statements from the prospect. These should be from the company's most recently completed fiscal year or accounting period. If more are available, at least the last two or three years are recommended. The more years that are available, the better it is. If financial statements are unavailable, income tax reports are possible substitutes.

The next step is to evaluate the quality of the statements provided. The report from an independent accounting firm states that the records were audited and to what degree. If the statements were prepared in-house, look for a signature of a corporate officer and determine if they are interim, year end or estimated.

Examine the package of statements, paying particular attention to the balance sheet and income statement. All the appropriate footnotes should be read and understood.

The next step is to examine and analyze the two primary statements. On the balance sheet, working capital, quick assets, and net worth are calculated and compared with current liabilities and total liabilities where appropriate. On the income statement, the examination is for profit or loss -- the bottom line. If statements from two or more years are avail-able, a trend analysis is performed. In the examination of working capital, net worth, sales and profits over a period of time, a steady positive trend of growth is desirable.

To complete the examination, a basic ratio analysis is performed. Using the data from the most recent statements, seven key ratios are calculated. These are compared with the rule of thumb standards, and if a reference of industry ratios is available, compared against them. If additional data are available, trends of the key ratios may provide some insight to the future.

Though not mandatory for this analysis, one comparison can be made for personal interest. Is the prospect's most recent rate of return on investment (ROI) in excess of the rate of interest for any borrowing for capital expansion?

With this analysis completed, the industrial development professional now possesses a greater understanding of his prospect's financial position. Now he can participate in financial discussions with authority. He can make more enlightened decisions and recommendations. He is better able to serve his prospect and his community.

Case Example

Table 3 contains a summary of the financial statements provided by a small manufacturing company during its site selection process. It is well suited to serve as an example of the financial analysis the industrial developer can perform. The pertinent data of the statements are summarized rather than complete reproduction of them in their entirety.

The summary of the prospect's financial statements appears in a form similar to a technique the banking community calls "statement spreading." In this case, it lists only the numbers from the statements necessary for the industrial developer to perform his analysis. The eight items in the first group are taken from the statements for the appropriate years, while the remaining items in the other two groups are calculated from these eight. The second group shows the prime components of a balance sheet analysis. The last group displays the seven key ratios to test liquidity, solvency, and profitability. Once the data have been calculated and arranged in this format, the industrial developer can make his analysis quickly and easily.

In 1988, both the current assets and quick assets were far in excess of current liabilities and even compared favorably against total liabilities. There was a large cushion of working capital for future contingencies. Net worth indicated the owners' interest in the company was much greater than the creditors. The company's operations showed a good profit with strong sales.

A trend analysis for the last three years reveals steady growth overall, with a fluctuation in 1987 and subsequent recovery in the following year. Without the later recovery, the loss of profits in 1987 could indicate a serious problem. The dip in working capital in that same year is, no doubt, the result of a four-fold increase in current liabilities, which were reduced the next year. Nevertheless, the strong showing of the company at the end of 1988 speaks well for management's ability to recover from the earlier fluctuations.

The ratio analysis verifies these initial conclusions. The company was extremely liquid, and could easily cover its current liabilities without the sale of inventory.

TABLE 3
Summary of Prospect
Financial Statements, 1986-1988

Statement item	1988	1987	1986
From Statements			
Current assets	$65,554	$58,593	$52,207
Current liabilities	11,112	20,054	5,751
Total assets	151,759	129,220	114,948
Total liabilities	29,612	46,054	32,151
Inventory	38,985	25,829	27,322
Receivables	14,048	14,704	12,731
Sales	333,743	173,049	162,867
Net Profit	39,837	367	19,906
Components from Balance Sheet			
Working capital	$54,442	$38,539	$46,456
Quick assets	25,164	32,764	24,885
Net worth	122,147	83,166	82,797
Key Ratios			
Current ratio	5.9	2.9	9.1
Quick ratio	2.3	1.6	4.3
Debt/net worth	.24	.55	.39
Sales/receivables	23.8	11.8	12.8
Sales/inventory	8.6	6.7	6.0
Net profit/net sales	.119	.002	.122
Net profit/net worth	.326	.004	.240

The owners' interest was 4:1 compared to creditors'. A high turnover of accounts receivable is evident with the average collection period (360 divided by sales/receivables), of approximately fifteen days. The inventory turned over rapidly allowing for more profit. The company realized almost twelve cents of profit for each dollar of sales. The rate of return on investment (net profit/net worth) was large enough to justify capital expansion even in times of high interest rates.

As for expansion by this prospect, due to its small size and relatively small net worth, leasing (as opposed to buying) a facility for its relocation was recommended. The debt necessary to purchase a building was larger than the company can afford and would cause the debt/net worth ratio to approach critical levels. Smaller capital outlays for items such as equipment was recommended.

The company's philosophy at the time was to plow all the profits back into the business rather than acquire real estate. Examination of the new profit/net worth ratio confirmed the wisdom of this approach, since every dollar of additional investment produced 32.6 cents of profit.

The bottom line was that this prospect represented a small, very healthy, growing manufacturing company with conservative management deserving of a good recommendation. With these statements and a lease commitment from the prospect, a local developer obtained building financing from a bank. A facility was built which the prospect occupied and the company today is thriving.

NOTES

[1]Three good sources of industry ratios for all segments of manufacturing are *Statement Studies* by Robert Morris Associates, *Key Business Ratios* by Dun and Bradstreet, Inc., and *Almanac of Business and Industrial Financial Ratios* by Prentice-Hall, Inc. All are available at most larger libraries and many banks have a copy of *Statement Studies*.

* Reprinted with the permission of the Southern Economic Development Council.

The Bank Community Development Corporation: An Underutilized Tool for Economic Development

Anne Nickel

The economic development community has not taken full advantage of a financing tool that has been made available by both the Federal Reserve Board (FDB) and the Office of the Comptroller of the Currency (OCC), regulators of bank holding companies and banks. That tool is the Bank Community Development Corporation (CDC).

A DEVELOPMENT TOOL

A bank CDC is unique because it allows banks and bank holding companies to venture into investment areas that are outside the scope of their normally permitted activities. The CDC program permits banks to make direct equity and other investments in community development corporations, business ventures, or community development projects which serve predominantly civic, community, or public purposes.

The key here is the purpose of the CDC investment. If it serves the public good, a CDC may purchase, own, rehabilitate, construct, manage, and sell real property. It also allows banks to make equity or debt investments in local business and development projects. Historically, banks only financed these activities. Through a CDC, banks can become directly involved in executing and benefitting from them.

National banks may establish wholly-owned bank subsidiary CDCs. They may also help form and capitalize multibank CDCs, invest in existing CDCs, or invest in qualifying community development projects or ventures. Bank holding companies' CDCs may buy, sell and manage real estate, take equity positions in small businesses, act as joint venture partners and deal in syndications. Although the CDC requirements of the FRB and the OCC are different, the regulators' reason for allowing nonbanking activities is the same. As long as the bank powers are used to revitalize economically distressed areas and to help the residents who live in the areas, bank CDCs are permissible.

A RECENT TOOL

Although CDCs have been around since the 1960's, bank CDCs are a fairly new financing tool. It wasn't until the 1980's that the federal regulators began to encourage their use as a method of financing economically depressed areas.

Trying to interest banks in participating in development of distressed areas was no easy task. " High Risk" is a label attached to these neighborhoods, a label incompatible with prudent banking practices. The role the CDC asks the bank to play does not fit the traditional and conservative role of banks. Banks rely on market forces to dictate worthy projects; CDCs claim that market forces tend to shun poor communities. Bank decisions are based on profit and economic benefits; CDC decisions are based on outcome and social benefits. It became the role of the CDC advocates to convince the banking industry that a significant market existed that could not be addressed through conventional banking practices; that the market existed in low-income neighborhoods; that there was and is economic payback through investments in this market. The problem was getting the banking industry to listen.

Fortunately, the Community Reinvestment Act (CRA), passed by Congress in 1977, serves as a strong reminder that banks are obligated to meet the credit needs of their community and must give a yearly account of how they implement this act. This became an effective aid in persuading banks to look at CDCs as an effective way to extend credit to depressed areas.

The lending industry got added encouragement when all their regulators issued a joint statement in 1989 defining their CRA expectations and recommending a process to be used. This statement urged lenders to use a process that defines their community, determines its credit needs and takes steps to meet those needs through appropriate and prudent lending efforts. The process requires input from the community and its development groups. The groups are invited to make suggestions on how the bank can be more successful in meeting the community's credit needs.

COMMUNITY DEVELOPMENT FINANCING

As a result of these efforts, a new banking concept, "community development financing", has emerged. Although similar to conventional banking, it has marked differences.

The major difference is the subordination of the principle of profit maximization. The focus of community development financing is on community needs and objectives. The challenge is to apply good banking principles to projects identified through a community process. The credit needs of these projects are usually not within the conventional limits of bank financing. The bank, therefore, had to create a mechanism or a service that utilized creative financing methods. CDCs fit the need.

EXAMPLES

Community development financing has taken many forms as lenders across the country tailor their programs to their community's needs. A good example is the Community Investment Fund (CIF) set up in 1985 by the Federal Home Loan Bank of San Francisco to assist its member institutions in financing their community lending and reinvestment activities. It made $500 million available. Eligible projects, from member institutions, state and local governments, and non-profits, had to directly benefit low or moderate income people or revitalize downtown areas or older neighborhoods. In the first year, $47 million in community investment advancements were made. This money facilitated over $100 million in projects indicating that the CIF was an active leveraging agent with other private, public, or foundation funding sources. Projects ranged from downtown redevelopment in San Diego to industrial development in Los Angeles Watt's area to housing projects throughout the state.

Not all CDCs are large. Small towns use them effectively. Key Bank in Chester, New York, formed a CDC in 1986, with $250,000 equity investment, to promote the revitalization of their community through acquisition, ownership, renovation, leasing, managing, mortgaging, selling or promoting of real estate from residential or commercial use.

In McAllister, Oklahoma, the local bank, First National Bank and Trust Company, capitalized its CDC with $150,000. The CDC provides financial and technical assistance for a variety of community projects in McAllister and smaller surrounding communities.

With the rise of CDCs, a variety of tools and techniques have developed. Their primary purpose is to package loans in such a way as to make as much as possible of the required financing qualify for conventional lending. Because the borrower usually has limited means, the cost of the loan and the monthly payments are a major consideration. The flexibility offered through a CDC can help by reducing the amount of conventional loans needed, by reducing the rate of interest (through a high risk fund or pool), or by lengthening the loan terms.

SUMMARY

The more banks become involved with community financing or CDCs, the more its advantages become obvious. Banks have a vested interest in where its loans have been made. A stable and economically healthy community helps protect the banks collateral used for its loans and the borrower's ability to repay the loan. Markets, once closed to lenders because of policies and perceptions, are opened and defined. New products are being developed to address these market needs, increasing profits for the lenders.

Bank CDCs can be an invaluable tool for the Economic Development professional. It brings together all the forces at play within the community, articulates development goals and a plan to reach those goals, and creates access to the capital necessary to implement the plan.

To see if a bank or savings and loan has a CDC, one should look at the annual CRA report. To find out how to get a CDC set up, one should contact any one of the lenders' regulators. Each regulator has a CDC specialist now on staff.

Advantages & Disadvantages Of Tax Increment Financing

Mark Royse

INTRODUCTION

Declining revenues from both federal and state funding sources are forcing communities to assume responsibility for financing economic development projects. State laws, fortunately, provide communities with mechanisms to raise the needed revenue. Typically, these mechanisms allow communities to raise existing taxes or impose new taxes. Given the wave of the "no new taxes" movement at all levels of government, local elected officials are placed in an unenviable position. Local leaders are attempting to find revenue sources without having to increase taxes. Tax increment financing is one option that communities have. Before pursuing tax increment financing, however, local elected officials and the public need to understand the advantages and disadvantages of this financing option.

BENEFITS OF TAX INCREMENT FINANCING

There are four benefits of using tax increment financing. First, tax increment financing is not a direct tax. Second, tax increment financing is a flexible tool. Third, tax increment financing debt is generally not included in debt limitations, such as Indiana's two percent debt limitation. Fourth, TIF is more controllable than other economic development incentives.[1]

Not A Direct Tax

In Indiana, as in most states, tax increment financing is one financing option identified that is not a direct tax on the income or property of the public. This does not mean that TIF is the best financing option. Since TIF is not a direct tax increase, TIF is a more acceptable type of financing to local elected officials. Although approval of a tax increment financing project in Indiana requires a public hearing, the process does not afford opponents the same ability to remonstrate as it allows for other financing options (e.g., general obligation bond financing).

Flexible

Tax increment financing is a flexible tool. Most states with TIF legislation now allow local governments to use TIF to finance more types of projects. The original intent of TIF was for urban renewal projects, but states are changing the legal definition to cover more than just slum and blight projects.[2] Also, TIF can finance projects in different ways. In Fort Wayne and Allen County, Indiana, tax increment financing revenues are repaying a state loan, retiring a bond, and covering lease payments.

No Impact on Debt Limitation

Tax increment financing relies only on the increased tax revenue of a designated TIF area. Tax increment financing debt is not backed by tax revenues from all real estate in a city or county. This means tax increment financing debt is not a general obligation of a community and does not fall under the two percent debt limit of the community. This is positive in two ways. First, if a community is at or close to its debt limit, TIF can be used as an alternative source of financing. If a community is not close to its debt limit, TIF can be used in order to save the community's general obligation bonding capability for the future or other capital projects that cannot be financed using TIF.

Controllable

Tax increment financing is more controllable than other economic development incentives. Tax increment financing is used for specific public improvements to serve specific economic development projects. The additional tax revenue generated from the increased assessed value in a TIF area pays for public improvements in that area. Paying off the debt issued for the public improvements precludes the need to capture additional tax revenues. The additional tax revenue is then available to the other taxing units within the taxing district. Also, the public improvements are usually road improvements or utility extensions. This means that others can benefit from these improvements. However, this is not the case with other types of economic development incentives.

Advantages over Incentives

The most common incentive offered to induce development in Allen County, Indiana is tax abatement. This type of incentive provides financial assistance to the company receiving tax abatement and does not provide a direct benefit to other taxpayers. Second, the total amount of the financial assistance a company receives is not known at the time the abatement is approved. Last, since the abatement period can last for a period of ten years, it is more difficult to determine the cost versus the benefits.

Like tax abatement, the Urban Enterprise Zone incentive is a tax deduction. The deduction applies to the inventory of businesses located within an enterprise zone. Again, this incentive provides direct financial assistance to a particular company, but does not directly benefit others. Also, the total amount of the benefit is unknown, and a company receives the tax break based on the location of the company. The company does not have to realistically provide any benefit back to the community.

DISADVANTAGES OF USING TAX INCREMENT FINANCING

Just as four benefits of TIF have been identified and explained, there are also four drawbacks of using tax increment financing.

The first disadvantage of using tax increment financing is its effect on tax rates. Second, tax increment financing affects certain taxpayers more than others. Third, tax increment financing is subject to higher costs compared to conventional forms of financing. Fourth, some question whether or not tax increment financing actually induces an economic development project.

Impact on Tax Rates

Tax increment financing relies on the property tax revenue generated from the *increase* in taxable assessed value in a designated area. This tax revenue covers the tax increment financing obligation (e.g., a bond, lease, or loan). In effect, the

149

taxable assessed value of a taxing unit is reduced by the assessed value deduction for tax increment financing projects. This precludes the *increased* property tax revenue from being distributed to the existing taxing units within a taxing district where a TIF deduction is in effect. Taxing units include the county's general fund, the airport authority, and the applicable school district's general fund.

Most taxing units in Indiana compensate for a lower net assessed value through having a higher tax rate. The difference between this higher rate and the rate without the assessed value deduction for TIF represents the effect on tax rates and the indirect tax passed on to property owners.

There are also certain taxing units that have a set rate that cannot increase to compensate for a lower net assessed value. Examples of these units include the cumulative capital development fund for Allen County and the cumulative capital fund for each of the school districts. These units lose actual dollars as the net assessed value is reduced by the deduction for tax increment financing.

Selective Tax Payer Impact

Tax increment financing also may affect certain tax payers more than others. In Indiana, local communities can either grant the State Property Tax Replacement Credit (SPTRC) or not. The SPTRC reduces a taxpayers rate by up to 20%. If a tax payer in a TIF area has an increased net assessed value, that increase may not be eligible for the SPTRC. The increase in net assessed value can result from a declining percentage of a tax abatement or from a general property reassessment. A community may not grant the SPTRC to assure the required debt coverage ratio for a bond or to reduce the term of a bond. This means that a property owner in a TIF area may pay higher taxes than other property owners within the same taxing district. This can occur even if the property owner does not make any improvements to the property.

Potentially Expensive

Tax increment financing may be more costly than other types of financing. For example, general obligation (G.O.) bonds are secured by property tax revenue generated from all property owners. TIF relies on revenue from a limited geographic area. Also, TIF requires an increase in assessed value which is not always guaranteed. This makes a TIF bond riskier than a G.O. bond, resulting in a higher interest rate and more total interest paid. Also, there are higher issuance costs, including feasibility studies, outside financial audits, and extra legal fees.[3]

Need

An additional drawback of TIF is one that is common to all economic development incentives. There are those who believe that an economic development project would occur without certain financial incentives. These incentives could include tax abatement, industrial revenue bond financing, infrastructure grants, and job training assistance. As TIF becomes a more common method of financing economic development projects, this issue is certain to be raised.

SUMMARY

Tax increment financing is a local revenue source available to communities for economic development projects. Before implementing a tax increment financing program, communities need to understand the advantages and disadvantages of tax increment financing. The major benefit of tax increment financing is that it is not a direct tax. The biggest drawback of TIF is that it affects the rates of taxing units.

RECOMMENDATIONS

The following recommendations apply not only to communities in Indiana, but also to those communities in other states that have tax increment financing legislation.

First, using TIF to finance economic development projects requires understanding the opportunities and limitations of the state enabling legislation that allows tax increment financing. Also, the economic developer must be able to explain simply the mechanics of tax increment financing to local elected officials and the public.

Second, the economic developer must have an understanding of the state and local tax system in order to show the effect of TIF on tax rates and taxing units. This understanding is necessary so TIF projects are presented based on facts and not beliefs. Also, this understanding aids in analyzing the effect of individual projects as well as the overall effect of using TIF.

Third, using TIF requires a continued evaluation of TIF's effect on tax rates and tax units. Depending on the amount of net assessed value reduced by the TIF deduction, the tax rates may be minimally or significantly affected. Policy makers need to identify the point at which they believe the use of TIF constitutes a burden on tax rates. Monitoring the overall effect of the TIF deduction on tax rates requires an annual evaluation of the use of TIF.

Fourth, a community must address the negative aspects of tax increment financing. A community should strive to limit the effect of TIF on tax rates and taxing units. This can be accomplished by guiding TIF developments to areas of a community where the effect will not be as great. Second, a community should find ways to offset any additional cost to taxing units and individual property owners. Third, a community must weigh the additional cost of TIF financing versus using other financing methods such as general obligation bonding.

Employing these recommendations should help in using tax increment financing in a fiscally responsible manner.

FOOTNOTES

[1]Maribeth Backman, "Tax Increment Financing for Indiana Municipalities," (unpublished paper, Institute of Government Finance, Indiana University-Purdue University at Fort Wayne), 1984, pg. 8.
[2]Tschangho John Kim, Clyde W. Forrest, and Karen A. Przypyszny, "Determining Potential Gains and Losses of TIF," *Tax Increment Financing*, Planning Advisory Service Report Number 389, July 1985, pg. 11.
[3]Maribeth Beckman, "Tax Increment Financing for Indiana Municipalities," (unpublished paper, Institute of Government Finance, Indiana University-Purdue University at Fort Wayne), 1984, pg. 9.

Incentives As a Public Business Investment

Kate McEnroe, MBA

The use of incentives as a marketing tool involves both the formulation of a policy or policy guidelines and the development of an incentive negotiation strategy. For the economic development practitioner, policy defines the tools to use and the negotiation strategy determines when and how these tools will be used. From the prospect's point of view, the incentive policy provides the tangible benefits that affect the timing and economics of a project, while the negotiation strategy provides the sense of satisfaction of having aggressively pursued the best available deal on behalf of the company.

RIGHT OR WRONG?

Whether it is "fair" to request or "right" to grant incentives are two of the most often debated issues in our industry today, and airing views on these issues is a familiar precursor to the formation of any area's incentive policy. From the community's perspective, those who object to incentive programs often cite the following positions:

❑ Business should not be receiving incentives paid for with dollars that could be going into education and other important programs.

❑ Businesses offer no guarantees that they will stay in the community or maintain employment after incentives are granted.

❑ Granting incentives to selected companies provides an open invitation to an escalating cycle of demands.

❑ Companies should display more loyalty to their communities and want to be good corporate citizens; they should not demand incentives as payment for staying in the community.

❑ States, cities, and counties should all agree not to give incentives and to compete on their merits.

On the other hand, those in favor of aggressive state and community policies believe that discussion of right or wrong is outweighed by the competitive realities of the marketplace and the pressure to announce attractive expansions and relocations.

From the perspective of the prospects and their advisors, requests for incentives are the logical result of tighter margins and a broader variety of good location choices. Their positions focus on the benefits that they bring to the community and a desire to share in those benefits themselves, as typified by the following perspectives:

❑ Communities should look upon incentives as investments, which carry some risk, but the potential for great reward.

❑ If businesses do not thrive, there will be fewer overall tax dollars for education; the community still gets the lion's share of the tax and employment benefits a new business generates.

❑ Loyalty to community is an important company value, but not at the expense of competitiveness; a business is worth nothing to its community if it goes under.

In much the same way that community politics affects an area's approach to incentive policy, corporate politics and culture affect the definition of a successful site location project and often create an environment which requires the prospect to be an aggressive negotiator.

THE INCENTIVE NEGOTIATION MINDSET

We live and do business in the United States today in an environment that encourages and rewards cost cutting and aggressive negotiating. In our personal lives we thrive on finding sales, factory outlets, and flea market bargains. Paying the sticker price for a car, for example, is generally regarded as naive. This same mindset has come to characterize many facets of the site location process. To be and feel successful, a site selector wants not only to find the best place to do business, but to make "the best deal". If the best deal means getting as much as or even more than anyone else has

gotten, it is easy to wind up in a situation of continuously escalating demands.

This situation is further complicated by the environment of imperfect information in which negotiations take place. Although many incentive programs are statutory, and well documented, prospects often have the lingering perception that other incentives have been granted, but are not publicly acknowledged for fear that they will have to be duplicated. As a result, prospects will use a number of methods, including hiring consultants, to uncover this anecdotal information and provide some assurance that nothing is "left on the table" because it was not requested. Prospects often perceive the statutory "as of right" programs as a starting point and measure success by the unique incentives above and beyond that they are able to secure. In this situation, the leaders who have access to discretionary funds will have the flexibility to respond creatively to individual situations.

The challenges of operating in the dark also affect the economic development practitioner and are unlikely to change. Full disclosure of a company's financial status and business plans are always desirable, but rarely are available early enough in the process to make the practitioner comfortable.

Even when information is provided, the pace of change is so rapid that the information may not remain constant even during the course of the project. At one time, during the era of the Bell System divestiture, several back office projects were ongoing for AT&T. Staffing projection changes were provided on a weekly basis which dramatically and repeatedly changed project specifications throughout the entire selection process. Although this may have been an extreme example, quite often if a prospect cannot be pinned down on specifics, it will be because the specifics are not yet completely defined. More and more often companies are adopting the Ford Taurus model for product development, which means that engineering, marketing, finance, manufacturing, and facility plans are all being developed simultaneously, and a change in one area can affect all areas.

POSSIBILITIES AND LIMITATIONS

Since the issue of incentives is fraught with both emotion and conflict, it is important to understand exactly what can be accomplished through their use. Incentives are typically used to increase prospect traffic to an area (a marketing tool) and/or to close a deal that has come down to a short list (a sales tool).

If incentives are used prominently in marketing programs, it should come as no surprise that many prospects will be focused on incentives from the outset. Promoting incentives to increase traffic can be very effective, however, if program elements are communicated clearly and accompanied by realistic portrayals of an area's other assets and liabilities. Kentucky's statewide incentive programs gained great exposure in a short time through a highly effective road show built around a simple one page worksheet showing the variables and calculations that determine incentive levels. Pueblo, Colorado is an often cited example of a community that used an incentive based marketing approach some years ago to draw prospects into a community industrial park. For a community experiencing significant unemployment and in need of a method of quickly increasing employment opportunities, marketing incentives proved to be the right strategy at the right time.

When used as a sales tool, if properly designed and implemented, incentives can help to swing decisions on expansions and relocations to a community by:

❑ Satisfying the need for negotiation.

❑ Differentiating among areas that are very similar.

❑ Meeting competitive standards for infrastructure readiness.

❑ Satisfying corporate financial benchmarks.

❑ Offsetting one-time relocation costs.

❑ Providing assurances in an unfamiliar environment.

Incentives also have their limitations, which should be considered before a great deal of hope is invested in these programs as a means to turn around an economic situation. In competition for projects that have short time frames, incentives will not be effective as a substitute for timely delivery of a site, building, or labor force. Incentives are also generally ineffective as a means of overcoming long term fatal flaws; for example, if the project requires access to an international airport, incentives may cause the decision maker to relax the requirement from one hour distance to one and one-half hour distance, but they will not eliminate that requirement.

States and communities should also listen carefully to the reasons that prospects give for requesting incentives and factor them into their response. Incentives can-

not, in and of themselves, make an unsuccessful company successful, nor are they likely to solve the problems of the high cost producer in an industry, since they eventually run out.

MATCHING INCENTIVE PROGRAMS TO PROJECTS

The most effective incentives for a project are those that target a key area of competitive advantage for the company or offset a disadvantage for the community (Figure 1).

For companies that are competing primarily in the area of product and service quality, training the workforce may be the most critical area of assistance. Companies that are in industries competing on cost will be attracted to incentives that reduce their land or facility cost, or their tax liability. Some projects, particularly those trying to beat a competitor to market with a new product, are very time sensitive; in these cases, incentives which save time or guarantee delivery dates, such as infrastructure preparation or permitting assistance, are particularly appealing. Since time is so often a critical location factor, incentives that delay a client's schedule will not be effective if alternatives are available. This situation often arises in the area of infrastructure. Commitments to clear and grade a site or build a road, for example, are only perceived as incentives if the project can wait for the work to be done and if the competition offers no faster-track alternative. Communities and states should review their target industries and make sure that the types of incentive programs they

are prepared to support match the needs of the industries being targeted.

When resource constraints are prohibitive, or creativity is called for, providing effective linkages for existing and new businesses can be a high impact, low cost, inducement strategy (Figure 2).

Acting as a resource to bring together employers and employees has always been a role for economic development professionals, but it will become even more critical and complex in the future. In addition to the connections to traditional full time workers, companies are looking for ways to connect with older workers, students, temporary workers or agencies, and small businesses or independent contractors that perform functions historically handled by in-house staffs.

There is also a role for economic developers to play in connecting prospects with suppliers and customers. Once companies are established, it is not uncommon for chambers of commerce and other business organizations to foster this type of networking. Engaging in this type of matchmaking before the decision is made can provide the prospect with one more reason to perceive an area as more attractive and better prepared.

For the future, the most valuable connection may be to users of a company's byproducts. Byproduct disposal is projected to be one of the fastest growing operating costs for manufacturing and service businesses alike. At the same time, commercial uses are being developed for a wide range of byproducts, including paper, oil, and rubber. The major stumbling block for many of these ventures is the inability to match

---

FIGURE 1
Matching Incentives to Need

NEED		INCENTIVE
• Quality	→	Training
• Cost	→	Land cost; tax reduction
• Timing	→	Infrastructure; permitting

FIGURE 2
Required Company Linkages

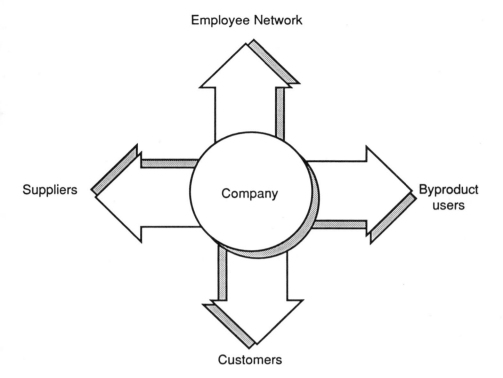

producers of byproducts with users. By playing a role in facilitating these matches, a community is also helping itself minimize its own waste disposal burden.

THE INVESTMENT APPROACH

At the foundation of any area's incentive strategy should be a well defined set of potential tools and a set of guidelines on when and how to use those tools. The single most important element of a successful incentive strategy is the willingness and ability to walk away from a project if the price is too high. The second most important thing to remember is that the price will be different for every area and for every project.

In the best of all possible situations, the components of an incentive program are designed based on the needs or desires expressed by prospect companies and lead to a win-win situation for the state, the community, and the company. In the real world, they are always heavily influenced by resource constraints and political constituencies. An investment approach can help to separate the incentive process from the political process, but it must be developed on a proactive basis; to expect to

develop such a concensus in the heat of the hunt for a large project is an invitation to failure.

Using an investment approach, the state or community should:

❑ Quantify the benefits of the project.

❑ Determine the required rate of return.

❑ Consider alternative investments.

❑ Determine the appropriate level of investment.

❑ Refuse to exceed this level of investment, without corresponding increases in benefits.

By contrast, an incentive policy that is ruled by a political approach allows the desire to win to obscure the judgment of benefits, and neglects to evaluate the "prize". Worst of all, because the process is transformed into a win-lose proposition, those who have staked reputations on the win leave themselves no room to back away from a project that has gotten too expensive to yield a net benefit to the community.

Quantifying the benefits of a project has always been one of the more difficult aspects of evaluating a prospect's attractiveness. There are many theories regarding the

correct multipliers to use which will accurately predict the spin-off jobs and revenues generated by projects, each with their own rationale. At the present time, there does not seem to be any one theory that will apply to every community and every situation. In the absence of specific, valid data, the best approach is to create a number of scenarios, supported by research in other similar projects wherever possible.

A successful incentive policy will not win all projects, but will win projects that are good for the state and good for the community. While the individual components will differ depending on the characteristics of the community and its economy, the ruling elements behind the policy should be:

❑ Applicable to all types of business.

❑ Contains a process for quantifying costs and benefits to the community (an impact model with scenarios).

❑ Pre-sets guidelines for investment and required return.

❑ Draws on benchmark research of business requirements and cost profiles.

❑ Displays a true understanding of competitive advantages and disadvantages.

❑ Contains a procedure for quick response.

❑ Exists before the prospect calls.

❑ Allows the community to walk away from bad deals.

❑ Contains safeguards to protect the community's investment.

There is virtually no way to guarantee that the jobs projected by a prospect will materialize. As has been seen in recent years, companies cannot guarantee anything to their employees about their futures, much less make guarantees to communities. It is possible, however, to attempt to build in safeguards for the state's and community's investments. The most logical and acceptable form of safeguards are to tie incentive awards to successive levels of job creation and investment.

KEY TRENDS IN
REQUESTS AND PROGRAMS

The key trends evident in prospects' requests for specific types of incentives reflect the rapid rate of change affecting business.

The issues prospects with large projects continue to look for assistance on are:

❑ Initial and ongoing employee training.

❑ Land acquisition and facility construction costs.

❑ Project timing.

❑ Reduction of tax liability.

❑ Control of future environment.

The heavy requests for intensive and ongoing training support, for example, reflect the United States' continuing advantage in knowledge-based manufacturing and service businesses. Noticeably missing from this list is access to low cost capital. Large companies with large projects have often developed sources of capital at rates competitive with those a state or community can provide. For the smaller companies, however, access to low cost working capital and venture capital remains very important. Although each project that comes from smaller companies does not represent as great an individual impact, they are projected to be the group that will generate the greatest number of jobs.

On the community side, new state programs are changing the balance of state versus community contributions to incentive packages, and raising the business community's awareness of the programs available to them. Oklahoma, North Carolina, Georgia, Ohio, Kentucky, and several other states have developed and implemented new program elements, and many more are on the horizon. Most of these programs are tied to job creation and offer training and tax benefits; however many provide for more discretionary power to negotiate and creatively use earmarked funds as appropriate for individual projects. While these newer programs continue to focus most incentives toward less advantaged areas, usually with some form of sliding scale of benefits, they show significantly more flexibility in the types of projects they consider eligible. Progress is being made, for example, in treating office-based prospects on an equal footing with manufacturing projects of similar impact for incentive purposes. Traditionally, incentive programs were developed to support manufacturing projects on the theory that they were most plentiful, highest paying, and had the greatest multiplier impact. Over the past several years, as office based projects have grown in number and economic impact, programs have begun to change accordingly.

FUTURE CHALLENGES

The argument that has been used to justify awarding incentives to any given project has been its ability to create jobs and generate tax revenue. A project's desirability is typically measured by the magnitude of its investment and the number of full-time, permanent jobs with benefits that are created. The challenge for the future will be to structure incentive programs that address the impact created by companies that use non-traditional staffing strategies, the so called networked businesses or virtual corporations. Many business experts are predicting that the model corporate organization in the future will contain only a small core of full-time permanent employees, supplemented by much larger cadres of temporary workers and outsourced services. Today, we do not typically "credit" a project with job creation unless the company is the direct employer; this approach may have to change if alternative staffing becomes the rule rather than the exception. Our traditional assumptions used in multiplier models hold that indirect employment resulting from a project generally consists of lower paid jobs than direct employment; in the case of employers who make heavy use of temporary agencies, the reverse may be true.

A second challenge will come from the projection that most new growth will come from small to mid-sized companies, and therefore from smaller projects. Small businesses and "lone eagle entrepreneurs" are also expected to be strong growth niches and will require new focus. Their need for access to low cost capital, as mentioned earlier, should lead to a renewed interest in incubators, small business programs, and venture capital corporations, perhaps with public investment. It would not be surprising to see a ranking among the best cities in which to start a business, gain the same prestige as a ranking among the best cities for business.

A third challenge will be to design incentive programs that respond to the borderless view of geography prospects hold. The positive economic impacts of a project are felt well beyond the boundaries of the city or county where it locates and strides are now being made to share the costs of investments and incentives required to attract these projects. Prime examples are the experiments in revenue sharing from multi-county industrial parks in South Carolina and the legislation pending in Georgia. Although they have had their growing pains, as all new endeavors do, they merit the time and energy to perfect.

CONCLUSIONS

The current environment seems to assure that whether right or wrong, incentive negotiation will remain a significant part of business attraction and retention programs. The challenge for companies and economic developers alike will be to ensure that incentives are accorded their proper role in site selection. Incentives should always be viewed and communicated as one line item in an overall project budget. Each community and state must decide for itself what it is trying to accomplish in both tangible and intangible benefits and approach incentive negotiations as an opportunity to make a business investment, not as a game to be won or lost.

Creative Efforts At The Local Level For Providing Business Attraction And Expansion Incentives

James E. Mooney

INTRODUCTION

Businesses are continually looking for that competitive advantage. As operating costs increase and competition holds prices for goods and services steady, the key to business success continues to be achieving the best profit margin possible.

Achieving that maximum profit margin starts from the selection of a competitive business location. Many factors, in fact an ever increasing number of factors, effect the site location decision.

Some factors are controlled at the national level. These include labor standards and minimum wage laws, transportation control legislation and trade/tariff costs when doing business across governmental borders.

Other factors at the state level have an effect on business location decisions. A leading issue today is the availability of workforce development programs. Other issues such as business, sales and income taxes, workers compensation and unemployment legislation and a state's attitude toward business all come in to play.

At the local level, the business perspective of the community is the key determinant effecting location decisions. Is the community ready for new business investment? Do they have a ready and willing workforce available? Are there construction ready sites for relocating or expanding companies? Does the community offer incentives which will work to create a win/win situation for the company and the community?

Site selection today is a process which requires balancing all of the costs and benefits in order to select the best fit situation for the firm. As the decision making process moves toward closure, the effective use of incentives can positively impact the location decision. Professionals working to facilitate the site location process need to be skilled in incentive negotiations in order to create successful site locations at the local level.

SOME INITIAL OBSERVATIONS

Once a business completes the state assessment, county and community reviews will quickly follow. It is at this level that community aggressiveness and creativity can make the difference between securing the project or being a runner up in the attraction effort.

Local governments should understand the company's objectives. A real estate project from the perspective of the investor involves the commitment of time, money, or other property today to earn income or profit on that outlay in the future. Therefore, the company considering the real estate investment would assess the quality of the investment by analyzing specific factors, such as the degree of risk, the amount and rate of return on the initial investment, and the amount of effort required to develop, renovate, market, and/or manage the project.

A municipality has control over a broad range of incentives, programs and services that can reduce risk, increase return, decrease front end costs and simplify management of the development process.[1]

PREREQUISITES

However, before a community can effectively get to the stage of using incentives, some key people and processes must be in place in order to facilitate the development process. These include simplifying the regulatory process, having trained staff on hand and conveying a readiness to work with the investor.

Simplified Regulatory Process

Control over development can be successfully achieved by the ease of local regulatory process. If local regulations, standards, review processes and procedures support and facilitate development, the private sector is more likely to conduct business in that city. If they are entangling, cumbersome and discouraging, the private sector can and will take its business elsewhere, particularly when the city with cumbersome regulations is also a weak market for new development.[2]

Communities can expedite the development process by offering one-stop-shopping. This allows the investor to have a single source contact for the development process thereby eliminating a great deal of the frustration often incurred when dealing with the multiple, unfamiliar departments of local government.

More importantly, the time it takes to get through annexations, site plan review, permitting and the various boards and commissions needs to be reviewed and improved if necessary. Projects can, and have been lost when the frustration level of the new investor reaches a level which justifies moving to new communities and starting over.

Trained Staff

Trained staff are the second prerequisite to the use of incentives. It is vitally important that professionals who have the ability to communicate effectively in both the language of the new facility owners or developers and the language of the community. These individuals are essential for ensuring that a smooth and as pain free as possible development experience is had by the newly locating project.

Readiness to Work

Finally, a readiness to work with the investor is an essential prerequisite to the development process. The commonly joked about persona of municipal employees has to be avoided in these scenarios. Friendly, outgoing, eager professionals are the community's welcoming party to new investment. Their place, and importance to the development scenario are essential to creating the public/private partnership needed when new investment opportunities come to the community.

The Prepared Community

Having secured these three essential elements, a community is then ready to provide incentives to the new investor. When providing incentives for new development, a community has the ability to impact three components of the site location decision:

❑ corporate expenses,
❑ workforce development expenses and
❑ relocating executives' expenses.

CORPORATE EXPENSES

The traditional role a community plays in the site selection process involves reducing the barriers in the development process. Here are some incentives which have proven successful with other development projects.

Land Preparation

Adjustment to Zoning.

Although simple in concept, it is surprising how many communities overlook achieving the proper zoning on a parcel of land that is being made available for development. By moving this parcel into the proper zoning category before the location negotiations begin, the company will sense an increased state of readiness from the competing community.

Land Acquisition/Eminent Domain/Land Banking.

All three of these tools allow the municipality to begin acquiring land in preparation for development. Obviously, the most preferred scenario is for an amicable sale of the property to the local municipality. In many, if not most situations, this is commonly achieved. However, in some situations the local municipality must take land for the public good through the use of eminent domain. When needed, eminent domain has allowed communities to complete development projects that later served the collective needs of the community at large.

Acquiring land can occur in many fashions. Fee simple purchase offers the ability of the community to acquire the land in advance of development. This approach is most common when a municipality finds it necessary to acquire a number of smaller parcels in order to provide a larger tract of land for future development goals.

Purchase options allow the municipality to gain a first right of refusal on a piece of property without taking ownership. Often, these options can be achieved at very low cost to the municipality and can easily be extended when needed. If purchase options are used, it is important to make them assumable. For example, a municipality may opt to option land in order to assist a new manufacturer with keeping their development plans quiet for a longer period of time. At the time the manufacturer is ready to go public, rather than having the municipality purchase the land and then resell it to the manufacturer, it would be easier to have the option assumed by the manufacturing entity.

Finally, land trades (or swaps) may assist in providing land for development projects. Few people will know the community as well as the local unit of government. This allows them to swap land in the community if a particular site is preferred by the investor, but the property owners are still interested in owning property. Under this scenario, comparable land can be provided through the municipality in order to make the development project feasible.

Enhancing Financial Feasibility

In general, obstacles to financial feasibility result from a developer's inability to meet one or more of the following needs: adequate front-end investment capital, positive cash flow and an acceptable level of perceived risk over the term of the project. A number of public incentives address one or more of these needs.[3]

Free Land/Free Rent

Many communities offer free land or free use of a building to qualified development projects. Free land is most commonly found in rural areas and free buildings in inner city projects which are aggressively trying to attract new investment. Exceptions can be found to both scenarios however. Most commonly, these incentives are assembled by the community using either general funds, tax increment financing or state and federal grant funds that make the project cost competitive with other sites under consideration during the site selection process.

Land Write-Downs

Land write-downs reduce the front-end capital costs of a project by subsidizing the difference between the actual cost of acquisition and clearance and the cost to the developer. General revenues, general obligation bonds, Community Development Block Grant funds and other funds might be a source of financing.

Land Leases.

Land leases require less initial capital than outright purchase by the developer. A land lease reduces the amount of debt that a project must support as a portion of the project cost as the land does not need to be financed. The equity needed for the project is reduced, thereby reducing the developer's risk. In addition, a land lease enables investment in aspects of the development that have favorable tax consequences - for example, in the structure, which can be depreciated rather than the land, which is deductible as a business expense and is nondepreciable.

Land and Building Leases

These leases are a variation of the conventional land lease but are more complex and require careful financial structuring, financial guarantees and legal safeguards. In this case, a private developer leases the land and a building to be built from the municipal government or one of its agencies. While in a legal sense the governmental unit is the owner of the property, the company is the constructive owner of the property. If the term and conditions of the lease are proper, it is possible for the company to depreciate the building and take other tax advantages as though the building were privately owned. Because the legal owner is a municipal entity, tax exempt financing is possible (if all the other state and federal requirements for tax exempt findings are met. This option may not be available in all states). If a municipal entity decides to pursue this route, the deal must be based on a very sound legal and financial structure. Adequate safeguards to ensure the continued financial participation of the development entity in case of financial problems with the project are also necessary to ensure that the municipality does not become the owner of a defaulted building with no recourse to outside financial remedies.

Equipment Leases

Equipment leases enable a developer to lease heavy equipment from a city and thereby avoid the costs of the purchase. This reduction solved the problem facing one hotel renovation project which was encountering difficulty remaining within the $10 million limit of the industrial revenue bonds. The developer was able to lease the elevators and other electrical mechanical equipment from the city and reduce its capital expenditures. The potential loss of tax exempt interest rates more than offset any increased costs of leasing.

Publicly Provided Infrastructure

Reducing project costs can be quickly achieved if infrastructure normally provided by the company is provided by the municipality. Water and sewer services are the most commonly provided infrastructure; however street lighting, gas, electrical service, parking facilities and storm water drainage are all possible infrastructure projects which may be needed to bring a project to fruition.

Other "Soft" Costs

All of the costs of a project should be carefully reviewed, because some of the (non-development) costs might be reduced, thereby reducing the capital cost of the project and the amount of financing required. For example, all public fees charged should be carefully scrutinized to ensure that they are necessary. These fees can be abated on a case by case basis to enhance the competitiveness of the incentive package.

Tax Increment Financing

Tax increment financing (TIF) helps finance the front end costs of development by allowing the incremental increase in tax revenues from new development pay for the public investments needed to realize the development. These public investments include land acquisition, building demolition, relocation, site improvement and various public improvements. Based upon the projected amount of the incremental tax, the municipality sells bonds to obtain the money necessary to pay for the public improvements.

Special Assessment Districts

Special Assessment Districts help finance infrastructure by raising property taxes for designated landowners by the amount needed to pay for the improvements. The district is created by act or vote of residents for a specific purpose with the power to levy taxes and float bonds for improvements. The special assessment(s) for improvements represents a long-term loan from the municipality to the developer at interest rates below those found in the conventional market. Merchants can also use special assessment districts to pay for private improvements and services, such as increased police protection or trash removal, the development of a pedestrian mall and improved lighting.

Lowering Debt Service Expenses:

Several tools are available, depending on local authority, for reducing debt service expenditures.

Industrial Revenue Bonds

Industrial Revenue Bonds (IRB's) are extremely helpful to businesses that need assistance in financing the acquisition of land, the construction of buildings and the purchase of equipment. Normally, the power to issue IRB's is vested in a local development authority. The authority assumes no financial obligation for repayment, so that a company must have sufficient financial resources to ensure prompt payment of principal and interest over the life of the loan.

Loan Guarantees/Subordinate Financing

Financial assistance can be provided by the municipality to enable a project to obtain beneficial financing terms - e.g. extension of the amortization period of a loan and reduction of the interest rate. Sources of such financing include CDBG funds, city revenues, foundations, tax increment financing (where allowable by law) and UDAG repayments to cities having previously received UDAG funds. Through these sources, a second mortgage at an interest rate lower than that charged on the first mortgage of a project can also be used to lower the total interest rate charged on a development.

Deferred Payment Mortgages

Deferred payment mortgages are another method of reducing the initial costs of debt service by allowing the first or second mortgages provided by the public sector to accrue principal and interest for a short period of time (perhaps 3 to 5 years).

Buying Down The Interest Rate

Buying down interest rates is a method used to reduce the interest rate charged on a longer term loan by making an initial payment. For example, a banker might agree to lend money at 12 percent over 10 years, rather than at 14 percent, if the project makes an initial payment that is roughly proportionate to the present value of the expected loss of interest over the term of the loan. Cities might be requested to provide a grant to accomplish this "buy down."

Lowering Operating Costs

Two of the most common forms of incentives are those which have been used to lower the operating costs of the incoming business.

Tax Abatements

Tax abatements can provide relief for overall financing costs of a project because a reduction in local property taxes will reduce operating expenses and result in an increase in net operating income. Because the financing of a project is directly related to NOI, an increase in the amount of the loan and a reduction in the amount of cash equity can be obtained through the use of this incentive.

Utility Incentives

It is very common for competitive utility agencies to offer rates which provide reduced rates for new investment or for high demand users. These rates are sometimes published incentives, or they are held for special negotiation situations where they are used as necessary.

Creation of Enterprise or Foreign Trade Zones.

Enterprise zones and foreign trade zones are made possible through federal and/or state legislation. They are vehicles which lower the cost of doing business essential through the elimination or deferral of taxes associated with the cost of doing business within the zone. Enterprise zones are commonly established as a revitalization tool for targeted areas of the community. Foreign trade zones are established to facilitate and encourage importing and exporting amongst the local industrial community.

Assisting the Project During Construction:

Public/private cooperation can ensure a project's success in many ways through development and construction. A little advance thought and planning will solve many potential problems.

Permits and Approvals

Permits and approvals should be obtained before construction starts, and cities can expedite the process for obtaining the necessary zoning, approvals and permits. For example, some cities have established "one-stop" permit counters or departments, where all necessary local approval agencies and staff are located. Other cities appoint a project manager responsible for following through and assisting each project.

In recent years, communities have elected to have sites pre-approved for environmental permits for specific uses. This pre-approval process accomplishes two objectives. First, it reduces the amount of time to move through the preparatory stage of development and second, it expresses a business like demeanor for the community using the pre-approval process to solicit targeted types of industrial development.

Compatible Scheduling

Scheduling of public and private ventures will aid construction; for example, major public roadwork around a key site should not interfere with the private development effort. Compatible construction schedules for complementary facilities are essential to ensure that they are completed at the same time. It is especially important to make a qualified person available to supervise the public portion of the project and to give that person the authority to make necessary on-site decisions about construction.

Selection of Contractors

Contractors selected by the city for projects with public and private elements can be an important factor in development and construction. Requirements for public bidding may result in two sets of general contractors, subcontractors and union representatives, working side by side on the construction of an integrated structure that contains public and private elements. This problem can be avoided by the retention of a construction manager responsible for the development of the city's portion of the site and coordination.

Non-Strike Agreements

Non-strike agreements can be negotiated to assist a site selection effort with the construction of a key project. Under such an agreement a strike that occurs while the project is under construction would not affect work on the project, thus resulting in significant savings and reduced risk.

WORK FORCE DEVELOPMENT ASSISTANCE

One of the most important incentives available to a business in the 1990's is the provision of a ready and willing workforce. In fact, it is becoming clear that above tax incentives and other gimmicks, good vocational training programs and a willing work force are among the best attractions, if not the best.

Across the country, increasingly, when a local work force doesn't have the skills and education that relocating or expanding manufacturers are looking for, the states are jumping in to cure the deficiency.

North Carolina pioneered such industry specific job training in the late 1950's. But a spurt of new programs in the 1980's put more than half the states into the business of training made-to-order work forces. It's a shadow school system that can spend thousands of dollars per student, focused

exclusively on meeting the precise needs of business.

Equally, it is a condemnation of the immensely costly U.S. educational systems which annually turns out 2.7 million high school graduates and nearly 1 million college graduates with a general education but does little to prepare young people for jobs in the real world. About 80% of Michigan's job training budget goes to companies that are trying to upgrade workers or processes or to install new technology. Up to 20% of the total is used for remedial training in reading and arithmetic.[4]

Pre-Employment Screening.

One of the most effective economic development incentives that can be offered to a new employer is for the local community to pre-screen any and all employees to be hired at the facility. Services can be provided through the local employment and training agency, community or vocational technical colleges or the state office of unemployment to ensure that those applicants reaching the human resource director's desk are the best qualified to produce in the new jobs. These services greatly streamline the hiring time and costs of the new employer.

On-the-Job Training Programs

On-the-Job training programs will typically allow for picking up all or half of the wages of the new employees during the start up training period. These funds are most commonly available through the local Private Industry Council, community college or vocational technical school.

Customized Training Programs

Customized training allows for employer specific training to occur which quickly moves new hires into productive new job positions. Customized training also allows for the upgrading of skills of the current work force of existing employers in the community.

Job Training Funds

Job training funds are one of the most popular incentives used in today's competitive attraction climate. They can be provided by a municipality to fund the cost of employee training at the new manufacturing facility. A properly structured job training program, with adequate administration and carefully targeted applicants, is often necessary to achieve these benefits. However, the cost can be viewed as a trade-off because savings realized as a result of employee's improved efficiency offset the

continuing operating costs of a project.

Technology Transfer Programs

Although not exclusively a work force development effort, tech transfer programs offered through state and university resources typically result in an increase in work force productivity. These programs are instrumental in transferring research knowledge at the university level to increased production capacity on the shop floor.

CORPORATE RELOCATION INCENTIVES

Providing assistance to relocating executives allows the community to focus on the "people" side of the site location decision. They are often secondary impacts to the decision making process, however they can be instrumental in helping the company look good to its relocating executives thereby helping to swing the site selection decision to the competitive community.

Community Presentations

Communities vying for competitive economic development efforts can offer to go to the parent facility and/or key branch facilities. These trips work very well to present the new community to potential employees who will have an interest in bidding for the jobs to be created at the new facility. This effort goes a long way for the site location decision team. By having a team of representatives offer to go and meet the incoming workers, a good faith welcoming effort is extended by the community. Also, this relieves upper level management from some of the pressures of enticing key individuals to accept the relocation offer.

Spousal Employment Programs

In today's two income economy, it is very important when relocating executives to help with the employment of their spouses. In the past, this often meant finding work for the trailing wife. However, today it means helping the husband find work more often than not. Regardless of the sex of the client, the ability of the community to expedite the re-employment of the spouse helps them to gain a leg up in the competitive site selection decision making process.

Temporary Housing for Relocating Executives

When executives make the relocation decision, it is not without costs. They will go through a period of living out of a suitcase. Everything the community can do to make this period as amenable as possible helps to increase the receptiveness of the executives to the new community. This, in turn, reduces their stress involved with the move, increases their productivity during the time of transition and reaffirms the decision of upper level management regarding the selection of the community for the new facility.

Temporary Transportation

Executive transportation while seeking new housing can be a problem during long distance relocations. The local car dealers or rental agencies in the community can offer a loaner car to corporate executives while in town seeking new housing or planning their move to the corporate facility.

Assistance with Acclimating Children to the Community

The most frequently overlooked component of the relocation is the children. They are leaving old friends behind and often are heavily challenged by the move. Assistance can be provided by the community to help them become oriented with their schools, become registered for sports or signed up with scouting and other activities. In short, anything that can be identified which will minimize the transition period will have value to incoming executives.

Discounts on Home Furnishings

New residents in the community mean new home sales which mean new carpeting, dishwashers, curtains, and a host of other finishing items. The competitive municipality can involve its retail community in the incentive ball game by soliciting discounts on durable goods to be sold to the new residents when they locate.

Moving Cost Reimbursement

Communities have been successful with closing economic development deals by offering the relocating executives reimbursements for their relocation costs. These funds often come from local pools of economic development dollars established to "do whatever it takes" to make the project happen for the community.

As stated earlier, relocation incentives often become secondary in nature to those involved with reducing corporate expenses or enhancing the productivity of the workforce. These incentives however, can be instrumental when used in closely contested site location decisions. Creativity on the part of the community and the site selection team will result in a package of incentives which will secure new jobs and investment for the successful community.

SUMMARY OBSERVATIONS, CONCLUSIONS AND RECOMMENDATIONS

There are two points which need to be emphasized. First, the front line in business incentives is created at the state level. States who fail to create a competitive business environment are out of the competition before they even get started in attracting new investment or encouraging existing businesses to expand. Second, there is a plethora of incentives available to even the smallest of communities if they choose to use them to attract new investment.

There are communities all over the United States, Canada and Europe that are willing to offer substantial incentives to attract new business or to retain the existing business community. These communities often fail to understand that incentives, although instrumental in closing the deal, are insufficient to overcome excessive business operating costs.

When state level operating costs are so cumbersome that they drive business away, there are very few things that an individual community can do to offset these costs in the long haul.

Having said that, the importance of the incentives as the project moves to closure need to be reemphasized. After the site selection process moves to the sub-state level, it is competition between communities which finally results in the site selection. Since all business costs within a state are constant with the exception of property taxes, permit fees and utility costs, it is at this level that business incentives become the most effective.

Incentives indicate the state of business readiness of the community being reviewed. Ultimately, it is not so much how much they are used, it simply is important that they exist. Stated differently, it doesn't make a whole bunch of difference if you have them, but it makes a difference if you don't. Those incentives, particularly the tax incentives, are a reflection of an attitude more so than they are an economic benefit.[5]

The use of tax incentives effectively creates the win/win scenario so commonly sought after in today's business climate. The company's site selection team can return to its upper level management with a report of having saved the company some front end costs while selecting a site which will prove profitable over the long haul.

The leadership of the community can report to its citizens that a new jobs and tax base have been created in the community which will allow for a strengthening of the local economy. Overall, everyone wins through the use of location incentives in the community.

The future of the use of incentives varies depending upon whom you consult. One perspective argues that the number of projects has continued to decrease over the past few years while the number of economic development organizations attempting to attract new investment has increased. This will certainly result in increased competition and incentive use to site an increasingly shrinking market of projects.

The other perspective argues that there is a paralleled decrease in resources for local governments to use incentives which are matched by their increased sophistication in making the incentive decision. The number you hear being tossed around is a return of $5 in indirect tax and economic benefits for every $1 that comes out of the treasury.[6]

At the same time, communities are generating their own economic impact statements in order to generate the return on investment to the local economy. This increased sophistication in decision making has led to increased scrutiny in the use of public incentives.

The end result will probably lie somewhere in the middle. Communities eager to attract new investment to their area will use every resource available to them to bring that investment home. The amount of incentives offered will be directly proportional to project size and community aggressiveness.

In order to guide the decision making process, it is generally recommended that the community adopt a policy statement in advance that determines when and where the incentives will be used. As a tool, the incentives have two uses to the community.

First, they offer the community a resource to effectively compete for new business investment. Second, they offer the community a tool to guide new investment within its jurisdictional boundaries. For example, an industry may be offered a tax abatement for locating in the industrial park, but not for a site which is located across the street from the industrial park. The readopted policy allows the community to make sound decisions as it negotiates with plants who want to locate within the community.

As long as states and cities continue to compete for new investment, companies will be able to use incentives to augment the return on their new plant investments. Like the end game in a chess match, incentive negotiations are the culmination of the site selection process. Success in negotiating, like winning at chess, requires skill, experience and mastery of the rules. But in the incentives game, there need be no losers. Both sides can win when negotiations are conducted with a clear view of the company's goals and priorities, and with sensitivity to the needs of the community.[7]

NOTES

[1]Stout, Gary E. and Vitt, Joseph E., "Public Incentives and Financing Techniques for Codevelopment", *Urban Land Institute Development Component Series*, 1982, pp. 2-5.

[2]Ibid. pg. 6.

[3]Ibid. p. 15.

[4]Weiner, Steve and Siler, Charles, "Trained to Order", *Forbes* Magazine, June 26, 1989, p. 73.

[5]Meyers, Greg, "Bidding Wars", *B&E Review*, Jan-Mar 1987, pp. 9.

[6]Ibid, p. 45.

[7]Shapiro, William M., "You Can Be a Winner in the Incentives Game", *Area Development* Magazine, July 1991, p. 58.

E. D. Practices:
The Best And the Worst

James H. Renzas

INTRODUCTION

Every once in a while, it is a good thing to sit back and take a look at where one has been, and where one is going. Some call it the mid-life crisis, others the retrospective, some, nostalgia. But I like to think that such a review is an important part of career development. I have been a consultant to site-seeking companies and economic development organizations for over 15 years now. I also have spent three years setting up and running an economic development organization on my own in Orem, Utah. I also serve on the Board of Directors of the Orange County, California Economic Development Consortium and am chairman of its response committee. Because I have an opportunity to work with ED organizations from across the nation on an almost daily basis, I have seen the best and the worst of the profession. By means of this article, I would like to share my observations with the community of ED practitioners.

BEST PRACTICES

Some practitioners have recognized that economic development as an institution is going to change dramatically during the coming decade and have created customer focused programs to meet the needs of the business community. Noted below are some characteristics of the best and brightest stars.

Long Term Perspective

Perhaps the single biggest distinguishing factor between the successful economic development organization and an unsuccessful organization is the perspective of the board and the community toward economic development.

Far too many communities wait too long to commit to a pro-active economic development program, often only after a major employer announces a reduction in employment or some such other "crisis" happens in the community. The result of this situation is often the need to create immediate results in economic development and the hiring of a professional "turnaround artist" who can make a major change in the economy of the community within a year's time.

Well, as anyone who has been in economic development for more than a few days knows, there are no "overnight sensations" in the world of economic development. Real long-term, lasting economic development requires a commitment to build an organization the right way, from the ground up, and build a product that can compete with the "best of class", not only in the state, but the country and the world.

Successful economic development organizations at all levels - state, local and regional - are those with consistent goals and objectives, consistent funding arrangements, and a long term commitment toward staff.

Product Development

Too many economic development organizations gather their four-color brochures and begin large-scale direct mail programs to thousands of companies without the slightest idea of what to do when an actual prospect comes to visit the community. Successful communities, on the other hand, have focused in on what industries they are best suited for, and prepare for those industry groups based on specific industry requirements and competitor surveys. They have isolated what that community does better than anybody else, and determined what needs improvement in order to compete for their industry targets. They know their strengths and weaknesses and have set up a plan of action to make their community into a "world-class" competitor.

This takes time, money and commitment on the part of the community. Commitment toward improvement - real commitment - is the critical thing that makes these economic development organizations successful. They have the commitment to be #1. For they know there can be only one site chosen for expansion or relocation. They want to make the short list and to close the deal.

Focus on Quality & Service

The most successful economic development organizations have not only prepared the way by building a world-class competitor, they have an almost single-minded focus on closing the deals that they have in-house as opposed to a focus on finding more prospects to fill the pipeline.

Once you have a live project, focus all of your resources on turning that live project into new jobs and investment for your community. It's amazing to me that economic development professionals can put so much work into generating a proposal and then let up on promotion and follow-up during the critical decision-making stages of the site selection process. Once your community has made the final cut - it's time to pull out all the stops (if you really want a project) to close the deal before it goes elsewhere.

Successful communities have frequent contact with the prospect and get the prospect away from thinking about the site selection decision and more about the day-to-day decision-making associated with relocation.

The most forward-thinking of the best of class are providing their prospects with services geared toward making the relocation a "risk reduced" transition by providing financing, architectural, engineering, facilities planning and group move services which are all necessary to ensure a successful relocation (but seldom thought about during the site selection stage by corporate managers or economic development professionals). In many cases this can make the difference between closing the deal or finishing in second place.

Relocation is the third most stressful experience in life - just after death and divorce. A Runzheimer study showed that over 75% of all managers responsible for completing a major relocation were no longer with their company two years after the move.

Your prospects should be scared to death, but they often don't realize the implications of managing a relocation or expansion project. To the extent that your organization can provide services geared to making that relocation or expansion project successful, in lieu of cash incentives, you will be able to close more of the prospects you currently have in the pipeline.

This service-related approach is probably the most revolutionary aspect of what the "best & brightest" are doing to capture more of the market. Often, this customer service approach can override a cost differential or other weakness your community may suffer that you are powerless to change. I liken it to going shopping at Nordstroms, where you pay more for clothing, but know that the organization is totally dedicated to making you feel like a king or a queen when you walk out of that store and where quality of the product is their number one concern. You can go to a lower priced store, but you suspect that the quality of the product is not always there and the clerks have little regard for how you feel about the experience.

Economic development is undergoing a similar revolution that retailing went through in the 80's. Quality and customer focus are what's important to site seekers nowadays, not just the lowest cost location. To the extent that you learn to provide the services that are necessary to ensure a smooth move - and that you can offer the highest quality location for the type of operation your community is seeking - you will be successful in the 90's.

THE WORST PRACTICES

There are, unfortunately, some practices that show the poor side of economic development.

No Story to Tell

As a site selection consultant in California -- I often get telephone calls from economic developers throughout the country who want to set up meetings in my office. This is without a specific project in mind. Often, this happens during the winter months -- with the majority of phone calls from economic developers in colder climates planning trips to Southern California. Just coincidence?

Well, I'm generally a pretty nice guy and, if I'm in town, I usually will try to make some time to meet with them. After all, I put some pretty heavy demands on the economic development community for information and assistance on site selection projects, and the least I can do is meet with them when they are in town.

The frustrating part is when we finally meet. Generally economic developers sit themselves down in our conference room, taking up my valuable time, and then have no prepared presentation, nothing new to discuss, and no meeting agenda. It drives me crazy, and I'm sure that all prospects must be frustrated from the unproductive time wasted talking with unprepared economic developers. Then, when I try to

stimulate the conversation by asking them some specific question -- they don't have a clue as to the answer!!

Our sales force -- including everyone in the organization -- spends more time preparing for a sales call than in getting appointments. Our logic is that "a bird in the hand is better than two in the bush". In other words, if you have a qualified prospect, you had better know as much as possible about that prospect including background on the company, the nature of the situation, what has been done thus far, key issues to be discussed, and who has decision-making responsibility.

In addition, we spend a great deal of time preparing professional looking presentations, which are specifically created for each prospect to show them in a meeting who we are, what we stand for, how we work and what benefits and features we have to sell.

Please don't waste your time or your prospect's time in holding meetings to introduce yourselves. When you meet with me, please have a carefully thought out agenda in mind, unless the meeting is for a specific project. I need to know specifically what new projects have announced in your area, what companies have moved out or are closing and why, and new programs and incentives which may make your community more interesting to our clients. That way, we can both save a little time in getting me up to speed on what is happening in your area. If you don't take this approach, in an exciting, enthusiastic way, I will assume that nothing is going on in your community.

No Product to Sell

Having no story to tell is bad, but having no product to sell is worse. You know, W. Edwards Deming said that 85% of a product's quality comes in the first 15% of the process. So many of you are out there beating on doors, printing brochures, and placing ads in magazines before you really have a well-thought out product to offer the world. You must think of what unique assets your community has, who are the "best of class" competitors, and how you can one-up them in the competition for new jobs and investment. Then you have to carefully select which industries your community or area is best suited for and prepare your community to be the best-of-class as a site for that particular industry. So many of you are out there trying to be all things to all companies that you have no focus on what you really are best suited for. You are seeking more prospects for the pipeline,

while all along you are unprepared to really compete for any of them.

A word of advice. Until you know *exactly* the type of company which is best suited for your location, and until you have made your community the ideal location for the type of company, save those hard to get dollars.

Premature Marketing Programs

How may of you have developed pretty brochures, bought a mailing list, sent out a million form letters, and waited for a response. Guess what? It's never going to happen that way!!

I receive stacks of unsolicited brochures, newsletters, flyers, etc. which I never read and most often get wasted. Just think of the number of trees and the postage dollars we could save if economic developers followed a more carefully crafted plan to target their audience with something meaningful and then followed up with a telephone call.

What's wrong with using the phone? I'm not going to hang up on you if you have something to tell me that I really ought to know and if your letter shows that you have spent some time understanding my company or client's needs. It's my job to be aware of all the useful opportunities that are out there and I can't possibly keep up with everything without your help. But please, don't just send unsolicited information without knowing my needs or following up with a telephone call. Most of this stuff will just be thrown away and the marketing dollars lost.

No or Poor Quality Research

Very few economic development organizations in this country have a capable staff of research professionals to answer questions, look into how the community could be doing a better job, study industry trends, or simply track changes in the community which could affect its attractiveness to new industry. Maybe that's because many of you have limited staffing budgets and not enough time in the day to undertake quality research which could help your organization be more effective. I liken this shortsightedness to the warrior who is too busy fighting the battle with bows and arrows to bother listening to a salesman selling guns.

If you spend time up-front with research related to knowing your community better and understanding your marketing targets better, you will be able to save money by better focusing your efforts on *only* those activities which are most productive, instead of chasing all over the country and selling to every Tom, Dick, and Harry. Your marketing and sales activities will be tightly focused and much more efficient. The result will be less wheel spinning and more deal making.

I am constantly amazed by the lack of good quality research about community attributes, incentives, wage rates, and everything else that a typical site selector would ask for during a preliminary survey.

Now, I realize that many consultants and businesses conduct a "beauty contest" where they are evaluating fifty or more communities and ask for everything under the sun -- the more obscure the better. But I encourage economic developers to call on these information requests and ask for the three or four things that are the most important factors for continued inclusion on the short list and then focus your efforts on providing *quality* information on these factors.

Quantity not Quality

Many economic developers are focused on one thing, prospect flow. They could care less if they ever close a prospect. Their objective is to "blow and go" -- in other words to get the maximum number of prospects in their pipeline before the next board meeting so that they can show their board members how effective they are.

This is because every time you actually close a deal, you are going to make a small group happy - the broker who got the deal, the realtor who sold the house, the banker who got the loan, the contractor who built the building -- but mostly, you are going to anger all those in the community who view themselves as working so hard for economic development and contributing to your budget, but did not benefit personally or professionally from their commitment.

So economic developers compensate through a "fear of success" syndrome which means that when a deal is close to closing -- where all that they have worked for is about to come true -- they panic when they realize that about half of their board members and about 80 percent of their contributors are going to be mad at them until *they* get a deal!

Consequently, economic developers concentrate on having the maximum number of prospects while closing the fewest amount of deals. This means that they will have job security, at least until the next board meeting, and that they will anger the fewest number of important people in their communities.

The only problem is, this mode of operations only lasts for a few years until somebody starts grumbling that no deals ever seem to close and maybe its the economic developer's fault, so you're back on the road again looking for a job.

Not Listening

What is it with the economic development profession? When I say I want specific information about available buildings or the number of new manufacturing employers in your area, don't send me a stack of brochures with a note stating that the information I am seeking is buried somewhere in these materials. This isn't a treasure hunt!! I need specific information now for active client projects. I frequently want to answer just one or two questions; instead, I get more information than I ever wanted or get information on a question I never asked.

The key to a successful relationship between you and your customers is to *listen carefully!* When you ignore my requests and send information that does not answer my questions, you make me or my research people have to call you back and ask again until the question is answered. Eventually, we are going to get the information we need and you will probably be the one we keep pestering until we get an answer, so you might as well listen closely the first time and save everybody time, money and frustration.

The "No Problem" Syndrome

One of the most pervasive areas of ethical abuse in economic development is what I like to call the "no problem" syndrome. When we are investigating sites on behalf of corporate clients, we are often given the response that any obstacles that we encounter can be overcome with "no problem". To me, this is code for "not my problem! – your problem". We steer our clients wide of communities that make these kind of statements without providing backup support and commitment to follow through on promises. One of the biggest areas of abuse is when it comes to environmental permitting. This is an area that is highly technical and the economic development professional has little influence on the state and federal laws regulating industry emissions.

Yet I often hear that environmental permits will be "no problem", that they will not slow down or inhibit a project. One of my favorite stories is in California where a large multi-national bank selected a large unzoned parcel of property for a major

corporate center. During land negotiations, this company was told that getting a rezoning would be "no problem" -- until, that is, when the company was actually ready to build and was told that entitlement fees would increase from $2.00 per square foot to almost $5.00 per square foot. Since the project was rather large and would take up 40 acres, this little "no problem" cost the company an additional $5.2 million dollars

Again, I would encourage economic developers to become much more familiar with the permitting and enforcement officials in their states and areas. In addition, economic developers need to become much more familiar with what potential industry impacts are likely given a particular type of facility locations. For example, if the company is a metalworking facility with painting and plating operations, it is critical that the technical experts be consulted at the onset to get reliable information regarding permitting requirements, timing and procedure.

This situation can work both ways as well. For example, many businesses either have no idea what environmental impacts their particular operation will have and what permits will be necessary or will try to deliberately downplay the environmental impacts in order to speed the site selection process. This approach can come back to haunt the business executive as well as the economic developer when it comes to actually putting the deal together.

No Implementation Skills

Relocation is a "bet the company" decision and those responsible for managing are more often betting their careers on the success of a move. The problem is that most managers have no experience in managing a major relocation and furthermore, have their own jobs to do while they are planning the thousands of details associated with moving.

The economic development community as a whole is guilty of enticing companies to move by showing them all the benefits of relocation without being honest about the risks associated with such a strategy and without providing adequate support systems in place to ensure that the company continues to function successfully during the disruption of a move.

I realized this when Paragon was being formed back in 1987 because, up until then, site location consultants would simply tell a client to relocate to a new community without providing any guidance with respect to the risks of a move or how to minimize those risks. Paragon was specifically formed to bring a "teamed" approach to relocation consulting and implementation where the risks and rewards were factored in early in the analysis and appropriate planning activities are undertaken to ensure the continued success of our clients. I am proud to say that, to date, we have never lost a client to a relocation nightmare, although we have had some close calls from those who decided to ignore our advice.

As noted earlier, sophisticated economic development organizations are now finding ways to assist not only with the provision of information, but also with the provision of relocation assistance services necessary to ensure smooth, disruption-free relocations. This is either done by building a local team of experts who work on each and every prospect inquiry or through the hiring of a relocation firm like Paragon Decision Resources who has the expertise to assist a company plan and implement what is often a difficult transition.

You see, economic development is no longer a game of finding prospects, deluging them with information, and hoping that they decide to locate in your community. The bar is being raised by forward-thinking economic developers who have figured out that the future of the profession lies in moving from an information provider to a service provider.

To keep up, you are going to need to learn a whole lot more about how to make an error-free transition of corporate facilities and personnel. Firms like Paragon can help you.

Meetings, Meetings, Meetings

One of the most wasteful practices is excessive, unproductive meetings. Almost invariably when I have a new project that I need to get information immediately for, the economic development representative is in a meeting and can't be reached.

What do you do in all of those meetings? You know - one of the ten most unproductive things that you can do with your time is to spend it in meetings -- especially with large groups. Surveys show that the average economic developer spends 50 to 60 percent of his or her time attending to administrative matters. This means that only 40 to 50 percent of the average professional's time is spent in finding and qualifying prospects and closing deals.

If you have to have meetings, spend your time working to resolve problems your existing employers have in the community or work to recruit new companies that have an interest in your community, but avoid, as much as possible, unproductive meetings with large groups. This is one of the biggest time wasters you can have. In the real estate brokerage industry, for example, some companies have created conference rooms with *no chairs and no tables*. This keeps meetings brief and to the point -- since nobody likes to stand up for two or three hours while someone else drones on and on about some administrative detail.

Ineffective Boards of Directors

It is impossible to have a successful organization with a board of directors that does not know the business of economic development or is too large to make a decision. You need a board of directors to protect you from political flak and to help you when it comes to deal-making time. Those board members should be influential in the community. But these boards with city council members who are housewives, shoe salesmen, and bureaucrats must stop. You will never be effective if you have to educate your board every time you need to make a move. They need to be savvy businesspeople in their own right to help you become the best deal maker out there.

Also, don't waste your time with boards over seven members. Few can make a decision with more than seven members on the board because human nature will override all logic and somebody on the board will raise an issue and no one else will want to offend that person and nothing will get done.

Please, - if you have to have a board of directors - and in most cases you will - make sure that the board is made up of doers that can make things happen in your community and not those who want to banter every single issue to death.

Now I realize, that many of you need to build and solidify your board members or develop a common strategic goal for your community and this process takes time - much of it in meetings. But this work should be accomplished early on in the process of establishing an economic development organization and should not have to be re-done constantly. Once a common strategic plan is agreed on, you should assign your board members some research assignment or other network building task which can be useful in getting their buy-in into the strategic plan and will also give them an appreciation of what you are trying to accomplish. The most effective organizations are run this way.

Taking/Distributing Credit

One of the last things you want to do as an economic developer is to have your face plastered all over the front page of the newspaper when a new company is announced. The want ads are filled with E.D. professionals who have become *too* popular and have threatened those who have power over their budget.

When you announce a new plant, a successful program, or other positive news, make sure that you give the credit to those who can use it the most at the moment. You will make friends forever and have a strong defender the next time your budget requests and your continued employment comes up on the agenda. Don't become such a "local hero" that the high and mighty cut you down and you have to pack your bags and leave town.

Turnover in the Profession

What company would survive in the private sector, if the chief executive officer and almost all of the management staff left office every three years to be replaced by another new chief executive officer and management team? Every new manager takes time to understand the community and wants to implement a new program which is unique to his or her management style. The constant start/stop cycle in economic development programs is the single most destructive force in the profession today. It's impossible to have a successful organization with a 33% turnover rate at the top.

Compensation

Most business executives know that in order to get maximum performance out of an employee they need to have specific goals and objectives which are tied to salaries and merit increases. Yet few in the economic development world have specific, measurable performance objectives and even fewer still are compensated based on performance. There seems to be very little relationship between performance and compensation in the economic development community. Those who work hardest and achieve results are often paid the exact same as those who work hardly at all and achieve nothing.

Whenever I see an economic development professional working hard and achieving real results for his/her community -- results which mean millions in tax revenues and personal income for his/her area, I am struck by the fact of how few are really compensated in relation to their value.

Conversely, whenever I see an economic developer spending all of his or her days in unproductive meetings, or worse, in political battles, while the poor and the unemployed live amid squalor with very little money, I am struck by how much these persons are paid in relation to what they are doing for their community.

In business, this practice is intolerable. Our consultants and salespeople are paid in direct proportion to the value that they bring to the company, either in revenues gained or in the satisfaction of our clients. No revenues or no satisfaction -- no performance bonus.

Few economic development organizations are structured this way, which is puzzling given the glut of economic developers out there and the tight funding most economic development organizations operate under.

The economic development world has to reflect the real world of business if it is truly to serve the needs of the community. Economic development is hard work and it is not always easy to get up every morning and push yourself to new levels of performance. But when your paycheck is either bigger or slimmer, depending upon your performance, it is amazing what it will do for your attitude.

SUMMARY

Relocation is an activity which is fraught with risk - both for the company involved, and its employees. Successful economic development activities in the 90's will focus more on the provision of services to reduce the risks associated with relocation, rather than the information-oriented focus of the past. This article outlines many of the "bad habits" of the economic development profession and describes how economic developers can be better prepared to service the needs of relocating companies and site selection consultants.

It's Marketing, Stupid!

Rodney Page
Patrick Topping

"We are being swept downstream by a torrent of change. Each year, each month, almost every week, the landscape alters. The familiar vanishes, and with it the effectiveness of the styles and tools we have used to make decisions...."
Robert Theobald,
British Economist and Futurist
"The Rapids of Change"

This quotation by Theobald applies as much to our field of economic development as it did to its original subject. The task of "creating wealth" or "expanding the economic base" or whatever we call it, has gone through dramatic evolution in recent years. The historical path towards economic vitality that once led to the traditional heavy industrial firms has changed. The path now leads to high tech companies, back office operations and incentive warfare. The most dramatic change in our industry, however, is on the horizon....the emergence of innovative marketing planning and the subsequent aggressive implementation of marketing strategies and tactics.

The key issue is how the successful economic development practitioners of the future will adapt to these changes and distinguish themselves from the pack. To examine this issue, lets first look at today's existing situation and how we got here.

WHAT *WAS* ECONOMIC DEVELOPMENT?

Economic development is defined as the process by which a community creates, retains and reinvests wealth. That definition addresses the key elements of economic development ....1) the need for investment (creates), 2) requirement to maintain the viability of existing wealth (retains), and 3) an obligation to seek continual upgrades (reinvests) to insure the sustained health of the whole.

Approaches taken by different communities to pursue these goals are as different as the communities themselves. Traditionally, economic development was, and in some areas still is, simply an effort to acquire and clear a piece of land, put up a sign with a phone number and wait for a prospect to drive through town and call. Perhaps the phone number has not faded beyond the point of legibility.

Then, the local development authority (Chamber of Commerce, elected officials, volunteers, etc.) would assemble the necessary data hopefully proving the low cost of land and labor, lack of union activity, low tax structure and plentiful infrastructure. Negotiations would begin. A few roads would be promised, the land amazingly becomes free, the local officials make a visit to a prospect's home office, and the deal is done.

With a little luck and a lot of blood, sweat and tears, in a few months the silver shovels are brought out, the media assembled and the mayor announces the location of a new "ACME" plant. Everyone is understandably proud of their accomplishment. The whole process then starts over again with the placement of a new sign on a new piece of property.

This scenario is not dissimilar from the realities of many economic development efforts today. However, the script has changed and will continue to change even more in the future. There are fewer and fewer "ACMEs" and more communities are pursuing them. "ACME" no longer needs just a good piece of land, lots of labor and minimal water waste treatment or disposal facilities.

They do require convenient access to major highways, rail yards and international airports. The potential labor force must possess technical skills and there must be access to ongoing training and education. Advanced data/voice communications facilities must be available. Today's projects sometimes involve investment in plant and equipment greater than that in human resources. This makes it harder for the local elected officials to judge the financial impact of the project and associated tax abatement issues.

WHAT *IS* ECONOMIC DEVELOPMENT TODAY?

Plant location selection today really seems to be more of a process of location elimination. Dis-qualifiers....demographic data, wage data, tax structure, labor availability, union activity, local political situations, cost of living information....all are readily accessible to consultants and in-house real estate professionals. They can access it from the comfort of their own offices through electronic data bases without the local economic development people knowing anything about it. The "personal touch" that once played a big part in initial site identification has disappeared.

Georgia, for example, has been extremely successful in recent years in its recruitment efforts. The state created over 170,000 new non-agricultural jobs in 1994, in large part due to the coordinated efforts of statewide organizations working with local communities.

The Georgia Power Resource Center (GRC), a high tech site selection facility, offers business prospects an overview of Georgia's communities complete with demographic data, available buildings and sites, and quality of life video presentations. The GRC brings together the economic development resources of Georgia Power, the Georgia Department of Industry, Trade and Tourism, Georgia Institute of Technology, Georgia Research Alliance, Atlanta Committee for the Olympic Games, and the state's cities and towns. Using cutting-edge computer technology, this consortia helps prospective companies fine-tune their search efforts.

Additionally, the state's other major players, Oglethorpe Power, municipal water and gas companies, the railroads and banks, have played major roles in the state's successful economic development program.

Even with the existing success and support economic development in Georgia has enjoyed, however, it, like all other states must face the fact that the rules of the game are changing. We all must move rapidly from the world of reaction to that of proaction. In a phrase, from now on: It's Marketing, Stupid!

In the remainder of this article concepts from the world of marketing as practiced in the private sector are presented. Most of the components of sound marketing planning and implementation that make for business success can be equally effective in economic development. Differences do exist, but there are many more similarities.

Many practitioners may be skeptical about these statements. Some perspectives may be: "We're not selling a product" or "We use a lot of volunteers" or "We don't want to be sales people" or "Marketing is irrelevant anyway....it all boils down to who is offering the best incentive package." These are legitimate issues which will be addressed in this article.

WHAT IS MARKETING?

....the entire planning and implementation process of communicating the benefits of a product/service (community) to potential customers (prospects) and delivering those benefits once they buy (select the community)....

To clarify further, it is very important to understand in more detail what marketing is and what marketing is not.

Marketing is not:

❏ Assuming that the community is going to be a high potential candidate for every business in the world that is considering relocating or building a new facility.

❏ Offering the most lucrative economic incentive packages.

❏ Developing the most expensive and flashy promotional materials.

❏ Running the most advertisements in the most trade publications.

❏ Having and utilizing a lavish prospect entertainment expense account.

❏ Adhering to the quick talking, back slapping high pressure sales image.

❏ Ignoring your existing base for the allure of new industry.

❏ And, in summary, marketing is not trying to be all things to all companies by throwing a lot of money at them.

Marketing is:

❏ Specifically defining the community's economic development goals and objectives.

❏ Completely understanding what the community has and does not have to offer.

❏ Understanding what types of prospects are more likely to have interest in the community.

❏ Developing a marketing message consistent with the goals/objectives and with what the community has to offer.

❏ Communicating that message to the targeted prospects and the community's economic development partners (development commissions, state level economic development, consultants, etc.).

❏ Effectively and professionally managing the relationship with each prospect.

❏ Delivering once the deal is done.

❏ And, in summary, understanding the needs of the prospect and fulfilling those needs to the satisfaction of both parties.

DEFINING THE COMMUNITY'S ECONOMIC DEVELOPMENT GOALS AND OBJECTIVES

It is useful to take a look at what marketing is and address some of the components mentioned above. All economic development efforts currently have visions/missions/goals/objectives. Few of them, however, possess the clarity to be very effective as part of a marketing effort. Some bad examples are: "Bring industry to 'X' county." "Improve the business environment in 'Y' city." "Increase the number of jobs in 'Z' region."

Why are these bad examples? Simply, to be effective in a marketing effort, goals and objectives must be:

❏ specifically defined

❏ realistic and achievable

❏ easily understood and communicated

❏ easy to determine if they were achieved or not (quantitative or time frame specifics).

With that in mind, the following would be better examples of goals and objectives:

❏ develop the light industry base of "X" county; add 250 skilled/semi-skilled jobs by 1997.

❏ reduce the business license fees in city "Y" 20% by 1996.

❏ increase available single family residences by 150 over the next 3 years by actively recruiting residential developers and making local government more "user friendly."

Planning at all levels and for any reason must be focused on clear and specific goals. More importantly, however, all of the members of the decision-making team must support them. Well defined goals that no one supports are not only meaningless, but destructive.

UNDERSTANDING WHAT THE COMMUNITY HAS *AND* DOES NOT HAVE TO OFFER

Most communities have a well-cataloged list of features....usually a litany of infrastructure capabilities and work force statistics. These are important, but we will not spend too much time discussing them because everyone already knows about them.

It is recommended, however, that communities unemotionally identify and address what they don't have to offer. Rather than wishing and hoping and/or avoiding the issue, recognize the fact that the community does not and will not ever have certain features and take that into account in the marketing planning. If the interstate highway is 35 miles away, it is not going to get any closer. If the water capacity of the community cannot be significantly increased without spending $80 million, it is not going to get significantly cheaper by hoping. If the existing work force is unskilled, no amount of good intentions will make them computer literate. A clear understanding of what the community offers or realistically might be able to offer is critical in implementing an effective marketing plan.

UNDERSTANDING WHAT TYPES OF PROSPECTS ARE MORE LIKELY TO HAVE INTEREST IN THE COMMUNITY

Not every new or relocating business is a prospect for every community. Many economic development professionals, however, act like that is the case. The best way to describe the critical need for target marketing is easy: the economic development budget. All economic development programs have finite resources with which to market the communities. Therefore, where is it decided to expend them? If we do not have many skilled workers, why waste resources creating leads for high tech industry? If it does not have water, why try to attract heavy users? Therefore, matching the capabilities and characteristics of the community with firms more likely to need them is the key.

A common marketing model is called the "Ideal Customer." We'll call it the "Ideal Prospect." It is suggested that each community describe its ideal economic development prospect based on what it has to offer. Build the "Ideal Prospect" by answering key questions about it. Some common questions are:

☐ What type business do we want (by SIC codes)?

☐ How many employees would we like the company to employ?

☐ What skill level would we want the company to need?

☐ Would we prefer a foreign or domestically owned company?

☐ Would we like the company to use an existing facility or build a new one?

☐ What type infrastructure would be important to the company?

☐ What type incentives would the company expect?

Congratulations! By answering these questions, the first step in the target marketing program has been completed. Once the critical questions have been answered and a full description of the "Ideal Prospect" created, one has a clear indication of the type of company that would be a good fit for the community. The next step is to find them.

With the "Ideal Prospect" defined, identifying targeted industries and specific companies now becomes a matter of research and good detective work. Many economic development practitioners, however, may be asking an obvious question; "All this stuff is well and good, but there was nothing in the 'Ideal Prospect' model that had anything to do with whether or not the company is moving or expanding. No matter how good a fit I may identify, if they are not moving or growing, it does not matter."

Earlier in this article it was said that a lot of disqualification of communities is going on around the country by people sitting at computers. Communities never even know they were in consideration nor have any opportunity to display their benefits. Well, targeted marketing allows communities to communicate pro-actively to firms with a much higher likelihood of a match.

In direct answer to the hypothetical concern stated above, communities simply do not know what companies may be prospects. *If communities wait until they know they are being considered, the number of opportunities they have to compete for will be extremely limited. They must identify their targeted industries and companies and mount aggressive marketing campaigns to increase the "times at bat." Those that wait for the phone to ring will be lost in the dust of others.*

DEVELOPING A MARKETING MESSAGE CONSISTENT WITH THE GOALS/OBJECTIVES AND WHAT THE COMMUNITY HAS TO OFFER

A community's marketing message will be the heart and soul of its marketing campaign. It must take into account the goals of the economic development effort, what the community has/does not have to offer, and who will be receiving the message.

The marketing message will be communicated in many different ways under many different circumstances and, though specific, must be flexible enough to fulfill many objectives. It must have a degree of permanence....it cannot be changed every six months. It should always have a "call to action." When prospects receive the message, there should be no doubt as to what the originator wants them to do. A message is not an advertising theme, even though advertising may be used to communicate the message. The marketing message captures the essence of the economic development objectives of the community and what the community has to offer.

Consider the following hypothetical community's situation. Its economic development goal: attract five new distribution centers employing 200-300 employees by 2000.

What the community has/does not have to offer:

☐ fifteen minute access to major interstate highway via upgraded 3-lane state highway

☐ main north-south rail line, secondary east/west line both with spurs to industrial park and large tracts of undeveloped land

☐ seven percent unemployment rate

☐ primarily an unskilled worker base

☐ water but no sewer service to potential site locations

☐ good community hospital

☐ high fire insurance rating

☐ low to moderate rated school system

☐ very little available single family housing

☐ limited incentives, but flexible and progressive local government.

Its "Ideal Prospect" Model:

☐ What type business do we want (by SIC codes)? Established or growing firms with national distribution; primary targeted SICs 22XX, 23XX, 36XX.

☐ How many employees would we like the company to employ? 40-50.

☐ What skill level would we want the company to need? Primarily unskilled.

☐ Would we prefer a foreign or domestically owned company? Does not matter.

☐ Would we like the company to use an existing facility or build a new one? Existing, 70,000 square foot facility available.

☐ What type infrastructure would be important to the company? Basic water, high interest in fire and medical, attractive property tax structure, low inventory taxes.

☐ What type incentives would the company expect? Limited, but would appreciate the flexibility and creativity offered to make the deal happen.

All marketing messages, utilizing any of the media explained in the next section should contain some combination of the elements listed above. Those items represent the core of the community's marketability and economic development goals. Why contaminate the marketing message with other extraneous, irrelevant data?

COMMUNICATING THAT MESSAGE TO THE TARGETED PROSPECTS

Once the elements of the marketing message have been identified and the message itself begins to take shape, the next task is figuring out how to communicate the message to the targeted prospects.

There are only so many ways to get the message to the prospects: 1) go see them, 2) call them, 3) send them something to read, and, 4) advertise. Therefore, the number of options is limited and rather straightforward, but coming up with the ideal mix is the challenge.

There is a direct relationship between the method of getting the message to the prospects and the effectiveness of the message. The most effective means of communicating the message (direct sales calls) is also the most expensive. The least effective (advertising) is also the least expensive. Is it being suggested that the economic development director be sent all over the country calling on targeted prospects? Of course not. What is being said is that a structured process be used to decide which channel is used to communicate the marketing message to various prospects.

Direct sales calls

These should be made on prospects that have been highly qualified and where specific information exists indicating a high potential for relocation or growth. Notice that the growth or relocation may not be known for sure. There are situations when the facts warrant a speculative sales call. Direct sales calls are very expensive, however, and should be used prudently.

Telemarketing

This is a much abused, but highly effective marketing communications channel. In the economic development industry it can be used to qualify companies to determine whether or not they are prospects. Of course the irritating tactics we all experience at home in the evening are not being proposed, but rather professional, highly targeted, well-prepared calls to develop information about a company's plans. As with all the channels, telemarketing can and should be used in combination with the others. Most often, telemarketing will be used in follow-up to a direct mail piece.

Direct mail

This is a very cost effective channel to reach targeted prospects. Since it has been concluded that communicating the community's message is the critical element, the assumption that expensive four color brochures must be a part of a direct mailing is no longer valid. The call to action of most direct mail is to prepare the prospect for further contact, usually by phone, or to stimulate the prospect to request additional information. The former is much more effective than the latter.

Advertising

This is perhaps the most extensively used communications channel and the most ineffective (particularly when the ads are placed in periodicals that prospects never see!) Advertising can and should play a role in the mix of communications to targeted prospects. Even with its low cost per target reached, advertising is expensive because it very often either does not have a call to action and/or never evokes one. Used in conjunction with other channels, advertising has a role. By itself, it is practically useless.

A marketing campaign will necessarily balance the desires for contacting prospects with the realities of the budget. Very effective marketing, however, does not require massive amounts of money. How much does it cost to prepare a well written letter, mail it to 100 highly qualified prospects and follow them up with a phone call? Counting postage, letterhead, long distance charges and everything else.... maybe $300-$400. The critical issues are carefully defining who gets the message and what the message is.

The available resources are different in each community, and the perceptive economic development professional will utilize all that are available. At the very least, resource partners, such as statewide economic development groups, utilities and banks should be briefed on a community's marketing programs. If the opportunity exists, the marketing plan should be coordinated with the partners to take full advantage of the synergy that might exist. Possible cooperative efforts include development of strategies to overcome community deficiencies and shortcomings, joint marketing trips and shared advertising. As they say, two heads are better than one, and multiple partners striving for the same objectives are more effective than uncoordinated efforts.

Managing the relationship with each prospect effectively and professionally

In the private sector, this is known as account management. Sales people in all industries and in all size companies constantly struggle with a classic challenge: discussing the product or service in terms of benefits to the customers.

Economic development faces the same challenge. Since economic development teams are made up of diverse and changing participants, the challenge is even greater. Economic development teams must articulate the characteristics of the community in terms of how those characteristics can benefit the prospect.

☐ The fact that the schools are terrible but are getting better is not of benefit to a prospect.

☐ Nor is the fact that the community has the capacity of supplying 200,000 gallons of water an hour if the prospect does not need it.

☐ It is not beneficial to prospects to know how bad the community needs the new factory. They don't care! This is a business decision based primarily on financial consideration.

When discussions are underway between the economic development team and a prospect, it is imperative that the team function as a well organized, professional and cohesive group. Despite all the talk of incentives and "bottom line decisions" the impression the economic development team makes can make a significant difference.

Key factors to success are:

☐ The Account Manager....somebody, not bodies, has to run the show. Somehow, the complications of politicians and volunteers must be managed to insure that one individual has the responsibility, authority and accountability to manage the team to success.

☐ Planning and Organizing....everything from orchestrating site visits and presentations to insuring the requested information is sent out on schedule, basic planning and organizing skills are critical.

☐ Presentation Skills....as illogical and unfair as it may be, how information is communicated can sometimes be more important than the information itself. Not everyone has the ability to make interesting, energetic presentations. Those that do not....keep them away from the podium.

☐ Writing/Editing....as with presentation skills, poor writing hurts the content of the message. Identify the team members that have the ability to communicate effectively in writing. Keep the amateur "Lou Grants" out of their way. Additionally, today's businesses are accustomed to seeing attractive, easy-to-read documents. If the team does not possess desktop publishing capability and someone who knows how to use it, find someone.

☐ Customer (Prospect) Focus....everyone on the team, from the switchboard to city hall, must understand the only reason the team exists is to communicate effectively the benefits of the community to the prospect.

DELIVERING ONCE THE DEAL IS DONE

Marketing does not end when the deal is done. Contrary to much popular belief, marketing should be intimately involved in delivering the product or service to the customer, or in the economic development world, the successful relocation/establishment of the incoming company. The conversion of the company from a prospect to a member of existing industry only means that a whole new set of marketing challenges await.

WHY "IT'S MARKETING, STUPID"?

....not because the Economic Development industry is stupid. The 1992 presidential campaign where the phrase "It's the economy, stupid" originated demonstrated how effective the highly focused efforts of a team of people can be. Economic development teams must become as focused on developing and growing the requisite marketing skills required in our changing world.

As with many things in business today, the economic development landscape is changing very rapidly. We think a key success factor in mastering this change is a new systematic emphasis on marketing planning. Happenstance and luck will not work. A lot of us have already figured that out. We not only need to react quickly, professionally and aggressively, we must actively identify new prospects, qualify them and go after them.

That's what marketing is all about.

Targeted Industry Marketing: Strategy And Techniques

Daryl McKee, Ph.D.

INTRODUCTION

No area can compete successfully against the rest of the world for every new business location. On most economic development budgets, marketing to every business in every industry means not making an impression on any businesses in any industry. Economic development managers realize intuitively that some industries are better prospects than others, and that this is where they should focus their efforts. The only question is which are the best prospects?

This is not a new question. It is the defining question for all organizational strategies, namely: Who is our market? By answering that question carefully and in detail, we can craft the basis for a full and complete strategic plan. La Quinta motel chain defined its market as mid-level business travelers, and created a consistently profitable service and promotional package around them. Southwest Airlines defined its market as the no-frills shuttle flight and has become the nation's most profitable carrier by serving that market with distinction.

Economic development markets are more diversified than those for most companies, but the benefits of focusing on high-potential markets is repeatedly demonstrated. Singapore has attracted more than 650 international manufacturing corporations with its focus on creating an information-technology culture. (The Singapore Economic Development Board refers companies in search of low-cost labor to Malaysia). Akron has become a national center for polymer-related manufacturing by focusing recruitment and investment activities there. North-central Mississippi has steadily gained market share in the upholstered wood furniture industry during the past three decades through focused development programs.

Strategies like these, developed for clearly and carefully defined markets, are more likely to be successful for two reasons: the media and the message.

First, communications media aimed at target markets are more efficient than those aimed broadly. Halving the "reach" of a communications effort doubles the "frequency" with which prospects can be contacted. Increasing the variety of communications within "vertical" channels, like direct mail, industry journals, and trade shows, reinforces the area's message in a way that broad "mass communications" efforts cannot. Most importantly, communicating to a group with similar interests generates more "word of mouth" support, the leverage point of all marketing efforts.

The second reason focused marketing strategies are more effective is message content. The product can be framed in terms of issues of importance to that particular market. Of course, this is particularly powerful when the "product" has been tailored to the interests of a particular industry niche. For example, Mississippi hosts upholstered-furniture industry trade shows, invests $1 million a year in R&D for the industry, and more.

But an important effect of intensive involvement with specific industry groups is a current understanding of strategic problems faced by the industry in general and specific firms in particular. This knowledge creates a framework for an effective industry niche marketing program. Marketers who use the same direct mail letter, the same display advertisements, and the same trade show booth displays for different market segments are wasting resources. The main point of marketing communications is to prioritize the message based on the concerns of the target audience.

The essence of strategy is focus. Targeted industry programs are not a substitute for basic community and economic development. Successful industry targeting requires this groundwork. But no area or business can compete successfully against everyone everywhere. Most areas must focus their limited development and marketing resources on the most attractive markets where they have the best competitive advantage.

There are a variety of techniques for answering the key question: Who is our market? These techniques have been developed, used, and refined in consumer and industrial marketing firms worldwide for decades. The best market-segmentation techniques, like the best marketing plans, are adapted to the specific situation. All other things equal, generic target markets and marketing plans that resemble those of competing areas cannot produce outstanding results. The purposes of this article are to: (1) develop a basic process for evaluating target industries; (2) examine alternative targeting techniques currently used by area economic development agencies; and (3) show how industry targeting fits into economic development strategic planning.

THE TARGET INDUSTRY SCREENING MATRIX

Strategic planners have evolved a number of analytic techniques to help executives evaluate markets. One of the most widely used techniques is the "Business Screen." The Business Screen allows managers to examine a portfolio of market opportunities visually in two dimensions: market attractiveness and competitive position. Each of those two dimensions is based on a "bundle" of factors. For example, market attractiveness may be based on growth rate, profitability, absolute size, market volatility, and other factors. Similarly, a firm's competitive position in a particular market may be based on its cost structure, distribution system, image, and other factors.

The purpose of the Business Screen is to guide executives in decisions about where to focus their efforts. In order to outperform its peers, any organization must focus its resources on the most attractive markets where it has the greatest strength. If it cannot strengthen its relative competitive position in attractive markets, then it will probably waste resources by investing there. On the other hand, a firm that pursues slow-growth or otherwise unattractive markets, despite competitive strengths there, may also be wasting resources. This is the basis of business strategy.

Geographic areas compete based on these same two factors: competitive advantage (i.e., how well the area meets an industry's needs) and industry attractiveness. Areas should focus resources on attractive opportunities where they have, or develop, a competitive advantage. In the section below, a simple (and hypothetical) target market analysis will be conducted in three steps. First, a set of industries will be examined in terms of their attractiveness. Second, the area's competitive advantage in serving those industries will be analyzed. Finally, a target industry matrix will be created from these two dimensions.

Industry Attractiveness.

A good fit between industry needs and area resources, by itself, does not qualify an industry as a high priority market. In order to qualify as an attractive focus of economic development marketing efforts, an industry must be attractive in terms of both its mobility and its fit with area development goals.

Industry mobility determines the potential return on an area's economic development marketing investments, aside from the fit between area resources and industry needs. Consider the situation of an economic development organization in an "oil patch" state during the late 1980s. Because of market proximity and area resources, the area might "fit" with the needs of the oil field machinery industry. But the oil industry was in a cyclical downturn at that time. As a result, capacity utilization in the oil field machinery industry slipped from 54

percent during 1984 to 35 percent during 1987. An extensive economic development marketing campaign targeted at the oil field machinery industry was unlikely to be productive at that time.

Indicators of industry mobility include factors like historical and projected industry growth rate, number of establishments, capacity utilization rate, and change in capacity utilization rate. As can be seen in Table 1A, these factors vary widely across industries and within industries over time.

Industry attractiveness can also be evaluated based on the extent to which an industry meets the community's development goals. Area development goals may include stabilization of local employment cycles, environmental protection, increasing the proportion of white collar employment, and the like. These goals imply use of measures like industry employment volatility, air, water, or other environmental emission rates, professional and clerical employment as a percentage of industry total, and similar measures. The importance of these measures is their fit with area development strategy. For example, if the area is attempting to offset substantial employment fluctuations associated with a high proportion of certain durable goods manufacturing employment, then it may seek to attract offsetting nondurable manufacturing and service firms.

These indicators can be used to assess industry attractiveness by: (1) weighting each criterion in terms of its importance; (2) ranking potential target industry on each attractiveness criterion (Table 1B); and (3) summing the products of the weighted rankings. This process is illustrated in Table 2 for SIC 3411.

First, the industry attractiveness criteria are weighted in terms of their relative importance. These weightings may reflect empirical research findings or expert judgments about the contribution of each factor to industry mobility, as well as local leadership judgments about the importance of each factor to community development strategy. The role of strategic vision here is particularly important. At its best, area strategic planning enacts a vision of community progress; it answers the question "What kind of community do we want to become?" The types of industry we seek are important parts of that vision and our decisions here affect the industry we can seek later.

Second, the potential target industries are rated on each criterion. (Here they are placed into five approximately equal groups, where 5 is a high rating). These ratings can be developed in a number of ways. One simple method is to array all industries on each criterion and then divide the list into ranked tiers. For example, in

TABLE 1A
Sample Industry Attractiveness Data

SIC	Historic Growth	Projected Growth	Number of Large Units	Capacity Utilizat'n	3 Yr. Change in Cap. Util.
3411	2.9%	3.3%	294	61%	-13%
3441	0.8%	0.0%	1,160	77%	25%
3451	4.1%	0.2%	644	88%	14%
3523	-8.6%	0.0%	620	26%	-16%
3544	4.3%	1.8%	1,322	81%	8%
3551	-0.4%	2.2%	316	87%	7%
3573	15.8%	10.0%	834	72%	-8%
3645	8.4%	2.9%	250	74%	-18%
3714	4.7%	2.5%	1,111	79%	2%
3724	5.1%	6.6%	223	94%	22%
3822	5.2%	0.0%	89	83%	10%
3823	9.0%	0.0%	288	56%	-5%
3824	-0.4%	-3.0%	69	93%	9%
3841	13.5%	9.5%	312	64%	-10%

TABLE 1B
Sample Industry Attractiveness Data: Ranked

SIC	Historic Growth	Projected Growth	Number of Large Units	Capacity Utilizat'n	3 Yr. Change in Cap. Util.
3411	2	4	3	2	2
3441	2	2	5	3	5
3451	3	3	4	5	5
3523	1	1	4	1	1
3544	3	3	5	4	4
3551	2	3	3	4	3
3573	5	5	4	2	2
3645	4	4	2	3	1
3714	3	4	5	3	3
3724	4	5	2	5	5
3822	4	2	1	4	4
3823	5	2	2	1	3
3824	1	1	1	5	4
3841	5	5	3	2	2

terms of historic growth rate, SIC 3411 is in the second lowest tier of the five groups, and thus receives a rating of "2" (Table 2). Ratings on the remaining factors are assigned in the same way.

Summing the product of the weightings and ratings results in an industry attractiveness score (in this example, "2.65"). This score reflects the attractiveness of the selected industry, relative to others under consideration, as an economic development target.

Competitive Advantage

While industry attractiveness is based on criteria set by local leaders, competitive advantage is based on criteria set by the market (i.e., industry executives). In order to have a competitive advantage relative to other areas in attracting and serving a target industry, the area must have resources and competencies that are both valuable to that industry and difficult for other areas to imitate. Competitive advantage is inherently unique. Location incentive packages and skilled labor availability are not advantages if competing areas possess the same factors to the same degree.

Competitive advantage is also dynamic.

The area that establishes an advantage over others in attracting industry will eventually lose its edge in either of two ways. First, competing areas will imitate the source of competitive advantage. This can occur in the short term with advantages that can be quickly imitated (e.g., location incentive packages) or it can occur in the long term if the source of advantage is difficult to imitate (e.g., educational innovation, infrastructure improvements). Second, an area's competitive advantage can be lost as an industry's needs shift toward capabilities that the area does not meet (e.g., from low-wage to skilled labor availability).

Strategic theory suggests that there are three basic sources of competitive advantage: (1) investments in capabilities important to the industry that other areas are reluctant to make; (2) an image, created in the minds of potential prospects within the industry, that other areas cannot match; and (3) operating costs to which the industry is sensitive that are lower than those in competing areas.

An area's competitive position can be assessed by: (1) identifying the needs (i.e., location criteria) of each industry; (2) weighting those criteria in terms of their importance; and (3) rating one's own area in terms of its performance on those criteria, compared to alternative areas in which the industry could locate. It is important to note that, unlike industry attractiveness criteria, location criteria and their relative importance will be different for each industry. For example, location criteria in the telecommunications industry tend to emphasize operating infrastructure while those in the food processing industry tend to emphasize market access (Table 3). Identification of industry location criteria and their relative importance can be accomplished by using either input-output tables or industry surveys.

Input-output tables identify the resources utilized by an industry as a proportion of its output. The advantage of using an input-output table for assessing an industry's needs is its precision. On the other hand, there are two major disadvantages to the use of input-output tables for identifying industry needs. First, input-output tables do not include intangibles (e.g., the need for proximity to a research university). Second, input-output tables do not tend to represent the resource requirements of new facilities. Input-output tables are prepared based on all facilities in operation, so they may not reflect efficiencies built into new facilities (e.g., labor may be less important in the new facilities). Also,

TABLE 2
Calculating Industry Attractiveness in SIC 3411

Criteria	Weight	Ranking	Score
Historical Growth	.25	2	.50
Projected Growth	.25	4	1.00
Number of Large Establishments	.15	3	.45
Capacity Utilization	.15	2	.30
Change in Capacity Utilization	.20	2	.40
Total	1.00		2.65

TABLE 3
Location Criteria for Selected Industries

Telecommunications (Hoch 1992)	High-Tech (U.S. Office of Technology Assessment 1988) *	Corporate R&D Facilities (Lund 1986)	Food Processing (Lopez and Henderson 1989)
Operating costs	Labor skills & availability (89%)	Proximity to headquarters	Market access
Assured supply of productive employees	Labor costs (72%)	Availability of scientific and technical personnel	Infrastructure
Suitable office space	Tax climate (67%)		Fiscal policies (e.g., taxes and development incentives)
Access to advanced telecommunications infrastructure	Academic institutions (59%)	Quality of life	
Reliable utility service	Cost of living (59%)	Proximity to manufacturing	Labor availability
Reasonable taxes	Transportation (58%)	Proximity to university or research center	
Favorable regulatory climate	Market access (58%)	Property costs	
Investment incentives	Regulatory practices (49%)	CEO preference	
	Energy Costs (41%)		

* percent responding factor was "significant" or "very significant"
** listed in descending orderr of importance

input-output tables are likely to be dated. Because construction of input-output tables is expensive and time-consuming, they are not kept current. They may not represent more modern facilities in operation, much less new projects.

Surveys are more likely to indicate current and intangible industry location needs and their relative importance. While it is usually impractical to survey all industries, it also isn't necessary. As will be seen below, not all industries are attractive from the standpoint of a particular area's development strategy. It may be simpler to identify attractive industries first and then assess the area's competitive advantage in terms the most attractive candidate industries. Economic development consultants, industry analysts, local executives within the industry, and others can then help prioritize location factors for each industry.

The final step in assessing competitive position, evaluating one's own area in terms of industry needs, can normally be accomplished based on objective criteria. Labor costs for specific skill categories, access to markets, tax structures and financial incentives, and similar factors can normally be measured directly or by proxy for the focal area and its competitors. These can then be expressed as relative ratings.

These three steps — assessing location criteria, their importance, and the area's competitive rating on each — result in competitive position calculations for each industry under consideration. A fictitious example is show in Table 4.

In this example, ten criteria have been identified as important to SIC 3411. Their relative importance has been assessed — and expressed as weightings based on subjective assessments and input-output data. Next, the area has been rated relative to its competitors on each criterion. As before, the summed products of the weightings and ratings produces a single score (3.10) measuring community competitive position.

Target Industry Assessment Matrix

Industry attractiveness and competitive advantage scores for each prospective industry are shown in Table 5. These can be shown graphically in the form of an area target industry matrix (Figure 1). This matrix can be used both for community development and marketing.

From an area marketing perspective, the current target industry matrix provides a rational basis for prioritizing investments. The area is most likely to receive a positive return on its investment, in terms of its strategic goals, by marketing to attrac-

TABLE 4
Calculating Area
Competitive Position in SIC 3411

LOCATION FACTOR	WEIGHT	RATING	SCORE
Market access	.25	3	0.75
Business Climate	.15	3	0.45
Labor Cost	.20	4	0.80
Trucking Access	.06	2	0.12
Rail Access	.04	3	0.12
Water Access (Y/N)	Required	Y	---
Air Transportation	.16	2	0.20
Electricity Cost	.05	5	0.25
Natural Gas Costs	.02	4	0.08
Water Availability	.07	3	0.21
TOTAL	1.00		3.10

tive industries where it has a strong competitive advantage.

In this (fictitious) case, the area has a strong competitive advantage in two attractive industries: surgical and medical instruments (SIC 3841) and special dies (3544). Aircraft engines and parts (3724) and screw machine products (3451) are both attractive industries, but the area has no competitive advantage here. On the other hand, the area has a relative advantage in serving firms that manufacture fluid meters (3824), but — based on local criteria — this is a relatively unattractive industry.

From a long-term community development perspective, local leaders can also conduct "what if" analyses to examine the payoff from investments in community change. For example, computing equipment (3573) is relatively attractive, but this area has only a moderate competitive advantage in serving the industry. By varying the ratings of area resources in the calculations assessing competitive position for this industry, local leaders can study how investment in those resources would affect their competitive position in it.

ALTERNATIVE METHODS FOR TARGETING INDUSTRIES

There are no magic formulas for selecting target industries. Different approaches can be equally valid, provided that they

identify strategically attractive industries for which the area has a unique competitive advantage. The techniques that an area uses to identify target industries depends on a number of factors. For small communities that are unable to form a regional development alliance, the state and utility company economic development departments may be the only feasible targets. For areas with a significant international market, more sophisticated approaches may be useful. Summarized below are techniques used recently to identify target industries in a number of U.S. communities.

Industry Location Quotient by Growth Rate Matrix

The Greater Cleveland Growth Association identified targets from 106 three-digit industry groups based on location quotients and U.S. growth rate (based on the U.S. Department of Commerce's *Industrial Outlook*). The location quotient (local percentage employment by industry/U.S. percentage employment by industry) serves as an indicator of the area's relative competitive advantage. The U.S. growth rate for each industry serves as an indicator of industry attractiveness. As shown in Figure 2, the matrix plot of these two factors provides Cleveland with a prioritized list of targets.

Existing industry/business formation/ area competitiveness screening

A study for a major mid-western metropolitan area screened target industries through three consecutive analyses. First, existing industry was analyzed to identify the primary industries and their growth potential (based on national forecasts by industry). Second, new business formations were analyzed. This included a study of both business climate factors that relate to new business formation and a survey of community attitudes toward entrepreneurship. Finally, area competitiveness with the nation, and then the region, was assessed on more than 40 factors for more than 500 business groups.

Industry attractiveness competitive position screening

A consultant for one southwestern U.S. metropolitan area screened industries first in terms of their attractiveness. The top-rated industries were then screened in terms of the area's competitive position.

Screening industries based on national and regional growth rates reduced the list from more than 700 to about 100 types of firms. Further screening, based on number of establishments, proportion of large es-

TABLE 5
Target Industry Scores for Selected Industries

SIC	INDUSTRY	INDUSTRY ATTRACTIVE-NESS	AREA COMPETITIVE POSITION
3411	Metal cans	2.65	3.10
3441	Fabricated metals	3.20	1.50
3451	Screw machine parts	3.85	1.35
3523	Farm machinery	1.45	3.20
3544	Special dies	3.65	4.40
3551	Food production machinery	2.90	4.25
3573	Computing equipment	3.80	2.75
3645	Residential light fixtures	2.95	3.80
3714	Motor vehicle parts	3.55	2.00
3724	Aircraft engines and parts	4.30	1.15
3822	Environmental controls	3.05	2.50
3823	Process controls	2.80	3.50
3824	Fluid meters	2.20	4.00
3841	Surgical & medical instruments	3.65	4.00

FIGURE 1
Target Industry Matrix

Target Industry Matrix (Industry Attractiveness vs. Area Competitive Position)

tablishments, number of employees per establishment, and location quotients reduced to under 70 types of firms. Examination of the area's competitiveness on the remaining industries' location criteria reduced the list to 19 four-digit manufacturing, wholesaling/distribution, and services industries.

Multiple-factor rankings

A mid-western state evaluated 440 manufacturing industries as target industries based on rankings of 51 variables. First, each industry was ranked based on its national performance for ten-year employment change, current level of employment and establishments, and number of establishments. Second, industry location requirements were assessed by industry average hourly wages and average gas and electric fuel bill/establishment. Next, the state's ability to meet the industry's location requirements was ranked based on payroll per employee compared to other states in the region and based on value-added per employer compared to other states in region. Finally, the industries were

ranked in terms of the state industry multiplier; industries with a higher multiplier have a greater impact, therefore a higher ranking. Values for each variable arrayed from low-to-high and given ratings relative to their rank. As a result of this process, 21 four-digit target industries were identified.

Industry, local, and competitive comparisons

An urban county in the Northeast U.S. identified 123 distinct four-digit SIC target industries in seven major categories. They assessed industry attractiveness based on historical and projected U.S. employment growth. They assessed competitive position based on historical regional employment change by industry (identifying the county's largest growth industries during the past five years), the number of firms and employees by industry moving into county during past six months (by place of origin), and historical local growth by industry, compared to growth of rival county.

Review of key issues

Planning at Southeast Texas, Inc., a three-county economic development alliance, was guided by consultants together with a steering committee with representatives from business, labor, minority groups, and geographic areas of the region. Initially, task forces were formed to identify the major issues affecting the area's economic development. Among the factors identified were the cost of doing business, education, infrastructure, finance, the labor market, and the quality of life.

The team of consultants prepared background papers on each of these issues with a preliminary list of action ideas to correct weaknesses. Research for the background papers included interviews with a cross-section of leaders from throughout the area. Next, the consultants received feedback on their preliminary findings from the steering committee and through a series of meetings throughout the region.

Finally, the accumulated information was used to identify and develop the key elements of the plan. Some 54 four-digit target industries, in nine two-digit groups,

FIGURE 2
Industry Targets

Using the methodology described earlier, 14 target industry groups were identified. The graph and table below lists the 14 industry groups identified in this study, their local employment, and the shipments compound growth rate (1988-93) for the fastest growing industry in each industry group. Detailed descriptions of the industries, location quotients, growth rates, and export potential can be found in Table I.

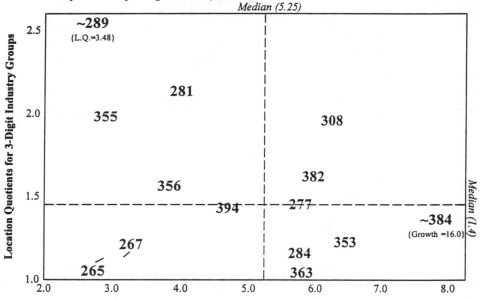

	SIC	Industry Group	Location Quotient	Shipments Growth '88-93(%)	High Growth Industry SIC
High	277	Greeting Cards	1.41	5.8	2771
	308	Miscellaneous Plastics Products	1.87	6.3	3088
	382	Measuring and Controlling Devices	1.68	6.0	3826
Good	281	Industrial Inorganic Chemicals	2.81	3.8	2812, 2813, 2816
	284	Soap, Cleaners, and Toilet Goods	1.16	5.8	2842
	289	Miscellaneous Chemical Products	3.48	2.6	2891
	353	Construction and Related Machinery	1.87	6.5	3533
	355	Special Industry Machinery	1.22	2.9	3554
	356	General Industrial Machinery	1.87	3.8	3565
	363	Household Appliances	1.07	5.8	3635
	384	Medical Instruments and Supplies	1.33	16.0	3844
Modest	265	Paperboard Containers and Boxes	1.13	2.7	2653
	267	Misc. Converted Paper Products	1.17	3.2	2676
	394	Toys and Sporting Goods	1.39	4.7	3949

Development Potential

were identified based on a review of previous studies.

Product-industry-area "Meatball"

The Beacon Council in Miami has developed a targeting matrix (Figure 3) based on three dimensions: (1) a Miami product line; (2) the target industry group; and (3) the target geographic area.

The Miami product line includes six different possible uses of Miami-based business assets, notes Dr. John Cordrey, Vice President for Research and Economics with the Beacon Council. These include: (1) Gateway, a platform for trade; (2) Entrepot, international warehousing and distribution; (3) Headquarters, primarily for Latin American regional offices; (4) Manufacturing and Assembly; (5) Tourism; and (6) Research, Education, Health, and Culture, specialized high value added services.

Miami's targeted geographic areas include: Dade County (i.e., its existing industry base), North America, Latin America, Africa, Asia, and Europe.

"We may go to Milan, Italy to market Miami as the entrepot for distributing Italian product to the U.S. and Latin America," notes Dr. Cordrey. "Our targeting is business location product by some targeted industry to some specific city. We call this 'the meatball.' Any business development trip must answer the three questions: What Miami business location are you marketing? What targeted industry are you emphasizing? What target city will you visit?"

The seven target industry studies described above, which were provided by members of ACCRA (the association of applied community researchers), provide examples of the variety of approaches in use to identify development markets. A variety of other methods are used, some involving computerized models and area mapping. But the ultimate test of any targeting methodology is whether it: (1) identifies attractive industry segments; (2) assesses the area's ability to compete for those industries; (3) fits within the larger context of the area's strategic planning effort.

THE ROLE OF TARGET INDUSTRIES IN AREA DEVELOPMENT STRATEGY

Marketing to target industries - even if the industries are carefully identified - cannot be successful if an area lacks a solid basic economic development structure. A targeted industry marketing program must be supported by three components: an area development alliance, existing industry satisfaction with the area business climate, and an entrepreneurial environment (Figure 4). For each component of this "Economic Development Pyramid" to be developed, the previous components must be in place:

❑ Attempts to retain and expand existing industry are unlikely to be successful without a cohesive development alliance;

❑ Start-up firms are unlikely to be created if existing industry is not satisfied with how the area serves industry;

❑ Attempts to attract or retain target industries are unlikely to be successful if all of the previous components of the pyramid are not in place.

Unless this structure is substantially in place, targeted marketing efforts are unlikely to be successful.

Economic Development Alliance

The Area Development Alliance is an umbrella organization of agencies that affect economic development policy and industry service. The purposes of the alliance

FIGURE 3
The Beacon Council Targeted Marketing Matrix

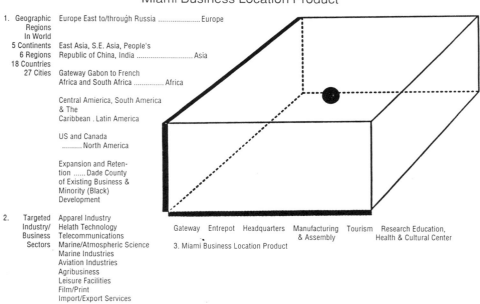

1
Geographic Regions in World
2
Industry/Business Sectors
3
Miami Business Location Product

1. Geographic
   Regions
   In World
   5 Continents
   6 Regions
   18 Countries
   27 Cities

   Europe East to/through Russia .... Europe

   East Asia, S.E. Asia, People's
   Republic of China, India .... Asia

   Gateway Gabon to French
   Africa and South Africa .... Africa

   Central Amierica, South America
   & The
   Caribbean . Latin America

   US and Canada
   .... North America

   Expansion and Reten-
   tion ...... Dade County
   of Existing Business &
   Minority (Black)
   Development

2. Targeted
   Industry/
   Business
   Sectors

   Apparel Industry
   Helath Technology
   Telecommunications
   Marine/Atmospheric Science
   Marine Industries
   Aviation Industries
   Agribusiness
   Leisure Facilities
   Film/Print
   Import/Export Services

Gateway   Entrepot   Headquarters   Manufacturing   Tourism   Research Education,
                                    & Assembly   Health & Cultural Center
3. Miami Business Location Product

---

are to: (1) develop a strategic vision for area economic and community development; (2) identify the core competencies that will be needed to attain that vision; and (3) coordinate the development of those competencies.

The basis for area development has changed as industry has entered a new information-based era. In this era, area services, the firm, its suppliers and markets, are seen as one system. The effectiveness of this system is based on how well its elements work together. Performance breakthroughs among firms that have reorganized around this way of thinking have rippled across industries. Firms no longer "hand off" projects between departments; they form inter-functional self-managed teams. They no longer inventory parts; they receive them "just in time" from single-source suppliers with whom they are linked through planning and "hard-wired" electronic networks. Emphasis in the information-based firm is on how functions are integrated.

Areas prepared to compete for the location (or retention) of firms in this information-based era have made a corresponding shift from isolated agency-based program planning to cooperative strategic planning. Educational programs in these areas do not "hand off" students with a generic diploma to local industry; they collaborate with industry to design curricula that lead to employable skills. Long-range infrastructure planning in these areas is not reactive to sins of past incremental growth, but anticipates problems and opportunities available to existing and future industry. The area is seen by its leaders as an integrated service system.

The foundation of this service system is the area development alliance. An area alliance is required for the same reason that companies are reorganizing into cross-functional teams. It is through this alliance — of schools, industry, city and county agencies, and other area organizations — that the vision for area development is articulated and attained.

The vision for area development is a broad and evolving statement of "what kind of area do we want to become." Filling out the details of that vision requires specification of the industries that a community wants to target for growth. Targeting industry is important because the mix of firms in an area is a central determinant of its character. Targeting particular types of firms — and building core competencies that service those industries — increases the likelihood of job growth. But without an effective alliance, targeting is superfluous.

Existing Industry

The primary leverage point for area development — and particularly for identification of targeted development — is existing industry. Most target industry efforts begin with an analysis of existing industry. Typically this analysis will include an examination of the concentration of industries in the local area compared to their concentration elsewhere (i.e., location quotient analysis), identification of suppliers and buyers that serve existing industry (i.e., industrial linkages), and monitoring of existing industry satisfaction with the area (i.e., the business climate survey).

Location quotient analysis assumes that particular industry groups that are disproportionately represented in the local area, compared to elsewhere, reflect basic area strengths. This should lead to further analysis — including interviews with executives in the over-represented industries — to identify those strengths. If a basis for local competitive advantage can be isolated in this way, area developers may then be able to identify other industries that value the same source of advantage.

Industrial linkage analysis assumes that out-of-area firms supplying or buying from local industry may consider a location in the area. Linkages can be determined by examining input-output tables or by surveying industry executives about the businesses they buy from and sell to. From the area perspective, this analysis is predicated on an attempt to capture more of the value chain involved in producing some good or service. A simple example of this is found in agricultural areas that try to move into food processing. The probability of industrial linkages resulting in new business locations appears to increase with the increasing importance of "just in time" and other rapid response systems.

From a marketing perspective, the most basic analysis is the existing *industry satisfaction survey*. Existing industry is the development agency's client base. Like other services, locations are "sold" by "word of mouth" between existing and prospective clients. This diffusion process has been documented among a variety of industrial and consumer product studies since the 1950s.

A recent illustration of the diffusion pro-

FIGURE 4
Economic Development Pyramid

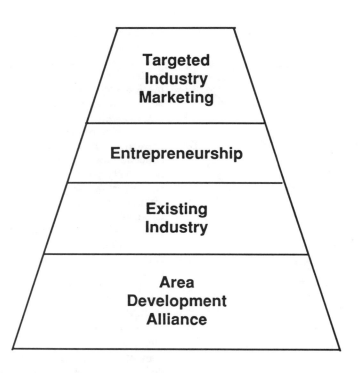

Targeted Industry Marketing

Entrepreneurship

Existing Industry

Area Development Alliance

cess in economic development is offered by a $1.5 billion travel agency, which has 2,600 employees in 400 offices worldwide, that located a branch in rural Linton, North Dakota. In describing the move, the CEO noted that executives from client firms have expressed an interest in his rural North Dakota "back office" operation.

"We share information on how we established the office and put them in touch with people who can help them get started. Just a year and a half ago, a large East Coast HMO accompanied us on one of our trips, and within a couple of months they hired over three hundred people in a town not far from our North Dakota site. They have since expanded their operation. Several firms who contacted us have opened similar facilities, including a hotel reservations company...a telemarketing firm...and a large airline's frequent flyer tracking operation...(Rosenbluth 1992)."

Existing industry is the gateway for communications to prospective new industry. Ultimately, neither advertising nor economic development sales calls "sell" an area; advertising merely generates interest and sales calls provide support information.

Only existing industry executives can sell other executives on a location. Because of this, it is important to monitor the satisfaction of existing industry executives with the area.

Satisfaction studies are widely conducted by service organizations among their clients. As competition has increased in the banking and health care industries, for example, the use of market research has increased dramatically. Such market studies — including focus groups, individual interviews, and surveys — provide the basis for continuous improvement in the services offered, and maintain or enhance client satisfaction.

Similarly, industry satisfaction studies can provide the basis for continuous improvement of the area service network. Such studies should serve as a focal point for alliance planning efforts, just as market research serves as a starting point for corporate plans. Properly conducted, industry satisfaction studies can help cross-functional area development planning teams design programs that address industries' existing and anticipated needs. Tracked over time, the results of these studies can

help the development planning team manage existing industry satisfaction with the area service network. In this process, industry retention and expansion becomes synonymous with industry attraction.

Satisfaction studies can also be used together with location quotient and linkage analyses to isolate industry-specific opportunities. Not all customers are equally satisfied with any firm's products; most firms develop their products so that they satisfy particular target customer segments. In the same way, not all local industry will be equally satisfied with any area service network. Effective development strategy requires a focus on particular industry segments.

Entrepreneurial Environment

The third level of the Economic Development Pyramid involves creating and maintaining an entrepreneurial environment. This is the catalyst for the growth of an economy. A study by Massachusetts Institute of Technology researcher David Birch concluded that 52 percent of all new jobs are created by independent businesses with 20 or fewer employees. A Small Business Administration study concluded that firms of that size generate about 63 percent of new jobs in rural areas. New businesses are not formed spontaneously, they require two ingredients: an economic context and individuals skilled in starting up a business.

Business creation is a learned activity. People whose parents owned their own business are more likely to start a business, much more likely than those whose parents were salaried employees. Creating an entrepreneurial environment involves more than providing the raw materials of business such as capital; it involves providing people who have marketable ideas with the business start-up skills needed to bring those ideas to market.

Entrepreneurs are a hidden economic development multiplier. When a basic industry (i.e., one that exports goods or services outside of the area and imports new revenue into the area) locates in an area, we calculate the "multiplier" effect based on the local-service jobs that firm will create in addition to its own direct employment. Most observers know that 10 new basic industry jobs will also mean additional jobs in local retailing, wholesaling, and services.

We do not calculate the entrepreneurial multiplier, the number of new businesses that will tend to be created in the same or related industries. The entrepreneurial multiplier is illustrated by the upholstered wood furniture industry that has grown in north-central Mississippi. That industry had its start in 1948 when the community of New Albany passed two bond issues to build a plant for a Chicago businessman (Mississippi Forest Products Utilization Laboratory 1988). He located in New Albany with two employees. Over time his apprentices started their own spinoff ventures, and so on. Subsequent investment by the state of Mississippi in research and development and trade shows specific to the upholstered wood furniture industry has lead to a steady increase in that state's market share of the industry.

The entrepreneurial environment as a leverage for target industry marketing is also seen in Waterloo, Canada. A town of only about 70,000 people, Waterloo is the fourth largest computer software producing area in Canada, after Toronto, Vancouver, and Ottawa. A key to this activity is the William G. Davis Computer Centre at the University of Waterloo, which graduates the largest concentration of computer researchers of any campus in North America. In the mid-1980s a four-community development alliance organized Canada's "Technology Triangle" to leverage this growth. By the late '80s, more than 75 companies in the region had been started by UW students, faculty, and staff (Powell 1990).

Entrepreneurial programs that are focused on key industries are growing throughout the U.S.. The Center for Innovation Technology in Herndon, Virginia, focuses on helping business start-ups that develop space-related technology. Two business incubators for ceramics-technology businesses have been launched in New York State. The "Entrepreneurial and Technology Group" in Orlando, Florida, launched a business incubator facility to provide low-cost real estate and business help to new high-tech companies. In each of these cases, the focus is on creating entrepreneurship in areas with significant job-creation potential.

Targeted Industry Marketing

The central premise of the Economic Development Pyramid is that targeted industry marketing is integrally related to a hierarchy of other development activities. Development will occur without targeted industry marketing; it is less likely to occur without an area development alliance, satisfied existing industry, and an entrepreneurial environment. Like an ecological "food chain," each level "feeds" the next one up; the elimination or reduction in lower levels diminishes the strength of higher levels.

Target identification is only an initial step in the targeted industry marketing program. A target industry study has no intrinsic value. Developers, like other executives, are too familiar with studies that became an end in themselves. The only time that a target industry study has value is when it is enacted. The next stage in the process involves in-depth research to: (1) understand the needs of the industry, and individual firms within the industry, in greater depth; (2) identify communications channels and media useful in communicating with industry executives; (3) prepare a variety of messages (e.g., advertisements, direct mail, trade show exhibits) framed in terms of industry- or firm-specific concerns; (4) track the most attractive prospects within the industry; and (5) continuously assess community resources and competencies in terms of the industry's evolving needs.

CONCLUSIONS

Targeting industry is not a cure-all. It is simply a more efficient way to attract new industry. Without a strong local community and economic development program, targeting industry is a waste of money. Areas that lack a solid Economic Development Pyramid to support the industries targeted are unlikely to attract them. If they do happen to locate a firm, they are unlikely to retain them.

A solid Development Pyramid becomes increasingly important as firms move toward the "boundaryless organization" envisioned by General Electric CEO Jack Welsh. These new-era firms are stripping themselves down to their core competencies, outsourcing all other components and services in the product's "value chain," and tying the entire system together through a "just-in-time" network. Area agencies — schools, highways, railways, and the like — are all part of this network. An area that is unable to adequately coordinate its services and satisfy its existing industry base is unlikely to become, or remain, part of such a network.

REFERENCES

Hoch, L. Clinton (1992), "Locating High-Performance Telecommunications Operations," *Telemarketing Magazine*, 11 (October), 70-77.

Lopez, Rigoberto A. and Nona R. Henderson (1989), "The Determinants of Location Decisions for Food Processing Plants," *Agribusiness*, 5 (November), 619-632.

Lund, Leonard (1986). *Locating Corporate R&D Facilities:* Report No. 892. New York: The Conference Board.

Mississippi Forest Products Utilization Laboratory (1988). *The Mississippi Furniture Industry and Its Use of Wood-Based Materials*. Research Report 13.
Mississippi State, Mississippi.

Powell, Doug (1990), "'Waterloo Becomes Hotbed for High-Tech Activity," *Computing Canada*, 16 (August 2), p. 12

Rosenbluth, Hal F. (1992). *The Customer Comes First*. NY: Quill.

U.S. Office of Technology Assessment (1988). *Technology and the American Economic Transition*. Washington, D.C.: Congress of the United States.

Industry Clustering For Economic Development

Gary Anderson

INTRODUCTION

Industry targeting—that is, the identification of specific industries or types of enterprises for emphasis in economic development activities—has become an important element in regional development strategies because it enables the developer to focus resources on a specific goal in order to increase efficiency and leverage efforts. However, targeting methodologies vary widely from practitioner to practitioner. This article discusses the use of industry clustering as a means for improving targeting efforts. Industry clustering is recommended for two reasons:

❑ The use of clusters captures the economic relationships among specific industry sectors, providing a far richer source of information about regional dynamics than is available in the typology of specific industry sectors inherent in the Standard Industrial Classification (SIC) system.

❑ The use of clusters provides a powerful set of tools for analysis, policy formulation, and regional organization and implementation to increase the effectiveness of economic development strategies.

To explain how industry clusters help achieve these goals and how the cluster approach can be implemented in practice, this article defines industry clusters, describes how they can support regional development strategies, and then discusses a methodology for identifying industry clusters in a specific region.

WHAT IS AN INDUSTRY CLUSTER

The concept of industry clusters has become fairly standard in economic development literature in the past five years. The precise origin of the concept is uncertain, but SRI International first used it in a consulting project for a southern California utility in 1988 to help the utility segment its commercial user market in a way that would allow the utility to define technical assistance services for groups of related customers. The concept was popularized by

Michael Porter in *The Competitive Advantage of Nations* (New York: Basic Books, 1990).

An industry cluster is a group of companies that rely on an active set of relationships among themselves for individual efficiency and competitiveness. These relationships fall into three general categories.

❑ *Buyer-Supplier Relationships.* This cluster structure is the one most frequently described in economic development literature. It consists of core companies that produce goods and services that are sold to final consumers and of companies at earlier stages in the value-adding chain that supply the inputs — intermediate goods and services and raw materials — that are assembled into or used in the assembly of final goods and services. Distributors of final goods and services, where separate from the producers, may also be a part of these clusters.

❑ *Competitor and Collaborator Relation-ships.* This cluster structure, consisting of companies that produce the same or similar goods and services at a specific level in the value chair, exists because competitors frequently share information (often unintentionally) about product and process innovations and market opportunities and may, in fact, formally collaborate to develop such innovations in precompetitive or strategic alliances.

❑ *Shared-Resource Relationships.* These relationships exist when firms rely on the same sources of raw materials, technology, human resources, and information even though they may use these resources to produce goods and services for very different markets.

An example of an industry cluster that has elements of all three of these relationships in it, the aerospace and advanced manufacturing clusters in southern California, is illustrated in Figure 1.

The common factor in all these relationships is the premise that such relationships benefit from geographic proximity. The premise is that such relationships will be stronger if the distances separating participants in the cluster are as short as possible. Physical movement of goods is obviously important. In an era where just-in-time inventory management and time-to-market responsiveness are standard elements of competitiveness and productivity, the shorter the distance from loading dock to loading dock or from desk to desk, the

---

FIGURE 1
Aerospace/Advanced Manufacturing Cluster in Southern California

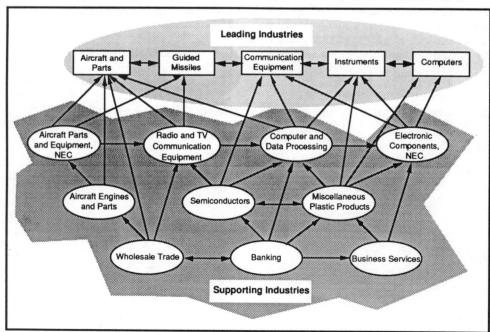

---

better. Similarly, the flow of information that directs the flow of goods and services improves as distance decreases. Although information technologies have reduced the impact of physical distances, many activities, ranging from product design to contract negotiations, can only be accomplished by face-to-face exchanges.

Geographic proximity is significant in economic development. If close physical relationships are important in the effective operation of a cluster, then it follows that industry clusters are important in regional development. To understand the dynamics of, say, a metropolitan area or state, the economic development professional needs to understand the region as an economic system, rather than trying to analyze the region and define strategies in terms of the region's individual elements.

The importance of geographic proximity to the existence and operation of industry clusters, has not gone unchallenged. Academic literature still views the geographic relationship within clusters as a theory based on observation, but not yet proven. However, the commonsense basis of the concept of regionally based industry clusters is sufficiently compelling to justify its consideration as an analytical and policy tool. In addition, success of its application in practice suggests that industry clustering is superior to more traditional approaches of industry targeting.

WHY IS THE CLUSTER CONCEPT USEFUL?

Practice has shown that the concept of industry clusters supports achievement of a variety of economic development goals. However, these goals do not include "picking winners and losers." Most economists and development practitioners agree that the effort to winnow industries doomed to fail from those fated to succeed is generally a mistake. Such efforts usually turn out wrong, and governments often inappropriately subsidize industries that they expect to be winners. Identifying industry clusters is different—it is a process to assess the "revealed preferences" of business communities and linkages among associated industries. This process is useful in providing guidance to industry attraction programs with limited resources and in surfacing areas for improvement in infrastructure and other resources needed by dominant industry clusters.

Potential applications of industry clustering, and their benefits, can be categorized in terms of their time horizons.

❑ Industry clustering is a valuable tool for short-term industrial attraction efforts that will pay off within one to two years.

❑ Industry clustering is also useful in strategies to retain firms and extend existing industry clusters that will pay off over a two-to-five-year horizon.

❑ Finally, industry clustering can be the basis for long-term efforts to establish new clusters and implement organizational efforts that will pay off over extended periods.

Short-Term Attraction Efforts

Attraction of companies to a region is generally the only means by which that region can achieve significant growth in employment opportunities in a relatively short period. Of course, economic development strategies in many regions no longer rely solely on attraction efforts (sometimes derided as "smokestack chasing" or "chip chasing"). Now, attraction efforts are usually balanced with strategies to retain and expand existing industry and strategies to establish new enterprises and clusters. Nevertheless, industry attraction continues to be appropriate as one of several economic development goals. In a small number of cases, enterprises find that the characteristics of a particular region no longer are adequate to help them sustain their competitiveness in global markets. These enterprises can be attracted to a different region that offers them the chance to regain the advantages they need for competitiveness. More often, firms that are expanding or replacing their production facilities can be encouraged to direct their new investments to a region that offers competitive advantages to the new facility.

How can the most likely target groups be identified? How can the region's comparative advantages be presented to them in an effective manner? Identification of existing clusters in a region and analysis of these clusters can answer these questions in two ways. The most direct way is to identify gaps in the value-adding chain that exist in the region's industry clusters. In Alberta, Canada, for example, forest products and petroleum production are two significant industry clusters. An analysis of the nature of firms and relationships in these industry clusters in other regions indicated that suppliers of tailored technology-based components, such as special-purpose software packages and specialized electronic control devises, had become an important element of competitiveness for the final producers. In contrast, it was found

through interviews with cluster companies in Alberta that the companies were having to go outside the region to obtain these components for their products and production systems. Companies that developed and manufactured these products were therefore identified as a prime attraction target. Their advantage would be that they would be able to find ready markets for their products in the province, and the close proximity would enable them to tailor their products more readily to the specific needs of the region's companies. Obviously the long-term goal of retaining large companies in this cluster would be served by strengthening the regional cluster with the addition of these critical supplier companies.

By determining why current companies in a cluster stay within a region, industry clustering can answer the second question of how to present the region's comparative advantages effectively to similar companies. Advantages that exist for a specific type of company in a region can be identified by talking to companies in the industry cluster. From this information, a focused marketing message can be defined to explain to companies similar to those already in the region why they should consider the region in their relocation and expansion planning. Such messages can emphasize, for example, particular work force skills, specific types of customers, specialized research assets, and focused education and training programs that are available to these types of companies. Such messages are much stronger than the generalized information that often characterizes regional marketing efforts. Brochures and advertisements that stress low-cost labor, generous tax incentives, easy access to recreation or culture, and an attractive community are much less effective than specific messages stressing particular advantages that are important to a targeted industry group. For example, to attract targeted electronics firms, Austin, Texas stresses the materials scientists, software engineers, and semiconductor technicians with pertinent training and experience who live in the region, and stresses the relevance to this industry cluster of the research programs at the University of Texas.

The key point is that attraction efforts are most successful when they rely on the opportunities inherent within existing clusters, and the advantages the region offers to firms similar to those in the industry clusters that already thrive in the region. Such methods are more effective in the short term—and more likely to produce lasting results—than are attraction efforts focused on types of firms that are outside the region's existing clusters and attraction efforts that rely on generic characteristics and expediencies such as tax incentives and training subsidies.

Medium-Term Development Strategies

Existing industry clusters are also an important analytical focus in defining development strategies that will require longer periods to pay off. In discussing the dynamics of economic development, current literature stresses the importance of helping small companies to become established in a region and discusses the importance of competitive foundations such as work-force preparedness and research institutions in sustaining economic growth. As relevant as these concepts are, initiatives to establish new firms and enhance economic foundations will require two to five years to begin producing measurable results. The important factor in defining these strategies is to determine which types of small businesses to target for support and which foundations to enhance in order to retain and support the growth of industry in the region.

The key to making these determinations again resides in the existing industry clusters in the region. The same analysis that worked in identifying attraction targets and defining attraction strategies is relevant here, though the applications are different. Here, the strategies will be more indirect. To achieve longer-term economic goals, the emphasis should be on initiatives that improve the region's ability to retain, establish, and grow industry.

Over a longer period, a region can strengthen its economy and create new employment opportunities by helping new companies to become established, either to fill gaps in existing industry clusters or to extend the existing industry clusters into new markets. To sustain its economic base, the region can also undertake efforts to address gaps and limitations in the economic foundations that support the ability of regional industry to compete in global markets.

A region can achieve significant leverage in the efforts to accomplish these goals by defining strategies that address a variety of objectives within integrated initiatives. Again, the key to defining these strategies lies within the region's existing industry clusters. Inherent in the concept of industry clusters that has been put forth by Porter and others is the existence of a set of core competencies that are shared throughout the cluster. For example, in a region like the central Midwest, with a cluster concentration in heavy manufacturing, core competencies in manufacturing processes, use of advanced materials, and production optimization are critical to success. In Omaha and Des Moines, which have established clusters in insurance and related financial services, knowledge of distributed data processing, large-scale real-time databases, and sophisticated data analysis methods is critical.

Once a region has identified a significant regional cluster, it can use interviews and analysis by industry specialists to identify the core competencies that are critical to the cluster's success. It can then identify those core competencies that are not as strong as industry executives would wish, and then define strategies to strengthen them. Such strategies can be structured in such a way that they support the establishment of new companies that specialize in these areas of competence, take advantage of opportunities to extend these core competencies into new markets through diversification of existing companies and establishment of new companies, and support the retention of existing companies by strengthening the region's ability to support these areas of competence.

Omaha's recent efforts provide one example of such an integrated strategy. Although Omaha is home to a variety of companies dependent on financial data processing, an analysis of the region indicated that, in the view of corporate executives, it was not adequately sustaining this core competence. In response, a number of corporations combined their efforts and established the Nebraska Applied Information Management (AIM) Institute in Omaha.

The AIM Institute designed its programs so that it could accomplish a number of important goals simultaneously. Its programs include improvement of the data processing curriculum at the local colleges and universities, establishment of a program of training seminars and continuing education courses for information processing managers and technicians in specific information processing technologies, and sponsor support for relevant applied research projects at the region's universities. The AIM Institute is now expanding its activities to include support for small service businesses that support the region's larger companies and sell to similar customers in other regions. Establishment of a business incubator for small software businesses similar to San Jose, California's Center for Software Development—is now being considered. Through its integrated program of activities, the AIM Institute is achieving a variety of economic development goals, ranging from retention and expansion of existing large and small companies to assistance in establishing new companies.

Long-Term Economic Development Goals

In discussions of the importance of existing industry clusters to a region's economic development with local organizations concerned with the region's growth, one objection is frequent: does this approach mean that a region is forever limited to the industry that it presently possesses? After all, wasn't Silicon Valley once just an expanse of prune orchards? And, wasn't Research Triangle in North Carolina once just a collection of sleepy Southern university towns?

The response to this objection is heartening, but must carry a large dose of reality with it. Over a long period, a region can give rise to a completely new set of industry clusters and can significantly change its economic base. Nevertheless, the particular developments exemplified by Silicon Valley and Research Triangle—one unplanned and the other the result of an explicit development program—took a long time to evolve. Silicon Valley, after all, traces its genesis to the invention of the vacuum tube in Palo Alto; its dramatic growth period started more than 30 years ago. Research Triangle was established in the early 1970s and has taken 20 years of sustained, focused development effort to reach its present stage of growth.

Economic development professionals and their sponsors should not ignore the long term in defining their strategies because, with sufficient time, the potential exists to reshape a region's economic base. Identification of present industry clusters can also be an important analytical and process tool in defining long-term goals and implementing long-term development strategies. The important point is that dramatic changes can literally require decades, but they start within the existing clusters of the region.

The most valuable application of industry clusters in achievement of these long-term goals is in providing an organizational framework and process that can support ongoing development efforts. Significant changes in the region's economic base must be rooted in a sustained, high level of collaboration among firms in the private sector, and between private corporations and public institutions. Leadership from within the existing clusters in a region can provide the basis for an organizational framework that can define and implement development strategies, and then review and refine these strategies as new challenges and opportunities arise.

Arizona's Strategic Planning for Economic Development (ASPED) project has employed this approach, defined in more detail in an article by Ioanna Morfessis in this issue of *E.D. Review*. The first step in that effort was to define the industry clusters that formed the foundation of Arizona's economy. Established (though by no means static) clusters included agriculture/forestry and food processing, aerospace, business services, health and biomedicine, information, mining and minerals, tourism and transportation. ASPED added optics, a small industry group but with high growth potential, after the initial survey/interview process. In a series of cluster meetings, managers from companies within each cluster then identified specific needs for future growth and defined strategic initiatives. They have now organized these clusters into formal ongoing groups that have taken the responsibility for initiatives from within each cluster and in collaboration with public organizations and institutions, coordinated through the Office of the Governor.

More recently, cluster groups provided the framework for a strategic assessment process in the region centered on San Jose, California. This project, Joint Venture: Silicon Valley, took a slightly different approach. Initial analysis identified a series of clusters including microelectronics, computers and communications, defense and aerospace, biotechnology and health care, software, and manufacturing. Volunteer representatives from each industry cluster became members of a series of working groups that met several times over nine months. With industry leaders as chairs and with the facilitation of SRI specialists, these groups first identified advantages and disadvantages of operating in Silicon Valley, then they agreed on strategic needs of the cluster and relative priorities, and finally they defined and developed preliminary business plans for initiatives to overcome high-priority deficiencies.

In contrast to the Arizona project, Joint Venture: Silicon Valley did not use the industry cluster groups as the organizational basis for implementation of strategic initiatives. Instead, it created formal organizations to implement those initiatives that required the ability to raise money, hire

staff, and contract for facilities and equipment; it organized continuing task forces to implement initiatives that could be carried out by groups of volunteers.

In the cases where a specific initiative was organized to meet the needs of a particular industry, the organization or task force was created out of the cluster working group. Initiatives of this type included, for example, a defense conversion task force, an environmental business incubator, a software industry organization, a biotechnology task force on university-industry cooperation, and a school-to-work internship program for the financial services industry.

In a number of cases, however, the identified need was broader than the concerns of a single industry and was beyond the resources of individual industry groups to implement. In these instances, Joint Venture organized "Flagship Initiatives." These initiatives ranged from the ambitious "Smart Valley" project—which has created a not-for-profit corporation with a full-time executive director and staff to undertake the technical and organizational planning necessary to create a Valley-wide telecommunications network—to the relatively straightforward Regulatory Forum, a task force of community regulators and corporate facilities managers that is collaborating to establish a simplified, consistent set of permitting regulations for new manufacturing and technical facilities across all the communities of Silicon Valley. Other initiatives include a K-12 educational improvement organization, an international trade center, and a multicorporation cultural foundation.

To coordinate the ongoing initiatives, the Joint Venture steering committee incorporated JV:SV Network. This umbrella organization will help raise money for small initiatives, provide a communication point for larger initiatives, and identify and organize new initiatives as required. JV:SV Network has a full-time chief executive and a small full-time staff working under the oversight of a board of directors from industry and government, with funding from a broad group of Valley companies.

Using clustering as the basis for this ambitious project was useful because it allowed individual groups to begin the process of identifying needs and responses on the basis of shared interests, and then only later begin to band together across industries on those specific issues that were important to more than one industry. Had the project been undertaken simply by holding town meetings at the outset, the project

participants may never have been able to agree on needs and priorities, much less establish a set of action-focused organizations that could design and undertake specific initiatives to response to high-priority needs.

HOW ARE INDUSTRY CLUSTERS IDENTIFIED?

The first step in any economic development strategy focusing on clusters is the identification of the core industry clusters that exist in a region. This process is not entirely quantitative, but rather relies instead on a combination of straightforward quantitative analysis of available data and evaluation of qualitative information. The process is no mystery; it is, instead, a commonsense approach to articulating relationships among individual firms in a region. The following steps are the ones that SRI employs in its economic development projects. They are similar to the methods in the case studies that Porter's book discusses.

Define the Region
The first step is to define, at least in rough terms, the economic region that will be the basis of analysis. An economic region is the geographic area within which most day-to-day relationships occur in a given industry cluster. Because industry clusters rarely stay within the neat boundaries of political jurisdictions, this task is not necessarily as simple as defining the jurisdiction of the economic development agency that is undertaking the strategy project. On the one hand, economic regions are almost never as small as a single city or county. On the other hand, they are rarely as large as a complete state. Furthermore, geographic and historic circumstances more often define the economic region within which a cluster operates than do political boundaries, so examples abound of economic regions that cross city, county, and often state lines.

The most practical approach is based on metropolitan statistical areas (MSAs). These MSAs represent concentrations of population that have generally arisen because of concentrations of economic activity, so they are generally a good approximation of an economic region. For convenience in collecting and collating information on MSAs, these areas are generally defined in terms of counties. As a result, a good first definition of an economic region is the set of counties that constitute an MSA. For example, the Gary, Indiana MSA consists of Lake County and Porter County in Northwestern Indiana. In addition to containing the city of Gary, this MSA includes Hammond, East Chicago, and several small communities. An analysis of Gary's industry clusters would start with this definition. In addition, attention should be paid to any MSAs that are contiguous to the area of interest. In the Gary example, the Chicago MSA abuts the Gary MSA, and might be included in the analysis. Similarly, an analysis of the Silicon Valley region would probably incorporate both the San Jose and San Francisco MSAs, and certainly would take notice of surrounding counties that have accepted the overflow from this industrial concentration.

One more caveat is that industrial clusters and economic regions may not be exactly the same, with clusters taking on different patterns within an overall region. For example, in the Silicon Valley project, although the computer/communications and the defense/space clusters were found to be concentrated primarily in the San Jose MSA, the bio-science cluster extended into San Francisco and Oakland. Effective cluster analysis does not depend on an exact definition of the economic region, and the definition can be refined further in qualitative analysis at later stages, but the MSA approach does provide a convenient starting point.

Calculate Employment Concentrations

Given a set of counties constituting an MSA as the first approximation of the economic region, the process can then identify the industries that ship goods and services out of the region and bring wealth into the region. Because few regions have accurate data about shipments out of the region, a proxy calculation is necessary. The standard approach that has been effective is to calculate employment concentrations, or "location quotients," based on data on employment by industry. The most effective source of this data is the *County Business Patterns,* published by the Census Bureau, which reports number of employees by industry annually, with a reporting lag of about three years. This data is useful in that it is reported in sufficient industry and geographic detail to provide insights into employment patterns in specific industry segments at a fairly small geographic level.

Employment concentrations or location quotients are determined by calculating the percentage of employment in an industry in the region to total regional employment as a ratio to the percentage of total employ-

ment in that industry nationally to total national employment:

$$\frac{(\text{Regional industry employment/Total regional employment})}{(\text{National industry employment/Total national employment})}$$

This calculation should proceed at the two-digit SIC level, with those industries that are significant employers in the region calculated at three-digit levels. If the ratio for a specific industry is greater than one, then we can make the assumption that the particular industry in the region is exporting some portion of its production to other regions. Using this ratio, all industry sectors in the region can be ranked in terms of their probable importance as exporters and wealth generators.

It is noteworthy when using *County Business Patterns* data that, below the two-digit level, the number of employees and the payrolls are not reported when they would compromise confidentiality. Generally this case will occur only when a very small number of companies make up the industry sector in the county. For these groups, size is reported in general classes, and income data is not reported. For these sectors, a midpoint can be used for number of employees, or data may be obtainable directly from the company or from other sources. Income data frequently can be estimated by interpolation using data from the next higher level classification or from the industry sector in a contiguous region.

Quantitative calculation of employment concentrations is not the only means by which significant regional clusters can be identified. Many examples exist of regions where industry sectors with a low current concentration are, nevertheless, producing products and services for markets outside the region and have the potential to become significant wealth generators for the region in the future. These emerging clusters, such as optics in Arizona and environmental technologies in Silicon Valley, are usually identified in interviews during the process of validating quantitative analysis described below.

Group Sectors into Preliminary Clusters

The third step is to group the key exporting industry sectors into probable relationships with one another. Here, no hard-and-fast rules exist. These cluster groupings will be based on general industry knowledge and general information about the region. Electronic instruments, for example, might be considered part of an aerospace cluster in one region of the country, whereas in another region they might be part of an

automotive cluster. Similarly, plastics and metals suppliers could easily be a part of either cluster, depending on the characteristics of the region. Input-output tables, such as the general table of input-output data for the United States and the tables of multipliers available for specific MSAs through the Department of Commerce Regional Industry Multiplier System (RIMS), can be an additional source of information to categorize industry sectors into specific industry clusters.

The objective is to identify those final suppliers of goods and services where employment concentrations are greater than one, and to group them with the suppliers of intermediate goods and services and raw materials that are related in the production chain. The employment concentrations should be at levels high enough to suggest that the final producer is getting most of its supplies of the component or service from within the region.

At this stage, the analysis should have produced anywhere from one to six groupings of clusters that appear to exist in the region. Examples of cluster groupings from projects in three different regions are shown in Table 1 below.

Validate and Refine the Clusters

Analysis of available data will provide fairly strong indications of the existence of clusters, but will not provide information on all important cluster relationships that exist in the region. Interviews with procurement and marketing executives of larger companies, supplemented, if desired, with broader surveys of smaller companies, will provide the additional detail that is needed to map and measure the region's industry clusters.

The questions are simple: Who are your major suppliers and who are your major customers by industry segment? What approximate percentage of your production needs come within the region, and what approximate percentage of your customer markets exist within the region?

To provide additional cluster information and support more strategic analysis that will be important at later stages in the economic development program, additional questions might be asked about why the individual company is located in this region. Proximity to markets? Proximity to suppliers? Transportation systems? Quality of available work force—managerial, professional, technical? Research centers? These questions might be elaborated on by asking whether these factors have been improving or weakening in the past five years.

TABLE 1
Examples of Industry Clusters

SOUTHERN CALIFORNIA	NORTHWEST ILLINOIS	ALBERTA, CANADA
Aerospace/Advanced Manufacturing	Manufactured Inputs	Energy
Process Manufacturing	Industrial Machinery	Agriculture and Food Processing
Light/Diversified Manufacturing	Electrical Equipment	Forestry and Forest Products
Heavy Manufacturing	Telecommunications Equipment	Telecommunications Equipment
Financial/Business Services	Transportation Equipment	
Health Serivces and Instruments	Health Services and Products	
Tourism/Entertainment	Financial and Retail Services	
	Transportation and Distribution	

FIGURE 2
Silicon Valley Cluster Changes

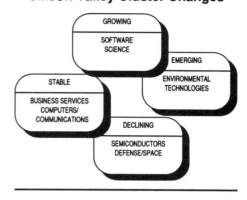

Map Each Industry Cluster

The most illuminating way of assembling and presenting the data and information that have been gained to this stage is to map the relationships that have been suggested in calculating employment concentrations, examining input-output relationships, and discussing buyer-supplier relationships. Figure 1 is an example of such a map—the aerospace/advanced manufacturing cluster that was developed for the Southern California region. This cluster map was part of a project to determine the potential effects of significant reductions in defense procurements on the industries and economy of that region. Similar information could have been obtained (and in fact was used in the project) from regional industry multiplier tables, but because the purpose of this study was to define responsive strategies, the visual presentation of the information was much more useful in illustrating the nature and extent of interactions in this key regional industry.

Calculate Importance of Clusters and Analyze Recent Trends

Having created a list of industry clusters and assigned individual industry sectors to their primary cluster, the final stage in this analysis is to calculate the relative importance of each cluster to the overall economy of the region and to determine growth trends in each cluster. This step is critical and underlines an important characteristic of industry clusters. Clusters are not static. Rather, they are dynamic and change in response to external forces and internal conditions. Relative sizes and growth trends of various clusters will be useful specifically in establishing priorities for various economic development strategies, and generally in understanding the overall dynamics of the region.

The calculation is again straightforward and is simply a matter of adding up the number of employees in each industry sector represented in the cluster and then calculating that employment as a percentage of total employment in the region. Similarly, the personal income produced in each industry can also be calculated. An additional piece of information is the growth trend in the industry cluster. It is generally useful to go back five years from the most recent data to calculate the employment and income importance of each cluster at that time, and then to calculate the rate of growth or decline of that industry cluster. The analyst may also wish to compare these growth rates to the growth rates of comparable industry groupings at the national level.

These calculations can provide a variety of useful information. For example, an examination of relative importance and growth trends in industry clusters in the Silicon Valley made a point that had largely gone unnoticed, illustrated in Figure 2. The region's economy had undergone a significant transformation that was likely to continue. Semiconductor manufacturing had been in decline through the recent past, whereas software and biotechnology had experienced significant growth and were rapidly replacing the traditional "silicon" base of the economy with a creative design base. The computer/communication, manufacturing and business services clusters had remained relatively stable but merited attention as mainstays of the region's economy.

In the analysis of the Southern California region, calculation of size and growth data emphasized several interesting points. First, the decline of defense procurement had already been having significant effects on total regional employment, and the rela-

tive importance of the defense and aerospace cluster indicated the vulnerability of the region's economy to continuation of this decline. Second, the furniture cluster had been a reasonably important cluster five years before, but (because of migration of this industry to Mexico) had declined to the point that it was rapidly becoming irrelevant to the region's future. By contrast, the financial services, international trade, and entertainment/tourism clusters had been showing significant growth in the region in comparison to national trends, and had become significant players in the region's future.

As another example, in Omaha, the insurance and financial services cluster was a significant employer and income producer in the region, though recent growth had been slow, particularly when compared with national trends. This low growth rate suggested that the cluster deserved emphasis in any economic development strategy, not only because its health was critical to the region, but also because it had not been growing at the rate national trends would have suggested.

WHERE THE CLUSTER APPROACH DOESN'T WORK

Use of industry clusters as a base of analysis and as a source of ideas for strategic development can be a powerful tool in most economic regions. However, in at least two types of economic regions, this approach cannot be directly used exactly as discussed above. It cannot be used where the defined economic region is too small to support the diversification inherent in the concept of an industry cluster, and it cannot be used where the region is too undeveloped and too isolated for clusters to survive.

In the first case, crude observations suggest that if a region has a population of less than, say, 500,000 people, a complete cluster is unlikely to exist. This lack is not necessarily a significant deterrent to definition of economic development strategies for the region. It may mean, instead, that the net has to be wider. For example, referring again to the Gary, Indiana region, the data and observations indicate that no complete cluster exists within its MSA. Instead, most employment in businesses producing tradable goods and services is concentrated in a small number of large steel mills. The remainder of exporting industry employment is represented by a relatively disparate group of other manufacturing firms.

However, the small size of the region does not mean that the clustering approach is not useful. In this instance, the appropriate region for consideration of development opportunities is at least the Greater Chicago region which encompasses the Gary MSA, and might even be extended to include the Detroit/Southern Michigan region, because this nearby region is easily accessible to and from Gary. While economic strategies would be concentrated in the Gary area, because this area is the target of concern, these strategies can be built on support for extensions of these clusters into the Gary area. For example, development strategies might include support for establishment of small manufacturers who supply goods and services to clusters centered in other parts of the region.

In the second case, that of rural and isolated regions, the tool of cluster analysis is also going to be limited if the work force isn't sufficient to support growth and sustain an autonomous cluster, and if there isn't any population and industry concentration close by on which to build, even if the boundaries of the region are expanded. Communities in parts of the western United States and in the Atlantic provinces of Canada are good examples of this problem. This issue is the conundrum of defining development strategies for rural areas that once had vital economies built on agriculture and natural resources. In these instances, a variant of the industry cluster

approach can be explored, though it may not work in all areas, at least not to a sufficient extent to provide employment for all the people who currently live in the region.

The approach is to explore the possibility that a "satellite" to an existing cluster in another region can be established. Such an approach is dependent on two factors. First, the region has to have other factors, such as a very attractive quality of life (climate, geography, and recreational opportunities, for example) that will attract professional workers in jobs that don't depend on continuing face-to-face contact. Second, the region has to have sources of infrastructure support to make it possible for these workers to do their jobs.

For example, the State of Oregon is exploring this "satellite" approach with regard to Western Oregon. In this instance, the state is mounting a substantial telecommunications program to support the establishment of small businesses in information technology development and support. The Oregon program is intended to provide the linkages, such as advanced fiber-optics systems, that are needed to provide information highways through which to ship information products to cluster centers in Portland, Seattle, and San Jose. In addition, this program will incorporate regional learning centers, so that professionals and their families can take advantage of remote educational institutions to maintain their skills and knowledge, and have opportunities for intellectual recreation to supplement the physical attractions of the area.

Information technology services are not the only application of this satellite approach. This approach is also applicable to manufactured goods, provided that they have a high value-to-weight ratio and a high technology content, so that shipping costs are a relatively small fraction of their final costs as delivered. For example, a manufacturing company in Fargo, North Dakota, was established by an entrepreneur to manufacture turbine fans and hous-

ings for automobile engines. These parts must be manufactured to very close tolerances, but their designs can be transmitted through telecommunications links to computer-aided flexible manufacturing centers, and their light weight and small size makes it possible to ship them to the turbine assembly company at very low cost. In this case, the low cost of living and consequent low wage costs for well-educated workers in North Dakota overcame the shipping costs even to Europe and Asia, and telecommunications links make it efficient to transmit designs and orders from customer companies in Japan and Germany.

CONCLUSIONS AND RECOMMENDATIONS

Several points from this discussion are worth emphasizing. First, the industry cluster approach can be a more effective analytical tool than traditional industry segmentation methods in understanding the dynamics of a region and identifying strategies for attracting, retaining, growing, and establishing industry in a region. Second, the very nature of industry clusters, with individual companies relying on their access to one another to sustain their competitiveness, indicates that the roots of new industry growth in the near term and the medium term will be found within the existing clusters in a region. Third, the strategies that can be defined in this method of targeting go beyond near-term industry attraction. In addition, they encompass medium-term strategies to foster the establishment of new companies and support retention and expansion of existing companies. Fourth, the long-term goals of sustaining the economic vitality of a region can only be achieved through a continuing process in which the clusters themselves become players in contributing to their own growth and supporting continuing improvements in the foundations that support them.

How to Create A Marketing Team

Jerry Heare, C.E.D.

BUSINESS LOCATION DECISIONS

Businesses make location decisions based on the opportunity to make a profit. Many factors affect the cost of doing business and the resulting profit. This article addresses those factors of profitability which are community related.

This discussion centers on reasons why one community may be selected over another. Once the issue of profitability is focused, using all available data, it is very likely that several communities can be found to be equally profitable.

Why, then, would a prospect "shop" for community locations? What makes the difference in one community over another? There is one big difference in each city — the people who live there. Furthermore, it is the attitude of the people who live in the community that makes a difference. The prospect must feel that he/she can operate profitably in that community and that the personality of the company will dovetail with that of the community.

VOLUNTEER SALES TEAM

How does the prospect determine the community's profitability and personality? He does so by meeting the people and measuring the community by them. Some communities have employed full-time industrial or economic development professionals. Most prospects value their input, but they really want to meet the community leaders. These are the volunteers who are interested in seeing that their community develops economically and generates new jobs.

One of the virtues of America's people that makes our country great is its history of volunteerism. Can you imagine an American hero like Benjamin Franklin saying "What we really need as Ambassador to France is a young man. I'm seventy years old! It's time a new generation took over!"

And what if Nathan Hale had said, "Me, spy on the British? Are you kidding! Do you know what they do with spies when they catch them? Read my lips, pal. They hang 'em!"

Today in every community in America, people volunteer their time, talent, money, and other resources in order to make life better for their neighbors as well as for themselves. This same spirit of volunteerism is an essential ingredient in a successful local economic development effort.

These volunteers operate as the sales team for the community. Each member needs to realize that he or she is placed in a sales position. The best salespeople are those who help the prospect solve his problem by selecting their community. As is the case for any salesperson, one must know the community — not only its strengths but also its weaknesses. The team members must be experts about the product — their community.

TEAM CHARACTERISTICS

In searching for the right team members, the primary concerns must be the prospective member's interest in economic development, enthusiasm for the community, and leadership position or potential. **There is no place on the community's sales team for an individual who seeks personal prestige or inside information.** A prima donna does not contribute to the overall team effort. The team member must be sincere in his/her efforts and dedicated to the task of building an economic future for the community.

Some other characteristics of good team members include:

❑ the opportunity to leave his/her normal occupation to meet with the prospect when needed. One local chamber of commerce manager had her best prospect in years come to town on very short notice. Imagine her consternation when the bank president wouldn't break his golf date to meet with the prospect.

❑ the ability to keep his/her mouth shut. Most prospects prefer to remain confidential for a number of reasons. They may not select the town and don't want the adverse publicity. The prospect probably does not want his competition to know what he's up to, so keeping information confidential is required. An enterprising journalist overhearing a conversation in a local restaurant can produce the next day's news headline.

❑ the modesty that one does not assume he/she "knows everything". Members should not be so expert they can't ask questions to improve their knowledge, or so confident that they can't learn more.

❑ possess a "can do" attitude. People like enthusiasm and a positive attitude. The prospect expects this - just don't overdo it. If the community has a problem, own up to it, then tell the prospect what you're doing about it.

❑ ability to have a good time. Teams get better the more they work together. They should not become easily discouraged, for economic development takes time. Members should expect to serve on the team for several years. At one time, Babe Ruth was the world champion home run hitter, but most people don't know he also held the record for most strikeouts. Zig Ziglar makes the point that one doesn't drown by falling in the water, but drowns by staying there! Team members will suffer disappointments, but those will be offset when "the thrill of victory" is experienced.

What follows is a description of the kinds of information the team usually will need. The number of team members depends on the needs of the community and the information the prospect may require. It is not necessary for the whole team to meet with the prospect on the initial visit, and there may be times when a local expert or specialist with expertise beyond the team's knowledge will be called in. These specialists should be informed in advance how the team works, the prospect's requirements, and how they should respond. The best teams get together ahead of time to discuss the agenda for the prospect's visit, the specific information required, and who will handle each part of the interview. A community fact book should always be available for the prospect to take with him.

Individual team members should be prepared to respond to inquiries about community resources and services, workforce training and education, labor supply, buildings and sites, utilities, government and tax policies, financing and quality of life.

COMMUNITY RESOURCES AND SERVICES SPECIALIST

Services available to industry can mean the difference in location of a plant in one city over another. Local suppliers of components, metal fabricators, tool and die shops, research and testing facilities, consulting engineers, motor repair shops, and other potential suppliers to an industry are a few examples. Some industries themselves locate because they are suppliers of such services to a local industry.

Transportation costs are also an integral part of production costs. A natural-resource oriented industry locates near the source of its raw materials primarily to minimize transportation costs. The team members should not overlook rail, truck, water, air and pipeline transportation for lower transportation costs. If a prospect has multiple plants around the country, he/she may specify that a new facility be no more than a one hour drive from an airport with commercial airline service.

Market oriented industries reduce transportation costs by locating near their markets. The availability of truck and rail transportation in important. The transportation team member should know what trucking companies have permits to serve the city, and what the delivery times are to major markets.

A stable year-round climate, a dependable or especially trained labor supply, an abundance of quality water, access to the interstate highway system, or a deep-water port or ship channel constitute other important resources for an area.

TRAINING AND EDUCATION SPECIALIST

Most states offer extensive training programs to help their citizens qualify for jobs that may become available. The training may be for pre-employment start-up training, retraining, or for continuing education. Such programs can be delivered through the public school system, community college system, special vocational schools, and colleges and universities.

What is the delivery system for vocational training for new or expanding industry in the community? Who can meet with the prospect and make a commitment for special training programs if necessary? What part of the cost is paid by the state? How are the trainees selected? Are they

reimbursed while they train? These questions and the answers are the type of details needed to meet the prospect's needs.

Once the prospect's training needs are known, the volunteer team member may need to set up an interview with the appropriate education official. It is best to establish rapport with these education officials ahead of the interview, in order to prepare the official for response to the client's needs.

A good public education system is an asset to every community's economic development efforts. The team member should know the local education system and how it compares with others, and be able to discuss the quality of the local public school system. The quality and level of education of the schools has a direct relation to the quality of the labor supply.

Management people who transfer to the community will be interested in the school system for their children. Such factors as the full accreditation of grades kindergarten through twelve, curriculum offered, number of teachers with advanced degrees, awards for interscholastic achievement, and teacher pay scales are factors that indicate the quality of the school system.

LABOR SUPPLY SPECIALIST

The individual providing labor information can be expected to perform yeoman service. Rarely does a site location involve the relocation of more than five percent of the total work force to be employed. The employer looks to the community to provide the bulk of the industrial workforce.

The state employment service is a good place to start. One of their labor analysts should be able to help the volunteer get an accurate picture of the labor situation in the city, county, or metropolitan area. This information should include the number in the work force, both employed and the unemployed who are looking for work. It likely will not include those who are not employed and not looking for work but who would work if a job were available. The state service should be able to help prepare a labor market analysis as a basis for developing projections about the available labor supply.

The state labor market analysis ought to be expanded with local information. If the city is large enough to have a personnel association, such a group could be of tremendous value; if not, such data will have to be compiled. This information should include wage rates for various skill levels, availability of specific skills within the

prospect's needs, customary work hours and fringe benefits, local commuting patterns, turnover rate and absenteeism, work attitudes, education levels, and labor union history, including the names of unions organized in the area and in what firms, the percentage of the workforce unionized at each location, and a history of work stoppages.

Often a prospect will ask that personal interviews with local employers be arranged. Sometimes the volunteer may suggest employers, while on other occasions the prospect knows which employers he/she wants to interview. As the labor volunteer specialist will be calling on employers gathering data, these visits provide ample opportunity to know the persons the prospect may want to interview. The volunteer should know their attitudes about developing new jobs so that he/she can steer the prospect to them or away from them. If the prospect insists on talking with an employer known to have a negative attitude, the volunteer should be prepared to counter any adverse impressions.

The team member also needs to be prepared to discuss worker's compensation and unemployment compensation. These are ordinarily established at the state level. If the prospect is from out of state, it is important to know how the state compares with others. If favorable, the volunteer will want to emphasize that; if the state has unfavorable rates or experience, one needs to be able to address this issue.

BUILDINGS SPECIALIST

Available buildings are an asset that will attract industrial prospects to the community when otherwise it might not be considered. In general, industrial buildings of 15,000 to 20,000 square feet are the minimum size that attract attention. Buildings smaller could be considered, but only if they are expandable or suitable temporarily.

The team member specializing in this subject should collect as much information as possible on each building. He/she should request the real estate broker to submit written information for the team's files. Most state departments of commerce and utility companies as well have forms for collecting needed information. If not already available, have the owner or real estate broker complete the forms. Make several copies for the team's files and also send them to the state department, utility companies, and other industrial allies who are in a position to market the community to potential industrial prospects.

Such forms generally provide the following information on each building:

❏ Address and description of location.

❏ Size of building including dimensions; interior clear heights; whether clear span, or bay sizes; amount of office, manufacturing, and warehouse space by square footage.

❏ Material used in the building, thickness of slab, type of roof, and insulation.

❏ The number of overhead doors, their sizes, and whether they are dock high, street level, or other heights.

❏ The previous use of the buildings, and any unusual features as a result of that use.

❏ The safety features of the building such as overhead sprinkler system, burglar alarm, hazardous materials storage area, emergency lighting, and fencing.

❏ The utility service to the building, including size of the water line and pressure for fire protection purposes, size of the sewer line, amount of electricity serving the building in transformer size, amperage available, and whether single phase or three phase, and size and pressure of the gas line serving the area.

❏ The size of site available with the building and its zoning, as well as availability of additional acreage for the expansion, and total amount of building that can be built on the site.

❏ The asking price of the building and any financing to be assumed.

SITE SPECIALIST

The team volunteer on available sites should develop a complete inventory of available industrial sites in the area, both those in an industrial parks as well as stand-alone sites. Documentation on each site should be prepared separately with information on the location, general description, utility status, zoning, easements, price, and name of owner or owner's broker.

A map of the locality with sites identified is helpful. A plat or survey of each site is the best way to present the site, especially if the survey shows dimensions, easements or right-of-way, and improvements. Aerial photographs are a great way to show a site in relation to the surrounding area. Topographic maps as well as soil maps are valuable. To gain access to this data, the volunteer will need to work with local surveyors and title company personnel.

The utilities available at each site need to be determined. The location of water and sewer lines as well as their sizes must be known. The city fees likely to be charged for connecting to the utilities, as well as the city's policies for extension of utility services for industrial purposes, should be documented.

It is helpful if the team member has walked each site and identified the corners and any other features. An added feature is to flag the corners and mow the site before showing it to the prospect.

UTILITIES SPECIALIST

While the community's water and sewer system are often taken for granted, only when they are lacking or deficient does the team think about planning and financing improvements. Most industries do not have large demands for either water or sewer service, but if the community does not have any available then it can't even supply basic necessities.

The team specialist should know the source of the water supply, the amount of treated water available daily, storage capacity, maximum daily use, average daily use, and pressure at the point of delivery. The prospect who uses water in processing will want more in-depth information. This may include a chemical analysis, or pH balance. One soup company was delighted to see how long the local lake water stayed muddy after a rain. It was an indication that the water would support and suspend the soup ingredients.

The same questions of capacity are important for sewerage. Industries with specific effluent problems will want to know more. The type of sewage treatment system used by the community may have an effect on a location decision. Policies of the city determining the kinds and amounts of effluent that can be placed in the system should be known as well as when the company must pretreat its effluent. Also, it should be determined if there are extra charges to treat unusual effluent.

The utility specialist needs to know who is the supplier of electricity in the city and what the rates are as well as rate projections for three to five years. If there is more than one source, similar information ought to be compiled. The utility's attitude toward cogeneration units for large industries can be another consideration. Information on the frequency and duration of outages, and what fuels are used to generate electricity should be documented.

Similarly, it needs to be established if natural gas is available as an industrial fuel and what company serves the area. Information should be readily available on rates, conservation policies, and sources, and if other fuels are available.

Computers have increased our ability to store and transmit data at a phenomenal rate. Much of the data is transmitted by the telephone system, so the capabilities of the telephone system may be a critical issue.

GOVERNMENT AND TAXATION SPECIALIST

Local elected officials must be viewed as partners in economic development efforts; to exclude them is to invite trouble. Elected officials with a business background or with a good understanding of business can be a real asset to a community.

Attitude is a key ingredient in the equation. The city council, county government, school district, or other taxing bodies must be aware of the local economic development efforts, and their support obtained. Once that support is gained, it must be extended to the staff or employees of each jurisdiction so that there is not doubt that an attitude of cooperation permeates these governing bodies.

If it appears that the prospect may have difficulties getting permits, inspections, or other governmental approvals, start at the top with elected officials who are sensitive to the needs of the electorate. Enlist their support, then ask them to communicate that support to the staff. Try not to irritate those whose job it is to work out the details of a location by appearing to "go over their heads". This simply causes resentment and can create problems somewhere else in the bureaucracy.

The volunteer responsible for this subject area should have a list of the taxing jurisdictions in the area and the tax rates levied by each district. This information should be coordinated with the site and building specialist to determine what taxes are in effect for each location. Each jurisdiction's policies on tax assessments and how the rates are set should be known, as well as what state law permits each jurisdiction in setting policies and if there is any latitude to provide tax incentives.

The volunteer should know how the community's tax structure compares with that of other cities that are its competitors. If taxes appear higher, he/she must be prepared to answer why. One city successfully convinced a prospect that the community's commitment to quality education justifies a higher tax rate — the rate paid for better facilities, a broader curriculum, and better teacher salaries. Another city placed emphasis on city parks and recreation facilities that enhanced the quality of life for all citizens as the reason for a higher tax structure.

FINANCING SPECIALIST

The team volunteer specializing in this subject should be prepared to answer questions about the availability of local financing. This includes programs that may be available through local banks or their correspondents, or available from state government, and the federal government programs such as the Small Business Administration. This is a very complicated subject area, so the volunteer should know how each of these programs works and what is required for the prospect to qualify. Other conventional sources of financing should be familiar to this specialist, including mortgage companies, investor/builders, banks, savings and loans, insurance companies, and trusts. Some non-conventional sources may be a local investor, a community investment group (profit or non-profit), and venture capital groups.

The best attitude to assume during a preliminary visit by the prospect to the community is that local financing will be based on adequate financial information from the prospect.

The local team should not be shy in asking for details from the prospect at the appropriate time; after all, this is a business transaction. Unfortunately, there are charlatans and con artists who will seek to take advantage of a community's hospitality and eagerness to generate jobs.

In addition to conventional financing assistance, the prospect may ask about incentives to encourage the firm to select the community. The community's policy on incentives should be established prior to the prospect's inspection trip. This may take the form of tax exemptions, subsidizing utility extensions, or low interest financing. Historically, incentives have been given when competition is most keen, when unemployment is high, and when the economy is weakened. Incentives are usually based on the anticipated economic impact from the project — the larger the impact, the larger the incentive.

Few plant locations are based on incentives alone. The community's attitude towards encouraging the prospect by offering incentives is often more important than the incentive itself. Some communities are effective in emphasizing the advantages of a location in their city which offset incentives offered by the competition. Those firms which will place great weight on incentives may be weak financially and move when the incentives expire!

QUALITY OF LIFE SPECIALIST

Every community has a certain intangible allure for the people who live there. It is often hard to express this to someone who is not familiar with the community. Many physical aspects of the community contribute to this quality of life. They often are attributes not directly involved with operating a business, except as they contribute to the overall well-being and health of employees.

Many facets of the community contribute to the quality of life. Among these are recreational opportunities, such as lakes, parks, golf, tennis, hunting, and fishing, and organized sports for all age levels. Cultural opportunities include those provided by the school system as well as opportunities available from area colleges and universities. Symphonies, ballet, musical performances, and theater all add to the quality of life.

Health services are also important. The peace of mind in knowing that medical help is available immediately contributes to the citizens' perceived well-being. It is a compliment to a community to have a variety of medical and dental specialists practicing locally.

The appearance of a community cannot be overlooked in economic development. Appearance reflects community pride. It is the single most important feature by which a community is judged without interviewing the residents. Most people pass through a number of communities each year and make judgements about them without ever meeting a person who lives there! A good program to improve the community's appearance is a terrific asset for economic development. After all, how can the community invite a new corporate citizen, if it's not proud enough to clean it up.

SUMMARY

The volunteers who serve as the marketing team make a genuine contribution in sustaining the economic development program of a community or an area. They are the contacts upon whom the representatives of businesses investigating locations will rely. The volunteers should be experts in describing their product — the community and the assets which it offers.

Team members must be versatile and knowledgeable. Most of all, they should be attuned to the needs of modern industry looking for the best locations in which to operate. The areas of expertise, and the subjects on which business facility location representatives will need specific details, include community resources and facilities, workforce data, utilities and government services, buildings, sites, financing, and, most importantly, the quality of life aspects.

Nothing can guarantee success in this effort, but without the knowledge, preparation and participation of the volunteers as a marketing team, the ability of any community to grow and to expand its economic base will be severely hampered.

Comparative Operating Cost Analysis: Bottom-Line Incentive for Expanding and Relocating Companies

Christopher A. Roybal, MBA

INTRODUCTION

As corporations around the globe compete for market share, they find themselves constantly seeking ways to lower their cost of doing business. Today, most competitive companies have reorganized through management reassignments, reduced marketing budgets, personnel cuts, redefined product lines, etc. Simultaneously companies have sought alternatives to improve operating costs efficiencies. In some cases this can be accomplished through utilization of more efficient equipment, more productive work assignments, just-in-time processes, etc.

This article will focus on other facets of operating costs that may be realized as a result of a corporate relocation, or expansion, to an area where cash flow improvements can be gained through lower workers compensation rates, utility rates, property tax rates, health care costs, construction and labor cost improvement. To be sure, there are other areas of cost savings, such as corporate income tax rates, as well as other tax benefits, but this analysis will focus only on areas where comparable data can be gathered on competing cities for a particular project. In other words, workers compensation costs can be compared for various communities by obtaining the number of projected employees and the workers compensation rates for a given industry. It is more difficult to project a company's net income over a series of years to indicate the savings in tax dollars.

As economic development professionals and consultants prepare data for companies seeking better and more accurate information to decide on a relocation or expansion, this operating cost analysis provides the corporate decision-maker with one more tool with which to make an informed decision. Further, as companies seek incentives from states and local municipalities, it allows public sector officials to make better informed decisions regarding the provision of incentives, if they can demonstrate that these indirect operating cost incentives benefit the targeted company relative to another community. What sets this process apart from other cost comparisons is the projection of the cash-flows relative to specific cost areas, as opposed to simply stating "cost indices". This allows the company to more fully visualize the anticipated cash-flow enhancement that may be realized as a result of operating their business in one community versus another.

COLLECTING DATA AND RUNNING THE NUMBERS (A CASE STUDY)

As opposed to relying strictly on index comparisons, this approach not only uses index rates, but also utilizes traditional approaches to compare costs. This case study is a variation of a real project that involved a manufacturing company seeking an expansion location where 150 new jobs would be created. Based on the company's marketing and sales regions, the competing community finalists were Salt Lake City, Utah; Phoenix, Arizona; and Tacoma, Washington.

The company provided the following data to initiate the process: estimated construction costs of a new facility were $5.5 million. Equipment was estimated to cost $9.5 million. The new facility would operate 24 hours per day and have utility usage requirements as follows: electric -2,560 kW/month demand, and 1,111 kWh usage; natural gas - 18,000 MCF/Decatherms per month with firm rate. After full capacity is realized in year 2, the electric and natural gas rates will increase by 5% thereafter. Average manufacturing wages were approximately $11 per hour. Fifty employees would be hired in year 1, and the additional 100 jobs will be added in year 2, with employment increasing by 3% per year thereafter. Healthcare costs were based on an existing Utah company with a similar profile paying $350 per month per job. Beginning in year 3, the health care costs are estimated to increase by 7% each year. Workers compensation classification code of 9014 was given for electrical manufacturing.

Workers Compensation Costs

Because up-to-date data can be collected from individual states' workers compensation commissions, no index rates were used to compare costs. Commissions were contacted in Utah, Washington and Arizona. Salt Lake City and Phoenix derive their costs on a rate per $100 of payroll for the classification code 9014; Salt Lake City is at $5.58, Phoenix at $7.99. Tacoma is based on $.0824 per hour for the given classification. The company has estimated that they will pay the same average wage in each market (otherwise the model would have different annual wage rates for each community). Because less than 5% of the workforce was classified under administrative/clerical pro forma, costs were developed with all 150 workers under the 9014 classification.

With this data the following calculation can be made and incorporated into a spreadsheet format. (See Table 6 for spreadsheet format)

Construction Costs

It was estimated that construction costs for this project in Salt Lake City would be approximately $5.5 million. Using this as a benchmark, other communities' costs can be determined by using the following conversion technique with index rates. (With any index comparison it is assumed that a benchmark will be developed from one of the communities)

Editor's Note: The Economic Development Corporation of Utah received the 1995 Outstanding Area Research Award of the Industrial Development Research Council and Conway Data for the process described in the article.

Equating these costs is similar to converting miles to kilometers, if one knows the ratio, the comparisons can be made. In this case, one is simply converting from Salt Lake City "dollars" to Tacoma and Phoenix "dollars". (See Table 2.)

Property Tax Costs

Most states calculate property tax differently. The goal is to "equalize" the various methods to indicate annual property tax payments that would be made by the company. Again, each community was contacted to obtain their respective property tax rates. A specific community (taxing district) was identified within Salt Lake County with a property tax rate of 1.924% at 100% of assessed value. Phoenix reports their rates for similar properties between 5.871% to 14.432% at 25% of assessed value. Tacoma indicates rates between $13.80 to $17.00 per $1,000 at 100% of assessed value. It was assumed that an average of the Phoenix and Tacoma rates would be used. If sufficient data cannot be collected, then index rates could be used to compare costs. No land costs were included in this analysis. Equipment costs are assumed to be purchased at the same price, regardless of location, at $9.5 million. For purposes of the spreadsheet, it is assumed that property tax rates will remain flat throughout the life of the project. (Projection increases may be incorporated, based on historical patterns.) (See Table 3.)

Utility Costs

In this case study, the regional electric company and natural gas companies provided in-house models to project utility costs for the three different areas. Their models are based on existing rate fees relative to demand and usage requirements. Otherwise, index rates may be used. Using the Edison Electric Institute one can, with the demand and usage factors, estimate annual electric bills. It was assumed by the company that electric and natural gas usage would increase 5% per year. The analysis was performed under full plant capacity, therefore, year one indicates one-third of the total cost, based on employment at one-

---

TABLE 1
Annual Workers Compensation Costs

Salt Lake City
(Number of Employees) multiplied by (annual wage) divided by (100) multiplied by ($5.58)
150 X 22,880/100 X 5.58 = $191,506.

Phoenix
(Number of Employees) multiplied by (annual wage) divided by (100) multiplied by ($7.99)
150 X 22,880 X 7.99 = $274,217

Tacoma
(Number of Employees) multiplied by (2080 hours) multiplied by $.8024
150 X 2080 X .8024 = $250,349

Sources: Workers Compensation Fund of Utah, Arizona State Compensation Fund, Washington Dept. of Labor and Industries

---

TABLE 2
Total Construction Costs

Index rates for Construction costs:
U.S. average 1.00; Salt Lake City - 0.87; Phoenix - 0.9; Tacoma - 1.05

Salt Lake City - $5,500,000 (Benchmark)

Phoenix - ($5.5 million) multiplied by 0.9/0.87 = $5,500,000 X 1.034 = $5,689,655

Tacoma - ($5.5 million) multiplied by 1.05/0.87 = $5,500,000 X 1.207 = $6,637,931

Source: "Means Square Foot Costs 1994", R.S. Means Co., Inc.

TABLE 3
Annual Property Tax Costs

Salt Lake City
($5.5 million + $9.5 million) multiplied by (.01924) = $287,130

Phoenix
($5.689 million + $9.5 million) multiplied by (.05871 + .1443)/2 multiplied by 0.25 = $385,438. The multiplication of .25 for Phoenix equates to 100% of assessed value.

Tacoma
($6.634 million + $9.5 million) multiplied by (.0138 + .0170)/2 = $248,524

Sources: Salt Lake County, Greater Phoenix Economic Council, Pierre County, Dept. of Community and Economic Development

---

TABLE 4
Annual Utility Costs

Electric Usage Assumptions:
Maximum monthly demand - kW   2,560
Monthly kWh usage - kWh   1,110,000

Estimated Annual Bills (Rate 6)
Electric Bills:
Salt Lake City $678,272
Phoenix $918,087
Tacoma $331,786

Natural Gas Usage Assumptions:
Monthly usage   18,000 MCF/Decatherms

Estimated Annual Gas Bills (Firm Rate):
Salt Lake City $603,551
Phoenix $897,084
Tacoma $1,049,237

Sources: Utah Power & Light Company, Mountain Fuel Supply Company, Southwest Gas Corporation, Washington Natural Gas Company.

TABLE 5
Annual Health Care Costs

Index rates for Health Care Costs:
Salt Lake City - 1.41, Phoenix - 1.53, Tacoma - 2.16

Salt Lake City - $350/month/job (Benchmark)

Phoenix - ($350)(1.53/1.41) = $350 X 1.085 = $380/month/job

Tacoma - ($350)(2.16/1.41) = $350 X 1.532 = $536/month/job

Source: PHH Fantus, *Places Rated Almanac*

---

third of the total. (See Table 4 and Table 6, Year 1 costs)

Health Care Costs

Again, a benchmark was utilized to develop the index comparisons. An existing Salt Lake City company with a similar profile was used. This company's health care costs were approximately $350 per month per employee. Using index rates, the following comparisons were developed. Based on data from the client company, health care costs were assumed to increase by 7% per year. (See Table 5.)

Pro Forma Format and Present Value Calculations

The pro forma spreadsheet shown in Table 6 is a compilation of the cost factors analyzed in Tables 1 through 5. The purpose of this final analysis is to show the cumulative costs for each competing city on an annualized basis. In addition, Table 6 calculates these costs over a ten-year period to give decision makers a long-term view of the impact of the project. Furthermore, the spreadsheet calculates the Net Present Value (NPV) of the cumulative stream of costs. The NPV is simply the value of the costs stated over a period of time reflected in today's dollars. Many companies want to know what the dollar value is today for a set of cash flows that may run over a series of years. In other words, each year's costs are discounted back to year 1 using a predetermined dis-

count or interest rate. Table 6 was created using a Lotus spreadsheet. NPV and other mathematical calculations can be performed with Lotus or other program spreadsheets.

For this analysis, the length of the pro forma was ten years. The ten-year timeframe was used based on local incentive offers that would be generated over this same time period. Because this company wanted to know the present value of future cash flows, present value calculations were included. The discount rate, which is the interest rate used to determine the present value of each of the ten years of cash flows, can be estimated by using several criteria. For this project, the company's corporate bond rate was used at a rate of 8%. The company's "cost of capital" can be deter-

TABLE 6
Manufacturing Company
150 Employee Operation
Comparative Costs - Cash Flow Improvement Pro Forma

FALL 1994

Year COMPARATIVE COSTS	1	2	3	4	5	6	7	8	9	10	Totals	Cumm. Net Present Value
WORKERS COMPENSATION (see Table 1)												
Salt Lake City	63,835	191,508	197,251	203,168	209,263	215,541	222,007	228,668	235,528	242,594	2,009,361	1,290,731
Phoenix	91,406	274,217	282,443	290,917	299,644	308,633	317,892	327,429	337,252	347,370	2,877,203	1,848,197
Tacoma	83,450	250,349	257,859	265,595	273,563	281,770	290,223	298,930	307,897	317,134	2,626,770	1,687,329
CONSTRUCTION COSTS (see Table 2)												
Salt Lake City	5,500,000										5,500,000	5,092,583
Phoenix	5,689,655										5,689,655	5,268,199
Tacoma	6,637,931										6,637,931	6,146,232
ELECTRIC POWER (see Table 4)												
Salt Lake City	223,830	678,272	712,186	747,795	785,185	824,444	865,666	908,949	954,397	1,002,117	7,702,840	4,895,484
Phoenix	302,969	918,087	963,991	1,012,191	1,062,801	1,115,941	1,171,738	1,230,325	1,291,841	1,356,433	10,426,315	6,626,369
Tacoma	109,490	331,787	348,376	365,795	384,085	403,289	423,453	444,626	466,857	490,200	3,767,958	2,394,698
NATURAL GAS (see Table 4)												
Salt Lake City	199,306	603,959	634,157	665,865	699,158	734,116	770,822	809,363	849,831	892,323	6,858,899	4,359,124
Phoenix	296,038	897,064	941,938	989,035	1,038,487	1,090,411	1,144,932	1,202,178	1,262,287	1,325,402	10,187,792	6,474,777
Tacoma	346,249	1,049,238	1,101,700	1,156,785	1,214,624	1,275,355	1,339,123	1,406,079	1,476,383	1,550,202	11,915,739	7,572,961
HEALTH CARE (see Table 5)												
Salt Lake City	210,000	630,000	674,100	721,287	771,777	825,801	883,608	945,460	1,011,642	1,082,457	7,756,133	4,879,351
Phoenix	227,872	683,617	731,470	782,673	837,460	896,082	958,808	1,025,925	1,097,740	1,174,581	8,416,229	5,294,615
Tacoma	321,702	965,106	1,032,664	1,104,950	1,182,297	1,265,058	1,353,612	1,448,364	1,549,750	1,658,232	11,881,736	7,474,750
PROPERTY TAXES (see Table 3)												
Salt Lake City	287,130	287,130	287,130	287,130	287,130	287,130	287,130	287,130	287,130	287,130	2,871,300	1,926,666
Phoenix	385,438	385,438	385,438	385,438	385,438	385,438	385,438	385,438	385,438	385,438	3,854,375	2,586,317
Tacoma	248,524	248,524	248,524	248,524	248,524	248,524	248,524	248,524	248,524	248,524	2,485,241	1,667,617

Total Salt Lake Costs	Gross Value	$32,698,533	Cumm. NPV	$22,443,947	
Total Phoenix Costs	Gross Value	$41,451,570	Cumm. NPV	$28,098,474	
Total Tacoma Costs	Gross Value	$39,315,375	Cumm. NPV	$26,943,588	

mined in a more sophisticated manner using the capital asset pricing model, which defines a company's blended rate of both debt and equity capital. Because, in this example, the company is privately-held, with no public equity, the company's internal bond rate, or cost of borrowing, was utilized to best represent the stream of discounted cash flows most accurately.

Year 1 costs were estimated from Tables 1 through 5 at one-third of the annual costs based on employment levels stated above. Beginning in year 2, employment is at full capacity (150) and reflects the numbers that were calculated in the first five tables. Thereafter, the yearly figures are indicative of the percentage increases stated above.

Conclusions

Although the spreadsheet in Table 6 calculates real values, "ranking" the three cities in terms of these six comparative cost categories is the preferred method of evaluation. As mentioned previously, other tools will be utilized in the final decision-making process; hence, the analysis should be used as a ranking system. However, for the categories indicated, this approach should give the company a reasonable outlook on several cost areas. Over the stated ten-year analysis, Salt Lake City's costs, gross value and net present value respectively, are approximately seven million and five million less than Tacoma, and approximately nine million and six million less than Phoenix. Based on this analysis, these operating cost breakdowns indicate a ranking of cost to the company as follows: Salt Lake City, Tacoma, and Phoenix, respectively. In addition, this analysis can be used by local and state governments with respect to incentive proposals.

SUMMARY

As corporations seek information regarding relocation and expansion projects, this operating cost analysis process described will enhance the ability of economic development professionals and consultants to deliver critical and useful data.

Unlike simply listing index rates, collecting hard data, when available, and running the cash flow projections is much more time consuming. However, as companies seek more detailed information with regard to relocations and expansions, our experience indicates that companies will increasingly continue to request this type of analysis. Obviously, this analysis only evaluated several key factors, and should be used as one of many tools available for corporate relocation and expansion decisions. The projections are limited by how accurate the input data is, and whether or not index rates have to be used. Nonetheless, companies make decisions based on operating cost projections, and can decide what weight to place on the various categories and the assumptions that accompany them. As models continue to be developed for various projects, economic development professionals and consultants can begin to establish a network of resources and data that make the analysis more accurate. Other index sources that can be used include: *American Gas Association; Edison Electric Institute; County Business Patterns, U.S. Department of Commerce; Employee Benefits, U.S. Chamber of Commerce; Cost of Doing Business Index; Places Rated Almanac, etc.*

Effective Prospect Presentations: Your Competitive Edge

Michael B. McCain, CED, FM

INTRODUCTION

The most successful companies today do not concentrate on selling a product or service. Rather, they focus on identifying and satisfying individual customer needs in a highly responsive fashion. The most effective economic developers do likewise.

From the standpoint of business recruitment, development practitioners can no longer place the top priority on marketing and follow up later with general information. Instead, the emphasis has to be on identifying the individual needs of prospective corporate customers and presenting project-specific information which shows how these needs are best fulfilled.

Competitive pressures in a global economy have affected how companies do business and the ways they make business location decisions. Manufacturers, for example, must produce greater numbers of higher quality products at a lower unit cost, while maintaining the flexibility to meet customer desires and schedules. Changes affecting service sector operations are equally dramatic.

To compete, companies are investing more money in computer-driven equipment and the skilled employees to operate it. Never before has the facility location decision had so great an impact on a company's bottom line. As a result, never before have corporate information demands on economic developers been so detailed, project requirements so stringent, or deadlines so restrictive.

At the same time, the number of areas worldwide which are seeking new facilities has never been larger. Just as companies change to meet competitive challenges, so must economic developers. A major difference is the way data is presented to prospects. Consider these scenarios:

❑ A prospect wants information about the community. Because of your prior research, printed copies of a thick statistical facts book are readily available. One is mailed the same day.

❑ On short notice, a prospect is coming to visit. You are prepared, armed with a video depicting every aspect of the community and a permanent sales team ready to go into action.

❑ You are finalist for a new corporate facility. Wanting to be certain company officials do not overlook anything before making a location decision, you follow up by sending another copy of the statistical facts book, quality of life brochures and a copy of the video.

Not too long ago, some considered this standard operating procedure. Respond in these ways today, and you risk losing to a community with more effective presentation capabilities.

WHAT IS A PROSPECT PRESENTATION

By definition, a presentation is a descriptive or persuasive account of something, such as a product. General information is not persuasive to prospective corporate customers. A prospect presentation should describe specific attributes as they pertain to a prospect's individual requirements. An effective presentation clearly shows how the requirements are fulfilled and explains why the product offered is the best choice.

Different service providers need to present different kinds of information to prospects, of course. Presentations by state development agencies, economic development departments of utilities and railroads, architectural and engineering firms, construction companies, industrial realtors, financial institutions and others, will differ from presentations by local development groups. The emphasis here is on community presentations, although some of the material that follows has applications for all.

There are several ways to present information to prospects: in face-to-face conversations; visually, using projected transparencies, videotapes and interactive geographic information systems; electronically, by phone, fax or modem; and written documents, such as booklets, reports and proposals. All these methods might be employed during the course of a project. They can be categorized into four distinct types of presentations:

❑ initial presentations about a community, usually in writing, tailored to project needs

❑ personal presentations during prospect visits, often using visual aids

❑ follow-up presentations, addressing specific questions and concerns

❑ formal proposals, which are a deal-closing mechanism.

Pre-printed statistical fact books, quality of life brochures and generic community videos are not prospect presentations; they are compendia of diverse information. Although they may incorporate the data a prospect is seeking, by their very nature they also contain non-essentials. It is time consuming, and often irritating, for a prospective customer to endure drivel just to find those items which are important to a project. In today's competitive environment, responsiveness to individual needs and tailored customer service are paramount.

Pretend being the prospect. When compiling a presentation, ask yourself, "Does this answer all my questions? What exactly is being offered? Is there an obviously good fit between what the project requires and what the community is presenting? Am I persuaded to consider this area further? Based on this information, would I locate this facility here?"

Keep in mind that companies do not

undertake a process of *selecting* a site. Rather, it is a site *elimination* process. When you're first contacted about a project, it's a good bet the company is screening thirty or forty other areas as well, if not more. Inundated with responses, their top priority is to narrow the locational options to a manageable number. They often develop an evaluation matrix to compare initial project costs and annual operating expenses from city to city and eliminate communities until they get down to three or four finalists.

The role of written, personal and follow-up presentations is to keep from being eliminated. The purpose of a formal proposal is to be chosen as the site. But in order to prepare either, there are five things you must know:

❑ your product

❑ your customers

❑ what they want

❑ the consultants who may be assisting them

❑ your competition.

PREREQUISITES FOR EFFECTIVE PRESENTATIONS

Know your product

Accurate information about what you have to sell must be available. There have been numerous articles, seminars and EDC/EDI classes about how to research, develop and maintain a community data base. Its importance cannot be overemphasized. Nevertheless, possessing this information will not do much good unless you have the ability to promptly access and modify specific items, format them appropriately and present them effectively.

Computer capabilities are a prerequisite. While individual economic development agency needs will vary, basic hardware might include a personal computer for each staff member, a file server to allow sharing of information, sufficient random access memory and a large enough hard disc storage capacity, a laser printer with automatic sheet and envelope feeders, an optical scanner and a color inkjet printer (which can be used to store and retrieve photos of sites and buildings), a CD-ROM drive, and a modem, permitting electronic communications. Software alternatives for presentation purposes are numerous. At the very least, you will need a strong word processing system, graphics package, spreadsheet, data base manager, desktop publishing and, perhaps, a project tracking system.

With these capabilities, it is possible to store and update volumes of information, select what is needed, modify whatever is necessary, and quickly print pages of text with graphics and photos, all with the same formatting, and having a professional appearance.

Not everything included in a project-specific presentation has to be output on a moment's notice. Such documents as lists of employers by SIC, utility rate schedules and analyses of job applications and wages by occupational category, can be placed in compartmentalized shelves for easy retrieval and compiling as required.

Knowing what you have to sell also predetermines the kinds of companies which will be your best prospects. But in this competitive environment, that is not enough. Although recruiting targeted businesses does help improve a community, a corollary is even more accurate: improving a community helps attract new businesses. Investments to improve your product will return multiple dividends by increasing the number of customers who will find it attractive.

Know your prospect

It is imperative to know your prospective customer. This includes the company, the subsidiary or division responsible for the project and the people with whom you will be dealing--the ones who will make the business location decision.

One way to obtain a great deal of company and industry-specific information is by accessing on-line data bases via computer modem. In a matter of minutes you can ascertain a company's size, financial strength, mode of operation, locations of facilities, biographical information on principals, as well as current trends in a prospect's industry.

A few examples include Dun & Bradstreet, Dow Jones News Retrieval, Dialog and Nexis. Alternatively, a service bureau could conduct a data base search. For instance, they can perform a key-word query of a company's name in trade magazines, provide synopses of articles written about them recently, and compile a report on what is happening in a company's SIC category.

Such information also may be found in public libraries, or preferably in your office library. *Who's Who in America, Who's Who in Finance and Industry,* D&B directories, *Standard & Poor's, Thomas Register, U.S. Manufacturers Directory,* and *The Directory of Corporate Affiliations* are standard reference publications. Such research will be invaluable in preparing a presentation to a company.

Know their real requirements

This is the most important aspect by far. To demonstrate, take out two sheets of paper. On one, list every community asset you have to sell. On the other, put down what the prospect, your customer, wants to buy. Invariably, the first page will have a lot more writing than the second. Find out what the prospect is really looking for.

Some project requirements are self-evident and commonly divulged, such as a ten-acre site near a major highway. There are also requirements which are not always volunteered, like a ten-acre site in a Class A business park, accessible to but not visible from a highway, served by fiber optics and near a pre-school day care center.

Go beyond the standard locational requirements questionnaires used to interview prospects. Ask for their evaluation checklist or comparative matrix. Sometimes, it will be provided. In conversation, find out all their locational criteria. Determine what is most, and least, important. Identify the real factors affecting their decision.

This is much easier said than done. It is difficult to develop the rapport necessary to get this level of detail and the requirements often will change during the life of a project; but without this information it is tough to put together an effective presentation. If this is impeded by confidentiality constraints, respond by saying you do not need to know the company's identity but would like enough information to enable a meaningful response. There will be times when they cannot or will not tell you. Then you must rely on knowledge and experience.

For example, you are having an initial phone conversation with a prospect, consultant or statewide developer who is not able to divulge anything about the company. All he or she can say is that it is a precision metal machining project to make a lightweight component for another product, and some preliminary data about the community is needed. Well, you justifiably can assume that skilled labor, such as CNC machine programmers, will be an important requirement. So will tool and die shops and related support services...pertinent education and training programs...motor freight carriers...the reliability and cost of electric power. You also can assume they will not be interested in such things as barge transportation capabilities or the number of food processing firms in the area.

It is much better to make such assumptions and tailor a presentation accordingly than to send a document consisting of a generic laundry list. Better yet, ask someone with a relevant background what the typical requirements and operating costs are for such a project. Input/output tables from the Bureau of Economic Analysis, U.S. Department of Commerce can be used as a guide. Computer software programs for industry targeting purposes can be helpful, too.

As an aside, do not waste the prospect's time or yours. If you cannot meet the requirements, or conclude other cities are a much better fit and you have no offsetting advantages, say so. You will eventually lose this one anyway, right? The prospect will appreciate your honesty and you can spend your time and money on more promising projects.

Know their consultants

On larger projects, a company may retain the services of a business mobility consultant, engineering firm, realtor, attorney, accountant and/or other technical assistance providers. In your initial conversation with a prospect, ask if outside consultants are helping with the location evaluation process. If the response is affirmative, send them copies of everything provided to the company. Keep the consultants informed and they may volunteer project details you otherwise might not learn about. Work proactively to make them an advocate of your location.

In the initial stages of a project, you may be dealing exclusively with a consultant who is performing a location analysis for a client. At this point, the consultant is the prospect. If a presentation does not con-

vince the consultant your location merits further consideration, forget about being given a chance to persuade company officials you have the right spot. There are three rules to follow:

❑ Provide exactly the information needed, in the precise order or format requested.

❑ Respond promptly, and continue to be responsive in handling follow-up queries.

❑ If confidential information is divulged, keep it confidential.

The same holds true when state development agencies, utilities, railroads and similar organizations call to obtain information for a prospect. On the other hand, if you're working with a company directly, you should have already involved these economic development allies. In many cases, the prospect contacted them before speaking with you or will eventually. Make sure your presentations do not conflict with the information they provide.

Know your competition

Ask prospects where else they are looking; many times, they will say. If you know who the competition is and can find out what they have to offer, you will have a competitive advantage. The purpose is not to learn their weaknesses, but to determine your comparative shortcomings so offsetting benefits can be identified.

There are several ways to get this information. Some economic development magazines publish annual synopses of state business costs and incentives. Although this is a questionable tactic, ask a friendly plant manager to respond to competitor ads in economic development magazines. Call the employment service offices, utilities, state revenue departments and similar agencies in competing areas. Conway Data's SiteNet, an on-line data base, is another way to ascertain what other cities offer in sites, buildings and incentives.

Never use this information to engage in negative selling. You will lose credibility by pointing out competitors' shortcomings. Emphasize your strengths instead, as well as advantages which offset comparative weaknesses.

It is perfectly acceptable, however, to compile business cost comparisons which objectively portray factual data about operating expenses in your community versus others. Be very careful about doing this,

because if your information about competing areas is inaccurate, incomplete or out of date, it will compromise the veracity of all the other material you provided.

So, you know your product and have the capability to present it; you know the customer, both the company and the decision-makers; what they really want to buy; their consultants; and something about the competition. Now you are able to put together an effective presentation.

TYPES OF PRESENTATIONS

There are four types of presentations: initial written presentations about the community, personal presentations to company executives, follow-up presentations addressing particular concerns, and formal proposals which show what the community will do to meet their needs and minimize project costs.

Written presentations

The first opportunity to make a presentation likely will be in writing. Remember, a standard statistical facts book and similar pre-printed publications are not presentations. Sending generic community materials is better than nothing, but that is about all.

Sure, it is quicker and easier to pull a facts book off the shelf and drop it in the mail. Preparing an effective written presentation may take several hours of concentrated effort and require the work of more than one person. But if sent the same day it will not take any longer for the prospect to receive it, and is a lot more effective. An emerging trend is to copy a presentation from a word processing file to a computer diskette for a prospect, or even to transmit it electronically, assuming hardware and software compatibility.

A custom presentation for a major project with unusual requirements may take days of full-time work to prepare. This is one instance where being the first to submit data is not necessarily the best. Take the extra time to do the job right, let the prospect know when to expect your package and ensure it is there as promised.

The elements of an initial community presentation will vary, obviously, according to the requirements of a particular prospect. Generally, they include:

- site descriptions, aerial photos, plot plans and topo maps
- specifications, floor plans, and photos of available buildings
- utility data, including capacities, service characteristics and costs
- materials on transportation attributes, with freight rate and transit time analyses
- details about raw materials, supportive services, and related inputs
- labor availability and wage rate information, by pertinent occupational category
- information describing education and training resources
- tax rates, financing programs and cost-reduction incentives
- quality of life factors, such as housing costs and recreational and cultural amenities.

Some of these materials will be obtained from others, such as your state development agency, utility companies and real estate developers. Check and double check every bit of data obtained from outside sources for relevance and accuracy; if it is voluminous or contains extraneous details, excerpt needed portions for a particular presentation. Above all, include only information which relates to the individual project's unique needs and make it easy for corporate decision-makers to see that you have what they want. Following are a few tips:

- Summarize pertinent advantages in an easy-to-read cover letter or executive summary.
- Use sections with tabbed dividers to make categories of information easy to find.
- Personalize it. Do not convey the impression of it being "off the shelf."
- Bind it appropriately. Image and appearance count.
- Do not send a presentation via regular mail. Express ship it, or better yet, deliver it personally.
- Provide extra copies. Get your materials in the hands of as many decision-makers as possible.

Personal presentations

The goal of an initial written presentation is to convince the prospect to inspect your community in person. Effective prospect handling during a community visit is a topic unto itself, but there are some guidelines as they relate to the subject of personal presentations.

When first meeting prospects face-to-face, the cardinal rule is, do not sell! Instead, listen. Ask questions. Look for cues in their facial expressions and body language, and react accordingly. Try to get more information about the project, its requirements, and how the location decision will be made. This new knowledge will be especially helpful during follow-up presentations.

If it can be circumvented, do not have one permanent sales team which meets with every corporate visitor. Each project is different and the composition of presentation teams should differ according to project needs. Include only those who have key information to impart--not from your perspective, but from the prospect's point of view. Here's a good example: normally, a prospect would not meet the entire city council during an initial visit. The development practitioner, though, in researching the backgrounds of company principals, learned the CEO had served on the city council at his headquarters location. Local council members were told in advance what to say, and the CEO met with them during the visit itinerary. He later said the cooperative, pro-business attitude of local government was a main reason he chose to locate in that city.

Your primary sales tool during a visit is the itinerary. By following it, prospects should be able to see that their requirements are fulfilled. The community literally should sell itself. Meetings with business owners or plant managers are a principal component of almost every itinerary and comprise one reason why a good existing industry assistance program is so crucial. Because of their knowledge of factors meaningful to visiting prospects and their perceived objectivity, they typically are the most important members of a community presentation team.

Visual aids are helpful when making personal presentations to prospects, because seeing graphic materials reinforces what is heard. A number of software programs are available which enable quick design of a presentation including computer slides, overhead transparencies, handouts and speaker's notes, all in one file. As you create slides you are automatically creating the presentation, in a format that carries through from beginning to end.

Videotapes are a frequently used visual aid and presentation tool. As a complement to one generic community video, consider having several, short videos. One might focus on quality-of-life attributes, another on education and training resources and another on location and transportation advantages. In this manner, you can visually present those subjects of most importance to a prospect, without spending time on topics that may not be of interest. Furthermore, the creation of a video library of individual subjects will enable the quick production of custom presentations.

Imagine the impact on a prospect viewing statistical data, maps, photos, graphics and video images, all the while listening to relevant narrative, simply by pressing a touch-sensitive VDT screen or clicking a mouse. Although some state development agencies and utility economic development departments are doing this today, interactive computer video presentations using laser disc technology require a budget and staff beyond the means of most local development groups.

However, CD-ROMs are becoming an affordable alternative. At a comparatively small cost, you can record written data, graphics, maps, photos and motion images on a compact disk and use a personal computer to quickly access and sequence the images and statistics of interest to your prospect. Emerging technology will soon permit the production of interactive, multimedia presentations with full-screen video and audio on a laptop in your office or a prospect's.

Follow-up presentations

No matter how professional your written and personal presentations may be, it is for naught if you do not follow up. Good economic developers are very responsive in fulfilling a company's additional information requests. The most effective ones try to anticipate needs and answer questions before they are asked.

If you learned of an important issue during the prospect visit, now is the time to address it. If the subject is involved and requires a lengthy explanation, maintain the same level of quality and attention to detail as in your initial written presentation.

Many follow-up presentations are brief. Only a few elaborative details may be needed on an item, but usually they are required immediately. A fax machine, therefore, has become a necessity in today's economic development office. Tomorrow, E-mail may become just as necessary.

There are varying levels of follow-up. An initial presentation contains material about a wide variety of subjects. After the first round of elimination, more specific information is needed on a select number of factors. As the candidates are narrowed to a fewer number, an even greater degree of specificity is required. Follow-up presentations on specific subjects are just as important as written and personal presentations about the community.

Some economic development agencies hire consulting firms to analyze local attributes for targeted operations. Such reports (for instance, *The Suitability of Yourtown as a Location for Distribution Facilities*) can lend a great deal of credibility to community presentations. They are particularly useful as a follow-up device.

Do all this and you may become a finalist. You will then have the opportunity to try and close the deal by preparing a formal proposal.

Formal Proposals

Face-to-face and in writing, you have presented information about what you have for a company. Now, it is time to emphasize exactly what you propose to do for them. A formal proposal does three things:

❑ It describes the ways you intend to reduce their initial project costs and annual operating expenses, in summary form and in a detailed explanation of each item.

❑ It contains letters of commitment, and even legal agreements, backing up everything that is promised. It also includes letters about non-cost factors the company deems important.

❑ It conveys the powerful image of a can-do community, having the commitment and capacity to serve the company and management team over the long term.

Rather than having sections with tabbed dividers, proposals often have numbered pages with a table of contents, making it easier to find any one item. To illustrate,

reproduced below are the main categories of a 70-page proposal that helped close the sale for a 1,200-employee plant; individual items under these categories were listed by page number:

❑ Project Expediting and Cost Savings

❑ Cost-Reduction Incentives

❑ Letters Pertaining to the Site and Utilities

❑ Letters Describing Tax Abatements

❑ Letters About Labor Availability, Cost and Training

❑ Letters Addressing Union Climate

❑ Letters Explaining Existing Industry Assistance Benefits

❑ Letters About Reducing Relocation Costs

❑ Letters Offering Favorable Home Loans for Transferred Executives

❑ Letters Describing Other Quality-of-Life Attributes.

It is common for proposals to be hard-bound and embossed with gold leaf lettering. In addition to written proposals, economic developers occasionally produce special-purpose videos outlining their unique locational advantages and financial inducements for major projects.

This brings up a subject that has caused a great deal of consternation in the economic development profession, namely the increased use of financial incentives, resulting in an escalation of the bidding war. Do not expect a truce. The competition (for companies seeking to reduce costs and the locations trying to attract them) is simply too intense. For instance, the corporate real estate executives who say they actively seek incentives jumped from twenty-eight to fifty-seven percent during 1988-1993, according to surveys by *Site Selection* magazine. At the same time, the number of states offering tax credits for new jobs rose thirty-eight percent and the number offering free land increased by twenty-eight percent. Basic kinds of financial incentives found in formal proposals are:

❑ cash grants directly to a company, or money paid to others to reduce a firm's project expenses

❑ low-interest-rate financing, using public funds

❑ giving away or dropping the cost of something that is already owned, such as property

❑ infrastructure improvements, usually benefiting a broad area as well as the company

❑ providing specific services, like free employee training, through existing program budgets

❑ tax exemptions, which involves giving up something that previously had not been received.

Some prospects will ask you and other finalists to submit a proposal that guarantees a free site, fully serviced and ready to build on. They do not consider this to be an incentive and they will not accept your cost to provide it as constituting money in their corporate pocket. They do not care if it costs you one dollar or million; it is simply their way of comparing such factors on an equal basis.

Economic developers must be both aggressive and prudent. It is imperative to deploy enough weapons to win the project, while avoiding the ricochet of excessive inducements. If you quantify what is available (even federal government incentives like JTPA) and the competition does not, you will have an advantage.

The benefits must exceed the costs, however, and you must be able to explain it in a way the average citizen understands. Some communities and states include a recapture clause in their proposals, where incentives have to be returned if job or investment promises are not kept. Of course, it is naive to offer incentives if a company would come anyway, but this situation is rare indeed.

There will be times when your financial incentives will not be competitive or when it makes no economic sense to offer some of them. Other locations will have the ability and propensity to offer more. Then, the only option is to "outwant" the competition. To that end, here are examples of other inducements which can be included in a proposal:

❑ the approval of all permits will be expedited

❑ building owners will provide free office space during the construction period

❑ spouses of transferees will receive help in finding jobs

- [ ] banks will extend home mortgage and bridge loans on favorable terms
- [ ] attorneys will donate their legal services
- [ ] hotels will comp rooms during house-hunting trips
- [ ] retail stores will offer discounts to all new employees
- [ ] hospitals will give free care for the first year they are in town
- [ ] colleges will provide free tuition to the children of relocated executives.

Do everything possible to portray a community wide commitment to save the company and its management team time and money. Convey the intent and ability to be immediately responsive to their business and personal needs, both initially and throughout the future. Create an atmosphere of trust, acceptance, personal concern and guaranteed performance. This can result in a very real comfort level, so great that a CEO will choose your community over one which offers larger financial incentives, but which lacks such a commit-

ment. Sometimes, this approach works; when everything else is equal, it invariably does.

The sole purpose of a formal proposal is to justify a corporate location decision in your favor. Contrasted to presenting objective information, as in an initial presentation, this is the time to sell. It probably will be the final opportunity to close the sale, so make certain your proposal is forceful and compelling. After all, there are no rewards for second place in this profession.

THE END RESULT

Project-specific presentations require a lot of thought, hands-on effort and investments in computer hardware and software. The end result indicates to a prospect not that the area is seeking new facilities of any type, but that it wants this one particular project and has the best location for it. It also demonstrates a commitment to customer service and responsiveness that will benefit them upon becoming a corporate citizen.

SUMMARY

To summarize, if you...

- [ ] contact prospects sooner than your competitors,
- [ ] present materials directly related to their unique interests more effectively,
- [ ] corroborate everything during their visits in a more professional manner,
- [ ] ensure all their questions and concerns are addressed better than your competitors do,
- [ ] show specifically how they can make more money in your area than anywhere else, and
- [ ] make it easier for them to reach this conclusion,
- [ ] while providing a community that is perceived more attractive...

Then you'll have a competitive edge—especially over those who mail a standard propaganda package.

"How to Interview The Industrial Prospect"

J. Martin Orr, C.I.D.

INTRODUCTION

From sharing information with a "suspect" to negotiating with a "live prospect," the interview, as a communication process, is the basis for our results as economic developers. The interview is the first step in turning an available building or site into a new facility with jobs for your community.

In actuality, no two interviews will be the same. Individual economic developers have their own styles. Individual local communities base their interviews to some degree on their strengths (which prospects will likely know in advance). Every prospect representative has his own individual approach. This diversity provides a great challenge and is a reason for economic developers to operate in a professional manner.

The prospect representative can come in all shapes and forms. Some will be company officials or officers. Some may be staff personnel (such as engineer, real estate manager, marketing representative) assigned the task of finding a location for the new facility. Or, in numerous cases, a consultant will be employed to do the initial investigation and screening. On the other hand, your community may be represented by a professional economic developer. In quite a few instances, however, local volunteer leaders will be performing as the community representatives.

The purpose of this "interview primer" is to emphasize the importance of the interview process. Regardless of individual approaches, the basic elements in preparing for and conducting an interview are consistent. Properly conducted, the initial interview with a "suspect" will often lead to detailed discussions with a live prospect. For that reason, each interview must be thorough. A complete interview will include: LISTENING to the prospect's requirements and desires; TALKING both to answer the prospect's questions and to sell your product and community; and WATCHING to be aware of facial and other reactions which may indicate the need for further information.

The "HOW TO" theme of this publication is designed to assist the economic developer to prepare for and to conduct a successful prospect interview. For either an existing business expansion prospect or a new business facility location prospect, you are representing your community.

PREPARING FOR THE INTERVIEW

Knowing Your Product

As the professional economic developer or the committed volunteer representing the community, the prospect expects you to know a broad range of details about your community. Thus, you are responsible for accumulating quantitative information about your community, your sites and buildings, and your services. The product also includes those qualitative attributes that you and your community are proud of and can sell to others.

Although developing a thorough knowledge of your product at first appears to be an ominous task, a good economic developer learns to utilize local and state resources. For information not easily maintained in your organizational files, being familiar with and having access to others becomes important. Other on-going resources would include: the city engineer and public works staff, city and county tax offices, university industry resource offices, state development organization and revenue department offices, and private realtors and developers.

Instead of saying "I do not know" to a prospect's question, it is better to say "I will get that information for you."

Know Your Prospect

If the name of the prospect company and the name of the prospect representative is known in advance, you have an opportunity to prepare for the initial prospect contact or interview.

A small amount of research can provide you with information on the company's current facilities, sales and profit history, and prior investment patterns. Familiarity with this information and names of the prospect's corporate executives helps the economic developer in two ways. With fewer questions to ask the prospect, you have more time to listen to the prospect and to respond to his questions. Secondly, the prospect will appreciate the active interest of the local community.

Sources of information include local libraries, chambers of commerce, and state development organizations. Types of information include annual reports, *Dun & Bradstreet, Moody's, Standard & Poors*, and other investment reports and business periodicals.

Frequently, the name of the prospect is not known at the time of the initial request for information. Prospects and site selection consultants will acquire information from many communities before selecting a limited number for more detailed analysis. In these cases, the economic developer must respond professionally to the specific questions asked. A part of the response may include asking the prospect's representative for more detail regarding some questions.

Knowing Yourself

Conducting an "interview" by face-to-face meeting, telephone conversation, or by letter requires confidence on the part of the economic development professional. The prospect's initial opinion of your community is directly influenced by the confidence you have in yourself and your product. This confidence is reflected in the ability to answer questions and to show enthusiasm.

In the interview process, some decisions have to be made, particularly whether the project appears to fit in with your community's environment and whether the proposed facility or expansion ought to be pursued vigorously.

Participating in professional economic development education programs and learning through experience provide the basis for your confidence. This, along with knowing your product and the prospect, puts you in the position to represent your community properly.

CONDUCTING THE INTERVIEW

Setting the Stage

As noted earlier, no two interviews will be the same. Your initial prospect communication may be limited to a telephone interview or to a written response from a prospect representative. However, for each case you have the opportunity to present professionally your community or to muff it completely. In each case, the purpose of the interview is to **respond to the questions of the prospect and to sell the benefits of your site and community.**

When limited to a written response, you have few alternatives. Short, concise but thorough, answers must be given to questions presented. Additional written response should be limited to an attractive community profile and/or organizational brochure along with your offer to provide further information. A site selection representative may request information from many communities; if multiple responses are being reviewed, the voluminous information packet may be quickly rejected.

The Telephone Interview

The telephone interview requires the same elements and attention you would give to a face-to-face interview. Your environment must be controlled to the degree that you will not have interruptions and that you will have information available. If you cannot devote adequate time or you must gather information from other areas in your office, it is advisable to ask the prospect if you can call back within a short period of time.

Listening to the prospect's requirements and questions is the crucial part of the interview. Prematurely attempting to lead the prospect to the attributes of your site without knowing the prospect requirements may shorten the interview. The prospect representative may feel that you cannot meet the requirements.

Although cordial conversation is expected, answers to individual questions must be to the point. If the prospect representative has a site selection evaluation form from which questions are being asked, superfluous discussion may indicate a "snow job." Asking for clarification during response to questions may further help you to document the requirements. Allow the prospect to end the "interview." Once you understand the requirements, offer to mail further information. Based on your feelings about the interview, you could invite the prospect to visit your community or

offer to visit the prospect at his office.

The Face-to-Face Interview

The face-to-face interview normally occurs in one of two environments — your office or that of your prospect. In either case, you must commit your time and your attention to the prospect representative. The face-to-face interview is very demanding because you must present yourself as an organized professional. At the same time, it can be most rewarding because you can visually see the response of and establish a rapport with the prospect representative.

In the interview in your community, you are in control of the environment. By setting aside time in your office or a private conference room, you are able to devote your attention to the prospect requirements. Although there may be pressure by local community leaders to participate in the initial interview, this contact should be limited to yourself and one or two key resource persons. At this time, you are primarily responding to the prospect's questions. The more people present and taking time to talk will reduce your ability to learn the prospect's requirements. A site/facility tour and a meal or cocktail with the prospect will provide an opportunity to introduce others to the prospect. However, it is very possible that the prospect representative will not want to meet with others. The desire to remain anonymous should be respected.

A team effort may be beneficial, with one person primarily responsible for listening to and recording the prospect requirements and a second person primarily responsible for answering questions and selling the product. In addition to benefiting you, the team effort may expedite the delivery of a good response to the prospect.

PROSPECT INTERVIEW INFORMATION

Prospect inquiries and interviews normally include four types of information. From the prospect, the purpose of the inquiry and technical requirements are received. From you to the prospect site/facility/community facts and community attributes and incentives are provided. An example "Prospect Information Guide" is included in Exhibit A; the following is a description of the information sought.

Purpose of the Inquiry

The general purpose of the inquiry should be identified to assist you in determining

your ability to respond to the prospect. This would include the proposed use of a facility and market/geographic factors of importance in considering your community. The type of facility is based on the proposed use, ranging from manufacturing to office purposes. Market service area factors include both geographic service area and type of customer information. Other geographic factors include time, distance, and shipping costs from suppliers or to customers.

The initial prospect inquiry will normally include the anticipated date by which a proposed site/facility is needed. Critical site/facility or service requirements are often identified initially.

The prospect's introductory information will provide you an overview upon which more detailed requirements will be based. This introductory information may indicate factors you will want to emphasize in future communication.

Technical Requirements

Specific site, building, utility, transportation, and employment requirements of the prospect are normally identified in general terms in the initial interview. Based on response to the initial requirements, more detail may be requested.

Site size my be but one consideration as other site information may include soil types, slope, shape, and expansion options. In addition to such location factors as transportation access and population area, consideration may include relationship to other business and planned industrial/business districts.

If an existing building is sought, the prospect will identify general facility requirements and specifications such as noted in the example form. Other special requirements such as heavy utility services should be noted so that you can investigate the community's capability of meeting them. If the prospect proposes new construction, factors for consideration may include building codes and recent cost comparisons.

Utility requirements vary in importance depending upon proposed type of use. In any case, however, special attention should be given to the terminology used — i.e., units per hour vs. units per day vs. units per month. Also, any special requirements or peak factors should be noted.

In addition to volume of water, other criteria may include pressure, alternate sources, and purity or mineral content.

Both existing and possible future sewerage requirements should be noted. Special

PROSPECT NO. _____
STAFF PERSON _____
INITIAL CONTACT _____19 _____

PROSPECT SOURCE:

Referral by: _____ **Existing Company**
_____ **Bank**

Response to:_____ **Advertising campaign**
_____ **Letter/direct mail**
_____ **Telephone contact**

_____ **Consultant**
_____ **State**
_____ **Realtor/Developer**

I. COMPANY INFORMATION

Company Name _____
Contact (Name) _____
Title _____ Phone (____) _____
Street _____
City/State/Zip _____
Principal Product(s)/Service(s)_____
Location of Headquarters _____
Location of Other Facilities _____

II. REQUIREMENTS: Occupancy by _____ 19 _____
A. FACILITY for:
Primary Function: manufacturing_____ , assembly _____
    distribution _____ , warehouse _____ , bulk processing _____ ,
    office _____
Primary Markets: local _____ , regional _____ , national _____
    international _____
Geographic Area based on: proximity to raw materials/suppliers_____
    proximity to commercial customers_____ , proximity to consumer markets _____ ,
    other _____

B. SITE: Acres _____ /soil bearing _____
Freeway access:No _____ ; Yes _____ : within _____miles
Metro area: Yes _____ ; population range _____
        No _____ ; but within _____miles

C. BUILDING: Size _____sq. ft.
    Available _____ or will construct _____
    Ceiling height _____ Bay widths _____
    Sprinkler _____ Air Conditioned _____
    Docks_____ truck high _____ Drive-in doors _____
    Type of construction_____
    Floor bearing _____
    Type of use: Office _____ sq. ft.
            Manufacturing _____ sq. ft.
            Warehouse _____ sq. ft.
            Number of parking spaces_____
    Other building requirements _____

D. UTILITIES
    Water (treated) _____ gals./day   (untreated) _____ gals./day
    Sewage _____gals./day
    Electricity _____ kw/peak   _____ kw/day
    Natural gas _____ cu. ft./day
    Coal _____ tons/day
    Other fuels _____
    Other waste disposal _____

E. TRANSPORTATION: Rail served: No _____ ; Yes_____ ; volume _____
  Trucking: private_____ ; local _____ ; interstate _____
  Commercial Air: No _____ ; Yes _____; within _____miles
  Barge: No _____ ; Yes _____ ; volume _____

F. EMPLOYMENT: Total Projected _____
  Transferred _____ New _____
  Professional_____
  Skilled _____
  Unskilled _____
  Training Assistance Desired: No_____ ; Yes_____
     Type of skills _____
  Organized Labor: No _____ ; Yes _____
     Union(s) _____

G. FINANCING: Assistance requested: No _____ ; Yes _____
  Approx. Investment $ _____Land/Building
                      $ _____Equipment

H. OTHER: Foreign Trade Zone: No _____ ; Yes _____ ; within _____ miles
  Bonded warehouse: No _____ ; Yes_____ ; within _____ miles
  Underground space _____

III. COMMENTS/FOLLOW-UP

_____
_____
_____

---

disposal requirements should also be noted, although special processing is normally the responsibility of the prospect.

Electricity requirements, in addition to base demand, may include available alternate sources and interruptible service factors.

Immediate and future natural gas and fuel requirements may include information about alternate fuels available. For coal users, content and source may be a factor.

For each type of utility service, the costs may be a factor based on volume of use. Additionally, pollution control requirements of your community may be a factor in response to some prospect needs.

Normal transportation requirements are easily identified. Special cargo handling requirements and zone information should be noted if an immediate response cannot be made.

Employment and skill level requirements should be collected so that available labor and training information can be provided to the prospect. Special considerations may include salary and wage comparisons, training assistance available, and union involvement in the prospect company and/or in your community.

Financing assistance by your state or local community may be requested. Depending upon your knowledge of the pros-

pect company, the general alternatives can be presented. Detailed discussions of financing should normally be deferred to the appropriate officials (for example, local or state financing authorities).

Other prospect requirements may include the need to have some or all facilities within or near a foreign trade zone or underground space. Also, bonded warehouse space information may be important.

Responding to prospect requirements may involve information readily available or, as previously noted, may involve calling upon local and state resources. In either case, the local economic developer is responsible for getting the answer to the prospect.

Your Response

The third type of information in the prospect interview is your response to the requirements given you. Having an available community profile or fact book is desirable during your verbal response to questions asked and a copy should be given to the prospect representative for possible unasked questions.

Community Attributes and Incentives

The fourth type of information in the prospect interview supports your extra effort to make the sale — if you can meet the

basic requirements. Information about community attributes, so-called livability factors, and other factors about which your community is proud should be available both verbally and in material to be given the prospect.

Written information about financing, training, and tax incentives should also be provided. Whether administered locally or by your state, you want the prospect to know you are aware of the services and prepared to help.

FOLLOW UP

The prospect interview does not end with a simple exchange of information. A follow-up letter should reinforce your interest in helping the prospect to locate in your community. Also, a prompt response to any unanswered technical questions should be provided — both by telephone and in writing.

Through cooperation with the staff of your state economic development office, use of their support and their contacts may be beneficial in attracting a new company from another state or country. For an expansion prospect within your state or community, use the support and contacts of other companies — unless the prospect inquiry is confidential.

How to Recruit New Manufacturing*

Robert L. Koepke, C.E.D., FM, HLM
Steven R. Warren

INTRODUCTION

The desire to improve the quality of life in their area is the reason why citizens of an area become and remain involved in economic development. This critical but elusive quality of life substantially is a result of the area's economic base, as measured by the area's tax and job bases.

The economic base of any area, in turn, results from investment or reinvestment. it is investment and reinvestment of capital which produces the tax base and the jobs. In the American economy, most of these crucial investment dollars come from the private sector.

One important source of this essential private sector investment is from manufacturing firms that are new to an area.

According to the Illinois State Chamber of Commerce, 100 new manufacturing jobs in a community can have a substantial impact on an area. For example, these new jobs can produce 315 additional related jobs, $12 million more in personal income per year, and $5,000,000 in additional bank deposits.

Given this impact, it is not surprising that manufacturing investment is sought by people in any area.

THE CHALLENGE OF RECRUITING NEW MANUFACTURING INVESTMENT

Recruiting new manufacturing investment, however, is a very competitive business. There are reported to be in excess of 10,000 economic development organizations in the United States, all competing for one or more of the just 200 major location decisions made each year.

To improve the chances of standing out — of winning the investment "race" — the leaders of an area must approach their job of stimulating private sector investment as a sales function, treating the potential investor as a client and the area as the product.

It has been said that the people who are successful in economic development are locally sensitive yet investor client driven. The challenges to the area's leadership are to develop and implement a recruitment strategy based on matching the area's desires and abilities with the investor's needs and interests.

THE FIRM'S NEEDS AND INTERESTS

A firm looking to invest in a new manufacturing facility has one thing — profitability — upper most in its business mind. The management of such businesses have to go before their board of directors regularly and report to them how the firm is doing. Certainly the board wants to know about recent sales and costs, but ultimately they are interested in how much money the firm made and may make in the future. Management is always asked "what are the profits?"

Profit, of course, is determined by revenues and costs. Easy access to current or potential new customers can affect a firm's revenues and is often a significant plant location consideration.

Costs, of course, are a major concern of any business and dominate most locational decisions. It is essential for local citizens involved in economic development to realize that businesses measure nearly everything in money terms. Businesses must know in detail the costs, revenues and resulting profitability of doing business in any location, especially when they are in the plant site selection process. They must have current and accurate data to use in making their investment decisions.

The investment decision makers in the firms are vitally concerned with tangibles. They pay particular attention to an area's track record in working with other businesses. No manager can afford to put his company at risk by betting on an area's hopes and promises.

Hence, local leaders must know what the area has that the business firm needs. Capabilities must be documented. In any business, before salespeople call on a prospective new account, they know their product inside and out. Selling an area is no different.

It is paramount for local citizens to think and act like business people. Citizens must be ready to respond to a prospective investor's business inquiries accurately, completely, and rapidly.

THE PROCESS OF RECRUITING MANUFACTURING

In order to improve their chances of being successful in the recruitment of new manufacturing, there are three sequential steps the citizens in an area should follow. These steps are: 1) creating the product (area) for investment, [preparing] 2) communicating the product's (area's) capabilities to targeted potential investors [prospecting] and, 3) facilitating the decision making activities of those investors who have expressed an interest in the product (area) [prospect handling].

Becoming Prepared

Once the leaders of an area understand what motivates an investor, their economic development need becomes to position themselves to respond to the business product and information needs of the potential investor.

The Product

The area must be in a position to meet the business needs of the firm. This means having in place such manufacturing requirements as the appropriate transportation network, facilities (land and/or buildings) with adequate services, and the necessary labor. If these requirements do not exist in the area, the only logical response of the economic development leadership of an area is to create them [or at least be in a position to do so].

* The contributions of Greg Nieman and Robert Treat to the content of this article and the support of Illinois Power are gratefully acknowledged.

Data

Data that address the cost of doing business and document the nature of the "product" in the area must be obtained, put in a usable form, and kept current. An area's data bank should include information on the availability, quality, and costs of labor, transportation, public services, (such as water, sewerage, and fire and police protection), and energy services — (electricity and natural gas). Community leaders must also be familiar with available industrial properties — land and buildings. They must know where they are, how much they cost and their quality.

Finally, the leaders must know what incentive programs are available, especially locally.

Some nonbusiness information should be in the data bank as well, such as recreational activities and educational programs.

Obviously a great deal of information must be collected. It must be current and accurate and kept that way. This is not a simple job. It requires a committed local leadership.

Presentation of Data

The next challenge in preparation is to decide how data should be presented to the potential investor client to document the capabilities of an area.

A variety of formats are available; they include: (1) a profile (that summarizes the information on the location); (2) a fact book (which provides back-up detail); (3) industrial site and building brochures; (4) labor statistics; (5) a multi-color brochure portraying the quality of life in the area; and (6) finally and least important, a video tape that gives visual information about the location.

In preparing information in any of these formats, it is useful to keep in mind that the firm's first need is quality information. Illustrations, while not irrelevant, are of secondary importance. Illustrations can make good information clearer, but they cannot make poor data good.

Throughout this entire effort, the local leadership must *think* and *be creative* because each client is different. Leaders cannot afford to make a purely mechanical response. Needs of prospective clients certainly must be anticipated, but unfortunately, no one can anticipate all the needs of a specific manufacturing investor. The local economic development leadership must be prepared to be as innovative as necessary and mentally ready to create special responses to meet special needs.

The leaders who are in a position to respond to a basic business request have done their homework. They have made their location more competitive in the business of economic development through their anticipation of the product and information needs of potential new investors.

The Organization

But one substantial requirement has not been addressed yet, namely *who* will collect all the prerequisite information, put it in the appropriate format, keep it accurate and up to date and present it to investors?

The answer, of course, is the leadership of the area through a local economic development organization. This organization will have the responsibility to assure that what is being done is consistent with the wants and desires of the people of the area as a whole. The economic development organization will also be the group that actually solicits and works with potential investors. The organization is a key component of an economic development program, for the job of economic development is too big and too important for one person or just a small handful of people in the area. Rather, it is most successful when it is the effort of a broad-based team composed of local people who have an interest and capability in economic development.

The organization may consider hiring an economic development professional to implement their program. This decision should be based on the sophistication of the program and the availability of funding. If it is impractical to hire a professional, the economic development organization of course will need to utilize committees to implement various aspects of the program.

With an operational organization in place and with the necessary data about the product collected and put into a useful form, the local leaders are well on their way to being "prepared" for economic development.

The evidence is clear that the prepared area has the best chance of success in the highly competitive business of economic development.

Generating Investor Interest

The second step in an economic development recruitment program is generating prospective investors.

There are two different ways in which potential investor clients may approach an area. Some clients will contact the local organization directly, without any solicitation effort on the part of the local leadership. Other clients result from a response to an outreach activity by the local group or other organizations.

Because it does not have to wait for the client to come to it, the well prepared organization has a major advantage in prospect development. Its leaders are able to take the message of its area's capabilities to prospective investor clients.

To generate prospects, a local economic development organization may contact investor firms directly or it may be referred to prospective clients. The leadership of an organization can use both of these approaches, along with responding to unsolicited inquiries.

Referral Organizations As Client Sources

Referrals generally come from economic development organizations that have an interest in the welfare of the area, such as the state economic development department, utilities, and railroads that serve the location. These potentially supporting organizations are commonly called "allies".

Referrals can also come from consulting firms retained by the investor. This group includes plant location consultants, along with realtors, especially industrial realtors.

The local economic development organization may choose to concentrate its energies on informing these referral groups of the business capabilities of the area and keeping such people informed. After all, they come into contact with more prospective clients than the local economic development organization ever will.

Referral groups can also be cultivated relatively inexpensively. The number of ally and consultant groups is very finite and the names of the key contacts in each are available. Often, moreover, they are commonly not a great distance away and thereby travel is affordable.

Positive relationships with referral groups, especially allies, also can be very beneficial to the local area, in that they can be of significant support in providing details of services to the area's prospect. There will be times — perhaps frequently — when the local leaders will need the help of the knowledgeable people in its referral network.

But a note of caution is in order. If the local leadership wishes to maintain a working relationship with this source of potential investors, such leaders must work with the referral group in a *professional manner*. The referral group, by bringing a prospect to the area, has put *its* reputation on the line.

They in effect have told the client that the location has the capability to meet their needs. The area's leadership cannot afford to let the referral group down.

Direct Generation

Prospects can also be generated directly by the local organization itself. This is done in one of two ways or a mixture of the two.

One is to make the capabilities of the area known to industries in general. For example, the local economic organization may place an ad in a general economic development publication.

The second approach is to focus on a select number of industries and associated firms, with the first step being the creation of a list of those industries whose probable needs match the area's interests and capabilities.

After the target industries have been identified, the local economic development organization must produce from this initial screening a more detailed list of targeted industries. Next it must identify specific firms within the industry group(s) to solicit actively.

Finally, decisions have to be made about how to contact the management of the targeted firms.

The alternative communication procedures are: 1) to promote the area in industry specific magazines, 2) to mail prepared marketing materials directly to the identified management, 3) to exhibit at trade shows, and 4. to use telemarketing.

Once interest is expressed by a particular firm, local leaders should look for opportunities to visit the firm's office to present the area's capabilities directly to the management or encourage the management of the firm to visit the local area.

An Expensive Undertaking

The economic development leadership of an area needs to recognize that most outreach activities are usually relatively expensive and, if conducted properly, are very time consuming. Prospecting for new business is neither cheap nor simple.

One way for a single location to reduce the cost of recruiting new business is to band together with others and, as a group of towns or a region, solicit targeted industries and firms.

Facilitating The Investment Process
Initial Response

If the people in the area have done their homework and are lucky, a business person, ally, or consultant/realtor will contact the economic development organization wanting investment information. What should the people in the organization do?

First, they need to continue to think in business-like terms from the vantage point of the investor. It is vital that the local leadership realize that their objective is to stay on the client's list of possible locations by addressing and responding to the contact's requests.

This third step in the recruiting of manufacturing process is often called "prospect servicing or prospect handling".

In preparing the community's initial response, the leaders need to determine as much as possible what the client wants. This will enable the leaders' to respond accurately and thoroughly to the prospect's needs. Ask how one can help. Listen!

Then the information that the client desires should be sent in the agreed-upon timeframe. At a minimum, a follow-up letter should be sent summarizing what is available and what will be done, and when.

After the initial response package has been sent, a telephone call follow up should confirm that the material arrived. Determine if the information sent was what was desired.

Finally state one's willingness to provide additional help as needed and determine when would be the best time for follow-up again. In the process, look for opportunities to have the client visit the local area.

On-Site Investigation

If the leadership is *very* fortunate, the client will eventually state a desire to make a business trip to the area. Leaders should treat this request in the same businesslike manner as they did the previous ones. Remember that the client is coming to confirm the information on the business product he or she has been supplied and to learn more.

The bad news is that the client is also continuing to try to find something that will eliminate the area. By this time, the prospect is also evaluating other locations. They have typically narrowed down a large number of locations from early in the process to a select a few to study in depth. Their job, at this point, is to select the best one, by eliminating the others.

The client is of course in the area to see the location. But before the business tour begins, the local leadership must confirm what the client wants to see and do. They also must confirm the amount of confidentiality the client wants. The leaders should not make assumptions — they should ask!

The responsibility of the leadership of the local economic development organization is to keep the visit on a business level by showing the client only what he/she wants to see and by keeping the local host group small, but composed of people who can make the necessary commitments and who can answer questions.

It is wise to keep the business trip low key. This means no press, no flashy meals at the country club, no banners, no press conferences. Maintain confidentiality always! A location can be eliminated solely on its inability to keep the company's name and intentions out of the newspapers and local gossip.

The leaders need to follow up as before with answers to the new questions raised by the client.

Closing The Deal

If the local leaders have created and documented a competitive "product" and are extremely lucky, the negotiations may proceed to the deal closing stage.

SUMMARY

Recruiting new manufacturing investment offers a potential way for any area to affect positively its quality of life.

Local leaders who choose this course, however, must recognize that a well developed economic development program is required, as is a significant commitment of the area's leadership resources and, depending on the activities chosen, a substantial commitment of financial resources as well.

They should also realize that a three step sequential process is available to increase the area's chance of attracting new investment.

Step one is preparing the area. There is homework to do and it must be done. The area — the product — must be known and its capabilities documented and even improved. The people of the area need to know whether or not they can compete competitively in the business of recruiting new manufacturing investment.

Step two is generating prospects. A realistic program to reach prospective investors must be created and implemented. This includes cost effective allocation of available local money, people and time.

Step three is handling or servicing the client. Local leaders must function as professional sales people, which means becoming knowledgeable about how to relate to a prospective investor.

Although utilizing this or any process or procedure does not assure the desired results, by following these three steps, the leaders of an area are doing what they can to increase their area's chances of success.

No location can expect to win them all. Attracting new industries is very competitive and successes are hard to come by. Expectations should not be set too high and instant results should not be anticipated.

The creation and implementation of a realistic plan, based on the principles that have been described, however, will certainly make success more likely.

Recruiting Retail Investment

Clifton Harald, MA

INTRODUCTION

Retail recruitment is an important part of the economic development effort in many communities, despite a history of neglect within the profession. The first section of this article identifies the reasons retail has been overlooked, and goes on to describe why retail recruitment is becoming increasingly important. The second segment summarizes the key elements of a retail recruitment program, including researching the local market, targeting specific retail businesses, generating qualified retail prospects. A case study of a successful retail recruitment project is presented as the third segment. Comments facilitating investment decisions conclude the article.

WHY RECRUIT RETAIL INVESTMENT?

Retail investment is traditionally viewed as a low economic development priority because it creates lower-wage jobs and usually re-circulates capital locally instead of creating it. As evidenced by well-publicized resistance to Wal-Mart's plans to open stores in some markets, retail development also can be controversial, for residents, government officials and businesses may oppose new projects.

Retail investment, however, can be very important to local economies. In many states it has tax base advantages over manufacturing or office uses. In these states, cities compete with each other to capture retail expenditures (and taxes) made by households and businesses. Restaurants, department stores, movie theaters, and other retailers are also amenities valued by most residents and businesses and can be important measures of a community's quality of life.

Retail also may be seen as a low priority because economic developers marginally influence retail investment decisions. The decision to open a retail business is based on narrowly-defined financial criteria; retail site selection is determined by the sales a retailer expects to generate within a local trade area. However, economic developers can accelerate retail investment decisions by drawing attention to a market that might otherwise be overlooked, and by facilitating the analyses and negotiations leading to investment decisions.

DEVELOPING AND IMPLEMENTING A RETAIL RECRUITMENT PROGRAM

Understanding Local Strengths and Weaknesses

Before implementing a recruitment program, a community's market should be researched and evaluated. A basic issue to be resolved at the outset is determining the community's economic need for retail through local area economic analysis. In particular, the importance of retail to local government finances should be evaluated. The level of local support for new retail development should also be assessed early in this process.

With these and other basic questions addressed, the specific information sought by retailers can be researched. Criteria important to retailers include demographics, especially population densities and income, and area growth trends, particularly residential development. Equally important is the availability of highly visible sites readily accessible from well-traveled streets. For each potential site, retailers will require demographics, traffic counts, and other data. They will also want to know the closest location of their competitors to a prospective site. For a complete description of the research conducted by retailers and developers in evaluating a market, refer to *Market Research for Shopping Centers* by Ruben Roca.

After completing this basic research, local strengths and weaknesses can be determined. Key sites with the best potential for retail development can be identified based on demographics, traffic counts, and the location of other retailers. At the same time, a community can anticipate and prepare responses to any concerns expected to be raised by retailers about weaknesses in demographics or other criteria.

Defining Targets: Retailer, Developer and Broker

The most complete directory of U.S. retail businesses is the *Directory of Leading Chain Stores* published annually by Business Guides. It lists nearly 10,000 retail companies managing over 600,000 stores nationally. The Directory categorizes stores by type and provides information about key personnel, preferred markets and expansion plans.

The first step in targeting specific retail prospects is to assess the likely retail development potential of each local site based on its demographics and other attributes. Is a site best suited for a stand-alone/pad retailer, a convenience center, community center, power center, regional center, or some other kind of project? Not all retailers have the same requirements, so it is important to understand the different kinds of retailers and their needs. A grocery store anchoring a community shopping center, for example, typically requires a smaller trade area than a discount department store in a power center. For a description of the typical criteria of different kinds of shopping ce1nters, refer to the Urban Land Institute's *Shopping Center Development Handbook*.

The next step in targeting retailers is to take an inventory of retail businesses already in the market. The inventory will help clarify retail voids in the market and identify categories of retailers that might be targeted to fill them. In conducting the inventory, it is important to include all retailers who serve the local market, even those located outside the community recruiting new retail. It is also important to include retailers committed to new development projects within the local market.

Another step in targeting retailers is to survey local residents and businesses to determine the perceived retail needs and preferences, as well as potential support for retail development.

In addition to retailers themselves, the targets of a recruitment effort should include developers and real estate brokers specializing in retail. Their contacts with retailers can be leveraged by providing them with site, demographic and other information about the local market. Names of developers and brokers can be assembled by contacting brokerage firms active locally and through the International Council of Shopping Centers, a New York based association of retail developers and retailers.

Generating Retail Leads and Qualifying Prospects

With a list of targeted retailers, economic

developers can begin the actual recruitment campaign. The initial goal of the marketing and outreach effort is to draw attention to a market that might otherwise be overlooked. The next step is to get retailers, developers and brokers to visit the community and evaluate its potential.

To prepare for the marketing campaign, organize the data assembled during the community analysis phase into a series of databases. These will include site information, demographics, housing construction trends, commercial/industrial construction trends, employment trends, major arterials and traffic counts, existing shopping centers and retailers. The information will be critical to retailers when they decide about investing locally, but it also may be used to produce marketing materials, and if warranted, advertising.

Retailers will often request information about a market before visiting it in person, so collateral materials highlighting market strengths must be available to them. The first materials produced should summarize local demographics, growth trends, traffic counts and existing retailers. Information about recent retail development will be particularly useful in attracting additional retailers. Maps will also be valuable, including a regional map, local area map, retail competition map, aerial site maps, conceptual site development plans, and development trends map (identifying areas of residential and non-residential development). Demographic information can be purchased from a number of private companies such as Equifax and Urban Decision Systems. These commercial reports typically describe key features of a defined trade area surrounding potential retail sites, including population, income, households, age, etc. Finally, brochures describing key features of potential retail sites such as location, size, zoning, and price should be prepared.

Advertising can complement a marketing program. Retailers, however, rarely use ads to find markets and sites so it is important to evaluate the benefits versus the costs of an ad campaign. Advertising should target a retail audience. Print media options include industry magazines such as *Shopping Centers Today, Stores, Chain Store Age Executive, Mass Market Retailers, Value Retail News,* and *Shopping Center World.* Local or regional business and real estate publications can be useful in reaching brokers or developers working in the area.

The most important element of the marketing effort is taking the community's message directly to retailers, developers and brokers through a marketing program integrating telemarketing, direct mail, trade show participation, and personal contact. The goal is to get retail interests to visit the community to evaluate its potential.

The least expensive component is a combination of telemarketing and direct mail. Begin by compiling or acquiring lists of retailers, developers, and brokers. Call them to introduce the market, mail them trade area data and information about positive growth trends, and then invite them to tour the community.

Retail industry trade shows and conferences offer a more direct means of contacting retailers. By joining associations such as the international Council of Shopping Centers, the National Retail Federation, and Value Retail News, contacts can be made directly with retail, developer and broker targets. Trade area information can be provided during these meetings and invitations extended to visit the community and tour the trade area.

The best outreach effort is to meet with retailers, developers and brokers at their offices. Again, trade area information (retail profile, maps, site brochures, demographics), should be presented and targeted prospects invited to tour the local trade area.

When prospects visit a community, they should be given a complete tour of the market including stops at possible retail sites, competitive retail locations, residential neighborhoods (especially new ones), and employment centers. When appropriate, involve local property owners, lenders, government officials, and even other retailers in welcoming retail prospects.

RETAIL RECRUITMENT CASE STUDY

The Project

In June 1993, Dayton Hudson announced that it would build a new Target store on the site of an aging shopping center in Broomfield, Colorado. Motivated by an eroding sales tax base, and a blighted city entrance, this affluent suburban Denver community spent years attempting to avert the death of its oldest shopping center.

The special significance of the project is the partnership between Broomfield and Target. The Broomfield Economic Development Corporation introduced Target to the local market, helped them evaluate the trade area and study development plan options, and facilitated negotiations with the property owners and the city's urban renewal authority. Broomfield's urban renewal authority developed the project, successfully relocating several existing retail ten-ants, razing the existing center, and delivering a clean site ready for development to Target. In addition to investing $5.5 million in building the new store, Target agreed to loan Broomfield $2.8 million for the redevelopment effort, to be repaid from incremental taxes generated by the store.

Target's decision was a "win-win-win" for Broomfield. It meant complete redevelopment of the aging retail center, creating a much improved image of Broomfield at the city's "front door." The new store significantly expanded shopping opportunities available to area residents and businesses. Perhaps most importantly, the Target store is conservatively expected to generate at least $17 million in sales annually once it opened in March 1995. This sales volume would produce $1.3 million in sales taxes each year, nearly half of which would be collected by the City. The City's share represents a 10% increase in the City's 1994 total sales tax collections, all from one store in one year.

FACILITATING THE RETAIL INVESTMENT DECISION

Economic developers can play an important role in facilitating the analyses and negotiations conducted by retailers in making an investment decision. During the analysis phase, the information required in market research and site analysis can be provided. In addition to the data described above, a community can underwrite market feasibility studies frequently required for larger development projects. Economic developers can also coordinate the participation of other interests in the analyses, including developers, brokers, property owners, and city government.

If market analysis indicates a feasible project, the most difficult phase of retail development begins, namely negotiating agreements. Here, too, economic developers can help produce a successful project by facilitating negotiations between retailer/developer and the property owner, between the developer and retailers, between retailer/developer and city government during the development review process, and between the retailer/developer and local residents and businesses affected by the new project.

After marketing the trade area, providing data and analysis, and facilitating negotiations, economic developers must acquire a sense about when to get out of the way. Like investment decisions made by office users and manufacturers, the success of a retail investment decision will depend on the analysis and judgment of private interests. But unlike most office or manufacturing projects, the sales volume projected for a specific store serving a defined trade area is the single most important factor determining the success of a retail project. More important than the availability of a competitive work force, favorable tax rates, or even generous incentives, retailers seek sites which will generate the sales they require. The wrong location will ultimately produce failure, regardless of any inducements a community may offer.

Despite these challenges, retail recruitment can be a valuable element of a community's economic development effort. It can provide tax advantages over manufacturing or office projects and it is an amenity valued by most residents and businesses. Economic developers can facilitate retail investment decisions by drawing attention to a market that might otherwise be overlooked, and by facilitating the analyses and negotiations leading to the investment decision.

The Retail Recruitment Effort

Target's decision was a direct result of the Broomfield Economic Development Corporation's (BEDC) retail recruitment program. BEDC was given a mandate by the Broomfield City Council to recruit new retail businesses. Beginning in 1990, BEDC developed and ran the most aggressive retail recruitment program in the Denver metro area. BEDC made the first contact with Dayton Hudson (Target's parent company) at the National Retail Federation Convention held in New York in January 1991. At the conference, BEDC's Executive Director spoke with the Chairman and CEO of Dayton Hudson about Broomfield's desire for a Target or Mervyn's.

BEDC addressed numerous concerns raised by Dayton Hudson and Target during their analysis of Broomfield's market. Two major issues raised were timing and sites. Dayton Hudson actively builds stores throughout the country and cautioned that Broomfield's project would have to be scheduled accordingly. BEDC worked to keep the project a high priority by providing data showing the rapid growth of the market and by keeping Dayton Hudson apprised of their competitor's (K-Mart, Wal-Mart, ShopKo) activity in the market.

Dayton Hudson raised issues about the suitability of local sites, particularly the accessibility and potential costs of the aging shopping center it eventually redeveloped. BEDC produced a Broomfield Gateway and Commercial Center Vision Plan to identify and illustrate specific access improvements, land uses, and landscaping recommendations for redevelopment of the shopping center site. The Plan was presented to Target early in their evaluation of the market and helped them better understand the site's potential. BEDC also explained the urban renewal/tax increment financing powers of the Broomfield Urban Renewal Authority, which could help make the cost of the shopping center site competitive with any alternative.

BEDC provided Dayton Hudson and Target with a constant flow of information; this included maps (regional, aerial, utility, land use/zoning, competition), site plans, demographics, information about growth trends, housing permit activity, urban renewal powers, developer and potential co-tenant contacts, testimonials, and other material.

BEDC had many meetings with Dayton Hudson and Target executives and staff after the initial contact in January 1991. In addition to meeting the Chairman and CEO of Dayton Hudson, meetings were held with senior officers and managers of the research and real estate divisions of the company. Meetings were held at Dayton Hudson's headquarters in Minneapolis, at conferences of the International Conference of Shopping Centers, and in Broomfield.

Lessons Learned

Target's decision offers several lessons about the process of economic development:

☐ The process is often lengthy. BEDC first initiated contact with Target's parent company, Dayton Hudson, in January of 1991. Target announced their decision in June 1993, and the store opened in March 1995.

☐ The process often involves many people. Since the initial contact with Dayton Hudson, BEDC worked diligently with several persons and departments of Dayton Hudson and Target to keep Broomfield's name and interest in their minds and on their desks. BEDC worked with Dayton Hudson's research and

planning staff, Target's real estate staff, and their project management staff. BEDC staff visited Minneapolis in January of 1992 to talk with five of the company's top executives about the Broomfield market. BEDC also hosted numerous tours of Broomfield for Dayton Hudson and Target executives, most of whom visited Broomfield repeatedly.

☐ The process requires enormous amounts of information. Since January 1991, BEDC provided Dayton Hudson and Target with demographic data, real estate information, BEDC's Vision Plan for the shopping center area, information about Target's competitors in the market, statistics about housing growth in the area, information about the City's powers to facilitate redevelopment of the site, numerous maps including site plans, regional aerials, land use and utility maps, newspaper clippings about growth trends in the area, testimonial letters from the Mayor of Broomfield and former Senator Tim Wirth, and a steady stream of letters keeping Dayton Hudson and Target apprised of local developments and the continued interest in them.

☐ Money spent on economic development is an "investment" in the community. Since BEDC was formed in 1986, the City of Broomfield has "invested" $1.3 million dollars in funding for BEDC. In one year alone, Target is conservatively expected to generate $600,000 in City sales taxes. This tax revenue does not include the economic benefits of money spent locally by Target employees or money spent by Target for real estate, construction, utilities, and supplies required to operate the store.

BIBLIOGRAPHY

"When Wal-Mart Comes to Town"; Edward O. Welles; Inc. magazine; July 1993.

"Why Wal-Mart is Worth it to Us"; Hank Gilman and Anetta Miller; Newsweek magazine; November 8, 1993.

Market Research for Shopping Centers; Ruben A. Roca, Editor; International Council of Shopping Centers; New York, NY; 1980.

1995 Directory of Leading Chain Stores; Business Guides, Inc.; Tampa, FL; 1994.

Shopping Center Development Handbook; John A. Casazza and Frank H. Spink, Jr.; ULI-the Urban Land Institute; Washington, D.C.; 1985.

Retail Targeting And Attraction Strategies

James A. Devine, CED, FM

INTRODUCTION

Retail attraction may seem to be an exercise on the margin to purist economic developers who pursue the "basic" industries. But in some communities, retail sales are a basic industry, just as tourism and retirees are basic industries in certain areas of North America. In California and Arizona, for example, large percentages of communities' *new* general fund revenues come increasingly from sales tax receipts. With the increasing taxpayer focus on limiting or stabilizing property taxes, these new sources of income must be pursued to meet increased demands for services. For example, in Glendale, Arizona, about 33% of the city's general fund revenues come from its 1.2% sales tax rate. Phoenix, Arizona recently approved an additional $.001 increase in sales tax to fund additional public safety officers. The City of Scottsdale is considering a sales tax increase to pay for construction of a major highway not funded by the state of Arizona.

Some practitioners may scoff at retail trade's lower, non-value added wage rates, fewer employee benefits due to retail's large part-time work force, and lower multipliers estimated to be about 1.0 as compared to manufacturing's multiplier of 2 to 3. The limitations of the retail industry are real, but nevertheless, people need full or part-time employment.

These revenue generated and job creation imperatives cause publicly funded economic developers, who report to cash-flow conscious city managers, to "follow the money," as suggested by Watergate's "Deep Throat." Thus, in the Southwest, economic developers are competing with their peers in neighboring communities to attract major sales tax generators such as new car dealers ($100,000+ per year), regional malls ($500,000+ per year), furniture stores ($100,000+ per year) and major discount stores ($150,000+ per year). By contrast, a manufacturer is not as lucrative to a city from a cash-flow perspective. In Glendale, a new 40,000 square foot manufacturing building's tax bill would be about $36,000. Only $1,400 of this goes to the City's general operating fund, while $3,360 is used to retire municipal bonds. The rest ($31,240) funds public schools and other special assessments.

GENERAL RESEARCH

Gathering, synthesizing, and packaging data into research studies and sales collateral materials is essential. Retail site seekers require current and projected demographic information. They seek a population threshold or the minimum number of consumers necessary in a trade area to provide an adequate sales volume for a particular type of retail business.

Typical demographic analysis considers:

- ☐ Regional population growth
- ☐ Net in-migration
- ☐ Age levels
- ☐ Job growth (as a barometer for a community's economic vitality)
- ☐ Educational attainment (as a proxy for buying habits and disposable income)
- ☐ Households
- ☐ Cars per household
- ☐ Average income
- ☐ Ethnic mix
- ☐ Traffic counts.

Retailers aggregate information into Trade Areas of 1, 3, 5 or even 10 miles, depending on their product(s) and customer mix. Trade areas can be radius-based or polygons created by roads and/or barriers such as bridges, railroad tracks, or multi-directional intersections.

There are many sources of research data. They include National Decision Systems, Claritas Corporation, DRI McGraw Hill and Woods and Poole. Most of these firms derive data from the most recent census and update it via proprietary models. For example, Claritas Corporation has developed consumer characteristics of market areas through a Consumer Lifestyle Cluster System. Forty dominant lifestyle types, or clusters, have been identified throughout the USA. Each consumer cluster is composed of households that tend to exhibit similar lifestyles and to act uniformly and predictably in the marketplace. Clusters are given names which describe their characteristics. Examples include Upper Middle, Child Raising Families in Outlying Areas; Owner Occupied Suburbs; Blue Chip Blues; Mixed Gentry and Blue Collar Labor in Low-Mid Rustic; Mill and Factory Towns; Golden Ponds; Pools and Patios; Young Influentials; Blue Collar Nursery; Old Yankee Rows and Hard Scrabble. These definitions help market researchers and tenants to visualize the customer and to develop sales strategies. National Decision Systems' Informark Express allows radius and polygon demographic research. Each site can be characterized on its demographics in detailed seven-page reports.

TARGET RESEARCH TECHNIQUES

Targeting retailers can be a time consuming and expensive research effort. In a dynamic retail market, it can be end-run by actively dealing with the marketplace suppliers, developers, tenants, and brokers. However, for the rigorous-minded professionals, or areas needing to document demand to make a market, a traditional target research technique consists of assessing the market demand through a retail gap or a leakage of study. Typically this analysis is based upon developing or purchasing average household expenditures for any of 150 retail category types. Examples of retail category types include appliances, clothing, fast foods, recreational, personal services, and restaurants. Examples of restaurant sub-categories include Italian, seafood, deli's, and fast-food restaurants.

By determining the average household expenditure for any of these sub-categories, a market feasibility study can forecast projected store sales by radius from any X, Y coordinate. These projected sales are then analyzed and compared to the existing number of retail sub-category tenants within a trade area to determine if the market is under- or over-served. Store specific variables such as creative pricing, marketing, or promotional activities are considered also.

Another targeting technique would be a supply-side analysis. This methodology divides the total population of the area by the total number of stores in any one particular retail sub-category. This result is the average population served per retail store type. This ratio can be compared to the subject trade area's ratio. Over- and under-served retail categories can be documented by this technique. Under-served categories can then be solicited. Economic developers can use either of these supply or demand analyses to develop a powerful argument to attract new stores to fit documented under-supplied niche markets.

Retail decision making, however, is as much art as science. Each retailer has its own demographic requirements. For example, a music store location is driven by age (mostly children in school), while restaurants are driven by age and disposable income. Retailers are not as sensitive to labor costs as manufacturers since the competition is likely to be paying the same rate of the trade area served. While retailers pay lower wages, many sales people are paid commission or receive tips, thereby increasing their effective hourly rate.

TRADE SHOWS

Trade show attendance is an important sales and reconnaissance technique. For national tenants, the International Council of Shopping Centers (ICSC) can be the biggest lead and market assessment activity. ICSC's regular attendees are the decision-makers. Deals are made at ICSC's national, regional and statewide conferences. Key additional ICSC members influencing tenant decisions include architects, developers, national franchise site selectors and brokers. The National Association of Corporate Real Estate Executives (NACORE) is another trade group frequented by national retail tenants.

FACE-TO-FACE SALES

This technique can include inbound familiarization tours for developers and/or site consultants, outbound blitzes to areas of high concentration of retail decision makers, and networking with local brokers and investors. Personal relationship building is essential, especially in

retail attraction. National chains generally have established relationships with brokerage houses, individuals, and architect and engineering firms throughout the USA. The local economic development practitioner may identify a site seeker, but chances are s/he will call a local broker or architect to get the inside story.

ADVERTISING AND PUBLIC RELATIONS

Advertising and public relations would be useful in publicizing or "making" an unknown market or reinforcing an existing market's image. Since the decision makers operate nationally (developers, national chains, partnerships, REITs, brokers, and architects), reaching them via advertising may be too expensive as compared to attending ICSC or NACORE. With a good list, direct mail also may be more cost effective.

SITE AND BUILDING DATA

Site seekers have many choices because every retail site competes for tenants with every other site in the same trade area. Many cities zone every corner "retail" in hopes of luring sales tax generators! (Frequently, this strategy can dilute the market, or competitors' profitability, as the neighboring communities have sites too -- "just across the street.")

Site-related data worth collecting and profiling include

❑ Roads

❑ Facilitators and barriers to street access

❑ Traffic counts

❑ Side of street in relation to traffic at rush hour

❑ Price

❑ Competitor locations

❑ Same-store locations (to avoid cannibalization of market share).

Price is extremely important as it is one variable which can be negotiated. Since retail is highly competitive, with low margins, the lease or mortgage rate and term impacts profitability year after year.

INCENTIVES

Most tenant locations are based on the numbers — price, population, income, traffic count, etc. in the prospective trade

area. If a decision is swayed by incentives rather than the integrity of the demographics, the retailer may be doomed to failure.

Low profit margins, ever-changing consumer buying preferences and decreased volumes due to seasonality, however, can be offset marginally with incentives which serve to lower out-of-pocket costs and increase returns on equity. Developers who build-to-suit, lease, and then sell after 3-5 years are especially grateful for incentives in their projects. Incentives can take the form of sales-tax rebates (state law permitting), tax-increment financing (the proceeds of which are funded by the project's projected sales tax revenues), grants, or loans. Incentives generally fund public right-of-way improvements such as enhanced landscaping, new curb and gutter, water and sewer upgrades, rehabilitated streets or intersections, and new signalization. These investments should be memorialized in a development agreement between the city and the developer/tenant or owner. The agreement should specify the level of sales tax performance to be expected for the privilege of using a portion (usually 30-50%) of the newly generated public funds. If threshold sales tax receipts are not met, the agreement can be voided and the offsite costs repaid with interest.

CUTTING RED TAPE

"Time is money," especially in retail. Christmas is the "make it or break it" season for many consumer goods businesses. Malls, downtown or redevelopment sites will survive or die depending on whether they make an October opening deadline. A city with a proven fast-track process for design review, building inspection, or tenant improvements may be favored over one with poor customer service. A list of satisfied fast-track retail customers and their phone numbers can make the difference between a store locating in one community versus another.

Other public sector regulatory concerns which site seekers evaluate include:

❑ Is the community overly zealous in trying to enforce its codes and rehabilitation requirements of marginal centers?

❑ Is the Americans with Disabilities Act religiously or realistically enforced, depending on the site and the economics of the deal versus the competition?

❑ In the case of rehabilitation, are there design and retrofitting standards which require an inordinate, startup budget-busting outlay?

❑ How much landscaping and infrastructure improvements do the tenant or developer have to pay for doing business in the city?

❑ Do the physical aspects such as site planning and urban design architecture affect the site/building rents and costs?

❑ Do the social aesthetic policy issues decided through review boards, neighborhood associations and planning commissions drag the process on so long that the window of opportunity closes and another site is developed in a competitor community?

All of these regulatory and subjective community values combine into a pro-forma budget which renders the site or building uneconomical or worthy of further investment of time and money.

DEALING WITH "MOM AND POP" RETAILERS

Caution: as in industrial development, the small projects tend to take as much or more time than the big ones. Dealing with "mom and pops" can be rewarding, but typically it is not. They are less sophisticated in making site decisions; their goals may be based on a dream, not a plan; they are undercapitalized, typically working off of savings and family loans; they may not know how to run a retail business and don't understand marketing. But they *DO* know how to complain and reach the elected officials for enhanced service demands. Their needs (politically endorsed) can occupy the economic developer's attention for all the wrong reasons, taking time from the bigger deals which offer more value to the community. This possibility has been dealt with in Glendale. The City Council has indicated that regional retailers which employ ten (10) or more employees shall be fully serviced by the City. Smaller ones are referred to the Chamber of Commerce for assistance.

TYPES OF RETAIL CENTERS AND SITES

The retail industry divides its centers into four (4) basic types of centers:

❑ **Regional shopping centers** (500,000+ square feet) with two (2) or more major department stores and anchors greater than 100,000 square feet each;

❑ **Community centers** (150,000- 350,000 square feet) include a discount department store or a junior department store and draw customers from outside the local area. Power centers with several "category killer" tenants ranging from 15,000 to 100,000 square feet (Ross or Walmart) are a subset of community centers.

❑ **Neighborhood centers** (80,000 to 150,000 square feet) include drug and/or grocery stores and multiple outlet types of tenants providing daily living needs of an area;

❑ **Strip/specialty centers** (50,000 square feet or less) usually have no anchors but can sometimes be united by a theme.

Each of these types of centers can be solicited using the tried and true sales tactics mentioned before, but in different combinations and intensities.

For example, when attracting a regional mall, pull out all the stops, especially if retail sales tax generation is the goal. Once enticed, the mall developer and leasing staff do the tenant attraction and the city manager and the economic developer can sit back and count the cash coming in.

In community level centers and power centers, the national brokerages and local brokers specializing in big-box users in excess of 30,000 square feet have an incentive (their commissions) to recruit tenants. In this situation, face-to-face networking with brokers and decision makers at ICSC and NACORE may be time well spent.

Neighborhood centers typically have smaller tenants, usually mom-and-pop stores serving the area. Successful attraction strategies here are directly proportional to the professional's regular communications with the local brokers and as good as their available site and building information.

Strip and specialty centers are difficult to attract and maintain. Frequently, their locations are mid-block, success is difficult and there are many competitor sites. Without anchors or themes, they are most in need of professional assistance and are mostly occupied by mom-and-pop tenants.

The community's most helpful stance for strip and neighborhood centers is to provide quick customer service for plan review and tenant improvement. A redevelopment plan may also be prepared to allow the site to be retrofitted for modern customer and facility demands. Typically, the tenant is considering several locations and the one that can come in on time and under budget becomes the winner.

There are several kinds of sites. They may be free standing, in-line and end cap. They may be corner or mid-block location. They may be pad sites in a masterplanned commercial center or a free standing site without a lot of architectural or thematic support from its surroundings. Once the demographics are worked through and the search is narrowed to a few locations, some of the typical site selection criteria include: concessions, tenant mix, image, style, charm, character, visibility, retail signage (wall/pylon/monument), competitors' name and physical location and condition, distances within proposed shopping center and to other competitors, ingress/egress, parking, trade area (current and projected), and real estate commission rate.

All these variables combine to make some sites and buildings better than others. The economic developer who knows and documents all the major and minor commercial locations, their tenants, and operating situations will be an invaluable market research resource for retail site seekers. Glendale, for example, maintains a database of all tenants, centers, and brokers throughout the county. All 1,600 centers and 15,000 tenants are geo-coded to allow radius-based searches and analysis for over 150 tenant categories. The database can track the exact distance in mileage of any tenant or site from any given site, provide lists of any tenant or broker by category throughout the county, and identify market niches. This tool, Glendale's Retail Opportunity Analysis Report (ROAR), is a comprehensive site, building and demographic market study for any of Glendale's 120 commercial centers. It has assisted more than 20 site decisions and has facilitated many market research meetings with tenants and developers.

CONCLUDING COMMENTS

Arm yourself with the proper research (demographic and collateral materials including sites and buildings), a proven, user-friendly regulatory process, and incentives (if necessary or appropriate), and communicate with all potentially affected decision makers. Network with the major national chain decision makers, the local or regional brokers specializing in retail, and architects, appraisers, lenders, investors and developers with track records in retail.

In a dynamic retail market, keep the communications lines open and then stay out of the way. There are more than enough brokers and developers to take the risk.

If the market needs to be "made" and publicized, as in rural or downtown or redevelopment retail attraction, the upfront face-to-face sales job is essential and time consuming. Generating market feasibility studies (demographics) is essential. National chains rank trade areas by their potential and enter into markets by investing in the most lucrative to the least lucrative. Inserting a community ahead of the pack requires good research and follow through. Remember, most brokers and developers pursue retail sites or buildings which can be operating ASAP and where demographics are, or appear to be, the best for the tenant in hand.

A Comprehensive Strategy for Rural Downtowns

Terry Lawhead

INTRODUCTION

America's commercial downtowns have undergone profound change and nowhere is this more evident than in its small rural communities. The problems faced by a small rural downtown are unique due to numerous economic and social factors. First and foremost is the significant leakage of retail sales to new shopping centers or retail power centers offering lower prices and located either outside of the downtown or in a neighboring city a few hours away.

Second is the management/ownership structure. A traditional business district is an economic entity which includes, and competes for, the office, housing and entertainment markets as well as the retail market of a specific community. By comparison, a retail power center, housing large chain stores providing competitively priced products at a volume unachievable by smaller operations, is a simplified version of the complexity of a traditional business district. Comparing its management to those faced by a retail power center store is revealing.

No single department of a store located in a retail power center is a stand-alone business. It must report directly to the overall management of the store, where decision making is coordinated and controlled from the top. To improve a department, one improves the management directing the department.

The challenge in revitalizing a rural downtown is that numerous small businesses are owned by an assortment of different individuals, all of whom have different strategies for success as well as often dramatically different rates of success. Consistency and the intent to standardize and sustain uniform quality throughout a single department in a power center is relatively easily achieved using conventional management techniques based primarily on lowering costs and moving products. Guiding a downtown coalition of enterprises is significantly more complex and requires creativity, flexibility and numerous, often fragile, partnerships based upon mutual interest.

Such partnerships make up the nucleus of an effective downtown management strategy modeled after the Main Street approach. The Main Street Program has proven that it has an excellent results-oriented process which can take action on decisions emerging from such partnerships and derive measurable results which provide great benefits to small communities.

BACKGROUND

The National Trust for Historic Preservation, long involved in the preservation of older, architecturally important buildings, launched the Main Street Program in 1977 to:

❑ study the reasons downtowns were dying

❑ identify the many factors that have an impact on downtown health

❑ develop a comprehensive revitalization strategy that would encourage economic development within the context of historic preservation.

Demonstration projects revealed the essential success factors of the Main Street approach, including:

❑ a strong public-private partnership

❑ a committed organization

❑ a full-time project manager

❑ a commitment to good design

❑ quality promotional programs

❑ a coordinated, incremental approach to economic development which produced achievable concrete goals.

By any standard of measurement, the Main Street approach to downtown preservation and revitalization was successful in developing stronger and more successful businesses. As a result, the National Trust established the National Main Street Center in 1980, locating it in Washington, D.C. It quickly expanded until today there are 900 individual Main Street programs in 34 states.

Measurable criteria are standardized throughout the United States to demonstrate achievement of the goals of the national program (see Figure 1). Using those criteria, the Arizona Main Street Program has also achieved great success. Since its inception in 1986, the Program has provided guidance for more than $149 million in local reinvestment. This represents a return ratio of $100 of investment for every state dollar spent. In addition, the Program has assisted in the attraction of 549 net new businesses, the creation of 2,899 net new jobs and the development of 1,030 building projects.

The Main Street Program is an economic development program designed to produce increased levels of reinvestment and jobs. But it also attempts something more. It intends to preserve and enhance the heritage of communities. Anybody involved in community development, tourism and quality of life issues can recognize the importance of these elements and their relationship to successful and sustainable economic enhancement.

The important role of preservation is often misunderstood. The renovation and subsequent utilization of historic or unique buildings in a community is a demonstration of commitment by residents of that community. Community pride and the development of a sense of place cannot be ignored in the effort to improve the quality of life for all ages. Fortunately, preserva-

---

FIGURE I

CRITERIA MEASURING ECONOMIC CHANGE IN BUSINESS DISTRICT REVITALIZATION

Number of Building Projects
Value of Building Projects
Number of Property Acquisitions
Value of Property Acquisitions
Number of Public Improvements
Value of Public Improvements
New Jobs
New Businesses
Reinvestment Dollars
(Total of above values)

---

tion values are present in many American communities and today it is rare when a community treasure is demolished without discussion. In some newer communities without a great number of older buildings, historic preservation may be described not as just protecting architecture but as the general effort to maintain good design which can help identify a special market niche for downtown.

MAIN STREET FUNDAMENTAL PRECEPTS

The Main Street approach to downtown revitalization is based on four fundamental precepts:

❑ Design involves improving the downtown's image by enhancing its physical appearance. Buildings, street lights, window displays, parking areas, signs, sidewalks, promotional materials and all other elements that convey a visual message about what the downtown is and has to offer are areas where design can make or break a downtown.

❑ Organization means building consensus and cooperation between the groups that play roles in the downtown. Many individuals and organizations in the community have a stake in the economic viability of the downtown, including bankers, property owners, city and county officials, merchants, downtown residents, professionals, chamber of commerce representative, local industries, civic groups, historical societies, schools, consumers, real estate agents and local media.

❑ Promotion involves marketing the downtown's unique characteristics to shoppers, investors, new businesses, tourists and others. Effective promotion creates a positive image of the downtown through retail promotional activity, special events and ongoing programs to build positive perceptions of the district.

❑ Economic restructuring means strengthening the existing economic base of the downtown while diversifying it. Economic restructuring activities include helping existing downtown businesses expand, recruiting new businesses to provide a balanced mix, converting unused space into productive property and sharpening the competitiveness of downtown merchants.

The elements interrelate. Without the design component, the Main Street approach resembles any other economic de-

velopment program. Without promotion or economic restructuring components, it resembles a museum project seeking only to preserve unique architecture for the sake of history. The precepts are not meant to provide a cookbook solution and they respect and work with local strengths and weaknesses. The magic is tailoring the mix to each community and in educating local leadership to understand the importance of not crippling the effort by emphasizing one component over another.

The key to success of the Main Street approach is adhering to its comprehensive nature. Underlying this strategy is the conviction that no individual business exists outside of the context of a downtown commercial district. By carefully integrating all four precepts -- design, organization, promotion and economic restructuring -- into a practical downtown management strategy, the Main Street approach can produce fundamental changes in the downtown's economic base. Activity in one area reinforces activity in the other three. Programs that have concentrated on just one precept have seen limited success in that area but without support from the others have been unable to build on that success to create long-lasting positive change.

LOCAL LEADERSHIP IS IMPORTANT

The education, training and empowerment of leadership is essential to producing

programs which successfully develop and reflect local influences. Due to growing skepticism of "experts," local leadership is preferred by residents to an influx of outside "specialists," although it is generally acknowledged that the fresh perspective provided by an informed "outsider" can be of inestimable value.

The Main Street approach is highly structured. It ensures that local community leaders are provided with enough information so that they can effectively run the program. Ideally, a local manager is fully qualified in understanding the process of economic development and can act as a liaison between numerous individuals and private and public groups but also is willing to take directions from a board of residents, business owners and elected officials (see Figure 2).

The immediate results of such a volunteer-driven, professionally-staffed structure is profound. Local leaders and volunteers soon realize they can take the credit for successes as well as be held accountable for mistakes. As new challenges arise, residents have more confidence in their ability to come up with their own solutions and not rely on outside consultants.

A useful analogy which illustrates the importance of devising a comprehensive downtown revitalization program can be taken from real estate. There is a common understanding in real estate appraisal that for a commodity to have value, it must have scarcity, purchasing power, desire (for the

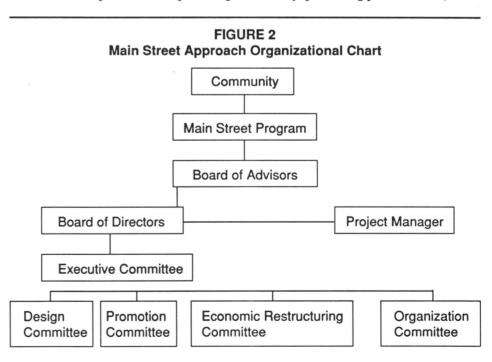

FIGURE 2
Main Street Approach Organizational Chart

Community → Main Street Program → Board of Advisors → Board of Directors — Project Manager; Board of Directors → Executive Committee → Design Committee, Promotion Committee, Economic Restructuring Committee, Organization Committee

object) and utility. For a retail business to have value, it must have sales (desire), a strong market (purchasing power), adequate parking and other physical maintenance items (utility) and a strategy of how to position itself to compete with other similar operations (scarcity). The goal is to reposition the business district in the marketplace so that it is capable of capturing a greater market share. That goal is accomplished by encouraging, developing and implementing strategies that bring about business retention, improvement, expansion and recruitment.

COMMON PROBLEMS OF DOWNTOWNS AND A FEW STRATEGIES

There are five common problems faced by declining small rural downtown commercial areas. They are:

❑ Sales leak out to surrounding shopping malls.

❑ Parking is consistently a problem, with limited space and accessibility.

❑ Direction to downtown planning is often lacking or absent.

❑ Marketing of existing businesses is non-existent or uneven to potential customers.

❑ Businesses are usually undercapitalized and have difficulty financing expensive programs.

No single small business has the resources to tackle such large problems. No single success can, in the longterm, overcome problems which are related to infrastructure, planning and public image. A community of businesses, however, can come together and reinvent and reinvigorate itself to solve its problems.

Any successful comprehensive strategy has these essentials. They are:

❑ It relies on quality, be it buildings or people. A town must focus on its best existing assets and make them as excellent as possible.

❑ It acknowledges, causes and incorporates changing attitudes. Attitudes reflect information and understanding, and the public must be educated.

❑ It implements changes one step at a time. Problems do not appear overnight nor do solutions. Small and steady improvements means that people can make changes and then see them cause other changes. Such activity empowers people to strive for more and thus achieve more.

FINDING AND STRENGTHENING ANCHOR BUSINESSES

Never forgetting the comprehensive emphasis of the Main Street approach nor neglecting continuous improvement on all four precepts, a close examination of business activity downtown reveals two obvious fundamental problems which fuel the multiple symptoms of decline requiring the strategy listed above, which are:

❑ existing businesses are struggling to survive;

❑ new businesses require encouragement to open.

If existing businesses are not strengthened, then customer loyalty, continuity of important goods and services and the need for credibility requires retaining existing businesses and improving their operating methods. Existing businesses are the building blocks toward a revitalized commercial center and if they are not doing well, no new businesses will consider opening in the area. Subsequent strategies may vary tremendously, however, depending upon dominant philosophies and convictions.

Facilitators of Main Street programs should understand that no program can retain all businesses and they must target the winners. They should also recognize that an individual failure does not signal failure for an entire district. Closures have their positive side as well for the surviving stores, suggesting gaps in the market that should be examined in the business recruitment program. The yardstick is not whether a specific business person was successful but whether the business is needed and whether customers are there to support it.

The first step is evaluating which businesses are competitive is to do research. The Retail Assessment Form is frequently used to establish a baseline assessment (see Figure 3). There are other instruments as well. A business inventory addresses the kinds of businesses present. It can be analyzed to understand and compare with the nature of the existing market served. A market analysis attempts to quantify supply and demand. It can reveal market niches and oversupply.

Any viable business requires an adequate market, adequate space and support facilities and a sense of local upward momentum. Again, the value of the market study should be repeated. It must be available to existing businesses considering leaving a downtown location and to new operations interested in locating there.

A market study should provide, in clear and understandable language:

❑ A historical understanding of the area, the functions it once served, the nature of its decline and the reasons why that decline occurred.

❑ A complete inventory of the existing space and businesses in the target area. This inventory should include the number of units, present usage, location, size, rent levels or sales prices, amenities such as shipping-receiving areas, storage rooms, etc., potential usage and current sales receipts.

❑ Data concerning the characteristics of the local consumer population including geographical determination of the primary and secondary market areas, population, age breakdown, number of households, household profile, household income level, number of workers per household, household movement trends (in or out migration), shopping habits and the preference of

---

The Example of Page, Arizona

When Page, Arizona joined the Main Street Program, the prevailing perception was that the city had adopted a policy of directing new development to an area "off the mesa" by providing infrastructure to a new Wal-Mart shopping center at the edge of town. After the Bashas grocery left the Uptown area for the new center, things looked bleak. However, the city, working with the Main Street Program, has reinvested in the Uptown, changed codes and ordinances that were restricting development and sought to attract private investment. The old Bashas is now an upscale outlet mall following extensive rehabilitation of the building and a new 140-unit Best Western Motel had been developed across from City Hall. This is in addition to numerous rehab projects of retail businesses, restaurants and the bowling alley. Downtown interest must concentrate on the developments on the outskirts.

FIGURE 3
Retail Assessment Form

Use this form to evaluate the quality and effectiveness of
existing small businesses.

Name of business _____

Address _____

Owner _____ Phone _____

Owner's address _____

Manager _____ Phone _____

Merchandise category _____ SIC# _____

Store concept _____

Type of Traffic: ❑ Destination   ❑ Impulse   ❑ Other

Date of assessment _____ Conducted by:_____

Physical characteristics

Size in square feet   (1) Gross: _____ (2) Sales area: _____

Quality of:

❑ Display fixtures _____ ❑ Lighting _____

❑ Signs (interior) _____ ❑ Signs (exterior) _____

❑ Layout _____ ❑ Window displays _____

❑ Point of purchase displays _____ ❑ Facade (exterior) _____

Target market/customer characteristics

❑ Age _____ ❑ Sex _____

❑ Area of residence _____ ❑ Workplace _____

❑ Income range _____ ❑ Other_____

Service characteristics

❑ Sales staff knowledge of goods/services _____

❑ Sales staff friendliness _____

❑ Store return policy _____

❑ Product/service guarantee policy _____

❑ Credit available _____

❑ Convenience of hours for target market _____

❑ Delivery services _____

❑ Other _____

Marketing/promotional characteristics

❑ Quality of advertising _____

❑ Frequency of advertising _____

❑ Overall advertising effectiveness _____

Inventory characteristics

❑ Breadth of merchandise available _____

❑ Depth of stock on hand _____

❑ Turnover frequency _____

❑ Overall quality/condition _____

Other comments: _____

_____

Suggestions: _____

the current population for the business district or competitive retail centers.

❑ Inventory of services provided by competitive retail centers profiled by types of services offered and typical rent levels or sale prices.

❑ Listing of nonretail-related functions such as transportation routes, office or housing located in the district, public improvements and parking.

Ideally the results of these instruments are used in conjunction with what is called a Resource Team Report. This is conducted by local individuals and selected "experts" and views the circumstances surrounding revitalization through the "lens" of the four precepts (organization, promotion, economic restructuring and design). A Resource Team Report is produced to be understood by the lay person and presented to the public for discussion. Afterward, more qualified economic development specialists can work with more technical information.

This mix of vernacular knowledge and technical data illustrates a rule of thumb of the Main Street approach, namely to never dismiss common assumptions in favor of "expert conclusions." On the other hand, it is well known that assumptions attesting to the longevity of a business may be misleading or seriously out of date. A balanced mix is required. Strict surveys and inventories restore often-repeated commonly held beliefs to the status of factual information (see Figure 4).

There are many operations in a downtown context: strong locally owned businesses, chain stores, marginal businesses operating on a close margin of profit, and "doomed" businesses. There is also always a core group of effective merchants and business people from that mix who realize that the long-term prospects for the district will have a direct effect on their own operations. These are the anchor proprietors to be brought together as the core group of an effective revitalization effort.

Anchor stores are best determined by having the practitioner conduct an Operating Method Assessment. Criteria include all aspects of operations, such as store presentation, lighting, selection of merchandise, demonstration of current retailing trends, cleanliness, and general skills of the merchants to serve their customers. Required next is an examination of merchandise depth, determined by evaluating if there is an assortment of goods in a

FIGURE 4
Assessing Public Perceptions of and Attitudes about Your Downtown and the Competition

Market Group:

Characteristics	Competing Shopping Alternatives		
	Your downtown	Mail Order	Other
Attractiveness			
Cleanliness			
Parking convenience			
Traffic flow			
Shopping hours			
Friendliness of salespeople			
Safety			
Variety of goods/services			
Cost of goods/services			
Quality of goods/services			
Special events and festivals			
Ambience			
Historic environment			

Rating Scale: 5 = Very positive, 4 = Somewhat positive, 3 = Neutral
2 = Somewhat negative, 1 = Very negative

variety of sizes. Merchandise depth is a selling tool to convince customers that a merchant has a broad selection of what they need. Finally, the quality of the customer service, easily the greatest reason for repeat customer business, must then be analyzed. Again, any conventional survey instrument can be used to obtain this data (see Figure 5).

At this juncture, it must be determined if business owners and operators truly have the ability to participate in a revitalization program. This can be realized in part by intuition and in part by viewing the information gleaned from the surveys. Revitalization activity requires financial and time commitments and the elusive quality of imagination. Many small businesses are under-capitalized and operators may be unable to expand. They may be misreading their market but defensive to new ideas. They may have become non-competitive for any number of reasons. Part of the goal of revitalization is to rekindle the spirit of the business people to ensure they are having fun in their workday and to promote this excitement to the market. If this spirit cannot be revitalized, goals must be carefully re-examined to determine whether or not they are achievable.

COUNSELING STRATEGIES

One-on-one sessions can offer insight into business management and provide practical techniques to business owners and operators. A brief selection which highlights some of those techniques follows below.

Merchandising

The practitioner should encourage retailers to look at their store as customers do. The windows and store layout are the first impressions a store makes on a potential customer.

❏ Displays also have to work fast. Studies indicate that businesses have eleven seconds to get walk-by customers into a store. A selection of ideas on visual display would be necessarily too specific for the purposes of this section because successful displaying depends upon attention to the fine details. Again, the Main Street approach provides volumes of suggestions, as do many other references.

❏ Windows can work in favor of the business by using attractive, up-to-date merchandise in displays that are changed frequently (at least once a month). Good windows can sell even when the business is not open. The program should encourage better utilization of these "silent salesmen" through putting display lights on timers,

---

A Willcox, Arizona Merchant

After long resisting suggestions from Main Street support staff, a Willcox, Arizona retailer of seventeen years standing finally availed himself of design assistance. He claimed he knew his business and his customers and that the changes would not make a difference, but went ahead and followed recommendations, giving his western wear store a complete make-over, inside and out. He maintained a customary cheerfulness and welcomed the attention he received as the work was conducted. After completion, the business was featured in a national magazine and consequences closely monitored. The owner reported an increase of gross sales of forty-one percent after the improvements, and became an even stronger anchor of the business district.

FIGURE 5
Summary Checklist for Evaluating the Level of Service to the Customer

Many of the changes that should be made in downtown businesses cost money. Improving the level of service provided to the customer can improve the profitability of a business without increasing costs. Ask yourself the following questions when rating the level and quality of service that a business provides.

Rating range: 5 = excellent; 4 = good; 3 = fair; 2 = poor; 1 = terrible

Business	1	2	3	4	5
1. Convenience					
• hours and days of operation					
• various methods of payment					
• customer parking					
• accessible to customers					
• quick transactions					
• standard prices					
2. Product knowledge					
• sales personnel understand product					
• awareness of competitive advantages					
3. Environment					
• business cleanliness					
• exterior appearance					
• friendliness, courteous sales personnel					
• personal security					
• adequate lighting					
4. Personal services					
• special services					
• first-name identification of customers					
• free delivery					

and crucial for the practitioners to roll up their sleeves and assist stores with interior layout. Some retail consultants recommend that store layout be changed a minimum of once a month. That means people need to be constantly thinking about new ideas. Retailers should be encouraged to study the practices of the competition, particularly the malls, to find a balanced approach. Characteristics of mall store layout are easily identified:

❑ colors are grouped together.

❑ distinct categories are outlined -- accessories are grouped, career clothes for women are set apart from sportswear, etc.

❑ interiors are clean and attractive, giving the feel of well-organized variety.

❑ the customer feels that what he/she wants is there and readily located. Friendly sales personnel with good product knowledge will reinforce this impression.

❑ high demand merchandise is toward the rear of the store encouraging a traffic flow through the store.

❑ impulse items are arrayed near cash registers to encourage last minute purchases.

Downtown retailers should strive to keep stock up-to-date and put merchandise which has not "moved" on the sales rack before the end of each season. Merchandisers should be encouraged to purge their inventory. If merchandise does not move when marked down, there are vendors who will take it at a greatly reduced price; or it can be donated to Goodwill.

However it is moved, outdated merchandise must go. If one new customer finds old merchandise, they will likely not return and will just as likely tell several friends that downtown is no good for anything but out-of-date merchandise. Again, this negative word of mouth advertising can negate a great deal of costly advertising.

Customer Service

Good service and hospitality should be encouraged and strengthened. Downtown retailers need to accommodate their customers since they are the reason the stores are in business. The customer is, in effect, their employer. Retailers should be encouraged to attend customer service clinics and send staff members.

This educational process can be furthered by planning customer service clinics. One survey offered the statistic that one

allowing them to sell to people coming through downtown at night. Most importantly, the program should encourage that windows be planned - they are the most cost-effective form of advertising and the least expensive way of selling a business. If they are not done well, they can effectively cancel other more costly forms of advertising.

Interesting Layout

It is implicit in the Main Street approach

satisfied customer typically mentions a positive experience to one other person, but a dissatisfied customer will typically relate the experience to thirteen other potential shoppers. That goes a long way to explaining why "friends come and go, but enemies accumulate".

Businesses should learn that making their hours meet customer needs ensures strong repeat sales. This is always an interesting proposal but it must be understood that the customer is the retailers' boss. Some factors to be considered in this effort are:

❏ staying open later need not mean more total hours. A business open from 9 -5 might simply move its hours to 10 - 6.

❏ who are downtown's customers and when do they shop? Statistically, most of America is now shopping evenings and weekends, up to 65% of all retail sales are made after 5 p.m. and on Saturday and Sunday.

❏ how many businesses will take part? Sometimes it is easier to look for a cluster to pioneer the concept rather than attempting it across the board. With retailing as small of a percentage of downtown use as it is in some places, it may be difficult to get enough businesses to stay open to make downtown appear open. If a few key businesses located in close proximity to one another could stay open, their example might serve to encourage others.

Management

Management issues reflect the emphasis placed upon organization, one of the four precepts of the Main Street approach. This can be a sensitive area as it involves both owners and employees and their technical and social skills. One of the larger questions to introduce is whether it may be required to reposition the business and add new goods and services to meet the needs of a changing customer base. Other criteria include:

❏ expanding inventories in current products, to create a wider range of buying opportunities in a range of products similar to current types of merchandise.

❏ adding new product lines, which can complement existing lines or even be competitive lines.

❏ relocating to a larger or more advantageous location (within the downtown, of course) to give more room and/or display to expanded lines or possibly to improve the cluster in a certain area of merchandising.

❏ assistance in locating loans (some revitalization programs even have loan pools to assist with purchasing inventory; some SBA programs are targeted at this, as well).

❏ assisting in locating new lease or purchase property to house the business. An improved location can significantly increase business if it is a well thought-out move.

❏ procuring assistance in preparing business plans. The lack of an effective business plan is a great deterrent to successful businesses. Local Small Business Development Centers are good sources for help.

❏ working with local education institutions to make sure that there is an adequate supply of trained staff available.

MAIN STREET'S SUCCESS MIRRORS TOWN'S DETERMINATION FOR SUSTAINABILITY

One resident once expanded upon the routine comment that "more jobs make a town better" by adding, "making a town better attracts more good jobs." Such an observation reflects the general priority of the Main Street Approach to have a balanced view of economic growth and community heritage. However, timing of the phases of a Main Street Program and all of its techniques is crucial. There are many efforts which failed because the analysis of a community was flawed. Common flaws include basing projections on assumptions which are no longer accurate, misreading the customer base, positioning businesses poorly relative to the competition and poor consensus building leading to fractured efforts to promote the district.

An ironic problem is that as a commercial district evolves and matures -- and becomes successful -- new programs must adapt to new needs and opportunities. In addition, when successes become commonplace, politics enter more significantly into any public policy question. The many partnerships implicit in any program which is organized to succeed in a timely fashion become vulnerable to unforeseen stresses when alliances reposition to reflect new agendas.

These are acceptable problems and any town would welcome the burden of successful revitalization. Attractive design, personal and public safety, a supportive infrastructure, management capability and a strong retail/reuse development strategy are all part of the revitalization package and are subject to subtle and extreme changes. The perceived popularity of these components will influence the opinions of local politicians and consensus must be sustained under constant threats of splintering. The city must be committed to public improvements, retail support facilities such as parking and business incentive programs such as storefront improvement financing programs. Then, even if it is generally committed, a city organization will also suffer from periods of benign neglect or errors in judgment. The private sector's support must be rock solid and willing to back controversial decisions to ensure the public that there is in fact a consensus and a vision.

The Main Street Program is committed to being rooted in the local population. It does not assume it can dictate a direction which conflicts with the aspirations of the residents it serves. In this way, the Main Street approach becomes transparent and is simply an outstanding, well planned locally-driven entrepreneurial effort integrated with concerns about the long term quality of life in a community. As a result, the economic development practitioner must also accommodate to a role of transparency, yet be assertive in a variety of areas to move the process toward its goals. Compared to power center management, the path of small town downtown retail redevelopment is strewn with unseen hazards, but the rewards are rich. Such business district revitalization is a return to community self-reliance and a restoration of traditional American values for participating families involved in retail and service operations. It encourages imagination, sharpens business skills and results in appropriately scaled solutions to present and future problems.

How To Implement Local Industry Development and Retention

Miles K. Luke, C.I.D.

INTRODUCTION

An effective local industry development program is becoming increasingly important. Communities now realize that more jobs, typically, are created by the expansion of existing firms in manufacturing and service industries than by attracting new industry.

Major corporations are not building facilities in new locations with the same frequency as they once did. In fact, major corporations have suffered a net loss in jobs in the past decade. Small business is creating the bulk of new jobs in most communities.

The U.S. economy is becoming more information- and service-oriented. In 1984, approximately 75% of all U.S. workers were classified as service workers by the Bureau of Labor Statistics. Forty years, ago, the work force was evenly distributed between the goods-producing and service-producing sectors.

The competition for new jobs is keen and the developer is well advised to recognize the importance of existing industry and its contribution to the local economy, and to be equipped to assist in the formation of "home-grown" start-up companies.

NEED FOR EXPANSION/ RETENTION

The bottom line for the economic/industrial development professional or volunteer is job creation and capital investment in the community. Job and capital creation may be accomplished in several ways: location of a new plant or facility in the community, expansion of an existing business, and entrepreneurial assistance programs to foster start-up firms.

The most glamorous activity is the public announcement concerning a new plant location. However, in planning an economic development program, consideration should be given to the cost of job creation and new capital formation. How much has been spent on advertising, marketing trips, etc. in locating a new plant vs. the cost of an effective local industry development program? After considering these kinds of factors, a balanced economic development program can be planned.

Local industry development offers an opportunity which should not be overlooked. Surveys show that most expansions occur at a company's existing location. Industry will locate where it is wanted and will stay and grow where it is well treated, market conditions permitting.

The best salesman for a community is the plant manager who has already found the area to be a profitable place to operate. If the existing industry is not happy, it is not likely to expand its local operation nor will it recommend the community to others.

If we care about the bottom line—jobs and capital investment in our community—we can not afford to ignore existing industry.

LOCAL ORGANIZATION

A local industry development program needs an organization consisting of people who are willing to work. This organization can be created within a Chamber of Commerce, or by a local government, an economic/industrial development corporation or interested business leaders.

Members should have business experience and comprise the backbone of community leadership, crossing as many areas of the local political scene as possible.

The organization will need to establish goals and objectives based on the needs of the community and the requirements of area industry.

After the organization has had an opportunity to formulate and evaluate its goals and objectives, it must develop specific work programs which should include a solid local industry development and retention program. A wide variety of programs and initiatives has been developed for the local organization to use in its existing industry program.

EXISTING INDUSTRY CONTACT PROGRAMS

Most contact programs involve personal and/or telephone contact with each firm at least once per year. These contacts are made as an information device. Quite often information of a confidential nature is revealed. The company's wishes on confidentiality should be protected. To do otherwise is to lose credibility.

If volunteers make calls on existing industry, they need to be trained. A questionnaire form to guide them through the interview should be available. A sample report form is provided in Exhibit 1. Finally, response mechanisms must be in place to respond to an industry's request. Nothing is worse than someone calling on a plant manager to offer help and then needed help not be immediately forthcoming.

Hopefully, the contact team can tour the plant and will have an opportunity to better understand the company's operations and products. This tour can provide first-hand knowledge of problems and opportunities. A sample questionnaire to use during the visit is included in Exhibit 2. Each organization should develop such a form for its use.

Frequently, the committee may have to approach local, regional or state government to address any problem or need that arises. If good records are kept of the visit and proper analysis is made of information obtained during the interview, the local organization will have the information necessary to assist the firm.

If the company has expansion plans, the ED/ID practitioner wants to know about it and where help can be offered. Company managers may not be aware of the federal, state and local incentives available to them for expanding. Programs which should be explained to company managers include:

- Training assistance
- Enterprise Zone program
- Tax incentives
- Various financing options available
- Assistance available through the Small Business Development Centers (SBDC's) — a program jointly sponsored by the Small Business Administration and local universities.

Many communities conduct an annual survey of all firms to determine the extent of the expansion of jobs and capital investment which have occurred. Besides providing valuable statistical data, it may yield information that should be publicized in the community. Of course, the survey is an excellent means of justifying a funding request for a local industry development program.

Some communities prepare an annual manufacturers directory which is distributed to industry and the community. It is a means of making other firms and individuals aware of products made in the area and a source of revenue when sold to sales people needing such information.

Industry visitations, surveys and directories are aimed at making industry aware that they are part of the community, that they have citizen support, and that there is a willingness to assist with their problems. The programs also provide a means of publicizing the impact of local firms in the community economy.

INDUSTRIAL RECOGNITION PROGRAMS

One of the most frequently used programs is an Industry Appreciation Day or Week. A wide variety of activities can be included in a program:

1. Invite plant managers and their wives to an appreciation dinner which can range from a cookout to a formal dinner. The program can include speeches by local officials, industrial development organization officers, and others expressing their regard for the industry. In other instances, speeches are held to a minimum and entertainment is offered.

2. Proclamations, certificates and plaques can be given to firms for various recognitions.

3. One city takes coffee and doughnuts to industrial plants for employees during Industry Appreciation Week.

4. Another city sponsors an Employee of the Year award at each plant.

5. Activities can include displays of the manufacturing firm's products in merchants' windows. This can be done on a large scale in a bank, airport or motel lobby. One community uses a large tent for product displays and slide shows on local firms.

6. Plant tours and open houses emphasize the impact industry has on the community and provide an opportunity for the public to express its appreciation to the firm.

7. In communities with unique economic activities, special activities can be designed that highlight industries involved in those aspects.

8. Many areas have agri-business dinners or a Town and Country Day when merchants sponsor farm families for a dinner. One community has an Egg Breakfast on behalf of community economic growth.

INDIVIDUAL RECOGNITION PROGRAMS

There are many ways to recognize individual accomplishments. Several directly related to economic growth are:

Present an award for Small Business Person of the Year. Winners compete at the state and national level. An award for Small Business Advocate of the Year recognizes an individual (non-industry) who has made a significant contribution to the community. Some communities have an "Entrepreneur of the Year" award. Quite often these awards will be given at the annual Chamber of Commerce banquet or other appropriate occasion.

The news media is extremely important to an effective industrial appreciation program. During a special period set aside for such activities, newspapers may have a special section describing local industry and its impact on the local economy. Radio and television stations can also do specials featuring firms from the area, discussing the number of jobs and payrolls of the various firms, etc. Some Chambers of Commerce have a special publication for Industry Appreciation Week describing each firm, while others cover one or two firms with each publication throughout the year.

The basic secret of any industrial appreciation program is the sincerity with which the appreciation is extended and the organization's ability to make it fit the special needs of the community. The old adage, that everyone enjoys a kind word, is also true of corporations. So a central feature of an appreciation program is to say kind, sincere words about the existing industry.

BUSINESS DEVELOPMENT INITIATIVES

The local industry assistance program must help existing employers develop new business and thereby influence expansion opportunities through increased sales. Implementing programs that will save companies time and money is equally important. Mechanisms available to assist economic development organizations in doing so include:

- **Federal procurement:** Helping local businesses sell to federal government agencies is basic to an industry assistance effort. A subscription to *Commerce Business Daily* will provide a variety of leads which can be passed on to local businesses for follow-up. Seminars about bidding on government contracts can be held for plant management. In addition, many federal agencies have Departments of Small and Disadvantaged Business Utilization, including the General Services Administration, Department of Defense, and others. Their information pamphlets should be distributed to local companies.
- **Export promotion:** As with federal procurement programs, assisting local businesses in penetrating foreign markets can lead to increased sales and employment. Many banks have full-service international departments whose personnel are anxious to help local businesses. U.S. Department of Commerce district office staff members welcome opportunities to work with economic development organizations in holding "How To Export" seminars and in providing individual assistance to existing industries. Universities are an equally valuable source of relevant data and technical aid.
- **Management seminars:** Tax laws, OSHA regulations, NLRB policies, environmental permitting, small business bookkeeping, and financing programs (to cite only a few examples) all provide additional seminar program topics which can directly assist business owners.
- **SBIR awards:** The Small Business Innovation Research Awards Program provides yet another opportunity for the economic developer to provide meaningful help to local businesses. Complete details are available from the Small Business Ad-

ministration, Office of Innovation, Research and Technology and can be presented to local plant management.

• **Market research:** Economic developers should communicate their willingness to help research potential new markets for their existing firms, products or services. Sources of such information which are readily available include mailing lists from commercial brokers, census data, *Sales & Marketing Management* magazine's "Survey of Buying Power," computer data bases like Dialog and Nexus, and ChaseOne and other providers of customized research.

• **Match-market analyses:** Simple or complex match-market surveys have one primary objective — the identification of existing and potential customers and suppliers of local businesses. Their subsequent attraction to the community provides jobs and investments, but also results in a tangible benefit to local firms.

• **Plant Manager's Association:** Should one not already exist, the creation of such a group by a development organization provides a convenient forum for idea exchange, common problem-solving, and shared information (such as wage rate and fringe benefit surveys) and can even lead to new business relationships among participants. It is an ideal adjunct to the individual contact visits described in "*Existing Industry Contact Programs*" above.

• **Labor relations:** Successful business assistance programs have historically emphasized alert systems to warn of union organizing attempts, and/or management-labor committees to help resolve disputes and improve the local labor climate.

• **Incentives:** Information on loan programs, employee training mechanisms, tax exemptions, site preparation assistance, grants and other available cost-savings programs should be provided in writing to local businesses.

Notwithstanding the success of these types of programs, plant closings due to circumstances totally beyond the control of a community will invariably occur. A local industry development and retention program ought to include economic adjustment strategies in the event of a shutdown.

BUSINESS INCUBATION CENTERS

The business incubation center, a relatively new concept, is becoming increasingly popular as an innovative approach for start-up companies and entrepreneurs seeking to get their idea to the marketplace.

Incubation centers provide flexible space at below market rates, offering shared office services and management assistance. As the fledgling company grows, additional space is made available and within three to five years the company should be ready to move out. The success rate for start-ups spawned in an incubator is around 85%. The national rate of failure for small business is 80%. Incubators are increasing the success rate of start-ups.

In most cases incubators are non-profit and can be controlled by the public or private sector or a combination of the public/private sectors. Incubator facilities range in size from about 20,000 square feet to over 350,000 square feet. Each incubator is the result of the economic conditions and leadership in the local area. Communities studying their potential for an incubation center need to make a careful analysis of building space available, sources of start-up funding, cash flow break-even, organization to operate, and market.

FINANCIAL ASSISTANCE PROGRAMS

Financial assistance is another major area where local industry can be helped. Local firms should be made aware of how industrial revenue bonds can be used. More communities are organizing venture/seed capital investment clubs. Entrepreneurial strategies differ, but essential to all start-ups is financing.

Local industries planning capital expansion and increased jobs are utilizing the long-term fixed asset financing available through the SBA-504 program. Local development companies (Certified Development Companies) are certified by SBA to operate this new program in designated geographic areas. Another financing method that can be offered to local expanding industry, is the Community Development Block Grant (CDBG) — Economic Development Activity Funds. These funds are administered by each state.

Some communities have established a revolving loan fund that can provide small loans at below market interest rates to leverage other financing. Some economic development foundations have incorporated the various financing capabilities mentioned into their services offered. The revenues generated from loans packaged will contribute to funding the organization's overall program.

Developers should know enough about the many financing alternatives so they can put the firm's executive in contact with the proper persons or agency to arrange their financing.

SUMMARY

It is appropriate to emphasize that industrial firms appreciate a kind word for their contribution to the community. It is equally important that the local industry appreciation group be prepared to provide assistance to firms when problems arise. Industry that finds a community willing to express its gratitude in the various ways discussed in this article and to help solve industrial problems will reward that community with its continued presence and probably its expansion.

When that next industrial prospect comes along and interviews local firms, it will be obvious that this community is a good place in which to locate. When an existing firm does fail, the community would want this failure to be due to external market factors — not to a community that didn't foster growth for its local firms.

The economic/industrial development organization's goal should be to become a "Single Point of Contact" for existing industry. Publish a brochure spelling out all the services you can offer and then publicize it to the community and industry.

By all means, be innovative. That's the key to success!

Name of Firm _____

Address _____

_____

Telephone Number _____

Year Began Operations Here _____

Products Manufactured or Type of Business _____

_____

_____

Number of Employees _____

Name and Title of Company Official Contacted _____

_____

_____

Projected Labor Requirements (one year, two years, five years) _____

_____

_____

_____

Labor Training Needs _____

_____

_____

_____

Labor Problems (turnover, productivity, union activity) _____

_____

_____

Skill Needs Not Met _____

_____

_____

Problems/Concerns That Government (Local or State) Should Address ___

_____

_____

List of Major Suppliers _____

_____

_____

Purchasing Requirements For Which Closer Sources Would Be Desirable _____

Does This Plant Export? _____ If Not, Is It Interested in Exporting? _____
Will Firm Want To Be Contacted By State Department of Commerce Representative on:

    Labor Training _____ Need For In-State Sources of Procurement _____

    Expansion Financing _____ Problems with State Government _____

    Export Assistance _____ Other (Specify) _____

What Type Employment Opportunities Does Our Community Need? _____
_____
_____

Are There Industrial Service Needs In The Area? (machine shops, plating, maintenance, etc.) _____
_____
_____

COPIES: One copy for local use

         One copy for state or regional office of Department of Economic Development

VISITATION COMMITTEE MEMBERS

_____   _____
_____   _____
_____   _____
_____   _____

EXHIBIT 2
Community Survey of Manufacturers
(Adapted from Mississippi Research and Development Center)

                      Date _____

GENERAL DATA

Name of firm _____

Address _____

Telephone Numbers _____ Date local operation started _____

Home office address _____

Name/title of local executive _____

Name/title of person responding _____

SPECIFIC DATA

1.   Type of manufacturing operation (List top four S.I.C.'s in order of importance)

    a. _____   c. _____

    b. _____   d. _____

2.   Products manufactured _____

_____

_____

3. What is your straight time hourly wage for all hourly workers (no overtime)? _____

_____

4. What is your starting wage for hourly workers? _____

5. What percentage of your payroll goes to fringe benefits? _____

6. Availability of Labor _____

    Is the labor supply in the area adequate to fulfill your current and future needs?

    Hourly skilled   ☐ Yes   ☐ No

    Clerical   ☐ Yes   ☐ No

    Supervisory and technical   ☐ Yes   ☐ No

7. How many workers have you hired during the past 12 months?

    Skilled _____   Unskilled _____

8. How many applicants do you now have for employment?

    Male _____   Female _____

10. In what categories are hourly workers hardest to find? _____

    _____

11. Future Labor Requirements
    What demand will you have for increasing the work force over the next five years?
    Indicate the number of additional workers.

	1991	1992	1993	1994	1995
Hourly skilled	____	____	____	____	____
Hourly unskilled	____	____	____	____	____
Clerical	____	____	____	____	____
Supervisory and technical	____	____	____	____	____

    a. Have you used the Department of Education's training program?

        Yes ☐   No ☐

    b. Are locally available (off-plant site) programs adequate to train workers to fulfill your job requirements?

        Yes ☐   No ☐

        At what work level are the programs most adequate? _____

    c. Do you think productivity could be improved through additional training to upgrade their work

        and/or management skills?   Yes ☐   No ☐

    d. Do you think your operations could be improved through motivational and attitude-type training of your

        employees?   Yes ☐   No ☐

    e. What training programs do you require in each of the following categories?

        Management, supervisory, technical training _____

        Skills training _____

        Motivational or attitude training _____

        Other _____

13. Are your employees represented by a labor union?   ☐ Yes   ☐ No

If so, name of union

Number of days lost due to union strike   Day/Year   Day/Year   Day/Year

_____

Percentage of workers belonging to union   _____

14. Major raw materials used in the manufacturing process:

Raw Materials Purchased	Location From Which Purchased	Approximate Annual Volume
_____	_____	_____
_____	_____	_____
_____	_____	_____
_____	_____	_____

15. Other materials, goods, or services used in the manufacturing process:

Materials, Goods, or Services Purchased	Location From Which Purchased	Approximate Annual Dollar Volume
_____	_____	_____
_____	_____	_____
_____	_____	_____
_____	_____	_____

Of the above materials, goods, or services purchased from outside the area, which would you purchase locally if made available at a competitive price?

_____

_____

_____

16. What is the market area served by your present operation?

Geographical Area	Percentage of total sales
Local _____	_____
County _____	_____
State _____	_____
National _____	_____
International _____	_____

TOTAL 100%

Providing Business Plan Assistance to Small Manufacturing Companies

Patricia A. Crawford-Lucas, C.E.D.

INTRODUCTION

A business plan is used for a number of reasons: 1) to raise capital for an expansion or start-up project; 2) to determine the direction a company is going and how it intends to get there; and 3) to be used as an internal document to show both short and long term goals of the company.[1]

In assisting small business concerns an economic development professional is often asked to provide assistance in the development or evaluation of a business plan. Economic developers should be prepared to discuss with a business the steps necessary to get started or expand. In doing so, it is important to be in a position to provide guidance to assist the manufacturer in the venture.

At other times, when a manufacturer/businessperson is asked to prepare a business plan in order to obtain financing or for an expansion, he/she may fail to see the necessity of going through the exercise of its preparation. The economic development professional should have the ability to explain the importance of a business plan and the multitude of uses it may provide to a business. There are a number of areas in which a manufacturer may benefit by preparing and using a plan, including financing, strategic planning and for everyday operations. It is important that an economic developer be well versed in counseling a business on these potential uses.

An economic development professional is also asked to make a recommendation on whether or not a proposed venture is viable. An economic developer may wish to avoid giving a direct answer, because evaluation of a venture is difficult. Instead, an economic development professional should encourage the manufacturer to thoroughly evaluate a proposed venture by developing a business plan. This article discusses the content of this valuable business assistance tool, a business plan.

THE BUSINESS PLAN COMPONENTS

The business plan consists of several components, which must be presented in order for the document to be complete. Each will be defined and suggested comments for an economic developer will be given for evaluation purposes.

Executive Summary

The executive summary gives a snapshot of a proposed project to a potential investor. It contains (or should) the following:

❏ A brief description of the product and its estimated market (describe the success ingredient that makes the product unique).

❏ A brief description of the management team and how that team will help the company achieve success, and other successful business ventures in which management has been involved.

❏ A capsule summary of projected financial data, such as annual revenue and net income, for two years.

❏ An estimate of the amount of capital that is needed and how the money will be used. Suggested terms of borrowing and repayment, with a description of available collateral, should be given.

❏ The name and address of the company should be included, along with the contact person for questions regarding the plan. This should be included on a cover sheet. A separate sheet should be used for each capital source in which the plan is submitted.

A well written executive summary allows prospective investors to decide within two or three minutes if the manufacturing business plan deserves further study.[2]

Statement of Purpose

The statement of purpose is a reflection of the goals of the proposed manufacturer stated as simply as possible. The proposed project and its use, the anticipated effects on the business, and how the loan will be repaid should be in the statement of purpose. This initial information should be supported by the rest of the business plan.

Table of Contents

The table of contents breaks the business plan into sections. By using the table of contents, the reader can easily find the areas in the business plan of particular interest. Each of the areas defined in this report should be included in the table of contents.

The supporting documents do not have to be included, but may help the manufacturer in getting the project financed.

History and Description of Business

This part of the business plan is the beginning of the body of the plan and provides a general description of the company.

The description of the business should answer at least seven basic questions:

❏ What business is the company in? What are its products? Who are its customers?

❏ What is the status of the firm? A start-up? An expansion of an existing business? A takeover of an existing business? A subsidiary or division of a larger business?

❏ What is the business' legal form: sole proprietorship, partnership, or corporation? (The economic developer is encouraged to refer the firm to an attorney and/or accountant to determine the best legal form for the proposed start-up. The economic developer may not be completely familiar with all the legal and tax implications involved in the complex establishment of a business.)

❏ Why is the business going to continue to grow and be profitable?

❏ When was the firm established?

❏ What hours of the day and days of the week will the company be in operation?

❏ Is the business seasonal or year round?[3]

In addition to the questions asked, the entrepreneur should state the goals and objectives of the business. It is important that the goals and objectives appear to the reader as being both realistic and attainable, with a clear indication of where the company is going and how it plans to get there.

Product

Defining the company's product(s) is a very important part of the business plan. The product being offered must have a certain appeal in the marketplace. When explaining the product the firm should give a clear, concise description. He/she should always keep in mind that the lender may not have the technical expertise about the product that he/she has. A benefit must be realized for the product by the market being targeted.

When describing the product the firm should concentrate on the product's physical description, use/appeal, and stage of development.[4]

When evaluating this section of the business plan, the economic developer should review the material to make sure it is in simple terms that can be understood by a potential lender.

Manufacturing Operations

An entrepreneur must explain how the product will be produced. If possible, it is a good idea to draw a floor plan that shows product flow. This will give a lender assurance that a firm has taken the time to make sure that the appropriate amount of space is sufficient to produce the product.

The discussion of manufacturing and operations should also concentrate on manufacturing costs. It is important for the manufacturer to know, at all levels of the production process, whether costs are what they should be.[5]

An economic developer should ask the manufacturer questions about the manufacturing costs and what sources are available for back-up raw materials should the need arise. In addition, the developer should encourage the entrepreneur to put a lot of thought into the costing process.

Marketing Information

The manufacturer should have a thorough knowledge of the market. When looking at markets, the entrepreneur has control over what market he/she chooses to enter. Entering or leaving markets is a major strategic decision; therefore, it is important to put a great deal of planning into the selection of a target market. This can be estimated by looking at how large a market is and what drives it. The purpose of the target market section is to explain how a prospective business intends to manipulate and react to market conditions in order to generate sales.[6]

The marketing section of a business plan is one of the most important and deserves a great deal of evaluation. An analysis of apparent evaluation trends in the market and how the product will fit into current attitudes should be completed.

Excellent sources of market data collection include trade associations, industry studies, trade literature, and industry "experts."[7]

Location Information

Selecting a location is very important to the business for serving its customer base. There are a number of sources of information for finding the ideal site. A local economic development professional should have the information on file regarding available sites and buildings, along with available infrastructure.

The entrepreneur should explain in detail the advantages and disadvantages of a location given the markets to be served. These should be described in terms of wage rates, labor unions, labor availability, proximity to customers or suppliers, access to transportation networks, state and local taxes, state and local laws, utilities, and zoning.[8]

Locational factors can play a strong role in overall operating costs. This is an important exercise that an economic developer should be certain that the entrepreneur has carefully considered before choosing a location, especially in the case of a start-up business.

Competition

This section of the business plan should be a comprehensive description of the competition and its product lines. An evaluation should consider who else is making this product and how it compares. How much of the market does the company have and what are their strengths and weaknesses? Also, how will the competition respond to changes? All of these should be answered by an entrepreneur, because these are real issues that will be tested in the marketplace. Too much competition creates a market saturated with the product being offered, which can lead to price cutting. The result can be reduced profits and even bankruptcy, with its consequent loss of investment. Too little competition, particularly with industrial products, can cause customer rejection. Customers are often afraid that products with too few suppliers might not be available in the required quantities at the right time and at the right competitive prices. Continued supply might be jeopardized if a manufacturer is acquired by a competitor or goes out of business.[9]

The economic developer should be sure the entrepreneur has reviewed the competition very carefully. This can and will be an area that can break a business if a proper strategic plan is not developed to handle changes as they occur.

Product Pricing

Most entrepreneurs will try to convince investors that they have a superior product that can be sold at a price less than what the competition is charging.

There is no magic formula for calculating the price; however, there are several factors that must be considered when setting a price or price range. A traditional formula is:

$$\text{Price} = \text{Product} + \text{Service} + \text{Image} + \text{Expenses} + \text{Profit}$$

The prices set for the manufactured product should be reflective of not only the product, but also an intangible image factor.[10]

When setting prices, there is always a chance that the competition will undertake a price cutting strategy in an effort to maintain market position.

Offering discounts should be considered when pricing products. This can dramatically improve cash flow when customers feel they are getting a bargain.

Pricing is a direct function of profit margin. A break-even analysis can also be helpful in determining the right price.

Distribution and Sales Strategy

A general starting point for developing a sales strategy is deciding how the product will be sold.

There are several alternatives available to an entrepreneur when selling products, including: 1) executive selling; 2) a company sales force; 3) utilizing sales representatives; and, 4) mass distribution.[11]

When an economic developer evaluates the selling and distribution strategies he/she should be certain that the entrepreneur considers the approaches available and determines which is the best for the product(s) being sold.

Management

Prior to financing a project, an investor

should perform an in-depth reference check on each member of the management team. If an investor has to choose between an excellent product with an average team or an average product with a superb management team, he/she is likely to choose the latter.

According to various studies of factors involved in small business failures, 98% of the failures stem from managerial weakness. Two percent are due to factors beyond the control of the persons involved.[12]

This section of the plan should introduce the key players of the manufacturing firm. An assessment of the strengths and weaknesses of each will help determine what, if any, player may be lacking in order to have a winning management team. If players are missing critical skills, the manufacturer should indicate what methods will be used in recruiting these people.

A balance of marketing operations, financial skills, and experience in a proposed venture are key ideas in promoting success for the entrepreneur. As a team, the management must work well together. The business plan should also include a copy of resumes of key management staff.

Organizational Chart

An organizational chart defines who is responsible for each of the key areas in the management of the business. The business should be operated in a way that tasks and responsibilities are addressed in the most effective manner for operational purposes.

The economic developer should evaluate the organizational chart to gain a level of confidence that the entrepreneur has a thorough understanding of the management reporting process.

FINANCIAL DATA

Sources and Uses of Funding

This section highlights how much funding will be needed and what it will be used for. It is important that the manufacturer get firm estimates. The list should be itemized, especially for equipment and major building components. A lender may be very interested in using the new assets as collateral for the loan.

The sources section should identify how the total project will be financed. The manufacturer will have to inject a certain amount of equity into the project, either from current cash flow, equity in assets or other sources.

An economic developer must make sure this component is included in the business plan. This is the most often forgotten part of the plan.

Financial Statements — Historical

An existing company should include historical statements in the business plan. These give a lender a good indication of past performance and trends that may have developed. Balance sheets are designed to show how the assets, liabilities and net worth of a company are distributed at a given point in time, whereas, income statements detail revenue and expenses for a period of time.[13]

An analytical review may highlight any trends or a one-time extraordinary item. This may prove that the entrepreneur is generally a good businessman, but may have had to deal with something unexpected on the financial statement during the year.

Ratio Analysis

Lenders will often compare the firm wishing to borrow money with the industry that he/she is in. This is done by using a book published by Robert Morris Associates (RMA). It is used to show how a firm is performing relative to its industry. Ratios are classified into four basic types: liquidity, solvency, profitability, and market tests. The ratios are listed below, and can be found by referring to the RMA publication or any financial accounting book.

Liquidity Ratios
They include:

Current Ratio	=	$\dfrac{\text{Current Assets}}{\text{Current Liabilities}}$
Quick (Acid Test) Ratio	=	$\dfrac{\text{Current Assets-Inventory}}{\text{Current Liabilities}}$
Receivables Turnover	=	$\dfrac{\text{Net Sales}}{\text{Average Receivables}}$
Inventory Turnover	=	$\dfrac{\text{Cost of Goods Sold}}{\text{Average Inventory}}$
Days Receivables	=	$\dfrac{\text{Accounts Receivable}}{\text{Net Sales}} \times 360$
Days Payable	=	$\dfrac{\text{Accounts Payable}}{\text{Purchases}} \times 360$

Solvency Ratios
Solvency Ratios show whether a company can pay all of its debts as they become due. These may be current or long term debt.

Debt/Equity	=	$\dfrac{\text{Total Liabilities}}{\text{Total Equity}}$

Profitability Ratios

Tests of profitability can show whether the amount of income generated is adequate.

Return on Sales	=	$\dfrac{\text{Net Income}}{\text{Net Sales}}$
Return on Total Assets Interest & Taxes	=	$\dfrac{\text{Earnings before}}{\text{Average Total Assets}}$
Return on Owner's Equity	=	$\dfrac{\text{Net Income}}{\text{Average Owner's Equity}}$

Market Test Ratios

Market test ratios show investors or shareholders how well a company is performing. These are important for public companies.

The economic development professional should evaluate the ratios to determine the general financial well-being of the company. A ratio that is too high may, for example, indicate a problem area. Not all ratios are included in this document; however, the key ratios for lender decision-making are listed.

When pro-forma statements have been compiled, the ratios should be applied to help determine project viability.

Breakeven Analysis

The basic break-even formula is as follows:

$$S = FC + VC$$

S = Breakeven level of sales in dollars.
FC = Fixed costs in dollars.
VC= Variable cost/unit x units sold.

The breakeven point is the sales volume level where profits are zero. The breakeven point will reveal how much additional sales volume is required to cover the cost of new debt.[14]

An economic development professional should make sure the manufacturer has determined the level of production necessary to breakeven. This is an often overlooked component in business planning. Knowing where the breakeven point is can be very helpful for a start-up.

Cash Flow

Cash flow statements can be the life and breath of a business plan. This document will let an entrepreneur know quickly whether costs are being maintained as planned. The cash flow reflects all increases in revenues and expenses as a result of the expansion and how these change the existing business activity.

The cash flow analysis will:

1) Show how much cash the business will need,

2) When it will be needed,

3) Whether the manufacturer should look for equity, debt, operating profits, or sale of fixed assets, and

4) Where the cash will come from.[15]

At least two years of projections should be included. It is not unusual for a lender to request three to five years of projected cash flow.

An important ingredient of the cash flow projections are the assumptions used for deriving the numbers. A lender will need this information to evaluate the believability of the projections. Items included in the assumptions should at least include the following:

1) Receivable collection period

2) Percentage of sales growth (most support required)

3) Labor required — increases in the labor force and affect on cost

4) Material Cost (%)

5) Fringe benefit changes

6) Real estate taxes (millage)

7) Debt service — principal and interest should be separated

8) Line of credit requirements (if necessary)

9) Insurance requirements

10) Trade discounts

11) Officer salaries

12) Any planned wage increases.

In the most concise manner possible the manufacturer should try to improve the confidence level of the lender regarding the company's ability to translate projections into operating reality.[16]

The economic developer should take care to look at the questions in detail and try to compare these with any historical statements. Projections and assumptions should be believable.

Pro Forma Statements

A pro-forma statement gives a future picture of what a company is expected to look like with the increased sales, expenses, debt, etc. Once the cash flow is completed, the pro forma statements should be prepared. Sales should be recognized when they occur rather than when collected.

For presentation, it might be a good practice to provide a spreadsheet with historical statements listed side by side with the projected statements. A ratio analysis

should be included.

An economic developer can look at pro forma statements and the ratios provided to determine whether a project has merit.

Personal Financial Statements

Commonly, the officers or owners of a manufacturing firm are required to submit personal financial statements as part of a business plan. This is especially true with a start-up venture.

SUPPORTING DOCUMENTS

If further supporting documentation is available it should be included in the business plan. This may include letters of reference, letters of intent, and/or copies of leases.

An economic developer should make sure the manufacturer includes these in the plan if they are available or attainable.

CONCLUSIONS AND RECOMMENDATIONS

Planning is the key to business success. A clear organization of thoughts should be the first step in the planning process. Once the organization is complete, a concise description of each of the components should be presented in the business plan document.

It is important that the manufacturer take the time to concentrate on each area of the plan. Usually, a plan is used to obtain financing, but in the long term it should be used as a guideline for the overall operation of the business.

A major component that an economic developer has in his/her job is the evaluation of project viability. This article has made an attempt to comprehensively review all components of a business plan and the respective importance of each.

An economic developer can greatly assist a manufacturer in the planning process by evaluating the plan before it is presented for financing. This may force the entrepreneur to probe further into areas of the plan that may not be complete. All developers would like the manufacturers to be as successful as possible. One tool to assist in this success is putting in place a well thought out business plan.

A good business plan can help make a business credible, understandable, and attractive to someone who may be unfamiliar with the business. Thinking through a good business plan before writing it will not guarantee success, but it can go a long way

toward reducing the odds of failure.[17]

NOTES

[1]David H. Bangs, *Business Planning Guide,* (Dover: Upstart Publishing Company, Inc., 1985), p. 3.

[2]Deloitte, Haskins, Sells, *Raising Venture Capital* (Fifth Printing, 1987), p. 20.

[3]David H. Bangs, Jr., *The Business Planning Guide: Creating A Plan For Success In Your Own Business* (Dover, New Hampshire: Upstart Publishing Company, Inc., 1988), p. 10.

[4]Eric S. Siegel, Loren Schultz, Brian Ford, *The Arthur Young Business Plan Guide* (New York, N.Y., John Wiley & Son, Inc., 1987), p. 53-54.

[5]Deloitte, Haskins, Sells, *Raising Venture Capital* (Fifth Printing, 1987), p. 30.

[6]Eric S. Siegel, Loren Schultz, Brian Ford, *The Arthur Young Business Plan Guide* (New York, N.Y., John Wiley & Son, Inc., 1987), p. 59.

[7]Eric S. Siegel, Loren Schultz, Brian Ford, *The Arthur Young Business Plan Guide* (New York, N.Y., John Wiley & Son, Inc., 1987), p. 62.

[8]Stanley Pratt, *How to Raise Venture Capital* (New York, N.Y., Charles Scribner's Sons, 1982), p. 107.

[9]Harold J. McLaughlin, *Building Your Business Plan* (New York, N.Y., John Wiley & Son, Inc., 1985), p. 20.

[10]David H. Bangs, Jr., *The Business Planning Guide: Creating A Plan For Success In Your Own Business* (Dover, New Hampshire: Upstart Publishing Company, Inc., 1988), p. 21.

[11]David Gumpert, *Business Plans That Win* (New York, N.Y.: Harper & Row Publishing Co., 1985), p. 93-97.

[12]David H. Bangs, Jr., *The Business Planning Guide: Creating A Plan For Success In Your Own Business* (Dover, New Hampshire: Upstart Publishing Company, Inc., 1988), p. 28.

[13]David H. Bangs, Jr., *The Business Planning Guide: Creating A Plan For Success In Your Own Business* (Dover, New Hampshire: Upstart Publishing Company, Inc., 1988), p. 50.

[14]Samuel S. Beard, *Business Credit Analysis* (New York, N.Y., The National Development Council), p. 25.

[15]David H. Bangs, Jr., *The Business Planning Guide: Creating A Plan For Success In Your Own Business* (Dover, New Hampshire: Upstart Publishing Company, Inc., 1988), p. 72.

[16]Eric S. Siegel, *The Arthur Young Business Plan Guide* (New York, N.Y., John Wiley & Son, Inc., 1987), p. 140.

[17]Eric S. Siegel, *The Arthur Young Business Plan Guide* (New York, N.Y., John Wiley & Son, Inc., 1987), p. 179.

BIBLIOGRAPHY

Books

Bangs, David H., Jr. *Business Planning Guide.* Dover, N.H.: Upstart Publishing Company, Inc., 1985.

Bangs, David H., Jr. *The Business Planning Guide: Creating A Plan For Success In Your Own Business.* Dover, N.H.: Upstart Publishing Company, Inc., 1985.

Gumpert, David. *Business Plans That Win.* New York, N.Y.: Harper & Row Publishing Company, 1985.

Luther, William M. *How To Develop A Business Plan In 15 Days.* New York, N.Y.: American Management Association, 1987.

McLaughlin, Harold J. *Building Your Business Plan*. New York, N.Y.: John Wiley & Sons, 1985.

Pratt, Stanley E. *How To Raise Venture Capital*. New York, N.Y.: Charles Scribner's Sons, 1982.

Siegel, Eric, Loren Schultz, and Brian Ford. *The Arthur Young Business Plan Guide*. New York, N.Y.: John Wiley & Son, Inc., 1987.

Articles

"A good business plan can set the foundation for raising venture capital." *CPA Journal*, December 1985, pp. 89-91.

Pendola, C.J. "The first time business plan." *CPA Journal*, September 1986, pp. 104-5.

Pamphlets

Deloitte, Haskins & Sells. *Raising Venture Capital — An Entrepreneur's Guidebook*. Fifth Printing. Deloitte, Haskins & Sells, 1987.

Miscellaneous

Beard, Samuel S. *Business Credit Analysis*. An advanced training manual for economic development financing presented by The National Development Council.

Guide to Starting a Business in Michigan. Guidebook provided by the Michigan Department of Commerce. 1987 edition.

Early Warning Signs of Risk Companies

Helga R. Weschke

It is very important in a business retention program to develop a means of determining at-risk companies, especially using qualitative early warning signs. This article is a list of early warning signs that may indicate downsizing or shutdown risk that may be observed by persons inside or outside a company.[1] The first thirteen signs are long term patterns indicating risk. The final five are immediate danger signals that could result in a plant shutdown.

LONG TERM PATTERNS

Declining Sales

☐ steady decline in sales, loss of market share

☐ general industry decline

☐ deterioration of key client relationships[2]

☐ inadequate analysis of markets and competitors[3]

Declining Employment

☐ steady or drastic decline of employment

☐ high employee turnover due to working conditions[4]

☐ in-house work being contracted outside

☐ excessive overtime instead of hiring

OWNERSHIP ISSUES

Changes in ownership, either through mergers and acquisitions

☐ consolidation, downsizing, or divestiture of units may become an issue. Questions to ask are:
 – where does plant fit in new owner's overall plan?
 – does new owner have same or similar products and does it create duplicate capacity?
 – does new owner have a history of closing other plants?
 – did the owner take on a lot of debt to make acquisition? Will debt be reduced by selling off parts of the operation?

☐ absentee ownership. Parent company residing outside of state.

☐ conglomerate ownership.
 – may show little loyalty to any one industry.
 – high rate of management turnover.
 – short term profit orientation.

☐ successorship. Family owned businesses face potentially several difficulties.
 – not having a family member available to take over the business.
 – no management or ownership provisions in the case of a sudden demise or incapacitation of an owner;

☐ sale of business may indicate any of the above.

Duplicate Capacity

May result from a change of ownership or creation of a sister plant. Changes in production capacity is important to observe in this instance.

Disinvestment

May result in a self perpetuating spiral of decline and can take on many forms:

☐ capital reinvestment

☐ inadequate share of profits put back into a plant for modernization and maintenance

☐ may indicate parent is milking the business

☐ low profits because of old inefficient equipment

☐ diversification. Companies drain cash from one division to buy another operation that may be more profitable

☐ excess dividends. Pay out of a third to a half of profits to shareholders.

☐ excess debt. High debt to equity ratio may indicate company is paying a lot of debt service and less money for reinvestment, typical result of a leverage buy out.

☐ wage and benefit concessions. If closure is inevitable, there may be a way to get extra cash out.

☐ sale of equipment.

Financial Management Issues

☐ lack of profitability over time

☐ late and inadequate financial and management reports[5]

☐ business is managed on the basis of profit and loss performance rather than on cash flow[6]

☐ leverage:
 – a deterioration of debt-to-worth ration showing that creditors have a larger financial stake than the company owners[7]
 – debt service: ability to cover it with earnings[8]
 – cash flow to total debt
 – new liens on assets: when lender was previously in a insecured position[9]

☐ liquidity: current ratio, the relation of current assets to current liability[10]

☐ fixed assets decline: may indicate that assets are being sold to meet maturing obligations or funding operation[11]

☐ difference between gross and net sales increase dramatically, may indicate increase in level of returns and allowances[12]

☐ cost of goods sold escalation[13]

☐ sales levels escalate and profits decline[14]

General Management Issues

☐ failure to diversity

☐ failure to reinvest

☐ failure to act on worker ideas

☐ inadequate quality control

☐ nepotism and cronyism

☐ poor labor relations

☐ short term vs. long term strategies

☐ inadequate R & D or new product development

☐ sales dependent on one or few customers[15]

☐ lack of clearly articulated and agreed-upon business goals and ineffective communication[16]

Management Instability

☐ management turnover

☐ new plant manager with a liquidator reputation

❑ executive's personality dysfunctions[17]
 – isolation: increasingly isolated and uncommunicative, may be fearful or depressed
 – obsession: locked in with a single objective
 – anger: abusive or violent to colleagues or outsiders, without provocation
 – indecisiveness: delays taking action
 – capricious: responds to circumstances in a arbitrary manner, needs a crisis to demonstrate worth
 – workaholic: excessive time spent working: only satisfaction, may burnout or collapse.

Changes in Management Behavior

❑ sudden change in labor bargaining, either adversarial or cooperative
❑ failure to negotiate with employees or unions
 Decline in Utility Usage - indicates changes in production levels.

"Business Climate" Complaints

❑ complaints about issues such as taxes, cost of living, business atmosphere
❑ hiring of a locational consultant may be a strong indicator of relocation plans

Changes In Land Use

❑ changes in zoning in surrounding area to office or residential
❑ increase in tax rates

Changes in Environmental Regulations[19]

❑ environmental standards and requirements become stricter

❑ cost prohibitive to meet new requirements

IMMEDIATE DANGER SIGNS

Removal of Equipment

❑ equipment is integral to plants overall production flow
❑ equipment is being shipped to another facility with lower wages or no union
❑ equipment is being shipped to a competitor

Cash Crunch or Irrational Cutbacks

❑ sudden layoffs
❑ suppliers are demanding C.O.D. payments due to delinquencies
❑ inventory levels drop severely
❑ payroll is not being met or paychecks are bouncing

Unusual Bargaining Positions

❑ shorter contract length
❑ negotiations are surprisingly easy with management
❑ company initiates proposal for severance pay that may affect shutdown benefits
❑ backloaded contracts - i.e. first and second year a modest increase and third year large increase, management may anticipate not being around to fulfill contract

Unidentified Visitors/Cosmetic Improvements

❑ sudden plant tours by unidentified people (such as Realtors)

❑ appearance of equipment and property appraisers
❑ cosmetic improvements to interior and exterior

Delinquencies

❑ taxes - real estate, sales, federal or unemployment
❑ utilities
❑ suppliers

NOTES

[1] Indicators listed in "Early Warning Sings" are based primarily from the "Early Warning Indicators" developed by The Midwest Center for Labor Research. Indicators from other sources are noted by separate footnotes.
[2] Thomas E. Cronan, "Early Warning Signals," *Small Business Reports*, Vol. 16, No. 9 (September 1991), p. 55.
[3] Ibid.
[4] Ibid. p. 54.
[5] Ibid. p.56.
[6] Ibid.
[7] A.Roger Bosma, "Diagnosing Credit Weakness: Some Early Warning Signs," *The Bankers Magazine*, Vol. 171, No. 6 (Nov.-Dec. 1988), p. 77.
[8] Subhash Sharma & Vijay Mahajan, "Early Warning Indicators of Business Failure," *Journal of Marketing*, Vol. 44, No. 4 (Fall 1980), p. 84.
[9] Bosma, p. 76.
[10] Subhash, p. 84.
[11] Bosma, p. 76.
[12] Ibid. p. 77.
[13] Ibid.
[14] Ibid.
[15] Ibid. p. 76.
[16] Thomas, p. 58-60.
[17] Ian Sharlit, "Six Early Warnings of Business Failure," *Chief Executive*, No. 56 (March 1990), p.28.
[18] Aurhor's indicator.
[19] Ibid.

Establishing A Local Manufacturers' Association: The Vaughan, Ontario Experience

Elise S. Back, M.A.E.S., Ec.D.

INTRODUCTION

The retention and growth of our existing industries are an important element in the economic health of our communities. It is a well known fact that between 65-80% of all jobs come from existing businesses, rather than new business development. Thus business retention and expansion are a vital facet of our local economic development program.

In response to this, the City of Vaughan has initiated a new and innovative program geared towards business retention and expansion through the establishment of the Vaughan Manufacturers' Association (VMA).

The purpose of this article is to briefly outline the steps involved in implementing a local manufacturers' association.

THE SETTING

Structural changes in the economy, high interest rates, the high Canadian dollar and other factors have resulted in the rapid decline of the manufacturing sector within the Greater Toronto Area. Given these realities of our local economy, the City of Vaughan and the Central East Branch of the Ministry of Industry, Trade and Technology (MITT) have taken the initiative to assist the local manufacturing industries to deal with their current situation and to respond to issues affecting their productivity and competitiveness, by establishing a local manufacturers association.

The concept behind a local manufacturers' association is based on the principle of SELF-HELP within the manufacturing community. Each manufacturing establishment would have the opportunity to share and resolve common difficulties and problems in a non-competitive environment.

Thereby, this networking system would lead to increased global competitiveness for the individual manufacturers.

The objectives of such an association can be summarized as follows:

☐ To foster cooperation and to facilitate those members within the community and surrounding areas to become organized.

☐ To provide an environment of cooperation among companies and various levels of government on trade, investment and other development activities.

☐ To stimulate the development of an outward looking international orientation of the City's industry.

☐ To strengthen the City's industrial base and to improve its international competitiveness.

☐ To enhance the productivity and performance of the City's industrial base by encouraging adoption of innovative technologies, industrial processes and human resource practices.

WHY VAUGHAN WAS CHOSEN FOR A LOCAL MANUFACTURERS' ASSOCIATION

In order to establish a local manufacturers' association, an environment conducive to its survival must exist. The following criteria should be considered if a local manufacturing organization is to be established in a given community. These criteria are set out as follows:

☐ The community should have a dynamic and growing manufacturing base.

☐ There should be a definite recognition by the community that a strong manufacturing sector is essential to the economic well being of the community.

☐ There should be a significant number of individual manufacturing firms that are relatively well off and growing. This is essential in order to maintain attendance and interest in the association.

☐ There should be a manufacturing base of 800-1000 individual firms that are potential candidates for membership. A targeted promotion program should result in 100 members over a period of time. It is essential for the survival of the association to have at least 20-30 members initially.

☐ The community should have a strong locally-based organization/individual that will become the leader in the establishment and development of the association.

The City of Vaughan provided the ideal setting for a local manufacturers' association because of its dynamic and diversified manufacturing base. There are an estimated 2,000 manufacturing firms located in Vaughan. The City is one of the fastest growing communities within the Greater Toronto Area and enjoys a relatively high economic growth rate. In addition, the recent establishment of the Economic Development Department indicates the commitment by the City to foster local economic development.

THE STEPS

There are a number of steps that must be undertaken in order to initiate a local manufacturers' association. These steps are:

Determining The Facilitating Organization

The success of a local manufacturers' association is clearly dependent upon the facilitating organization or group acting as a catalyst. This facilitating organization could be the local Chamber of Commerce, the Economic Development Department, or the provincial Ministry responsible for economic development. The facilitating group does not have to be limited to just one local organization. In the case of Vaughan, the City's Economic Development Department worked in conjunction with the local branch of the Ministry of Industry, Trade and Technology.

Identifying The Community "Spark Plugs"

It is paramount to the success of the association to identify key players ("spark plugs") within the community who would assist in the promotion, development and organization of the association. These individuals could consist of the CEOs, or top executives of the major manufacturing industries within the community.

Establish A Founding Board

Once the "spark plugs" have been identified, the facilitating group should organize a meeting with the "spark plugs." At this meeting the "spark plugs" and the representatives from the facilitating group would act as the founding board of the association. After all, it is imperative that you have an association to promote.

Brainstorming Session

After the Board has been established, some basic principles must be determined. Those would include: setting up an executive committee and an organizational structure in terms of reference, mission statements, promotional strategy, membership eligibility and method of financing. With reference to Vaughan, it was determined that the Association's executive group would consist of: the Chairperson, Vice-Chairperson, Secretary and the Treasurer. There are eight Board of Directors, and four Ex-Officio Board members from the City and MITT. It was also decided that there would be a Program and Membership Committee. In terms of financing, both the City and MITT provided $2,500 each for seed money.

Council Endorsement

For any local program to be successful, Council's endorsement is a must.

Promotional Strategy

The hardest task that the new association will encounter is trying to sell itself to the local community. First, some sort of promotional strategy will have to be devised. The strategy should address such marketing tools as: direct-mail, telemarketing, press releases, flyers, letters from the Mayor and cold calls. The VMA's membership drive included a letter from the Mayor, and a flyer, followed up by telephone calls. As a result, there are over 50 local manufacturing firms that belong to the Association.

Inaugural Dinner Meeting

Once the association is underway, an inaugural meeting should be held to officially launch the association. This meeting could be in the form of a dinner, with a keynote speaker used as a drawing card. The association's goals, mission statement, and action plan would be unveiled at the same time.

Follow-Up

After the inaugural meeting, a follow-up survey should be undertaken of the members to determine the success of the association. To determine their future needs, a survey of the association is a good idea. The survey could address the future promotional activities, dinner or workshop suggestions, preference of meetings, and whether the members are interested in exhibiting their products at the association's functions.

TO DATE

The Vaughan Manufacturers' Association (VMA) is one of a kind in Canada. The membership is over 65, and the Association's Board of Directors are continuing their membership drive. The VMA's inaugural dinner meeting was held in October of 1991, with the Honourable Ed Philip, the Ontario Minister of Industry, Trade and Technology as the guest speaker. The VMA has also hosted a number of other successful events including dinner meetings with guest speakers as Catherine Swift from the Canadian Federation of Independent Business, Frank Stronach of Magna International Inc., and Howard Levitt from Howard Levitt and Associates. In addition, there have been a number of breakfast seminars and workshops on such topics as "Workmen's Compensation," "ISO 9000 Quality System Executive Workshop," and "Government Services and Programs."

CONCLUSION

The future looks bright for the VMA. There are a number of new initiatives planned for the future including a membership directory and newsletter. The success of the Vaughan Manufacturers' Association is a result of the commitment of the City of Vaughan's Council and the constant hard work by the VMA's Board.

In order for an association to be successful there has to be two important elements: the human and the financial resources. In terms of the human resources element, there should be an individual who will devote at least one day a week to the association. If the Economic Development Department is the facilitating organization, the Economic Development Professional would be the individual responsible to help the association.

With respect to the financial resources, the facilitating group would be responsible for providing the initial "seed money" to cover the start up costs.

It took just over a year for the Vaughan Manufacturers' Association to get off the ground and so far it has proven to be a great success. It is strongly recommended that communities across North America consider this new and innovative approach to business retention and expansion modelled after the VMA experience.

Understanding and Encouraging The Entrepreneur

Joseph A. Yarzebinski, C.I.D./C.E.D.

INTRODUCTION

As economic developers move towards implementation of job generating programs involving incubators, technology transfers, import substitution, and the like, the search for the entrepreneur appears to be a central focus and common theme. The success of these programs seems to depend upon the community's ability to uncover, discover, or stimulate the entrepreneur. The entrepreneurs' ability to innovate makes them the pivot point in these types of programs. Incubated businesses, new technologies transferred from the lab to the marketplace, or a new manufacturing line to replace products imported into the community all have innovative entrepreneurs as their cornerstone. The entrepreneur can innovate *provided* the correct atmosphere exists.

Just as communities assess their suitability for certain targeted businesses, they must assess their suitability for entrepreneurs. A community's ability to meet the needs of the entrepreneur increases that community's chances for successful job generation programs. Understanding the traits of entrepreneurs as well as some of their unique needs can help communities assess whether a climate for entrepreneurs exists locally. If such a climate does not exist locally, the community may fail in its efforts to generate new jobs. Simply starting a program such as an incubator prior to completing the assessment will not, on its own, produce entrepreneurs; and it may not produce any net new businesses either.

The community must endeavor to understand the entrepreneur. It must determine what an entrepreneur is and how can one impact the local community. Then the community must decide if the entrepreneur is worth pursuing. For some communities the pursuit of the entrepreneur may be a lower priority than other issues. If the entrepreneur is deemed important, the community must determine what costs it can incur to establish and implement programs aimed at fostering an environment for the entrepreneur. It is a concerted community effort which is needed to create and maintain an atmosphere appropriate for entrepreneurs.

DEFINING "ENTREPRENEUR"

It is difficult to pick up a current article on economic development without running across the word "entrepreneur." It is not a new word but it certainly has become an overused buzz word. But, as often as it is used in articles and titles, one rarely sees a definition of the term. Authors tend to jump into discussions of the inherent value of entrepreneurs in our economy without solidly identifying an entrepreneur. This creates a problem. Authors assume readers have the same biases and predispositions they have regarding entrepreneurs. Of course, rarely do author and reader have precisely the same understanding.

Since the entrepreneur is both spoken of so frequently and identified as being so valuable to programs such as technology transfers and economic growth, it is thought best that at the outset of discussions a definition be established. In this manner, further discussions can be firmly grounded in one definition of such a key term.

Volumes of articles, reports, papers, and books have been written about or around entrepreneurs. For a definition of an entrepreneur one must abandon the economic development literature and look into the business world — into the discipline of management. Peter F. Drucker, who is said by some to be one of this country's foremost authorities on management theory, reminds the reader that entrepreneurs were identified centuries ago. Drucker indicates that around 1800 J.B. Say, a French economist defined entrepreneurs.

The entrepreneur…"shifts economic resources out of an area of lower and into an area of higher productivity and greater yield".[1]

But Drucker immediately notes for the readers that "…since Say coined the term almost two hundred years ago, there has been total confusion over the definition of entrepreneur."[2]

Not only has there been confusion over the definition of an entrepreneur, but confusion has also reigned over the place the entrepreneur has in society. Perhaps one problem gives rise to the other. Assisting that confusion is the idea that entrepreneurs do not fit into classic economics. The classic economists developed theories about maximizing or optimizing the use of resources to attain equilibrium. Introducing a new technology momentarily upsets that equilibrium. Technology, then, becomes an external force to the classic economist's equations for equilibrium. The entrepreneur, because of his/her direct relationship to the development of new technology, and being the force that has delivered that technology, also is an external force.

ENTREPRENEURS AND CHANGE

External forces rarely become institutionalized, for entrepreneurs are not an institutionalized concept. The act of being an entrepreneur is more a behavior. As a behavior, being an entrepreneur is not confined simply to economic spheres. Entrepreneurs can be found in banking, health care, tourism, and even in government. Entrepreneurs can be found in any environment or industrial sector where higher productivity and greater yield can be gained. Although not always obvious, there is a common theme that is responsible for linking these environments. That link is change.

"Entrepreneurs see change as the norm and as healthy. Usually, they do not bring about the change themselves. But — and this defines the entrepreneur and entrepreneurship — the entrepreneur always searches for change, responds to it and exploits it as an opportunity."[3]

Exploitation of change is firmly rooted in innovation. Innovation is the tool all entrepreneurs utilize across their environments, be that banking, government, industry, or others. It is innovation that creates value in resources as that resource is lifted from a lower to higher productivity. The rocks and liquids under the Alaskan mountains and valleys have no value and create no wealth for the local economy until the entrepreneur innovates. The entrepreneur then determines how to dig those rocks and change their productivity and yield.

Innovation is easily defined as adopting new technologies. This is the key link between entrepreneurs and programs, such as technology transfers. By adopting new tech-

239

nologies in an inherent organized, purposeful, systematic manner, the entrepreneur innovates. The creation of wealth and value through elevation of resources does not occur as Drucker calls a "flash of genius."

"...contrary to popular belief in the romance of invention and innovation, "flashes of genius" are uncommonly rare. What is worse, I know of not one such "flash of genius" that turned into an innovation. They all remain brilliant ideas."[4]

During times of economic growth, communities often incur development or establishment of "me-too" businesses. That is, one sector will thrive and many people will jump on this bandwagon. The 86th tanning parlor opening in a community creates no net new wealth, exploits no change, elevates no resources, and adopts no new technologies. The economic developer and the community must differentiate between the entrepreneur and the "wanna-be." There are similarities between entrepreneurs and people that want to be entrepreneurs, but simply running a business does not an entrepreneur make.

TRAITS OF THE ENTREPRENEUR

The key to effective utilization of an entrepreneur for adopting those new technologies, and for elevating resources, is the creation of an environment allowing for the personal strengths of the entrepreneur to be maximized. The traits of the entrepreneur include:

❑ ...unusually well-developed ego, believing in his ability to accomplish what he sets out to do.

❑ They are detail oriented and — in many ways — perfectionists. Much of the time they are sources of frustration to their subordinates. They are open and problem/solution oriented, they rarely develop personally vulnerable openness or intimacy in their relationships.

❑ ...endowed with an inexhaustible reservoir of energy.

❑ Nothing is done soon enough and everything is a crisis.

❑ ...tend to be contingency thinkers, generally six months or longer ahead in their thinking... They always maintain options, moving...at a moments notice, even reversing themselves frequently.

❑ In the final analysis, they are unwilling to surrender the need for complete control.

❑ They are above average intelligence

and tend to see things in a "holistic" sense, that is "the big picture." They are able to conceptualize a task or problem quickly, frequently arriving at the solution well in advance of others.

❑ They are pragmatists, dealing with the world as it exists not as they would have it. They are...calculated risk takers, not gamblers. The entrepreneur takes those risks where he or she can...establish a high probability of achieving a set goal.

❑ Entrepreneurs have a higher than normal threshold of emotional stability... They manage emotion in a fashion that minimizes its impact on their efforts.

❑ They must have a strong desire to succeed, enthusiasm about the product and business, perseverance, creativity and competitiveness. Most detrimental to their success is their inability to work well with others, unwillingness to communicate freely, disruptive, inability to delegate, and obstinacy.

❑ ...other characteristics such as personal fitness, high energy level, alertness, ability to endure stress, analytical ability, a history of personal hardship, and experiences in leadership.

❑ ...an entrepreneur is usually the first-born child, a male, and begins his first company between the ages of 30 and 35...married...well educated, possessing at least a bachelor's degree and frequently a master's, but seldom a PhD... The primary motivation for starting his own business is that he simply does not like working for someone else. He has difficulty following someone else's direction and seeks independence.[5]

As much as the reader may want to hold fast to these traits, there is no universal pattern or formula to identify the entrepreneur when he/she walks in the office. It takes one to know one. All the indicators from various psychological interviews should only serve as a guide or comparison for the local community to help determine if the local demographic characteristics reveal an environment that exists where a seed may be planted and the entrepreneur nurtured and coaxed along. The entrepreneur has needs. The traits reveal many of the needs. If the community is such a setting where these needs can be met, fulfilled or challenged, that community stands to gain new technologies, added wealth, and more jobs through innovation by the entrepreneur.

Taffi summarizes the common factors

among entrepreneurs. These factors include the need for:

❑ achievement
❑ recognition
❑ avoiding control by others
❑ change
❑ tangible and meaningful rewards
❑ satisfying built-in expectations (generally insatiable).

It is important to note that contrary to the popular stereotypical association of an entrepreneur and risk, Taffi does not include risk-taking in the final analysis. Entrepreneurs do not have a propensity for taking risks. Their aim is to define the risks early in the process and minimize those risks to every extent possible. Through systematic analysis of the sources of innovation opportunities the risk is reduced.

The tool linking entrepreneurs across their environments is innovation. Drucker lists five principles of innovation. Innovation develops through systemic, organized, purposeful analysis. First, "...innovation begins with the analysis of the opportunities."[6] Timing and location are the key factors when attempting to identify the importance of sources of innovation. Analysis is done on a case by case basis.

Second, ". . . innovation is both conceptual and perceptual."[7] There is an analytical analysis of the innovation and opportunities. Then the human side, values, habits, and expectations, are also identified and brought into defining the innovation and opportunities. If both sides are not included, the right innovation may take the wrong form.

Third, ". . . an innovation . . . had to be simple and focused . . . The greatest praise an innovation can receive is for people to say "This is obvious. Why didn't I think of it?"." [8]

Fourth, ". . . effective innovations start small." [9] Small is easier, cheaper, and requires fewer people and resources. As any idea needs changes once underway, small helps to apply those changes quicker, easier, and cheaper.

Lastly, ". . . successful innovation aims at leadership" in the market.[10] A lack of leadership invites competition. The entrepreneur and the new innovation both face enough hurdles. Aiming high for leadership helps to stave off competition thus helping to ease if not eliminate at least one hurdle.

Through innovation the entrepreneur offers the community change. The entrepreneur offers what too few want, since people resist change. But change is what everyone needs since change is the means to the end of getting from point A to point B. As is the case with Anchorage, diversification and development of the economic base are what has been identified by the community as priority needs.[11] The diversification can only come from change. The community needs to be changed. The entrepreneur is identified as a key element of the change formula. It will be the entrepreneur seizing the opportunity to create new values and new technology. It is the entrepreneur creating wealth for the community by elevating resources. In fact, until there is a market for the resource it is not a resource. Productivity, values, habit, behaviors, expectations, wealth, jobs, and technologies all changed after the first entrepreneur raised the resource from a lower to a higher level of productivity.

HOW COMMUNITIES SHOULD RESPOND

Simply stated, the community will stagnate and deteriorate without the entrepreneur. One way to ensure continued economic growth is to keep the challenge in front of the entrepreneurs. One method for challenging the entrepreneur or developing new entrepreneurs is to create or maintain a community which fulfills the needs of entrepreneurs. Community and economic development leaders should review the traits and needs of the entrepreneur. If a community is not a place which appears to be able to meet those needs or enhance those traits, but in fact community leaders want it to be such a place, then local economic developers can develop the community attitude which welcomes and supports entrepreneurs.

Legislation, policies, programs, and the like are ways economic developers can help to create a haven for entrepreneurs. Creating jobs is largely the province of the private sector, and the role of the public sector is to establish the framework in which these jobs are created. Development of the community as a haven for entrepreneurs is, in part, dependent upon legislation and policies.

First, the economic developer should lead the community in legislative reform. Local tax laws can be modified to benefit select economic sectors or types of businesses. Economic in-fill strategies can select under-developed sectors, targeting them for select legislative assistance. "Buy local" preferences can be established for government, military, and school district contracts. Entrepreneur zones can be defined to allow application of incentives to select geographic areas of the community. Tax holidays may be granted on select personal property, such as computer equipment. Tax credits can be granted if local businesses invest in technology transfers, additional research and development, or new machinery and equipment.

Depending upon the community needs, economic conditions, and overall long-term strategic economic goals, these legislative reforms do not have to be radical, universal, or permanent. Sun-set clauses can ensure a limited period of life for new legislation. Impact thresholds can be written in the policies so that incentives are suspended when the threshold is met. Pilot, or test, policies can be established prior to community-wide regulations being created so that extensive economic impact analyses and assessments of the new programs can be completed. Specific and targeted economic or social sectors can be identified as the recipients.

Second, beyond legislative and policy reform, the economic developer can design specific programs. A community education program can teach politicians and taxpayers the value of entrepreneurs. Inventor appreciation rallies can draw other entrepreneurs out. Special loan pool programs can help raise the level of capital available to entrepreneurs locally. Industry appreciation luncheons can help entrepreneurs discover opportunities. Public relations campaigns can communicate the entrepreneurial message to those in the community as well as those around the nation. Arrangements with the university extension service, public television station, local vocational-technical schools, and the like, can provide introductory classroom-like sessions to challenge residents to assess their entrepreneurial potential. Peer courts can bring similar businesses together to discuss ideas, technologies, and opportunities in confidence. Executive loan programs exchange new blood and new ideas between local companies, revealing potential opportunities.

CONCLUSION

The entrepreneur is credited with shifting economic resources out of an area of lower and into areas of higher productivity and greater yield. This is more than value-added processes. The entrepreneur is cred-

ited with always searching for change, responding to it and exploiting it as an opportunity. This is more than being a catalyst or a change agent. The entrepreneur adopts new technologies and innovates. This is more than plagiarism or copying. The entrepreneur makes possible the growth and expansion of existing businesses, and the future development of technologies not yet marketed.

The act of being an entrepreneur is a behavioral response. It is a way of conducting oneself. Not everyone has that behavior nor does everyone appreciate that behavior. Lest a zealous economic developer think that entrepreneurs are a panacea for job development strategies, remember, entrepreneurs see change as the norm and as healthy. Politicians and government officials thrive on stability. Change creates instability. Private sector businesses attempt to maximize profits by minimizing costs. Change is expensive to implement. The programs to stimulate the entrepreneur, as well as the entrepreneur himself, can upset the public and the private sectors, alike.

Getting communities to become havens for entrepreneurs can be costly. There is supporting logic for incurring these costs. Communities want economic growth. Communities want new jobs, added tax base, and increasing wealth. Existing businesses are responsible for more than eighty percent of a community's new jobs. That means business expansion programs are inherently reliant upon local entrepreneurs. Some businesses expand because their market is growing and demand for their product is up. However, if a community allows its growth to be based solely on existing market shares, that community will experience some drastic economic swings and cycles. Basing that growth on new technologies or on new innovations — essentially on the entrepreneur — can help the community develop and maintain a stable process for continued growth during the good times and the bad. It's the difference between being a market leader and being lead by the market.

Without the entrepreneur, the community will stagnate and economically regress. Without an atmosphere of innovation, the entrepreneur will not survive.

The entrepreneur is a key to the success of job generating programs such as incubators, technology transfers, and import substitutions. But not every community is a place where entrepreneurs thrive. The traits of the entrepreneur are threatening to some communities. The anti-change attitude of certain communities is intimidating to some entrepreneurs. When a community decides that it desires to be a haven for entrepreneurs, it can implement specific legislative and policy reforms, along with implementing specific programs. The economic developer should be cognizant of the costs of developing or not developing a community into a haven for entrepreneurs. The short-term costs for implementing the programs catering to the entrepreneurs are high. The long-term costs are very low. The benefits far exceed the costs.

Communities with strong entrepreneurial atmospheres, or those willing to accept and harbor the entrepreneur, show that maintaining or developing a haven for entrepreneurs is economically profitable. These communities have researched and understood the value of the entrepreneur. They have defined a place in the community for entrepreneurs. They have fulfilled a portion of the entrepreneurs' requirements through legislative reform, development of new policies, and implementation of special programs. These communities have growth patterns and business attraction/development rates that are incomprehensible to communities which have not targeted the entrepreneur.

FOOTNOTES

[1] Peter F. Drucker, INNOVATION AND ENTREPRENEURSHIP (New York: Harper and Row Publishers, 1985), p. 21.
[2] Ibid.
[3] Ibid., p. 28.
[4] Ibid., p. 133.
[5] Donald J. Taffi, THE ENTREPRENEUR: A CORPORATE STRATEGY FOR THE 80's (New York: American Management Association, 1981), pp. 24-28.
[6] Drucker, INNOVATION AND ENTREPRENEURSHIP, p. 134.
[7] Ibid., p. 135.
[8] Ibid.
[9] Ibid.
[10] Ibid.
[11] Joseph A. Yarzebinski, "Anchorage Target Business and Industry Program: Basic Sector Analysis. An Explanation of The Methodology," (Anchorage: Municipality of Anchorage, 1984).

Guidelines For Incubator Development

Rhonda P. Culp

INTRODUCTION

The small business incubator is an innovative development tool used to foster growth and diversify the economic base. It is a facility, sponsored by private and/or public concerns, in which young companies co-exist in a nurturing environment until they are able to survive independently. This nurturing environment is created by providing on-site support services and flexible rental space at below-market rates.

Small businesses generated all of the net new jobs in the U.S. economy between 1980 and 1982. But it should be noted that small businesses experience a high failure rate of nearly 50 percent within the first five years. A national study conducted in 1985 revealed a favorable survival rate for incubator tenants. This indicates that the incubator concept, if applied correctly, can be a potentially effective means of off-setting the high failure rates of small businesses.

When a development group begins to express interest in establishing an incubator facility, an initial feasibility study needs to occur to test the applicability of the concept against local economic conditions.

A general methodology for this study is prepared in this article. The methodology is derived from recommendations of existing and planned incubator projects throughout the United States. It is composed of a series of nine steps. The nine steps are:

1. Establish a working group to initiate development,
2. Assess the small business support network,
3. Analyze the level of entrepreneurial activity,
4. Analyze the local market economy,
5. Real estate analysis and potential site identification,
6. Financing for the facility and tenants,
7. Planning for start-up,
8. Marketing the incubator,
9. Evaluate and re-define goals.

STEP ONE: ESTABLISH A WORKING GROUP

The first step for the project director or initiator is to establish a working group whose purposes are to direct development activities and provide expertise in various aspects. The Small Business Administration recommends the group should be comprised of six to eight persons (U.S. SBA, 1984).[1] Recruitment should be from economic development or planning agencies, engineers, banks, universities, real estate, accountants, and architects. The working group will be responsible for establishing general goals to serve as a guideline to development. The goals may be obvious or may become apparent after initial research. For example, for a general goal of "promoting economic growth" the focus may be on recruiting out-of-area businesses to supply local corporations and to recruit labor-intensive firms.

Initially, the group should divide research duties among the members who have expertise in that field. Steps one through four are considered the feasibility stage. The expenses for these steps may be covered by donated time and supplies from the working group members. If their services cannot be donated, then arrangements for defraying these costs must be made. However, the critical focus at all times should be on obtaining the financing for acquisition of the facility. Although actual cost estimates are determined at a later step in the process, sources for capitalization should be sought from the beginning of the project.

STEP TWO: ASSESS SMALL BUSINESS SUPPORT NETWORK

It is important to identify sources of help for small businesses because incubators complement and draw upon other small business support programs. At the same time, this assessment helps determine if local businesses and public officials endorse the concept. School officials, bankers, and others should be contacted to identify potential support, financial and otherwise. Local, state, and federal support agencies such as the Small Business Administration, Small Business Development Centers, economic development agencies, local chamber of commerce, and industrial development authorities should be used.

STEP THREE: ANALYZE LEVEL OF ENTREPRENEURIAL ACTIVITY

An analysis of the entrepreneurial activity in the area helps identify growing sectors of the economy. The following procedures are recommended.

1. Determine the number of start-ups and failures of small businesses for the last several years. Employment Security Commissions usually tabulate these data. Also check with city permit officials for the number of business permits issued within a given period. It is useful to determine the total number of business births and deaths for the county or area and find the ratio of births to deaths. This indicates the percentage of failure or growth the area is experiencing. Compare this ratio to those of surrounding areas and the state. Next, determine the types of business failures and start-ups. At what age do most businesses fail? The types of business started can give an indication of the orientation of the incubator. Also, the amount of building permit activity in an area is a useful economic indicator as are residential and commercial vacancy rates and sales data.

2. Examine the percentage of professional and technical workers in the area using the Bureau of Census Labor Statistics (U.S. 1984).[2] This gives an indication of the job skills of the workers in the area and helps determine the type of incubator needed. For example, if a high percentage of technical workers exist in the local market, then a "technology-oriented" incubator is possible.

3. Check attendance at local business seminars and similar organizations. Obtain a mailing list of participants, if possible, to determine what they need in regard to business support services.

4. Ask local bankers and developers about inquiries regarding new business ventures. This will help give an indication of what types of businesses are being started in the local area and the overall economic health of the community.

STEP FOUR: ANALYZE THE LOCAL MARKET ECONOMY

An understanding of the economic base of the area is essential to help target specific industries and determine the skills of the labor force. The study should focus on the local scale as this will be the prime area from which entrepreneurs originate. The incubator should rely primarily on conventional businesses currently existing in the market. For example, it would not be feasible to start a high-tech incubator if the existing base is traditional manufacturing or if there is not a substantial percentage of technical workers in the area.

The economic base data may be gathered with two separate surveys, but if the area to be surveyed is less than 50,000 in population, then only one is needed. For larger areas, more detailed data can be generated utilizing two surveys. Help in administering the surveys may be solicited from local chambers of commerce, city government, or others. As an added incentive to gain help, the surveys can be designed to generate useful information beyond the scope of planning for the incubator. For example, the list of out-of-state suppliers can be useful for a targeted industry effort.

Business Needs Survey

The first survey combines both mail-out questionnaires and telephone or personal interviews. It is designed to reveal information concerning the needs of small businesses in the area. First, a mailing list of small businesses (less than 20 employees) in the local area should be obtained through manufacturers' directories or similar publications. The sample to be surveyed can be narrowed by choosing those businesses linked to specific industries or by age of firms. For example, "firms under two years of age are found to fail quite frequently, then firms over this age may be examined to indicate "survivability traits." A cover letter should accompany the survey form, and a telephone call requesting a 30-minute interview may follow. Usually, additional comments otherwise unobtainable may be gathered during personal interviews. Sample survey questions are listed below:

1. How did the company owners train for their job as founder? (i.e., was this a "spin-off" industry where founders gained training and management expertise from another company?)

2. Did the first customers originate from the local area and are present customers within the community? (Note which major companies in the area are not customers of applicable small businesses.)

3. How often has the company moved, what type of facility is required, how much can it afford to pay for it, and did the company originate from the local area?

4. What were the first sources of financing, and what are the capitalization sources today? What obstacles did the company face in obtaining financing? (This indicates the availability of local funds.)

5. Have these businesses grown in employment and sales?

6. Do they have a written business plan?

7. Are the major suppliers outside the area?

8. Are there problems in obtaining quality labor, and what are the average wages paid?

9. What are the perceptions regarding city officials, development organizations, chambers of commerce—do these agencies provide needed support for these small businesses?

10. What are the major obstacles to growth?

11. Which of the following services would be most useful to the business if they were available at affordable rates?

a. Market opportunity identification (such as assistance with government contract procurement, etc.).

b. Clerical services (word processing, answering service, photocopying).

c. Fixed-asset, long-term financing and sources of working capital funds

d. Legal and accounting services.

Potential Markets Survey

The survey of potential markets may be sent separately to large companies in the area, or combined with selected questions from the first survey. Addresses of respondents may be obtained from manufacturers' directories. Analyzing the characteristics of local large companies can provide insights into potential markets for small businesses. Topics to be addressed in the questionnaire may include the following.

1. The amount and product type of services or supplies obtained out-of-state. This will indicate if a significant amount of products are imported and therefore potential markets for local small businesses. Market opportunities should be more thoroughly examined, but the list generated may indicate several products or service groups to explore. It is helpful to divide the supplier names into two-digit Standard Industrial Classification (SIC) groups to de-

termine which need further examination. Also, it is helpful to check parent/subsidiary relationships which may mandate supplier-buyer agreements, with which local businesses cannot compete.

2. Check to see if there is a substantial amount of sub-contracting or spin-off industry activity. Examine any primary sources for these activities. This will help indicate potential incubator tenants.

STEP FIVE: REAL ESTATE ANALYSIS AND POTENTIAL SITE IDENTIFICATION

Real Estate Analysis

The purpose of step five is to assess the demand and supply for rental commercial and manufacturing space in the local area. This will indicate if existing space is adequate for entrepreneurs, or an unfilled demand exists. An effective method of surveying is to telephone local realtors and developers. If opposition to the incubator concept is expressed (below-market rental rates may not be viewed favorably by local realtors), explain that firms move into incubators to survive the first crucial start-up years and then graduate into the community better able to compete in the local market. Also, point out that it is a better risk to rent to an established business able to commit to a lease than to a start-up business which may fail within the first year.

The survey can ask realtors to respond to the following type of issues.

1. Rate the level of demand for office space, light manufacturing and service space, and commercial space

2. Rate the level of supply for the same types of space

3. Market rates for each type space

4. Typical lease agreement for each type

5. Services included in rental rates.

Potential Site Identification

After completing the real estate analysis, potential sites can be investigated. Information from the business needs survey should indicate the general types of rental space demanded. The key is to acquire the facility as inexpensively as possible in order to pass the savings on to tenants in the form of cheap rental rates. The building must have the flexibility to adapt to adjustable space partitions, loading docks, conference rooms, etc. Consider soliciting donations from public entities for vacant buildings such as schools, post offices, university building, etc. Private corporations may lease or donate underutilized manufacturing space for a specified time.

STEP SIX: IDENTIFY FINANCING FOR THE FACILITY AND TENANTS

The initial research or "feasibility" study should be completed at this stage. Although new data will continue to be gathered, there is enough preliminary information to determine if the concept is applicable in the area. Goals and objectives should be redefined and clarified to reflect the nature and scope of the project as relevant data are revealed.

The focus now turns to identifying sources of financing for the acquisition of the facility. Any reasonable leads should be thoroughly investigated. It is essential to keep acquisition costs low in order to pass the savings on to the tenants in the form of low rental rates. First, estimate costs for acquisition and renovation for the potential sites chosen. Working group members with expertise in architecture, construction, or engineering may be delegated this task. Second, establish rental rates to be charged as part of the estimation of operating costs. Generally, rent is the greatest source of income for public facilities. It is used to cover operating expenses and is usually not sufficient to cover building acquisition and renovation costs. This "gap" in financing is filled by federal, state, and local public funds in conjunction with private funds which average over 30 percent of the total capitalization of public facilities. Also, fund-raising efforts to help with acquisition costs can be an advantage. Private incubators typically charge the highest rental rates (averaging $9.10 per square foot) in order to cover amortization of the building (McLean, 1985).[3]

Public facilities charge the lowest rates (averaging $2.50 per square foot) because the facility is typically financed with public funds to offset high acquisition costs.

After determining project costs, every avenue of possible funding should be explored. Federal monies are becoming more limited and harder to obtain, but should be investigated. The following is a list of recommended sources that have been utilized in financing incubators.

1. Private/public partnerships, highly encouraged by the federal government, could utilize Community Development Block Grants and Economic Development Administration (EDA) Title IX, funds. EDA grants have been used to finance over fifty incubators.

2. Explore state agency funds, Industrial Revenue Bonds, and if relevant, Appalachian Regional Commission funds.

3. Solicit local corporations for donations and loans of funds, equipment, and vacant buildings.

4. The SBA recommends obtaining a grant from foundations to help finance incubator development. The *Foundation Directory,* published annually by The Foundation Center of New York, is a good reference source. University libraries often can conduct a computer search of relevant information. To identify foundations with related funding interest, use key search phrases as "jobs for the unemployed," "small business assistance," "community revitalization," and "community economic development." A letter of inquiry should be sent which includes these aspects: (a) problems addressed and objectives, (b) program for pursuing objectives, (c) qualifications of persons involved, (d) budget, (e) current sources of funding, and (f) Internal Revenue Service classification.

Projects for which other sources of financing are readily available are generally not considered. Aspects of incubator development likely to be eligible include salaries of the staff, fees for professional assistance to tenants, centralized office equipment, marketing programs, or an innovative feature to facilitate success of tenants.

5. Real estate syndication can be a method of financing an incubator facility. A limited partnership is established with a one percent general partner (local governments, non-profit groups) and a 99 percent limited partnership/ownership. The limited partners are passive investors seeking a shelter against an investor's taxable income. The general partner seeks cash flow and management responsibilities. Fees for services can be granted to increase cash flow from the limited partnership to the general partner.

6. Consider holding a fund-raising event in the community either as a one-time effort or an on-going source of funds.

7. The National Cooperative Bank (NCB) of Washington, D.C. and its affiliates provide financing to operative businesses. Provided the incubator was established as a cooperative, it could be eligible for funding from NCB.

Financing for Tenants

Not only should financing for the facility be of major concern, but financial sources for tenants should also be identified. Tenants need affordable financing for equip-

ment and working capital. Incubators act as a broker between new businesses and investors, often by introducing lenders and venture capitalists to the businesses. Sometimes this process entails formulating proposals and packaging loans. The Advanced Technology Center in Atlanta sponsors an annual two-day venture capital conference at the incubator which helps bring attention to new businesses. It is recommended that funds from the Job Training Partnership Act be utilized for customized employee training. Equity financing is also possible, with the private sector paying operating expenses in exchange for equity shared in tenant firms. Some incubators have established revolving loan funds for their tenants. Funding for these programs usually originates from public sources, such as EDA Title IX grants. An initial pool of money is secured from donations, grants, fees, and rental charges. Tenants repay by conventional methods or through equity shares.

STEP SEVEN: PLAN FOR START-UP

Six to nine months before opening the facility, the working group should set overall operational policies. The five policy elements below are usually considered.

1. Leasing agreements should be flexible. Some facilities offer longer leases to larger firms, and shorter terms (even on a month-by-month basis) to smaller firms. This allows internal expansion within the facility. Some facilities renegotiate leases, and the rent owed is spread out or deferred until cash flow increases. This approach is especially important when firms enter a rapid growth phase entailing a negative cash flow even though the firm is growing.

2. Tenant screening and selection policies need to be established. A board of knowledgeable businesspersons may be appointed to screen prospective tenants. Many incubators require the tenants to have a written business plan to present for review to the screening board. If they do not have a plan, they are referred to the appropriate agency for assistance. The business plan provides the foundation for the business and it helps the board to uncover any deficiencies and assess the long-term profit potential. Questions the business plan usually covers include: Is the product marketable? How will it be manufactured? How much capital is needed? Does the entrepreneur possess the necessary skills to commercialize this product? A major advan-

tage in having screening criteria and a board is that political influences are reduced.

3. Graduation policies should be set. Public firms tend to have explicit graduation policies which average three years. Private firms generally do not detail graduation policies. Most incubators offer tenancy as a temporary situation. Rents are simply raised to market values as firms become more successful and are able to compete in external market conditions. Some facilities recommend allowing permanent anchor tenants to serve as role models for younger companies.

4. The basic staff needs to be identified. Typically, the staff consists of a director, a clerical person, and a part-time maintenance person. The director must be capable of establishing rapport with tenants. The director must be able to foster a supportive environment and have a mutual commitment to succeed with a new venture or idea. He or she will provide ongoing business assistance to the tenants and should periodically monitor their financial situation such as cash-in, cash-out. The director is also responsible for coordinating all technical and financial assistance and for promoting the incubator and its tenants. Generally, this person should possess the following attributes: (a) effective communication skills, (b) working knowledge of accounting and marketing, and (c) proven management expertise.

The clerical person provides services such as word processing, overall, phone answering, filing, and billing for the incubator management and tenants either as part of the rent or for a small fee. Often, clerical service firms are invited to reside in the incubator at reduced rates in exchange for providing management and tenants with services. Maintenance can be part-time as tenants are usually responsible for light maintenance of their rental space. Maintenance may be traded for rent as is the case with clerical services. Overall, (1) services needed by the tenants should be identified, (2) generally, the majority of the facilities provide centralized services to help reduce overhead costs of new businesses, (3) some service needs will become apparent in the surveys and interviews previously conducted, (4) other services will be implemented as the incubator begins operating, (5) typical centralized services include photocopying, data processing, typing, phone answering, and bookkeeping.

Costs for some of these services can be included in the rental rates, others may be provided for a small fee. It is recommended that incubators should capitalize on their own services, allowing excess capacity to be available to tenants. It is important to offer only those services needed by tenants at affordable rates. Utilize support networks for technical and business assistance that is beyond the skills of the incubator manager. Services such as legal, accounting, and advanced financial counseling are usually contracted out for below-market rates. Private companies generally offer less services or allow tenants to structure a "package" to suit their needs.

Conference and luncheon rooms are usually made available, and a library is highly recommended. Information regarding sources of financing and business assistance programs should be available. The Small Business Administration produces a series of useful publications, available free of charge or for a small fee.

STEP EIGHT: MARKETING THE INCUBATOR

Promotion of the incubator is an ongoing effort. Promotion efforts should begin well before the facility opens. Although the facility cannot be expected to be fully pre-leased before opening, tenant targeting efforts can be initiated after establishing initial policies such as screening criteria are determined. Recommended elements of a marketing campaign include the following.

1. Alert media regularly of any developments throughout the project.

2. Develop brochures and other printed materials to respond to requests and mail-outs.

3. Begin a direct mail campaign to potential tenants as identified in previous research. Mail out information to college staffs, vocational-technical centers, support agencies, and bankers.

4. Promote the incubator through speeches with civic clubs and other groups.

5. Stage a "grand opening" and invite public officials, private businesses, media, and others.

6. Develop a newsletter to send to tenants. Copies can be sent to bankers, chambers of commerce, and manufacturing associations.

7. Hold seminars, not only for tenants, but for businesspersons in the community as well.

8. Conduct tours for business and technical students and civic clubs, etc.

STEP NINE: EVALUATE AND REDEFINE GOALS

As the facility begins operations, objectives and goals will have to be reassessed. The key is to remain flexible to accommodate changes. Continue to evaluate development plans.

SUMMARY

It is recommended that a group considering the development of an incubator thoroughly examine the area to test the applicability of the concept. Despite its many advantages, the incubator concept is not a cure-all for the economic ills of every community. Therefore, a careful assessment must first occur to determine the correct application. The steps outlined in this article should be helpful in conducting this assessment.

NOTES

[1] U.S. Small Business Administration, Office of Private Sector Initiatives. 1984. *Small Business Incubators: New Directions in Economic Development.* Washington, D.C.

[2] U.S. Small Business Administration, Office of Private Sector Initiatives. 1984. "Incubator Times." Washington, D.C.

[3] McLean, Mary. 1985. "Different Approaches to Incubator Development." *Economic Development Commentary,* 9 (Winter): 8.

Targeting International Business: Strategies for Expanding Local Economies

John B. Cordrey, Ph.D.

INTRODUCTION

Almost every community can benefit from international business development. International economic development may be direct or indirect. Direct international economic development occurs when business activity increases a community's output and the increase is paid for directly with foreign currency. Indirect international economic development occurs when the increase in output is paid for with domestic currency obtained from another community's international sales.

There are many avenues to increasing international business including: a) increasing foreign sales, b) providing services that facilitate international business, c) increasing intermediate components sales or d) encouraging foreign investment.

Developing a community's strategy begins with two fundamental questions:

❑ What is demanded by global markets?

❑ What does the local community have to offer these markets?

The global demand for goods or services can be gauged by two factors, namely country demand indicators and commodity demand indicators. The country demand indicators can be assessed by the growth in the country's Gross Domestic Product, inflation rate, foreign investment, trade policy changes and foreign aid. Commodity demand indicators can be tracked by observing increases or decreases in commodity trade flows.

The two-fold purposes of this paper are to explore some of the research techniques that have been used to target international business and to report some of the successful programs used to expand international business in Miami/Dade County, Florida.

THE RESEARCH APPROACH

Before targeting an industry or visiting an international city, economic development professionals need to consider and assess international business options.

To determine the best option for an international business development program, the following should be addressed:

❑ Establish international development goals

❑ Identify the community's international assets

❑ Target industries

❑ Target global markets

❑ Consider economic development tools

❑ Complete a general economic analysis.

Establish international development goals

An economic development professional should consider at least five different goals:

❑ Increase the two-way flow of international merchandise trade processed through the local U.S. Customs District

❑ Increase local manufactured export products

❑ Increase local service export

❑ Increase forward investment

❑ Increase reverse investment.

Identifying a Community's International Assets

Depending upon a community's economic make-up, the following business assets may serve as the community's platform from which international business is conducted.

❑ An international transportation network

❑ Geographic location

❑ International business organizations (consulates, trade offices, bi-national chambers)

❑ International education

❑ International services (finance, freight, forwarders, importers/exporters).

Target Industries

Generally a community identifies the strengths of its local economy and targets these strengths as industries to export:

❑ Manufactured Products

❑ Regional Office Operations

❑ Services
– Business
– Technical/Professional
– Health Care
– Education

❑ Research and Development.

Target Global Markets

The specific global region chosen will depend on the established goal. For example, if the goal is to increase the flow of merchandise trade through the area, then one would target countries within global regions where large volume of trade occurs.

If the goal is to increase local manufactured products, one would target countries that are growing and have a demand for your products.

Economic Development Tools

After establishing the goals and selecting the targets, the next choice is which economic development tool should be or could be utilized.

Examples of economic development tools include:

❑ Export seminars

❑ Export financing

❑ Import financing

❑ Local/international business matchmaking

❑ Outbound market visitation

❑ Inbound market visitation

❑ Strategic alliances and cooperative agreements

❑ Selected media promotion; direct mail, advertising, collateral materials.

Economic Analysis

Each international economic development option can be assessed in terms of its cost, probability of success and economic impact. The ideal option would have relatively high probability of success and a relatively high economic impact at a relatively low cost.

INCREASING INTERNATIONAL TRADE

One of the goals of an international business program may be to increase the flow of merchandise trade processed through the area. What research is required to assist this strategy? Does a community have a comparative advantage in the transporting of products to specific countries? The answer is that certain U.S. city regions have an absolute economic advantage as the hub or gateway through which U.S. goods are processed and transported through Customs to foreign destinations.

To serve as a hub or gateway, U.S. cities also must have the optimum geographic location via global regions. Major in-land U.S. cities may have great transportation systems but may not serve as gateway cities. The transportation economics favor coastal cities because it is less costly to transport merchandise by land to the coastal city then either transport it by air or sea to its destination.

By studying merchandise trade flows, gateway cities can be identified. The Beacon Council's research staff has analyzed merchandise import and export trade flow patterns through all 44 U.S. Customs Districts (Table 1). The U.S. Customs data can be obtained by contacting the U.S. Department of Commerce, Bureau of the Census (301) 763-4100.

For example, in 1990, thirty-seven (37) percent of U.S. merchandise trade with Canada is processed through the Detroit Customs District. Forty-three (43) percent of all U.S. trade with Mexico is processed through the Laredo, TX Customs District. Miami Customs District processes 18 percent of all U.S. two-way trade with South America, 43 percent of Caribbean trade and 47 percent of Central American trade.

This research reveals a powerful conclusion regarding the Miami area, namely most U.S. trade with three global regions, South America, Central America and the Caribbean, is processed through the Miami Customs District. The Greater Miami Area has an absolute comparative advantage in processing and transporting merchandise trade between the U.S. and these three global regions.

Using the 1990 U.S. Customs data on CD-ROM, The Beacon Council's research staff identified the type and volume of products cleared and transported through this gateway (See Table 2 for data on South America).

The top five export products identified by four digit Harmonized Code, processed

TABLE 1
U.S. Gateways To Global Regions

Global Region	U.S. Gateway	U.S. Trade Processed Through Gateway Percent
United Kingdom	New York, NY	23
Germany	New York, NY	20
France	New York, NY	26
Canada	Detroit, MI	37
Japan	Los Angeles, CA	25
South Korea	Los Angeles, CA	32
Mexico	Laredo, TX	43
South America	Miami, FL	18
Caribbean	Miami, FL	43
Central America	Miami, FL	47

Source: U.S. Department of Commerce, U.S.Customs data, prepared by The Beacon Council Research Department.

TABLE 2
Top 10 Commodity Exports to South America
Through Miami Customs District
Millions of U.S. Dollars, Non-Petroleum

Commodity	Exports by Commodity	1989	1990	1991	1992
1	Automatic data process machines: magn reader etc.	$366	$379	$595	$704
2	Motor cars & vehicles for transporting persons	32	57	210	599
3	Parts etc. for typewriters & other office machines	281	291	389	572
4	Aircraft, powered spacecraft & launch vehicles	314	227	308	256
5	Parts & access for motor vehicles (head 8701-8705)	129	181	211	236
6	Parts for machinery of headings 8425 to 8430	147	158	178	176
7	Parts of balloons etc, aircraft, spacecraft etc.	269	314	209	176
8	Trans appar for radio telephone etd; tv cameras	50	73	115	171
9	Parts for engines of heading 8407 or 8408	142	156	170	163
10	Electric apparatus for line telehone etc. parts	73	70	86	137

Source: U.S. Department of Commerce, prepared by The Beacon Council Research Department.

through Miami Customs District were:
1. Data processing equipment
2. Automobiles
3. Parts for office equipment
4. Aircraft parts and machinery parts
5. Auto parts.

Knowing the types of products exported to or imported from selected countries provides the basis for developing a program to increase merchandise trade through the Customs District. This Miami research lead to a number of program activities directed towards increasing trade flows to and from the U.S. and South America.

Specifically, to increase U.S. exports

through the Miami Customs District, The Beacon Council has targeted U.S. businesses that manufacture the products listed in Table 2. Personal visits and briefings are scheduled with these targeted businesses. The message includes: 1) the large volume of similar products exported through Miami to South America; 2) the details of the local international transportation system; 3) the availability of international trade services (freight forwarders, finance, insurance, foreign government and business representatives).

The message concludes that Miami is the least-cost and thus most profitable geographic location through which to distribute international merchandise with South American businesses.

Gateway cities can also consider increasing imports as a method of increasing economic activity. The United States is the world's largest market. Foreign businesses seek ways to access this market. Utilizing similar research, international regions and businesses can be targeted for both import expansion, as well as reverse or foreign investment.

To increase imports, the economic development program can organize and conduct outbound market visitation programs to deliver the gateway message to international business. A key to this message should include how to use the gateway as the entry or access point to the U.S. market.

This import development program offers international businesses a good reason (increased sales) to become familiar with the area. Thus, increasing the probability of future foreign investment.

The economic development option of increasing exports/imports within gateway areas has a relatively good probability of success; however, this option has a relatively low economic impact. Generally, an employment multiplier of 1.1 is used; i.e., if 10 direct additional import/export related jobs are created, one indirect job is also created.

INTERNATIONAL DISTRIBUTION CENTER

Another economic development strategy is to focus on the flow of trade and convince the exporters to use the community as a world-wide distribution center.

Becoming an international distribution center requires excellent international transportation systems plus international warehousing, such as, free trade zones or bonded warehouses.

The message is to utilize the community's assets as a platform to re-route or perform final product preparation prior to destination shipment. This strategy uses the same basic research to identify the targeted industries and geographic regions. The probability of success decreases. However, the employment multiplier increases (a 1.25 employment multiplier is common) because of the value added.

INCREASING LOCAL EXPORTS

Exporting products has a high employment multiplier effect. The U.S. Department of Commerce estimates that for each one billion dollars of U.S. exports, between 20,000 to 22,000 jobs are created. The employment created at the local economic level will not be this large; however, increasing local exports will have the similar multiplier effects as the attraction of new manufacturers into the region, i.e. local employment multipliers of 1.5 to 2.0. The exact multiplier would depend upon the industry expanded.

Many U.S. Department of Commerce and state export development programs exist to assist local manufacturers. The basic questions a research program should answer for the local manufacturing businesses are:

☐ What specific product(s) should be exported?

☐ What is the foreign demand for this product?

☐ What international government or business will buy my product?

The U.S. Department of Commerce provides annual updated information in its Country Reports and Country Marketing Plans. These reports indicate what products are in greatest demand from each country and serve as one of the information sources. These reports can be obtained by contacting the local U.S. Department of Commerce in the community.

A country's Gross Domestic Product (GDP) or GDP growth rate serves as another measure to identify potential markets. Countries with steady growth in GDP create growing levels of income and thus provide a greater opportunity for international sales.

Identifying local manufacturers that export, or have the capacity and interest in exporting, can be developed through local research. Business organizations such as chambers, world trade centers and economic development agencies prepare and produce local manufacturers directories or international trade directories. These publications serve as a primary listing of local businesses that could be your potential exporting team.

Another source of information on local businesses that export can be obtained through business information organizations such as Dun and Bradstreet. A sample listing from D&B for the Miami area medical devices and pharmaceutical manufacturers is shown in Table 3. (contact number : 1-800-526-0651)

Using U.S. Department of Commerce Country Studies or the knowledge of local business, one can identify the country and city to visit. Using the local manufacturers directory or business listing, one can identify the specific businesses that could serve as your industry team. The task is to match local businesses with international buyers.

One of the successful methods for matching local and international buyers and sellers is to form strategic alliances with selected business organizations in global regions. In most countries these organizations are funded through a national business tax. These organizations represent business interest much as local chambers of commerce in the U.S.

The Beacon Council has entered into a number of these strategic alliances to assist in our international business program. The agreements call for both organizations to assist in matching local and international business interests.

For example, The Beacon Council has a strategic alliance agreement with an Italian business association, Assolombarda from Milano, Italy. When outbound development trips are planned, Beacon Council staff seek assistance from this organization to host joint meetings, develop itineraries, and set up business-to-business meetings

TABLE 3
Exporting Businesses in Dade County's Medical Technology Industry

Business	Export Products
Al-Site Corp.	Opththalmic goods
Althin CD Medical	Artificial kidneys
Baker Cummins Laboratory	Pharmaceutical
Baxter Diagnostic, Inc.	Diagnostic equipment and reagents
Cordis Corporation	Angioplasty
Coulter Corporation	Blood cell counting instruments
Diamedix	Reagents
IVAX Corporation	Pharmaceuticals
North American Biologicals	Blood analysis
Noven Pharmaceuticals	Medical trans-thermal devices
Royce Laboratories	Pharmaceuticals
Symbiosis	Medical instruments
Telectronics Pacing Systems	Heart pacemakers

Source: Dun and Bradstreet, 1993

while in Italy. The reverse process is set in motion when Italian businesses visit the Miami area.

To assist in match-making, The Beacon Council's research staff has surveyed local businesses to determine their interest in meeting with international businesses (Exhibit 1). These responses provide the basis for introducing the local business to the international business. Strategic alliances provide a number of advantages to local economic development organizations. First, they increase the probability of success by providing a network of people through which your organization can reach selected businesses. Two, they provide a low-cost method of keeping your community's business assets in front of a large number of international businesses. This tool also permits an excellent way to provide the continuous follow-up required in developing or promoting your region's international economic development program.

Another major advantage of strategic alliances is that research is shared between organizations, thus the research capability is expanded. Research from the international partner is made available to the organization for future program planning.

SERVICE EXPORT

Trade in services represents approximately 20 percent of total U.S. trade. However, as the U.S. economy moves towards a service economy, the role of trade in services will increase. The local economic impact of service exports is large and should be considered comparable to product export.

Trade in services includes: foreign tourism/visitors, education, business, financial and technical services, health care and telecommunications. Information on the dollar volume of trade by these industry sectors and by country receiving U.S. services, exists only at the national level. No readily available service data, similar to the merchandise trade data, by U.S. Customs District exist. Thus to initiate service trade development programs requires local research. The research process is similar to identifying a merchandise trade export development program. First, identify what services represent a major strength to the economy, then determine if they are currently providing or would be interested in providing export services. For example, based on Beacon Council research, more than 8,000 international students are enrolled in the five universities in Dade County. This represents an export service

EXHIBIT 1
The Americas Campaign
Greater Miami: Business Capital of the Americas
Business Contact Program

The Business Contact Program is an electronic database made up of companies in Greater Miami/Dade County who have indicated their interest in investment, joint ventures, distributorships, or trading with international business groups that come to Miami through the offices of The Beacon Council.

Companies from Greater Miami/Dade County interested in investment opportunities and international commerce and investment opportunities will have a company profile on record with the Council. Through our strategic alliances, The Beacon Council connects foreign companies with Miami businesses and assists them with business appointments and handling inquiries.

This Program affords an excellent opportunity for companies to expand their customer base and enables firms to find suitable partners overseas. This Program is another means by which The Beacon Council will continue to assist in creating new business opportunities for Greater Miami: The Business Capital of the Americas.

To Connect with Foreign Companies
and incoming Business Development Missions

• If you are interested in an appointment with a foreign company that meets your requirements, please complete the registration form.
• When we receive notice of an incoming business delegation or an inquiry, you will be contacted by fax or telephone with details on the participants, such as: industry, their interests and date of visit.
• It is extremely important that you always confirm you appointment via fax - 24 hours in advance - in order for us to assist you and our international partners and their business delegations.

---

of approximately $120 million annually and provides a targeted industry from which an economic development program (i.e. attract more international students) can be launched.

Yet another example of services that local areas could export is research and problem solving. The Beacon Council research staff recently completed a study of our area's environmental science research conducted at area universities and federal agencies. One of the findings was that South American governments are seeking expertise at reducing their oceanographic and atmospheric pollution. This example presents an excellent opportunity for economic development organizations to market their community's scientific assets to international governments or businesses.

As stated earlier, the exporting of local services, except for tourism, has not been a major component of most economic development organizations' strategies. However, adopting a service export strategy has simi-

lar economic development impacts as strategies for exporting merchandise. Employment multipliers range from 1.3 to 1.7.

CAPITAL INVESTMENT

Does investment follow trade? This issue has been debated among economic development professionals for years. The Beacon Council's experience clearly points to a positive answer to this question. Miami tends to be a gateway area for exports to South America, Central America and the Caribbean, and many regional headquarters operations have been established within the area. Therefore, Miami's message to North American businesses doing business in Latin America is **"Miami is the Business Capital of the Americas."** Not only does Miami provide the most cost effective and easily accessible transportation routes to South America but businesses can also establish their Latin American headquarters in Miami and maintain U.S. stability.

BUSINESS CONTACT PROGRAM/COMPANY PROFILE/REGISTRATION FORM

Company Name: _____

Second Name: _____

CEO: _____

Title: _____

Other Contact: _____

Street Address: _____

Telephone Number:_____ Fax Number_____

Total Number of Employees:_____ Year Company Established:_____

Line of Business:_____

Type of Business: [ ] Mining/Agriculture/Forestry/Fishing [ ] Construction
                 [ ] Manufacturing [ ] Services
                 [ ] Transportation/Comm./Utilities [ ] Retail Trade
                 [ ] Finance/Insurance/Real Estate [ ] Other
                 [ ] Wholesale Trade

Internation Interest
Import   [ ]
Export   [ ]
Trade   [ ]
Subcontract   [ ]
Searching for Joint Venture Partner   [ ]
Commercial Partners (Agent/Distributor) [ ]
Receive Subcontract   [ ]

Main Markets Interested In   Main Markets Currently Representing
[ ] United States   [ ] United States
[ ] Canada   [ ] Canada
[ ] Caribbean   [ ] Caribbean
[ ] Central America   [ ] Central America
[ ] South America   [ ] South America
[ ] Europe   [ ] Europe
[ ] Asia   [ ] Asia
[ ] Africa   [ ] Africa

Specific Country: Specific Country:

Name of person completing this profile:

                      Title: _____

               Telephone: _____

                       Fax: _____

                    Date: _____

To develop a listing of U.S. businesses that could profit from establishing their international headquarters in your location, one uses the same trade flow research that is used to expand international trade or establish distribution centers.

Attracting investment, which leads to the creation of additional employment, continues to have the greatest employment multipliers. Gateway cities have a natural advantage for attracting distribution centers and regional headquarters.

Economic development professionals can also target reverse foreign investment by identifying existing international manufacturers that may provide a magnet for international manufacturing suppliers. For example, in the 1970's the Honda Motors Corporation built an auto assembly plant in Western Ohio. This one investment encouraged a number of Japanese automotive parts manufacturers to relocate in the same region. Economic development organizations targeted automobile suppliers and marketed their community's business assets to Japanese businesses.

SUMMARY

Targeted international research provides the foundation for international business development. Fundamental research includes knowledge of trade flow patterns, understanding your local export base (both merchandise and service), and your international business infrastructure (transportation, culture, foreign consultants and trade organizations.)

In the final analysis one must judge the probability of success, the economic impact, and the economic development cost.

Before any international business development trip is undertaken, a firm understanding of where you are going and what you offer international businesses is essential. Your research program should provide these answers.

The Professional Development Challenge Of The Next Decade

Harry G. Foden, CED, FM

INTRODUCTION

Economic, technological, and social changes of the past decade illustrate the need for economic developers to exert every effort to reflect these changes in their daily activities. As recently as 1984 and 1985, for example, few economic developers were facile with computers; the seminars on computers, offered by the AEDC Educational Foundation at the Hilton Head and Boston conferences, attracted only the "daring." The Boston conference addressed the importance of technology to economic development and led to special projects on the utilization of technology by economic developers to assist existing businesses -- an area of concern of few economic developers at that time.

The traditional focus of many economic developers on manufacturing facilities alone has given way to a realization that a broader focus on any economic activity that brings new wealth to the community is appropriate. As a result, we have seen heavy competition for such activities as the United Airlines maintenance facilities. Retailing and tourism also have emerged as targets for many economic developers, a situation unheard of not too long ago. The importance of back office activities in the thinking of economic developers is reflected in the very high attendance at AEDC's special course offerings on attraction of back office operations. The large number of people at the courses on economic impact analysis suggests that many economic developers see the need to evaluate the impact of many types of activities on their community and the need to convey this information to their employers and the community at large.

Throughout the decade we have also seen a rapid increase in the speed with which developments occur. Federal Express and other overnight delivery services had hardly established a foothold when the high speed fax made it possible to provide same-day -- or even same-hour -- transmission of material. And now E-mail and the Internet have opened up even broader areas of communication. Clients and prospects expect immediate responses to their inquiries. We are either prepared to do so or we lose our competitive position.

As fast as things have changed during the past decade, the likelihood is that they will change even faster in the next. All business is under tremendous pressure to perform in the global economy. Economic development is no exception.

OUTLOOK FOR CHANGE -- CHALLENGES FOR THE ECONOMIC DEVELOPER

Total Quality Management (TQM), Business Process Redesign of Business, Re-engineering and Downsizing (or "rightsizing" as some like to call it) are all responses of business to the challenge of operating in the global environment. These responses pose multiple challenges for the economic development practitioner. The number of new plants, for example, is likely to be less (and probably more likely to be outside the United States), the size of the establishment will be smaller, the need for less skilled personnel much less, and the allegiance by business to the community much more tenuous. There will be the need for more small firms to grow and prosper and to adopt more advanced methods, and to have the ability to respond quickly to the market changes. Communities will become more concerned about the lack of quality job opportunities for their young people, as companies, in the growing information society, seek more highly skilled and well-educated personnel and have a reduced need for less-skilled personnel.

The economic developer, as a result, is likely to be besieged on all sides -- trying to demonstrate to new and existing businesses that his or her community can meet the needs of globally competitive business, identifying ways to help the community's small and medium-sized businesses acquire the assistance needed to grow, and helping the community attract or hold onto businesses that can provide jobs for those in the community who do not have the capability or skills for the new age economic activity.

CAN WE MEET THE CHALLENGE?

Have we as economic developers managed to meet the challenges of the recent past as well as we could have? Will we be able to meet the challenges ahead as effectively as we should?

In some areas we appear to have done well. Whereas in 1984 and 1985, only a few economic development organization were equipped with computers, desk top publishing, etc., there has been great progress since that time. When, in 1986, a key speaker at the conference in Hamilton, Ontario said that he preferred to receive videos rather than written material because of the ease of reviewing them, not too many organizations were well equipped to produce their material in video form; today that has changed drastically. As organizations began to use computers more extensively, software was developed to permit economic development organizations to send material to clients in disc form. As faxes became more widespread, economic developers adapted their material to this new communication form.

Larger, well-funded organizations have experimented with advanced technology to display site and building information. While developments such as these are beyond the financial resources of small organizations, they hold promise for utilities, state development agencies and major chambers of commerce who can incorporate in their data base information about the smaller communities in the region.

While large organizations are the only ones that can afford many of the complex, sophisticated technological advances, presentations at the 1995 Annual Conference of AEDC indicated that even one- and two-person offices can take advantage of technology. The availability of a wide variety of software, coupled with the willingness to experiment a bit, has enabled economic development practitioners to enhance the effectiveness of their efforts.

Educational opportunities for economic developers have increased dramatically during the past decade. The availability of fundamental educational offerings has become widespread, to the point that 18 Economic Development Courses are offered each year in various parts of the country. The Economic Development Institute held at the University of Oklahoma for 34 years, has been expanded to an additional site at Indianapolis, making it more convenient for a larger number of economic developers to take advantage of the educational program. Numerous seminars and short courses are offered at various locations throughout the country. Exploration of courses by mail and by video is underway.

The 1995 Annual Conference of AEDC and the focus on technology in both program offerings and exhibits, was a very appropriate response to the great interest of economic developers in the application of technology. A optional session on computers, held on a sunny afternoon in the area of Disney World and other attractions, was filled to overflowing. Other sessions were equally well attended, demonstrating the awareness of those economic developers in attendance that they must be abreast of new techniques if they are to succeed in their profession.

In other areas, we have moved more slowly than we should have. For example, following the Boston conference and its them of technology, a special task force was set up by AEDC and, with the aid of an EDA grant, developed a handbook and sponsored two seminars with the AEDC Educational Foundation on how the economic developer could help his/her local businesses gain access to technology. In spite of initial interest, there was little follow through by economic developers. Yet, today the need is even greater and there are many small and medium-sized businesses in desperate need for help. The Narragansett Electric Company, the Greater Providence Chamber of Commerce and other private companies in Rhode Island, recognizing this need, have just established a well-funded alliance to help small manufacturers tap into the network of universities and state agencies that have the capability to help, but have never been well

enough connected to business to do so effectively.

In another instance, the importance of existing industry to the community was pointed out in the early to mid-1980's, yet it was several years before such activities were included in the programs of economic development agencies and made part of the curriculum at the Economic Development Institute and the Economic Development Courses.

The recently announced AEDCNet, which will enable economic developers to gain quick and easy on-line access to information and professional expertise, is a significant advance, but required two or three years of discussion and evaluation to bring about, and even then had to build upon an existing system that had been working well for the U.S. Chamber of Commerce.

WHAT OF THE FUTURE?

As we move toward the beginning of the 21st century, are we sufficiently prepared for what economic development will require? Businesses have found it necessary to re-examine their basic operations, utilizing total quality management techniques, business process re-design or re-engineering, leading in many cases to severe reductions in the number of employees. Have we prepared ourselves for the following implications of such business changes?

❑ The loss in our communities of hundreds, if not thousands of jobs (many of them high paying) as companies close plants or severely reduce their labor requirements.

❑ The significantly reduced demand for less skilled personnel and the call for more highly educated and trained personnel to operate in the information society.

❑ The need to respond to the community's call for jobs for the less skilled.

❑ The interest of companies in total quality communities.

❑ The ability of many companies to locate operations in lower cost communities, relying on telecommunications to connect these facilities to other operations.

❑ The new location requirements brought about by flexible manufacturing (see my article "Responding to Changes in Traditional Manufacturing", in the Summer 1994 issue of *Economic Development Review*).

Have we re-examined our own opera-

tions to see that they are as competitive as they ought to be? Have we considered the application of TQM techniques for our own operations, large or small? It is fascinating to me to note the value of applying TQM techniques to even simple operations, finding that we easily fall into habits of doing things over and over again, failing to recognize the potential for simplification.

Are we still focusing too heavily on business attraction -- and the potential for a big hit -- and neglecting to pay sufficient attention to the smaller local businesses that, with help, might add (or retain) significant jobs in the community?

Can we respond to requests -- be they from outside prospects or local companies -- as quickly as the inquirers expect? Are we utilizing the technologies that are available?

SOME APPROACHES TO PROFESSIONAL DEVELOPMENT

The successful economic development practitioner is one who acquires and maintains a broad perspective on developments in our economy and society. He or she tries to anticipate development in business, knows how to work with local companies and the community at large, responds to the needs of volunteer boards, and markets the community to a broad audience. Given such a broad mandate, how does today's economic development professional keep abreast of developments? Following are a few suggestions:

❑ Stay abreast, through the business press, of new developments in industry. A regular reading of such publications as *Business Week, The Wall Street Journal*, and *Forbes* can give one clues on the latest techniques being used by business - and some of the implications of such applications. Each year, it seems, companies explore new techniques -- strategic planning, shareholders' value, business re-engineering -- put forth by academics or consultants to try to improve their operations. While you need not be familiar with the details of such techniques, you should try to understand how they might affect business operations and, ultimately, your community.

❑ Take advantage of educational courses. Build into your budget sufficient funds to enable you to do so. If you do not, your successor will. Those responsible for economic development -- be it the volunteer board of directors, the VP of Marketing or other responsible supervisor -- must be educated to understand how important such education is.

❑ Strive for Certification. Not only will certification provide an indication to your present or future employer that you are highly qualified and up-to-date, but the very effort involved in preparing yourself for the Certified Economic Developer exam will also broaden your perspective, provide a structure for your experience and enhance your ability as an economic developer.

❑ Join your professional organization at the state, regional or national level, as your budget permits. Participation in such organizations will broaden your knowledge, make you more aware of your competition, and acquaint you with the latest techniques. Your participation and expression of your needs will help your professional organization to do a better job of serving you.

And what should you expect from your professional organization in the years ahead? In my opinion, it is appropriate to expect the following:

❑ A continuing flow of information about sources that you can tap to stay abreast of the latest developments in the economy.

❑ Rapid response to your requests for assistance. If your organization cannot provide the assistance itself, it should be able to direct you to the appropriate source.

❑ Educational courses, by mail and video as well as in seminar form, at various locations, on topics that are current and relevant. Such courses should cause you to stretch your mind and your experience.

❑ Making available to you at moderate cost new developments that only a larger organization can provide -- particularly as new technologies emerge.

❑ Annual conferences that provide opportunities to stay abreast of the latest developments, presented in such a manner that members can select the information that is appropriate to their stage of development and the needs and budgets of their particular organizations.

Responding to The Challenge of Professional Development: The Programs of AEDC

Gene Handley, Ph.D., CAE

INTRODUCTION

This article presents a brief overview of the origin and nature of the professional development activities of the American Economic Development Council. The long history of the Council with its beginnings in 1926, and the limited length of this article allow only partial treatment of this topic. The reader is encouraged to review the *50th Anniversary History of the Council (1975)* and the *History of the Council (1961)* for a more complete understanding of the history.

Briefly stated, the Council's founders and leaders have consistently viewed the *professional development* of its membership as their primary mission.

Furthermore, from its beginnings, the Council convened for the purpose of the professional development of its members and its efforts have evolved from an annual meeting to the current full range of programs.

CURRENT PROGRAMS

The Council now has in place a four-part education program for economic developers. These efforts provide (1) introductory knowledge regarding the profession (Economic Development Courses), (2) intermediate knowledge (Economic Development Institute), and (3) advanced knowledge (AEDC professional development courses). In addition, the Council provided education services to those at all levels (4) through the Annual Conference, Washington Briefing, CED Summit, self-directed learning, and other programs and services to meet the wide range of needs of economic developers. Figure 1 displays the continuum of AEDC services currently available to the profession.

These programs currently are presented in a variety of ways. (Figure 2). AEDC

Sponsored programs are those developed, financed and promoted by the Council. AEDC Co-Sponsored and Accredited programs are those whose primary sponsors are other organizations that have met the Council's accreditation standards to sponsor an Economic Development Course, Economic Development Institute, or On-

Site Program. The Council provides continuous oversight for these programs in terms of periodic review and accreditation maintenance as well as curriculum modifications. Finally, AEDC Accredited programs are those sponsored by other organizations that meet AEDC accreditation criteria on a per offering basis but for which the Council has no on-going oversight responsibility.

EVOLUTION OF AEDC PROGRAMS

Professional development is the central mission of the American Economic Development Council. As stated in its by-laws, the Council's mission is to "advance the profession of economic development, foster the interchange of ideas and educational experiences, and enhance the career growth

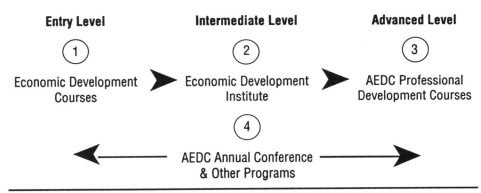

FIGURE 1
Types of AEDC Education Programs

Entry Level — (1) Economic Development Courses → **Intermediate Level** — (2) Economic Development Institute → **Advanced Level** — (3) AEDC Professional Development Courses

(4) AEDC Annual Conference & Other Programs

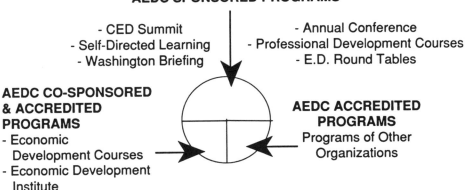

FIGURE 2
Sponsorship of AEDC Educational Programs

AEDC SPONSORED PROGRAMS
- CED Summit
- Self-Directed Learning
- Washington Briefing
- Annual Conference
- Professional Development Courses
- E.D. Round Tables

AEDC CO-SPONSORED & ACCREDITED PROGRAMS
- Economic Development Courses
- Economic Development Institute
- On-Site Courses

AEDC ACCREDITED PROGRAMS
Programs of Other Organizations

of professionals employed in the field of economic development." Three of the ten enumerated objectives commit to "provide continuing education programs," "disseminate information regarding the profession," and "(maintain) a certification program." In this regard, AEDC is not unique in that most professional societies include professional development as their primary mission. What is unique is the manner in which the Council has pursued that mission. The following is a brief chronology describing the evolution of AEDC professional development programs.

Annual Conference (1926)

The Chamber of Commerce of the United States sponsored an annual meeting of industrial developers from 1926 through 1929. At the annual conference in 1930 those in attendance adopted the constitution that founded the American Industrial Developers Council and assumed sponsorship of the Annual Conference that continues today. Through the 1960's, attendance at the conference was a requirement of membership and attendance at the meetings exceeded 500.

Economic Development Institute (EDI) (1962)

Initially developed by the Southern Industrial Development Council, AEDC became co-sponsor of and a financial contributor to the University of Oklahoma's program including the formation of a Board of Regents for Education that provided oversight for the program.

District Meetings (1965)

Initiated in California as part of an effort to increase local involvement, annual meetings were sponsored in six of the then ten Council's districts. This effort later was discontinued.

AIDC Journal/Economic Development Review (1966)

In 1966, the Council published the first edition of the *AIDC Journal*, which later became the AEDC Journal and which is now the Economic Development Review. This professional journal continues today to serve as the Council's primary vehicle for the "professional development" of economic developers. AEDC members view *ED Review* as the single most valuable benefit of membership. Most editions of the journal address a special topic, as well

as an ongoing series of featured components. Practitioners and consultants write many of the practical and informative articles.

Economic Development Courses (EDCs) (1967)

Developed in response to comments by EDI faculty that participants were ill prepared to attend the Institute, the first "Basic Industrial Development Course" (now EDC) was offered at Texas A&M. The number of programs accredited by the Council has grown to offerings at twenty universities. Approximately ten percent of those who attend EDCs are members of the Council.

Certified Economic Developer® Program (1970)

In 1970 the AEDC Board of Directors established the Certified Industrial Developer® program, now known as The Certified Economic Developer® Program. The purpose of the program is to create a professional standard of practice for the profession based on established criteria that include years of practice, peer nomination, adoption of a code of ethics, and the successful completion of an oral and written examination of professional knowledge. In addition, Certified Economic Developers® must submit evidence of continuance of service and continuing education every three years in order to maintain their certification. To date, more than 1,100 individuals have earned the Certified Economic Developer® (CED) designation. The Certification Board is responsible for the development and management of the examination process and the appropriate administration of the certification process. Organizations and communities with increasing frequency are including the CED designation as a requirement for candidates for leadership positions in economic development.

Washington Briefing (1985)

The conference focuses on changes at the federal level that have an impact on the profession. The meeting is also the occasion for participants to meet with federal agency staff members and congressional delegations.

AEDC Professional Development Courses (short courses) (1980s)

Throughout the years the Council has

offered occasional "short courses" of one- or two-day duration. In the late 1980s, AEDC offered a fixed calendar of two-day courses at locations throughout the United States. Those offerings continue today through the Council's *Regional Course Offerings* and the *On-Site Program*.

On-Site Programs (1993)

Relying on "partnerships" with other organizations, the "On-Site" program offers local, state and regional organizations the opportunity to present AEDC professional development courses at dates and locations of their choosing. Ten such programs are scheduled for the current year.

CED Summit (1993)

The Council identified a need for Certified Economic Developers® to meet annually to discuss the strategic issues facing the profession and to network with other CEDs. AEDC created the *CED Summit* to meet those needs. More than 100 Certified Economic Developers® are expected to meet in Phoenix, Arizona this year to continue the dialog.

Self-Directed Learning Programs (1995)

In response to those individuals unable to afford the resources to attend the Annual Conference or other AEDC programs, the Council is producing print materials that permit the economic developer to acquire and apply new knowledge and skills. In their final stages of development are programs on the topics of "Economic Development Finance" and "Managing Economic Development in Rural Settings." These print materials will permit self-paced learning while providing individuals who complete and return an application exercise with credit towards certification maintenance.

HISTORY OF SELECTED PROGRAMS

It is instructive to examine the history of selected AEDC professional development programs in that doing so reveals both the original purpose of the program as well as its evolution. The history of the Annual Conference, the Economic Development Institute, the Economic Development Courses, and the Education Committee will each be described.

Annual Conference

The first comprehensive written history

of the Council published in 1961 reports that the Chamber of Commerce of the United States convened an annual conference from 1926 through 1929 of industrial developers employed by local chambers of commerce. The National Chamber was of the opinion that such a meeting "might lead to a better understanding of the work of industrial bureau managers and bring their work to a higher degree of proficiency." They stated frankly that "some managers were guilty of making most extravagant claims concerning their work and results gotten, to the extent that the entire chamber of commerce movement was being jeopardized by a few who set no limits to their claims." At the close of the fifth such annual conference in 1930, those in attendance elected officers and adopted a constitution thus establishing the American Industrial Development Council.

These first annual conferences were strictly informal, the chairman not being elected until the opening day of the meetings. It was not until 1949 that the Council prepared and distributed verbatim reports of the meetings to the members. Members devoted entire sessions of the conference to "The Question Box." Those with questions would deposit them in a box and a panel of more experienced members would supply answers. Initially, the leadership scheduled all annual conferences in Washington, DC with the exception of 1933 when the meeting was held in Chicago. Beginning in 1956, the leadership decided to rotate the location of the annual conference to other parts of the United States and Canada. In 1957, the National Chamber of Commerce ended its policy of providing support for such associations and the Council established its own office in Newark, Delaware.

The Council's principle activity continued to be the Annual Conference. Although previous conferences had exhibits of industrial development literature, it was not until 1958 that the Council conducted an actual awards program.

Economic Development Institute (EDI)

The Southern Industrial Development Council formed an Education Committee that lead to the creation in 1962 of the Industrial Development Institute, (now the Economic Development Institute), a three-year, one-week-a-year program. The University of Oklahoma sponsors offerings each year in Norman, Oklahoma and Indi-

anapolis, Indiana. In 1963, AEDC became the accrediting co-sponsor of EDI.

The Council formed a semi-autonomous body known as the Regents for Educational Programs to provide oversight for the Institute. Since then, this body evolved into the Council's Board of Regents which in turn recently became the Education Board, with responsibility for AEDC's education programs.

An important part of the EDI experience is the thesis program. As a condition for graduation from EDI, a candidate must produce an original work of research in an area of economic development, thus adding to the literature of the profession. On average, twenty percent of those who attend EDI are members of the Council. In the absence of available undergraduate degree education programs in economic development, EDI has generally served as the equivalent program to prepare new professionals for the field of economic development.

Economic Development Courses (EDCs)

It became apparent to the administrators of the Economic Development Institute that a number of individuals lacked the basic knowledge regarding economic development to benefit from this program. The Council subsequently developed a curriculum for a one week "Basic Industrial Development Course" and solicited universities to sponsor the course. In 1967, the Council accredited the Texas A&M program as the first approved course. Renamed "Economic Development Course," twenty universities now sponsor these introductory programs in the United States.

Education Committee

In 1963, a Council request to a national foundation for financial assistance was summarily dismissed with the comment that "the practice of industrial development was categorized as little more than hucksterism and piracy." This rebuff led the Council leadership to institute a long-range educational program that would raise the practice to the level of a profession. That year the Board of Directors established an Education Committee and an Education Foundation. The Executive Director, Richard Preston, "was instructed to consider ways and means for formal and informal industrial development education to the end that practitioners would be better prepared to

face the rapidly changing needs of the emerging profession." "The Education Committee assumed as its long-range objective the creation of an industrial development profession based on formal education media at both the collegiate and continuing education levels.

MEMBER OVERSIGHT

A body of members oversees each of the Council's professional development activities. The Education Board, composed of regional representatives and the chairs of related committees, has oversight responsibility for AEDC co-sponsored and accredited programs. The Education Board is responsible for on-going strategic planning in education. The Annual Conference Committee is responsible for development of the Annual Conference. The Certification Board is responsible for the Certified Economic Developer® program. The Education Board, Annual Conferences Committee, and the Certification Board report to the AEDC Board of Directors. Potential volunteers are encouraged to call AEDC for further information.

CURRENT EFFORTS TO DEFINE THE PROFESSION

The Certification Board, in collaboration with the Economic Development Institute, Economic Development Course directors, and the AEDC Education Board, are examining the nature of the economic developer. The task force's intents are to focus the content of the CED examination and to assist those responsible for the continuing education of economic developers in developing their programs. The efforts of this joint task force are described elsewhere in this issue. In addition to defining the profession, the task force is describing the core body of knowledge underpinning the practice of economic development. The task force will next conduct a random sampling of the opinions of the total membership regarding the definition of the profession and body of knowledge.

FUTURE PROFESSIONAL DEVELOPMENT ACTIVITIES

It is anticipated that the following factors will play critical roles in future AEDC professional development activities:

❑ Partnerships - working in cooperation

with other organizations to provide services.

☐ Technology - employing emerging technologies to deliver education programs, products and information.

☐ Career Assistance - establishing the most comprehensive base of information regarding the careers of economic development professionals.

Partnerships

The first factor, partnerships, addresses the fact that AEDC cannot and should not be "all things to all people" in professional development. There exist programs of excellence offered by other organizations that AEDC can recognize and support to avoid expensive duplication of effort. An example of this is the AEDC "accreditation" of programs offered by other organizations, thus lending our endorsement and support. The Economic Development Institute and the numerous Economic Development Courses represent programs developed in partnership with universities nationwide. The AEDC On-Site Program, based on working in cooperation with regional, state, and local organizations, can deliver programs closer to the "customer," thus reducing their travel costs. The newly initiated "Economic Development Regional Course Offerings" demonstrates an application of this approach as Council programs are offered in each of the four AEDC Regions in cooperation with regional, state, and local organizations. The Council anticipates that the next area for partnership will be to expand its partnership efforts with other national economic development organizations.

Technology

The second critical factor is technology. The technical resources available to deliver education products and services to AEDC members are rapidly expanding. The new AEDCNet on-line service has great potential for professional development programs. The Council is also investigating the viability of live computer conferencing, video and audio teleconferencing, computer assisted instruction, and pre-recorded interactive media. The decision of AEDC to use such technology will be determined first by the technology's ability to facilitate education and second by the availability of the technology to our members at an affordable price.

Career Assistance

The third factor will be the ability of AEDC to provide career assistance. The Council intends to increase its ability to serve as the source of information of the highest quality regarding the careers of economic developers, e.g. optimizing career paths, compensation practices, education needs, career counseling, employment assistance, and personal financial planning. The Council will strive to provide the economic developer with easy access to this information. The hallmark of AEDC's professional development will be *that AEDC provide programs and services for economic developers that are essential to their success and that the services are of the type and quality not avialable elsewhere.* In order to do so, such services will have to be offered in *partnership* with other organizations, employ the most cost effective *technologies* available, and reflect a comprehensive understanding of the *career needs* of our members.

CHALLENGES TO PROFESSIONAL DEVELOPMENT

The Council faces the following challenges to providing professional development programs of high quality:

☐ *The profession of economic development still lacks a clear definition, and therefore, a clear understanding of the knowledge, skills and abilities required to prac-* *tice effectively.* The Council is currently addressing this challenge through its "defining the profession" project.

☐ *Little comprehensive information exists regarding the demographic and other characteristics of economic developers, the career paths they have followed and the changes that have occurred in both over time.* The Council's updated computer system and expanded member data base will greatly expand knowledge in this area.

☐ *The nature of their work places many economic developers in the position of having little time for professional development and few resources available to participate had they the time.* The Council must employ a wide array of delivery mechanisms to provide access to new knowledge in a cost efficient manner.

☐ *It is not economically feasible for the Council to offer a full array of professional development services to meet all the needs of each of the various types of its members.* While the diversity and needs are great, the Council must define and serve the areas of need common to all economic developers and work in partnership with other organizations to meet other needs.

CONCLUSION

The profession of economic development continues to change rapidly in form and function. Keeping pace with such changes requires that economic developers work continuously at maintaining and enhancing their knowledge and skills. The American Economic Development Council is committed to serving the economic development profession as its partner in career-long learning. If you would like additional information regarding the programs, products and services of the Council, simply contact the AEDC Professional Development Department.

The Economic Development Institute

Nancy Thompson

THE BEGINNING

The idea of an educational program for economic developers was conceived by the Southern Industrial Development Council. The Site Selection Committee chose the newly constructed Kellogg Center for Continuing Education at the University of Oklahoma to be the site of the first Industrial Development Institute. SIDC and the University of Oklahoma jointly sponsored the program, both contributing to the curriculum development and project financing. SIDC subsequently suggested that the sponsorship be given to the American Industrial Development Council and the University to give the program a national focus. The Institute continues to be a partnership between the University of Oklahoma as the provider and the American Economic Development Council as the professional accrediting agency. The first Industrial Development Institute Year I Class met August 19-25, 1962, with 39 participants attending.

PROGRAM STRUCTURE

IDI was designed as a three session program consisting of one week-long class for three consecutive years. The original curriculum typically consisted of 1/2 day sessions taught by one instructor. Classes began on Monday morning and ended with a luncheon the following Saturday. Evening sessions were held Monday through Friday. The thesis requirement has been a part of the program since its inception and has gradually been strengthened to the present stringent standards. The first Advanced Symposium was a three day class on investment held in 1965.

During the early years, the Institute was run with a minimum of staffing, which included the Director of the program from the University, who dedicated about one-third of his work time to IDI, and volunteer staff who were mostly from SIDC or AIDC. Classes were monitored by participants se-lected from each class. The University presently has two full time employees who work solely with EDI and one with a fifty percent time commitment. The volunteer staff is a dedicated group of economic development professionals who work with the program as needed throughout the year and full time during Institute week. Many of them say that this in one way they can "give something back" to the profession. This staff includes the Dean, two Assistant Deans, five Class Directors and twenty Thesis Advisors/Discussion Leaders.

The Institute continues to utilize a Curriculum Committee which meets annually to review the evaluations of the program and individual instructors, and to introduce new topics into the agenda. This group has grown from the original five to six members to approximately twenty-four. Those people presently involved in curriculum strategy include the EDI Director and Associate Director and the Program Assistant from the University, the Dean, the Assistant Deans, the Class Directors, Chair of the Thesis Advisors, and representatives that are elected by the participants from each class in each site. The Curriculum Committee includes representatives of AEDC accredited Economic Development Courses, the AEDC staff, and the Educational and Certification Boards to provide appropriate linkages among the various education courses and between AEDC's education and certification programs.

GROWTH

In 1964 the Institute began full 3 session operations with sixty-eight participants; it has grown gradually to the largest enrollment of 614 participants in two locations in 1991. On September 10, 1993, an article in *The Wall Street Journal* on Executive Education rated "EDI the second most popular public-enrollment executive-education offering in the nation according to 1992 total enrollment figures." The graduating class of 1964 consisted of 17 graduates (all male). The largest Year III Class graduated in 1991 with 133 participants, 85 males, 48 females. Through 1994, the Institute has graduated 1,851 participants.

MAJOR CHANGES

☐ In 1980 the name was changed from the Industrial Development Institute to the Economic Development Institute in recognition of the continuing trend away from just "smokestack chasing" to a broader definition of economic development.

☐ Breaking up of 1/2 day topics allowed the introduction of more new subjects including computer applications, environmental issues and community consensus building. Also, with the introduction of elective classes, participants were given curriculum choices and were able to relate the curriculum more closely to their individual needs.

☐ The first Advanced Symposium was held in 1965 to allow IDI graduates the opportunity to continue their professional education. The number of classes gradually increased from one offering to four offerings. In 1989, the Advanced Symposia were integrated into the Year III curriculum and as many as 10 choices are now offered.

☐ The rapid rise in enrollment in the early 1980s led to unusually large class sizes in Years I and II. EDI responded by offering the core course two times and breaking up each year into "A" and "B" groups. In 1986, the Institute expanded to a second site. The Year I session was held in Cleveland, Ohio, for three years. In 1989, with the addition of Year II, it was moved to Indianapolis, Indiana, where the program has almost reached maximum capacity for the facilities there. The first group to attend the entire Economic Development Institute program at a location other than Norman, Oklahoma, graduated in Indianapolis in 1993.

☐ Conducting the Institute at two sites each year has allowed participants to "fast track" through the program. Conceivably, a participant can begin in Norman in August, attend Year II in Indianapolis in the Spring, and graduate in Norman the following August.

☐ At the present time, the Economic Development Institute staff is having preliminary discussions with the economic development community in California concerning the possibility of a third site for the Institute.

The Certified Economic Developer Program: A Quarter Century of Evolution from Practice to Profession

J. David Wansley, CED

The Certified Industrial Developer program, which finally became a reality in 1970, was initiated in 1967 when the AIDC Board of Directors designated a committee chaired by Past President Everett Tucker, Jr. to study the feasibility and make recommendations to institute the system. As originally envisioned, the C.I.D. program, as set forth, included a qualification procedure and examination designed to recognize the professional developer and to maintain a standard of excellence for the profession. The first 182 individuals certified were "grandfathered" based on a minimum of fifteen years experience in industrial development. The first written examination was held on May 9, 1971 and has been held every year since.

Since then, the profession and the program have undergone several changes, including its name. In 1981, the Council members voted to change its name to the American Economic Development Council. From then until 1993, the Certification Board allowed members to use either the C.I.D. or C.E.D. (Certified Economic Developer) designation. In 1994, the Certification Board officially adopted the CED designation as the only proper designation.

THE PROGRAM

Certification is designed to recognize the professional economic developer and to establish the standard of excellence for the profession. A professional economic developer, who is certified as having attained compliance with the professional competency standards adopted by the American Economic Development Coun-cil, demonstrates a commitment and interest in providing only the highest quality professional economic development services available. The Council's Certification Program, which is voluntary, provides more than an ordinary assurance of professional quality services; the certification designation "Certified Economic Developer®" (CED®) is recognized as the sign of achievement of excellence.

The mission of the Certification Program is to advance and help assure a high overall quality of professional services in the economic development field. The specific goals of the Certification Program are:

❏ To improve professional practice in the economic development field.

❏ To identify a body of knowledge and skills necessary to the practice of the economic development profession; and

❏ To recognize those individuals who have demonstrated a level of excellence in the practice of the economic development profession.

As of April, 1995, there were 623 active CEDs. The Certification Board believes that there are a significant number of economic development professionals who are qualified to sit for the exam. Efforts are being made to aggressively invite them to apply.

IMPROVEMENTS

A number of issues have been addressed by the Certification Board as it works to upgrade the status of the CED® designation:

❏ To ensure the administration of the Council's Certification Program is uni-form and equitable, the Certification Board wrote a Procedural Guide for the information and guidance of the participants.

❏ In 1994, a psychometrician was hired to develop new short-answer questions and to assist in validating the existing questions. So far 26 new questions have been added to the "pool", with another 32 under evaluation.

❏ Professional Competency Standards, similar to those developed for other professions (law, accounting, engineering), including education, experience, performance and other criteria, have been developed and are being reviewed annually.

❏ The Board has approved Standards of Professional Conduct for CEDs, to which all CEDs are required to adhere.

❏ Policies have been approved and implemented concerning accommodations for disabled persons who want to take the exam.

❏ The Certification Board installed a new Code of Conduct of the members of the Certification Board. This Code is designed to establish high ethical standards of professional and personal conduct and developed penalties for a breach.

❏ The Board convinced the Council to sponsor an annual educational meeting exclusively for CEDs, called the CED Summit.

❏ The increase in the number of candidates taking the exam has required that the Certification Board be expanded, because the Board not only sets policy for CEDs but serves as examiners at all exams.

The other half of the Certification Board's job is to review the maintenance of certification by CEDs. What professional achievements should qualify a CED® to keep his/her certification?

Currently, there are a number of professional continuing education programs and activities which contribute to the profession which are required. Additional study is taking place to refine these criteria.

FUTURE ISSUES

The Certification Board is also busy studying issues which will impact the future of the Certified Economic Developer Program. Several of these issues will be affected by the results of the on-going study by the CED/EDI Task Force. A few of these issues are:

❑ The Board is working to update exactly what measurable criteria should be met in order for a candidate to be eligible to sit for the CED exam. The purpose is to help potential candidates "pre qualify" themselves before they spend money and time taking an exam for which they may not be prepared.

❑ The Board is working to identify the core body of knowledge, which must be obtained by an individual in order to function professionally. Included in this study is determining the primary specialty areas in which one might practice.

❑ Improvements are being implemented in the training of graders and grading procedures to ensure consistency of grading of all components of the exam.

❑ The Board is working to enhance the professional standing of the CED® designation among peers, employers and clients.

❑ As more economic development professionals join the ranks of the American Economic Development Council from Canada, Mexico and other countries, should the criteria and methodology of exams and certification maintenance change?

The Certification Board invites the constructive comments and ideas of practitioners on these and other issues facing the future of the economic development profession.

Passing The CED Examination

Edward M. Krauss, CED

INTRODUCTION

In April, 1995, I had the challenge of taking and passing the CED examination on my first try, something that I have since learned is done less than twenty percent of the time; I was one of two who succeeded out of fifteen, which is only thirteen percent.

In these notes I will share with you my study techniques, which I hope will prove helpful to you in preparing for the examination. Since some readers may be re-taking one of the three parts, I want to discuss not only the total study and testing process but also offer hints regarding each of the three sections.

SOME INITIAL SUGGESTIONS

First and foremost, take the examination seriously. Be a little scared, somewhat intimidated. Do not assume that just because you work daily in the world of economic development that you can pass a test on its finer points or write essays on its several facets.

An example: we all know what a car is and how to drive one. But if you wrote an essay test on driving and left out, "Put the key in the ignition lock and turn the key," you would lose points; and you might gain some points by briefly describing what an ignition lock is and does. A few more omissions, such as saying to step on the gas pedal but neglecting to say which pedal that is, or to turn on the lights [which lights?] at sundown without saying how to turn them on, and you, a driver for many years, might flunk that essay exam.

Another example: we ride on radial tires, and we know what those are. But I am sure a question could be created on a multiple choice test, asking what the word "radial" means, and that many of us [this author included] would flunk.

STUDY PROCEDURE

OK, how to start. First, begin as soon as you get the materials from AEDC. I studied for at least eight weeks, some time every weekend and occasional hours during the week. Order the recommended books right away.

As I read, I forced myself to go slowly, re-read certain portions, and I highlighted or noted certain items and sections. Short phrases or key words [more on which later] were highlighted, longer sections had brackets or exclamation points written in the margin. Where appropriate, I wrote "list" [lists of steps or items] and "def" [definition] next to the section.

What I did next involved a word processor, but it could be done by hand. I went back over the study materials and copied all the underlined and noted sections except for the longer lists, which I marked with those "yellow stickies" found in every office.

A word of advice at this point. It would be easy for those of us with skilled secretaries to ask that all noted sections be copied for you. Don't do it! Copy the information yourself. This is slow and time consuming and occasionally aggravating, especially if you type as poorly as I do. But reading the words again, and performing the physical act of recording them, will drill them into your brain most wonderfully. Using a fourteen font for these aging eyes, I ended up with about fifty-five pages for my study guide. I then read through this guide and read the tagged lists many times.

I urge you to identify your areas of weakness. None of us is an expert in everything. I could talk knowledgeably about labor supply and vocational education and wage rates and industrial training for hours, but would not last long in a discussion of sophisticated banking and financing procedures. Recognizing that, I obtained additional materials which addressed Community Development Corporations, let-

ters of credit, linked or pooled bond financing, 504 and 7[A] procedures, and related information. Do the same for yourself. Do not confuse familiarity with a subject with knowledge of it. If, as you read the materials provided by AEDC, you recognize that you have been using these terms without truly grasping the concepts, study those sections extra hard. In addition, seek out supporting materials from sources such as the US Department of Commerce, your state's economic development office, your local Community Development Corporation, your chamber of commerce, and the library and bookstore. Finally, find an expert in the field where you are weak—perhaps someone you have worked with on projects—and conduct an hour or so interview, asking questions and taking notes. The information is readily available, but you must first identify within yourself the need for that information.

The test was on a Saturday. I took vacation days Wednesday and Thursday and read my study guide and the lists and skimmed through the books. I also did some special things to prepare for each of the three parts. I will take them in reverse order of how they are actually given, and also [as indicated by pass/fail scores] in level of difficulty.

ORAL

The CEDs quizzing you do not expect you to be an expert on everything that could come your way in the course of your work, but do expect that you have a strong working knowledge of most of it. I am not giving anything away, since the list of items is published in the study guide, but you should be able to talk about:

❑ Development in your area: the pace, the price of land, outstanding projects, special assets to promote or liabilities to overcome.

❑ How your community markets itself to the world: techniques, costs.

❑ Economic development organization, structure and management.

❑ Sources and types of financial assistance available in your area.

❑ Permits: what is required for new or expanding facilities, which agencies administer, how long does it take, how do you [help] make it happen.

❑ Detailed discussion of labor, training,

wage rates, unions, benefits, and related employment issues.

❑ Why you want to become a Certified Economic Developer.

If there is something that you never do that is always handled by another agency, then know how to refer people to that agency, what the hand-holding or follow-up procedure is, how long the process takes, what you can do in the meanwhile to help the process, etc.

MULTIPLE CHOICE

Two items require emphasis. The first is to make sure you read the questions carefully. They are not tricky but neither are they obvious. Make very sure you understand what is being asked and that the answer you choose is complete....partially true may mean false....and that it says what you think it does. Do not allow yourself to skim.

The second item is that, when studying, note and record all unusual words, phrases, and organization structures. Remember the "radial" example? Let me use a real term, which may or may not be on the test you take. The term is "non-basic." These are common English words in a unusual formation, and for that reason should jump off the page at you yelling, "They sure will ask about me!" Note the note-worthy.

ESSAY

After it was announced that I had passed, many people were kind enough to congratulate me, and a gentleman from Louisiana bought me a drink. In the course of these conversations I asked people who had failed the essays how they had prepared, and all responded with some version of "I studied the material." What follows is what I did differently, and what should make an enormous difference from just reading.

Few of us have held a writing instrument and written for two straight hours for years and years. When you take the test you will use either pencils or pens. [I strongly recommend pencils over pens, along with one of those small in-a-case sharpeners and a quality eraser.] There is a certain pace to this activity and only so much you can write in that time. OK, now my secret.

I identified areas that I was concerned with and studied them hard during the last week. I then wrote out a question for myself and left it there, along with paper and pencils and sharpener and eraser when I went to bed. Then on Wednesday, Thursday, and Friday morning [I had a noon Friday flight] I set the alarm for about 6:00, got up and did all the usual morning things including eating breakfast and getting dressed, and about 7:30 I sat down and answered the question, writing for at least half an hour each time. After that I graded the test and reviewed the material as indicated.

The point was to achieve a muscle-memory pattern that said to my body that I would get up and get ready and then sit down and write with a pencil about economic development early in the morning. Thus, when the real thing happened Saturday shortly before 8:00, it was the fourth day in a row for that activity.

Be aware of how much you can write in thirty minutes, and have your watch off your wrist and sitting right next to your bluebook staring at you. I wrote lots on the first question, somewhat less on the second, and barely made it on the third. The two hours flew by. Some people told me that they ran out of time on the third, and

that is easy to do. Know your pace, and watch the clock.

Be aware that you will be thinking and working hard writing essays for two hours, then after a brief break take the short answer exam. You might be well served to keep your energy up by having available an apple or some cheese to eat during the break.

Finally, memorize a mnemonic or two, a list or two. Let's say you want to remember [this is not from the material, just an example] three concepts of innovation: generation of ideas, application of concepts, production of product. The first three letters gives you GAP, and you might jot that inside the cover of your bluebook as soon as you get it. I had a mnemonic of three short words that proved very helpful. Concerning lists, there is one from the materials that I memorized because I thought it would keep me from missing something if there was a question concerning site development. I expect to be able to do this list if I live to be a hundred....product, site, building, labor, freight in, freight out, scrap, solid waste, gas, electricity, water, sewer, noise pollution, special services.

The essay portion is the most difficult, with by far the highest fail rate. Do not depend on the fact that you have plowed the fields for years or that you have read the books. Practice writing, preferably several times, and certainly in the days before the test. Grade yourself, and be a tough grader. Then study what you need to improve upon.

CONCLUDING COMMENTS

Achieving this goal of earning the CED designation is a wonderful feeling. You will be proud of your investment when you receive your CED. Believe in yourself, work very hard, and be a little scared.

Growing Your Organization Through the Accredited Economic Development Organization (AEDO) Designation Process

Mark S. Davis, Esq.
Elizabeth A. Neu, CED

INTRODUCTION

How can you further the credibility of your economic development organization? Consider going through the Accredited Economic Development Organization (AEDO) review process. This new program, recently adopted by The American Economic Development Council (AEDC), certifies that a specific organization has demonstrated ability to effectively run and manage economic development activities for that community.

THE PROCESS

The process of becoming designated as an Accredited Economic Development Organization (AEDO) consists of two parts: 1) A review of relevant documents; and 2) An on-site peer review.

Documents

A list of necessary documents is sent to the applicant, who in turn submits them to the AEDC office (Table 1). AEDC staff reviews the documentation and contacts an AEDO team leader to arrange for the on-site review. The team leader also reviews the documentation. If any material is missing, the AEDC office contacts the applicant and asks for an explanation as to why it is missing or to provide some other

similar material in is place. For example, if a city-managed Department of Economic Development Program contracts with another organization to provide marketing, the relationship to this entity must be established and explained. Once the documentation review is completed, the on-site visit is scheduled.

On-Site Review

The criteria used for the on-site review is available to the applicant prior to the visit so they know what to expect. This allows the applicant to do a "self-evaluation" and determine whether or not they may even want to go forward at this point. The criteria examined are listed in Table 2.

Audit - Accreditation

The audit process is virtually the same, except it is only a review, to offer suggestions on possible improvements. The community makes the choice, with consultation from the AEDC office, as to whether or not they are ready for accreditation or would prefer an audit review.

PEER REVIEW CONSULTANTS

The AEDO Committee has trained several professional economic developers to act as "peer review consultants." This allows the organization seeking the designation to be reviewed by those of us who practice this profession on a daily basis. A team leader is selected and two others form the "AEDO Review Team." At least one member selected to serve on the team

TABLE 1
Documentation Review

- articles of incorporation and bylaws
- mission and goals statement
- last annual report
- recent organization newsletters
- recent press releases
- minutes of last four Board of Directors meetings
- roster and position descriptions of officers
- staff policy and procedures manual
- organizational chart and job descriptions of employees
- marketing plan
- marketing materials used within last year
- annual budget
- last audited financial statement, compilation, review or equivalent financial disclosure
- IRS Letter of Exemption
- most recent IRS Form 990
- commitment of support to CEO and other evidence of multi-year

will work for a similar agency. For example, if it is a Chamber of Commerce seeking accreditation, at least one member will be from a Chamber or have had recent Chamber staff level experience. Likewise, if the applicant is a not-for-profit local economic development organization, at least one member of the team will have that experience.

ON-SITE REVIEW

The two-day on-site review is scheduled to meet the needs of the community and the review team members. The team members are volunteering their time and welcome the opportunity to visit another community in a friendly and non-threatening manner. They are here to provide a service, not to cause problems for the organization's CEO. However, it is recommended that the host organization treat the review team members like they would treat a prospect coming to their city. Make hotel reservations in advance, show them the best the community has to offer, and make the appointments in advance with community leaders.

Editor's Note
This article and the two that follow it are included to present different perspectives from people involved in the start-up of the AEDO program.

TABLE 2
On-Site Visit Criteria

Internal Environment
  Office Resources
    Offices
      appropriate offices for e.d.
        organization
      functional, well-kept,
        accessible
      privacy for conferences
    Computer
      adequate hardware
      adequate software
      LAN
    Phone/Fax
      adequate phone service
      fax capability
      modem, voice mail
  CEO
    Professional Experience
    Professional Credentials
      CED
      other
    Commitment and Range of
    Compensation
      contract/letter of agreement
      comparability of salary/
        fringes
    Continuing Professional
    Development
      AEDC membership
      Regional/state e.d. organiza-
        tion membership
      Resources to attend
        seminars, courses
      EDC graduate
      EDI graduate
  Management and Support Staff
    Professional Experience
    Professional Credentials
      CED
      other
    Compensation
      comparability of salary/
        fringes
      personnel policies
    Division of Duties and
    Responsibilities
      current job descriptions
      clear reporting relationships
    Continuing Professional
    Development
      AEDC membership
      regional/state e.d. organiza-
        tion membership
      resources to attend semi-
        nars, courses
      EDC graduates
      EDI graduates
  Turnover History

Leadership
  Volunteers
    Orientation
      formal session
      orientation materials
      word-of-mouth
    Regular Meetings
      agenda and minutes
      ongoing schedule
    Structure of Volunteer
    Leadership
      continuity
      clear delegation of duties
      appointed/elected board
      appointed/elected officers
      term limits
      leadership development
      community representation
        (women, minorities, etc.)
  Direction and Vision
    Goal Setting Process
      existence of strategic plan
      date of last update
      how implemented
      involvement of leadership/
        volunteers in process
      evaluation of outcomes
    Budget Process
      one year or multi-year
      reflects strategic plan/
        goals and objectives
      reflects leadership input
      presentation of budget
    Commitment to Strategic Plan
      year-to-year continuity
      periodic updates
      evaluation of results/method
        of measurement
    Linkage Between Strategic
    Plan and Program of Work
      periodic review
      review vis-a-vis budget
      comparison with staff
        distribution and priorities
External Environment
  Liaison With Public Officials
    Method of Communications
      With Public Officials
    Representation by Public
      Officials on Board of
      Directors
    Utilization of Public Officials
      in Prospect Tours, etc.
  Marketing
    Marketing Plan Timely
    Target Audiences Selected
    Adequate Resources
      Committed

    Marketing Goals Tied Into
      Overall Strategic Plan
  Relations with Community
  Opinion Leaders
    Means of Communication
    Liaison/Access When
      Appropriate
    Participation in Decision-
      Making
  Prospect Handling
    Identification of Prospects
    Qualification of Prospects
    Identification of Customer
      Communities
    Confidentiality Issues
    Follow Up Procedures
    Closing Process
Financial Resources
  Budget
    LInkage with Strategic Plan
    Involves Volunteer Leaders
    Reevaluated As Fiscal year
      Progresses
    Includes Appropriate Fiscal
      Controls
  Sources of Incomes
    Keep Pace With Growth of
      Organization
    Numbers and Type of Sources
    Annual or Other Commitment
    Fund Raising Program
Special Issues

Interviews

The AEDC office provides a recommended list of "community stakeholders" who will be interviewed during the on-site visit. The key leader would be the chairman of the board of directors, for a not-for-profit corporation, or the mayor in the case of a city managed organization. It is also recommended that other economic development "players" be included, such as utility providers, planning directors, Chamber of Commerce executive, SBDC directors and bankers. A minimum of six interviews should be scheduled for the team visit. These visits can be scheduled concurrently so that one team member can be interviewing the banker while another visits with someone else. Who on the team makes the interview is decided after the team arrives. The three team members arrange a conference call prior to the visit to go over the visit agenda; however, a team "overview meeting" should be scheduled upon the arrival of all team members to go over the final agenda. The final agenda is discussed with the CEO of the organization being reviewed, along with his/her perspective of key issues in the community and/or organization. This gives the CEO an opportunity to highlight areas of concern (whether they are board, community-wide or personnel related issues) in a confidential manner and alerts the team members of things to look for more carefully.

It is important to be flexible in scheduling the stakeholders meetings because we all know that unexpected situations can arise causing someone to be unavailable in your community. If arranged, a few extra interviews can sometimes be conducted jointly. It is also highly recommended that a dinner is scheduled with the Board Chairman (or highest elected official) so that all team members have an opportunity to meet him/her in a casual atmosphere. At least one team member interviews the other economic development office personnel. The professionalism of the staff, office environment and meeting space are all factors included in the evaluation.

Processing The Information

Once a tour of the community and all interviews are completed, the team members meet to draft the evaluation. Prior to the team members meeting privately, a "debriefing" is held with the CEO to alert him/her of any unusual criticisms or compliments made during the interviews. A decision is made "on-site" before the team members depart as to whether or not the organization is to be recommended to become accredited. The review team results are collected by the team leader and sent to the AEDC office. The review team's decision is a recommendation to the AEDO Board. The recommendation is reviewed and voted on at the next scheduled AEDO Board meeting and then sent to the AEDC Board of Directors, where the accreditation vote is made at a formal board meeting.

Awarding The Designation

The CEO and/or the organization's Board Chairman are presented with an engraved plaque designating the organization as an Accredited Economic Development Organization. This is given at either the AEDC Annual Conference or it can be arranged to be delivered at a community event if the organization so de-

sires. AEDC is also available to assist with any media announcements.

CREATING THE AEDO PROGRAM

Now you know the criteria and the process, but how did the creation of the AEDO Program come about? How do you start a new project or program in the American Economic Development Council? Talk it up and write it down. We hope the somewhat humorous (but accurate) description below encourages you to try something new and to get "accredited" or "audited"!

Desires

What happens if your local economic development program does not obtain accreditation after applying for it? If economic development is to become a profession, do we need to establish professional standards for organizations, as well as individuals? What are the appeal procedures for organizations? Frankly, the Board of Directors of the American Economic Development Council (AEDC) asked these kinds of realistic questions before adopting the Accredited Economic Development Organization (AEDO) program in 1994.

The Board instructed the team of volunteers and AEDC staff to design a program that was positive and helped economic development organizations grow, while recognizing our responsibility to not cause harm to either community efforts or the professional staff. Individual AEDC members and several elected AEDC Officers and Board members had discussed the need for some sort of professional accrediting program for several years prior to its adoption in 1994 by the Board of Directors. The idea had been talked up, but not written down.

Fleshing-out The Details

It takes a leader to make things happen, and Michael Olivier, a leader in both AEDC and SIDC, stepped up to this unmet challenge. At the first ever CED Summit in December 1993, Olivier sat down with AEDC board member Mark Davis and they wrote the first draft of what became the AEDO program. (Actually, Olivier got mad about it not getting done and dragged Davis along to lunch because he had expressed interest in helping out and, as all good attorneys do, had a legal pad of

paper handy!) Ever alert and gracefully helpful AEDC President, Jim Ahr, soon got this project organized (i.e., back on track). Ahr arranged a series of conference calls with a small committee that was quickly established under Olivier's leadership to nurture the program along.

Miracles do happen, because after the first draft was turned over to Ahr, a structured second draft appeared that had enough detail to spark several vigorous discussions. For example, who would pay for and how much would these services cost? If AEDC began an accreditation or audit process, would we talk with the media in the local community if asked to do so? Were we more interested in serving state level economic development organizations and utilities or local economic development organizations? Would an experienced local economic developer be required on each site visit, not just a state level official or consultant? Could a consultant participate on a site visit and subsequently try to sell services to the community? Must all site team members be CED's? The answers are: keep it low cost for the organizations, avoid the media, serve *local* organizations, an experienced *local* person is required, consultants cannot try to sell services to the community for at least one year, and we encourage but do not require all team members to be a CED.

Initial Efforts

After vigorous debate and discussion, a draft report was made to the AEDC Board of Directors in the Spring of 1994, and the first two "test run" organizations were visited. At the October 1994 AEDC Board meeting, a slightly modified program was unanimously adopted. The Hamilton County, Indiana Alliance was granted accredited status and the Parkersburg/Wood County (West Virginia) Development Corporation was recognized for having completed the audit process. Following the official adoption of the program by AEDC, Birmingham, Alabama also applied and received accredited status as the first city-managed organization to go through the AEDO process.

SUMMARY

What are the advantages of becoming an Accredited Economic Development Organization? It can play a variety of roles. First and foremost, we want to assist economic development organizations with independent authoritative feedback on their operation, structure and procedures. Many times the CEO of an organization may need "validation" to prove to his board that he/she is needed. Also, it can heighten awareness as to the contribution made by the economic development organization in its community. In addition, besides benefitting the individual organizations receiving the accreditation, we are looking to recognize excellence in local economic development organizations on an "industry-wide" basis.

Evaluating the Next Position: Successful Career Advancement In Economic Development

Timothy L. Martin, CED, CCE

You are working in economic development and doing a great job. Someone in another city or organization has heard of your excellent work and has asked you to consider becoming a candidate for an open position. Or, you have learned of a vacancy which interests you. Either way, you would like to know more about the position and the opportunity. What information should you ask for to help you analyze the situation and make a decision?

This article will discuss several items common to economic development organizations, whose careful study can be quite revealing. Likewise, the absence of these documents tells a great deal, as can the reluctance or refusal to provide them.

PRE-INTERVIEW

The Position

First of all, let's discuss pre-interview materials one should consider. Of course, the first item you would request is information about the position (Table 1). The position description should tell you the title, minimal qualifications and responsibilities of the position. Be very careful if a job description is not available.

Do not be shy about asking for information on the selection committee. Names, titles, relationships to the organization, special interests, and timing can all be important facts to include in your deliberations.

If an employment contract will be offered, you may want to review a draft copy of it. These details will help you shape your answers as you respond to questions from the community about your skills, background experiences, and interests.

The Organization

A second area of interest to you will be the organization itself (Table 2). The U.S. Chamber of Commerce and the American Economic Development Council conduct effective and comprehensive accreditation review programs for local chambers of commerce or economic development organizations. Accreditation provides an overview of the organization and also demonstrates a willingness on the part of the organization to improve and develop itself via a formal evaluation process. If the organization you are looking at has gone through this process, they will have ready answers and documentation for most of your issues of concern. In fact, just ask for a copy of their most recent evaluation report.

Another revealing document is the Program of Work or similar document addressing the organization's short term goals. As such programs typically provide only a one year picture, you may want to view the past three to five years to have a true sense of progression. Past annual reports should be able to determine whether or not progress is being made in addressing specific goals and community needs. Long range or strategic plans demonstrate a willingness and ability to be involved in the planning process and indicate a conscious attempt to identify the anticipated future course of the organization.

Budgets, both current and historical, can clue you in on past revenue sources and amounts as well as past expenditures. They should also point out financial trends that may impact the future success of the organization. I believe it is good advice to always look at audited financial statements. Request at least a Balance Sheet and a Statement of Income and Expenses, though cash flow projections can also be very valuable. Financial statements give you a snapshot of the financial condition of the organization and a series of financial statements gives you a moving picture. They will also point out assets, liabilities or obligations, and membership equity. Note if the statements are audited according to generally accepted accounting procedures. This is important not only because it is more reliable, but, because it demonstrates that the organization takes its fiduciary responsibilities seriously.

Manuals

A Policy Manual highlights the positions the organization has taken on a variety of issues down through the years or at least the recent past. Often the past is prologue to the future. Here again, whether or not they have one, you'll know something about the seriousness of the commitment of the individuals involved in the organization. Of course, every situation is different and there may be mitigating circumstances.

A Procedures Manual and an Administrative or Personnel Manual can be extremely valuable to you as these two documents will state standard operating procedures and considerations for that organization and will cover such items as vacations, sick leave, holidays, and other employment benefits and practices. Your questions concerning such items as the formal organizational structure, eligibility of members, selection of directors, election and term of officers, limitation of methods and duties and roles of committees will be answered in the constitution and bylaws. Remember to ask for them. Minutes of past board meetings can often be quite informa-

---

TABLE 1
Information about the Position

1. Position description
   a. Title
   b. Responsibilities
   c. Authority
   d. Accountabilities - chain of command
   e. Minimum/preferred qualifications/requirements to fill job
   f. Date when last reviewed
2. Composition of the selection committee
3. Salary range
4. Fringe benefit package
5. Method and timing of selection
6. Willingness to sign an employment contract
7. Other decision makers/negotiators

tive and give clues to both content and process; what the organization gets accomplished, who does it, and how it gets done. Information on the chain of command and the delegation of the work load is addressed in the Organizational Chart.

Staff

Information on staff -- names, titles, responsibilities, qualifications, interests, salaries, etc. is also important. This may not be an item you would solicit upon the first contact, but keep it in the back of your mind that it may be crucial to know about those with whom you will have to work.

Membership

Membership lists from the past three years and a membership investment schedule provide a feel for retention and the amount of money coming in from membership. This information can and should be cross referenced back to the financial statements and budgets.

Other Organizations

Some organizations, in addition to their basic economic development functions, manage, administer, or staff other organizations. Get a list of these. This will point out potential additional responsibilities as well as potential conflict of splinter groups. Go in with your eyes open.

I also think it is wise to check on other business organizations which may be located in that community. Those organizations may be allies or competitors to the organization you are reviewing. It would be good to know about that up front before you make your move. It might be wise to ask about the potential for mergers.

Community Information

General community information can be very valuable (Table 3). Ask for current economic profile data (ACCRA Cost of Living Information, if available), and a copy of the most recent community magazine. You might also be able to borrow an AV presentation of the community. If there is time, subscribe to the local newspaper. Otherwise, pick up a couple Sunday issues. Remember, you and your family will have to (get to) live in this new city and this is the place you are going to "sell".

Other Information

In addition to pre-interview materials, obtain pre-interview information which probably is not in written form (Table 4). For example, what happened to past CEO's? Who were they? Why did they leave? Where are they now? This information may have a

---

TABLE 2
Information about the Organization

1. Overall
   a. Latest U.S. Chamber of Commerce Accreditation report
   b. Latest AEDC Accreditation report
2. Activities
   a. Programs of work
   b. Annual reports
   c. Long range or strategic plans
   d. Marketing plans
   e. Property development plans
   f. Fund raising requirements
   g. Examples of printed promotional material, newsletters, brochures, catalogs, directories, pamphlets, etc.
3. Financial
   a. Audit reports
   b. Membership investment schedule
   c. Budgets
   d. Financial statements - Balance Sheets, P&L's, Cash flow projections
   e. Financial operating protocols
4. Policy, procedures, organization
   a. Constitution and bylaws
   b. Articles of incorporation
   c. IRS application for exemption, determination letter, current 990, 990T, 1099, etc.
   d. Organizational chart
   e. Policy manual
   f. Procedures manual
   g. Minutes of past Board meetings
   h. List of officers and directors and their professions
   I. List of subsidiary organizations
5. Personnel
   a. Personnel manual
   b. Job descriptions
   c. Resumes of staff
   d. Salary administration plan
6. Membership
   a. Membership directory
   b. Investment schedule
   c. Trends
7. Associated organizations
   a. List of other local business organizations
   b. Contracts for services

TABLE 3
Information about the Community

1. Current economic and demographic profiles
2. ACCRA Cost of Living information
3. Recent community magazine
4. Local newspaper; subscribe or Sunday issues
5. Healthcare, schools, housing, shopping, recreation, cultural, church, etc.
6. Information on climate
7. AV presentation
8. Maps
9. List of major employers
10. List of headquartered firms
11. Other existing economic development information, such as site sheets, spec buildings, puff pieces
12. Spouse employment

direct bearing on whether or not you would be interested in a job with this organization. You may want to contact previous CEO's directly and ask them questions about the organization or the community.

THE INTERVIEW

So, you have gathered your pre-interview materials and information and are still interested in the position and the selection committee has granted you an interview. I believe answers to some key questions will guide you further in making a wise decision regarding a move (Table 5). Remember, an interview is two-sided. As you are being interviewed, interview. Find out expectations now, not after you have been hired and cannot perform the job. Express concerns now, not after disrupting your family and career by moving.

It is appropriate to take questions with you to the interview. Do not be afraid to ask quality, probing questions prompted by your review of documentation and research. They show you cared enough to do some prior homework, thinking, and planning. Ask questions regarding philosophy, thrust, programming of organization, and "vision for future".

The process continues and you have been contacted for further interviewing. Do not accept a second or further interview if you cannot/will not accept the position if offered. Be professional enough to not waste either your or the organization's time. See Table 6 for questions for use in later interviewing.

CONCLUDING COMMENTS

There are many other factors to consider, for each situation is unique. Do not be afraid to ask about or for what you think is important. As a rule, the salary and benefits should be twenty or thirty percent more than your current level to make a major move profitable. Expect to experience an emotional let down whether you accept the job or not. You will expend a tremendous amount of psychic energy through this process and cannot help but have second thoughts about your decision.

We've explored in detail what you should look and ask for from an organization. Be prepared to provide to the selection committee all of the above items from your current organization. They want to find out about you every bit as much as you want to find out about them. As it has been said, the best marriages are those made when both parties go into the partnership with their eyes and their hearts open!

TABLE 4
Pre-Interview Information (probably not in written form)

1. Other organizations -- potential turf rivalries
2. Potential mergers
3. List of and what happened to past CEO's?
4. Staff morale
5. How are goals set and by whom?
6. Community's potential
7. Leadership capability and potential?
8. Organizational power structure?
9. Linkages to political structure?
10. Community's perception of organization? (especially the newspaper's)
11. Issues facing the community, i.e.,
    a. No growth city council
    b. School board problems
    c. Waste management/ landfill problems
    d. Single industry control
    e. Under-integration of minority population
    f. Labor unions
    g. Major infrastructure needs

TABLE 5
Questions for Initial Interview

1. What is the financial status of the organization?
2. Do you have sufficient funds to do everything you need to do?
3. Can you raise more money?
4. How? Who?
5. What are the strengths of the organization?
6. What are the weaknesses of the organization?
7. What have been the most significant results over the last 3 years?
8. How are the existing industry relations?
9. Are strong community leaders involved in the program?
10. How's the political climate? Cities/County?
11. What's the 5 year strategic plan?
12. What's the marketing plan?
13. How is targeting done?
14. Is organization ready, willing, and able to expand/accelerate programming?
15. Are the current facilities, equipment, and staff adequate?
16. What's the relationship of the board to the staff?
17. Are there opportunities for personal and professional growth and training?
18. Is there a formal performance evaluation program?

TABLE 6
Questions for Later Interviews

1. Is there an infrastructure improvement program?
2. How's the school, healthcare, housing, spouse employment situation?
3. What's the community's potential?
4. What/How can the organization work to meet those expectations?
5. What is the organization's role in the community?
6. Personal issues:
    a. Moving expenses
    b. House hunting assistance
    c. House selling assistance
    d. Mortgage assistance
    e. Closing costs
    f. Bridge loans
    g. Incidental expenses
    h. Family travel expenses
    i. Temporary living quarters
    j. Spouse job assistance
7. Any other unanswered questions or concerns

There's a "Magic" In Tupelo-Lee County, Northeast Mississippi

Harry A. Martin

INTRODUCTION

My first introduction to Tupelo came in 1936 when it was reported that the worst and most destructive tornado in the history of our nation had virtually wiped out Tupelo, a Mississippi city 165 miles north of where I grew up on a farm in East Central Mississippi. It was reported that several hundred people had been killed. This event and the name of the town stuck in my mind because of my background in growing up in rural Mississippi. At the time the tornado struck Tupelo, I was a boy of ten. I had heard my father and his friends relate scary stories of smaller but very destructive tornados they had witnessed in the Clarke County area. Around the campfire, the adults would tell stories and talk about tornados where a 2 x 4 timber was driven through an oak tree and where the storm was so strong it drew all the water out of the open wells or cisterns used commonly for drinking water. The name Tupelo was indelibly placed in my mind.

The next introduction I had to Tupelo came when I was a junior at Mississippi State University. Dean E. B. Colmer, whom I worked for as a student, asked if I would like to spend six weeks in Tupelo in the summer of 1947 to study a new program that was being initiated called the Rural Community Development Council (RCDC) program. The program was supposed to expand the economy in this rural Northeast Mississippi town. I accepted the Dean's offer and came to Tupelo in June of 1947 to begin my study of the new program.

Having a genuine interest in economics and population and demographics, I became acquainted with statistics that were not impressive at all. The per capita income was lower than the State's average. The literacy level was lower than the State's average. Mississippi had the lowest level of per capita income and literacy of the nation at that time and holds to that position today. The economy was definitely based on agriculture with cash income received primarily from dairying and cotton. The farms were small and the farmers numbered 5,200 in Lee County, where Tupelo is the county seat.

There was no resemblance of "magic" in this area in the late forties. It was primarily farm worker drudgery where entire members of the family worked seven days per week to make a living. There were less than 2,000 people employed in manufacturing. Most of the employees were female and worked in "cut and sew" apparel plants for near minimum hourly wages. The first predominately male-employing industry was opening and extreme competition was evident for the available jobs. The facts showed that the area was poor and obtaining a good education was not the highest priority in town. During the 1930's and early 1940's, Tupelo was the center of the poorest part of the poorest state in the country.

I finished my report in August and returned to Mississippi State University in September to complete work on my degree with graduation in May of 1948. In September of that year I received a call asking if I would like to return to Tupelo to work for the Cooperative Extension Service which embraced the new rural community development movement.

From October 1, 1948 to 1956, I learned the process of economic development and in 1956 was asked to assume the Executive position at the Community Development Foundation (CDF), a non-profit corporation that consolidated and focused economic and community development efforts. The past 46 years have been extremely enriching and rewarding for me and my family. I have experienced the dynamics that the Tupelo leaders' "magic" exemplified. This is what happened.

RESULTS

CDF's impressive statistics on economic and community growth are not illusions or "magic"; they are for real (Figure 1). Over the past 11 years, the CDF has helped create more than 13.5 million square feet of new manufacturing floor space, and 11,572 new jobs (Figure 2). In 1993, retail sales in Tupelo/Lee County, Mississippi reached an all-time high of $1.1 billion, and represented a 50% increase since 1986 (Figure 3)(. There are more than 92,000 manufacturing jobs within the retail trade area of Tupelo (Figure 4). The total employment for the Tupelo trade area is 341,767 (Figure 5). For each of the past five years, Lee County has averaged 30 acres of under-roof expansion and annual capital investments have averaged $100 million (Figure 2).

This is the sum of accomplishments some call "magic," which many seek, and which Tupelo has found. Two hundred and two industries, with forty-two of them Fortune 500 or large international companies, are in Lee County with 635 industries in the trade area. It is unheard of that this large number of plants could be located in a remote area such as Tupelo.

A recent chapter in the story is related in milestones achieved during the most recent year, which is yet another in the continuing string of "Most Successful," with companies such as Action Industries, Norbord Industries, Tecumseh Products, North Mississippi Medical Center and others becoming larger employers of more advanced professional and technology based positions.

It's a "magic" that is found in the vitality of the region, which for more than four decades has been heralded as an international model for community development, a record recently noted by *The U.S. News and World Report*, *The Wall Street Journal*, National Public Radio, John Naisbitt's *Trend Letter* dealing with the global net-

Editor's Note

The Wall Street Journal on March 3, 1994 carried on its front page a story entitled "Tupelo, Miss., Concocts An Effective Recipe For Economic Health." Since it is not every day that economic development receives this kind of exposure, the editor decided to follow up on the newspaper report and determined that what was said was accurate. The program at Tupelo truly was a success story. This article, which describes this widely recognized program, was prepared at the request of the editor.

work and other prestigious media.

The record in its totality is unbelievable to most, amazing to others, but nevertheless, the record stands.

Other visible results are the happy faces of thousands of families who live, work and enjoy a high quality of life -- where they pursue realistic dreams which they have been taught to expect as part of their birthright.

When community leaders from around the world come to Tupelo-Lee County to see firsthand what a highly respected national corporate recruiter called the "Best Small City in the South," they're hoping to capture a portion of our economic "magic" to take back to their own hometown. Frequently when they depart, like the Queen of Sheba describing King Solomon's splendor of old, they say "the half has not been told."

CURRENT EFFORTS

Perspective

Our hearty forefathers taught us more than campfire stories, including that there is merit in hard work and honor in doing a job well. We owe much to goal-oriented visionaries who have blazed the trail before us, but simply talking today about yesterday's accomplishments will not guarantee tomorrow's success.

Tupelo-Lee County has moved into the pole position in the race to get and hold companies which are on the cutting edge of technology. The Community Development Foundation (CDF), twice chosen to be included in the top ten economic development organizations in the U.S., has provided the vital ingredients that have been necessary for success and progression in the quality of economic growth.

The most critical issue since globalization that began here in the late 1970's has been keeping the human capital capacity in line with the technology being used in the economic activity in the community.

Human Resource Development

The task of educating and training a world class work force that can think for itself and outperform the rest of the world is formidable. The stakes have never been higher nor the potential rewards greater, because we know that if Northeast Mississippi fails to develop a work force that can compete successfully in the global economy, it will be unable to provide a standard of living to which the citizens have become accustomed. Family income will decline. Accomplishments of the region will degenerate. On the other hand, if the region responds effectively to this challenge, it can reasonably expect continuing growth and enjoy higher than average per capita income. This is a legacy which began in the 1940's. It is a birthright of future generations of Northeast Mississippians. It is the force which produces "magic." Our people began this journey well behind the State and Nation in literacy. To "play catch up" we must make a much greater effort than others.

Dr. Mike Walters, Superintendent of the Tupelo Public Schools, cited by National

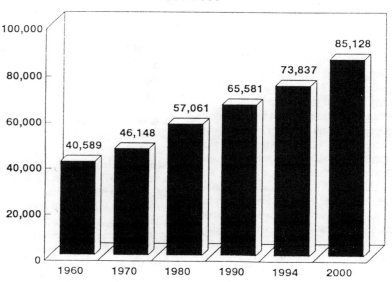

FIGURE 1
Lee County Population
1960-2000

Source: U.S. Census of Population 1990, Staff Calculations, March 1994

FIGURE 2
New & Expanding Industry
Lee County, MS
Eleven Year Summary

Total New Manufacturing Jobs: 11,572   Total New Manufacturing Space: 13,527,364

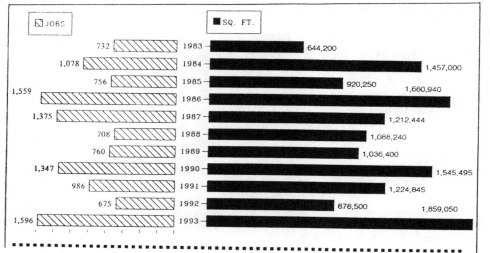

Source: Community Development Foundation, 300 W. Main Street, P.O. Drawer A, Tupelo, MS 38802-1210

FIGURE 3
Gross Retail Sales
Lee County, MS — 1986-1994

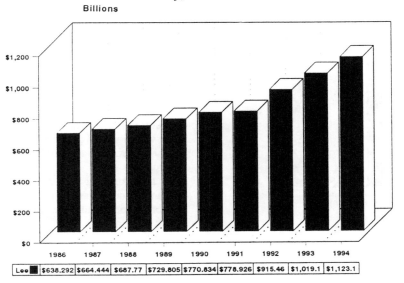

Billions

	1986	1987	1988	1989	1990	1991	1992	1993	1994
Lee	$638.292	$664.444	$687.77	$729.805	$770.834	$778.926	$915.46	$1,019.1	$1,123.1

Source: Mississippe Business, July, 1994,
Volume 52, No. 7, Pg. 2.

FIGURE 4
Trade Area Employment
Mississippi, Alabama, Tennessee

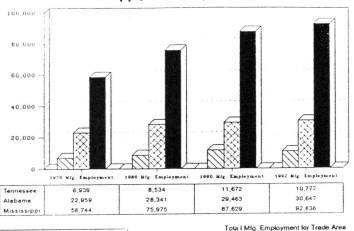

	1970 Mfg. Employment	1980 Mfg. Employment	1990 Mfg. Employment	1992 Mfg. Employment
Tennessee	6,939	8,534	11,672	10,777
Alabama	22,959	28,341	29,463	30,647
Mississippi	58,744	75,975	87,629	92,836

Total Mfg. Employment for Trade Area

1970	1980	1990	1992
88,642	112,850	128,764	134,262

Source: MS data from MS Employment Security Commission, AL data from AL Dept. of Industrial Relations, TN data from Dept. of Employment Security Research and Statistics Division, 1992.

Education Association as a model system, is proud of the innovative private-public partnership which exists in Tupelo. Substantial amounts of private monies have been given to local schools.

"Technology -- the new tool for the artist and the engineer will pervade the world in which our students live and work. The Tupelo

School District is responding to this challenge by putting the technologies of the 21st century into the hands of our students today. A comprehensive technology has begun. Tupelo students in grades kindergarten through 12 have access to computers in a ratio of one computer to every six students. In the

Tupelo Middle School Center for Applied Learning all 8th grade students are leading academic content by using lasers, programmable robots, CAD systems, pneumatic and hydraulic equipment. They are developing an understanding of engineering, aerodynamics, graphics and animation. They are using the technology of the 21st century to apply the academic of the classrooms. A similar program is planned for Tupelo High School.

However, the application of technology goes beyond a facility. These 21st century tools must and will be an integral part of every subject and program -- the media center, visual arts, English composition, history, foreign language, mathematics. We understand that our mission must be to equip our students to be academically sound, but even more than that, be prepared to do the job in the 21st century workplace.

The citizens of our community are making these things possible in Tupelo -- and our students are loving it."

The leadership of the CDF has been sensitized to the emergence of the global economy for more than a decade. Despite the fact more than one-third of all manufacturing jobs in Mississippi are located within a 50-mile radius of Tupelo, the region remains a state leader in developing new work opportunities in both manufacturing and service sectors. The potential for these jobs to be placed at risk is very real as issues of quality productivity, profits, and competitiveness drive the restructuring of corporate America. Locally, this often translates into a redefining of the work place, new applications of technology, and the need for worker retraining. Heavy investment in worker training has been a major factor in bringing all segments of the population within the sphere of the region's economic success.

Two years ago Itawamba Community College (ICC) Tupelo Campus set up a Computer Integrated Manufacturing Center (CIM), where companies can train their employees. Dr. David Cole, ICC President, explains how college officials work with area companies on plant specific training programs.

"One of Itawamba Community College's missions is the chosen delivery system for skills train-

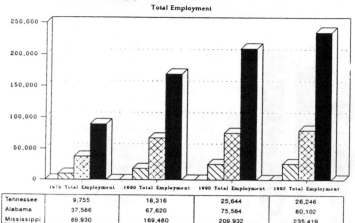

FIGURE 5
Trade Area Employment
Mississippi, Alabama, Tennessee

Total Employment

	1970 Total Employment	1980 Total Employment	1990 Total Employment	1992 Total Employment
Tennessee	9,755	18,316	25,644	26,246
Alabama	37,586	67,620	75,584	80,102
Mississippi	89,930	169,480	209,932	235,419

☐Tennessee ☐Alabama ■Mississippi

Total Employment for Trade Area			
1970	1980	1990	1992
137,271	255,416	311,160	341,767

Source: MS data from MS Employment Security Commission, AL data from AL Dept. of Industrial Relations, TN data from Dept. of Employment Security Research and Statistics Division, 1992.

ing to prepare persons for the workplace or to upgrade the skills of personnel in existing industries. Laboratories on the college campus are used in conjunction with plant site facilities to integrate classroom and real-world experiences into meaningful instruction.

The Computer Integrated Manufacturing Center (CIM), for example, is a place where people can see the future at work, utilizing technology, information systems, quality principles and teamwork. It's a real-time, full-scale production line that gives students a realistic perspective of plant floor operations in an automated setting. It's a place where students see, touch and feel an automated factory of the future, and bring what they have studied together in a systems approach.

The CIM Center creates a vision for the future...providing a glimpse of what will be necessary for our companies to stay competitive...vital information that residents will need to remain players in the work force of the future.

Also as a result of our partner approach, the Furniture Technology Center assists Northeast Mississippi manufacturers in meeting their education needs for the '90s and beyond. The Furniture Tech-

nology Center is a modern learning space that offers companies the rare opportunity to study traditional manufacturing principles in conjunction with the latest in automated furniture manufacturing technology.

ICC offers state-of-the-art instruction in both vertical and horizontal CNV machining and computerized EDM machining to meet the potential needs of some 400 manufacturing firms in the ICC district. The college can now provide local firms with 2-D and 3-D manufacturing assistance that qualifies its worker against a national standard for work with computerized machining tools and sets an important pace for the development of progress at the college."

With encouragement from various corporate leaders, the CDF commissioned several studies which suggest a bold, new education initiative is needed to prepare the region for the changes occurring in the work organizations. Contents of this document provide a blueprint for the development of an education continuum that can develop academically talented, technically competent employees needed for the new high performance manufacturing centers of Northeast Mississippi.

A Master Plan for the development of a World Class Skill and Technology Program has been and still is one of the top

priorities of the Community Development Foundation and its members. It has been clear for more than a dozen years that a key for the greater Tupelo/Lee County area should be education. CDF has consistently supported education at the public school, community college, and university levels in carrying forward its mission of economic and community development.

In April 1991, the CDF in partnership with the Tennessee Valley Authority, initiated action to develop the guide for a program which would produce high performance workers for the high performance workplace.

A task force of nationally recognized engineers and managers conducted a professional, independent evaluation of the area's training capability and needs. this multi-dimensioned review included educational and industrial interviews, plant tours, private sector strategic thinking and other research and analysis. In December 1991, the task force reported to CDF officials and guests.

Since the select committee's report, much has been accomplished but work remains to be done. Mr. Oliver Benton of Signal Mountain, TN, Chairman of the 1992 Evaluation Team and Consultant in Technical Education, has continued to work with the CDF and area entities to further define recommendations for the greater Tupelo/Lee County area. The purpose of these plans is to consolidate all that has taken place, all that is planned and all that needs to be done to create a World Class Skills and Technology Program that can and will meet the needs of Northeast Mississippi well into the 21st century.

While it is generally acknowledged that the United States faces a serious challenge to its competitiveness in the global economy, a consensus has emerged that one key to ensuring the nation's economic position in the world is the development of a work force that can compete successfully with any around the globe.

A national effort to define and support a comprehensive and coordinated program of work force training is still fragmented, although some progress is being made. In the meantime, Northeast Mississippi cannot afford to wait.

THE "MAGIC"

It's this combination of impatience, vision, and determination that creates the atmosphere that has been called the Tupelo-Lee County Northeast Mississippi "Magic."

Ben Franklin spoke of the invention of compound interest as a great discovery. There is no "magic" in numbers, but there is merit in the compounding process of economic development. Economic development is the transfer of wealth from one place to another through creative and innovative methods and techniques. The Tupelo plan allows compounding in two directions, the first is horizontal or geographically and the second is vertically. The vertical compounding is achieved by improved human capital and improved and more efficient community infrastructure. The "magic" in the Tupelo way is that we have achieved them both and not lost our original principal investment we started with. There are two other "C" words that have had a lot of influence on our growth besides Compounding. They are Consistent and focused efforts and Committed leadership. Volunteers and professionals including dedicated officers are important elements of the "magic" in Tupelo and the success of the economic development efforts that have become world renowned.

WHERE TO FROM HERE

The strategic plan calls for the completion of a World Class Skills and Technology Center with Itawamba Community College and the University of Mississippi at an estimated cost of $6 to $10 million. The public schools of Tupelo and Lee County are to be among the best in the nation with science and technology as a part of the K-12 agenda. Also there is the improvement in the quality of life including community appearance. Efforts will continue to develop wholesome and constructive leisure time opportunities for all segments of the population.

Last and foremost, the goal is to continue to increase the number and quality of jobs by 2,500 annually so that the per capita income, which moved from the bottom in the State and Nation to second in the State, will in this decade become comparable with that of the Nation. It is not "magic." It takes hard work, aggressive marketing and staying on course to become a part of the fast emergence of a global economy.

For More Information on Community and Economic Development Strategies and Organization Contact:
Harry A. Martin
Community Development Foundation
300 West Main Street -- P.O. Drawer A
Tupelo, MS 38801 - 1-800-523-3463

For More Information on Public Schools Contact:
Dr. Mike Walters
Tupelo Public Schools
P.O. Box 557
Tupelo, MS 38802 - 1-601-841-8850

or

Dr. David Cole
Itawamba Community College
Fulton Campus
Fulton, MS 38843 - 1-601-842-5542

Community Economic Development: A New Fashioned Approach

June M. Wilmot

ome along on a journey of a community toward its strategic plan for economic development. The community is Winchester, Virginia which is surrounded by the County of Frederick with the Blue Ridge Mountains to the east and the Alleghanies to the west. The combined population totals 67,000. Its location is approximately 75 miles northwest of Washington, D.C., but far from the bustle of the Nation's Capitol, its relationship is more comfortable with the northern Shenandoah Valley, a legend in music, Civil War history, apples and of course, the River. This is a place where, a new resident once related, "heaven is a local call."

It is also a business community, having claimed as one of its early support services the establishment of a surveying company by a 19 year old, George Washington. Economic development circa the 1700's. He was Winchester's first "Congressman", too, by having been elected twice to Virginia's House of Burgesses.

Why is this Winchester story of interest? Why is it legitimate to present it as an example of a success story? After all, it is a community in which many others can find a piece of identity. And, yet, there are both subtle and significant differences. The actions which made this effort special include the following:

❑ The strategic planning effort was overlain on top of what was a successful typical industrial development effort.

❑ There was a specific education component which preceded the actual development of the plan.

❑ Flying in the face of most caveats, staff played a central role in facilitating and moderating the interests of a variety of organizations.

❑ The stereotype of an all-encompassing economic development office was overturned in favor of contractual relationships between the office and other community organizations to implement the program areas.

❑ The strategic plan serves not only as a vision, but an actual workplan and funding document.

The story here is that this experiment in community implementation of an economic development strategy tests the traditional role of an economic developer. And so far, there are meaningful results as measured in the traditional sense.

THE EARLY COMMISSION

The trip begins in January, 1982 when the Winchester-Frederick County Economic Development Commission was formed by joint action of the Common Council of the City of Winchester and the Board of Supervisors of Frederick County. The industrial development effort was first begun here just after World War II by a private Industrial Development Corporation which developed an industrial park and then followed by the Chamber of Commerce which incorporated industrial development as part of its program of work. The city and county governments saw the impacts of increased population growth of the early 1980's and determined that a more aggressive effort was necessary.

The Commission membership, as formed in 1982, is comprised of seven representatives as detailed in Table 1. In Virginia, cities are independent of the counties, so the Commission's membership mirrored each other between the two jurisdictions. Also, in Virginia, industrial development authorities are formed for the purpose of issuing industrial development bonds only and are not usually involved in program development.

Although separate jurisdictions, Winchester and Frederick County have been economically tied for centuries. While the interests of the City and County have had different priorities, they came together in the past in the development of a good deal of infrastructure such as the Winchester Regional Airport, the Opequon Wastewater Reclamation Facility, the Frederick County Landfill, and the Handley Library. A joint effort for economic development was also perceived to have benefit for both jurisdictions.

The Commission was created "for the purpose of fostering an efficient and cooperative effort towards establishing economic development goals and strategies to meet these goals for the Winchester-Frederick County area" (Joint Resolution, January, 1982). From that time until February, 1991, the effort concentrated principally upon industrial attraction, and staff consisted of two persons, a part-time director who is a well respected retired corporate executive vice president and a full time coordinator.

Officers of the Commission include a Chair, Vice Chair, and Secretary. These officers are elected from among themselves, and the representative from the County Industrial Development Authority served as Chair from the inception of the Commission until 1992 when he was elected as Chair, Board of Supervisors. The Chair then became the representative from the City Council.

The early budgets were very modest and relied totally on public—city and county—funding on a two to one basis. However, bolstered by the infrastructure in place, the location of the community, and five privately owned, ready-to-go business parks, the program of business attraction was successful in attracting a variety of manufacturing operations including printing, plastics, woodworking, computer systems, metalworking, and laboratory equipment.

TABLE 1
Economic Development Commission Membership Roster

Member, City Council

Member, County Board of Supervisors

Member, City Planning Commission

Member, County Planning Commission

Member, City Industrial Development Authority

Member, County Industrial Development Authority

Member, at large, elected by the Commission

In February, 1991, the then director retired and a full-time director, the author, was employed.

STRATEGY DEVELOPMENT

While informally meeting the intent of its mission as stated in 1982, the Commission determined that it was time to develop a more formalized strategic plan which encompassed a broader vision of what comprised economic development. Certainly, experience in economic development strategic planning comprised a large part of the job interview. While no specifics of what that plan should encompass had been determined, it was obvious that there was a manufacturing base in place that needed attention, tourism efforts were fragmented, and agribusiness development had received a modicum of support.

The development of the strategy, as well as the challenge of bringing more people into the process, was the first assignment given to staff by the Commission. The motivation for this task came from not only the charge to the Commission in 1982 but the result of the work of a two-year visioning effort begun in 1989 entitled *2020 Vision Project: A Citizens Commission Report on the Future of Our Community*. A proposal by the then Mayor of the City, it was a joint city-county effort involving over 150 citizens, including Commission members. They worked on fifteen areas of concern of which economic base, demographics, education, utilities, local agriculture, utilities and quality of life were directly related to an economic development strategy.

Certainly from the community preparation as evidenced above, the community's readiness for a strategic plan was way beyond the starting stage. A successful industrial development program, a good start on a tourism program by a very effective Chamber of Commerce (now 1,300 members) but which had fragmented support and funding, the visioning process, an entrepreneurial public mindset as evidenced by the infrastructure development, and an expectation of business participation starting with George Washington all created an advanced jump-off point. The challenge to staff was how to incorporate these activities and organizations into something broader that worked—together.

Initial activities combined both administrative and program efforts. By-laws were established for the Commission which elevated its activity to policy direction and legislative issues rather than the day-to-day operation of the industrial development program. A monthly meeting date and participation requirements were established. The staff was given the responsibility to develop the strategy. A general time frame and plan for the development of the strategy was discussed with the Commission and the process began.

During the first three months of the project, staff identified organizations and individuals with investment of some sort and amount in an economic plan and visited with each. The list was developed based on a review of organizations, community documents, newspaper reports, and conversations with Commission leadership and staff experience. In fact, except for the results of conversations with the Commission leadership, the nucleus of the list was prepared prior to reporting for the job.

The variety of persons who met with staff included the executive director of the Chamber of Commerce, elected officials from both the city and county governing bodies, city manager, county administrator, planning commissioners, school administrators, local university president, preservationists, bankers, airport manager, planning department heads, industrial park owners, executive director of the Downtown Development Board, public utility officials, electric and natural gas utility representatives, publisher of a local daily newspaper, presidents of existing manufacturing companies, and president of the local regional hospital. A total of approximately 40 persons was contacted.

The discussions were informal, but each person was asked seven questions which were developed by staff from a combination of strategic planning documents:

❑ What do you see as the community's biggest asset?

❑ What do you see as the community's biggest liability?

❑ What makes the community unique?

❑ If you could name three of the most active leaders in the community who would they be?

❑ If you could name the three most influential leaders in the community who would they be?

❑ What would you like to see an economic development program achieve?

❑ Would you be willing to serve on a task force to assist in developing an economic development strategy?

This process gave staff a good deal of insight into whom the leadership of the community was (sometimes the most active are not necessarily the most influential) and the expectations of the strategy. What were the hoped for results of an economic development plan? Was an expansion of the program elements possible? What should they include? Who could help? Who would work? What organizations have economic development agendas? How could the agendas mesh? The answers helped in deciding *how* to implement, not necessarily *what* to implement. The end of the process identified the organizations which had a stake in the strategy and the individuals in those organizations who had an interest in participating.

Based on these interviews and conclusion reached in the *2020 Vision Project*, staff recommended to the Commission that four "export" business development areas should be first addressed in the strategy. They were existing industry development, travel, agribusiness development, and business attraction. While these program areas are the more traditional in terms of economic development programming, they were identified as important elements to the community. It was perhaps not as traditional to combine them into one strategy.

STRATEGY WORKING GROUPS

In June, 1991 four working groups, comprised of representatives of the organizations from the interview process which had an interest in one of the four program areas, were formed to develop the four strategies. Each organization's leadership was consulted by staff in the selection of the person to represent it, although generally, the persons interviewed and the organizational representation remained the same. The importance of this representation cannot be overemphasized. Organizational interests, not individual interests were the driving force behind the selection for inclusion in the process. The Strategy Working Groups are given in Table 2.

Based on the interview process and other strategic planning experiences, staff recommended to the Commission that these interests take a major role in developing the goals and strategies appropriate for each of the identified program areas. Even more importantly, at the outset of the process it was stated that the organizations were expected to have a role in implementing portions of the strategy, as appropriate. This was staff's judgment, and it hinged on the history of participation in the past.

The membership of each of the four working groups averaged seven persons representing the like number of organizations. Each was assigned the challenge of identifying what set the Winchester-Frederick County community apart from the competition (but within their respective program area) and how to use the goals of the program area to build toward what had been identified as the goals of the community. The role of staff was to assist each group in defining goals and identifying effective strategies, with corresponding measures of attainment. A member of the Commission served as liaison with each working group.

ADVISORY COMMITTEE

While a number of organizations had specific interest in specific programs, there were four persons representing four organizations which had an interest in the comprehensive effort and stood to participate in most of it. Rather than place them on one of the working groups, staff recommended to incorporate those interests into an Advisory Committee to the Commission. Formed at the beginning of the process, the Committee includes the city manager, the county administrator, the executive director of the Chamber of Commerce, and the executive director of the Downtown Development Board. They joined in the process of the strategy development and revision process by the working groups as their schedule allowed. They can almost be considered an extension of Commission staff and provide valuable liaison to both the public and private sectors. They are copied with communiques to both the Commission and the working groups.

TASK FORCES

In addition, the real estate and banking communities have a stand in most of the activity. To incorporate those interests, both groups were formed, also at the beginning, into Task Forces. The Commercial Brokers Task Force, an operating group of the local Board of Realtors, meets monthly for information exchange as well as to keep the Commission's inventory of sites and buildings updated. The Commercial Bankers Task Force meets on call and responds to project financing as needed. A Community Development Corporation has been formed, and a Directory of Financial Services has been developed. The Chairs of both Task Forces serve on the Business Attraction Working Group.

PREPARATION FOR THE PLAN DEVELOPMENT

Each of the four working groups was provided a notebook of information which provided a common knowledge base about the community and the process they were launching. A good portion of first meetings of each group was spent reviewing the information, but its importance was that it served almost as testimony that could be referred to once the strategy development was underway.,

Ranging from 75 to 100 pages in length, the notebooks consisted of four segments. Segments one through three were the same materials for each of the working groups. The three common segments were Economic Development (General), Strategy Development, and Community Analysis.

The fourth segment was comprised of materials which dealt with that program area, i.e. Existing Industry Development, Travel, Agribusiness Development, and Business Attraction. Where appropriate, information from the *Vision 2020* project was inserted which helped in relating what they were about to do to what the community had already accomplished. The remainder of the materials came from a variety of sources, with the *Economic Development Review* a major resource.

WORKING GROUP ACTIVITY

For the next five months each of the working groups moved along at its own pace, some meeting more frequently than others. The role of staff was to take groups through the process. Staff reiterated at a variety of places in the varying schedules that the community would identify where it wanted to be, and the staff could suggest some of the techniques of getting there. At the first session, a mission statement was hammered out by each group. The goal was to come out at the other end of the process with one document describing four program areas.

There were some general guidelines:

❑ We would get done what's effective; that is, what set us apart from the competition.

❑ We would get done what can be measured; that is, accountability.

❑ We would use our resources wisely; that is, people and money.

TABLE 2
Economic Development Strategy Working Groups

Existing Industry	Travel	Agribusiness Development	Business Attraction
Development • Plant Managers Committee Business Development Center - Lord Fairfax CC Shenandoah Valley Manufacturers Association Shenandoah University School of Business Dowell J. Howard Vo Tech Center • Business Assistance • Frederick County Public Schools • City of Winchester Public Schools	**Winchester-Frederick Co.** **Historical Society** **Preservation of Historic** **Winchester** • Group Tour Marketing Council (Marketing) • Tourism Committee • Apple Blossom Festival	Extension Service Apple Growers Association Farm Credit Bureau Livestock Association Farmers Market Association National Fruit Prod. Co. Fruit Research Lab • Agribusiness Committee	• Economic Development Committee C & P Telephone Shenandoah Gas Co. Winchester Regional Airport Commercial Brokers Group Industrial Parks Association Industrial Development Corporation Commercial Bankers Group Ex-officio: Va. Dept. of Econ. Dev. Potomac Edison CSX Corp.

* Chamber of Commerce Committee

After the development of the mission statement, each group went through discussion of the following seven subjects developed by staff. The mission statement was revisited repeatedly during these discussions, and when the discussion wandered, the mission statement served as a plumb line to get back on track.

Subjects for discussion for each program area:

❑ Review of where the community was, and what organization was doing it.

❑ Identify where we wanted the community to be; how to raise our level of expectations.

❑ Identify assets and liabilities.

❑ Suggest strategies, alternatives, actions in support of the mission and goals for each area.

❑ Identify the likely organization(s) to carry out strategies; who would have responsibility.

❑ Identify where the resources are or were likely to be.

❑ How would the program be evaluated; how would we know we had made a difference.

PRESENTING THE STRATEGY

By November, 1991 the four working groups had completed their tasks. The Winchester-Frederick County Economic Development Strategy, first edition, came to fruition. For each program area there were included the mission, objectives, activities, and impact measures, all of which were supported by other working materials which provided more details on the specific programs.

The next steps were approval by the Commission as a whole, which was accomplished at the December meeting, and, since the Commission represented the public bodies involved, presentation to the City Council and Board of Supervisors. Through the representation on the Commission, the Strategy also became either a part of or referenced in the city and county planning documents. The unveiling of the plan took place through a variety of media including newspaper, local cable television, service club presentations, and other opportunities as presented.

BUDGET DEVELOPMENT

With the acceptance by the Commission, the Strategy became the basis for budget development by staff. The sequence is important here, because no effective activity would be discarded because of budget considerations. By the end of December, the budget was also developed *and incorporated by program area* into the final Strategy document. The addition of the budget was approved by the Commission in January, 1992. The Strategy became the basis for all funding requests. Another change to reflect the all-community effort was that it would be a public/ private effort, and that included funding. Requests to the public bodies were on a 2 to 1 basis using population as the formula (45,000 for the County; 22,000 for the city). The private sector participation was pegged to 25% of the budget.

REVISION PLAN

Also adopted in the Commission's By-Laws was an annual cycle by which the review process by each group would begin in June with the completion by November. That cycle reinforces the importance of changing the document, and it also places the Commission in a position where it is looking one year ahead in terms of budget support. At the writing of this article, the Commission has been asked by staff to present at its next meeting suggestions for a 1994-95 Strategy, the third edition.

RESULTS

The record of achievement in a very short period time has been significant. Some of these are noted in Table 3. Specific highlights include:

Business Attraction

❑ Over $100 million in new manufacturing developments in the past 18 months.

❑ Targeting outreach program to three SIC codes identified as "putting a white coat on top of a blue collar" to diversify job opportunities and increase income.

❑ Funding for an Alternative Work Center where Federal employees can work several days per week rather than making the 70-mile commute to within the Washington area.

❑ A 50% increase in the number of new prospect inquiries.

Existing Industry Development

❑ Over $55 million in manufacturing expansions.

TABLE 3
Winchester-Frederick County Commission Overview

	1990-91	1992-93
Programs	Industrial Development	Business Attraction Travel Existing Industry Dev. Agribusiness Dev.
Staff	Part Time Director Full time Coordinator	Full-time: Executive Director Existing Industry Dir. Research Analyst
Funding	$156,000 (all public, 33% city, 66% county)	$426,760 (3:1/public:private)
External contracts/ agreements for program delivery	$750	$116,400
Organizations participating	Agric. Extension	Agricultural Extension Chamber of Commerce Preservation of Historic Winchester Downtown Development Board

❏ An active industry call team which has called on each of the manufacturing companies within a calendar year.

❏ An annual calendar of industry recognition with an event monthly.

Agribusiness Development

❏ A Harvest calendar of consumer crops for retail purchase or pick your own.

❏ A metropolitan list of retail markets for wholesale producers.

Travel

❏ Funding of a full time tourism marketing professional.

❏ Funding and development of "Shenandoah: Crossroads of the Civil War", a regional Civil War information center located in the Kurtz Cultural Center in downtown Winchester.

❏ A coordinated and cooperative marketing program for both the leisure traveler as well as group tours.

❏ A 50% increase in the number of tourist inquiries.

OBSERVATIONS

The advantages of the process in the Winchester-Frederick County experience are that it built on what was a successful organization in one aspect of economic development, expanded the breadth of the program, and incorporated other organization in the implementation phase. The Commission brought the table and organizations gathered around. The strategy became a *community* strategy, not just a Commission strategy. It also used the existing structure to involve more people, rather than inventing a structure to accomplish the same goal. From a seven-member Commission, the strategy process through its working groups, now Committees, Advisory Committee and Task Forces, involves more than 55 people in the annual cycle of strategy implementation and revision (See Figure 1). By incorporating the budget into the strategy, it became a vehicle for funding and re-emphasized that, although there are different constituencies, Existing Industry Development, Travel, Agribusiness Development and Business Attraction are all intertwined. The funding process now incorporates both public and private dollars on a 3:1 ratio. With the funding successes, other organizations now see the strategy as a big plus and have joined the table of participating organizations. The public sector sees the advantage of not having multiple funding requests relating to economic development. Accountability in terms of achievement has become effective organizational peer pressure.

From the staff perspective, the challenge is to be cautious in terms of reassuring partner organizations that the strategy component for which they have responsibility is in their (and the community's) best interest rather than appearing that the strategy is driving their agenda. For the economic development professional, it takes a lot more management and orchestration than in-house program implementation. If economic developers can walk the talk that it really makes no difference who or what gets the credit, then letting the *community* implement an economic development program is a very rewarding, and so far, effective process. It might be the economic development effort of the future.

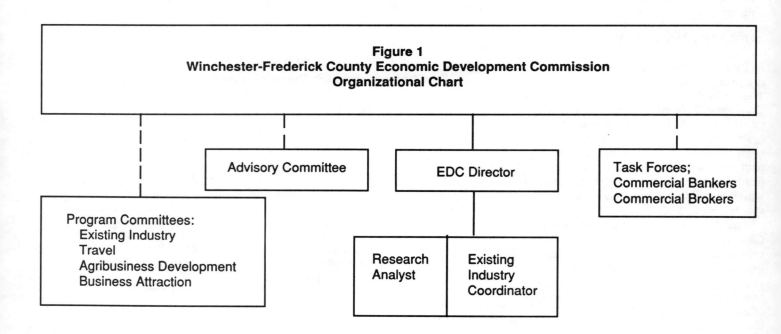

Figure 1
Winchester-Frederick County Economic Development Commission
Organizational Chart

The Evolution Of Economic Development In Broward County, Florida

James A. Garver, C.E.D., F.M.

INTRODUCTION

I came to Broward County, Florida in 1982 at the request of a search committee made up of several business leaders in the area who felt it was time to make changes in their approach to economic development. Broward County was beginning to experience significant changes. It was emerging from being an area which had catered to tourists and retirees to a metropolitan area with the potential to be a thriving business community and they felt that strong leadership by an experienced professional was needed.

During the past twenty years, the economic development process in the county had changed numerous times in attempting to keep up with the dramatic increase in population and change in business environment. The program had begun as a quasi-governmental organization with a mission to attract new business, specifically manufacturing and related industries, to the Broward County area. It continued with that limited mission for fifteen years.

A few years prior to my joining the organization, it was becoming evident that Broward County was not competing successfully for business relocations with other areas such as the Greater Miami/Dade County region, Orlando or Tampa. While the population increased in the years from 1960 to 1980 measurably, very few meaningful jobs had been created. The majority of the residents remained in the retiree sector and the jobs were still in the service area. It became clear that economic development had become a sophisticated process and that a professional in that field was needed.

A national search was conducted, and that was when I took the reins of this organization. The mission given to me by the Board was to make the changes necessary to become a competitive force in the economic development arena.

EARLY NINETEEN EIGHTIES

My first recommendation was to change the name of the organization from the Broward Industrial Board to the Broward Economic Development Board (BEDB). This recommendation became very controversial as the leadership felt that this would take away from their desired mission of attracting only manufacturing type businesses. My proposal was to attract all types of businesses including service, financial organizations, national headquarters and various types of technological industries.

I believed that it was also time to recognize the need for nourishing existing companies for growth and expansion. This concept also met with raised eyebrows by the leadership. The Board felt that the changes being proposed were too radical; that the organization was moving too fast; that its mission should be more singular and should not compete with the 15 area chambers of commerce which traditionally served local business growth and expansion.

Having worked with both private and public sectors, I realized that I would need to recruit several of the Board members to my way of thinking or nothing would ever be changed. After a period of time, I was able to convince two of the members that the field of economic development had changed and we were dealing in the "dark ages." Once they realized I was right, I was able to continue with my recommendations with the support and confidence of at least a few members of the Board. Their challenge was to convince the others that economic development was indeed a new ball game.

Walking very softly at first, I was finally able to introduce a few new programs, but I still felt that we needed further guidance in determining a direction that would put us on the map as an economic development agency. This would necessitate utilizing a professional consultant. Although, I knew which way we wanted to go, I realized that I would have to have the back-up of a consultant to convince the Board. This would not be the first time I would hire a consultant to assist in selling my programs.

It was determined that the direction of the organization had been delegated to the public sector and that there was only a limited role for private sector leadership except for local business people representing various chambers of commerce. A recommendation was made by the consultant that a private sector arm of the Board be created. This resulted in the formation of the Committee of 100 which became the private sector partner of the Broward Economic Development Board.

With the addition of the private sector which included representatives from local businesses, we began a more aggressive marketing program. We had started targeting specific types of businesses for attraction purposes. However, once again, I wanted professional assistance to determine which businesses would be best suited for our area. Therefore, another economic development consultant was contracted to develop a list of desired business sectors for both the manufacturing and service industries.

With the recommendations in place, it was time to seek professional advice in creating an effective advertising campaign. This, too, was difficult to get by the Board based upon the cost of a campaign such as this. Keep in mind that these techniques had not been utilized in the past and the Board was unaware of the steep costs attached to such a campaign. Based on my past experience with other programs, I was committed to the idea that this was the right way to go and it was the only way to become competitive. Once again, I had to fight for my beliefs, but with the help of a few loyal Board members, we were able to continue with the programs.

With the development of these collateral pieces, we had to take stock of our resources within the county. What were our pluses or minuses as far as being able to provide the services and facilities needed by potential businesses? We wanted to attract high technology industries, but did we have the educational system needed to train the workers? While there were twelve universities and colleges in the area, very few had developed programs that were geared toward high technology or business in general. The K-12 education system was very weak and vocational-technical and adult education was being addressed on a very superficial level. This had to change in order to be able to attract the types of business we were seeking.

To address these problems, I believed that all Broward County citizens needed to become involved in our overall problems. The local educators must become partners with the business people in the community to be able to evaluate education on all levels. As a result, an organization, called "Broward Compact," was formed. This group would study the educational needs of the business community and make recommendations as to which direction our educational system should be heading. Representatives from the school board worked closely with business in the area of course development to ensure that a work force could be trained that would match the requirements of our new Broward businesses.

As to problems in the K-12 education levels, another organization called "Partners in Excellence" was formed. This program, also supported by our organization, provided for the adoption of a school by a business which resulted in a "hands on" partnership between the businesses, the educators and the students. Businesses would be responsible for raising funds for needed equipment, supplies or facilities to bring our schools up to the level needed to produce graduates that could either go directly to higher education or join the workforce armed with the knowledge to obtain employment in Broward's new technologies.

One of the major infrastructure needs after education was transportation. Our roads were not adequate for the growing population and we had no major mass transit system to speak of. However, work had begun on a major interstate expansion project which included an east-west thoroughfare which was badly needed for distribution to the west coast of Florida. Here again, I felt that our organization must be involved in the process. We created a subcommittee of our Growth and Assistance Committee to address the relocation problem faced by local businesses which might be condemned due to the need for additional land for the I-95 expansion and creation of I-595.

Plans for a new state of the art international airport were on the drawing board. Our Board supported and became involved with the planning process for this new facility.

Our Sea Port, which is the deepest port south of Norfolk, Virginia, was also being expanded to prepare for future shipping and cargo business as well as for a thriving cruise ship business.

I believed that we had to become cognizant of all of the changes being made around us and be involved with them. It was our job to sell our area and we could not do this without knowing everything that was happening with our infrastructure, and with the changes occurring, it was time to, once again, prepare a strategy for marketing the area for business development.

MID NINETEEN EIGHTIES

Since the growth of our area was so far-reaching, we felt it was time to reassess our area and make sure that we were going in the right direction. However, I felt that we needed the involvement of more citizens than just the Economic Development Board. I contacted the Broward Workshop, which is an organization comprised of approximately 60 CEO's of local corporations, to ask for their assistance in convening a long range planning study. The group, which convened in 1984, entitled their study "Project Horizon." Its mission was to identify future needs of the County in various areas.

The study identified several key issues that would have great impact on the county's future growth and development. These issues included community identity, image, attitude, infrastructure, minority business development, tourism, and of course, economic development. Although all of these issues together profiled a full community, our organization was primarily concerned with the recommendation concerning the economic development organization. Up until this time, besides the Economic Development Board, there were approximately 109 different organizations in Broward County carrying out a program of economic development. The list included every organization from the State of Florida to railroads, utilities, municipalities, chambers of commerce and federal agencies. Our goal was to have all of these efforts consolidated into a more effective, functioning countywide economic development program.

After 350 business, civic and public leaders spent over 35,000 hours identifying and studying the issues, they delivered their overall recommendations. The one which affected our organization was that a single, private, countywide economic development organization be created. The Broward Economic Development Board and the Committee of 100, the private arm of The Board, were designated the county's official economic development agencies to deal with attraction and retention of business. This left the chambers of commerce to programs

of work in the areas of transportation, education, health services, small and minority business development and other infrastructure support for business development.

Simultaneously, the Committee of 100 began reorganizing to strengthen the private sector participation in the organization. I have always felt that to be successful, "ownership" of the economic development process was needed by the business community. This began our campaign to invite select business people for their commitment to enhance the economic climate of Broward County by working together to bring in new businesses in order to create jobs. A representative group bought into this concept and a new Broward's Committee of 100, Inc. was born replacing the original private sector arm, the Committee of 100.

During the first year, various members of the original group and I contacted other businesspeople and asked for their support to continue with an aggressive economic development program. After the first year, the membership swelled to over 200 people — each contributing their time and financial resources to the furtherance of our programs.

By 1986, the Broward Economic Development Board's budget had increased to nearly $500,000, while Broward's Committee of 100 raised approximately $350,000. The two organizations contracted with each other to parallel the two budgets along with their facilities and staff as no personnel or equipment were covered in the Committee's budget. All funds from that budget would be for business development — the attraction and retention of business. Those activities would be carried out by private sector members through seven committees and task forces which included: Membership, a committee to increase the membership of the Committee of 100 and to develop its policies and procedures; Growth and Assistance, a committee to address the growth and expansion needs of local businesses; Programs, a committee to promote awareness of the Committee to the local community through forums and showcases; Outreach, a committee which actually travelled outside the State of Florida to promote the area for business development; Theme Development, a specific committee to create the theme for the Board and the Committee resulting in the theme, "We're Building a Future for your Family and your Business. Broward County Florida.", which has been utilized by many of Broward's municipalities and the Broward County Government to name a few; Advertising & Communications, a committee to develop advertising plans and all collateral materials; and Motion Picture and Television, a committee charged with promoting the area for film production.

With the Committees and Task Forces in place, Broward's Committee of 100 began establishing an enviable track record. A program of business attraction targeting specific businesses within the manufacturing and service sectors had been developed and was being carried out.

The Committee also undertook a program of business retention and expansion. Keeping in mind that there were over 750 new occupational licenses each year, we felt that it was important to make sure we retained them. Previously, very little had been done on an intensified level to retain existing companies. In the past, there had been programs which addressed major employers and their expansion capabilities which was done at the staff level, but it was limited in scope. The new program was to involve Committee of 100 members who would personally call on existing companies on a peer to peer basis. This was a new concept which worked very well as many local businesses had no knowledge of our organization and that there was assistance available to them.

With our two major programs — attraction and retention — being handled successfully, I felt it was time to go back to the County and ask for additional funding. We had made great strides with the limited funds provided from the County's general fund, but I believed that it was now time to approach the County Commission and ask for additional financial support. Other economic development agencies had received funding from the respective counties based on the occupational license fees, and I believed we could do the same thing. After many hours of meetings and conferences our funding request was approved by the county which resulted in a significant increase in our budget. With this new funding under our belt we could then seek new programs that would benefit the development of Broward County.

One of the first programs we considered adding was a sports development program. Due to an increasing number of local sporting events in the area and the sizable economic impact achieved, it was decided that a program was needed to handle inquiries and to aggressively market the area for potential sporting events. The question was whether this should be handled by establishing a Sports Authority or be included under the Development Board. It was in-cumbent upon me to remind the Board of the recommendations of Project Horizon to eliminate fragmentation and duplication of organizations. This resulted in the position being created under the Development Board. In the past several years, the Sports Committee has been successful in its efforts to lure the Whitbread Round the World Race for the only stopover in North America in 1990 and again in 1994. It has also been involved in procuring the 1995 Super Bowl for the area and assisted in the creation of the Blockbuster Bowl. The Committee also assists with The Honda Classic Golf Tournament, promotes the International Swimming Hall of Fame and assists the municipalities with numerous amateur events.

EARLY NINETEEN NINETIES

In 1990 all programs were underway and the goals of the well oiled economic development machine were being realized. In fact, Broward's Committee of 100 was being recognized for its programs as it was named one of the Top 10 Development Organizations for four years in a row by *Site Selection Magazine* and Conway Data, Inc. Due to this, Broward's Committee of 100 and the Broward Economic Development Board were gaining recognition in the community for the development of the Broward County business base. However, having two agencies under one roof handling development began causing confusion in the marketplace. Questions arose as to which agency was the lead agency and which was truly doing the work. The public sector agency, composed of all chamber representatives, was taking a back seat to the private sector organization which was run by local business leaders who were personally carrying out the mission of both organizations. The relationship between the two organizations had to be defined and redefined repeatedly.

Once again, I felt it was prudent to seek professional advice and a management consultant firm was contracted to assess the roles of the organizations and to make recommendations. Collectively, the organizations were doing an outstanding job, however, the cohesiveness of one Broward County organization as declared by Project Horizon, was not being fulfilled.

In 1991, a recommendation was made by the consultant that a single not-for-profit sector economic development organization be created. A plan was then devised to consolidate the two organizations merging the Broward Economic Development Board with Broward's Com-mittee of 100, Inc. This merger resulted in a new organization — The Broward Economic Development Council, Inc. The new organization retained the funding from a portion of the county's occupational licensee fees along with monies emanating from membership dues. The new organization adopted the logo of the former Development Board and operating procedures and policies of Broward's Committee of 100 while fulfilling the missions of both organizations. The Board of Directors of each group was retained and two more representatives were added swelling the number to 38 board members. From that an executive committee was selected which would meet more frequently and be the final word on policy and procedure.

The first year of operation of the new Council was spent in blending the two former organizations together. All procedures and policies, collateral materials, and job descriptions were reviewed and revised to fit the new agency. When these tasks were completed, it was then necessary to address the mission, goals and objectives, programs and activities in light of the new organization.

During the year of re-alignment, outside forces were at work that created changes in the national, state and local economies. Nationally, there was a recession which trickled down to the States and local communities. Jobs were being lost at a rapid rate and businesses were failing. I knew that all of these things collectively were having an impact on our effectiveness as a development organization to carry out our mission of creating jobs. I also felt it was time to measure the progress of the recommendations made by Project Horizon as they related to the community. Now that all pieces were in place, I was concerned about whether we were attracting the types of businesses we should be and if we should change our direction or our techniques.

To address these questions, a steering committee comprised of a few board members was formed. It was determined by them that the Council must begin planning for the future and, thus, the Long Range Planning Committee was formed. This group was made up of approximately 40 Council members and was guided by a facilitator/consultant.

The study was conducted over a period of five months. Issues regarding both Broward County and the Broward Economic Development Council were considered. The Council was still in its infancy, being only one year old, and it was important to the committee that the new organization start

FIGURE 1
Organizational Evolutions of the Economic Development Program Broward County Florida

PUBLIC SECTOR	PRIVATE SECTOR

Broward Industrial Board (1978)

❑ Public corporation affiliated with county government.
❑ Funding through county general fund.
❑ Responding to inquiries, business only — Manufacturing Industry was the main focus (not pro-active).
❑ $225,000 budget — staff of five.

None

Broward Economic Development Board (1982)

❑ Public Corporation that remained affiliated with county government.
❑ New CEO hired to direct organization.
❑ Responded and targeted specific industries and was not limited to the manufacturing sector.
❑ Initiated a Target Industries Study.
❑ $233,000 budget — staff of six.

Committee of 100 (1982)

❑ A committee partner of BEDB.
❑ A membership based organization.
❑ Began targeting specific types of businesses through the use of advertising and direct mail.

Broward Economic Development Board (1986)

❑ Reorganized by contracting with BC100 to cover both attraction and retention while reinforcing existing Broward County businesses.
❑ 1988 funding was switched from County government fund to a portion of Occupational License fees.
❑ Budget grew to $500,000 — staff of 13.

Broward's Committee of 100 (1986)

❑ Reorganized to strengthen the private sector participation with a separate Board of Directors budget paralleled with BEDB budget.
❑ Membership grew to over 200.

PUBLIC/PRIVATE PARTNERSHIP

Broward Economic Development Council (1991)

❑ Formed by merger of BEDB and BC100. All programs and functions now under new organization.
❑ A contracted agency of the County with funds continuing to come from Occupational License Fees.
❑ Membership 400.
❑ $1.1 million budget — staff of 15.
❑ 1993 $1.5 million budget staff of 16.

out on the right foot in its future economic development programs. We needed to know how we were perceived in the community. It was equally as important to the committee to know what changes were occurring in Broward County and how they could be dealt with.

From this study it was learned that Broward County was indeed undergoing changes. The demographics were changing. The population was getting younger and there was an increase in immigration from other countries. This would mean a change in the type of workforce which would be available.

It was also determined as a result of the study that Broward County's infrastructure had improved. Our highway system was almost complete with one interchange left to be finished on the north-south interstate. We now had I-595, a much needed east-west interstate which connected with I-75, a direct route to Florida's west coast. We also had the Sawgrass Expressway which encircles Broward County and meets with other interstates, and the Florida Turnpike had been improved. We also now had a tri-county rail system, a commuter train providing mass transit from Palm Beach County from the north all the way to Dade County (Miami) to the south. As of 1988, we had a new international airport which is a state of the art facility with major national and international flights. The cruise ship business at Port Everglades had increased considerably as well as the shipping capacity of that facility. Our transportation services had indeed caught up with our business needs and that fact had to be communicated.

Although we were working diligently with educators to create a bond between business and education, we still had a way to go to have the type of educational system we felt was needed to compete. It was also discovered that there was still fragmentation in the business community and governmental structures and it was a detriment to attracting businesses to the area.

When considering new ways in which to market Broward County as a prime business location, the concept of a sole economic development organization was reinforced, but with a strong partnership with the 18 chambers of commerce. It was fur-

ther found that Broward needed more higher paying jobs and that efforts should be made to attract the type of businesses that would provide those jobs. Due to the recession, a heavy emphasis was placed on retention and survival of local companies.

With the findings of all of the committees, came solid recommendations. These recommendations would form the blueprint for the Council's direction for the next five years.

It was recommended that the Council should be a leading participant in the county charter review process so that the problem of fragmentation could be addressed. To ensure that the Council could be considered in a leadership capacity, it was recommended that the awareness and image of the Council must be increased.

Target industries for future attraction would include health care, information services and high-tech manufacturing. A strong emphasis was placed on international trade and investment. The Committee agreed that the Council must answer the need for international trade guidance in the community and the need to showcase the area for possible international headquarters locations or other business locations.

Education would remain a high priority with a continuing partnership between business and education. It was discovered through the study that Broward's education system is in definite need of attention. Primary and secondary education must be improved, and there must be further attention to adult education and job training programs to retain the skilled, higher paying jobs.

As for retention of existing businesses, it was recommended that the Council assist Broward businesses by improving their awareness and access to sources of capital and expedite the process by which they obtain it.

FUTURE BUSINESS PLAN

It was from these basic recommendations that I formatted a business plan for the next five years. To date, task forces have been formed to address health care, education and the marine industry which was found to need assistance for pure survival. A communications staff person has been hired for the purpose of developing pro-

grams to enhance the Council's image, reviewing and improving advertising placement and upgrading collateral materials to present a better picture of Broward's and the BEDC's assets.

Planning is underway for reassessing the way in which we market the area for business attraction. It must be determined which is the most effective way — whether it be advertising or direct mail or a combination of both.

The Council has become involved with various trade shows relating to the health care industry and the international market. Numerous foreign delegations have been hosted by the Council in an effort to showcase Broward County for the improvement of international trade.

A liaison program with the Chambers of Commerce has been established in order to create a better working relationship with those organizations.

These are just a few of the accomplishments which have occurred based on the Long Range Plan. In 1992, during the long range planning process and during the restructure, we were recognized by *Site Selection Magazine* and Conway Data, Inc. once again. This time we received Honorable Mention for the progress we had achieved with our new programs.

CONCLUDING COMMENTS

As the President of the Broward Economic Development Council, I feel an obligation to provide the best services available to the business community while seeking to attract the most desirable businesses for the area. It wasn't an easy task convincing the different boards over the past ten years that economic development doesn't just happen, that it has to be planned and formulated and nurtured, and that the economic development organization needs to evolve (see Figure 1). However, I was able to persevere with the help of local representatives from our business and governmental sectors. They have given me the support I needed to turn our economic development program into an aggressive one. My challenge now is to keep this progress moving in a positive direction. I look forward to that challenge and hope that I will be around for the next twenty years to make sure that our programs keep up with the times.

Bibliography

Richard Preston, "Principles of Total Community Development" *Economic Development Review*, Volume 9, Number 3, Summer, 1991, pp. 61-62.

Mark D. Waterhouse, "Building Viable Communities -- The Essence of Economic Development" *Economic Development Review*, Volume 9, Number 3, Summer, 1991, pp. 14-22.

Jerold R. Thomas, "Skills Needed By The Economic Developer" *Economic Development Review*, Volume 13, Number 3, Summer, 1995, pp. 9-11.

Phillip D. Phillips, "Site Selection: Corporate Perspective and Community Response" *Economic Development Review*, Volume 9, Number 2, Spring, 1991, pp. 4-11.

J. Craig Davis and Thomas A. Hutton, "The Role of Service Activity in Regional Economic Growth" *Economic Development Review*, Volume 11, Number 1, Winter, 1993, pp. 54-60.

Robert H. Pittman and Rhonda P. Culp, "When Does Retail County As Economic Development?" *Economic Development Review*, Volume 13, Number 2, Spring, 1995, pp. 4-6.

Robert W. Shively, "Community Power Structures" *Economic Development Review*, Volume 12, Number 3, Summer, 1994, pp. 13-15.

Eric P. Canada, "Power, Influence and the Development Professional" *Economic Development Review*, Volume 11, Number 2, Spring, 1993, pp. 42-45.

William T. Whitehead and Robert M. Ady, "Organizational Models For Economic Development" *Economic Development Review*, Volume 7, Number 1, Winter, 1989, pp. 8-12.

David R. Kolzow, "Public/Private Partnership: The Economic Development Organization For the 90s" *Economic Development Review*, Volume 12, Number 1, Winter, 1994, pp. 4-6.

Paul J. Greeley, "Energizing Boards, Commissions, Task Forces, and Volunteer Groups" *Economic Development Review*, Volume 13, Number 3, Summer, 1995, pp. 24-27.

David R. Kolzow, "Smooth Sailing With Your Board of Directors" *Economic Development Review*, Volume 13, Number 3, Summer, 1995, pp. 20-23.

Michael A. Lanava, "Creating Your Own Economic Development Team" *Economic Development Review*, Volume 12, Number 2, Spring, 1994, pp. 85-87.

Gene B. Lawin and Donald G. Chaplain, "Obtaining Technological Resources For the Economic Development Office" *Economic Development Review*, Volume 13, Number 1, Winter, 1995, pp. 11-18.

Rick L. Weddle, "Preparing Tailored Fact Books And Prospect Proposals" *Economic Development Review*, Volume 13, Number 1, Winter, 1995, pp. 32-36.

Michael L. DuBrow, "Exploring The Internet For Economic Development Opportunities" *Economic Development Review*, Volume 13, Number 3, Summer, 1995, pp. 89-94.

Mark M. Miller, Lay James Gibson and N. Gene Wright, "Location Quotient: A Basic Tool For Economic Development Analysis" *Economic Development Review*, Volume 9, Number 2, Spring, 1991, pp. 65-68.

Richard F. Celeste, "Strategic Alliances For Innovation: Emerging Models of Technology-Based Twenty-First Century Economic Development" *Economic Development Review*, Volume 14, Number 1, Winter, 1996, pp. 4-8.

Jerry L. Wade, "Economic Development and The Small Community" *Economic Development Review*, Volume 7, Number 1, Winter, 1989, pp. 45-48.

Joseph H. Nies, "Providing Community Support" *Economic Development Review*, Volume 12, Number 2, Spring, 1994, pp. 93-94.

Eric P. Canada, "TQM Benchmarking For Economic Development Programs: "Good Is Not Good Where Better Is Expected" *Economic Development Review*, Volume 11, Number 3, Summer, 1993, pp. 34-38.

Barbara Francis Keller, "Using Strategic Planning In Economic Development" *Economic Development Review*, Volume 8, Number 2, Spring, 1990, pp. 20-24.

Patricia L. Plugge, "Self-Help Strategic Planning For Small Communities" *Economic Development Review*, Volume 11, Number 2, Spring, 1993, pp. 14-17.

Raymond B. Ludwiszewski, "The Interdependence of Economic Development and Environmental Protection" *Economic Development Review*, Volume 10, Number 3, Summer, 1992, pp. 5-7.

Hans Neuhauser, "Tips On Creating An Environmentally and Economic Successful Project" *Economic Development Review*, Volume 10, Number 3, Summer, 1992, pp. 63-64.

Economic Development Administration, "How To Make An Industrial Site Survey" *Economic Development Review*, Volume 9, Number 4, Fall, 1991, pp. 65-68.

Mark D. Waterhouse, "Principles of the Real Property Development Process" *Economic Development Review*, Volume 9, Number 4, Fall, 1991, pp. 25-28.

Rick Thrasher, "Prospects, Realtors and Economic Developers: A New Partnership" *Economic Development Review*, Volume 9, Number 4, Fall, 1991, pp. 10-13.

James Halverson, "Planning and Developing A Speculative Industrial Building" *Economic Development Review*, Volume 9, Number 4, Fall, 1991, pp. 31-34.

James A. Devine, "Creating a SIMPLE Spec Building Program: The Example of Glendale, Arizona" *Economic Development Review*, Volume 11, Number 3, Summer, 1993, pp. 83-84.

Lay James Gibson, "Labor Force Surveys and The Economic Development Program" *Economic Development Review*, Volume 5, Number 2, Summer, 1987, pp. 24-30.

Steven R. Warren, "Obtaining Comparable and Reliable Community Labor Data" *Economic Development Review,* Volume 10, Number 1, Winter, 1992, pp. 26-28.

Patrick Vercauteren, "Career Fair For High School Sophomores" *Economic Development Review*, Volume 14, Number 1, Winte, 1992, pp. 48-50.

Mark Barbash, "Emerging Trends and Opportunities in Economic Development Financing" *Economic Development Review* , Volume 10, Number 2, Spring, 1992, pp. 4-6.

Henry L. Taylor, Jr., "How To Analyze Financial Statements" *Economic Development Review*, Volume 7, Number 2, Spring, 1989, pp. 62-67.

Anne Nickel, "The Bank Community Development Corporation: An Underutilized Tool For Economic Development" *Economic Development Review*, Volume 10, Number 2, Spring, 1992, pp. 80-81.

Mark Royce, "Advantages and Disadvantages of Tax Increment Financing" *Economic Development Review*, Volume 10, Number 2, Spring, 1992, pp. 84-85.

Kate McEnroe, "Incentives As A Public Business Investment" *Economic Development Review*, Volume 12, Number 4, Fall, 1994, pp. 12-15.

James E. Mooney, "Creative Efforts At The Local Level For Providing Business Attraction and Expansion Incentives" *Economic Development Review,* Volume 12, Number 4, Fall, 1994, pp. 52-57.

James H. Renzas, "E.D. Practices: The Best and The Worst" *Economic Development Review*, Volume 12, Number 4, Fall, 1994, pp. 83-87.

Rodney Page and Patrick Topping, "It's Marketing, Stupid!" *Economic Development* Review, Volume 13, Number 4, Fall, 1995, pp. 62-66.

Daryl McKee, "Targeted Industry Marketing: Strategy and Techniques" *Economic Development Review,* Volume 12, Number 2, Spring 1994, pp. 4-12.

Gary Anderson, "Industry Clustering For Economic Development" *Economic Development Review*, Volume 12, Number 2, Spring, 1994, pp. 26-32.

Jerry Heare, "How to Create A Marketing Team" *Economic Development Review*, Volume 9, Number 2, Spring, 1991, pp. 42-46.

Christopher A. Roybal, "Comparative Operating Cost Analysis: Bottom-Line Incentive for Expanding and Relocating Companies" *Economic Development Review*, Volume 14, Number 1, Winter, 1996, pp. 53-56.

Michael B. McCain, "Effective Prospect Presentations: Your Competitive Edge" *Economic Development Review*, Volume 13, Number 3, Summer, 1995, pp. 83-88.

J. Martin Orr, "How To Interview The Industrial Prospect" *Economic Development Review,* Volume 9, Number 2, Spring, 1991, pp. 47-51.

Robert L. Koepke and Steven R. Warren, "How to Recruit New Manufacturing" *Economic Development Review*, Volume 9, Number 2, Spring, 1991, pp. 38-41.

Clifton Harald, "Recruiting Retail Investment" *Economic Development Review*, Volume 13, Number 2, Spring, 1995, pp. 43-45.

James E. Devine, "Retail Targeting and Attraction Strategies" *Economic Development Review*, Volume 12, Number 2, Spring, 1994, pp. 47-50.

Terry Lawhead, "A Comprehensive Strategy For Rural Downtowns" *Economic Development Review*, Volume 13, Number 2, Spring, 1995, pp. 75-81.

Miles K. Luke, "How to Implement Local Industry Development and Retention" *Economic Development Review*, Volume 9, Number 1, Winter, 1991, pp. 16-22.

Patricia A. Crawford-Lucas, "Providing Business Plan Assistance To Small Manufacturing Companies" *Economic Development Review*, Volume 10, Number 1, Winter, 1992, pp. 54-58.

Helga R. Weschke, "Early Warning Signs Of Risk Companies" *Economic Development* Review, Volume 12, Number 3, Summer, 1994, pp. 66-67.

Elise S. Back, "Establishing A Local Manufacturers' Association: The Vaughan, Ontario Experience" *Economic Development Review*, Volume 11, Number 1, Winter, 1993, pp. 70-71.

Joseph A. Yarzebinski, "Understanding And Encouraging The Entrepreneur" *Economic Development Review*, Volume 10, Number 1, Winter, 1992, pp. 32-35.

Rhonda P. Culp, "Guidelines For Incubator Development" *Economic Development Review*, Volume 8, Number 4, Fall, 1990, pp. 19-23.

John B. Cordrey, "Targeting International Business: Strategies For Expanding Local Economies" *Economic Development Review*, Volume 12, Number 2, Spring, 1994, pp. 55-59.

Harry G. Foden, "The Professional Development Challenge Of The Next Decade" *Economic Development Review*, Volume 13, Number 3, Summer, 1995, pp. 6-8.

Gene Handley, "Responding To The Challenge of Professional Development: The Programs of AEDC" *Economic Development Review*, Volume 13, Number 3, Summer, 1995, pp. 12-15.

Nancy Thompson, "The Economic Development Institute" *Economic Development Review*, Volume 13, Number 3, Summer, 1995, pp. 74-75.

J. David Wansley, "The Certified Economic Developer Program: A Quarter Century of Evolution From Practice to Profession" *Economic Development Review*, Volume 13, Number 3, Summer, 1995, pp. 71-72.

Edward M. Krauss, "Passing The CED Examination" *Economic Development Review*, Volume 13, Number 3, Summer, 1995, pp. 72-73.

Mark S. Davis and Elizabeth A. Neu, "Growing Your Organization Through The Accredited Economic Development Organization (AEDO) Process" *Economic Development Review*, Volume 14, Number 1, Winter, 1996, pp. 22-25.

Timothy L. Martin, "Evaluating The Next Position: Successful Career Advancement In Economic Development" *Economic Development Review*, Volume 13, Number 3, Summer, 1995, pp. 59-61.

Harry A. Martin, "There's A 'Magic' In Tupelo-Lee County, Northeast Mississippi" *Economic Development Review*, Volume 12, Number 4, Fall, 1994, pp. 78-82.

June M. Wilmot, "Community Economic Development: A New Fashioned Approach" *Economic Development Review*, Volume 11, Number 2, Spring, 1993, pp. 81-85.

James A. Garver, "The Evolution of Economic Development in Broward County, Florida" *Economic Development Review*, Volume 11, Number 3, Summer, 1993, pp. 85-89.